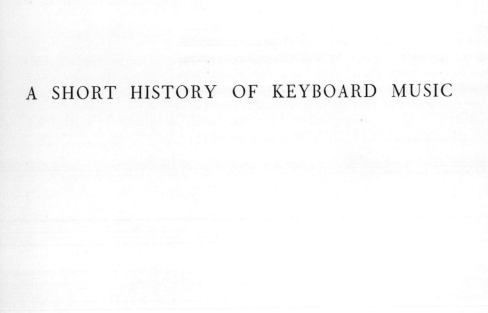

A SHORT HISTORY OF KEYBOARD MUSIC

F. E. KIRBY

A Short History of
KEYBOARD
MUSIC

THE FREE PRESS, *New York*
COLLIER-MACMILLAN LIMITED, *London*

Collier-Macmillan Canada, Ltd., Toronto, Ontario

Library of Congress Catalog Card Number: 66-23081.

printing number
2   3   4   5   6   7   8   9   10

TO *Emily*

Preface

In recent years, there has been much interest in keyboard music on the part of scholars in music history. Doubtless the most important and comprehensive project undertaken in the recent past is the *Corpus of Early Keyboard Music* published by the American Institute of Musicology under the general editorship of Willi Apel, who intends to bring out new and reliable editions of all keyboard music composed up to 1700 (excluding what has already been adequately edited). Along with numerous other recent publications of early keyboard music, there have been important dissertations and other studies, such as Göllner, Lord, and Southern on the fifteenth century; Burns, Jackson, and Slim on the sixteenth and seventeenth centuries in Italy; White on Lublin, and Curtis on Sweelinck; Young's work on sixteenth-century German organ music, as well as his survey of all keyboard music up to 1600; the important source studies on seventeenth-century German music by Riedel and Schierning; and the several studies and editions of Hoffmann-Erbrecht. See the Bibliography for complete citations. Established scholars, among them Apel, Newman, Plamenac, and Stevens, have also continued to make important contributions. There is also the handbook of Alker.

This interest on the part of scholars, however, has been concentrated on the keyboard music of the Renaissance and Baroque periods and, to a large extent, neglects that of the eighteenth, nineteenth, and twentieth centuries. It thus happens that there are but few scholarly works on precisely those historical periods that are of the greatest general interest and whose music—except for organ and harpsichord music—forms the basis of the present-day repertory. A notable exception to this general state of affairs is Frotscher's large book on the history of the organ and organ music, which has recently been reprinted.

Still another aspect of the literature on keyboard music is that, most often, the music for each of the keyboard instruments is dealt with separately. Frotscher's

vii

book on organ music has been mentioned, and we can also refer to Kenyon's work on harpsichord music along with a number of books on piano music, such as those by Georgii, Hutcheson, Dale, and the Friskin-Freundlich handbook. But, in this approach, the essential unity of the field is lost. And while this unity is most important in connection with earlier music up to around 1750, where, for instance, the distinction between harpsichord and organ music is often not very clear, there are nevertheless basic mutual relationships between piano and organ music that run right on up to the present day.

The present book is intended as a corrective to this situation, in a small way at all events. It attempts to deal with the whole repertory of keyboard music from the historical point of view. It will readily be conceded that this is a large and possibly impossible undertaking in which whatever success may be achieved will be only partial. But it is nonetheless hoped that scholars, students, and music teachers of all kinds, and even many of those who just listen to music, will derive some benefit from the book.

There has been in English but one book dealing with keyboard music as a whole—Willi Apel's *Masters of the Keyboard* (1947), which was the outgrowth of a series of public lectures addressed primarily to amateurs and music listeners in general. The present work, generally speaking, is an expansion of Apel's plan; it is a historical survey of music composed for all the keyboard instruments (organ, harpsichord and/or clavichord, and piano). There are, at the same time, several important differences. This work is much bigger than Apel's book, and a much larger proportion of its content is given over to keyboard music since 1750; on the other side, it has not been possible to follow Apel's procedure of reproducing complete compositions as illustrative examples. A historical anthology of keyboard music is planned as a sequel to this volume.

The emphasis here has been placed on music for solo keyboard instruments. Important compositions for piano duet, for two pianos, and so on, are mentioned and on occasion, where their stature demands it, given more detailed consideration. But music for a keyboard instrument with orchestra (concertos and the like) has had to be excluded, since its inclusion would have greatly enlarged the work and because such music has frequently been dealt with in other books, some on symphonic music in general and others specifically dealing with concertos. Another omission has been chamber music in which a keyboard instrument has an important part, the inclusion of which again would have enlarged and greatly altered the plan of the book.

This book, then, is a historical interpretation of keyboard music. As such, it relies on standard editions of music and on the standard scholarly literature and references in the field. The hope has been to provide a comprehensive overview of the field, drawing, as far as possible, on the results of the most recent research. The facts presented—the raw material, as it were, of the book—do not present anything new. But it is hoped that the historical interpretations resulting from the study of the whole repertory of keyboard music will be suggestive and will at times open up new lines of thought and opportunities for further scholarship. It goes without saying that any interpretation of this sort requires selection, and here opinions will surely differ on what ought to be included and what not and on what ought to be emphasized and what subordinated. The writer can only say that he has tried to be objective and fair and to follow where the direction of the evidence seemed to lead. One can echo Arthur Mendel, who concluded his address to the New York Congress of the International Musicological Society (1961) by quoting Cromwell's warning to the Church of Scotland: "I beseech you, in the bowels of Christ, think it possible you may be mistaken." In any case, a book of this kind is fated to suffer from new work in the field that will render it in various ways obsolete. Finally, it is hoped that the book will have some value as a reference or handbook, by virtue of its extensive bibliography and index.

A constant problem has been the relationship between the proper subject of the book, the history of keyboard music, and the changing relative position of keyboard music in various historical periods. There have been but few composers of major significance who wrote principally for keyboard (as outstanding examples, we can name Frescobaldi, Froberger, Domenico Scarlatti, Clementi, and, especially, Chopin), so that, in most cases, account had to be taken not only of the position of keyboard music in a given composer's output, but also of the general position of keyboard music in the repertory of the given historical period. Another not unrelated problem concerns the relationship between music for keyboard and music for other media in a given historical period; as is emphasized in this work, keyboard music is often dependent on forms and procedures indigenous to such other instrumental media—as examples we can mention the influence of orchestra music on French organ music generally or of lute music on French harpsichord music.

For any project of this size, an author requires assistance of all kinds; in the present case, such assistance has been both timely and competent. Work was materially advanced by a grant from the Faculty Senate of West Virginia University for the year 1962–1963, for the administration of which thanks are due to the Provost of the University, Dr. J. F. Golay, and to the Dean of the School of Music, Dr. Richard E. Duncan. Acknowledgement is also made to Lake Forest College for other assistance, in particular, to the Provost and Dean of the Faculty, Dr. William L. Dunn. The book owes a good deal to the untiring efforts of Mr. William C. Watson (now of Wichita State University), who did much to correct errors of fact, interpretation, typography, and diction, and to the extraordinarily competent typing and checking of Mrs. Leland B. Golay. My wife Emily assisted in additional checking of large portions of the manuscript. For help in assembling the music examples, thanks go to Mr. James Miltenberger of West Virginia University and to Miss Ann Bowen and Mr. Robert Huhn of Lake Forest College. Recognition is due the following libraries, where much of the work was done and that have cooperated in many ways: the library of West Virginia University, with special thanks to its then Associate Director, Mr. Michael M. Reynolds (now at Indiana University); the Carnegie Free Library of Pittsburgh; the music library at the University of Texas; the library of The School of Music at Northwestern University, with special thanks to its librarian, Miss Jean Kauffman; and, last but by no means least, the Newberry Library in Chicago. Finally, thanks are due the following publishers for their kind permission to reproduce copyrighted material as illustrations: Associated Music Publishers, New York; Bärenreiter-Verlag, Kassel (West Germany); Ernest Benn, Ltd., London; Boosey & Hawkes, New York and London; Elkan-Vogel Co., Philadelphia; the Encyclopaedia Britannica, Chicago; Éditions Max Eschig, Paris; Wilhelm Hansen Edition, Copenhagen; Leeds Music Corporation, New York; G. Schirmer, New York; and Universal-Edition, London.

F. E. K.

Lake Forest, Illinois

Contents

List of Examples

xiii

Note

For ease in securing illustrative examples, from the earlier periods in particular, reference is made throughout to a number of standard historical anthologies of music that are readily available and generally inexpensive. These, with their abbreviations, are:

GMB *Geschichte der Musik in Beispielen*, edited by A. Schering (Leipzig: Breitkopf & Härtel, 1931; New York: Broude Brothers, 1950).

HAM *Historical Anthology of Music*, edited by A. T. Davison and Willi Apel (2 vols.; Cambridge: Harvard University Press, 1949–1950).

HMS *History of Music in Sound*, edited by Gerald Abraham (10 vols.; New York: Oxford University Press and RCA Victor). Records with explanatory handbooks.

MPM *Masterpieces of Music before 1750*, edited by Carl Parrish and J. F. Ohl (New York: Norton, 1951). Recorded by the Haydn Society.

TEM *A Treasury of Early Music*, edited by Carl Parrish (New York: Norton, 1958). Recorded by the Haydn Society.

Other collections to which reference is frequently made are:

Willi Apel, *Masters of the Keyboard* (Cambridge: Harvard University Press, 1947).

Walther Georgii, *Keyboard Music of the Baroque and Rococo* (3 vols.; Cologne: Volk, 1960).

———, *400 Years of European Keyboard Music*, Vol. I of *Anthology of Music*, edited by K. G. Fellerer (Cologne: Volk, since 1958).

Willi Kahl, *The Character Piece*, Vol. VII of *Anthology of Music*.

W. S. Newman, *Thirteen Sonatas of the Eighteenth and Nineteenth Centuries* (Chapel Hill: University of North Carolina Press, 1947).

Erich Valentin, *The Toccata*, Vol. XVII of *Anthology of Music*.

xvii

For editions of any composer, treatise, or manuscript discussed or referred to in the text, consult the Bibliography, Part One, second section. In the identification of secondary literature on any topic, the last names of authors who have written relevant books or articles are given in parentheses right in the text itself, and the reader should again check in the Bibliography, Part Two, under these names for full citations. This shorthand procedure is used in the footnotes as well.

Other devices used in the book are: major keys are indicated by capital letters and minor keys by lower case letters; in the text, Arabic numerals are used for a whole work or opus and lower case Roman numerals for individual pieces or parts within an opus, e.g., Beethoven's Sonata in d (op. 31 ii); in references to the *History of Music in Sound*, the volume number is given in Roman numerals followed by an indication of the record side (s.) and band (b.) on which the selection is to be found, e.g., *HMS*, III, s. 4, b. 4.

CHAPTER ONE

The Keyboard Instruments,
Their History and Construction

In the classification of instruments, the principle that determines which instruments belong in a group usually has to do with *how* the instruments make sound, that is, *how* their tone is produced. Thus, stringed instruments generally form one group, wind instruments another, percussion instruments yet another, and so forth. But, with keyboard instruments, this is not the case. Here, the common bond in the family does not have to do with *how* the tone is produced, but rather with *how* the instruments are played, that is, the means by which the notes that are to sound are controlled—the keyboard.

Apart from the presence of the keyboard, these instruments differ greatly from one another, especially in the crucial question of how the sound is produced, and it is the differences in this respect that determine the various branches of the family. There are four main divisions recognized among keyboard instruments. First, there are various kinds of organs, instruments whose tone is produced by wind vibrating in pipes; then, there is the clavichord, in which strings are touched by tangents; there is the harpsichord family, in which strings are plucked; and, finally, there is the piano family, in which the strings are struck by felt hammers. The organ with its pipes, then, is the only member of the family that does not make use of strings. Each of these four types may be regarded as a separate family group, since, except for the clavichord, each has several subdivisions or types of instrument that properly belong to it. Furthermore, from time to time, efforts have been made to create individual keyboard instruments that combine in various ways characteristic features of the organ and harpsichord (*clavichordium*) or, going outside the family altogether, to combine the keyboard action with that of the bowed stringed instruments (*Bogenflügel*).

It may occasionally appear that certain keyboard instruments have affinities to other string and wind instruments that are stronger than their bond to other

1

members of their own family. This is true, for instance, in the case of the harpsi-chord, which had close connections to the lute and to lute music, especially in the sixteenth and seventeenth centuries. Since the structure of the instruments, especially in regard to the question of tone production, has an important bearing on the music written for and the musical style best suited to a particular instru-ment, we can commence with a brief discussion of the various groups within the keyboard instrument family, emphasizing technical and historical aspects.[1]

The Organ[2]

Since the organ's tone is produced by air being caused to vibrate in pipes, it is evident that all organs (pipe organs) must have, in one form or another, three elements: a set of pipes, a supply of air (wind), and a means of controlling which of the pipes are to sound at any given time. Most important for the actual sound of the instrument are the pipes themselves, their various types, and their organiza-tion or disposition in the instrument as a whole.

Broadly speaking, there are two types of organ pipes: flue pipes and reed pipes. In a flue pipe, the air column itself simply vibrates in the pipe and thus produces the sound, while in a reed pipe, there is a vibrating tongue, usually of metal, at the lower end of the pipe that sets the air in motion. This produces a different tone quality; the flue pipes operate as simple whistles, while in reed pipes the upper partials are attenuated, thus giving such pipes a more "biting," more characteristic tone color.

In general, however, tone quality in organ pipes is a function of the scaling, that is, of the relation of the diameter to the length of the pipe; the wider the pipe with respect to its length, the fewer the partials produced, the more "neutral" the tone quality, and, conversely, the narrower the pipe in relation to its length, the more partials are produced, the more sharply defined or coloristic the tone quality. Another method of causing alteration in the tone characteristics of a flue pipe is stopping it, i.e., closing the upper end (*gedackt*), which has the two-fold effect of eliminating the odd-numbered partials and of causing the pipe to sound one octave lower than would an open pipe of the same length. Tone quality can therefore vary considerably among organ pipes. Common varieties among flue pipes are principal (or diapason), flute, and string sounds; and the reed pipes are often made to imitate the sound of certain woodwind and brass instruments.

In an organ, the pipes are organized by ranks or registers, that is, full sets of pipes of the same type covering all notes from the lowest to the highest (see especially Mahrenholz). Apart from the tone quality, ranks are also distinguished

---

[1] On instruments generally, see the standard works of Sachs, Geiringer, and Donington; on the keyboard instruments, see, among others, Galpin, Hipkins, Hirt, James, and Krebs.

[2] On the organ generally, see Sumner, the most up-to-date and reliable, or, more popular, Klotz; older works are Dufourcq, Schweitzer, and Williams. There are many special works of all sorts.

by the pitch level at which their pipes sound. That is to say, a rank in which the pipes all sound at normal pitch (with respect to the keyboard) is said to be at eight-foot (8′) pitch, so called because the length of a pipe sounding the C two octaves below middle C (C), the "great C," is about eight feet. Let us assume an organist playing one note, middle C; when the 8′ rank is operative, middle C will sound. But there would also be another rank of the same kind of pipes at 4′ pitch sounding an octave higher, and the organist could, if he wished, employ

EXAMPLE 1

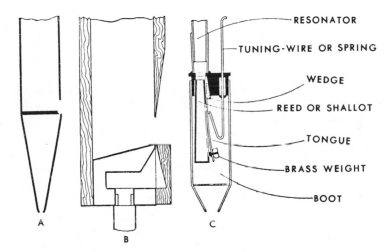

RESONATOR

TUNING-WIRE OR SPRING

WEDGE

REED OR SHALLOT

TONGUE

BRASS WEIGHT

BOOT

A

B

C

Principal types of organ pipes: A. Section of metal flue pipe; B. Section of wooden flue pipe; C. Section of reed pipe (trumpet) and its component parts.

From the *Encyclopaedia Britannica* (1962). Reproduced by permission.

both ranks at the same time, so that pressing the key middle C would produce two notes, middle C and the C an octave above it. A rank at 2′ pitch would produce the C two octaves above middle C, while one at 16′ pitch would sound the C an octave lower than middle C. Thus, by merely playing middle C, the organist, by allowing additional registers at 4′, 2′, and 16′ pitch to sound, could produce four C's, each in a different octave.

Also to be mentioned are two kinds of stops that are never used by themselves, but only in conjunction with others, mutation and mixture stops. The mutation stop is the simpler of the two, since it sounds the fifth or twelfth above the fundamental note. The mixture stop, on the other hand, is "compound" in that it does not present a continuous scale from the bottom to the top of its range, but rather shifts its relation to the fundamental note; the first twelfth of its range is two octaves above the fundamental, the next octave is a twelfth higher, the third octave is one octave higher, and the last octave is in unison. These stops are employed to strengthen the partial tones and thus provide an enrichment of the tone color. When one takes into account this aspect of the various pitch levels and adds to it the various different kinds of pipe, along with the possibility of ranks of open and stopped pipes, it is easy to appreciate the countless combinations that are possible on this instrument.

A rank or register, then, is a set of pipes of the same kind. A stop, strictly speaking, is the lever or control by which the organist causes a certain rank to sound or not to sound; but the term "stop" is loosely used to mean the same as register or rank. The keyboard or keyboards are called manual(s); and there is also a keyboard to be played by the feet, the pedal keyboard or, simply, pedals. Originally, particular manuals controlled certain registers, but most later organs are made so that all registers are available from any one manual.

While it is difficult to make generalizations on what is normal in the disposition of an organ, a few leading principles at least may be mentioned. Large organs are usually designed so that there is a basic section (the "Great organ") that emphasizes the more usual types of flue and reed pipes and a number of subsidiary smaller sections that employ more characteristic registers and, in some cases, special devices of various kinds. The number and disposition of these subsidiary sections varies a good deal from instrument to instrument. Most organs have a section consisting of "solo" registers (called by the names of various orchestral instruments; the term *récit* was used to denote an organ stop—any "solo-type" stop—in nineteenth-century France), using registers with highly characteristic tone qualities that the organist can use for stressing individual lines that he desires to stand out from the other voices. Another common section is the so-called "choir organ" (or "positive organ"), which has a small number of more unobtrusive registers that make it useful for accompanying soloists or choruses; the choir organ may also be totally enclosed to muffle the sound even more. Many organs also have a "swell organ," which is totally enclosed but the enclosure has movable panels that can be gradually opened, thus increasing the outward radiation of sound and causing a crescendo. The term "swell" comes from the name "Venetian swell," so called because the movable panels operate in a fashion similar to Venetian blinds. Finally, most organs have coupling devices so that various sections of the organ are available from several manuals in many different combinations.

For these reasons, one of the most important aspects of organ playing has to do with registration: which registers or combinations of registers should be used in the performance of a composition or sections of a composition, how they should be assigned, and so on. In modern times, composers have specified the registration of their works, but, in the past, except for French composers, this was left to the performer. The problem becomes critical when one wishes to perform an early composition intended for an organ of modest proportions on one of today's large concert organs. An injudicious use of the vast tonal resources of a large organ can produce serious distortions in a work composed for a smaller instrument.

We can now turn our attention to the history of the organ.[1] The oldest type of organ known to us is the "hydraulis" or water organ, which dates from the third century B.C. (see MacLean). Philo's *Pneumatica*, also of the third century B.C., explains the instrument and attributes its invention to an engineer of Alexandria named Ktesibius; a later description is found in Vitruvius' *De Architectura* (c. 14 B.C.). (See the translations in Sumner, pp. 17–18, 20–1.) It appears that in many respects the hydraulis was quite similar to later organs; it had an air pump, a wind chest, and eight pipes, all of the same diameter. Apparently, there also was a key mechanism; depressing the key caused a slide with a hole in its center to move, bringing the hole into alignment with the pipe, thus permitting the wind to flow through. There have been serious misconceptions concerning the use of the water in the hydraulis; actually, the water was simply an ingenious way of converting the fluctuating pressure of the air from the pump into the constant air pressure needed to make the pipes sound properly. Briefly, the method was as follows. The container filled with water was between the pump and the wind chest; in this container was a bell-shaped chamber into which came a tube from the pump and from which went another tube to the wind chest; the air from the pump, on its down cycle, forced water out of the bell while some of the wind went directly into the wind chest, and, as the pump returned to begin another stroke, the water rose in the bell, thus continuing to force air into the wind chest. There would thus be constant bubbling in the water, a fact noted in early descriptions of the instrument.

The hydraulis was popular in classical antiquity. There are several pictorial representations which have come down to us as well as numerous literary references to the instrument. In 1931, a hydraulis was unearthed near Hungary; this instrument had four ranks of pipes with thirteen pipes in each; others have also been found. It appears that the hydraulis existed in many forms, large as well as small, loud as well as soft, crude as well as refined. The large instruments had their place in such outdoor events as the circus and the gladiator combats, while the smaller instruments would be used in the palatial residences of the nobility. We have a picture of a Carthaginian hydraulis, with three ranks each of eighteen pipes, all of the same diameter, and equipped with two air pumps; since a person is shown in this picture, we can estimate that the instrument was about twelve feet high and six feet in width. The hydraulis may also have existed among the Hebrews under the name *magrepha*, although the exact meaning of this term remains uncertain (see Yasser).

[1] See Apel, "Early History of the Organ," an often neglected article; older and in some ways out of date are Farmer and Bittermann.

References to the hydraulis cease at the end of the fourth century A.D., and another type of organ, the pneumatic organ operating without water, appeared on the scene, apparently first in the Byzantine Empire, which held the lead in

EXAMPLE 2

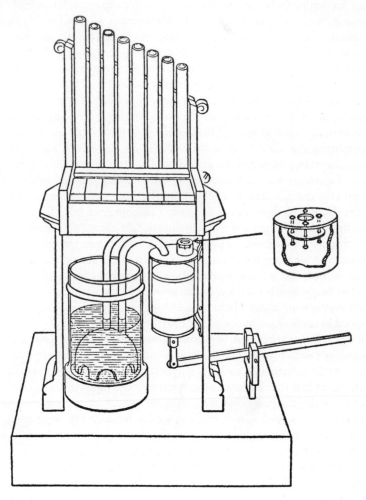

The hydraulis.

organ building until roughly A.D. 1000. The pneumatic type of organ was also known among the Arabs of the time. The earliest evidence of a pneumatic organ that has been found is in the *Onomastikon* of Pollux (*c.* A.D. 120); better-known but later examples date from the fourth century, especially the passage in Julian the Apostate comparing the organ to a field of reeds. The earliest pictorial representation of a pneumatic organ is found on the obelisk of the Emperor Theodosius in Constantinople, also from the fourth century, which shows an organ with eight pipes all of the same diameter with air pressure supplied by a bellows system operated by two men. These Byzantine pneumatic organs apparently could be built in very large sizes, as can be seen from an account formerly attributed to St. Jerome that refers to an organ in Jerusalem whose sound could be heard on the Mount of Olives about one mile away; this account describes another organ as having "twelve brazen pipes" and "a grand sound like thunder" (*magna murmura* and *tonitrus*).

It is not known just when organ building commenced in Europe. The instrument is mentioned as far back as the sixth century in European sources, in a poem by Venantius Fortunatus, and there are several others, so that it can be assumed that the organ (in some form or other) was widespread in Europe. We have the reference in the riddles of Aldhelm (seventh–eighth centuries) to an organ possessing great tonal resources whose sound is compared to bugles, harps, and trumpets. It also appears that the key action of the earlier hydraulis had been supplanted by a slider action (*linguae*): here, instead of depressing keys, the player had to push in a flat, thin piece of wood to make the air pass through to the pipes. This action was cruder and more cumbersome than the older key mechanism had been.

Even though the organ in some form or other was current in medieval Europe, a sensation was caused when, in 757, Emperor Pippin of the Franks received an organ as a gift from the Byzantine Emperor Constantinus Copronymous and, also later, in 812, when representatives of the Byzantine Emperor Michael I Rhangabes brought another of their organs to the court of Charlemagne at Aix-la-Chapelle. The sound of this latter instrument was described at the time as having a tone that "equalled the force of thunder, the liveliness of the lyre, the sweetness of the cymbal"; Charlemagne wanted to have the instrument copied, but it was not until some time later that his son Louis the Pious actually had the organ constructed. From the description quoted, it appears that these Byzantine organs possessed considerable tonal resources, and Apel conjectures (arguing from the obelisk of Theodosius and from a picture of an organ in the eighth-century Utrecht Psalter) that these instruments were double organs, played by two organists. In any case, they seem to have differed greatly from the organs to which Europeans had been accustomed (see, in addition to Apel, Degering and Perrot).

An important account of a European organ deals with the very large instrument at Winchester in England, built in the tenth century, that was fully described by the monk Wulstan. This organ had four hundred pipes arranged in a single row and forty sliders each of which controlled ten tones; to operate the bellows

required the labor of seventy men. The ouput of sound evidently was tremendous; listeners had to stop their ears, "being in no wise able to draw near and
hear the sound." Other accounts refer to the thunderous quality of the instrument: "to what purpose, pray, is that awful roar of the bellows, which is more
like the rumble of a thunderstorm than the sweetness of the voice?" (See the
translations in Sumner, p. 36, and Apel, "Early History . . .," p. 206.) A con-
tributing factor was that pipes controlled by the same *lingua* sounded not only
the fundamental note, but also the octave and the twelfth, so that a mixture
resulted.

The Winchester organ, then, was a large instrument, and there were other
such giants in Rheims, Limoges, Erfurt, Fécamp, and elsewhere; similar large
instruments continued to exist throughout the Middle Ages and the Renaissance.
In the fifteenth century, we hear of an instrument in Barcelona with 1,400 pipes,
another in Blois with 2,500 pipes (built in 1429), and other very large organs
existed in Germany, in Salem, and in Bamberg (the latter built in 1475). But
there was little in the way of a technical development taking place; the keyboard
range remained small, the keys were difficult to operate, registration possibilities
were few, the mixture arrangement predominated, the volume was loud, and the
tone was coarse.

The development of the organ as a musical instrument is connected with its
smaller form: the positive (see Bornefeld and Quoika), a small, stationary
organ that employed mainly flue pipes (the type of small organ using reed pipes
was the regal, which dates from the sixteenth century). Closely connected with
the positive is an important improvement in European organ building, the re-
introduction of something possessed by the early hydraulis: the slides (*linguae*)
were replaced by keys (*lamina*), thus greatly simplifying the operation of the
instrument. The earliest European reference to organ keyboards is found in the
so-called *Berner Tractat*, an anonymous treatise on organ building from the
tenth century, entitled *De fistulis organicis quomodo fiant*. An organ in Magdeburg (eleventh century) apparently possessed a keyboard.

A famous representation of a positive organ is to be found in the painting on
the Ghent altar by Jan van Eyck. Several observations may be made from this
reproduction. There are on the instrument two ranks of twenty-one pipes each,
so that the keyboard range may assumed to comprise a thirteenth (assuming a
full chromatic disposition, as seems evident from the painting); moreover, all
pipes have the same diameter, and, since the timbre of organ pipes varies by the
ratio of the length to the diameter, there would be a gradual change over the
gamut from the string quality of tone in the lower tones to the flue tone of the
treble (a quality that Apel designates as a tonal spectrum). There are many other
depictions of positive organs from the late Middle Ages and the Renaissance (see
Sumner, Plates II, V, VI, VII, and VIII).

The two types of organ, small and large, existed side by side. Along with them was a third kind of organ: the diminutive portative, or organetto (see Hickmann), an instrument that existed from the tenth century until it went out of use in the sixteenth century. It was played by one person, one hand working the bellows and the other playing the keyboard. The portative, then, was capable only of performing one part; it was a "monophonic" instrument used in ensembles with other instruments and singers in the performance of polyphonic music. Hence, there is no musical literature for the portative organ.

Returning to the "polyphonic" organs we find that, towards the end of the Middle Ages, a *rapprochement* between the large form of the organ and the positive gradually took place; features of the smaller positive organ were included among the resources of the large organ. In other words, beginning in the fourteenth century, a decisive step towards the modern organ was taken; the organ came to be regarded as a composite of several instruments of varying capabilities and functions, its resources controlled from several different manuals. Particularly important was the use of sets of the more highly characteristic solo registers, which players could employ to render more important voices in a composition. Other advances in organ construction made at this time included the development of a real keyboard in the larger instruments by virtue of the Tracker action (a mechanical arrangement of rods and levers by which the motion of the keys causes the valves of the pipes to open and close), the chromatic adaption of the keyboard, two manual instruments, and the addition of pedals (this last may go back to the previous century).

By the end of the fifteenth century, the organ had attained a form that does not differ principally from the instrument as it is today. This can be seen in an important treatise on organ building from the early sixteenth century, Arnolt Schlick's *Spiegel der Orgelmacher und Organisten* (1511), which describes an organ in great detail. The instrument with three manuals and pedals (having a compass of three octaves and a third) was organized in three sections each with its own characteristic sets of registers. There was a manual, which was the main part of the instrument, with eleven registers using both flue stops along with a few of the more characteristic "solo" reeds and mixture stops like the *Zymmel* and *Raus Pfeiffen*; a positive, with four registers of flue stops; and a pedal, again with four registers, among which the 16′ flue register as the lowest was important. Schlick gives detailed information on the use of the various registers and of the instrument in general. Finally, he explains the system of mean-tone temperament, based on a fifth that is slightly smaller than the perfect fifth, which produces near-perfect thirds and fifths in the keys using one or two sharps or flats but which causes serious discrepancies when carried into more remote keys (see Kendall).

Organ building in Germany continued much in the style of this instrument (see Pietzsch, Quoika, and Eberstaller). A twofold distinction in the organization of the registers was established in the sixteenth century; the "thin" registers

—narrow, bright, and open, producing a light and transparent sound—formed the principal part of the organ, while the "wide" registers—using particularly reeds and mixtures—served as the more characteristic "solo" stops (see Flade and Gurlitt). These divisions were carried out on each section of the organ; the wide registers were to be used sparingly in conjunction with the thin registers to produce the light and pleasing sound quality that we associate with the Baroque organ. Important organ builders in Germany at this time include the members of the Scherer family, Hans the Older, Jacob, Hans the Younger, and Fritz. The most important organ builder of seventeenth-century Germany was Arp Schnitger (1648–1719) and, somewhat later, members of the Silbermann family, Andreas (1678–1734) and Gottfried (1683–1753), whose organs were esteemed by J. S. Bach (see Flade and Wörsching). Important writings on organs from seventeenth-century Germany include the third part of Michael Praetorius' work on music (*Syntagma musicum*), called *De Organographia*, of 1618–1620, Athanasius Kircher's *Musurgia* of 1650, and two works of Andreas Werck-meister, the *Orgelprobe* of 1681 (revised in 1698) and the *Organum Gruningense redivum* of 1705.

In France, from the sixteenth century on, we find a prevalence of the large type of organ, divided generally into three sections (*grande orgue, positif*, and *pedale*), each equipped with a considerable variety of registers. An important source of information on French organs of the sixteenth and seventeenth centuries is Marin Mersenne's *Harmonie universelle*. In Italy, on the other hand, the preference until the eighteenth century remained with the smaller positive organ with but one manual and using mainly flue stops (see Sartorio). Important organ builders in Italy were the Antegnati family of whom Constanzo wrote a treatise, *L'arte organaria* of 1608. Another contemporary Italian work on organs was Girolamo Diruta's *Il Transilvano* in two parts, the first in 1593, the second in 1609. The smaller form of organ was also favored in England until the eighteenth century.

The history of the organ in the eighteenth and nineteenth centuries is dominated by the expansion of the instrument's tonal resources in direct emula-tion of the rapid development of the instruments of the orchestra. This was noted in 1795 by the German composer—organist—organ builder Justin Heinrich Knecht (1752–1817) in his treatise the *Vollständige Orgelschule* of 1795–1798 in which he states, "the organ can be regarded somewhat as the imitation of a large orchestra" (quoted by Sumner, p. 205). Expansion of the organ's resources had been especially cultivated in France since the seventeenth century, and this was avidly pursued in the eighteenth century, particularly in instruments built by the Clicquot family of whom François-Henri (1732–1790) is regarded as the most outstanding. Of fundamental importance was an encyclopedic treatise, François Bédos du Celle's *L'art de facteur d'orgues* (1766–1778). Another effort to make the organ resemble an orchestra, with a reduction of certain registers and an emphasis on crescendo devices, appears in the work of Georg Joseph Vogler (1749–1814), known as Abbé Vogler, an acoustician, composer, teacher, and instrument builder.

The great impetus towards the development of the large symphonic organ came in the nineteenth century. A chief problem that had to be overcome had to do with the increase in the amount of wind pressure needed for such large instruments and the consequent difficulty in the action of the keys. This was solved by the Englishman Charles Spackman Barker (1804–1879), the inventor of the pneumatic lever, who went to France where he worked with the most prominent French organ builder of the time, Aristide Cavaillé-Coll (1811–1899). The first of these symphonic organs was the result of their joint labor—the organ at St. Denis built in 1841. Cavaillé-Coll was preoccupied with increasing the dynamic possibilities of the organ as well as with the development of new "orchestral" reed registers. He also increased the resources of the swell organ and extended the range of the various manuals to include sixty keys. His organs, of which there were some six hundred, provided the medium for the influential nineteenth-century French school of organ composition including Guilmant, Franck, Vierne, Widor, and Dupré.

Organ building in the twentieth century shows several tendencies. There is, as would be expected, the continuation of the nineteenth-century French symphonic organ, which attained its most extreme manifestation in the "world's greatest organ" in Convention Hall at Atlantic City, New Jersey, built in 1932. Its disposition and resources are staggering. Then there are electronic organs in which the characteristic tone of the pipe organ is imitated by electronic audio generating devices; these instruments can be made much smaller and less expensively than pipe organs, and the possibilities for creating new tone colors are legion. The imitation of orchestral instruments and of the more normal organ registers is rarely convincing except in the largest of these electronic instruments.

Another important trend in organ building in the twentieth century may be seen in part as a by-product of the growth of musicology in the nineteenth century: the publications, for instance, of the *Bach-Gesellschaft* (the collected critical edition of the works of Bach). The necessary researches involved in this and similar projects brought about an interest in seventeenth- and eighteenth-century organs, and instruments by Schnitger and Silbermann were restored and put into operating condition. In 1921, the description of an organ found in Praetorius' *De Organographia* was followed in the construction of an instrument by Oscar Walcker, carried out under the guidance of a prominent German musicologist, Wilibald Gurlitt. The American organ builder Walter Holtkamp has also constructed instruments closely modeled on those of the Baroque, with reduced wind pressure, far fewer registers, and even with the re-introduction of the mechanical Tracker action. Most other builders, however, have preferred to produce what may be termed an eclectic instrument, either combining many of the stops developed in the symphonic organ with those found on earlier types of organ or by using mainly the resources of the Baroque organ but incorporating all of the most modern methods of wind supply, key action, and manufacturing.

A small form of organ that gained a certain popularity in the late nineteenth century was the harmonium (see Mustel and Hartmann particularly). It attained its characteristic form in the work of Auguste Debain of Paris in 1840, but other features were added from time to time as the century wore on. This is a single manual instrument using reed pipes; the wind pressure is supplied by bellows operated by the player by means of pedals. The important features are the expression, by which the player can directly control the wind pressure and thus readily effect dynamic gradations, crescendi and decrescendi, impossible on the larger organ; the percussion, a device enabling the instrument to respond instantly to the pressing of a key; the prolongement, enabling a note to be sustained after its key has been released; and two devices to increase the loudness level of the upper or the lower part, the melody attachment and the pedal substitute respectively, both of English origin. Related to the harmonium is the so-called "American organ," developed chiefly by the Mason and Hamlin firm of Boston, in which the wind is drawn through the reeds by suction. The harmonium enjoyed wide use as a domestic instrument and a rather large body of music has been written for it. In recent years, its place has been taken, not entirely successfully, by the small forms of the modern electronic organ.

The Harpsichord[1]

The remaining types of keyboard instruments employ vibrating strings for the production of tone. The most important among the earlier instruments of this type is the harpsichord in which the tone is produced by plectra, devices that pluck the strings. Each plectrum, originally a quill of some sort (since the eighteenth century, leather has been used), is fastened to a flat piece of wood called the jack, and mounted on a movable tongue in the center of the jack. When the key is depressed, the jack rises and the string is plucked by the projecting plectrum. On the return of the jack, the tongue moves back so that the plectrum bypasses the string. A spring (formerly hog's bristle was used) forces the tongue back to its original position flush with the jack. A damper mounted above the plectrum stops the string's vibrations when the jack returns to its normal rest position. The whole row of jacks is mounted in a long narrow tray, the jack slide, and over the whole row of jacks is a long, narrow piece of wood, the jack rail.

[1] For a brief survey, see Neupert; more detailed are Russell and Boalch (the latter in dictionary form); see also Winternitz.

Since the tone is produced by plucking, there is little dynamic variation possible on a harpsichord, at least in its simpler forms. Whether the key is struck hard or soft, it produces neither a louder nor softer tone. Although some slight

EXAMPLE 3

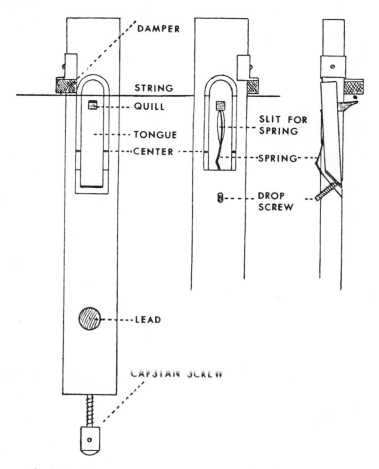

A harpsichord jack.
From H. Neupert, *Harpsichord Manual*. Reproduced by permission of the Bärenreiter-Verlag, Kassel, publishers.

alterations of this sort are certainly possible, their effect may be regarded as negligible. Therefore, other means of providing variety in and enrichment of the harpsichord's tone were sought, and the model used in this pursuit was the organ. Additional sets (or choirs) of strings with their own sets (registers) of jacks were employed; the name for an individual set of strings and its jacks is "register," a term borrowed from the organ. There is a basic register at 8' pitch with additional registers at 8' (unison), 4' (an octave higher), 16' (an octave lower), and, rarely, at 2' (two octaves higher). While the smaller models use a single manual with one or two registers (one at 8', the other at 4', or two at 8'), larger instruments employ two manuals (in some few cases, even three) and occasionally also a pedal keyboard (which includes a 16' register). While each manual is associated with certain choirs of strings, generally there is also a coupling arrangement to make the full resources of the instrument available from one manual. A frequently employed disposition would have two choirs of strings, at 8' and 4' respectively, played from the lower manual, and one at 8', played from the upper, with coupling to make all choirs available from the lower manual. It should be emphasized that, from the evidence, it appears that instruments with the 16' register were rare even in the eighteenth century.

Other common devices for introducing variation into the sound of the harpsichord have to do with tone color, the buff stop, and the lute stop. The buff stop (also called the harp stop) consists of a strip of felt mounted along the bottom of a bar that is lowered so that it rests across the strings of a register, thus damping their tone and producing a harp-like quality. The lute stop produces a similar effect by providing an 8' register with a second row of jacks mounted to pluck the strings near the bridge. There is some confusion in terminology between these two arrangements, so similar in effect yet so different in operation, the term "lute stop" often being used for what actually is a "buff stop." Dynamic variations were introduced in the eighteenth century by placing shutters flat over the strings and providing a means of opening them gradually, thus producing a crescendo of sorts. By analogy with Venetian blinds and a similar device in the organ, this was called the Venetian swell (in German, *Jalousieschweller*).

Most of the registers (apart from the swell and the two coloristic stops) operate by a sliding device in which the row of jacks is mounted, the jack guide or jack slide; sliding in one direction moves the jacks in a given row so that their plectra lie immediately below the strings, enabling plucking to take place, while sliding in the other direction moves the plectra away from the strings so that no plucking occurs. Various methods of controlling these registers are employed: manual (hand) stops, knee levers, and pedals, the latter being the most common on modern instruments. Manual levers were generally used for the similar mechanism of the buff stop.

There has been a good deal of confusion and uncertainty regarding the different members of the harpsichord family, particularly with regard to terminology. It is possible here to give only general explanations of what the various terms mean, and one should always exercise caution when dealing with Renaissance or Baroque writings on these instruments. The harpsichord may be regarded as the standard large member of the family, shaped in the wing form characteristic of the modern grand piano but narrower. For the smaller members of the family, two terms are used—"virginal" and "spinet." The virginal is a small oblong or square instrument; the spinet is a small, wing-shaped instrument.

A good deal of discussion has been occasioned by the term "virginal." It has been associated with virginity, with the Virgin Queen, Elizabeth I (but the term is found before her time), with the fact that young ladies often played the instrument (as is testified to in many pictures from the sixteenth and seventeenth centuries), or with *virga*, meaning thorn, that is, jack, in reference to the characteristic plectrum action, as has been argued by Sachs and, after him, Geiringer. There are etymological difficulties with this last, since *virgo-virgalis* (related to rod, thorn, or jack) could not be the same as *virgo–virginalis* (related to virgin). Therefore, one can hold with the earliest reference to an explanation of the instrument, found in the *Tractatus de musica* of Paulirinus of Prague (*c.* 1460): *Virginale dictum quod uti virgo dulcorat mitibus et suavissimis vocibus*; that is to say, they are called virginals because of the soft, sweet, and mild quality of their tone, like the voice of a young lady (see Neupert). This view was later held by Adlung in the eighteenth century. The origin of the term "spinet" is either *spina* (thorn), thus quill or, perhaps, the jack itself, or Giovanni Spinetti, the Venetian instrument builder (*c.* 1500).

There have been many other names used for members of the harpsichord family, e.g., "exaquier," "symphonia," and "buonaccordo," whose meanings are not always immediately clear. Furthermore, in England the word "virginal" was used generically for all members of the harpsichord family. Other types of harpsichord are the smaller instruments with one choir of strings at 4' pitch, called "spinettino" or "octavina," and the upright form of the instrument, called *cembalo verticale* in Italy or, more generally, "clavicyterium."

The harpsichord is generally thought to have derived from the psaltery, a plucked stringed instrument common in the Middle Ages, something on the order of the zither. It was normally in trapezoid form, and the resemblance in shape to a pig's head was not overlooked in various names given the psaltery, the German *Schweinskopf* and the Italian *istromento da porco*. Another name given the psaltery was "cymbalum." The relation of the psaltery to the harpsichord was stated as early as 1511 by Sebastian Virdung in his *Musica getutscht*; he wrote that keys (which, as we have seen, developed in the twelfth and thirteenth centuries in connection with the positive organ) were added to the psaltery, thus producing the harpsichord. The harpsichord, then, may be described as a psaltery with keys, a circumstance that is reflected in the terminology, since "clavis" means key and "cymbalum" means psaltery, the combination being "clavi-cymbalum," or harpsichord. This root is still current in the German and Italian word for the instrument, *cembalo*, as well as in the French *clavecin*. An alternative German designation, *Kielflügel*, makes reference to the plectrum (*Kiel*) action and the wing shape (*Flügel*).

While it is not known when keys were added to the psaltery, we have references to instruments with plectrum action from as early as the fourteenth century and many well-known pictorial representations from the fifteenth century, such as the *Très belles heures* of the Duke Du Berry (1409) and the Weimar *Wunderbuch* of around 1440. Also from the fifteenth century are accounts in musical treatises of which the most detailed is by the Burgundian Henri Arnault de Zwolle (see Le Cerf). It appears that, although the earliest extant harpsichords date only from the sixteenth century, we can conclude that the basic members of the harpsichord family had been developed by the fifteenth century.

In the sixteenth century, the building of harpsichords was centered in Italy, particularly Venice. Prominent builders were Giovanni Antonio Baffo (1523?–1581) and Alessandro Bertoletti, as well as Domenico of Pesaro and the Rossi family who were active in Milan. Sixteenth-century Italian harpsichords existed in both the oblong and in the wing shape with a usual disposition of two 8′ registers or an 8′ and a 4′ register; most had one manual. The oldest extant dated harpsichord of Italian origin was built by Jerome of Bologna (Hieronymous Bononiensis) in 1521 and is now in the Victoria and Albert Museum in London. The authenticity of a spinet built in Perugia ostensibly in 1493 has been questioned.

In the latter part of the sixteenth century, Antwerp became an important center of harpsichord building (see Curtis). The leaders here were several members of the Ruckers family, Hans the Elder (*c.* 1550–*c.* 1625), Hans the Younger, or Jean (Jan) (1578–1643), Andreas (1579–*c.* 1654), Andreas the Younger (1607–1667?), and Christoph (dates not known).[1] Another family of harpsichord builders in Antwerp in the seventeenth century were the Couchets. The Ruckers instruments were made in all sizes and shapes, along with clavichords, spinets, and virginals. Most of their harpsichords had one manual and one or two sets of strings (1 × 8′, 1 × 8′ and 1 × 4′, or 2 × 8′); but a great many had two manuals, the lower with registers at 8′ and 4′ and the upper having one at 8′, with coupling to make all playable from the lower manual. Other features of the Ruckers' instruments included the following: the lower manual was transposing, that is, its strings were tuned a fourth lower (see Marcuse) to facilitate transpositions that players were frequently called upon to perform; the bass range of each manual, which had usually ceased at the F in the second octave below middle C, was extended by the expedient of the "short octave," that is, by adding one note for the C and by adjusting the F♯ and C♯ keys so that they would sound D and E respectively; the bass F♯ and G♯ were not missed, because in the mean-tone temperament of the time they were unsatisfactory as fundamental notes since they were excessively out of tune with their fifths (see Kinsky).

---

[1] See the detailed article "Ruckers," the joint work of A. J. Hipkins, F. W. Galpin, and R. Newton in *GD*, VII (5th ed., 1954), pp. 299-324, with a catalogue of all extant Ruckers instruments by R. Russell; see also Pols.

Many of these Ruckers instruments were lavishly decorated by famous artists (Vermeer, Rubens, and Watteau, to name only a few). Most surviving Ruckers harpsichords had been subjected to later alterations both inside and out so that the original decorations, as well as many features of the original mechanism, have not been preserved. Italian instruments, too, were highly decorated; a most lavish instrument, built in 1577 by the Milanese builder Annibale Rossi, is ornamented with countless jewels.

Another great center of harpsichord building was London. From the sixteenth and seventeenth centuries, literary references exist in abundance, but only a few instruments have actually come down. That there was activity is indirectly demonstrated by the fact that London was the place where the first music for virginal appeared in print—the *Parthenia* of 1612 or 1613. It is clear also that, along with the virginal, the large forms of the harpsichord were known and widely used, as is testified to, for instance, by the title page of a second publication, *Parthenia In-Violata* (c. 1614). Although it seems that most of the instruments built were spinets, there were larger forms as well since Thomas Mace's *Musick's Monument* of 1676 has a reference to pedals on harpsi-chords. Two prominent instrument makers were Charles Haward and John Player.

English harpsichord building came into its own in the eighteenth century when it reached an excellence that made it second to none. The initiative for this development went back to Hermann Tabel (d. 1738), who had worked with the Ruckers firm in Antwerp and then established himself in London in the early years of the century. None of his instruments has been preserved so that for us his influence is felt through the work of his disciples, Burkat Shudi or Tschudi (1702–1773) and Jacob Kirkman (1710–1792). Shudi later was joined by John Broadwood (1732–1812) who became his son-in-law and partner, establishing a firm that is still in existence (see Dale). A characteristic feature of these English harpsichords was the great bulk and solidity of construction, which gave them a considerably more powerful tone than that possessed by other instruments of the time—even those of the Ruckers. The single-manual harpsichords normally had three choirs of strings, two at 8′ and one at 4′, while the two-manual instru-ments used four choirs, two at 8′ and two at 4′. In 1769, Shudi patented the Venetian swell mechanism (see Halfpenny).

Turning to Germany, the period prior to 1700 is characterized by many treatises on harpsichords and harpsichord building, but only some twenty instruments survive to the present time. The following firms may be listed: that of the Hass family in Hamburg, especially the work of Johann Adolf Hass in the middle of the century, who built some very large and elaborate harpsi-chords; the Strassburg firm of the Silbermann family, already mentioned in connection with organ building; the Dresden firm of the Gräbner family; and the Augsburg firm founded by Johann Andreas Stein (1728–1792) who had worked with Silbermann (see Hertz) and was succeeded in business by his son-in-law, Johann Andreas Streicher (1761–1833), who ultimately moved the operation to Vienna.

A famous German harpsichord of the eighteenth century is the so-called *Bach-Flügel* in Berlin. Whether or not this instrument was actually owned by Bach has been disputed, and the latest opinion is inclined to the negative (see Russell and Ernst). In any case, it is an example of the largest and most elaborate type of harpsichord: two manuals, 8′ and 16′ registers on the lower, 8′ with buff stop and 4′ registers on the upper, and coupling. But the point must be made again that such large instruments were not usual in the eighteenth century; the vast majority of harpsichords employed one manual with one, two or three sets of strings (often two at 8′ or one at 8′ and one at 4′), and even the disposition with three sets of strings (two at 8′ and one at 4′) was something unusual. These large instruments, then, were regarded as something extraordinary; the very elaborateness of their resources has caused them to receive much consideration and emphasis in the histories of keyboard instruments, an emphasis that has obscured the fact that quantitatively they were in the distinct minority in the seventeenth and eighteenth centuries.

An important source of French harpsichord making from the seventeenth century is Mersenne's *Harmonie universelle*. But very few French-built harpsichords have come down to us, and Russell conjectures that most instruments used in France were imported from Italy and the Netherlands. Among the French instrument builders from this period are the Denis family of Paris (Jean and Philippe), Nicolas Dumont, and Pampes (of whom little is known). There is more evidence of activity in the eighteenth century, when there occurred an increase in the number of harpsichords with three registers of strings and two manuals. Important builders of the eighteenth century are Jean Marius, who also made a portable harpsichord, the Blanchet family of Paris (especially François Etienne, *c.* 1705–1774?), and their successor, Pascal Taskin (1723–1793), who employed leather for the plectra, and Sébastien Erard (1752–1831).

In Italy, it was the small form that was preferred, and one disposition is by far the most frequent—a single manual with two choirs of strings, both at 8′ pitch (see Shortridge). There are only a few examples of larger harpsichords with two or three manuals, and instruments with pedals were evidently not known there at all.

It may also be mentioned that there was some interest in harpsichords and harpsichord building in the colonial United States. As would be expected, much of this involved the importation of European instruments, especially those made in England. We have, for instance, the correspondence of George Washington in 1793 and Thomas Jefferson in 1786 with harpsichord builders, dealers, and friends, all in connection with Kirkman instruments (reprinted in Russell). Then there are several European-born instrument builders who came to this country and produced harpsichords: Johann Klemm or Clemm (1690–1762), who worked in New York; the Englishman Charles Trute, who was associated with Wiedberg in Philadelphia in the 1790's; and John Harris, who came from England in 1768 and worked in Boston. Finally, we can mention two native American harpsichord builders, Samuel Blythe of Salem (1744–1795) and Francis Hopkinson (1737–1791) of Philadelphia.

In the latter part of the eighteenth century, the piano attracted more and more favorable attention at the expense of the harpsichord. After 1800, harpsichord building gradually came to a complete halt. But sporadic interest in the older instrument continued here and there all during the nineteenth century, with recitals being constantly given in England, for instance, by Moscheles, Salaman, Pauer, Hipkins, Engel, and Bonawitz, and in France by Diémer. Greater interest in harpsichords was aroused by the newly developing studies in musicology, again largely in connection with projects like the *Bach-Gesellschaft*. It came to be realized that it was desirable to perform early music on the instruments for which it was written. The universities played a large role in this through seminars in music history and collegia musica. In 1888, the Parisian firm of Erard and Pleyel commenced the manufacture of harpsichords on a limited scale, and the Pleyel harpsichord, of large dimensions and tonal capabilities, played an important part in the modest re-establishment of the harpsichord in the musical life of the twentieth century. Since then, this movement has grown considerably, and more and more firms began to produce harpsichords (such as Neupert, Dolmetsch, Hubbard, Dowd, Gough, Challis, Sperrhake, Wittmayer, and so forth). This growth has increased sharply since World War II. Contemporary composers have even seen fit to compose music for the harpsichord, and it has become possible for a few concert artists to make careers as harpsichordists (Wanda Landowska, Ralph Kirkpatrick, and Fernando Valenti, to name only a few). Modern technology has even managed to produce an electronic harpsichord.

The Clavichord[1]

The clavichord is mechanically the simplest of the stringed keyboard instruments. We have seen that the harpsichord is descended from the psaltery, a zither-like instrument whose strings were plucked by hand. The clavichord, on the other hand, in its fundamental operation represents an elaboration of the monochord, another instrument prominent in the Middle Ages and used for carrying out acoustic measurements. This was a wooden resonator with a single string that was damped at one end and had a movable bridge, so that the pitch sounded by the string would vary with the distance at which the bridge was

[1] See Neupert, Russell, and Goehlinger.

located from the front of the instrument. There is some indication from medieval sources that the monochord was elaborated by the use of several strings (perhaps as many as nineteen) and thus became a polychord. It is this development that lies immediately back of the clavichord, which, as Russell says, may be regarded as a "set of monochords" operated by means of a keyboard. Depressing the key causes a narrow blade of wood to strike and rest against a string—thus, the term "tangent action." The strings, as in the monochord, are damped at the far end, so that only the length of string between the blade of wood and the wrest plank or pin block sounds. Because of this, it was possible to have two or three adjacent keys arranged to strike the same string, since, in the bass range of the keyboard, notes next to one another would never be played simultaneously; such an instrument was called a fretted or *gebundener* clavichord, and instruments in which each key had its own string, which became more common in the eighteenth century, were called unfretted or *bundfrei*.

EXAMPLE 4

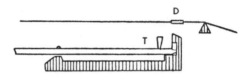

Clavichord action: T. tangent; D. damping.
From F. W. Galpin, *A Textbook of European Musical Instruments.*
Reprinted by permission of Ernest Benn, Ltd., London.

Because of this simple action, the clavichord shows neither the variety of form nor the great changes that characterized the development of the harpsichord or the organ. But also because of this direct action, by virtue of which the player is in intimate contact with the vibrating string, the clavichord has certain features that set it apart from the other stringed keyboard instruments. Chief among these is that the player, by a judicious shifting of the pressure of his finger on the key, can cause the string not only to maintain its vibrations, but can also cause slight variations in its pitch. This effect, known as *Bebung* (tremolo and balancement), is doubtless responsible for the great popularity of the clavichord in late eighteenth-century Germany. Furthermore, the volume of a clavichord's tone may be controlled to some extent by the force with which the keys are struck, so that, in this respect, the instrument bears some resemblance to the piano.

It is not known when the clavichord was invented. But since we know from the history of the organ and the harpsichord that the keyboard apparently became standard in the fourteenth century, it seems reasonable to assume the same for the clavichord. Again, we have a number of descriptions and pictures of the instrument from the fifteenth century, among them the treatises of Henri Arnault de Zwolle and Sebastian Virdung. At all events, the earliest extant clavichords date from the sixteenth century. Although, by and large, all firms engaged in the manufacture of harpsichords also produced clavichords (and this holds true today as well), there was a pronounced concentration on clavichords in Germany, to the extent that some three-quarters of the surviving clavichords were built in Germany; the instrument remained popular there well into the nineteenth century, long after the harpsichord had gone out of fashion.

Forkel states that J. S. Bach favored the clavichord "for study" and "for private musical entertainment" and "for the expression of his most refined thoughts," because of the "variety in the gradation of tone" that "on a small scale [was] very flexible." Bach's son Carl Philipp Emanuel was a great champion of the instrument, and several descriptions of his manner of playing it have come down to us, particularly, those of Charles Burney and Johann Friedrich Reichardt. It would seem that the instrument's very simplicity, smallness, and inexpensiveness played an important role in its popularity.

The Pianoforte[1]

This youngest member of the family of keyboard instruments was, like the harpsichord and clavichord, also descended from an instrument used in medieval Europe, the dulcimer; but the development did not take place until the eighteenth century. The dulcimer was roughly similar to the psaltery but was played with blunt clobbers with which the strings were quite literally struck. In a piano, then, the tone is produced by hammers striking against the strings—thus, the term "hammer action." The piano is unique among keyboard instruments in that the volume of tone produced depends entirely on the force with which the hammer strikes the strings and, thus, on the force with which the player strikes the keys; dynamics are a function of touch. This is the significance of the designation "pianoforte" (or "fortepiano," a term used in the eighteenth century), the instrument which readily plays either loudly or softly.

While from the Renaissance and Baroque periods there have come down isolated references to keyboard instruments using some sort of hammer action (Henri Arnault de Zwolle mentions keyboard instruments with *ictus* and Kircher in 1673 speaks of a similar instrument with *marculi*), the earliest concrete evidence of the existence of these instruments comes from the first decades of the eighteenth century. The invention of a viable hammer action and the construction of instruments based on this is credited to the Italian harpsichord builder Bartolomeo Cristofori (1655–1731) in 1709; his method was thoroughly described in 1711 by Scipione Maffei (his instrument was called a *gravicembalo col*

[1] See Harding, Closson, Rimbault, Paul, Schlesinger, Dodge, and Loesser (popular).

piano e forte), and two instruments built by him have survived. At about the same time, a German, Christoph Gottlieb Schröter (1699–1782), also worked out a hammer action, citing as his inspiration Pantaleon Hebenstreit (1669–1750) who had made a reputation for his performances on an elaborate type of dulcimer. And, in 1716, the Parisian harpsichord builder Jean Marius reported on a *clavecin à mallets*. It will be noted that in the eighteenth century the piano was built and developed by firms normally engaged in the manufacture of harpsichords.

The hammer action was—and is—a complicated mechanism with a great many component parts; the proper activation and return of the hammer, so that it is instantly ready to go again with a minimum effort needed in depressing the key and the damping, all require many parts. It is perhaps somewhat paradoxical that the stringed keyboard instrument in which the player's touch has the most control over the quality and loudness of the tone is at the same time the one in which the mechanism is the most involved, in which the player's finger is, as it were, the farthest removed from the vibrating string.

A most important element in the hammer action is the escapement, a means of allowing the hammer to fall back into its normal rest position ready for operation even though the release of the key may not have been completed; this feature is necessary for the rapid repetition of the same note. Cristofori had surmounted this difficulty in a clever fashion. Instead of having but one hammer between the key and the string, he used two, one of which was hit by the key lever which, in turn, impelled the other against the string; but, upon striking the second hammer, the hammer (called the hopper, or, in Cristofori's terminology, *linguetta mobile*) immediately fell back into its normal rest position; in other words, it escaped so that the second hammer was free to do the same regardless of whether or not the key was still depressed. But this mechanism had the drawback of being excessively bulky, so that, on many instruments of the eighteenth century, no escapement was used at all. Cristofori also employed a check, a means of securing the hammer once it fell back to rest position to keep it from rebounding and hitting the string an unwanted second time. Cristofori's work was not immediately influential, and it was not until later that it was taken up again and developed.

Much of the eighteenth-century development of the piano took place in Germany where some important builders were Gottfried Silbermann and Johann Andreas Stein, both of whom were prominent in the construction of harpsichords and clavichords as well. After much experimentation, Silbermann adopted something very much like Cristofori's action. There were two principles followed in these German instruments, which, in the tradition of the clavichord, were small and square. In one, the hammer was either mounted on or else directly connected to the key (the so-called *Prellmechanik*); in the other, it was detached from the key, and the two were mechanically connected by a hopper (the so-called *Stossmechanik*). The latter, as we have seen, had been employed by Cristofori. In the former, the hammer is mounted on a pivot on a fork on the key itself, its rear end under an overhanging edge at the back of the interior of the instrument; when the key is depressed, this overhanging edge trips the back of the hammer causing its front to rise quickly and strike the string forcibly. In the second type, each hammer is attached to a pivot mounted on a rail that runs along the back of the instrument, and the back part of the key strikes either the base of the rear of the hammer or a rod or pusher (the jack or hopper) which, in turn, causes the hammer to rise quickly and strike the string. Both types were eventually provided with escapements; in the case of the former (*Prellmechanik*), this was effected by a jointed bar at the back end of the hammer, while, in the latter (*Stossmechanik*), it was accomplished by a notch on the underside of the hammer into which the hopper or jack slid when the hammer rebounded from the strings,

EXAMPLE 5

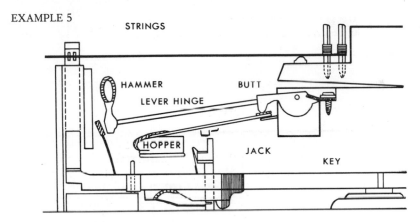

Cristofori's piano action.
From the *Encyclopaedia Britannica* (1962). Reproduced by permission.

and a spring forced the hopper or jack back into its original position once the action was completed. Escapements were a particular feature of pianos built by Stein, whose instruments were highly praised by Mozart on this account. In the 1790's, the Stein firm moved to Vienna, Stein's daughter having married Johann Andreas Streicher in 1793; their pianos became renowned for the lightness, delicacy, and transparency of their tone. Since their instruments generally employed a *Prellmechanik* with escapement, this combination came to be known as the German or Viennese action. Following the practice in harpsichords, these pianos were provided with a few characteristic coloristic stops: a harp stop (like the buff stop on harpsichords), a swell, a stop to lift the dampers (the so-called "forte" or "loud" stop), a bassoon stop (heavy paper laid over the string to produce a rustling sound), and Turkish music (tambourine and cymbals that beat against the sound board).

Besides Germany, the most important center for the building of pianos in the eighteenth century was London, especially after 1760 when a number of German instrument makers moved there. Johann Christian Bach gave the first public recital on the new instrument in London on June 2, 1768. As in harpsichord building, the Shudi-Broadwood firm was the most important, producing pianos from 1773. These early Shudi-Broadwood instruments followed the designs of

EXAMPLE 6

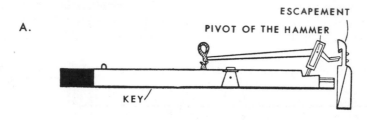

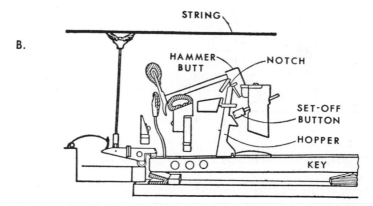

A. Stein's Viennese action. B. Broadwood's English action.
From the *Encyclopaedia Britannica* (1962). Reproduced by permission.

Johann Christian Zumpe, who popularized the square piano employing a single action (that is, one without an escapement). But, after 1781, the Broadwood firm came out with a different type of piano that was to prove most influential. Its characteristic was a double-action *Stossmechanik* (with escapement) the so-called "English action," and this made possible a heavier instrument with a much stronger tone. It is noteworthy and characteristic that while Mozart praised the Stein piano for its lightness and delicacy (see Brunner and Broder), Beethoven came to prefer the Broadwood piano, a much larger and more powerful instrument. Unlike the Stein-Streicher pianos, these Broadwood instruments did not employ coloristic stops beyond what was to become standard—the pedal raising the dampers and the *una corda* pedal.

Further changes were made throughout the nineteenth century. For the most part, these involved increasing the instrument's power by the use of heavier strings and strengthening the case and frame. Although metal had been used to brace the piano frame as early as 1777 by the Erard firm in Paris, as well as later by Broadwood, the step to a full single cast metal frame was the accomplishment of an American, Alphaeus Babcock of Philadelphia in 1825; but it went into general use only in the second half of the century. The firm of Erard likewise developed in 1821 a double escapement that was even more effective than what had been in use and that gave the player much greater ease in repetition, the rapid reiteration of the same note. A decisive improvement of the quality and power of the piano's tone was produced by cross-stringing. Instead of having all the strings running parallel to one another, they are arranged in two layers with the treble strings in a fan underneath and the bass strings on top; this not only allowed more strings to be over the highly resonant central portion of the sound board, but also, by bringing the treble and bass strings close together, facilitated the production of partial tones, thus making a far richer sound quality. Although this had been used by Pape in Paris as early as 1828 and by Babcock in 1830, it did not come into general use until the latter part of the century. The combination of cross-stringing and the full metal frame along with consistently high standards of workmanship was what distinguished the products of the Steinway firm, founded by Heinrich Engelhard Steinweg (1797–1871) who came from Braunschweig to New York in 1849. One other feature of Steinway pianos since 1874 has been the sostenuto pedal by means of which it is possible to catch and hold up the dampers for the notes of a chord that has been struck and sustain them against subsequent notes or chords whose sounds are damped in the usual way. Thus, the modern form of the piano was attained.

As with the harpsichord, many other forms of the piano developed, most of which were adaptations to make the instrument more suitable for use in the home. Most important are the various kinds of upright pianos, which have been in existence since the early nineteenth century and which generally have been manufactured by the same firms that made the larger grand pianos.

By way of conclusion, reference may be made to some of the more unusual types of keyboard instruments that have been devised from time to time. We have already pointed out that the family tie among keyboard instruments is not based on how the tone is produced, but rather on a common way of causing the tone to be produced—the keyboard. This very situation has given rise to numerous attempts to combine not only the various kinds of keyboard instruments, but also different methods of tone production into one and the same instrument. A few of these attempts do not venture very far afield since they represent an effort to make the harpsichord sound like a lute, thus retaining plucked strings as the means of tone production. Examples of this from the eighteenth century are Fleischer's *Theorbenflügel* and *Lautenclavecin* and Hildebrand's *Lautenklavizymbel* (*c.* 1740), which was known to J. S. Bach.

But other attempts were far more adventurous. The oldest is the idea of providing a harpsichord with one or more ranks of organ pipes, thus creating what was generally called "claviorganum." This had been known in some form or other since the fifteenth century, since it is described in the treatise of Paulirinus of Prague, and it is also discussed by Praetorius. It happens that the oldest extant example of English harpsichord building is such an instrument, built in 1579 by an emigrated Netherlander, Ludwick Theeuwes. From the eighteenth century, Kirkman harpsichords were also equipped on occasion with ranks of organ pipes. From the later eighteenth century, when the vogue of the piano was commencing, there were attempts to combine the hammer action of the piano with the plectrum action of the harpsichord in the work of two of the foremost instrument builders of the time, Stein of Augsburg and Erard of Paris. Going one step further, there was even an instrument that combined the hammer action and plectrum action with the tangent action of the clavichord—the *Tangentenflügel* built by the Regensburg firm of Späth and Schmahl.

Very often, attempts were made to overcome the inability of the harpsichord to sustain tone, which was felt at times to be a serious deficiency of the instrument. To do this, stringed keyboard instruments were produced with some sort of bowing mechanism—either rotating wheels that were pressed against the strings after the manner of the hurdy-gurdy or some sort of endless rotating belt of horsehair that could be brought into contact with the strings. Although such an instrument is mentioned by Leonardo da Vinci, the earliest extant example dates from the seventeenth century—Hans Hayden's *Nürmbergisch Geigen-werck* of 1610, which was described by Praetorius (see Kinsky). Other examples from the eighteenth century may be mentioned: Cuisinier's *clavecinevielle*, Gleichmann's *Klaviergambe* of 1709, and Hohlfeld's *Bogenflügel* of 1754. More unusual and somewhat different is Schnell's *anémocorde* of 1789 in which a bellows forces air against the strings causing them to vibrate, thus incorporating the old principle of the Aeolian harp; a similar instrument is Herz's *Piano éolien* of 1851.

The existence of such instruments provided the basis and indeed the impetus for even more grandiose endeavors, since it made it possible, at least, for one to envision a sort of "universal" instrument that incorporated within it all manners of tone production and was capable of imitating, to some degree, all other instruments, string and wind alike. The combination of strings (both plucked and bowed) with ranks of organ pipes in a keyboard instrument appears first in the *Denis d'or* built by the Bohemian Procopius Diviss (1696–1765) in 1730, a large instrument with some 130 different registers. Other such instruments are Plenius' *lyrichord* of 1742 and, on a lesser scale, Virbès' *clavecine harmonieuse et celeste*.

Of a quite different order are experimentations with varying the organization of the keyboard itself and using additional strings so that different ways of tuning and different types of temperament become possible, particularly so that microtones could be accurately produced. An important experiment of this type took place in sixteenth-century Italy in the work of Nicola Vicentino (1511–1572), who, in his preoccupation with the study of the Greek scale system, devised a harpsichord capable of realizing the chromatic and enharmonic genera along with the more usual diatonic genus. Other such instruments are Vito Trasuntino's *archicembalo* and the *clavicymbalum universale* described by Praetorius, both from the seventeenth century.

CHAPTER TWO

Keyboard Music to the End of the Sixteenth Century[1]

One of the most difficult questions that arises in connection with medieval and Renaissance music concerns performance practice. How was the music played, and what sonorities were employed? Here, we can limit ourselves to the use of keyboard instruments or, for practical purposes in this period, to the use of the organ. The manuscript sources do not clearly indicate media, a circumstance that caused at least one scholar, Arnold Schering, to attempt the admittedly difficult task of establishing *a priori* criteria for music to be played on instruments, as opposed to vocal music. Factors such as extreme range, lack of text, unusual intervals, extensive figuration with repeated sequential rhythmic patterns, and so forth, were adduced, but, on closer examination and comparison with the general repertory of medieval and Renaissance music as it has come down to us, they are not conclusive.

Two things must be kept distinct. The first is the use of monophonic instruments in the rendition of a polyphonic ensemble composition, and the other has to do with a polyphonic composition intended for performance on a solo keyboard instrument. These are almost completely mutually exclusive. This fundamental difference is expressed in the form of notation employed for the composition (see especially Apel). In the first case, we will have to do with compositions notated in choir-book format, i.e., each part is written separately, and they are then distributed about the page. For instance, the triplum (the uppermost part) might run down the left-hand side, the motetus (the middle part) down the left, with the tenor (lowest part) across the bottom, so that we have a form of part notation. In the second case, we find compositions notated in tablature, a specifically instrumental notation in score format. It differs from the normal mensural notation of the time in that it employs letters and numerals. Of the two types of tablature notation in most common use up through the seventeenth

---

[1] See, generally, the recent extensive discussion by Young; an earlier account is by Bedbrook.

and into the eighteenth centuries, the German either combines letters (used for the upper parts) with the normal signs of mensural notation (used in the lower parts) or else uses exclusively letters, while the Spanish operates entirely with numerals that designate diatonic steps of the scale. Tablature notation of this type does not appear in French and Italian keyboard music, both of which employ the normal mensural notation arranged in score format. This appears in one of two forms: either in something like our piano score, where the music is notated on two staves (known in Italy as *intavolatura*), or in what we call open score, where each voice is notated on its own staff (known in Italy as *di partitura*).

The style of notation, therefore, clearly indicates which of the two types is involved in a particular composition. Should a keyboard instrument be used in the performance of a work notated in choirbook format, it would in all probability be a portative organ (or organetto) that could take over one of the parts, as would a vielle, a flute, or even a singer for that matter. There are some indications that organs were used to accompany polyphonic ensemble compositions in which the organ is played polyphonically itself, and this would call for a positive organ since the portative organ is a monophonic instrument. In any event, this option is not expressed in the notation. Only those pieces that appear in tablature or in some sort of score format, therefore, are keyboard compositions in the usual sense of the word: polyphonic music to be played by a keyboard instrument.

Once we have decided that a certain work is for a keyboard instrument, the question arises, Which keyboard instrument is to be employed? This is a difficult question to answer. While a classification between sacred and secular music and the corresponding use of the organ for the former and the harpsichord or clavichord for the latter would hold in a general way, there are numerous and important exceptions. Chief among these is the portative organ, frequently used in secular performances. On the basis of musical style, again nothing definite can be stated. Hence, most of the keyboard music of the Middle Ages must be regarded as for keyboard instruments in general, equally suited for organ, harpsichord, or clavichord or, at least, with no specific stylistic traits that would associate it with one or another. This, in a general way, holds true for much keyboard music composed up to and even into the eighteenth century, as J. S. Bach's *Well-Tempered Clavier* eloquently demonstrates. At the same time, however, from the sixteenth century on, we will meet here and there with compositions that are specifically intended for a particular instrument.

It can be assumed, however, that the organ was employed in the performance of strictly liturgical music. There are several reports of the use of an organ during services in the fourteenth century and many others from later periods (see Rietschel and Gombosi), and its use even earlier is indicated by the opposition to the organ voiced by Thomas Aquinas in the thirteenth century. Three main uses of the organ in the liturgical music of the Middle Ages have been established: providing instrumental preludes, accompanying the choir, and performing in alternation with the choir. The first and last of these involve full-scale improvisation and possibly composition in our sense of the term. We shall see that these do indeed provide the main types of early keyboard music.

For the present, therefore, we can limit ourselves to a consideration of music for keyboard instruments in general as it has been handed down in some form of instrumental notation, either tablature or some type of score. We find only a few such sources from the fourteenth century but more from the fifteenth and sixteenth centuries. From then on, the material accumulates rapidly and in bulk.

In the fourteenth century, as has been seen, there occurred important developments in the history of keyboard instruments—the first diatonic keyboard with chromatic half steps and the invention of the harpsichord. To these, one more may be added—the first works written for keyboard instruments in tablature notation (see Wolf). There are three such sources that transmit music of this kind:

The Robertsbridge Codex (Ms., London, British Museum, Add. 28550)

The Reina Codex (Ms., Paris, Bibliothèque nationale, nouv. acq. 6771)

The Faenza Codex (Ms., Biblioteca Communaria 177).

The Robertsbridge manuscript is the earliest. It is a fragment containing six works on two leaves, of which the first and last are incomplete and the provenience of which is not known. The type of notation employed, using mensural note forms for the upper part and letters for the lower, is like that used in German keyboard tablatures of the fifteenth and sixteenth centuries, a circumstance which has led Apel, in his history of notation, to describe it as an example of German tablature notation. On the other hand, the mensural notation that appears in the upper part is clearly related to Italian *trecento* (fourteenth century) notation, so that the qualification "German" here is somewhat misleading.

The content of the Robertsbridge manuscript, however, has nothing to do with either German or Italian music. The manuscript contains three *estampies* and three transcriptions, two of motets from the *Roman de Fauvel* (*Adesto*— *Firmissime*—*Alleluya Benedictus*, and *Quoniam secta*—*Tribum quem*—*Merito*), and an incomplete work, apparently a hymn, *Flos vernalis*. While the *estampies* are for two voices, the transcriptions accurately reflect their models except that some ornamentation has been added. Stylistically, we notice a strange contrast between the transcribed motets and the dances; the former are examples of a new large form of composition, the isorhythmic motet, and the latter are dances showing a curiously archaic and primitive style with many progressions involving simple parallel fifths and octaves (*HAM*, I, 58, excerpts only). Right at the very beginning of keyboard music, therefore, we run into features that are characteristic of it and that remain so for some time: on the one hand, the emphasis on intavolaturas and, on the other, a curious anachronism of style in music written directly for the keyboard instrument. We will constantly be running into these features.

The next source for keyboard (organ) music in the fourteenth century is the famous Reina manuscript (see the general study of the manuscript by Fischer). This is an important source of French and Italian secular music from the very late fourteenth and early fifteenth centuries containing mainly polyphonic ensemble compositions. Among them are two keyboard pieces notated in tablature: a transcription of the ballata *Questa fanciulla* of Landini and a textless fragment that is thought to be another transcription of a ballata as yet unidentified.

Far more comprehensive and, for this reason, more important is the third manuscript, the Faenza Codex, the true significance of which has not been appreciated until rather recently through the work of Carapetyan, Plamenac, and Pirrotta. It dates from the fifteenth century but contains a large body of keyboard music from the fourteenth century, and is notated in score format employing the usual forms of mensural notation. More than half of the manuscript is occupied with these keyboard compositions, most of which are intavolaturas, organ transcriptions of polyphonic ensemble works, by French and Italian composers of the fourteenth century. Sixteen of these are anonymous; among the composers named, we find Jacopo da Bologna, Francesco Landini, Bartolino

EXAMPLE 7

Robertsbridge manuscript: *Estampie*—beginning

da Padova (three works each), and Guillaume de Machaut (two works). As an example of what is involved in the processes of intavolatura, one can refer to Landini's *Non aura pieta*, since both the original and the keyboard arrangement are readily available (see Fischer, *Variation*, p. 12). Among the cantus firmus settings is an anonymous Kyrie based on the plainsong *Kyrie Cunctipotens genitor*; the Gregorian melody appears in the lower part in relatively long notes, while the upper part engaged in figuration (*TEM*, 15).

In looking over these three sources, it seems apparent that Italy played a larger role in the development of keyboard music than is generally realized. All three manuscripts have Italian associations, especially in regard to provenience and repertory. In this connection, it is well to remember that the earliest extant harpsichords were built in Italy. Italy continued to be prominent in keyboard music, particularly in the sixteenth and seventeenth centuries.

From late fourteenth century England comes a single piece preserved almost by accident; it appears in a manuscript that had been used to bind a collection of sermons. It is a *Felix namque* in a manuscript at the Bodleian Library of Oxford University (Ms. Douce 381). Like some pieces contained in the Faenza manuscript, this is a setting based on Gregorian chant, the offertory for Saturdays in honor of the Blessed Virgin Mary, that appears in long notes as the lower part; over it move the upper parts in a rhythm suggestive of the old modal patterns

EXAMPLE 8

FAENZA MANUSCRIPT: Kyrie—beginning

Kyrie

of the thirteenth century (see Dart). This piece, therefore, is yet another indication of a certain primitive quality in early written keyboard music.

While sources for keyboard music are more numerous in the fifteenth century than they are in the fourteenth, their number still remains far from impressive. The scene clearly shifts from Italy to Germany, where we find four main sources (general accounts are Young, Apel, and Rokseth, along with Schrade and Feldmann):

> Tablature from a Dominican monastery in Breslau (Ms. Breslau, Staatsbibliothek I F 687)
>
> Tablature of Adam Ileborgh of Stendhal, 1448 (Ms., Philadelphia, Curtis Institute of Music)
>
> Conrad Paumann, *Fundamentum organisandi*, 1452 (Ms., Berlin, Staatsbibliothek 40613; bound with the *Lochaymer Liederbuch*)
>
> *Buxheim Organ Book, c.* 1460 (Ms., Munich, Staatsbibliothek Cim. 352b).

Along with these main sources go a number of smaller manuscripts, some discovered only recently (see Göllner), that are either fragments or else contain very few musical compositions. These comprise manuscripts in Breslau (Staatsbibliothek, Ms. I Qu 42, and I Qu 438), Vienna (Nationalbibliothek Codex 3617), Munich (Staatsbibliothek, Codices lat. 7775 and 5963), Berlin (Staatsbibliothek theol. quart. 290), Hamburg (Staatsbibliothek ND VI 3225), and Erlangen (Universitätsbibliothek 554); the Breslau manuscript I Qu 438 is known as the Sagan manuscript (from a monastery in Silesia), while the Berlin manuscript is known as the tablature of Ludolf Wilkin, presumably of Windesheim.

Five of these sources are treatises, instruction manuals on organ playing, that contain musical compositions largely as illustrative material; such are Paumann's well-known *Fundamentum organisandi*, the Hamburg manuscript, which contains a *Fundamentum* by Wolfgang de Nova Domo (or Neuhaus) along with examples of standard figures of ornamentation, the Munich manuscript 7775, and the two Breslau manuscripts. Two other manuscripts contain music incidentally—one is tempted to say, accidentally; the Wilkin tablature is primarily a collection of sermons, while the Munich manuscript 5963 is a collection of treatises on various subjects. There are only two that emerge as *bona fide* collections of keyboard music—Ileborgh's tablature and the *Buxheim Organ Book*. The Sagan and Erlangen manuscripts each contain but one piece. It might be mentioned that the Ileborgh tablature and a Breslau manuscript (I F Qu 42) contain the earliest music specifically calling for pedals.

While we know but little concerning the lives of Wilkin, Ileborgh, and Wolfgang de Nova Domo, Conrad Paumann (*c.* 1410–1473) clearly was a figure of international importance at the time. The seat of activity of this blind organist was the St. Sebaldus Cathedral in Nürnberg; later in his life, he was active in

Munich. Many heard him play, and his reputation extended to Italy and France. His treatise is among the earliest devoted to organ playing. The names of other musicians appear from time to time in these manuscripts. But it must be remembered that many works preserved here are intavolaturas of pieces by well-known composers (Dufay, Dunstable, Legrant, and Frye, among others) whose names are sometimes given but more often not. Occasionally, other names appear whose identities are not always certain, and one cannot always determine whether they are the composers of works that have been arranged for keyboard or whether they are in fact real composers of music for keyboard instruments; among these are Georg de Putenheim (appearing in Paumann and the *Buxheim Organ Book*), Götz (in *Buxheim*), and Paumgarten or Boumgarten (in Paumann and in *Buxheim*), while the Breslau manscript I F 687 mentions Leohardi and Petri.

The repertory of music presented in these German keyboard tablatures represents a considerable expansion over what we found in the fourteenth century. There, we had a mere handful of compositions, while here there is much more. We will see that some of the musical types are preserved and maintained, while others appear for the first time. In general, three types can be distinguished: the intavolaturas, the cantus firmus settings of sacred and of secular melodies, and, finally, the preludes. We will consider each of these briefly.

The intavolaturas of sacred as well as secular compositions still form the bulk of the repertory. We find a good many examples of motets, rondeaus, virelais, and ballades arranged for keyboard instruments. A leading source here is the *Buxheim Organ Book* (see Eitner, Schnoor, Booth, Lord, and Southern), the vast majority of whose 258 works are keyboard transcriptions of pieces by leading composers of the time—John Dunstable, Giles Binchois, Walter Frye, Guillaume Dufay, and others. This tradition plainly has been carried on from the fourteenth century. It may, however, be questioned whether such pieces can properly be regarded as keyboard music. While it is certainly true that certain kinds of alterations, generally involving ornamentation, are frequently made, the fact remains that such works were not originally keyboard pieces. We will see later that this arranging of polyphonic ensemble works for keyboard gives rise to original and independent forms of keyboard music.

Turning now to the second group of compositions, the cantus firmus settings based on plainsong, we find that the procedure followed is much the same as we have seen and thus closely resembles what was followed in the motet of the time. The cantus firmus melody generally appears in the lower part, usually in rather long note values, as a tenor, while the upper part or parts move in smaller note values and frequently engage in figuration. These works in principle have a distinct resemblance to the organum compositions of the twelfth and thirteenth centuries upon which they were modeled, as has been made clear in several studies by Schrade. Even the terms "organum" and "clausula" appear in German manuscripts associated with these compositions.

Prominent among these liturgical cantus firmus settings are individual move-
ments from the Ordinary of the Mass (see Siebert) and settings of the Magnificat.
Mass movements appear in the Sagan manuscript, the Wilkin tablature, and the
Buxheim Organ Book. A characteristic feature of these works is their sectional
form. The Sagan Codex contains parts of an organ Gloria in three sections—
Et in terra, Benedicimus te, and *Glorificamus te;* the rest is not preserved. The
Wilkin tablature also presents a Sanctus, also in three sections—*Sanctus,*
Dominus deus, and *In excelsis*—along with a fragmentary Credo that is also
sectional. An important feature is that not all of the Gregorian chant melody is
set for the organ; those sections not polyphonically elaborated for organ were to
be sung, presumably in unison, by the chorus. For instance, in the Gloria of the
Wilkin tablature, the full order in performance would be as follows: *Gloria in*
excelsis Deo (chorus, plainsong), *Et in terra* (organ, polyphony), *Laudamus te*
(chorus, plainsong), *Benedicimus te* (organ, polyphony), *Adoramus te* (chorus,
plainsong), and *Glorificamus te* (organ, polyphony); the rest of the work is not
extant. This procedure applies generally to such strict liturgical compositions for
organ and is often referred to as "alternatim practice," a term introduced by
Schering (see also Gombosi). A few organ Magnificats also show the same procedure; one example contained in Conrad Paumann's *Fundamentum organisandi*
is readily available for study (*Magnificat sexti toni,* in Fischer, *Variation,* p. 13).
Similar works appear in the Vienna and Hamburg manuscripts.

In the case of the secular cantus firmus settings, the procedure is much the
same. The result, however, is rather different, for the secular song melodies, unlike the plainsong melodies, have their own rhythms, so that the archaic quality
is not quite so evident. Most of the settings transmitted in these manuscripts are
of German songs, so that the keyboard version is principally the same as a polyphonic German *Tenorlied;* the song melody as cantus firmus appears in the middle,
and two contrapuntal accompanying parts are added to it, usually one above and
the other below; sometimes, the cantus firmus is the lowest part (see Schrammek).
Works such as these appear in most of the manuscripts. The best known among
them appears following Paumann's *Fundamentum organisandi,* the song *Mit*
gancʒem Willen wünsch ich dir (*HAM,* I, 81; also *HMS,* III, s. 4, b. 4). It is three-
voice composition; the song melody is the lowest part, the florid upper part
clearly attracts the most attention, and the middle part acts as a mere accompanying
voice. Another such work is also in Paumann's treatise, the song *Elend, du hast*
umfangen mich (*GMB,* 48).

Thus far, all the types of keyboard music discussed are closely related to
polyphonic ensemble forms, either as direct transcriptions (intavolaturas) of
motets, ballades, and the like, or as strict cantus firmus forms in which the
principle of composition is analogous to that used in ensemble polyphony.
It remained for the fifteenth century to introduce the first type of idiomatic keyboard music conceived without reference to pre-existent forms and in terms of

the keyboard medium. This is the prelude, or praeambulum (see Hibberd). The first examples appear in the Ileborgh tablature, whose title states, "Here begin preludes in various modes [keys] written in the modern style skillfully and carefully compiled with various *mensurae* added by Brother Adam Ileborgh. . . ."[1] The qualification "modern style" (*modernum modum*) refers to the use of all the meters commonly employed in the polyphony of the time. The use of meters, however, is more important for the three *mensurae*, which are all settings of a German song (*Frowe all myn hoffen*) than for the preludes, which exhibit "free rhythm," not strictly metrical at all. In some respects, these pieces resemble the liturgical cantus firmus compositions; we notice the lower part often proceeding in long held notes, the upper moving rapidly in scale patterns. But there is a critical difference: there is no cantus firmus used here. Furthermore, the figuration patterns in the upper voice, as well as the high degree of metric freedom, are not paralleled in the liturgical cantus firmus settings (see *HAM*, I, 84 and 84b). Another feature of these Ileborgh preludes is that they are transposable and can be used in various keys. This, along with the designation *praeludia*, indicates the purpose of these pieces: they are intended to introduce a polyphonic ensemble

[1] *Incipiunt praeludia diversarum notarum secundum modernum modum subtiliter et diligenter collectae cum mensuris diversis hic inferius annexis per fratrem Adam Ileborgh. . . .*

EXAMPLE 9

Iʟᴇʙᴏʀɢʜ: *Prelude* in C—complete

work to be performed during the service, a motet or part of a Mass. Such introductory pieces were generally improvised by the organist, and it is to this fact
that the unusually free meters are to be attributed. This improvisational quality
likewise marks the preludes—to some extent, at least—as the earliest idiomatic
keyboard compositions that have come down to us.

Similar preludes appear in Paumann's *Fundamentum organisandi*, the
Buxheim Organ Book (some of Paumann's, in fact, are included in the *Buxheim*
manuscript along with others), and the Hamburg and Erlangen manuscripts. In
Paumann and *Buxheim*, while the rhythmic freedom found in Ileborgh is not
preserved, the form itself is expanded. Two types of writing make their appearance. The first is like that which has been described, a slow-moving lower part
with a rapid and figured upper part; the other is chordal or, in the parlance of the
time, *nota contra notam*—all parts move simultaneously in equal note values.
(The parallel between this and the Notre Dame organum, with its alternation
between sustained-tone and melismatic style, on the one hand, and the *clausulae*
in *discantus* style, on the other, may be noted, although here of course, we are
not dealing with a cantus firmus form.) These two types, then, alternate with
each other. Nothing of the improvisational quality has been lost (*HAM*, I,
84c and 84d).

A feature of this music that strikes one immediately is its curiously archaic
quality. This is particularly evident when one recalls that this is the period of
Dufay, Binchois, Ockeghem, Obrecht, and even early Josquin des Prez, to
name only the leaders. Yet, these keyboard compositions show but little of this
quality; indeed, they might even seem almost primitive by comparison. There are
several possible explanations. One might involve a conscious attempt to maintain
the old Notre Dame organum, particularly in the liturgical cantus firmus settings.
Another would have to do with the rather peripheral nature of these sources.
But then another question can be raised. Why are there so few examples of keyboard music from this period that otherwise is quite rich in music manuscripts?
The answer to this, doubtless, is the fact, already mentioned, that, at the time, most
keyboard music was improvised. The practice of improvisation clearly lies back
of the preludes; it also lies back of the cantus firmus settings. A basic element
associated with composition in the period is the task of improvising a part or
parts to a given cantus firmus, as we know from many examples the most famous
of which is the account of the teaching methods of Josquin by the sixteenth-
century theorist and composer Adrian Petit Coclico. That it is also basic in keyboard composition may be seen from the treatise of Conrad Paumann, which
teaches an organist to do exactly the same thing. This explains why so few organ
compositions were written down. And, from the other side, it may be pointed
out that the bulk of the keyboard compositions that are written down are those
that do not arise directly from improvisation at all—the transcriptions of
polyphonic ensemble works for keyboard.

Speaking in the most general terms, a striking fact concerning the small body of keyboard music that has been preserved from before the sixteenth century is its geographical localization; it is limited largely to Italy in the fourteenth century and to Germany in the fifteenth. With the coming of the sixteenth century, however, the situation changes, and we are confronted with keyboard music in all the major countries of Europe. Many of the traditional types are maintained, and new forms and types develop from them. Our procedure will be to present the complex of sixteenth-century keyboard music country by country—Germany, Italy, France, Spain, England, and The Netherlands, in that order. In this way, many relationships will be come clear that otherwise might be obscured in the mass of musical compositions. (See, generally, Wasielewski, Kinkeldey, and Rokseth.)

The first figure of significance in sixteenth-century Germany is another blind organist and theorist, Arnolt Schlick (*c.* 1455–*c.* 1525) of Heidelberg. His famous treatise *Spiegel der Orgelmacher und Organisten* has already been mentioned (see p. 9), but there remains his large collection *Tabulaturen etlicher Lobgesang und Lidlein auff die Orgel und Lauten ʒu spielen* published by Peter Schöffer in Mainz in 1512, the first collection of keyboard music to appear in print. (The first keyboard music to be printed was an illustrative example in Virdung's treatise, *Musica getutscht*, 1511.) This collection consists of fourteen organ compositions as well as twelve lute songs and three lute pieces. The notation is in German tablature with the normal forms of mensural notation used for the upper part. These organ works are mostly cantus firmus settings based on plainsongs and show, in the main, the features already noted. A famous example from this collection is the *Salve regina* (*HAM*, I, 100) in which the famous Marian antiphon melody appears in the tenor part in the usual long extended notes accompanied by three other parts. There is considerable parallel motion in thirds and sixths, a common feature in fifteenth-century music, but the upper part is elaborately figured and attracts attention as the leading voice. Except for this last feature, the work is very much like a cantus firmus motet of the fifteenth century. Other works in the collection include a *Benedictus*, a *Christe*, an *Ad te clamavi*, an *O dulcis Maria*, and three settings of *Da pacem*. Ten other such works by Schlick, composed for the coronation of Charles V, have recently been discovered and published (see Kastner).

Schlick's *Tabulaturen* is also noteworthy for settings based on song melodies with vernacular German texts. His best known and often performed work of this type is *Maria ʒart von edler Art* (*HAM*, I, 101), a religious song. Following the procedure current in the fifteenth-century cantilena (or ballade) motet, this is a three-voice composition with the cantus firmus placed in the upper part rather than in the tenor or bass, and, as is also customary from vocal music, the borrowed melody is greatly embellished. Here and elsewhere, we can observe that Schlick is more elaborate in the treatment of the accompanying parts than the composers previously discussed. This new elaboration is polyphonic in nature and chiefly has to do with an approach to imitative counterpoint that was developing in the ensemble polyphony of the time. Schlick's compositions abound in scattered references of an imitative nature, but nothing systematic is presented. One of his more noteworthy efforts in this direction is represented by *O dulcis Maria.*

Another German musician to attain international significance was the Swiss organist Paul Hofhaimer (1459–1537); he was principally connected with the Hapsburg court and had associations with leading composers of the time, among them Heinrich Isaak, Heinrich Finck, and Ludwig Senfl (see Moser and Fuhrmann). The few works of his that have come down ill accord with his great reputation, a situation that lends support to the contention that, at the time, improvisation was given precedence over actual composition, at least as far as keyboard music was concerned. Readily available is a piece called simply *Carmen* (meaning "song") preserved in a Polish keyboard tablature; it is a short imitative composition in which the upper part is greatly ornamented (see Kahl, *Character Piece*, 4). Other works include an intavolatura of Barbireau's chanson *Een vroylic wesen* and two liturgical cantus firmus compositions, a *Recordare* and a *Salve regina* (see Moser, *Frühmeister der deutschen Orgelkunst*, pp. 9, 16, and 48).

Other composers of organ music in early sixteenth-century Germany are the following:

Hans Buchner (1483–1538)

Hans Kotter (*c.* 1485–1541)

Fridolin Sicher (1490–1546)

Leonhard Kleber (*c.* 1490–1556).

All were associated in one way or another with Hofhaimer, a circumstance that has caused them to be referred to as the "Paulomimes." Their compositions and arrangements have come down to us in manuscript tablatures, of which Sicher's is especially large (see Nef), and Kleber's contains pieces by Hofhaimer (see Löwenfeld and Kotterba). Buchner is the exception (see Päsler, Werra, and Schmidt), since his works are contained in a large treatise, the *Fundamentum,* an instruction manual on organ playing similar to those of Paumann and Wolfgang de Nova Domo from the previous century. This treatise contains instructions on the technique of keyboard playing, including fingering, from which it is evident—contrary to popular belief—that the thumb was used.

The repertory presented here is varied. As in the fourteenth and fifteenth centuries, intavolaturas are in the lead and appear chiefly in the works of Kotter and Kleber. Cantus firmus settings based on plainsong are important in the output of Buchner and Sicher, but also make their appearance in the tablatures of Kleber and Kotter (see Merian). Kotter's *Us tieffer Nodt* (*Aus tiefer Not*) and Buchner's *Quem terra, pontus,* both readily available for study (*GMB*, 82 and 83), are examples of this genre. Buchner's *Fundamentum*, being an instruction book, contains teaching pieces similar to those found earlier in Paumann's *Fundamentum organisandi*. The prelude type is also represented in these tablatures, mostly in Kleber, but some are in Kotter (*HAM*, I, 84e, 84f, and 84g; Georgii, *400 Years*, p. 11). These show the features we have observed in the preludes of the *Buxheim Organ Book*: there are sections employing mainly scale figuration passages alternating with sections that are primarily chordal.

One additional category of keyboard music appears in these tablatures, a type we have not yet had occasion to notice but that ultimately is of great importance—dances (see Merian). These are quantitatively of importance in the work of Kotter. Dance music had long been a prime type of instrumental music, polyphonic as well as monophonic. In the fifteenth century, a leading type was the basse danse associated with the Burgundian court at Dijon. This dance was in moderate 6/8 time (or, in the terminology of the time, *tempus imperfectum cum prolatione major*), and the term "basse" apparently refers to the gliding and thus low nature of the steps used. What is important about the basse danse, however, is that the original dance music is monophonic and its melodies appear in notes that are not differentiated as to rhythmic values. (In this respect, there is a resemblance to plainsong notation.) This means that there is a set group of basses danses that are employed as cantus firmi in polyphonic settings, treated in much the same way as plainsong melodies (see Southern). A German example of a basse danse for keyboard is found in the Kotter manuscript, *Il Re di Spagna* by Hans Weck (*HAM*, I, 102b [transcribed in 3/2 time instead of 6/8]), based on one of the familiar basse danse tunes that appears ornamented in the upper part.

In the fifteenth century, it was the practice to have the slow basse danse followed by a rapid dance in triple time. This custom of associating dances in pairs was continued throughout the sixteenth century. In Germany, the second dance was known as the *Nachtantz* (the dance after or following) or the *Proportz*. The latter name is explained by the second important feature of these dance pairs; the second dance frequently is a variation of the first, presenting the same thematic material but in triple time. Thus, it is related to the system of proportional notation, which explains the term. The practice of variation in the dance pairs can be found in many tablatures of the early sixteenth century. Standard pairings are the French pavane and galliard and the Italian passamezzo and saltarello. Easily available for study are German examples for lute (*MPM*, 22) and keyboard (Fischer, *Variation*, 5, p. 16; Georgii, *100 Years*, pp. 11–12). It has been conjectured that these dances by Kotter and others represent the earliest extant music specifically composed for harpsichord.

A center of German organ music in the mid-sixteenth century was Poland, especially Cracow where several German composers worked and where music in the German manner was composed. Apart from one tablature from the Order of the Holy Ghost in Cracow and another associated with the organist Martin

Leopolita, there is the extensive tablature of Johannes de Lublin (see Chybinski, Jachimecki, and White), which begins with a treatise on organ playing and improvisation and then presents works of the types associated with organ music: intavolaturas, sacred cantus firmus compositions, preludes, and dances.

In the second half of the sixteenth century, a certain decline took place in German keyboard music. This is the period of the so-called "colorist" school, famous for their use of embellishment. Their activities concentrated on keyboard transcriptions of polyphonic ensemble pieces (mostly motets and chansons) and outright improvisation. The older form of the liturgical cantus firmus setting based on plainsong is not present, but we do find such settings based on Protestant chorale melodies, so that we have here early contributions to what later became the repertory of the Lutheran organ chorale. The prelude type is likewise absent, but we do find much attention accorded dances (see Apel, *Masters*, 41 and 42, pp. 72–3; Georgii, *400 Years*, pp. 11–12). The later collections show an Italian influence. A positive contribution of the school is a result of the coloration itself: the attention given to the development of technique in keyboard playing, proper fingering, and the execution of standard types of ornamentation. In view of this, it may strike one as odd that this group evolved the so-called "new" and drastic form of German tablature notation, in which the mensural note forms were completely eliminated and letters were used exclusively. This kind of tablature remained dominant in Germany until the eighteenth century. Prominent representatives of the school, as discussed by Young, are Elias Nicolaus Ammerbach (1530–1597, see Wustmann); Bernhard Schmid the Older (1520–*c*. 1592); Johannes Rühling; Jacob Paix (1556–*c*. 1617, see Schuler); August Nörminger; Bernhard Schmid the Younger (1548–date of death unknown, see Young); and Johann Woltz (see Hug). Ammerbach is the compiler of the earliest printed German keyboard tablatures, the first of which appeared in 1571.

There exists a large gap in the history of Italian keyboard music; we have nothing between the Faenza manuscript of the fourteenth century and the printed collection *Frottole intabulate da sonare per organo* issued by the Roman firm of Antico in 1517. This gap, then, embraces the whole of the fifteenth century. In the sixteenth century, on the other hand, we find a great deal of Italian keyboard music and considerable development of musical forms (see, generally, Jeppesen and Lunelli). A great portion of this music appeared in print.

The most important Italian composers of keyboard music in the sixteenth century are the following:

Marcantonio Cavazzoni da Bologna

Girolamo Cavazzoni

Andrea Gabrieli (*c*. 1510–1586)

Annibale Padovano (d. 1575)
Claudio Merulo (1533–1604)
Giovanni Gabrieli (1557–1613).

Most of these were connected with the great cathedral of San Marco in Venice, which became an important musical center after 1527, the year in which the famous Netherlands musician Adrian Willaert was appointed *maestro di cappella* there. His presence quickly attracted other musicians both from Italy and elsewhere, among whom were the two Gabrielis, Merulo, and many others. Although this group of composers is chiefly known for the development of the concertato style through the exploitation of the double chorus medium (*cori spezzati*), its members devoted much attention to keyboard music.

As far as the general repertory is concerned, we find much that is quite traditional: cantus firmus settings, the prelude type, intavolaturas, and dances. But these standard forms are varied and made more elaborate, more important, so that, actually, types that are quite new were developed from them.

Among the liturgical cantus firmus settings, three categories stand out: the Mass, the Magnificat, and hymns. Hence, such keyboard music is restricted to two services, the Mass and Vespers. The procedure in these compositions is exactly like that we have encountered in other works of this type; the liturgical melody appears in one part while the others form an accompaniment that makes use of contrapuntal imitation and figuration. In some instances, the cantus firmus moves from one voice to another. Cavazzoni is the composer of the period who emphasizes these types to the greatest extent; good examples are his *Missa Apostolorum* (*HAM*, I, 117) and his setting of the hymn *Ad coenam agni providi* (*GMB*, 103). Another large organ Mass, by the Netherlander Jacques Brumel, appears in the manuscripts at Castell'Arquato near Piacenza (see Jeppeson), and later a set was published by Merulo (see, generally, Keller); finally, in 1598, an *Intavolatura d'organo* containing versets for the Magnificat made its appearance (see Kastner).

More important from the historical standpoint is the development from what, on the face of it, would seem to be the least promising category of all—the intavolatura, or keyboard transcription of a polyphonic ensemble composition. As we have seen, the first printed Italian tablature of keyboard music was of this kind, the *Frottole* of 1517. It is this type of transcription for keyboard that lies back of the canzone francese (or simply canzone; sometimes canzona). Works with this title originally were simply transcriptions for keyboard of popular French chansons. Since the chanson was a rather modest polyphonic work, generally of a joyful and "light" character but still employing the principle of contrapuntal imitation, it follows that its keyboard version would also show the same essential features. Hence, we find a sectional composition, with each section employing its own theme treated in imitative counterpoint. The only real change

lies in the addition of idiomatic keyboard figuration. Two examples of this
earliest stage in the development of the keyboard canzone may be referred to
here: Thomas Crecquillon's *Pour ung plaisir* was arranged for keyboard by
Andrea Gabrieli (*MPM*, 20 and 21), and the famous chanson *Fault d'argent*
by Josquin des Prez was freely worked out by Cavazzoni (*HAM*, I, 91 [Josquin]
and 118 [Cavazzoni]). There are other examples found in the work of most
Italian keyboard composers of the time. Those of Marcantonio da Bologna show
the repetitive schemes that often appear in chansons, such as *A B A*, *A A B*,
and *A A B A*.

The next step in the development finds the keyboard canzone breaking
away from its source. We begin to find free and independent keyboard compositions, called canzones and closely resembling canzones in the sense just described

EXAMPLE 10

A. GABRIELI: *Canzone alla francese* on *Petit Jacquet*—beginning

but which are actually original compositions. It is in this fashion that the vocal model gave rise to a new and idiomatic category of keyboard music; thus, we reach a real imitative contrapuntal form specifically for keyboard instruments, and we find it first among the Italian composers of the sixteenth century, particularly those at Venice. The original source of the form, however, continued to be reflected in certain stereotyped thematic types that are often used in canzones, particularly in the opening sections. Generally, these themes are sharply defined rhythmically and make use of repeated notes and leaps of a fourth or fifth. Figuration continues to play an important role.

The situation is much less clear with another form that is frequently associated with the canzone—the ricercare (see Apel, Murphy, Eggebrecht, and Slim). Even the very term itself is far from having a plain meaning. It seems to come from the Italian word meaning "to search" or "to seek out." We find it applied to various kinds of instrumental music of the early sixteenth century, first to lute music, especially in the prints of the Venetian firm of Petrucci between the years of 1507 and 1511, and then to keyboard and ensemble music. Since most compositions bearing the name "ricercare" are composed in imitative counterpoint, it has been maintained that the ricercare is in effect an instrumental motet, thus, a "serious" counterpart of the canzone.

Several difficulties arise here. Not the least of these is the fact that no one has yet found a ricercare which is an arrangement of a motet, although, in the earliest source to contain keyboard ricercares, Marcantonio's publication of 1523 (see below), they do precede intavolaturas of motets while at the same time being separate compositions; there are, however, thematic relations between the ricercares and the intavolaturas that follow them. Furthermore, the earliest keyboard ricercares do not show imitative counterpoint at all, but resemble rather the earlier lute ricercares and are similar to the keyboard prelude. Apel has suggested that the term be regarded in the sense of "study" and that, seen in this fashion, the discrepancy in style may be resolved; but no contemporary evidence for this can be cited, and hence the question must remain open for the present.

The earliest keyboard ricercares, then, appear in 1523 in a publication by Marcantonio da Bologna with the title *Ricercari, motetti, canzoni*; it contains two ricercares, two transcriptions of motets, and four transcriptions of French chansons. The two pieces called "ricercare" are, as we have said, like lute ricercares and have more in common with the quasi-improvisational form of the prelude than with the strict contrapuntal form that later goes under the name. These compositions are quite long and, one is tempted to say, rambling. The usual form-giving devices of repetition, variation, and imitation are absent; the chief characteristic is an alternation between sections of different character—scale figurations, on the one hand, and chordal passages, on the other. For this reason, they seem related to the prelude type. The difference is their considerably greater length. Similar are a number of ricercares contained among the manuscripts at

Castell'Arquato by Jacopo Fogliano, Guilio da Modena, the Netherlander Jacques Brumel (see Jeppesen), and the madrigalist Claudio Veggio (see Slim); some of Marcantonio's are also found here.

The first keyboard ricercares to be written in imitative counterpoint—and hence the first to employ the term in the sense in which it is generally understood —are by Marcantonio's nephew, Girolamo Cavazzoni. They appear in his publication *Intavolatura per organo,* issued in two volumes in 1543, which also contains the cantus firmus compositions already mentioned. In the four works bearing the title "ricercare," the rather free form used by Marcantonio is replaced by the systematic application of imitative counterpoint; the form is sectional, with five to nine parts each of which has its own theme that is treated in imitation. At the end, there is in some of them a free passage using scale figuration to make an impressive close. Many of these features can be observed in a ricercare by Cavazzoni in the Lydian mode (*HAM,* I, 116). This work has some seven themes each of which is treated imitatively; between the various sections are free, nonimitative passages.

The decisive shaping of the form, stamping it with all the features generally associated with the category, appears in the work of the Venetian composers. While there are some ricercares by Willaert, these are actually ensemble compositions, although they have been arranged for keyboard. It is rather the work of Andrea Gabrieli that must be looked on as having the greatest importance here.

EXAMPLE 11

A. GABRIELI: *Ricercare arioso*—beginning

In five publications containing the keyboard works of Andrea Gabrieli that have been preserved (all of them, be it noted, published posthumously, 1593–1605), there are seventeen ricercares. The contrapuntal approach we observed in Cavazzoni is maintained here as well as the sectional organization. The difference lies in the number of sections, which is reduced, and, as a result, the number of themes used is also reduced. Indeed, seven of these ricercares are monothematic while several others employ only two or three themes. At the same time, an increase in complexity takes place. The contrapuntal procedures become more involved; often the theme itself is broken up, and its second part is systematically used to accompany the entrance of the theme in another voice—hence, the use of a countersubject. Furthermore, the devices of "learned" counterpoint—inversion, diminution, and augmentation of the theme—as well as closely staggered entries (strettos), also appear in Gabrieli's ricercares. The traditional idiomatic keyboard figuration is still quite prominent. As an outstanding example of Andrea Gabrieli's keyboard ricercare composition, we can mention the famous *Ricercare arioso* contained in the collection of 1605 (*HMS*, IV, 3, s. 4, b. 2).

Several important observations can be made here. The first is that, with the monothematic form and the use of "learned" counterpoint, all the essential features of the later fugue are present, in principle at least. The second has to do with the alleged relation between the ricercare and the motet, a subject already mentioned. It is obvious that the development of the ricercare as seen in the work of Andrea Gabrieli has no parallel in the history of the motet, which retains essentially the same form throughout the sixteenth century. The ricercare, on the other hand, develops in terms of instrumental music without relation to vocal forms.

From the latter part of the sixteenth century, we have ricercares by Jacques Buus (1505–1564), Annibale Padovano, and Claudio Merulo. It must, however, be pointed out that most of the ricercares by Buus (see Sutherland) and Padovano are actually ensemble compositions not really intended specifically for keyboard. There are, at the same time, two by Padovano that are genuine keyboard compositions, both to be found in the posthumous collection published in 1604. These ricercares employ four and five themes respectively. The interesting feature here is that the principle of thematic variation is introduced into the category; the subject of the original imitative section is varied to form the themes employed in the subsequent sections. Hence, a tendency towards the monothematic form is again evident. Merulo, one of the most prominent keyboard composers of the time, is best known for his toccatas (see below), but he did publish three volumes containing ricercares for keyboard. In these, we seem to find the earliest type represented, for there is a tendency to a multiplicity of sections and of themes; two have as many as seven and eight sections while only one is monothematic. At the same time, the element of variation is present, which we have just noted in the work of Padovano, so that the trend towards unification in the form is not entirely absent. Other composers of ricercares from the end of the century are Sper'in dio Bertoldo and Antonio Valente.

There is some difficulty in relating the two forms, ricercare and canzone, to one another. Both are imitative contrapuntal forms (with the exception of the early ricercare in which successive sections employ various themes that may or may not be related to one another). It is tempting to generalize and maintain that the canzone is "light" while the ricercare is "serious." While this may hold true to some extent in a good many cases, at the same time, we occasionally meet with canzones that are eminently "serious" compositions, even liturgical, as well as ricercares that exhibit features usually associated with the canzone.[1] This distinction between the forms, therefore, does not really work, and, as we will see, the later fugue is the product of a combination of the two forms.

One further imitative contrapuntal form that is developed in sixteenth-century Italian keyboard music by the Venetian composers is the fantasia (see Reimann). Like the name "ricercare," "fantasia" is current in the lute tablatures of the time. Its first application to keyboard music occurs in Germany, in the tablature of Hans Kotter. In Italy, there does not seem to have been any real difference between the fantasia, on the one hand, and the ricercare, on the other. The sixteenth-century keyboard fantasia has nothing resembling a "free flight of the imagination"; rather, it is a work in strict imitative counterpoint (see Deffner, Murphy, Launay, and Slim). The rhapsodic elements appear later, in the fantasia of the seventeenth century.

Turning now to the last major category of keyboard composition in sixteenth-century Italy, the prelude, we find a considerable expansion from what we have previously encountered. It will be remembered that these preludes developed from pieces improvised before the performances of polyphonic compositions during church services, and hence we find them usually associated with specific keys by which they are identified. This is the explanation of the name given them in sixteenth-century Italy—*intonazione* (or "intonation"). There are several examples of *intonazioni* in the work of Andrea Gabrieli, and in these the features of the prelude can be observed; for instance, his *Intonazione settimo modo* (in the seventh mode, i.e., Mixolydian, G) opens with a short chordal passage and then continues with much scale figuration (*HAM*, I, 135).

A significant outgrowth of this form in Italy is the toccata (see Schrade, Gombosi, and Clercx). Here, the quasi-improvisational style is clearly in the background, but the whole composition has been greatly enlarged. The alternation between sections in contrasting styles is still the basis, but all have been extended, and passages employing imitative counterpoint have been introduced. Hence, the toccata is brought about by combining elements from the old prelude (or *intonazione*) with the ricercare or canzone. The most prominent composer

---

[1] *HAM*, I, 136, a ricercare in the style of a canzone but one that is an ensemble rather than a keyboard composition; see also the canzone in the style of a ricercare for organ, *MPM*, 26.

here is Claudio Merulo. A ternary scheme is used in most of his toccatas: first, a section employing massive chords and brilliant scale runs; then, a middle part in which imitative counterpoint is prominent, and finally, in the last section, the virtuoso elements characteristic of the beginning are brought back. Others have five sections in which three parts in the virtuoso "toccata" style are separated by two in imitative counterpoint (*HAM*, I, 153; *TEM*, 29; Valentin has examples by the Gabrielis and Bertoldo as well as Merulo).

Dances for keyboard also existed in sixteenth-century Italy. There are apparently three main printed tablatures: an anonymous collection, *Intabolatura nova di varie sorte di balli*, of 1551 and two other collections both called *Intavolatura di balli d'arpicordi*, the first by Marco Facoli in 1588 (see Apel) and the second by Giovanni Maria Radino in 1592. The dances represented are the passamezzo, the large dance in variation form employing both the *antico* and the *nuovo* or *moderne* form of the melody; the saltarello; the pavane; and the galliard. There is some linking of pairs of dances through the use of the same thematic material in each. Facoli's tablature also contains seventeen works similar in style, most of which are called arias; they are short homophonic pieces that apparently are harpsichord arrangements of short polyphonic songs of the villanella and napoletana type that became popular towards the end of the sixteenth century. Scale figuration and trills are prominent in them.

EXAMPLE 12

Merulo: *Toccata*—excerpt

Thus, we see that, in sixteenth-century Italy, several categories of keyboard music were developed: on the one hand, the imitative contrapuntal forms of the canzone, the ricercare, and the fantasia, and, on the other, the virtuoso toccata and dances, a type closely connected with the lute, also appear for keyboard. All play a role of great importance in the subsequent history of keyboard music.

In sharp contrast to the activity in Italy, we find relatively little going on in France, although that little is at the same time highly characteristic of the general keyboard repertory of the time. The sole French publications in the field of keyboard music consist of a series of prints issued by the Parisian firm of Pierre Attaingnant between 1529 and 1531. There are seven books in all; three contain sacred music (cantus firmus settings of Masses, Magnificats, and the *Te deum*, along with keyboard arrangements of motets and preludes), and four are secular works containing dances (see Apel). The latter is a genre that takes on increasing importance in the development of keyboard music (*GMB*, 91; *HAM*, I, 104)

Although none of the Attaingnant pieces presents much that is unusual, certain features call for some comment. They use the normal forms of polyphonic ensemble mensural notation in open score. The liturgical cantus firmus settings present the cantus firmus in one voice with highly figurative accompaniment in the other parts. One full organ Mass is presented, a *Missa Cunctipotens genitor* (for the Sanctus, see *GMB*, 92). Here, the practice of composing only the odd verses for keyboard is maintained. With reference to the motets many figurational elements are worked into the transcriptions; leaps of fifths and larger intervals are changed into scale runs and long notes are broken down into smaller. These procedures often alter the character of the work being arranged to a considerable extent. Good examples are the transcriptions of Compère's *O vos omnes* and Obrecht's *Parce domine*; the extent of the alteration is particularly evident in those motets that are primarily homophonic, such as Gascogne's *Bone Jesu dulcissime* or passages in Févin's *Sancta Trinitas*.

In Spain, we find more (see Apel and Kastner). Under the Hapsburg emperors Charles V and Philip II the Spanish court became an international music center. Especially important was the group of Netherlands musicians, the *capilla flamenaca*; and, for keyboard music, it is important to note that Arnolt Schlick provided the music for the coronation of Charles V at Aachen in 1520 (see Kastner) and that his music was well known at the Spanish court. In 1554–1555, members of the Spanish *capilla* accompanied Philip II to London for his wedding to Mary of England, and a lively exchange between Spanish and English musicians has been assumed, especially between Cabezón and Tallis.

Instrumental music was widely cultivated in sixteenth-century Spain and numerous tablatures have come down to us. Most of these are for lute (*vihuela*) or harp (*arpa*), but several contain music for keyboard instruments, for which the inclusive term *tecla* was used in the same way as the German *clavier*. But, as was true elsewhere, relations between lute and keyboard music were often very close (see Jacobs). There are two large printed collections in tablature devoted primarily to keyboard music: the *Libro de Cifra Nueva para tecla, harpa y vihuela*, edited by Luis Venegas de Henestrosa, published in 1557, and the comprehensive publication of the works of Antonio de Cabezón (1510–1566), the blind musician who was the outstanding Spanish organist of the day, the *Obras de musica*, posthumously edited and published by his son Hernando de Cabezón in 1578. There are also two treatises that deal extensively with both the composition and performance of keyboard music: the *Declaración de instrumentos musicales* of 1549 (revised in 1555) by Juan Bermudo (*c.* 1510–*c.* 1565, see Stevenson) and the *Libro llamado arte de tañer fantasia assí para tecla como para vihuela* by Tomás de Sancta Maria (*c.* 1520–1570), published in 1565 (see Harich-Schneider); both of these contain keyboard compositions as illustrative examples.

The anthology edited by Venegas de Henestrosa (see Ward) contains 138 compositions notated in a type of tablature regarded as new (*cifra nueva*) in which notes of the diatonic scale are indicated by the numerals 1 through 7; this was subsequently employed in the Cabezón *Obras* as well as in the early seventeenth-century publication of Correa de Arauxo. The composers represented are mainly Spanish, among them Francisco Perez Palero, Pedro Vila (1517–1582), and Pedro de Soto, as well as Cabezón himself; many pieces are anonymous. Ward has shown that the editor occasionally made drastic changes in the compositions printed in the anthology. The types of keyboard music found here are those we have previously encountered, particularly in Italy. There are liturgical cantus firmus settings: *himnos*, *salmos* (psalm versets), and *faburdones*, of which the latter are of two kinds, *llanos*, using simple block chords, and *glossados*, ornamented with scale figuration. Then there are arrangements of secular songs, variously known as *romances*, *villancicos*, and *canciones*, along with transcriptions of *vihuela* pieces. Also represented is the larger form usually in imitative counterpoint, the *tiento*, which generally corresponds to the Italian ricercare or fantasia. (The term *tiento* indeed conveys some of the same meaning as ricercare.) Many of these *tientos* and fantasias are original compositions, while others are elaborations based on other works, even including Mass movements and motets by noted Netherlands musicians. Finally, there are simpler works that are intavolaturas in the usual sense of the word.

Two important characteristics of this collection may be noted. The first has to do with the conception of variation and ornamentation, the *glosa*, which generally has the same meaning as diminution, i.e., replacing long notes of a piece with rapid scale figuration. In practice, a keyboard piece of this kind may carry the process of variation much further, extending the piece by making free and elaborate use of the themes, so that one could almost say that the piece has been recomposed. Ward has been led to apply the term "parody" to this procedure, which is, in principal, identical with that found in the parody Mass of the time; in Ward's own words, "the Spaniards developed out of the barren *glosa* a variety of forms which made of borrowing a vital form-principle" (Ward, p. 111). In addition to Cabezón, Palero emerges as an important representative of this art. The second feature of the collection is actually an outgrowth of keyboard settings of secular songs and dances, in which, as the melody is repeated over and over again, the accompaniment is varied, thus producing a theme and variations form known as *diferencias*. (On the history of the variation form generally, see Nelson, Gress, and Horsley.) England is the only other country to produce extensive keyboard works in variation form in the sixteenth century; this is noteworthy in view of the visit of leading Spanish musicians to London in 1554–1555. But it seems clear that the form had been established in lute music long before any of the keyboard examples known to us were written.

The great master of Spanish Renaissance keyboard music is Cabezón (see Kastner, Barber, Carpenter, and Hughes), who, from 1543, was the *Músico da camera y capilla* at the court of Philipp II. In his work, we find the same repertory of forms as encountered in the *Libro di cifra nueva*, so that the difference is one of quality rather than of kind. Cabezón is often ranked among the greatest of all keyboard composers. Prominent among the liturgical cantus firmus settings is the *verso*, in which a psalm recitation tone is set polyphonically, the organ settings then performed in alternation with a choir (see Speer), a practice already mentioned several times. A good example is the *Versos ad sexto tono* (in the sixth mode, Hypolydian, F; *HAM*, I, 133); in each of the four sections of this *verso*, the Gregorian chant appears in a different voice accompanied by restrained imitative writing in the other voices. The hymns show similar features, but, on occasion, the Gregorian melody is paraphrased, i.e., treated imitatively, while, in others, something akin to theme and variations comes about. The imitative form, the *tiento* (*GMB*, 113), is an elaborate composition stressing the learned aspects of contrapuntal writing and of thematic variation (see Howell). Cabezón is particularly associated with the technique of *glosa*, and not infrequently what appears to be a simple arrangement of another piece turns out to be an elaborately extended composition; a famous example is the *tiento* on the *Cum sancto spiritu* of Josquin's *Missa de Beata Maria Vergine*. Finally, reference may be made to the variation form, in which Cabezón composed several examples. Two of the best known are the *Diferencias sobra la pavana italiana* (Apel, *Masters*, 29, pp. 46–8) and the *Diferencias Caballero* (*HAM*, I, 134). The former employs a well-known Italian pavane melody to provide an ostinato, the accompaniment changing with each repetition. The *Diferencias Caballero* consists of five variations on a popular song of the time, in which the song melody serves as cantus firmus; in the first two variations, it appears in the uppermost voice, then it moves to a middle voice, and at the end comes to the bass.

Recent investigations (see Apel) have revealed an important successor to Cabezón in Francisco Peraza (1564–1598), who enjoyed a great reputation all over Spain as an organist. Although but one of his works has come down, a piece with the title *Medio registro*, we find in it several interesting features. First, there is the wealth of figuration, scale passages, or diminutions (*variedad de flores*), peculiarly idiomatic for the keyboard, a practice for which Peraza was celebrated in his time. Second, as indicated by the title of the work, there is a specification of the stops that the player is to use for the proper performance of the work. Here, the basic distinctions are between the "solo" and "choir" stops, on the one hand, and between the upper and lower halves of the keyboard, on the other; the designation *medio de alta* implies that solo stops are to be used for the upper and choir stops for the lower, while *medio de baxo* indicates the reverse: solo stops are to be used for the lower half of the keyboard range and choir stops for the upper.

Thus, all in all, the work of Spanish keyboard composers of the sixteenth century reveals several elements that came to be of great importance in the literature of keyboard music: the cultivation of the theme and variations form (by Cabezón), the emphasis on idiomatic keyboard figuration, and the effort to "orchestrate," to indicate how a piece is properly to be registered, or, put another way, to compose a piece with specific registration possibilities in mind. It would seem that Spain's role in the development of keyboard music is of greater significance than had long been thought.

It might also be mentioned that there are two Portuguese manuscripts containing keyboard music (see Kastner), one of which has largely intavolaturas of various kinds while the other gives prominence to dances and contrapuntal types. Among the Portuguese composers named are Heliodor de Paiva, Antonio Carreira, and Monoel Macedo.

English sources have been mentioned just twice thus far in our survey: the Robertsbridge manuscript, the earliest known source to contain keyboard music notated in tablature, and a *Felix namque* from the early fifteenth century. So far as is known, there are no other English sources of keyboard music until the the sixteenth century, when there was considerable activity of widespread proportions. While the power of Spain was beginning to decline in the latter part of the century, that of England was clearly on the rise during the reign of Queen Elizabeth (1559–1603). And, as often happens, political power stands behind an extensive cultivation of the arts. In keyboard music, two main areas can generally be separated from one another—organ music and harpsichord or virginal music.

The principal manuscripts of sixteenth-century England containing mainly organ music (see Lowinsky, Steele and Stevens) are presently in the British Museum: Mss. Add. 15233, Add. 29996, Add. 30513, Roy. App. 56, and Roy. App. 58. The oldest of these is Ms. Add. 29996, and the largest is Ms. Add. 30513, more commonly known as the *Mulliner Book*. Among a number of composers the following are the most important:

Philip Ap Rhys (or Rhyce)

John Redford (d. 1547)

Thomas Preston

Thomas Tallis (*c.* 1505–1585)

William Blitheman (d. 1591)

Thomas Tomkins (1572–1656).

The repertory is largely sacred, even liturgical, consisting as it does mainly of cantus firmus works. Most numerous are settings of certain plainsong melodies: the Offertory *Felix namque*, the antiphon *Miserere* [*mihi Domine*], for which several melodies were used, and *In nomine*, from the Benedictus of Taverner's Mass *Gloria tibi trinitas*. Such works not infrequently attain a considerable length, as is seen in Preston's *Felix namque*, or Blitheman's *Gloria tibi trinitas* and *Eterne rerum conditor*. It might be noted that, in this extended form, such works become sets of variations in which the accompaniment and style is varied with restatements of the cantus firmus, and, in this form, they are no longer strictly liturgical and often appear in collections given over to secular music. Of Redford's cantus firmus works (see Pfatteicher), which are small and liturgical, three are readily available: the hymn *Veni redemptor gentium*, the antiphon *Lucem tuam* (*HAM*, I, 120a and 120b), and the hymn *O Lux on the Faburden* (*HMS*, III, 2, s. 4, b. 3). This last represents a typically English procedure. In the normal practice in vocal ensemble performance of improvising against a plainsong, the faburden is that part moving at sixths and octaves below the plainsong; this faburden part is then taken and used as cantus firmus for an organ composition; as Bukofzer puts it, these keyboard faburden compositions are cantus firmus pieces "once removed." Some twenty hymn settings of this kind appear in Ms. Add. 29996.

Compositions for the mass are also found in Ms. Add. 29996. Rhys has a group for the Ordinary of the Mass for Trinity Sunday, while Preston has a set containing pieces for the Proper of the Mass for Easter Sunday, which includes the large and elaborate setting of the sequence *Fulgens praeclara* (see Miller and Stevens). Other pieces related to the Mass appear in Ms. Roy. App. 56. These organ Mass compositions, and many of the other liturgical cantus firmus works, are alternatim compositions, intended to alternate with a chorus that performs a plainsong those portions not composed for organ; this practice, however, is not common in the contents of the *Mulliner Book*.

There are few secular works in these sources. Ms. Roy. Add. 58, dating from the early 1530's, contains, along with a number of court dances, two well-known pieces: Hugh Aston's *Hornpype* (Apel, *Masters*, 37, pp. 62–4) and *My Lady Carey's Dompe* (*HAM*, I, 103), both of which are built on short harmonic progressions repeated over and over again in ostinato fashion. The term "dompe" or "dump" (see Ward) appears to have been given to pieces composed to commemorate the passing of persons of note (like the later French *tombeau*). In the *Mulliner Book*, there are intavolaturas of secular songs (two by Tallis) and a number of dances. In such works, it is by no means certain whether organ or the virginal (harpsichord) was the intended instrument.

Finally, there are works associated neither with the cantus firmus nor with dance types. Among these are the imitative pieces; there are short compositions called "points," each of which treats a single subject in contrapuntal imitation, as well as larger works using several themes, called "fancies," the English equivalent of the continental fantasia. The two voluntaries in the *MullinerBook* are related to the prelude type and emphasize figuration in their thematic material. Ms. Add. 29996 contains duets for keyboard by Tomkins and Nicholas Carleton (see Miller).

It is, however, in the realm of virginal (or harpsichord) music that we find a really distinctive English contribution to the keyboard music of the time (see generally Borren, Andrews, Jacquot, Niemann, and Ward; also Dart). While the few dances of the *Mulliner Book* are clearly virginal pieces, most such works are preserved in sources specifically devoted to this type of music. There are several of these, of which the most important are:

Benjamin Cosyn's Virginal Book
Will. Forster's Virginal Book
My Ladye Neville's Book
Parthenia
Fitzwilliam Virginal Book
Elizabeth Roger's Virginal Book
The Dublin Virginal Manuscript (the *Dallis Virginal Book*).

Of these, the Fitzwilliam manuscript is the largest and the most comprehensive; *Parthenia* has the distinction of being the first printed collection of virginal music (1612 or 1613); *My Ladye Neville's Book* is not, like the others, an anthology, but presents exclusively works by the most famous English composer of his day, William Byrd (1543–1623, see Tuttle). Three other virginal manuscripts are in the New York Public Library. Apart from Byrd, the main composers of virginal music are:

Giles Farnaby (*c.* 1560–*c.* 1620)
Thomas Morley (1557–*c.* 1603)
John Bull (*c.* 1562–1628)
Thomas Tomkins (1572–1656)
Orlando Gibbons (1583–1625)
John Munday (d. 1630).

Many of these are known for other contributions to the musical life of the time. Morley, for instance, wrote many madrigals as well as a famous treatise, *A Plain and Easy Introduction to Practical Music* (London, 1597). Gibbons, in particular, was one of the best of the English composers of choral music. On the other hand, others, like John Bull, a pupil of Blitheman, and Giles Farnaby are known chiefly for their keyboard compositions.

Particular interest attaches to *Parthenia* as the first printed music for virginal. The date is usually given as 1611, but it seems likely, in view of the dedication, that it appeared in 1612 or 1613. Its full title is, *Parthenia, or the Maydenhead of the first Musicke that ever was printed for the virginalls*; since *parthenos* is the Greek word for virgin, some Elizabethan humor is present (as is even clearer from the sequel, *Parthenia In-Violata* of 1614 for virginal and bass viol). In *Parthenia*, the three leading composers of virginal music are represented: Byrd, Bull (see Mellers), and Gibbons (see Hendrie). Dances are the most prominent, especially pavanes and galliards, after which come preludes. The only work in a larger form is Gibbons' *Fantasia in foure parts*, in which a number of themes are successively introduced and treated in imitation. Here, however, we will emphasize the contents of the *Fitzwilliam Virginal Book* (Ms., Cambridge, Fitzwilliam Museum, Mus. 32 G 29) as the largest and most representative collection of virginal music. The repertory is broad and embraces dances, variations on popular songs, preludes, fantasias, liturgical works using Gregorian chant cantus firmi, direct transcriptions of polyphonic ensemble compositions, and a few programmatic works.

The dances are the most numerous. Most are pavanes and galliards. Here, we can observe the practice that developed in the sixteenth century of presenting dances in pairs: first a slow and dignified dance in moderate duple time, then a rapid dance in triple time. We have also noted that, in many cases, this second dance is a variation of the first. The most usual combination in the virginal repertory is a pavane followed by a galliard. In general, these dances are simple. Reference can be made to William Byrd's pavane *Earl of Salisbury* (Apel, *Masters*, 39, p. 68), a short piece in duple time with the accent on what would normally be a weak beat. The work is homophonic, the chord progressions simple, the upper part clearly the most important. Also readily at hand is a much more extended pavane by Byrd's contemporary, Bull (*TEM*, 30).

Artistically more elaborate than either of these is the paired pavane and galliard by Orlando Gibbons, which also bears the title *Lord of Salisbury* (*HAM*, I, 179). The title relates to the person to whom the piece is dedicated and does not refer to a specific dance melody. Here, the pavane in particular is greatly transformed; we find long and irregular phrases and long rising sequences, much use of chromaticism with unusual and expressive intervals, and considerable contrapuntal detail, all of which make this one of the masterpieces of early keyboard music. Such stylization of an originally simple dance type continues to play an important role in the history of keyboard music. The galliard is a variation of the pavane.

Other types of dances in the *Fitzwilliam Virginal Book* are the alman (allemande), a dance in moderate duple time; the coranto, or courante, in moderate triple time; and, of lesser significance, the jig or gigge (gigue), in very fast triple time, and the branle (or brawl), in either duple or triple time. An unusual group is formed by the dompes (or dumps), which as already mentioned are built on the ostinato principle (see Ward).

Another important group in the repertory of virginal music is the variations, many on popular songs (see Neudenberger). England and Spain share the distinction of being the countries in which the variation form for keyboard was first developed (on earlier variations for lute, see Horsley). Like the Spanish examples, the English variations are of the cantus firmus type so that the melody used as the basis of the piece is repeated over and over again in ostinato fashion. Should it appear most often in the bass part, it becomes a basso ostinato, or, as the English called it, a ground (or ground bass). Since the melody was almost always a popular song of the time, it was not stated in simple form at the beginning; the work just begins with the first variation. The principle of variation used

EXAMPLE 13

GIBBONS: *Pavane, Lord of Salisbury*, from *Parthenia*—excerpt from second part

here involves altering the character of the accompanying parts, and this is done in such a way that a certain amount of contrast between the sections is achieved. Common devices are the operation with small motives that are worked out in the accompanying voices, and the employment of extremely rapid scale-passage work in one hand punctuated with sharp chords in the other. Well-known and readily accessible examples of this type of composition are Byrd's *The Carman's Whistle*, John Munday's *Goe from my Windoe*, and Giles Farnaby's *Loth to Depart* (see, respectively, Apel, *Masters*, 38, pp. 66–7 [first four variations only]; *HAM*, I, 177; and *MPM*, 29). Others with enticing titles are Farnaby's *Put up thy Dagger, Jemy* and Byrd's *John, Comme Kisse Me Now*. A major example is Gibbons' *The Woods so Wilde*.

A different class of compositions may be seen in the liturgical cantus firmus settings. These are of the same type as those encountered in English organ music of the time—variations on well-known plainsong melodies, each variation having a different style or character and using different and contrasting motives and types of figuration in the voices accompanying the plainsong melody. Even the repertory of melodies used as cantus firmus is the same as that found in the manuscripts containing organ music: *In nomine*, *Felix namque*, *Miserere*, and *Veni sancte spiritus*. In such works, the liturgical theme is used as the basis for an abstract keyboard work that in itself is neither sacred nor secular and indeed seems as much for harpsichord or virginal as for organ. We will meet with a similar situation in the chorale partita of the seventeenth century. John Bull, in particular, is noted for his *In nomine* compositions.

In regard to the imitative contrapuntal forms, inspired evidently by the work of Italian composers, the fancy or fantasia is dominant in England, a genre quali-fied by Morley in his treatise as the largest form of purely instrumental music. Here, as in Italy, none of the features later associated with the genre is present. Rather, the contrapuntal working out is strict. Many of these English fantasias have subjects based on scale segments, as indicated by such titles as *Ut re mi fa sol la* and the like, by Byrd, Bull, and others. The two most important composers of fantasias in England at this time were Bull and Gibbons.

Another traditional genre that retains its old character in the hands of the English virginal composers is the prelude (Georgii, *400 Years*, pp. 12–13; *HAM*, I, 178), which was described in the seventeenth century by Mace as "a piece of confused-wild-shapeless-kind of intricate play . . . in which no perfect Form, Shape, or uniformity can be perceived" (quoted by K. Stone in his edition of *Parthenia*, p. v). Noteworthy are those of John Bull, which exploit the virtuoso qualities inherent in the quasi-improvisational style particularly evident in the many scale figuration patterns. It must also be noted that these preludes are short; English composers did not take the step to the larger and more elaborate toccata that the Italians did.

An unusual body of compositions in the *Fitzwilliam Virginal Book* are the descriptive works. Some of these are related to dance types, while others are free compositions. There are, for instance, such characteristic dances as William Tisdall's *pavana chromatica* in which a particular affection, sadness or lamentation (generally associated at the time with chromaticism), is portrayed in a dance. Other titles make even more explicit reference to a "program"; Peerson's *Fall of the Leaf*, a pavane; Bull's *The King's Hunt*; Farnaby's *A Toy*; Byrd's *The Bells*; and others. Among the more ambitious works of this genre is John Munday's fantasia representing changes in the weather; the piece commences in rather noncommittal imitative counterpoint for "fair weather," then we get brilliant arpeggio and scale figuration on "thunder" and "lightning," followed by a return to the style of the beginning at "a clear day." Similarly ambitious is the cycle of three pieces by Farnaby, *His Humour*, *His Dream*, and *His Rest*, which constitutes a sort of musical self-portrait. *His Dream* is an example of a programmatic piece combined with a dance form, an allemande. John Bull also has a composition of this type, *My Selfe*, a gigue. Compositions such as these have no real parallel in previous keyboard music (see the selections in *HMS*, IV, s. 4, b. 2, first group).

Finally, lesser significance may be attached to the intravolaturas. The Fitzwilliam manuscript does, however, contain arrangements of very up-to-date Italian madrigals, such as works by Marenzio, Lassus, Striggio, and Caccini, the last-named being the famous musician associated with the *camerata* of Florence.

EXAMPLE 14

BULL: *Prelude*, from *Fitzwilliam Virginal Book*—excerpt

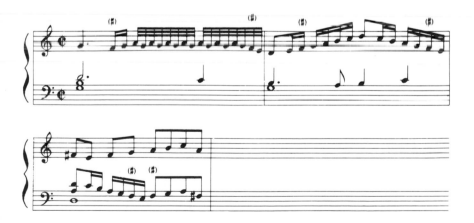

As examples of this art of transcription, Peter Phillip's arrangements of Lassus' *Bon jour mon coeur* (both original and transcription in *HAM*, I, 145a and 145b) and of Caccini's *Amarilli mia bella* (both original and transcription in *GMB*, 173 and 174) may be mentioned.

One of the most important features of English virginal music is the development of an idiomatic harpsichord style. For the first time in keyboard music, we have a large body of a compositions specifically intended for particular instruments and not, as in the past, written for keyboard instruments in general. Likewise, we can call attention to the development of secular forms in keyboard music, something we have seen before but not with the great emphasis that is placed on it here.

This survey of sixteenth century keyboard music can be concluded with a brief account of Jan Pieterzoon Sweelinck (1562–1621), the organist of Amsterdam whose work in many ways represents a summary and a combination of Italian and English developments in keyboard music (see Borren, Sigtenhorst-Meyer, Tusler, and Curtis). There is a report that he had been in Venice and was associated with the famous theorist Zarlino, but the validity of this is by no means certain. We do know of his close contact with English composers, especially John Bull. Indeed, Sweelinck is even represented in the Fitzwilliam manuscript. But the Italian as well as the English influence on his keyboard music is quite plain.

Three main categories make up his output in keyboard music: the fantasia, the toccata, and the variations. All connotations we have observed with each of these are maintained. It is noteworthy that the standard Italian categories of ricercare and canzone are lacking. Their place is taken by the fantasias, which exhibit most of the same features; one of the fantasias even bears the designation ricercare in one of its sources. Two of Sweelinck's fantasias employ the scale-segment themes identified by the solmization syllables (*Ut re mi fa sol la*), as has been observed among the English virginal compositions. One of the Sweelinck fantasias is particularly chromatic, following the experimental direction then current in Italy, and this feature is reflected in its title—*Fantasia chromatica* (*GMB*, 158); unlike his other fantasias, this one makes extensive use of augmentation, diminution, and also employs several countersubjects. A stronger case of the Italian inspiration of Sweelinck in the fantasias may be made on the basis of the six echo fantasias. Here, the resources of the several choirs of the organ are drawn upon, and short phrases, frequently nothing more than short scale runs, are repeated on different parts of the organ, first loudly and then softly (*HAM*, I, 181). This procedure is clearly related to the polychoral style associated with the composers at San Marco in Venice.

Sweelinck's toccatas likewise adhere to the Italian form, particularly that employed by Merulo. They are sectional, usually in three parts, and have the same alternation between the imitative passage in the middle and the virtuoso opening and closing sections in toccata style. Echo effects also make their appearance (Valentin, pp. 24–5).

The third category in Sweelinck's keyboard music has no Italian background at all, but leads rather to England—the variations. (There is nothing to suggest an influence from Spain.) What is quite important, however, is that Sweelinck uses sacred, even liturgical, as well as secular song melodies as the basis for his variations. This use of sacred melodies is clearly an outgrowth of the older cantus firmus procedure, except that the borrowed melody is usually embellished. Many of Sweelinck's sets of variations are based on Protestant chorale or metrical psalm melodies (see Breig and Gerdes), hence the term "chorale variations" that is often used in referring to them. These chorales are strophic, and each of the keyboard variations corresponds to a strophe of the original. Such is the set of variations of *Ach Gott vom Himmel sieh' darein* (*HMS*, IV, s. 4, b. 2, fourth group), which is spurious according to Breig. This group of Sweelinck's works takes on greater importance when viewed against the development that takes place in the seventeenth century. Among the seven sets of variations on secular songs, the best known is the group on *Mein junges Leben hat ein End* (Apel, *Masters*, 43, pp. 74–5, variations one, two, and six only). As these would not have been used in connection with worship, but to please visitors to the Amsterdam church, they may be called recital pieces.

The tremendous changes in keyboard music that took place in the sixteenth century may now be summarized. In a general way, the old dominion of polyphonic vocal and/or instrumental ensemble music over keyboard music, which had obtained since the very outset, is maintained, but it takes a very different form. While the old cantus firmus setting exists just as it had in the previous two centuries, we find that the direct keyboard transcription of polyphonic ensemble compositions became the source of one truly independent form of keyboard music, the canzone. At the same time, there appeared the related forms of ricercare and fantasia. These new forms then developed in their own way: increasing unity by reducing the number of different themes, and in the ricercare, increasing the contrapuntal complexity. The old prelude became greatly expanded in Italy and gave rise to the toccata. Dance music also became an important part of the keyboard repertory. And from Spain and England come examples of the theme and variation form. Last but not least, reference must be made to the gradual development of an idiomatic style in keyboard writing, notably in the hands of the English virginal composers. Possibly the greatest achievement in the sixteenth century was the establishment of independent categories and forms of keyboard music.

CHAPTER THREE

The Seventeenth Century

The year 1600 is generally assumed to represent one of the greatest and most far-reaching turning points in the history of music. The main aspect of this change is the rise of the monodic soloistic style in Italy and the decline of the older contrapuntal art associated with The Netherlands. The new Italian art found its ideal expression in an important new musical form—the opera. Hand in hand with this change went a new interpretation of the art work, which was now thought to exist for the purpose of expression or the artistic representation of human emotions. And, with the innovation of the solo style, came a new role for keyboard instruments: a new type of accompaniment the basso continuo (also known as the thorough bass or, sometimes, the figured bass), that usually consisted of an organ or harpsichord playing along with a bass string instrument (see Arnold and Bergmann).

Most of the changes associated with the arrival of the Italian Baroque had their origins in the Renaissance. There is considerable evidence in Renaissance music of solo songs and of the use of keyboard instruments in accompaniment, particularly of the organ in the accompaniment of motets and Masses during church services. In this respect, therefore, the changes are quantitative rather than qualitative. As far as the main aspect is concerned, the new aesthetic ideal of the art work and its function, we find that this also developed from the humanistic conceptions of the sixteenth century, when it took the form of a suitable musical setting for a text. Although this first may be observed in the work of the Netherlands composers themselves (Josquin des Prez being perhaps the first example), it received full development in the hands of the Italian madrigalists in the latter part of the sixteenth century who, to be sure, were first stimulated by such Netherlanders working in Italy as Willaert, Rore, and Wert. The intent was to give each line, each intimation in the poetic text, full value, and this goes hand in hand with the exploitation of novel and surprising effects. Great contrasts occur

63

even within a rather short composition between types of melodies, declamation, textures, range, and the like, all in keeping with the new principle of "espressivo." But the main device was chromaticism, both melodic and harmonic, as the one best suited to achieve the surprises that were sought. Chromaticism plays an important role in the works of most madrigalists near the end of the sixteenth century and on into the early seventeenth; its most extravagant manifestations may be seen in some madrigals by Monteverdi and, especially, the well-known accomplishments of Gesualdo.

Keyboard music occupied a curious position with respect to the alleged innovations that came with the seventeenth century. On the one hand, the monodic soloistic style naturally had but little effect on keyboard music *per se* beyond the increased use of keyboard instruments for accompaniment. Indeed, much keyboard music, as we shall see, shows precisely the opposite; many categories of keyboard music do in fact retain the older contrapuntal procedures and forms all through the seventeenth and into the eighteenth centuries, long after the celebrated "war on counterpoint" launched by the famous *camerata* group in Florence. On the other hand, the increased interest in expression and the achieving of surprises and sudden contrasts is quite common in certain types of keyboard music; and frequently the two were combined in one and the same work, strict counterpoint appearing along with the expressive style.

As in the preceding chapter, we will proceed by countries, treating in order Italy, Germany, France, England, and the countries of the Iberian Peninsula.

The chief characteristics of the repertory of seventeenth-century Italian keyboard music (for a general account, see Pannain) are foreshadowed in the work of a group of composers working in Naples in the late sixteenth and early seventeenth centuries. The earliest Italian composer of the school was Antonio Valente, who published his *Intavolatura de cimbalo* in 1576 (see Caravaglios and Burns), a work containing mainly ricercares, but also a fantasia, some galliards, variations on ostinato bass melodies, and intavolaturas. The ricercares and the fantasia incorporate, along with contrapuntal imitation, much virtuoso figuration. A second tablature by Valente, the *Versi spirituali* of 1580, contains liturgical cantus firmus compositions. The leading innovator in Naples, however, was the italianized Netherlander Jean (or Giovanni) Macque (d. 1614) who, like his associates, made many contributions to the madrigal literature. In his keyboard works, which remained in manuscript during his lifetime, we find the expressive attitude otherwise associated with the madrigal of the time, particularly the use of chromaticism, as can be seen from his *Consonanze stravanganti* (*HAM*, I, 174) and a piece called *Durrezze e ligatura* (meaning dissonances and suspensions). Other members of this group were Rocco Rodio (*c.* 1535–*c.* 1615), Ascanio Mayone (d. 1627), and Giovanni Maria Trabaci (*c.* 1580–1647), each of whom published two comprehensive collections of keyboard music (see Apel).

Mayone published two books called *Diversi capricci* in 1603 and 1609 and Trabaci, two books of ricercares and canzones in 1603 and 1615. Both volumes contain works in the representative genres of keyboard music: ricercares, toccatas, galliards, and variations on ground bass melodies (called *mutanze*). Mayone is noteworthy for his cultivation of the capriccio, an imitative type related to the canzone but indulging in sudden contrasts and exploiting chromaticism. Trabaci's most notable works are his toccatas and ricercares; among the former are two pieces in the manner of Macque, a *Durezze e ligatura* and a *Consonanze stravaganti*. Generally, the ricercares and canzones are conservatively treated (see *HAM*, II, 191, for an example by Trabaci), but there is a tendency to employ one theme in all the various sections, as well as various countersubjects, thus indicating a certain preoccupation with the over-all cyclic unity of the composition (see Podolsky). Another composer to be mentioned here is Giovanni Salvatore.

The central figure in Italy in seventeenth-century keyboard music, however, is one of the greatest Italian keyboard composers of all time, Girolamo Frescobaldi (1583–1643). Although born and trained in Ferrara under the inventive composer Luzzasco Luzzaschi (d. 1607), most of Frescobaldi's life was spent in Rome as organist in several cathedrals; he did make a journey to Flanders in 1607 and worked in Florence between 1628 and 1634 (see Ronga, Redlich, and Machabey).

His output of music for keyboard, most of which apparently is for organ, is large and comprehensive and clearly represents the most important part of his total work. It is somewhat difficult to survey, since the various volumes usually exist in different editions that vary somewhat in content and in title (here, the date of the first edition is given). There is a book of fantasias of 1608, two books of toccatas and other works of 1615 and 1627, four books given over to the various imitative forms (ricercares, canzones, and capriccios) of 1615, 1624, 1626, and 1645. While liturgical works appear in the second book of toccatas, the main publication is the *Fiori musicali* of 1635. Dances appear in both books of toccatas.

Frescobaldi's involvement with the expressive ideal and the link to the madrigal is made clear in the preface to the collection of *Toccate e partite* that appeared in 1637, in which he states that the toccatas should not be performed in strict time, but rather that the meter should be varied, just as it is in the rendition of madrigals. Here, it is the proper expression of the affections that is the main point. Similar sentiments are expressed in the preface to the *Fiori musicali*. It can also be noted that in several works we find tempo designations, adagio and allegro, particularly in the *Fiori musicali*, and they are employed several times within a composition. A preoccupation with the effect of a piece on the listener is evident from the instructions on the performance of imitative works. "The opening phrases should be played slowly so that the succeeding passages appear more spirited," is the instruction in the collection of *Capricci, Ricercari e Canzoni* of 1626; and the same is implied in the toccatas of 1637 and the *Fiori musicali*. The basic intent, therefore, is quite plain. Other directions given by Frescobaldi involve the execution of the embellishments.

Most characteristic of the extreme expressive attitude are the twenty-odd toccatas. The external form is much the same as that developed by Merulo. The difference is rather one of quality, and this is largely due to the use of extreme chromaticism and sudden contrasts, both from the madrigal. In this respect, Frescobaldi follows directly in the path of the Neapolitan keyboard school mentioned earlier. His toccatas are, therefore, virtuoso display pieces in which figurational passages in "toccata" style alternate with sections in imitative counterpoint. Frequently, however, the counterpoint operates with short motives that are treated imitatively between the various parts and accompanied with figurative material so that instead of strictly separating the two procedures, as the normal course would have been, we find them combined. Sectional in the old sense is, on the other hand, Toccata IX from the collection published in 1637 (*HAM*, II, 193). Instead of the broad plan of Merulo's toccatas, we find a larger number of shorter sections contrasting sharply with one another, so that the effect produced is one of restless discontinuity. Virtuoso elements are present in abundance. An accumulation of figuration comes near the end to make an impressive conclusion, and in the score we find the remark, "the end will not be

EXAMPLE 15

FRESCOBALDI: *Toccata* (Book I, No. 6)—excerpt

reached without difficulty."[1] While most of the toccatas of Frescobaldi show the use of chromaticism, there are a few that capitalize on it. The best known of these is the *Toccata di durezze e ligature*, the eighth in the toccata book of 1637. This piece is closely related to similarly named pieces by Macque and Trabaci of the Naples group. Here, the emphasis is on harmonic surprises, chromatic changes, and dissonance.

On the other hand, there are some toccatas that are liturgical works in the sense that they are assigned to a position in the service. The *Fiori musicali* and the collection of 1637 both contain toccatas that are to be played during the Elevation of the Host in the Mass: *da sonarsi alla Levatione.* Here the composer becomes moderate. These are shorter compositions, and the striking effects generally characteristic of the toccata are used sparingly; instead of many contrasting sections, we find that essentially one character is established and maintained throughout.

The next important group of Frescobaldi's keyboard compositions to be discussed are the imitative contrapuntal forms. These are present in great variety; not only do we find the old established types of canzone and ricercare, but also the fantasia and, particularly, the capriccio. It is difficult to distinguish

[1] *Non senza fatiga si giunge al fin.*

EXAMPLE 16

FRESCOBALDI: *Toccata di durezze e ligature* (Set of 1637, No. 8)—excerpt

between all three types with any real precision. In the preface to the collection of 1624, Frescobaldi states that the capriccios "are not so simple in style" as the ricercares, but it is not clear in what sense the qualification "simple" is meant. Generally, the ricercares are strictly imitative works uniform in character throughout, while the canzones and capriccios display greater variety with contrasts of different sorts between the various sections and figurational elements prominent.

The ricercares, then, are the most modest, but, at the same time, they tend to be more strictly contrapuntal. This can be seen in several ricercares of the 1615 collection that actually treat one of the voices as if it were a cantus firmus; it has a short phrase in abnormally long note values repeated over and over during the composition. In a similar vein are a group of ricercares that use scale themes designated by the solmization syllables, a device used in the fantasias of the English virginal composers and by Sweelinck. There is, then, a certain conservative, almost deliberately archaic element in many of these works.

The canzones, for their part, are more elaborate and freer in the use of figurative and other elements. Several of them are related to popular songs of the time—not, as in the early sixteenth century, in the sense of an intavolatura, but rather in that they use phrases from the song that are developed and treated in imitative counterpoint. Such pieces are prominent in the 1645 collection.

The canzones and ricercares continue the trend towards unifying the form by decreasing the number of sections and increasing the importance of each, as well as using one theme throughout. This is especially true of the 1645 collection of canzones. Variation is important in these works, for variations on the main theme often provide the thematic material of the different sections. This procedure can be seen in a canzone in the *Fiori musicali* (*GMB*, 196). The other procedure is much like what is found in Sweelinck where the main theme remains the same while the countersubjects are varied from section to section. Another important feature that appears in these compositions is the tonal answer, so important from the harmonic standpoint in the development of contrapuntal keyboard forms.

A typical and popular canzone that does not employ the variation principle is the one in F from the 1637 publication (*HAM*, II, 194). This work is in five sections. The first, in duple time, is strictly imitative with the tonal answer based on a typical canzone-type theme: a leap up of a fifth, repeated notes, then a continuation by rapid sixteenth-note scale figuration patterns. Next, there is a change to 6/4 time with slower, scale-wise phrases. From then on, the piece is dominated by a constant accumulation and acceleration; first, a sharply defined dotted motive is tossed from voice to voice and is followed by a still more rapid motive that finally dissolves into sixteenth-note scale figuration culminating in full chords, and just before the very end is a quiet respite, in 6/4 time again, consisting of broken chords and suspensions. There is little expressive chromaticism in this work, and this is generally true of the canzones, although the third canzone in the 1637 collection is a notable exception.

Quite unusual and noteworthy among these imitative contrapuntal works are those in which a solo voice, a singer, takes over one of the parts. There are two such works in Frescobaldi's output; one is the Capriccio No. 10 in the first book of capriccios (1626), and the other is in the *Fiori musicali*. This second piece is the ricercare before the *Toccata alla Levatione* in the *Messa della Madonna*, where the sung voice is used as a cantus firmus consisting of a short phrase repeated in ostinato fashion at regular intervals. Since this type of cantus firmus treatment is not uncommon in sixteenth-century ensemble music (a famous example is the motet *Miserere mei Deus* of Josquin), this work is yet another instance of the conservative attitude that prevailed in much of the keyboard music of the seventeenth century. (A similar work by Monteverdi, but for instrumental ensemble and sopranos, is the *Sonata sopra Sancta Maria* from the *Vespers* of 1610.)

The most characteristic of Frescobaldi's imitative contrapuntal works are the capriccios. This is doubtless because the contrapuntal stringency is considerably relaxed in these works to allow for many passages in a freer style, particularly figurative elements in toccata style. There is a great deal of variety in these works. Some employ subjects based on scale segments identified by the solmization syllables; others use the same theme throughout, presenting it in variation (*HMS*, IV, s. 4, b. 2); another group employs standard dance melodies of the time, like *Ruggiero*, *La Spagnoletta*, and *La Bassa fiamenga*; and still another group may best be described as characteristic pieces, like the *Capriccio cromatico con ligatura al contrario* and the *Capriccio di durezze*, both of which exploit dissonance and chromatic surprises, or the *Capriccio di battaglia*, one of many examples of this genre. There is, then, no set scheme or form for the capriccios; each piece is quite individual, and it is doubtless this great freedom and willfulness that underlies the designation "capriccio."

The next group of Frescobaldi's works to be looked at briefly here are the liturgical compositions. These are mostly to be found in the *Fiori musicali*. The organ Mass is dominant, the collection containing three: a *Messa della Dominca*, a *Messa delli Apostoli*, and a *Messa della Madonna*. But we do not find what might be expected. Of the usual items of the Ordinary of the Mass, we find here only the Kyries, which are cantus firmus settings based on plainsong, identified by the titles as follows: *Kyrie Orbis factor*, *Kyrie Cunctipotens genitor*, and *Kyrie Cum jublio*, respectively. The remainder of each Mass consists of canzones, ricercares, and toccatas associated with four important parts of the Mass—the Epistle reading, the Credo, the Elevation of the Host, and the Communion. The toccatas go with the Elevation, the ricercares with the Credo, and the canzones with the Communion. The *Messa della Madonna* has an additional ricercare before the *Toccata alla Levatione*. In addition, all three have introductory toccatas before the Kyrie, and there are two additional toccatas preceding ricercares in the Masses *delli Apostoli* and *della Madonna*.

In these works, the flamboyant attitude manifest in many of the works already mentioned is absent. All is restrained and sober in keeping with their liturgical character. These toccatas, as already mentioned, are short and lack the great extremes that are otherwise associated with the category. Chromaticism remains important, but it is not used for its surprise value; this can be clearly seen in the well-known *Toccata chromatica per L'elevazione* in the *Messa delli Apostoli*. This restrained attitude goes over into the imitative contrapuntal forms as well, although, again, chromaticism is used in the same careful fashion. An example is the frequently performed *Ricerare dopo il Credo* from the *Messa della Madonna* (*MPM*, 34). Here, the intensely chromatic subject provides the basis for the whole composition, appearing in augmentation in the second section, while the countersubject is inverted. The piece is representative of the collection as a whole.

Other cantus firmus settings by Frescobaldi are in the collection of toccatas and canzones of 1637. These comprise settings of hymns and Magnificats strictly based on plainsong; they reveal the alternation between polyphony on the organ and plainsong sung by the choir, a practice we have frequently observed in works of this type.

Of lesser importance in Frescobaldi's work are the dance compositions. Most of these appear in the collection *Toccate e partite* of 1637, while one other, a *Bergamesca*, is contained, oddly enough, in the *Fiori musicali*. Although there are some dances proper, mostly correntes, more important are the large sets of variations on popular dance melodies of the time called "partitas." The term "partita" thus designates a composition in sections (parts) related to the dance, on the one hand, and to variations, on the other. Frescobaldi's partitas are based on standard dance melodies: *Romanesca* (*HAM*, II, 192, not complete), *La Monachina*, *Ruggiero*, and the famous *La Follia*, which has become particularly well known through the famous set of variations for violin and continuo by Corelli.

Not the least important general characterization of Frescobaldi that can be made is the constant seriousness of purpose that is revealed in his keyboard output. This is closely associated with a didactic aim, which is constantly mentioned in the prefaces to his various publications. The object plainly is to raise the quality of organ music and of organ playing in general. Particular emphasis is placed by Frescobaldi on the use of an open score (*partitura*), and several of his publications, including the *Fiori musicali*, appear in this format. It is noteworthy that much of this was accomplished by strict imitative contrapuntal forms, thereby continuing traditions established in the sixteenth century.

It must be emphasized that Frescobaldi was primarily a composer of keyboard music. This is true of only a few of his contemporaries and predecessors, insofar as can be judged from the works that have come down to us. Of the important composers, only Cabezón seems to rival him in this respect. Frescobaldi's best effort is devoted to keyboard music, and, in this sense, he may be regarded as the first really great composer for the keyboard. He had a tremendous international reputation that was firmly established well within his lifetime. His numerous public appearances attracted great attention, and many accounts of them have come down to us. Interestingly enough, it was his remarkable ability at improvisation that aroused the most comment, which indicates that this basic element in keyboard music still retained its old importance. Frescobaldi's fame naturally brought him many pupils, and his influence was particularly strong in Germany; among his direct pupils can be numbered Johann Jakob Froberger and Franz Tunder, both composers of decisive importance in the development of keyboard music in Germany. Much later, another composer took the trouble to become intimately acquainted with the *Fiori musicali*, copying it by hand for his own use—J. S. Bach.

There can be no doubt that Frescobaldi is far and away the most important figure in the Italian keyboard music of the Baroque period; indeed, he can be regarded as Italy's outstanding composer of keyboard music. It is paradoxical that his immediate influence was not great in his native country, and, while some successors carried on his tradition to some extent, it was largely German composers who seized on the more suggestive and bolder aspects of his art and employed them in new and larger varieties of keyboard composition. In this respect, the contrast with his great contemporary and compatriot Monteverdi— with whom he had much in common—is striking. As far as Italy is concerned, the interest was given to the opera, the cantata, and the oratorio, and, somewhat later in the century, to the newer instrumental forms, chamber and orchestral, so that all in all, keyboard music took secondary position. At the same time there were interesting developments that took place in Italian keyboard music to which we can briefly direct our attention (see Sandberger, Fellerer, and Monroe).

Of a large number of composers active in seventeenth-century Italy and involved to some extent with keyboard music, but generally in a secondary way, we can list three as possessing the greatest historical and artistic distinction: Michelangelo Rossi (1600–1674), Bernardo Pasquini (1637–1710, see Haynes and Heimrich), and Alessandro Scarlatti (1660–1725).[1] The genres are the same as those handed down from the generation of Frescobaldi: the toccata, the capriccio (and canzone) and ricercare, the sacred cantus firmus works, and the works related to the dance and dance forms. But to these was added a new genre— the sonata.

The cantus firmus settings, which appear in Giovanni Battista Fasolo's *Annuale, che contiene tutto quello che deve far un organista per rispondere al choro*

---

[1] For a comprehensive list, see Frotscher, Georgii, and Newman.

tutto l'anno of 1645 and Guilio Cesare Arresti's *Partitura di modulationi percettive* of around 1664, are, as would be expected, conservative works in the tradition of the *stile antico*, which maintained a place for itself throughout the Baroque period as "proper" for church music. Other collections containing such pieces are Antonio Croce's *Frutti musicali di messe* of 1642, which has organ Masses along with canzones and ricercares, and Giovanni Scipione's *Intavolatura di cembalo et organo toccate, capricci, hinni sopra il canto fermo* of 1650; both of these are similar in content to Frescobaldi's *Fiori musicali*, to which Croce's title in particular seems indebted. Hymn versets composed by Francesco Seghi near the end of the century appear in an anthology published in 1699.

It is rather in connection with the older imitative forms, here represented chiefly by the capriccio, and with the toccata that changes are to be observed. The ricercare, for its part, appears as the vehicle for strict imitative contrapuntal writing, the "learned" form of keyboard music (see, generally, Douglass). This can clearly be seen from the ricercares of Fasolo's *Annuale* and those of Fabrizio Fontana, dated 1677—which are described as being *in stile antico e grave*—as well as in the ricercares of Luigi Battiferri written in four to six voices and using one to six subjects. Chromatic ricercares after the fashion of Frescobaldi appear in Croce's *Frutti musicali*. The canzone pure and simple is not common, having apparently been superseded by the capriccio. While the canzone still looms large in the work of Fasolo and Croce, it is not important in the work of the other Italian keyboard composers of the time; the capriccio, on the other hand, was eagerly taken up and is given a prominent place in the work of Scipione, Bernardo Storace, Gregorio Strozzi, and Pietro Andrea Ziani.

Closely related to these forms is the toccata. It has been seen that, by the end of the sixteenth century, the toccata had been altered by the addition of lengthy sections in imitative counterpoint (ricercare style) that alternated with sections in the virtuoso toccata style, so that a combination of the two had been practised for some time. The toccata as such continued as a main form—perhaps the main form—of Italian keyboard music of the period. It is prominent in the work of Michelangelo Rossi, whose sole publication is *Toccate e correnti d'organo e cimbalo* (first published in 1637, a second edition appearing in 1657); here, the toccata is much as it had been, except that polyphonic imitation appears even in the figuration of the sections in toccata style; the extreme chromaticism found in the *toccata di durezze e ligatura* is not lacking here, as Rossi's *Toccata septima* eloquently demonstrates. Then there are toccatas by Giovanni Scipione (in his *Intavolatura* of 1650 and his *Partitura di cembalo* of 1652) and by Francesco Foggia (*c.* 1604–1688), who was active in Germany and Austria as well as in Italy, as also was Alessandro Poglietti. More important are the toccatas of Pasquini and Scarlatti, both of whom are better known for their vocal works, oratorios, and operas. Pasquini's toccatas were published in 1704 in an anthology also containing works by Kerll and Poglietti. A toccata in c (Valentin, 11, pp.

30–2) begins with arpeggio chords after which the main part of the work proceeds with constant sixteenth-note figuration, mainly scale segments, accompanied by chords.

Alessandro Scarlatti's toccatas—long considered spurious but whose authenticity now seems established (see Shedlock)—are similar, and, while virtuoso considerations are uppermost, these works also have an expressly didactic intent. The *Toccata sesta* (Valentin, 14, pp. 34–7) can serve as an example: one section with constant sixteenth-note figuration throughout, mostly arpeggios, with many modulating sequences. Several of these Scarlatti toccatas reveal another feature that came to have great importance for the keyboard music of the time— the employment in keyboard music of a specifically orchestral style. This is to be seen in two ways. As far as the thematic material is concerned, it can be seen in the relentlessly driving rhythms of the theme, in which figuration is of great importance. And it can be seen in the form, which resembles the ritornello organization so common in the concerto grosso of the time; that is to say, in between the several statements (three or more) of a principal section there appear episodes contrasting in character. This can be found especially in Scarlatti's Toccata in A (No. 8) and, to a lesser extent, in his Toccata in g (No. 9). This type of toccata, generally speaking, can be viewed as a consistent development from what had been usual in this genre of composition. But, on the other hand, since the *Toccata settima* is in the form of a theme and variations, the genre cannot really be said to have acquired a fixed form in Scarlatti's work.

A new term is introduced in keyboard music in the seventeenth century— "sonata" (see Newman)—which at this time means quite literally a piece to be played, as opposed to "cantata," a piece to be sung. The term is first used with reference to keyboard music by Adriano Banchieri (1567–1634) in connection with the musical examples found in the several editions of his popular treatise on organ playing, *L'organo suonarino*, beginning in 1605 (see Newman). Here the sonatas (or *suonatas*) present a varied group; while some are imitative, others resemble toccatas, and this stylistic ambivalence remains with the sonata throughout the century. Sonatas that resemble the toccata have come down from Bartolomeo Monari and Giovanni Paolo Colonna (1637–1695) in an anthology edited by Arresti and published in 1687. On the other hand, a set of sonatas by Gioanpietro del Buono, published in his only known work, a collection that appeared in 1641, are cantus firmus settings of the vesper hymn *Ave maris stella* (see Newman and Apel). Still another unusual situation is found in the sonatas for two harpsichords of Pasquini, composed in 1704, which have come down in manuscript; each is in three movements, all in the same key but in different meters, but the composer wrote out only two figured-bass parts so that these sonatas evidently had to be "realized" by their performers.

At the same time, it seems that the sonata generally was thought of as related to the canzone. From around the middle of the seventeenth century, we have a *sonata chromatica* by Tarquinio Merula which shows such a relationship; it is in four sections (or movements) that employ imitation throughout and rather unexpectedly use both inversion and diminution. Pieces called "sonatas" by Bernardo Pasquini are also fugal in style. Even more indicative is a collection by Gregorio Strozzi, his op. 3, *Capricci da sonare cembali et organi* of 1687, which, despite its title, contains pieces called "sonatas" of a kind that, as is stated in the preface, are "improperly called *canonze francese* by other people" (see Newman and Apel). Notated on three staffs and in the church modes, these sonatas are in three or four sections (or movements) contrasting in meter and using the same thematic material throughout. Here, several features of the old canzone are retained: imitative counterpoint, sectional organization, and thematic variation. Likewise, in the work of Carlo Francesco Pollarolli, the terms "capriccio" (related, as has been seen, to the canzone) and "sonata" are employed for one and the same type of composition—imitative works in one section with chordal passages providing a measure of contrast. The close relation between the canzone and the sonata is also apparent from chamber music, and a single instance may be drawn in by way of example from the work of Massimilio Neri, who, in his publications after 1651, called his works "sonatas," whereas before he had used the name "canzone" for the same type of composition (see Newman). It is rather in chamber music that the sonata reaches its greatest development in the seventeenth century, and, generally speaking, the keyboard sonatas of the Baroque period are strongly under the influence of the trio sonata.

Dances, traditionally associated with the harpsichord, also exist both as individual pieces, including the larger variation forms, and as suites. Important contributions are Giovanni Picchi's *Intavolatura di balli d'arpicorda* of 1621; Rossi's collection of 1637, which contains *correntes*; Bernardo Storace's *Selva di varie compositioni d'intavolatura per cimbalo et organo* of 1664, which emphasizes the large variation forms (see Apel); and the anthology *Toccates et suites* published by the firm of Roger in Amsterdam in 1704, containing works of Poglietti, Pasquini, and Kerll.

In France, as in Italy, we find both old and new forms in keyboard music. Although a strong influence was exercised on French music by Italian composers, in France there was a more definite line of demarcation between styles and types: between sacred liturgical works for organ, on the one side, and secular pieces intended for harpsichord (or clavecin), on the other. Generally, those works in the older contrapuntal forms turn out to be for the organ while the newer types of music are in the secular realm and associated rather with the harpsichord. This sharp split between the two was, it will be remembered, characteristic of the Attaingnant prints of the early sixteenth century. At the same time, however, there are still many compositions extant for keyboard instruments in general (in the sense of the German term *clavier*); the split must, let it be emphasized, be taken to have only a general validity. We shall have occasion to note instances in which secular features are found in liturgical works for organ, so that a certain amount of caution in dealing with such matters is necessary. Let us first take up the organ music of France in the seventeenth century and then the very important corpus of music for the harpsichord.

The most important French composers of organ music at this time were:

Jean Titelouze (1563–1633)
Nicolas Grigault (1624 or 1625–1707)
Nicolas LeBègue (1631–1702)
Jean-Henri d'Anglebert (1635–1691)
François Roberday (1624–1690)
Nicolas de Grigny (1672–1702).

The first French keyboard composer of stature since the Attaingnant prints in Titelouze, who was organist in Rouen from 1585. There is a possibility that he was in contact with Catholic musicians from England who were in exile in France during his adolescence, a circumstance that would have made him familiar with English music, especially the virginal style. In any case, his output is strictly liturgical and is contained in two publications issued by the Parisian firm of Ballard, *Hymnes de l'église* of 1623 and *Le Magnificat suivant les tons* of 1626. The preface to the former work states that these hymns represent the first printed organ music in France *hors de la suivance des hommes*, a statement confirming the paucity of such music in France at the time.

Titelouze's hymns are cantus firmus settings of hymns important in the church year. They are strophic compositions, and those versets composed for organ are intended to alternate with those sung by a chorus. The first verset is in rather strict cantus firmus style, the Gregorian melody, with some variations, being given in long notes in one part while the other voices engage in an elaborate contrapuntal accompaniment using phrases from the cantus firmus for the thematic material. An easily accessible example is the hymn *Pange lingua* for Corpus Christi, where the Gregorian melody appears in the bass part (*HAM*, I, 180). Then there follow settings in which the hymn melody provides the themes, which are successively treated in imitation. A particularly vigorous fugue of this type may be seen in the fourth verset (the fourth strophe) of *Veni Creator spiritus*. In settings of this type, the form comes close to the strictly imitative ricercare, of which there are several examples using themes from standard melodies. In both cases, be it noted, the cantus firmus does indeed permeate the entire composition, exactly as was the case in many Masses and motets of the sixteenth-century Netherlands composers. In most instances, the technique of imitative counterpoint is dominant, the style strict, and the atmosphere sober. Yet, there are places where a change may be observed that involves the introduction of figurative elements from the toccata, as is the case in the third versets of the hymns *Pange lingua, A solis ortis cardine,* and *Urbs Jerusalem.*

The Magnificats, in accordance with long-standing custom, consist of eight cycles, each composed of seven versets, based on each of the eight Magnificat recitation Tones; as earlier, the practice of alternation between the organ settings and the chorus singing the plainsong is maintained. The characteristics noted in connection with the hymns are also found here in the Magnificats. An association with the ideal of expression makes itself evident occasionally, particularly in the *Deposuit potentes* sections in which there frequently appear highly rhythmical figures with much use of sixteenth-note figuration patterns, although plainer alternate versions also appear.

Titelouze's successors did not follow him in the cultivation of the strict cantus firmus types, even though their organ music did remain largely liturgical. But these cantus firmus forms did not go out altogether, as may be seen from the

EXAMPLE 17

LeBègue: *Basse de trompette*—beginning

work of François Couperin whose *Pièces d'orgue* of 1690 contains cantus firmus organ Masses. The general trend, however, is away from this type of composition, and we get something quite different (see Howell). Unlike composers in other countries, the French tended to emphasize the element of tone color in the organ. LeBègue's pieces, then, indicate what stops the organist is to use in performance: *trompette, tierce, cromhorne, taille, bourdon*, and the like, and the pieces then take the form of duos (dialogues) and trios as well as fugues. A common form is a suite or cycle of such pieces of differing registrations, customarily ending in a piece that calls for everything—*plein jeu*. Such explicitness in regard to registration may be seen, apart from LeBègue, in the work of Couperin, d'Anglebert, Raison, and Dandrieu (see Dufourcq, Tessier, and Gillespie). The instance on the importance of tone color remains a basic characteristic of French organ music. Readily at hand is a *Dialogue* by LeBègue (*HMS*, VI, s. 2, b. 5, a).

In LeBègue's organ pieces, Book I, we find what may be called "organ suites": sets of compositions contrasting in character but all in the same key with no external unifying factor such as the use of a cantus firmus or common thematic material in all the movements. Instead, they commence with a short prelude, continue with various shorter compositions, and conclude with an impressive *plein jeu*. The same thing is found in LeBègue's organ Masses. Unlike what we have met up to this time, these are not cantus firmus compositions at all; rather they are sets of pieces, and consist of a Kyrie, a Gloria, a Sanctus, and an Agnus Dei. The Kyrie and Agnus settings are the only ones to employ a Gregorian cantus firmus;

EXAMPLE 17—*continued*

Basse de Tr.

significantly enough, it uses the *Kyrie Cunctipotens genitor* that, as we have often seen, was used in organ settings of the Mass. The long Gloria movement adheres to the established alternatim practice, a fact that in itself would indicate close conformity to strict liturgical requirements, although a cantus firmus is not used. The situation can be seen even more clearly in LeBègue's cycle of Magnificats, which appears in Book II of his organ pieces. Here the old form is completely neglected. We find sets of eight compositions that commence with a section called "Magnificat," which is in the nature of a prelude; this is followed by a group of pieces with characteristic titles, and they conclude with an impressive finale marked *plein jeu*, invoking the full tonal resources of the organ. The old cantus firmus form is replaced by the new conception.

LeBègue's Book III contains still other liturgical works that show the same situation. Chief among these in importance are the Offertories. These works are long and sectional and are written in a free and quasi-improvisational style, but they do avoid the brilliant display of the toccata with which they otherwise have much in common. Still another important related group of compositions are the Noels, organ pieces based on Christmas melodies (*HAM*, II, 231), and the *simphonies*, which turn out to be in the form and style of the so-called "French overture" developed by Lully: a slow, pompous, impressive chordal first section that frequently exploits dotted rhythms, followed by a fast fugal section with a dance-like subject. Finally, there is a group of short compositions in a free form to be played during the Elevation of the Host at Mass, thus related to similar compositions by Frescobaldi and others.

Forms such as those used by LeBègue are characteristic of French organ music of the seventeenth and eighteenth centuries and, indeed, play a role in the formulation of the French organ school of the nineteenth century. Among other composers associated with this type of organ composition, with the emphasis on suites of pieces either for the Mass or Magnificat or else simply as suites, we should mention Henri Dumont, Nicolas Grigault, Nicolas de Grigny, and André Raison.

On the other hand, the influence of Frescobaldi makes itself felt particularly in the work of François Roberday, the Parisian organist who had been Lully's teacher (see Hardouin). His main contribution is the collection *Fugues, et caprices, a quatre parties mises en partition pour l'orgue* of 1660. His use of the open-score format is characteristic of Frescobaldi. But more important is the use of Frescobaldi's particular forms and types of compositions. Although the term "fugue" is used here, these works are much like Frescobaldi's canzones and ricercares while the term "capriccio" probably comes directly from Frescobaldi. There are compositions here that employ themes of Frescobaldi along with those of Couperin, Cavalli, and Froberger, as well as entire pieces by Frescobaldi, Froberger, and Ebner. Furthermore, the principle of variation is important and in an unusual fashion; we find the fugues and capriccios presented in pairs, united by the use of common thematic material submitted to various sorts of variation and development.

Also of great significance is the large body of music for harpsichord (clavecin) that was written in seventeenth-century France (see Mereaux and Pirro). While the organists we have mentioned also made contributions to this repertory, most composers of harpsichord music are not particularly noted for their organ compositions (the main exceptions are d'Anglebert and LeBègue). Most of them were associated with the magnificent court of Louis XIV. The chief among them are:

Jacques Champion de Chambonnières (*c.* 1602–1672)

Louis Couperin (*c.* 1626–1661)

Jean-Henri d'Anglebert.

Apart from printed collections, a large body of this music is preserved in the important Bauyn Manuscript in two volumes (Paris, B. N. Rés.[7] 674 and 675).

The repertory of harpsichord music differs significantly from that of organ music, as would be expected. It centers around the dance and forms related to the dance; the imitative contrapuntal types are neglected, as are the liturgical categories. This emphasis on the dance is related to lute music in the sixteenth century. Indeed, the importance of lute music is such that it may be regarded as the true source of the harpsichord art of the time in terms of style as well as of repertory. Lute music flourished in France in the sixteenth and seventeenth centuries, and, as it declined in the latter part of the seventeenth century, its traditions were transferred to and maintained in harpsichord music.

The forms and types that appear in harpsichord music are those of popular dances of the time. We have seen that, in the sixteenth century, there was a tendency to group dances in pairs. In this lies the origin of the practice of having a whole group of dances all in the same key, a form known as the "suite" or "dance suite." It must be emphasized that the incorporation of the principle of cyclic form by means of thematic variation is not a characteristic of seventeenth-century French harpsichord music. The appearance of a suite comprising three or more numbers seems to have been the main contribution of French composers of the seventeenth century to large forms in keyboard music, although there are contributions from elsewhere, and the form quickly attained international standing. The following dances are the most prominent.

allemande: moderate duple time

courante: moderate triple time

saraband: slow triple time

gigue: fast compound triple time (generally 6/8).

It should be pointed out that the designation "suite" was used but infrequently in seventeenth-century France with reference to harpsichord music, and, when used, it meant only a succession of pieces of different sorts and carried no implication of a particular genre (see Reimann). Three different kinds of arrangement have been found in this music, all based on the use of one key throughout: first, the "loose" form, consisting of a number of dances arranged by types, any number of dances in each group; second, the opposite of this, a series of single dances, one of each kind; third, a combination form, some dance types represented by individual dances and others by groups. The suites of Chambonnières are of the third variety; here, we can find, for example, an allemande, one or more courantes, and a saraband followed by an indefinite number of other dances. The suites of Louis Couperin (see Bouvet), on the other hand, are of the first kind, the dances being arranged by key and then by types; first there is a group in C, then one in d, followed by groups or suites in D, e, F, G, and so on, and, within each group or suite, all the allemandes are together, then all the courantes, and then the sarabands, as well as occasional other dances. The preludes appear together as a separate group at the beginning. Such freedom in the suite of the time is also found in the large and important output of d'Anglebert. Here there are groups or suites of some thirty to forty pieces, each arranged by key (C, g, and D). Each suite commences with a prelude that is followed by an allemande, several courantes, a saraband, a gigue, a number of galliards, then other dances and dance forms; this has been called the "open" form. Much the same situation can be found in the work of LeBègue. By no means infrequent is the succession allemande—courante (one or more)—saraband; but the gigue as finale is not common in seventeenth-century France, and, instead, we find the minuet, or chaconne, passacaille, or tombeau. It is not until the eighteenth century, in Dieupart (who worked in England), that the succession allemande—courante—saraband—gigue, each represented by one piece (the second type), appears with any regularity. (The single work of Hardel, or Hardelle, in the Bauyn manuscript is to be regarded as an isolated exception.) This being the case, it seems evident that, in the seventeenth century, the player was to make a selection of numbers in the same key and to play these as a suite. From the stand-point of the French composers, the emphasis was on the dances as individual compositions and not on the attempt to establish a large over-all form to which the individual dances are subordinate.

In these suites, the normal form of the individual dance is maintained. In most of them, the form comprises two parts, each to be repeated $\|{:}a{:}\| \ \|{:}b{:}\|$ with a modulation from the tonic to the dominant (or relative major) in the first section and a return, often passing through other keys to the tonic. Frequently, the second section employs the same thematic material as the first, or the second section commences differently and then restates, with changes, the first; this latter is often called "rounded" binary form. Often found, especially with the courante and minuet, is the double, a second dance of the same species, after which the first is played again. (Sometimes, the double is also a variation of the

first; for an example by Chambonnières, see *GMB*, 218; see also Reimann.)
This practice is maintained through the eighteenth and nineteenth centuries in
instrumental music as the trio section in a minuet or scherzo movement of a
sonata, symphony, or other genre. There are, however, some dances whose forms
differ principally from these. Important here is the rondeau, which has a refrain
like a ritornello that is repeated throughout and separates sections of contrasting
character called "couplets," the number of which is not fixed. The passacaille
and chaconne are both variation forms based on short ostinato patterns. But at
times we find examples of the *chaconne en rondeau*, a chaconne treated in rondeau
form. (See the example by Chambonnières, *HAM*, II, 212). Similarly, d'Anglebert
composed a *La Follia* in twenty-two parts.

Many of these dances and other pieces were given descriptive titles. Although,
in some cases, such titles are ceremonial, in many they indicate the specific program or affection for the music to represent. Examples in the work of Chambonnières readily available are the *Allemande dit l'afflige* and the piece *La
drollerie* (*HMS*, VI, s. 2, b. 1). Other pieces to be mentioned here are Chambonnières' *Les barricades*, representing a battle scene, the gigue *La villageoise*;
but there are innumerable examples. D'Anglebert's harpsichord dances, on the
other hand, do not bear any descriptive titles.

Serious lyric expression will be found in the saraband, as is particularly true
in the work of Louis Couperin. But there is another highly characteristic genre

EXAMPLE 18

L. Couperin: *Saraband* in d—beginning

that is taken over from lute music—the tombeau, literally, a gravestone or monument. Such works are restrained lamentations, an instrumental equivalent of the old planctus. All the leading composers of the time made contributions to this repertory. Particularly noteworthy are one by Louis Couperin (for a Monsieur Blanchecroucher) and another for Chambonnières by d'Anglebert.

Several groups of pieces exist quite apart from the forms and patterns of the various dances. Chief among these are the preludes which loom large in the work of Louis Couperin and d'Anglebert (see the example by d'Anglebert, *HAM*, II, 232). These carry on the old tradition of the prelude without bringing in elements added by the Italian composers in the latter part of the sixteenth century. The prelude, therefore, remains a small form in a quasi-improvisational manner exhibiting great freedom of rhythm. These pieces do not have time signatures; all notes are written as being equal in value, and the shape of our whole note is used for all. Hence, meter and rhythm are purely at the discretion of the player. The melodic material consists largely of arpeggio patterns. Louis Couperin's preludes are in two parts; the first is like that just described, but the second, with the designation *changement de mouvement*, is fugal, so that there is a similarity to the important orchestral form, the so-called "French overture." It might be mentioned here that d'Anglebert included in his suites transcriptions for harpsichord of compositions by Lully, of which important examples are transcriptions of the overtures to *Cadmus et Hermione* and *Alceste*; there are other overtures and also other numbers from the operas and ballets.

Several general features of this music may be discussed in conclusion. The style, on the whole, is quite simple, and most of the pieces are "light" in character, although there are a number of exceptions. Usually, there is a simple melody presented in the uppermost part accompanied by simple harmonies. The relationship to lute music can easily be seen, on the one hand, in the extensive ornamentation, chiefly of the melodic part, and, on the other, in the frequent use of broken-chord patterns, which is connected to the *style brisé* of lute music—the term refers to the judicious breaking up of chords so as to create the impression of a contrapuntal texture. Although there are but a few pieces that are really in imitative counterpoint, reference can be made to a canonic gigue by Chambonnières and to a similar saraband by Louis Couperin. In most of the dances, an extreme delicacy, lightness, and clarity may be discerned. An exception to this may be seen in the work of d'Anglebert, who was associated with Lully and carried characteristics of the orchestral style into harpsichord music. This is accomplished mainly through the consistent use of full chords with much doubling; driving, insistent rhythms; and an avoidance of the lute-like quality usually found in this music. We have already noted, in this connection, the transcriptions for harpsichord of Lully's orchestral compositions made by d'Anglebert.

The role played by ornamentation in this music is of great importance. The simplicity of the melodies as they are written is deceptive; the ornamentation must be considered as a fundamental part of the melody. This is no peculiarity of French harpsichord music, but is a regular feature of Baroque (and even Renaissance) music, which apparently derives from practices in vocal music. In fact, it seems that such ornamentation is an essential characteristic of Baroque art in general. So important is the ornamentation in the French harpsichord music of the seventeenth century that we find full instructions for the execution of the various ornaments given by Chambonnières, d'Anglebert, LeBègue, and others in their several publications. There are, however, many details in which we find

EXAMPLE 19

COMMON ORNAMENTS

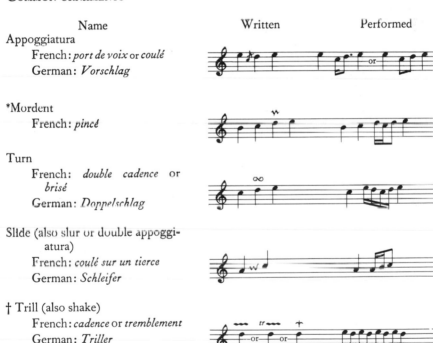

Name	Written	Performed
Appoggiatura French: *port de voix* or *coulé* German: *Vorschlag*		
*Mordent French: *pincé*		
Turn French: *double cadence* or *brisé* German: *Doppelschlag*		
Slide (also slur or double appoggiatura) French: *coulé sur un tierce* German: *Schleifer*		
† Trill (also shake) French: *cadence* or *tremblement* German: *Triller* Italian: *trillo*		

* The inverted mordent (*Schneller*) was of German origin.

† The trill could be prefixed with an appogiatura, producing the *tremblement appuyé* or *vorbereitete Triller*, and terminated with a turn-like figure (the *Nachschlag*). The short trill consisting of but four notes (the *Pralltriller*) went out of use at the end of the eighteenth century.

no agreement among the various sources. This lack of agreement involves not only what the various symbols stand for, but also in what the various ornaments actually consist. The most important of these ornamentations (or *agréments*) are the following (see Brunold; also Dannreuther and Dolmetsch; convenient is Donington's article in *GD*, VI, pp. 384–448).

The musical scene in seventeenth-century Germany presents a confused picture, considerably more so than elsewhere in Europe. Much of this is to be traced to the political disturbances that were ultimately the result of the Reformation, chief among them the incredible devastation wrought upon Germany by the Thirty Years' War (1618–1648) during which French and Swedish armies marched across Germany; some two-thirds of the German population perished during this war. At this time, musical culture was, to say the least, severely inhibited. But the political confusion was also parallel to the artistic situation; in both spheres, foreign influences dominated. Although some characteristic musical forms do indeed come into existence in Germany and Austria at this time, they plainly owe their existence to the music of Italy and France: Italy, particularly in the works of Frescobaldi, who was influential all over but especially in Austria and Bavaria; France, the harpsichordists and Lully, again noticeable especially in Austria and Bavaria. Still another influence is to be seen in Sweelinck, with his English and Italian background, particularly effective in the middle and northern parts of Germany.

Several different types and styles of keyboard music exist in seventeenth-century Germany. But added to the customary division between sacred and secular music was another: whether Catholic or Protestant. In general, the South (Bavaria and Austria) remained staunchly Catholic while the North, except for the Rhineland, embraced the Protestant faith. Each religion had its characteristic liturgy, although there were some correspondences between them, and each had its own types of music and musical forms. Along with religious music, there is a large body of secular keyboard music, particularly cultivated in the South but certainly present in the North as well, and here the foreign models are transformed into something new and different.

The following composers, all of them connected either with a cathedral or with a court, are the most important. In the South, we find at Vienna, Johann Jakob Froberger (1616–1667), Ferdinand Tobias Richter (1649–1711), Alessandro Poglietti (d. 1683), Franz Matthaeus Techelmann, and Johann Kasper Kerll (1627–1693); in Bohemia, Johann Kasper Ferdinand Fischer (*c.* 1665–1746), a name used evidently by two composers, father and son. In central Germany, we have Samuel Scheidt (1587–1654) in Halle, Johann Ulrich Steigleder (1593–1635) in Stuttgart, Johannes Klemme (*c.* 1593–*c.* 1657) and Nicolaus Adam Strungk (1640–1700) in Dresden, Johann Christoph Bach (1642–1703), the most celebrated among J. S. Bach's ancestors, in Eisenach; in Augsburg, Christian Erbach (1573–1635); in Nürnberg, Johann Pachelbel

(1653–1706) and Johann Erasmus Kindermann (1616–1655); in Frankfurt am Main, Franz Xaver Murschhauser (1663–1738); in Braunschweig, Delphin Strungk (1601–1695), father of Nicolaus Adam; in Erfurt, Johann Heinrich Buttstedt (1666–1727); in Passau (and also in Vienna and Salzburg), Georg Muffat (1653–1704); and in Bayreuth and Zittau, Johann Krieger (1652–1735).

There was particular activity in the Protestant North. Here, the most important centers included, first, Hamburg, where we find Heinrich Scheidemann (c. 1596–1663), Melchoir Schildt (1592–c. 1667), Jan Reincken (1623–1722), Jacob Praetorius (1586–1651), Matthias Weckmann (1621–c. 1691), and Vincent Lübeck (1654–1740); and, second, Lübeck (see Stiehl), where the most important organists were Franz Tunder (1614–1667), Johann Nicolaus Hanff (1665–c. 1711) and the great Dietrich Buxtehude (1637–1707). Other organists active in the North include Nicolas Bruhns (1665–1697) in Kiel, Paul Siefert (1586–1666) in Königsberg and Danzig, Georg Böhm (1661–1733) in Lüneburg, and Peter Heidorn about whom but little is known (see Riedel); and, in Leipzig, was one of the more illustrious of J. S. Bach's predecessors as cantor at the Thomasschule, Johann Kuhnau (1660–1722), a man of peculiarly broad talents and sympathies.[1]

Before the various musical types and forms themselves can be taken up, there are two general matters that call for special attention. The first of these concerns notation. Until this period, the form of the German tablature was employed in German keyboard music, a type of notation characterized, as we have seen, by the use of letters. This old form of notation clung on and was used in some parts of Germany all through the seventeenth and even down into the eighteenth century. The Italian form of the keyboard score, using the standard forms of mensural notation, made its appearance in the southern part of Germany where the Italian influence was the strongest. The impressive first occasion of its use in Germany was the important and influential publication of the Halle organist Samuel Scheidt, his *Tabulatura nova*, the three volumes of which appeared in 1624. This form of notation was also employed seven years later in a publication of Johannes Klemme.

The second matter has to do with the curious fact that little keyboard music was printed in Germany in the seventeenth century; most of it remained in manuscript. The list of composers whose keyboard works existed only in manuscript during their lifetimes is long and includes, among others, Weckmann, Tunder, Scheidemann, Böhm, and even Buxtehude. (Two recent studies on the

---

[1] A general study of Sweelinck's pupils in Germany is by Seiffert; among works on individual composers we can list (alphabetically by composer): Böhm (Wolgast and Waldschmidt), Bruhns (Kölsch), Buxtehude (Buszin, Hedar, Lorenz, Pirro, and Stahl), Fischer (Hofmann-Erbrecht), Froberger (Seidler, Bauer, and Somer), Kerll (Riedel), Kuhnau (Clercx), Murschhauser (Vogeleis), Reincken (Stahl), Scheidemann (Breig), Scheidt (Mahrenholz and Hünnicken), Steigleder (Emsheimer and Hirtler), Tunder (Stahl), and Weckmann (Ilgner and Roth). On keyboard music in Nürnberg, see Rumohr. See also Apel.

source materials of keyboard music in seventeenth-century Germany are by Schierning and Riedel). An especially important group of manuscript tablatures containing a large and comprehensive repertory, secular and sacred, representing the leading German composers, particularly those working in the North, is presently in Lüneburg.

The organ music that was published generally served one of two purposes— music for use in the service or music for teaching. Organ pieces based on Protestant chorales are most important in the first group, and the following publications may be mentioned: Scheidt's *Tabulatur-Buch* (Gorlitz, 1650) and Pachelbel's *Choräle* (Nürnberg, 1693). Catholic liturgical music is represented by Kerll's *Modulatio organica* (Munich, 1686), Muffat's *Apparatus musico-organisticus* (Salzburg, 1690), and Murschhauser's *Octi-Tonium novum organicum* (Augsburg, 1696). Among the didactic collections we may count Scheidt's *Tabulatura nova* (Hamburg, 1624), even though it contains liturgical music suitable for both the Catholic and the Protestant service, along with other compositions, and Klemme's *Partitura seu tabulatura italica* (Dresden, 1631), which contains thirty-six fugues arranged in order by the twelve church modes.

The publications of secular music for keyboard present a more uniform picture in that they by and large represent one category of composition—the suite. The following are the most important: Froberger's *Suites de clavecin* (Amsterdam, 1693); Fischer's *Pièces de clavessin* (Schlackenwerth, 1696); Krieger's *Musicalische Partien* (Nürnberg, 1697); and Pachelbel's *Hexachordum Apollinis* (Nürnberg, 1699). The one new category here is the sonata for solo keyboard instrument which appears in Kuhnau's two publications, the *Frische Clavier-Früchte* (Leipzig, 1696) and the *Biblische Historien* (Leipzig, 1700).

Apart from these, there is a group of publications that reveals a more composite and general character. Not only are many types of music for various purposes included in these collections, but also the instrumental medium is frequently indicated as clavier in general, thus not restricting the performance to any particular keyboard instrument. In a way, Scheidt's *Tabulatura nova* is of this type. Often, such collections contain a variety of imitative contrapuntal works, such as Steigleder's *Ricercare tabulata organis et organoedis* of 1624, Kindermann's *Harmonia organica* (Nürnberg, 1645), Froberger's *Partite di toccate, canzone, ricercari* (Mogart, 1693; second volume, 1696); and Fischer's *Ariadne musica* (Schlackenwerth, 1702; also Augsburg, 1715). We even find publications like Pachelbel's *Musicalische Sterbensgedanken* (Erfurt, 1683), a group of organ chorales that is clearly as much intended for "secular" performance on a harpsichord or clavichord as for performance on an organ in the church. Collections bearing the title *Clavier-Uebung* (keyboard practice or exercise) are of this type as well.

We may now turn to the various types of compositions found in the seventeenth-century German repertory. Our discussion will commence with the cantus firmus compositions, Catholic and Protestant, and then, move on to what might be described as the "free" forms in organ music, the toccata-type works and the fugue, and will conclude with harpsichord music, the suite and the sonata.

The old form of the cantus firmus composition continues to be of basic importance even though its application in seventeenth-century Germany results in forms that are quite different. It is here that the religious question takes on considerable importance, and our main interest will center on the Protestant service—on its departures from the Catholic liturgy and its maintenance of various features of the Catholic service, at least as far as the use of keyboard music is concerned.

In the Catholic liturgy, as has been seen, the organ had been used chiefly in connection with the Mass, the Magnificat, and certain hymns, generally those associated with Vespers. These were usually cantus firmus compositions based on the plainsong proper to the occasion, and the principle of alternation between the chorus singing the (monophonic) plainsong and the organ playing poly-phonically was preserved, although other combinations occurred. Apart from these, we also met with forms like the ricercare and the canzone and, particularly, the toccata, all of which were at times associated with the Mass. Compositions exclusively intended for Catholic use are not prominent in the work of the composers under consideration here. In fact, the most comprehensive publica-tion in this field is not by a Catholic composer at all; it is the third part of Scheidt's *Tabulatura nova* of 1624, which contains compositions for the Mass, a full cycle of Magnificats in all the church modes, and a group of hymns—in short, the whole Catholic organ repertory is represented. These compositions are examples of the purest and strictest kind of cantus firmus writing.

The situation, however, is complicated by the fact that Lutheran cathedrals in the larger cities frequently used Masses, Magnificats, and even certain hymns in their Latin texts. Especially common in Protestant churches was the Magnificat, with Latin text, so that one cannot immediately be sure whether a collection con-taining a Magnificat was either Catholic or Protestant. Hence, we find that the Magnificat is well represented in the work of the Protestant German organ composers; apart from the settings already mentioned, we can list those of Kindermann, Murschhauser (*Octitonium*, 1696), Buxtehude, and Kerll, whose *Modulatio organica* of 1686 is devoted exclusively to this genre. In the same spirit, we find an organ *Te deum* in the work of Buxtehude.

The surprising fact is the lack of Catholic organ music even in the work of composers active in the Catholic cities of the South, such as Munich and Vienna. These composers, instead, emphasized, on the one hand, the imitative con-trapuntal forms and, on the other, the secular genres, notably the suite. The old organ Mass practically disappeared.

In great contrast is the considerable activity among Protestant organists and composers in the cantus firmus settings based on the great body of chorale melodies that form the musical basis of the Lutheran service (see Dietrich, Kittler, and Scheide). The chorale is of fundamental importance in the Protestant liturgy; as in the Catholic plainsong repertory, there are chorales proper to specific seasons and particularly festivals—some for Advent, Christmas, Epiphany, Lent, Holy Week, Trinity, and the like—so that each chorale has its specific liturgical character, function, and significance. Moreover, certain chorales corresponded to items of the Ordinary of the Mass; e.g., for the Gloria, *Allein Gott in der Höh' sei Ehre* and for the Credo, *Wir glauben all' an einen Gott*. But, unlike the Catholic plainsongs, chorales are congregational: they are sung in German, and the melodies themselves, occasionally taken from popular songs of the time, are simple and easy to sing. It was their incorporation into organ music that provided the greatest area of activity among Protestant organ composers of the time.

The types of organ setting of chorale melodies, for which the generic term "organ chorale" may conveniently be employed, bear similarities to cantus firmus compositions in general. Briefly, there are three general types. The first is the chorale variation or chorale partita, a strophic composition in which the chorale melody is presented in each strophe but with variations; we have already noted examples of this in the work of Sweelinck and of the colorist school of the sixteenth century. Then, there is the so-called "chorale fantasy," an imitative contrapuntal type in which the chorale, instead of being given as a cantus firmus in one voice alone, is broken up and used in all parts so that this type takes the form of a fugue using themes of the chorale; either all the phrases of the melody are treated successively in imitation or only a few are selected; the emphasis, in either case, usually falls on the first line. The third type is at once the latest to develop and the simplest of the three, the chorale prelude; it is a short composition presenting the chorale melody as a cantus firmus in one voice with an accompaniment in the other parts, designed to precede the congregational singing of a chorale during the service.

The oldest of these is the first, the chorale partita. This is because it is directly analogous to the procedure in composing Magnificats and hymns, as well as that used in the variations on secular songs that appear in sixteenth-century keyboard music. Of interest here is the relation between the sacred and the secular, since the form is a mixture and can be used in either context. The terminology, however, differs; in a secular setting, each of the various sections is called "variatio" or "partita," while, in the case of sacred melodies, the plainsong terminology is followed and the term "versus" is used for each variation. Although the technique is basically the same for each, there was, in the early seventeenth century, a tendency to treat the chorale melody plainly and not to submit it to extensive alterations and variations, especially in regard to adding notes. Scheidt, in particular, was careful in this. In the secular variations, on the other hand, variations in the song melody are freely employed.

A number of such chorale partitas appear in the first two volumes of Scheidt's *Tabulatura nova: Wir glauben all' an einem Gott* (four versus); *Da Jesus an dem Kreuze stund* (six verses); *Christ lag in Todesbanden* (five versus); *Gelobet seist du, Jesus Christ* (eight versus); and *Herzlich lieb hab' ich dich* (two *versus*). As an example, *Da Jesus an dem Kreuze stund* may be briefly considered. Here, the chorale melody is strictly followed and appears *absque ullo colore* ("without any ornamentation") in long notes and in one part, which, however, varies from versus to versus. The variation, then, takes place in the accompaniment, whose character changes from section to section. This accompaniment often draws on phrases of the chorale melody for its thematic material, treating it either in imitation or motivically; or the accompaniment may be wholly figurative, consisting of many running scale passages after the example of Sweelinck and the English virginalists and of the German coloristic school of the latter sixteenth century.

The chorale partita is an important type of organ chorale setting and appears in one form or another in the work of many composers of seventeenth-century Germany. It dominates the output of Weckmann and Strungk and is important in that of Murschhauser and Buxtehude. An important publication is by Johann Pachelbel, the *Musicalische Sterbensgedanken* (Erfurt, 1683) which contains three chorale partitas: *Ach was soll ich Sünder machen, Werde munter mein Gemüthe*, and *Alle Menschen müssen sterben* (see Seiffert). In each case, a simple setting of the chorale melody is given first and is followed by the variations, of which there are from three to six. In general, these are contrapuntal variations that treat the chorale after the fashion of the chorale-fantasy. Others have many scale passages in the style of Sweelinck and Scheidt that border on virtuosity; an example is the first variation of *Alle Menschen*. These are not really liturgical compositions, and it is by no means certain that they are even organ pieces; rather, they seem intended as clavier works, that is, for keyboard instruments in general.

As the century goes on, the sacred-secular split so clear in Scheidt tends to break down, so that elements of the secular style play an increasing role in the sacred compositions. This may be seen in one of the most notable examples of the chorale partita, the *Tabulatur-Buch* of Johann Ulrich Steigleder published in Stuttgart in 1627. It also becomes more noticeable as time passes, until we encounter a complete lack of discrimination between the two in the chorale partitas of Georg Böhm. Most of his works in this genre show that the secular approach had completely taken over; we find chorale partitas in which each variation is called "partita" or, in one case, "variatio." The secular hallmark of extensive variation of the melody is used here. Yet, there is a small group of chorale partitas in the work of Böhm that retain the terminology "versus" and with it show the old, disciplined contrapuntal art in its elaborate grandeur. As a striking instance of this encroachment of secular elements in the chorale partita, we might mention the existence of a suite, ostensibly for harpsichord, in which the several dances all are variations of a chorale melody—Buxtehude's *Auf meinen lieben Gott* (see Georgii, *400 Years*, pp. 46–8).

The second type of organ chorale setting, the so-called "chorale fantasy," likewise goes back to Renaissance forms particularly the paraphrase treatment of a cantus firmus. As we have seen, many cantus firmus settings of Masses and hymns in France and Italy made use of this principle, at least in some sections. Its application to the Protestant chorale, however, is particularly emphasized in the work of the organists in the North of Germany: the work of the Lübeck organist Franz Tunder and the Hamburg organist Jan Reincken are exclusively of this type; also important here are Ahle, Henrich Bach, Georg Böhm, and Buxtehude. Some of these works, such as Buxtehude's *Wie schön leuchtet der Morgenstern*, are elaborate compositions; this is an extended work that commences with a slow section presenting the chorale melody in cantus planus style, then offers several fugal passages interspersed, and concludes with passages in typical virtuoso and impressive toccata style.

The third type, the chorale prelude, is the one that is exclusively liturgical. This is easily seen from the fact that several early collections of pieces of this type present them in a liturgical order, in accordance with the seasons and feasts of the church year. One of these is Scheidt's *Tabulatur-Buch* (1650), which commences with a group for Advent and continues through Christmas, New Year's, Purification, Holy Week, Trinity, and St. Michael's, after which come various other groups such as funeral compositions, catechism chorales, and some psalm settings. This order is the same as that followed in Johann Hermann Schein's *Kantional*. These are simple settings; in each, the chorale melody is prominently placed in the uppermost part while the other voices engage in simple contrapuntal accompaniment. Another important collection of this type is Pachelbel's *Choräle welche bey währenden Gottesdienst zum praeambuliren gebraucht werden können* (Nürnberg, 1693), which represents only part of a projected series. Still another cycle is by Johann Christoph Bach, which existed only in manuscript and has practically the same title as the Pachelbel collection.

It is usually necessary that a chorale prelude be short (fifty or sixty bars on the average) and not too elaborate. While most of them observe these strictures, there is at the same time variety in the treatment of the chorale melodies. Usually, the chorale is presented in one voice in the long, extended notes characteristic of the old cantus planus style, as may be seen, for example, in Pachelbel's *Vater unser* (*HAM*, II, 190c) or, even simpler, *Durch Adams Fall* (*HMS*, VI, s. 2, b. 3, a). Should the chorale melody be placed in the uppermost part, it is likely to be embellished. A not uncommon practice was to present the chorale melody in two-part canon, a practice often found in Pachelbel. In settings of this rather simple type, some attempt is often made to have the accompaniment express the affective connotation related to the subject of the chorale text or the liturgical occasion for which it is employed. As an example, Scheidt's *Aus tiefer Not*

(*Tabulatur-Buch*, the first version) has a highly chromatic accompaniment traditionally associated with sorrow and despair.

Some chorale preludes, on the other hand, follow to some extent the procedures of the chorale fantasy and treat the chorale imitatively, phrase by phrase, in all parts, as in Zachow's chorale prelude *Ich ruf zu dir* (Fischer, *Variation*, pp. 17–18) as well as in the work of Kindermann, Böhm, and many others. In the work of Pachelbel, we find a type that represents a mixture. The chorale prelude is divided into two sections. The first is a fugal treatment of the first line of the chorale; this completed, the setting continues as a cantus firmus setting of the remainder of the chorale. A readily accessible example by Pachelbel is *Ach Herr mich armen Sünder* (*GMB*, 243). Many chorale preludes by Johann Christoph Bach show the same scheme. It might be added that this procedure was used earlier, as, for instance, in Scheidt's *Vater unser* (*HAM*, II, 190a).

Buxtehude composed some thirty chorale preludes, which, along with his six chorale partitas and eight chorale fantasias, makes him one of the leading contributors to the repertory of the organ chorale. In these works, the features mentioned as characteristic of the type are clearly observable: the over-all brevity, the simple statement of the chorale melody, and the use of motives from the chorale in the accompanying voices (which, however, are somewhat more elaborate than in most chorale preludes by other composers of the time). The chorale melody itself is given an unusually elaborate embellishment in *Ein feste*

EXAMPLE 20

Scheidt: *Aus tiefer Not*, from *Tabulatur-Buch*—beginning

Burg ist unser Gott. More typical are his *In dulci jubilo* and *Vater unser* (respectively, *HMS*, VI, s. 2, b. 4, a and *HAM*, II, 190b); in both the chorale melody in the uppermost part is highly embellished and there is a characteristic figure developed throughout in the accompaniment. Also typical is his *Nun komm' der Heiden Heiland* (*TEM*, 41), which also brings the chorale melody embellished in the uppermost part with an accompaniment that is largely harmonic or homophonic.

It was in connection with what we might call the "free forms" of organ music that a remarkable development took place in the hands of the seventeenth-century German organists. The repertory as handed down to them consisted of the toccata and its related forms and the various types of pieces in imitative counterpoint, the ricercare, canzone, fantasia, and capriccio. In the works of the German composers, what we see is a tendency for them to come together and combine with one another so that a larger form results. The larger toccata and the organ prelude and fugue became largely indistinguishable from each other, while the various forms characterized by imitative counterpoint generally became known under one generic designation, "fugue." Most interesting, on the other hand, is the development of the fantasia; until then, in keyboard music this term had designated a piece using imitative counterpoint, either strict or rather free, but, from then on, it was used for a genre in no way distinguishable from the toccata.

In the early part of the century, the old forms dominated the scene (the old fantasia, the ricercare, the canzone, and the capriccio), and the influences were chiefly those of Sweelinck and Frescobaldi. Sweelinck's type of fantasia is preserved in the work of Scheidt and even in that of the Viennese Froberger. We even find compositions here using subjects based on scale segments, designated by the solmization syllables. (One by Froberger actually has a text in the same spirit, "So la re lascia fare mi," which, however, is not to be sung.) Such works are sectional compositions using the same theme throughout but varied and with new counter- and accompanying material. A few are based on pre-existent melodies, as Scheidt's *Fantasia super Ich ruf zu dir*, which is an example of the chorale fantasy already discussed. Scheidt also continued in the fantasy tradition. The ricercare also lived on well into the seventeenth century in the work of Froberger, Poglietti, Pachelbel, and Krieger, that is, composers in the southern part and middle of Germany. It maintained essentially the same character with a distinct leaning towards the learned features associated with it since the work of Andrea Gabrieli. The old canzone likewise maintained the same features and appeared again, largely in the work of the same group of composers (see Podolsky), particularly that of Froberger and Kerll, but also in the work of the Northern organist Buxtehude.

The capriccio came into its own in seventeenth-century Italian music, chiefly in Frescobaldi. Its cultivation in Germany generally was limited to the Viennese group of composers—Froberger, Kerll, and Poglietti. Again, the character was maintained: essentially contrapuntal and sectional, featuring thematic variation, and making use of figurational elements. Important is a distinct tendency to the surprising and the striking, the use of unusual and sharply characteristic themes, as may be seen in several examples by Froberger: the unusual subject of rapidly repeated notes in his Capriccio in F (No. 13) or the highly chromatic Capriccios in C and g (No. 6 and No. 8, respectively).

For these reasons, it is not surprising that the capriccio frequently became the vehicle for programmatic music, abounding in pictorial effects, as indeed can be seen in Frescobaldi. In the capriccios of Kerll, we find, among others, the *Capriccio Cücu*, which exists in three somewhat divergent versions, whose subject may easily be imagined; there is a *battaglia* (battle) piece that makes use of fanfare-like themes, rapidly repeated notes (*via* Monteverdi's *stile concitato*), "martial" dotted rhythms, and scale runs; and, finally, there is a piece with a pastoral subject, *Der steyrische Hirt*. A better known and readily available work of this kind is Poglietti's *Capriccio über das Hennengeschrey* (*TEM*, 49 or Georgii, *400 Years*, pp. 22–3), where the cackling of the hens and general barnyard noises are suggested by the use of rapidly repeated simultaneous seconds in the subject.

The interesting historical process—and one that is deserving of further study —is how these forms all came together to produce what came to be known as the fugue. This is not to imply that the various species completely died out, but it is certainly true that they declined, particularly towards the end of the seventeenth century, and were replaced by the fugue, which we might be tempted to regard

EXAMPLE 21

Kerll: *Battaglia*—excerpt

as a sort of combination form. Symptomatic is an uncertainty of terminology; Kindermann has a piece called *Fuga sive Fantasia* and Murschhauser has two, each of which he called *Fuga sive Canzona*, both of which show how the new term "fugue" was gradually asserting itself.

The designation "fugue" had been in use since the late fifteenth century with several meanings, all of them related to the procedure of contrapuntal imitation; in the fifteenth and sixteenth centuries, it often meant canonic imitation. The term then came to designate generally a composition employing imitative counterpoint usually, but by no means exclusively, for a keyboard instrument. The first important publication in which this occured is Scheidt's *Tabulatura nova*, Part II. Here, we find two pieces called "fugue," both closely related to the ricercare, especially as far as their subjects are concerned. But the imitation is not strictly maintained throughout; rather, figurational elements are introduced, and, in one instance, there is an effort to imitate the typical violinistic figuration patterns (*imitatio violistico*). One of these pieces is a *Fuga contraria*, with contrary motion.

That the term fugue had only a rather general meaning, and this related to the technique of imitative counterpoint, may be seen from the fugues in Kindermann's *Harmonia organica* (Nürnberg, 1645). While some of these are fugues as the term is now understood, others are based on pre-existent melodic material and, thus, are chorale fugues; virtuoso examples of this are his *Christ lag in Todesbanden*, *Christus, der uns selig macht*, and *Da Jesus an dem Kreuze stund*, whose themes are then combined in a triple fugue (*dreifache Fuge*).

Pachelbel composed several groups of fugues, some for harpsichord and others for organ; most of them are quite short, cast in one section, and monothematic. In general, they seem modeled loosely on the canzone, and their subjects reveal the use of figurational elements such as scale segments and trill patterns, often employing repeated notes and striking rhythmic configurations. One interesting aspect of the contrapuntal treatment is that, in Pachelbel's fugues, it often happens that the subject is broken down into component motives that are separately taken and developed. The devices of learned counterpoint, however, are avoided.

One group of fugues by Pachelbel has been the subject of some discussion: the Magnificat fugues of which there are ninety-four (see Nolte). These are short, monothematic fugues that show the features just described. They are arranged in groups according to mode; thus, the first twenty-three are under *Magnificat primi toni*, the next ten constitute the *Magnificat secund itoni*, and so on. One would expect them to be Magnificat compositions of the type already discussed were it not, first, for the large number of pieces in each group and, second, for the fact that they do not seem to be based on the Magnificat recitation Tone formulas. It seems, rather, that these fugues are intended as preludes to the performance of the Magnificat more than anything else, especially to introduce the congregational singing of alternate verses (for example, see *HAM*, II, 251).

The features found in Pachelbel's fugues became typical of the genre. Most important is the formulation of the theme itself, especially the use of figurative elements in the fugue subject. Also of importance is the breaking down of the theme into component motives during the unfolding of the composition. This type of fugue appears in the work of many other composers, such as Krieger and Buxtehude. Learned devices generally are absent, but Krieger does have a series of four fugues in C whose themes are then combined into one quadruple fugue.

Just as important as the fugue is the development of the toccata and the genres historically associated with it. Here, as might be expected, the Italian model especially as it grew in the hands of Frescobaldi, was decisive. Most of the toccatas were composed by organists in Vienna: Froberger, Kerll, and Georg Muffat whose famous *Apparatus musico-organisticus* (Salzburg, 1690) is largely given over to such compositions. The form was sectional. Froberger used generally three sections—a fugal part in the middle surrounded by typical passages in toccata style with several changes in meter. Muffat, however, used six or seven

EXAMPLE 22

PACHELBEL: *Fugue* in C—beginning

shorter sections that generally commenced slowly with full, impressive chords. Those by Kerll usually fall into four or five sections, differing in character, but they make virtually no use of imitation.

It is noteworthy that several typically Italian types of toccata appear in the work of these composers. Froberger, for instance, in two compositions, maintained the tradition of the liturgical *toccata da sonarsi alla Levatione* (to be played during the Elevation of the Host), resembling pieces of Frescobaldi. Kerll, for his part, has characteristic toccatas; one features arpeggios throughout (*Toccata tutti de salti*), another emphasizes the pedals (*Toccata per li pedali*), while yet another carries on the tradition of using dissonances and intense chromaticism that we saw in Macque, Trabaci, and Frescobaldi, even using the same designation, *Toccata cromatica con durezze e ligatura*. Shorter toccatas that limit themselves to the representation of but one affection—one theme or motive, texture or figuration pattern—are to be found in the work of Pachelbel. Available examples are the one in g and one in e (see, respectively, Valentin, 13, pp. 33–4, and *MPM*, 27).

The two forms associated with the toccata, the prelude and the *intonazione*, are present in the work of these composers but in small quantities. All may be seen in Murschhauser; the toccata is as we have seen it while the prelude and *intonatio* are much shorter and generally restrict themselves to working with but one motive or figuration pattern. In the work of Kindermann, we also find both types, but here the preludes are extremely short and are arranged by keys of which there are two for each of the modes, one authentic, the other plagal; the *intonazione* are somewhat longer and have a two-sectional form, the first in typical prelude style and the second fugal.

The combination of the two types, the toccata and the fugue, into a single genre was at least potential in the sixteenth-century Venetian toccata, which had sections in ricercare (fugal) style between those in the more brilliant toccata style. Also the form of the toccata and its expansion, as it was cultivated in seventeenth-century Germany, was prominent in the development of the new large form (see Valentin). But, at the same time, there is another tradition that developed of simply combining a prelude or toccata with a fugue in the same key, as can be seen in a modest way in a Prelude and Fugue in D by Heinrich Scheidemann (*HAM*, II 195b). Thus, there are two categories: the large toccata with fugal sections, on the one hand, and the prelude and fugue, on the other, both of which somehow came together. Along with this goes the quite unusual change that took place in regard to the fantasia. As has been seen, the fantasia was one of the strictest among the imitative contrapuntal forms; it now altered its character completely and became similar to the toccata. It is not always possible to distinguish between the three types.

The large toccata type was developed chiefly in the North of Germany. Here, we meet not with toccatas preceding fugues, but rather with the old sectional form of toccata in which the sections, however, are somewhat expanded. Most usual is the division into three sections, as had been frequently used in the toccata since the work of Merulo: first a section in typical toccata style, then a fugal section, and, finally, a return to the toccata style. In the North of Germany, these were endowed with a new degree of brilliance, particularly in the toccata style passages which abounded in striking effects: unusual progressions; striking figuration patterns, especially in the pedals; sudden harmonic changes and changes of texture; and, especially, a consciousness of the dramatic value of the pedal point in heightening the conclusion. Many examples of this highly characteristic art are readily accessible. Typical and not very well known is the work of Franz Tunder (see Stahl), who may be looked upon as an important initiator of this category in Northern Germany; his Prelude and Fugue in g shows the three-part structure that has been described (*HAM*, II, 215). Also important is Georg Böhm of Lüneburg, whose preludes and fugues show the same form. This form may also be seen in a Prelude and Fugue in E-flat by Johann Christoph Bach (*HAM*, II, 237), a work that had mistakenly been regarded as by J. S. Bach and included in the old standard collected edition of his works (the *Bach-Gesellschaft* edition).

Of the other Northern organists who contributed to this development, Tunder's son-in-law Buxtehude is clearly the most important. His Prelude and Fugue in e shows the same tripartite form, but the fugue section itself is in two parts, each with its own individual subject and a short interlude in toccata style (*GMB*, 249); thus, we see the close links between the prelude and fugue and the old sectional toccata. The same three-part form may be observed in Buxtehude's Prelude and Fugue in E (*HAM*, II, 234) and in a Toccata in g (Valentin, 16, pp. 38–40). More elaborately, Buxtehude had used the chaconne in conjunction with this genre; a work in c consists of a prelude, fugue, and chaconne. Other works in this genre employ an ostinato form in their concluding sections.

The other related form, the prelude and fugue in the same key, is less easily traced. It does not seem to have come about earlier than the latter part of the century, and, even then, the idea seems not to have been precisely formulated. Two sources from this period are Krieger's *Anmutige Clavier-Uebung* (Nürnberg, 1699) and Murschhauser's *Prototypon organicum longe-breve* (Nürnberg, 1703 and 1707). In both works, the idea of associating the two forms seems clear. In Krieger, we find examples of a Prelude and Ricercare in E or a Prelude and Fugue in G: but we also find examples in which the order is reversed, as in the Ricercare and Prelude in F and another in G or the Fugue and Fantasia in D. The situation is also ambiguous in Murschhauser; here again, the pieces are unified by being in the same key, but the order is by no means fixed by the composer. Instead, we find a group of works in the same key, and the performer is evidently supposed to make a choice. For instance, there is an *intonatio*, a *praeambulum*, three fugues, and another *praeambulum* constituting a group, all in the same key. A forerunner of Bach in the exploitation of even temperament is the *Adriadne musica* by Johann Kaspar Ferdinand Fischer (according to Hoffmann-Erbrecht, the father and not the son) that first appeared in 1702; it is a collection of short preludes and fugues in nineteen different keys (see the Prelude and Fugue in E [*HAM*, II, 247]).

The repertory of seventeenth-century German harpsichord music stands generally under French influence, and the category of the suite is the most important (see Epstein). Contributions were made from all over Germany, but the most significant are associated with composers in Vienna and in Southern and Central Germany. Along with the suite, there are not only the related stand-ard variation forms (chaconne and passacaglia), but also the various fugal forms that, in many, resemble those found in organ music and, finally, the solo keyboard sonata.

As far as the evolution of the keyboard suite in Germany is concerned, we have seen that the establishment of the various dance types and the idea of associating them into a fixed succession was a French idea but one that did not develop there into anything approaching a definite form. It was different in the hands of the German composers, and it is possible to indicate rather definitely the steps that led to the final, one might say "classical," form of the keyboard suite. In passing, it might be noted that these compositions were designated *Parthien* or *Partien*, related to partita, and that the term "suite" was not used in this connection in Germany until Buttstedt's *Musicalische Clavier-Kunst und Vorrathskammer* of 1713.

The move towards uniformity in the suite may be seen in the works of Kindermann, which existed in manuscripts and date from the middle of the century. Most of his dances, which are rather simple, appear in groups of three—allemande, courante, and saraband; in several instances, a dance in triple time, a ballet, replaces the allemande. The suites of Weckmann and of Pachelbel like-wise reveal a fixed succession of dances—allemande, gigue, saraband, and, at the end, courante.

The important figure in the development of the German harpsichord suite is Froberger, who alone composed almost thirty suites. These exist in two ver-sions, the first in manuscript and the second in a posthumous publication, *Suites de clavecin* (Amsterdam, 1697), containing ten. In the manuscript version, the order observed is allemande, courante, gigue, and saraband; but, in the print, which appeared almost thirty years after Froberger's death, we find that annotation on the title page *mis en meilleur ordre* (put in better order), and the succession is allemande, courante, saraband, and gigue with some other dance between the last two, which thereafter is standard. This order can be observed in most suites published in the late seventeenth century: in those of Poglietti; in Kuhnau's *Partien* (Leipzig, 1695) and his *Neue Clavier-Uebung* (Part I, Leipzig, 1689; Part II, Leipzig, 1692); those of Murschhauser, Böhm, and

Buxtehude; in Krieger's *Musicalische Partien* (Nürnberg, 1697); and, finally, in the suites of J. K. F. Fischer, the *Pièces de clavessin* (Augsburg, 1696; second edition, as *Musicalisches Blumen-Büschlein*, Augsburg, 1698; see *HAM*, II, 248) and the *Musicalischer Parnassus* of 1738 (see the prelude in Georgii, *400 Years*, p. 52).

Needless to say, the succession will not be found without fail in all keyboard suites of the time since substitutions, omissions, and additions are quite often made. Important among the dances that thus appear in suites are the minuet, the bourrée, and the gavotte, as well as the variation forms of the chaconne and passacaglia or sometimes an aria. Often, we find a double, that is, a second dance of the same kind, after which the first dance is repeated (see Reimann). This custom is the origin of the dance trio developed in the late seventeenth and most of the eighteenth centuries. Many of the suites in Kuhnau's *Clavier-Uebung* have introductory pieces called "preludes" before the succession of dances proper commences; these are either sectional pieces as we are accustomed to but on a smaller scale or else they are short and work with one motive or type of figuration. This practice is followed in Fischer's suites and is common in the early eighteenth century.

Particularly interesting departures occur in the suites of Froberger. These are in the French lute tradition of the tombeau, and, in two instances, they replace the allemande. Otherwise, the tombeau is an independent composition. There are four of these keyboard laments by Froberger. Two are for members of the house of Hapsburg, the *Lamento sopra la dolorosa perdita della Rea Majesta di Ferdinando IV, Rè di Romani,* etc. (in Suite No. 12) and the *Lamentation faite sur la morte très douloureuse de Sa Majesté Impériale Ferdinand le Troisième . . . Anno 1657*; then there is the *Tombeau faite à Paris sur la morte de Monsieur Blancheroche* and the *Plainte faite à Londres pour passer le Mélancholie* (in Suite No. 30; see Kahl, 8, pp. 28–9; *HAM*, II, 216; and Georgii, *400 Years*, p. 39). All these involve the expression of sadness, and in this all the traditional procedures are used with great effectiveness; chromaticism is most important, but we also find unusual chord progressions, expressive arpeggio passages, sudden pauses, outbursts, and irregular meters and rhythms. Noteworthy is the fact that these pieces are to be played, according to the composer, slowly and *avec discretion* (with great care), and, in the lament for Ferdinand IV, the player is enjoined to play *sans observer aucune mésure* (without observing any meter) thus revealing a link to certain works of Frescobaldi and Monteverdi.

These suites are, as has been observed, patterned after the French harpsichord music of the time. The various dances all retain the same characteristics, especially the gigue which is usually treated contrapuntally. The German suite does differ in several respects from the French. First, it differs in the fixed order of dances, which is not found in the suites of French composers. Second, it differs in the matter of style; the characteristic French delicacy and clarity are not present, and the rhythms tend to become more regular or "square," the harmonies fuller, and there is less emphasis on the *agréments*.

But more important is the conception of the suite as a unified work of art, a large composition consisting of a series of component and related parts. An important point here is the German insistence on the designation "partita," which, as we have seen, carries with it the idea of variation. What happens is related to the old practice we have already observed of the dance pairs in which the second is a variation of the first. Many of the German seventeenth-century harpsichord suites show a tendency in this direction. Most often it affects the allemande and the courante, the thematic relationship between which is easily observed, as reference to works like Froberger's Suite in e or Pachelbel's *Suite ex Gis* (G♯=A-flat [*MPM*, 35; *HAM*, II, 250]) will demonstrate. The suites of Kuhnau show the same feature.

In addition to suites of dances, there are also variations. These are of two kinds: the set of variations on a melody, either a popular aria or song of the time or one of the standard bass melodies, and the variation dances, the chaconne and passacaglia. The former is known under the designation "partita," so that this becomes a counterpart to the chorale partita already discussed. Sets of variations were often included with dance suites. This is the case with Froberger's cele-

EXAMPLE 23

FROBERGER: *Lament on the Death of Ferdinand IV* from Suite in C —beginning

brated variations on *Die Mayerin*. Other well-known sets of variations from seventeenth-century Germany are Reincken's set on the aria *Schweiget mir vom Weibernehmen*, Buxtehude's set on an aria from Lully's opera *Rofilis* (Fischer, *Variation*, 11, pp. 25–6), and Poglietti's *Aria allemagne con alcune variazioni* (*HAM*, II, 236). The last-named is remarkable for the presence of characteristic variations: the *Alt Weiber Condukt*, the *Französische Baislemans*, and the *Polnischer Sablschatz*. But the major collection of variations is doubtless Pachelbel's *Hexachordum Apollinis* (Nürnberg, 1699), a set of six variations of which the most famous is the last, *Aria Sebaldina*.

Unlike these variations, which are intended primarily for harpsichord, are the larger dances in variation form intended for either organ or harpsichord—the passacaglia and the chaconne. There does not seem to have been any general distinction between the two in the Baroque period (see Fischer), and both show the same basic features: the slow triple meter, dotted rhythms, and the association with variation (ostinato) form. This last would relate them to Italian partitas on *Ruggiero*, *Romanesca*, *Passamezzo moderne*, and others. In Italy, the chaconne was much more closely connected with the ostinato principle than was the passacaglia, and there was also a difference in key, the chaconne being major and the passacaglia minor. In France, on the other hand, it was the passacaglia that was often associated with variation form, the chaconne usually appearing as *chaconne en rondeau*. Both traditions appeared in Germany. The convenient distinction proposed by Apel, according to which the passacaglia employs a melody as the ostinato element while the chaconne uses a harmonic progression as ostinato, is not borne out by the examples of the forms that we have, as, for instance, in Buxtehude and Muffat.

One final development in seventeenth-century German keyboard music concerns the solo sonata. This is usually associated with one composer, Johann Kuhnau, and it appears first in the second part of his *Clavier-Uebung* which came out in 1689. This collection is devoted mainly to harpsichord suites, as has been seen, but the very last work is a Sonata in B-flat. This piece is in four sections (one might be tempted to call them movements except for their brevity) in the order Slow—Fast—Slow—Fast with the first slow section repeated at the very end, *da capo*. The fast sections are fugal while the third section is aria-like in the slow triple meter characteristic of the *bel canto* style. This suggests that the Italian *sonata de chiesa* is in the background, and this assumption seems to be correct. Further proof is the strong influence from the trio sonata ensemble style. Kuhnau's sonata, in several of its sections, could almost be a keyboard arrangement of such a composition; the bass clearly resembles a basso continuo line while the upper parts are solo voices that often move in parallel thirds and sixths. The fast fugal second section has figuration that seems quite violinistic.

This composition has attracted a great deal of attention, especially from German historians of music eager to claim it as the first solo keyboard sonata.

Actually, as has already been seen, there are Italian pieces called "sonata" for keyboard instruments by Gioanpietro Del Buono of 1641 and Gregorio Strozzi of 1687. Reference must also be made to a toccata-like Sonatina in d for organ by the Dresden organist Christian Ritter (*c.* 1650–*c.* 1725) preserved in manuscript; the exact date of this piece is uncertain. Apparently, the first use of the term in Germany in reference to keyboard music is in a harpsichord suite by Johann Heinrich Schmelzer (*c.* 1623–1680), the first movement of which has the name (see Newman). Other early examples of keyboard pieces called "sonata" are by Sybrandus van Noordt (d. 1702) of Amsterdam, published in 1690; these pieces, like those of Kuhnau, show the influence of the *sonata de chiesa*, that is, from the chamber music of the time.

These sonatas, however, are isolated, so that Kuhnau's distinction is to have made many contributions to the new genre, which was not to become a leading one until the middle of the eighteenth century. Kuhnau, in fact, issued two collections devoted entirely to the solo keyboard sonata: the *Frische Clavier-Früchte* (Leipzig, 1696) and the celebrated *Musicalische Vorstellung einiger biblischen Historien* (Leipzig, 1700; there are many other editions; the one with the title in Italian dates from 1710), known as the *Biblical Sonatas*. In all, we have some fourteen compositions by Kuhnau called "sonatas," so that he certainly deserves to be credited with having played the most prominent role in the establishment of the genre.

In the seven sonatas of the *Frische Clavier-Früchte*, there is some variety so that generally it can be said only that there is a succession of movements (three to six) that contrast in key, thematic material, tempo, and character. The over-all form is not unrelated to that of the earlier Sonata in B-flat, except that, in the five-movement works (the Sonatas in g, D, and F), a fast movement is added at the beginning making the succession Fast—Slow—Fast—Slow—Fast; in the four-

EXAMPLE 24

Kuhnau: *Sonata* in B-flat—excerpt

movement works there is no such scheme; the Sonatas in c (No. 4) and a (No. 7) present the order Fast—Slow—Fast—Slow; the Sonata in e (No. 5) has the most unusual succession Moderate (apparently)—Fast—Fast—Slow; noteworthy is the Sonata in B-flat (No. 6) with a chaconne at the beginning and repeated (*da capo*) at the end and two slow movements with a fast one in between. Here, the fast movements, whether fugal or homophonic, are clearly italianate; and the slow movements, equally italianate, in some cases are only rather short transitions featuring cadenza-like passages. The emphasis in these sonatas, as we have observed in other compositions, is on expression, as is here testified to by the abundant dynamic and tempo markings supplied by the composer.

Much more attention has been aroused by the six *Biblical Sonatas*. These are programmatic compositions whose subjects are taken from famous stories in the Old Testament. In each case, the whole sonata is representative of the story, and each movement portrays a particular episode or situation, usually embodying the expression of one affection. The number of movements varies from three to eight, so that, in this respect, the form does not differ from that in other sonatas by Kuhnau. At times, the musical representation operates with conventional forms: the *battaglia* piece, in all its traditional glory, appears in *Il Combattimento trà David e Goliath* (No. 1) and in *Gideon Salvadore del Populo d'Israel* (No. 5); the fugue, in both instances, represents the headlong retreat of the opposition (in which case *fuga* here literally also means flight). Unusual is the symbolic use of chorale melodies, *Aus tiefer Not* for the prayer of the Israelites before the battle in the David and Goliath sonata, and *O Haupt voll Blut und Wunden* in the Hezekiah sonata (*HAM*, II, 261; or Georgii, *400 Years*, pp. 42–5), so that these movements are not unrelated to the chorale prelude. It might be mentioned that these works may be regarded as instrumental equivalents, to some extent at least, of the oratorio.

In the seventeenth century, then, German keyboard composers drew together forms from all over Europe and used them as the basis for new and larger categories of composition. These new types have retained their importance down to the present day; the organ forms are related to the chorale—notably the chorale prelude, as well as the larger prelude and fugue (and the closely related toccata and fantasia and fugue)—the harpsichord suite, and, finally, the solo keyboard sonata.

Keyboard music in the Netherlands in the seventeenth century represents to a large extent the outgrowth of the work of Sweelinck. This is clear from the works of Pieter Cornet, organist at Brussels from 1593 to 1626, who worked especially with the strict imitative type of fantasia; Charles Guillet (d. 1654); Gerard Scronx; Hendrik Speuy; and various members of the van den Kerckhoven family, particularly Abraham (1627–1702). In the same tradition is the *Tabulatuur-Boek* published in 1659 by the Amsterdam organist Anthoni van Noordt (d. 1675), which, in addition to six fantasias, contains ten psalm settings

in variation form (roughly the equivalent of the chorale partita [see Seiffert]).
On the other hand, the *Pièces d'orgue* of 1694 by Lambert Chaumont are in the
French tradition of seventeenth-century organ music.

Until recently, the history of keyboard music in Spain and Portugal in the
seventeenth century was but little known. Between the time of Cabezón and
that of Cabanilles lay a period of something over a century of which we had little
knowledge, a situation that is well reflected in Frotscher. This has changed
somewhat thanks to the efforts of Higini Anglès and, particularly, Santiago
Kastner, who have been responsible for the publication of much of this music
and have thus provided the basis for several recent studies (Speer and Apel;
see also Hudson). Yet, this work is far from complete and what follows must
be regarded as the most preliminary and tentative kind of survey (see also
Eslava).

In the work of Cabezón, we noted, in some contrast to keyboard music
elsewhere in Europe, that the emphasis was on the forms of sacred music, cantus
firms settings of hymns, Magnificats (*versos* or *versillos*) and the Mass, or to a
conservative imitative type, the *tiento*; it was only in the historically important
but quantitatively relatively insignificant category of the variations on popular
songs (the *diferencias*) that secular elements made their appearance. This situation seems to have prevailed in the seventeenth century as well.

Until the middle of the century, the main composers of keyboard music in
Iberia were:

> Bernard Clavigo del Castillo (*c.* 1550–1626)
>
> Sebastian Aguilera de Heredia (*c.* 1565–*c.* 1620)
>
> Francisco Correa de Arauxo (*c.* 1575–*c.* 1663)
>
> Manuel Rodrigues Coelho (1583–*c.* 1623 or after).

While we possess only scattered individual works of Clavigo del Castillo and
Aguilera de Heredia, Arauxo and Coelho both are represented by large collections: Arauxo's extensive treatise with many musical examples, the *Libro de
tientos y discursos de musica practica y theorica de organo, intitulado facultad
organica* of 1626, and Coelho's *Flores de musica para o instrumento de tecla e arpa*
of 1620, which has the distinction of being the first music printed in Portugal and
the title of which has a striking similarity to works published in Italy (especially
Frescobaldi's *Fiori musicali* of 1635). (For other composers, see Frotscher.)

The cantus firmus or variation forms continue to play an important part in
the repertory. The *verso* (or *versillo*), the old liturgical cantus firmus type, exists
in great abundance, and often individual composers produced a hundred or more
such pieces. Most often composed were the antiphon *Salve regina*, the hymns
Ave maris stella and *Pange lingua*, the sequence *Lauda Sion*, and the Magnificat.

In Coelho, we also find settings of the Kyrie and the Benedictus from the Mass, as well as elaborations of the psalm recitation Tones (*HAM*, II, 200). In many cases, the liturgical melody is stated in breves (even notes) in one voice, certainly an old-fashioned procedure, while, in others, it is either given a rhythmic shape or is treated imitatively. Prominent in the secular variations are works called *Susanas grandas*, which appear in the work of Coelho and Arauxo; these are keyboard elaborations of the famous chanson *Susanne un jour* that Coelho adopts from Lassus' five-voice setting.

The most characteristic genre of Spanish and Portuguese keyboard music of the time, however, was the *tiento* (*tento* in Portuguese). As has been seen, while the *tiento* is usually interpreted as corresponding to the Italian ricercare, it actually is a freer form with more features in common with the toccata or the fantasia. The *tiento* may be described as a long sectional form beginning with a subject treated in imitation and followed by passages featuring scale-passage figuration or diminutions (*flores*) over slowly changing harmonies. This emphasis on figuration establishes the family resemblance between the *tiento* and the toccata. Individual *tientos* invariably are assigned to specific church modes and in some cases are even grouped in this way, as in Coelho's *Flores de musica* which contains twenty-four *tientos*, three for each of the eight church modes. The indication of organ registration, which we saw in the sole surviving work of Peraza in the sixteenth century, is likewise maintained here. In Arauxo, the designation used is *tiento de medio registro de baxon* for the solo stops used in the bass and *tiento de medio registro de tiple* for the use of solo stops in the upper (treble) range of the keyboard.

Yet another important type of *tiento* established in the sixteenth century retained its importance in the seventeenth—the *tiento de falsas*. This genre has much in common with the Italian *toccata di durezze e ligatura* with the emphasis on chromaticism, dissonances, and suspensions. The sole surviving work of Clavigo del Castillo is of this type, and works by Aquilera have also come down. Arauxo, in his *Facultad organica*, called attention to the *curiosidades* and *cosas neuves*, the *falsas y licencias*, that appear in these works; reference is also made to the use of proportions, which also are called "new," although they of course were common in the sixteenth century and earlier, if not in keyboard music (see Apel).

The outstanding figure in the Spanish keyboard music of the period is Juan Cabanilles (1644–1712), the principal composer of organ music after Cabezón in Spain (see Anglès). Organist at Valencia, he was also known in France where he made occasional appearances; he was also a celebrated teacher. His many works, in which all categories of Iberian keyboard music are represented along with some specifically Italian types, existed in numerous manuscripts mainly in Spain; none appeared in print until rather recently. There is a large body of versos. In the *tientos*, the traditional features are to be found: the adherence to

the church modes, the strict imitative opening, the extended passages in figuration, and the *tiento de falsas*. Several of his *tientos* are elaborations of hymns
(*Ave maris stella* and *Pange lingua*), so that this genre shows from time to time a
link with cantus firmus composition, as also happened occasionally in Italy. In
the toccatas, which are also in church modes, the influence of Frescobaldi is
again clear, as also in the passacaglia. Most striking are the *batallas*, equivalents
of the Italian *battaglia* compositions, using martial dotted fanfare-like themes and
rapid figuration and culminating in a quasigrandiose conclusion.

When we turn to seventeenth-century England, we find a situation in some
respects similar to that in Germany. The life of the country was severely disrupted
by civil and religious conflicts: the rise of Puritanism under Oliver Cromwell,
the execution of King Charles I (1649), and the eventual restoration of the
monarchy in 1661 with the ascent to the throne of Charles II. While all this
necessarily had an influence on music, the effect was not what one might expect.
The Puritans were opposed to the use of music in the church, and this opposition
was carried to the systematic destruction of organs in churches. While liturgical
music ceased, there was, at the same time, considerable cultivation of secular
music, so that the chamber organ and the virginal, along with small instrumental and vocal ensembles enjoyed great popularity. The secular forms, then,
were maintained seemingly in spite of the inhospitable atmosphere. During
the Restoration, there was a new wave of activity to construct organs in the
churches in order to replace those instruments destroyed under the Puritans.
As everywhere—except in Italy—influences from abroad were of decisive
importance. In England, it was the Italian style but with a most significant
element of French influence, due doubtless in some measure to the long-enforced
exile in France of the man who was to be Charles II.

Some of the leading English composers of keyboard music of the time (excluding Henry Purcell) were:

William Lawes (1602–1645)
Benjamin Rogers (1614–1698)
Matthew Locke (*c.* 1630–1677)
John Blow (1649–1708)
John Eccles (1668–1735)
Jeremiah Clarke (*c.* 1674–1707)
William Croft (1678–1727).

To these may be added a German emigrant, Gerhard Disener, who came to
England in 1670.[1]

In organ music, two types were important—the psalm verse and the volun-

[1] See, generally, West and Frotscher; on Purcell, see the thematic catalogue by Zimmerman.

tary, both of which, as has been seen, had their origin in the sixteenth century. The former can be regarded as representative of the old cantus firmus setting; it was strictly liturgical and, hence, not cultivated much in the seventeenth century, although there are examples in the work of Blow. The voluntary, on the other hand, presents a different situation, for, although properly its setting is also the church service, it was intended as a showpiece, a sort of concertato solo piece, for the organ; hence, it had much in common with the Italian toccata, particularly as that genre was treated by the North German school of organists. In its general plan, a voluntary resembled a toccata; sections featuring block chords and rapid figuration alternated with those in which imitative counterpoint was the principle of composition. This can be seen in the seven organ works in Locke's *Melothesia* of 1673 (a treatise on music, especially on basso continuo realization with extensive musical examples; see Kooiker) and in voluntaries of John Blow and William Croft. Those of Blow, for instance, deliberately exploit particular registers of the organ, drawing upon coloristic and echo effects; in this, we may see a relation to the French organ music of the time.

As has been indicated, the greatest activity had to do with secular music, and here it was, of course, dances for the harpsichord or virginal, either individually or arranged in groups, that occupied the leading position. Dances in groups, forming what we now call suites, at that time were known rather as "lessons" or "airs." The general arrangement of an English lesson would be a succession of usually three or four dances—the allemande (alman), a courante (corante), and a saraband (or sarabrand, as many sources of the time have it); at times an ayre (a modest piece in moderate duple or sometimes triple time with regular accentuations), a minuet, a "Round-O" (the English equivalent of the rondeau, usually with two episodes or couplets), or a hornpipe would be used either in addition to or instead of one of the more regularly used dances. Such are the suites of Blow and Clarke, as can be seen in the latter's *Choice Lessons for the Harpsichord or Spinet* (1711). Several of the suites of William Croft, found in his *Choice Collection of Ayres for the Harpsichord* (1700), on the other hand, add a prelude (sometimes rather elaborate) in the figurational style we have seen in French harpsichord music particularly. By and large, the dances found in these lessons or airs are simple in form and in compositional procedure, most of the interest being given to the uppermost part which, in the French fashion, is ornamented. The allemande usually is the most highly stylized of the dances, the corante is generally of the Italian variety (*corrente*), and the saraband forms the slow movement. Clarke's Suite in A (Fuller-Maitland, V, pp. 11–12) concludes with a two-voice gigue very much in the French vein, complete with imitation and even with inversion of the theme in the second part.

The greatest figure in English music of the seventeenth century, however, is Henry Purcell (*c.* 1659–1695), the celebrated "Orpheus Britannicus," perhaps the greatest of all native-born English composers. His talent was such that his teacher, John Blow, resigned from his position as organist at Westminster Abbey so that Purcell could have the post (a favor he also extended to his less talented pupil, Jeremiah Clarke, resigning his post as chorus master in St. Paul's in 1693). As is true of many composers of the time, keyboard music is relatively unimportant in Purcell's output, and there is relatively little of it: a few organ pieces, eight suites for harpsichord, a toccata, a few independent preludes, a number of individual dances, and several sets of variations on a ground. Of these, only a few suites appeared in print during his lifetime—in Playford's *Musick's Hand-Maid*, Part II; a collection of suites appeared posthumously in 1696, *A Choice Collection of Lessons for the Harpsichord.*

The organ pieces (see Downes), actually related to the voluntary, show a close relation to Italian music; they are sectional with imitation and figuration. The two pieces in d are similar to one another and commence with energetic subjects related to the Italian canzone-type. The work in G is more like the quiet toccatas found in Frescobaldi's *Fiori musicali* except that it lacks chromaticism. An exceptional work is the so-called Voluntary in A on the one-hundredth psalm tune, a cantus firmus setting of *Old Hundred* and hence much like a chorale prelude; the piece is notable for its exploitation of the cornet stop. Related to these organ works is the Toccata in A, evidently intended for harpsichord, which again displays the Italian form; it commences with figuration, then has a fugal passage with the characteristic canzone theme employing repeated sixteenth notes and an octave leap of that gradually dissolve into figuration, followed by a long crescendo passage over a pedal point that culminates in a quasimaestoso with full chords in dotted rhythm at the end.

The eight suites of the *Choice Collection* are similar to the suites already described. The dances are usually three or four in number; the allemande, the corrente, and the saraband are the most common; other dances used are the minuet and the hornpipe. All but one of Purcell's suites are preceded by a prelude that works with the same motive or figuration pattern all the way through. Of the dances, the allemande is the most stylized; this is particularly evident in the chromatic allemande of the Suite in g (No. 2) or the highly figured melodic line in the allemande of the Suite in d (No. 7). Again, these dances are by and large simple pieces in which the embellished upper voice draws the most attention. Thematic variation with cyclical relationships between the various movements is not present here. Of the other harpsichord pieces of Purcell, mention can be made here of the well-known *Trumpet Tune* that is short and dance-like with typical "trumpet-like" phrases not unlike those found in Italian *battaglia* pieces, the *Overture* that is much in the French manner, several grounds, a chaconne, and other individual dances of various sorts.

In the seventeenth century, the expansion of keyboard music continued, in the quantity of music as in the variety of types. Certain older forms declined. The old intavolatura ceased to exist, and the liturgical cantus firmus forms fell out of favor, except for those related to the Protestant chorale; this decline of the cantus firmus forms is particularly pronounced in France where organ Masses and Magnificats became nothing more than suites. The toccata, which developed in the latter part of the sixteenth century, continued its existence and became the large form of organ music, especially in the hands of the North German composers. Then there is the establishment of two larger forms of harpsichord music, the suite and the sonata. Throughout the century, in the midst of all the changes, the old imitative contrapuntal forms based in principle at least on the art of the sixteenth century were cultivated, chiefly in association with keyboard music (ricercares, canzones, or fugues) and frequently presented in publications whose intent was didactic. In this respect, then, the curious conservatism we have noted in the keyboard music of earlier centuries was not lacking in the seventeenth century.

CHAPTER FOUR

J. S. Bach

One of the most striking features of Baroque music, an art that was developed chiefly in Italy, was its essentially secular roots. From the twelfth century to the middle of the sixteenth, the main forms of music, generally speaking, were sacred; the secular categories were both subordinate to and dependent on sacred music. In sixteenth-century Italy, under humanistic auspices, this situation changed, and the main bearer of the change was a secular form, the madrigal. Humanistic activities also produced what was to become the leading type of Baroque music, the opera. This means that, in the seventeenth and eighteenth centuries, the relation between sacred and secular forms had changed completely; secular forms were in the lead, and sacred music in turn became to a large extent dominated by developments in secular music. An important aspect of the history of music in Germany in the seventeenth century is the adaptation of the modern Italian procedures associated particularly with secular music to the traditions of Protestant music. At the same time, there was considerable cultivation of secular forms, instrumental as well as vocal, in which influences from France joined those from Italy.

The distinct separation of sacred and secular forms found here is reflected also in the professional possibilities for musicians in seventeenth-century Germany. In the main, a composer had two choices: either he could devote himself to the church, in which case he would aspire to the position of cantor, and his duties would involve the composition of music and the preparation of performances for the church services along with responsibility for the education and general oversight of the choir boys; or, on the other hand, he could be connected with a court and become a Kapellmeister, in which case his duties, while including religious music, would emphasize the composition and performance of secular music, operatic or instrumental, for the entertainment of the court. The position of cantor, therefore, brought with it largely a local reputation while that of

Kapellmeister was involved with works of international standing and was the vehicle for the composer to achieve a wide reputation.

The conflict between the two may easily be seen in the life and work of Johann Sebastian Bach (1685–1750). Since he was trained as an organist, Bach was oriented to the way of the cantor, to which he devoted himself for the greater part of his life. Yet, from time to time, he seemed to regret this decision, seeing the greater recognition and remuneration that would have been his had he chosen the other way. Such feelings were especially characteristic of the latter part of his life. If we look over the positions he held during his life—member of a church choir in Lüneburg (1700–1703); organist at Arnstadt (1703–1707), at Mühlhausen (1707–1708), at Weimar, where he also became chamber musician (1708–1717); Kapellmeister at Cöthen (1717–1723); and, finally, cantor in Leipzig (1723–1750)—we find that only two were connected with courts, at Weimar and Cöthen. Much of his instrumental music (chamber music, orchestral concertos, and suites) dates from the years at Cöthen (1717–1723). For the rest of his career, Bach held to the way of the cantor. But a turn back in the direction of seeking an international reputation was made after 1735, when troubles with the Leipzig authorities became critical and resulted in the curtailment of his musical activities.

There can be no doubt, however, that Bach felt himself fundamentally related to the church. This comes clearly to expression in the letter of resignation he submitted to the Mühlhausen authorities when he received the appointment to the court at Weimar; in it, he stated his intention to work toward what he calls a "well-appointed church music" that was to embrace not only the composition and collection of better compositions for use during services, but also higher standards to be maintained in performances.

Bach's keyboard compositions reflect the situation just outlined; while the sacred music for the Lutheran service has the lead, there is a significant amount of music for secular purposes. To a large extent, this division corresponds to that between organ music and clavier music (harpsichord or clavichord). An important exception to this may be found in the didactic compositions, which are clavier works in the old sense of the term—for a keyboard instrument without specification, either organ, harpsichord, or clavichord, although some individual pieces may seem more suited to one instrument than to another.[1]

The consequences of Bach's choice in his life work can be seen also in the publications of his keyboard music. As might be expected, only few of them were

[1] The standard edition of Bach's music remains that of the *Bach-Gesellschaft*, here abbreviated *BG*; a completely new edition is in progress, the *Neue Bach-Ausgabe*, in which the organ music is to appear in Series IV and the harpsichord music in Series V. A standard reference is the thematic catalogue by Schmieder, whose numbering of Bach's works is used in this chapter for identification. Among many general works on Bach's life and works are those by Spitta, Pirro, and Schweitzer (see also Geiringer); on Bach's keyboard music, see Emery, Florand, Grace, Keller, Klotz and Frotscher on the organ music and Bodky, Keller and Roethlisberger on the harpsichord music. Aspects of performance practice are discussed by Aldrich, Donington, and Kreutz, among others.

published during his lifetime. Almost none of his many organ compositions, destined to form the mainstay of the organ repertory, are among them. The same holds for the organ settings of chorales with several exceptions, especially the so-called Schübler collection, which, as will be seen, contains arrangements for organ of what originally were movements in cantatas. The most famous work of Bach, and the one on which his reputation in the late eighteenth and earlier nineteenth centuries was based, likewise remained in manuscript—*The Well-Tempered Clavier* (S. 846–93), of which the first part was completed in 1722 (the second part was not completed until 1744). The most comprehensive publication Bach personally undertook of his keyboard music is the *Clavier-Uebung*, which appeared in four parts. Part I of 1731 contains the six partitas (S. 825–30); Part II of 1735 contains harpsichord compositions, the *Concerto nach italienischem Gusto* (*Italian Concerto*, S. 971), the *Overture nach französischer Art* (Suite in b or *French Overture*, S. 831), and several toccatas; Part III of 1739 contains organ music, chorale preludes, and a large prelude and fugue; and Part IV of 1742 contains the *Aria mit dreissig Veränderungen* (*Goldberg Variations*, S. 988). The title *Clavier-Uebung*, it will be recalled, had also been used by both Krieger and Kuhnau.

It is in Bach's organ music, as well as the cantatas, that we can best observe his creative contributions to the "well-appointed church music." The chorale preludes (see Tusler, Taylor, and Fischer) are of the greatest significance here. A most important collection is the *Orgelbüchlein* (*Little Organ Book*, S. 599–644, *BG*, XXV), which he began in Weimar and completed at Cöthen (see Huggler). It contains some forty-five chorale preludes arranged in accordance with the church year. Along with this liturgical propriety, it is a didactic work presenting organists with various types of chorale treatment and emphasizing work with the pedal. The other collection of Bach's chorale preludes that is organized in accordance with liturgical considerations is the third part of the *Clavier-Uebung* (S. 669–89) containing "different preludes based on the Catechism and other hymns, for organ" (*BG*, III). Here, the chorales used are associated with the five parts of the Lutheran Catechism (the Decalogue, the Creed, the Lord's Prayer, Baptism, and Communion) to which are added, at the beginning, chorales associated with the Kyrie and Gloria (common parts of the Lutheran *Hauptgottesdienst*, the main service) and, between Baptism and Communion, one for Confession. Because the whole in a way corresponds to the Lutheran *Hauptgottesdienst*, it is often referred to as the German Organ Mass (*Deutsche Orgelmesse*). The chorales involved are: *Kyrie, Gott Vater in Ewigkeit* (for Kyrie I), *Christe, aller Welt Trost* (for Christe), *Kyrie, Gott heiliger Geist* (for Kyrie II), *Allein Gott in der Höh' sei Ehr* (for Gloria), *Dies sind die heil'gen zehn Gebote* (for the Decalogue), *Wir glauben all' an einem Gott* (for the Creed), *Vater unser im Himmelreich* (for the Lord's Prayer), *Christ unser Herr zum Jordan kam* (for Baptism), *Aus tiefer Not* (for Confession), and *Jesu Christus unser Heiland* (for Communion). All of these appear in one or more versions, one for full organ and others simply *manualiter* (for the keyboards only), and exhibit different compositional procedures. Also included are four two-part pieces called "duets," possibly intended for harpsichord. The whole is framed by the famous Prelude and Fugue in E-flat

EXAMPLE 25

BACH: *Aus tiefer Not* (S. 686), from the *Clavierübung*, III—beginning

(S. 552), known as *St. Anne,* the prelude standing at the beginning and the fugue at the end.

There are several other collections of Bach's organ chorales. The six in *Choräle von verschiedener Art* (S. 645–50), published by Schübler of Jena between 1746 and 1750, were the only other ones to appear in print during Bach's lifetime (*BG*, XXV, 2). The collection contains transcriptions for organ of movements from Bach's cantatas (one has yet to be properly identified), and thus represents a revival of the old practice of intavolatura. Bach planned at the same time to publish a set of eighteen organ chorales, *Choräle von verschiedener Art* (S. 651–68), but this plan did not work out, and they remained in manuscript (*BG*, XXV, 2). The other large collection of Bach's chorale preludes is that copied by Joseph Kirnberger in the second half of the eighteenth century. A number of individual chorale preludes by Bach have also come down.

These compositions show considerable similarities in matters of compositional procedure. They represent the culmination of the art we examined in the last chapter. All the types encountered there appear in the work of Bach. These are, then, cantus firmus type settings of chorale melodies. The chorale appears more frequently in the uppermost voice while the other parts form a contrapuntal accompaniment; in some cases, the chorale melody itself is ornamented with trills, turns, and passing tones. In a few instances, we find the chorale melody treated canonically, a procedure used in the more elaborate chorale preludes found in the *Clavier-Uebung* (*Dies sind die heil'gen zehn Gebote*, S. 678, and *Vater unser*, S. 682), but also present here and there in the *Orgelbüchlein*.

We also find examples of the chorale fugue, in which the various phrases of the chorale are employed as subjects for a fugal working out. In some cases, like the virtuoso *In dir ist Freude* (S. 615) of the *Orgelbüchlein* or the impressive *Wir glauben all' an einem Gott* (S. 680) from the third part of the *Clavier-Uebung*, the subject is merely the first line of the chorale melody; in others, as in the six-voice *Aus tiefer Not* (S. 686) from the *Clavier-Uebung*, each line of the chorale melody is successively treated in imitation. Many of the alternative settings in this last collection are of this type.

In the *Orgelbüchlein*, the settings in the main are short and simple, in accordance with the practical liturgical intent of the collection, so that in many cases the result is little more than a modestly embellished harmonization of the chorale melody. Examples of this are *Jesu meine Freude* (S. 610), *Da Jesus an dem Kreuze stund* (S. 621), *Christ lag in Todesbanden* (S. 625; see *MPM*, 47), and *Alle Menschen müssen sterben* (S. 643). In the other collections, and occasionally in the *Orgelbüchlein*, however, the procedure is frequently more elaborate, an elaboration that principally involves the accompaniment; these compositions also are usually much larger.

This brings us to a most important aspect of these chorale preludes, one that is, however, by no means restricted to them but applies to Baroque music in general. Earlier, in the discussion of Frescobaldi, reference was made to what is called the "theory of affections," the idea that music is capable of stimulating certain emotions (or affections) in the listeners. This notion was worked out in broad systematic fashion during the Baroque period, especially in relation to vocal music and particularly in the opera. By analogy, it appears also in the instrumental music of the period. It is evident that such an intent exists in Bach's chorale preludes, manifesting itself in the keys, types of figuration, harmonic progressions, and textures employed. A few characteristic examples drawn from the *Orgelbüchlein* will have to suffice in the present context as indications of this. The representation of joy, for instance, in *Der Tag, der ist so freudenreich* (S. 605) and *In dir ist Freude* (S. 615) is accomplished by the employment of a concise and highly characteristic motive accompanying the chorale melody and the key of G. The quieter joys of the Nativity are celebrated in *In dulci jubilo* (S. 608) in A and with smooth stepwise triplet figuration throughout (chorale melody in canon; see *HMS*, VI, s. 2, b. 4, b). The representation of praise is similar to that of joy and involves rapidly moving figuration often outlining triads or making octave leaps, as may be seen from *Lob sei dem allmächtigen Gott* (S. 602), *Gelobet seist du* (S. 604), and *Lobt Gott ihr Christen* (S. 609). Sorrow, on the other hand, is associated—as would be expected—with the minor keys, slow tempos, and often with chromaticism, as in *Ich ruf zu dir* in f (S. 639) or in *O Lamm Gottes unschuldig* in F (S. 618, chorale melody in canon), which has an accompanying figure consisting of "sobbing" appogiaturas (which can be compared, by the way, to the closing chorus of the *St. Matthew Passion*). A famous and often cited example of this is *Durch Adams Fall is ganz verderbt* (S. 637) with its diminished

EXAMPLE 26

BACH: *Da Jesus an dem Kreuze stund* (S. 621), from the *Orgelbüchlein*—beginning

sevenths in the bass suggestive of Adam's fall from grace and the long chromatic
inner part representing sin (*HMS*, VI, s. 2, b. 3, b). As it is usual to have but one
affection expressed in a work of this kind, the same material runs throughout in
the accompaniment, so that musical unity is also imparted to the composition
by this means. Of many discussions of this question, a very famous one that in a
way pioneered studies of this kind is by Albert Schweitzer.

Along with the chorale prelude, Bach cultivated the genre of the chorale
variations or chorale partita, which had also come down from the repertory of
seventeenth-century German organ music. Bach composed six such sets, the
number of variations in each ranging from seven to seventeen (*BG*, XL).
Usually the chorale melody is presented first in simple form, homophonic, and
is then treated as a cantus firmus with various countermelodies going along with
it. Most of these chorale partitas are composed for an instrument with one
manual and hence can be rendered either on harpsichord, clavichord, or organ;

EXAMPLE 27

Bach: *O Lamm Gottes unschuldig* (S. 618), from the *Orgelbüchlein*—
beginning

but there are individual variations here and there that call for pedals, especially in the partitas on *Sei gegrüsset Jesu gütig* (S. 768) and *Allein Gott in der Höh' sei Ehr'* (S. 771). The canonic chorale partita *Vom Himmel hoch* is discussed below.

Apart from the chorale preludes and other works based on the chorales, the most important group of organ compositions by Bach are those related to the large toccata that are variously known as preludes and fugues, fantasias and fugues, and even, erroneously, as toccatas and fugues (see Fuller-Maitland). Bach's chief contributions to this genre, chronologically arranged, are the following.

Lüneburg or Arnstadt (1700–1708):
> Prelude and Fugue in c (S. 549; *BG*, XXXVIII, No. 1)
> Prelude and Fugue in a (S. 551; *BG*, XXXVIII, No. 3)

Arnstadt or Weimar (1708–1709):
> Toccata in d (S. 565; *BG*, XV, Toccata No. 2)
> Toccata in E (S. 566; *BG*, XV, Toccata No. 3)
> Prelude and Fugue in C (S. 531; *BG*, XV, No. 1)
> Prelude and Fugue in D (S. 532; *BG*, XV, No. 2)
> Prelude and Fugue in e (S. 533; *BG*, XV, No. 3)
> Prelude and Fugue in G (S. 550; *BG*, XXXVIII, No. 2)
> Prelude and Fugue in g (S. 535; *BG*, IV, No. 5)

Weimar (1709–1716):
> Toccata in C (S. 564; *BG*, XV, Toccata No. 1)
> Prelude and Fugue in f (S. 534; *BG*, XV, No. 4)
> Prelude and Fugue in A (S. 536; *BG*, XV, No. 6)
> Prelude and Fugue in c (S. 537; *BG*, XV, No. 7)
> Prelude (or Toccata) and Fugue in F (S. 540; *BG*, XV, No. 10)

Cöthen (1717–1723):
> Prelude (or Fantasia) and Fugue in g (S. 542; *BG*, XV, No. 12)
> Prelude (or Toccata) and Fugue in d (S. 538; *BG*, XV, No. 8; this work
> possibly was composed in Leipzig)

Leipzig:
> Prelude and Fugue in a (S. 543; *BG*, XV, No. 13; the prelude dates from
> Weimar; the fugue exists in an earlier version from Cöthen)
> Prelude and Fugue in d (S. 539; *BG*, XV, No. 9)
> Prelude and Fugue in G (S. 541; *BG*, XV, No. 11)
> Prelude and Fugue in C (S. 545; *BG*, XV, No. 15; the fugue was composed in
> Weimar)
> Prelude and Fugue in c (S. 546; *BG*, XV, No. 16; the fugue was composed in
> Weimar)
> Prelude and Fugue in b (S. 544; *BG*, XV, No. 14)
> Prelude and Fugue in e (S. 548; *BG*, XV, No. 18)
> Prelude and Fugue in E-flat (S. 552; *BG*, III)
> Prelude and Fugue in C (S. 547; *BG*, XV, No. 17).

The dating here is frequently uncertain and is made difficult by the fact that Bach often reworked earlier compositions while he was in Leipzig, either adding a prelude to a fugue he had composed in Weimar or the reverse. In other cases, the date can be ascertained only in a general way. It is clear that Bach composed in this genre at all stages of his artistic career, but, during the long period at Leipzig, the output declined, especially towards the end; only two works of this type were composed after 1736—the ones in E-flat (S. 552) and C (S. 547).

We have seen the development of this genre—the toccata—in the seventeenth century from the Italian ricercare and canzone and its particular cultivation in the hands of the North German masters Buxtehude and Reincken. Bach's interest in this music is well documented; his enthusiasm for Buxtehude caused him to overstay a leave of absence granted him in 1704 by the authorities in Arnstadt and he also esteemed Reincken, the organist at Hamburg. This Northern influence is particularly strong, especially in the earlier organ works of Bach.

What we have in these preludes and fugues, then, is, for the most part large works for organ that feature the typical toccata style, here at its most magnificent, and the keyboard fugue. The conventional designation "prelude and fugue" obscures the fact that, particularly in the earlier works of this kind, the distinction between the two is not great; there are fugal episodes in the so-called "preludes" and brilliant toccata passages along with very free episodes in the fugues. This is especially true of the works called "toccatas." At the same time, a certain change can be seen to commence during the Weimar period (see Krey); the tendency in the later works—those composed after 1716—is to separate in all respects the prelude from the fugue, to increase each in size and complexity, and to avoid the use of similar thematic material or of musical styles in each (see Frotscher, II, p. 872). Furthermore, the terminology is inconsistent in regard to the preludes themselves. While most of the works use the designation "prelude," in several cases, the sources do not agree; either "prelude" or "toccata" is used for the work in F (S. 540) from the Cöthen period and the work in d (S. 538) from Cöthen or Leipzig, while either "prelude" or "fantasia" is the term used for the pieces in c (S. 537) of 1716 and g (S. 542) from Cöthen. Other designations used are "toccata" and "fantasia and fugue." It seems that there is no real systematic difference between these various designations, a contention that is also supportable on stylistic grounds.

In the early works, those composed up to the Weimar period, the impetus towards virtuosity is paramount. This is seen from the figuration that is used as well as in the ornate, long, and difficult pedal solos. These solos, which apparently are to be associated with the organ in Arnstadt, appear in preludes and in fugues, and prominent examples may be seen in the Preludes and Fugues in c (S. 549) C (S. 531), D (S. 532), G (S. 550), and the Toccata in E (S. 566). These works abound in figuration of all kinds, often over dramatic pedal points, massive chords in dotted rhythms, and sudden changes of harmony. A particular feature often found in Bach is the rhythmic energy—the insistent, driving repetition of a rhythmic pattern using either concise motives or figuration or motives that are themselves compounded of figuration.

A characteristic example of these early preludes and fugues would be the Prelude and Fugue in C (S. 531) with pedal solos and a prominence of martial,

EXAMPLE 28

BACH: *Toccata* in d (S. 565)—excerpt

fanfare-like motives, triadic and in dotted rhythm. Another would be the well-known Toccata in d (S. 565) in which there is no real break between the toccata and the fugue and that ends with a return to the toccata style of the beginning. In this work, the fantasia element is prominent, especially at the end with its pronounced quasi-improvisational character, the explicit tempo changes indicated by Bach, and the designation *recitativo*. This last indicates that the performer is to play with a certain rhythmic freedom and with great expression, as has been seen in Frescobaldi and Froberger; the term is associated with the *recitativo accompagnato* of the *opera seria* in which a heightened form of expression was essential. Rather unusual among these earlier works is the Toccata in E (S. 566) composed at Arnstadt around 1707. This work is in four sections. The first is in typical toccata style with much figuration and a long pedal solo; the second is a fugue with a long subject employing much figuration that, in its use of repeated notes and leaps, is in the tradition of the old canzone; the third is a short transition in toccata style; and, fourth is another fugue, also with a canzone-like subject featuring dotted rhythms and, at the end, a return to the toccata style. The over-all model for this work is to be found in similar compositions of Buxtehude.

This type of toccata (or prelude and fugue) is maintained by Bach in the works he composed at Weimar. In fact, it is made even larger and more elaborate, the virtuoso element still very much in the forefront. Here, we still find the characteristic intermingling of the toccata and fugal styles in both main parts of a work. It should be noted that in these pieces, as in earlier ones, the fugue is not treated as a strict contrapuntal form; while there are many strict fugal expositions in which the fugue subjects are successively stated in all voices, there are also many episodes that are not fugal at all, but involve either figuration (alone or

EXAMPLE 28—*continued*

accompanied by chords) or echo effects of different kinds. In such episodes, there is a close relation to the concertato style of the Baroque period, which at the time was being used in Italian orchestral music and culminated in the concerto grosso. The concertato (or, as one is tempted to say, "orchestral") style plays an important role in these works, as will be seen. In two cases, it even appears in eighteenth-century sources: the Toccata in E (S. 566) and the earlier Fantasia and Fugue in G (S. 571), the latter of somewhat doubtful authenticity. Passages in this style may also be found in Buxtehude.

The Prelude and Fugue in D (S. 532) is a particularly brilliant example, composed around 1709 either in Arnstadt or Weimar. The prelude is in three sections. The first seems stylistically like a French overture or the beginning of a *concerto da chiesa*, a slow basic tempo with rapid up-beat scale runs and heavy chords in characteristic dotted rhythms; the second, *alla breve*, is in the style of a *sonata a quattro* with continuo, three voices working out the same thematic material over an evenly moving bass; then, at the end, there is an adagio with typical toccata-like figuration. The fugue is long and brilliant with many free episodes closely related to the orchestral concerto, in which a "solo" line of figuration is accompanied by regularly moving chords. The subject of this fugue is striking, very long, made of scale figuration, and full of rhythmic drive; it has been associated with a fugue of Pachelbel in the same key (see Oppel).

The influence of Italian orchestral music extends even further, to the point of governing the over-all form of the toccata or prelude and fugue. This can be seen in the Toccata in C (S. 564) whose three sections parallel the plan of a concerto grosso. Indeed, the first movement uses short motives that are treated in concertato fashion between the various voices featuring a rapid alternation of short "solo" lines with chords on the "full" organ, all very much like a concerto of Corelli. The Adagio, in a, is actually an instrumental aria, a single rhythmic pattern underlying the whole; then follows a short Grave consisting of chords with suspensions in the tradition of the old *toccata di durezze e ligature*. The fugue is in free virtuoso style, its subject related to Georg Böhm, abounding in concertato effects and closing in brilliant toccata style in which the violinistic quality of the writing is particularly evident.

Towards the end of the Weimar period, around 1716, Bach commenced to alter the disposition of his toccatas. The two parts, the toccata or prelude and the fugue, tend now to become more independent of each other. Each becomes larger and more complex. The change is particularly evident in the fugues themselves, which now eschew the concertato and "orchestral" episodes in favor of a stricter contrapuntal working out of the subject. Although the canzone type is still continued, as in the Prelude (or Fantasia) and Fugue in c (S. 537) but with a sober effect, it appears here with a second subject that is chromatic and moves in even, slow notes; the two subjects are not combined. In two other works composed at the same time, the Prelude and Fugue in f (S. 534) and the

Prelude (or Toccata) and Fugue in F (S. 540), the subjects are in the tradition of the ricercare—slow, moving, and with leaps; the Fugue in f, in five voices, is strict throughout, while the Fugue in F is an excellent example of the double fugue in which a second subject is introduced and given a full fugue exposition after which it is used in combination with the first subject.

EXAMPLE 29

BACH: *Prelude and Fugue* in D (S. 532)—fugue (beginning)

An impressive and often-played work of the Cöthen period is the Prelude (or Fantasia) and Fugue in g (S. 542), composed around 1720. Here, the direction established in the later Weimar works is continued; both parts are made longer and are kept separate from and independent of one another. The prelude, a good example of the large form, uses a scheme that goes back to the toccatas of Merulo; there are five sections in all in which passages in the virtuoso toccata style alternate with sections in what we might describe as *sonata a quattro* style, i.e., three voices over a supporting bass line. The fugue is correspondingly elaborate and employs a long subject that operates with sequential patterns and is related to the canzone type. This subject apparently was often used as part of the examination for prospective organists and is quoted as an example in this connection in substantially the same form by Mattheson; it also bears a resemblance to a movement in a sonata of Reincken's *Hortus musicus* as well as to works of Zachow and Pachelbel. In one respect, this work departs from Bach's new direction; it employs free nonfugal episodes, but these free episodes employ thematic material that is closely related to the fugue subject.

On the other hand, the Prelude (or Toccata) and Fugue in d (S. 538), composed either at Cöthen or Leipzig, clearly shows the new trend in all respects. Although sectional, the prelude employs the same thematic material throughout, operating a great deal with the contrapuntal treatment of a motive; some quasi-orchestral concertato writing is also in evidence. But the fugue, in most respects, is an archaic composition. It is a four-voice ricercare with a long subject in slow notes and suspensions, written in d but without the usual signature of one flat (hence, the popular designation "Dorian"); only at the very end does the coda, with its antiphonal chords over a pedal point, break the aura of strictness.

In the Leipzig works, we find that, while preludes and fugues in the new style predominate, the old virtuoso and concertato element is never entirely lacking. There is a fine example of the older type among the Leipzig works, the celebrated Prelude and Fugue in a (S. 543), a composition with a complex history since the prelude goes as far back as 1709 and the first version of the fugue was composed in Cöthen. The theme of the prelude, with its emphasis on broken chord patterns, suggests the violinistic style of Corelli and Vivaldi, and quasi-orchestral passages are also present; the same is true of the fugue with its long, sequential subject, the free concertato episodes, and the florid close in toccata style. Particularly violinistic is the Prelude and Fugue in d (S. 539), in which the fugue is a direct transcription for organ of the fugue from Bach's own Sonata in g for Unaccompanied Violin (S. 1001), so that the work is known as the "fiddle fugue" (this fugue, however, may be spurious; see Killian). The prelude is written for the manual only (*manualiter*) and is in one section, much in the style of a lyric aria, with the suggestion of a *da capo* at the end employing melodic sequences, suspensions, and chromatic modulations. The concertato style also appears in the first movement of the Prelude and Fugue in G (S. 541).

In general, the new direction can best be seen, as before, in the fugues. The ricercare type again is prominent, as in the Prelude and Fugue in C (S. 545) and in c (S. 546), of which the latter may be regarded as a double fugue. And the devices of learned counterpoint, augmentation, and inversion are used in the fugue of the Prelude and Fugue in C (S. 547). On the other hand, episodes in concertato style appear in the Prelude and Fugue in e (S. 548), whose theme, on account of the successive appearance of ever-widening leaps, has been nicknamed "the wedge."

The Prelude and Fugue in b (S. 544) can also be regarded as an example of the newer type of toccata. In the prelude, the old virtuosity is largely abandoned, and, although figurative material is used, it is treated motivically and contrapuntally. The prelude is large and in alternating sections, but the element of contrast is not great. In the fugue, an unusually uncharacteristic subject consisting of step-wise motion in even eighth notes is accompanied by a countersubject; apart from a few episodes using a motivic working out of the subject, the treatment throughout is strictly contrapuntal.

The most elaborate work by Bach in this genre is the Prelude and Fugue in E-flat (S. 552), which appears along with the chorale preludes in the third part of the *Clavier-Uebung* of 1739. In the prelude, three separate elements are to be identified: the typical opening with scale runs and dotted figures treated motivically, not unrelated to the French overture; a second part, homophonic with echo effects that then move on with a figurative phrase using syncopations; and a fast theme using violinistic figuration patterns. The first of these is used as a ritornello, appearing at the beginning and the end as well as between the two contrasting episodes. The fugue, in five voices, is in the strict style that became common in Bach's later organ preludes and fugues. There are three sections. The first introduces a subject somewhat in the ricercare style (which is similar to the beginning of the familiar hymn called *St. Anne*); in each of the two subsequent sections (the first in 6/4, the second in 12/8), this subject, in varied form, is contrapuntally combined with a new countersubject, the first of which is presented in inversion. This composition, then, is a revival of the old variation ricercare, and it stands among the most complex of all Bach's fugues for organ.

Apart from the preludes and fugues, there are a number of independent works —preludes, fantasias, fugues, and other compositions. A Fugue in g, (S. 578), composed in Weimar or Arnstadt around 1709, has become popular as the Little Fugue in g. Of some interest are the Fugues in c (S. 574) and in b (S. 579), based on themes of Legrenzi and Corelli, respectively, a circumstance that makes the link to Italian instrumental music clear from yet another standpoint. Then there is the Canzone in d (S. 588) of 1709, a work in the tradition of the old variation canzone in which variations of the main subject are treated contrapuntally. The authenticity of the eight Little Preludes and Fugues (S. 553–60), allegedly composed in Weimar around 1710, has been questioned, and they are thought to be the work of Johann Ludwig Krebs or possibly his father, Johann Tobias.

It should be pointed out that many of the organ preludes and fugues use thematic material taken either from other works of Bach or from works of other composers. Several instances of this have been mentioned already: the fugues on themes of Legrenzi and Corelli; the canzone on Frescobaldi; the fugue from Bach's own Sonata in g for Unaccompanied Violin (S. 1001) in the Prelude and Fugue in d (S. 539); the Mattheson-Reincken, *et al.* "examination" theme in the Prelude (or Fantasia) and Fugue in g (S. 542); the Prelude and Fugue in D (S. 532) connected with Pachelbel; and the fugue in the Toccata, Adagio, and Fugue in C (S. 564) connected with Böhm. Aside from these, there are at least three prominent instances in which themes from Bach's cantatas appear in the organ preludes and fugues: the first movement of *Tritt auf die Glaubensbahn* (Cantata No. 152) in the Prelude and Fugue in A (S. 536), the first chorus of *Ich hatte viel Bekümmernis* (Cantata No. 21) in the Prelude and Fugue in G (S. 541), and the last number of *Aus der Tiefe* (Cantata No. 131) exists also as an organ fugue in g (S. 131a). Such correspondences are not uncommon in the works of Bach and are interesting and important not only for the opportunity they provide to observe different treatments of the same theme or similar themes, but also for the operation of the all-important theory of affections and its application to purely instrumental music.

Mention has frequently been made of the influence of the Italian concertato, orchestral, style in the organ works of Bach. The concertato style has been noted not only in the episodes of fugues and passages in the preludes, but also in the over-all disposition of a large work like the Toccata in C (S. 564), in which a slow movement is inserted between the traditional prelude and fugue. In the same spirit, we find also that Bach made effective transcriptions of six orchestral concertos for organ (S. 592–7), the authenticity of some of which has been questioned. Especially noteworthy are three arrangements of concerti grossi of Vivaldi—those in a (Vivaldi's *L'estro armonico*, op. 3 vi, S. 593), C (Vivaldi's op. 7 v, S. 594), and d (Vivaldi's op. 3 xi, S. 596); two others are arrangements of concertos by Johann Ernst of Saxe-Weimar—those in F (S. 592) and C (S. 595), respectively; the original of the remaining work (S. 597) has yet to be identified.

This influence is also to be seen in the six sonatas for organ (S. 525–30), the so-called Trio Sonatas, composed in the early Leipzig years for Wilhelm Friedemann Bach (*BG*, XV). These are original compositions in the style of the Italian trio sonata but are composed for organ or, in Bach's own designation, for *2 claviere ed pedal*, which would also apply to the large type of harpsichord. These works, however, in their three-movement form with a slow movement between two fast movements, are also related to the concerto grosso. The Italian violinistic style is prominent in the fast movements of these works; the slow movements seem modeled after arias.

Related to but different from the preludes and fugues for organ is the famous Passacaglia and Fugue in c (S. 582), composed either in Cöthen or Weimar around 1716–1717 (*BG*, XV). Although generally thought of as an organ work and treated as such, in the score, Bach's annotation *cembalo ossia organo* makes it clear that the work is equally intended for harpsichord, although a large one would be necessary since the work has a pedal part. The passacaglia, originally a dance, became in the seventeenth century the largest of the variation forms. As has been seen, especially in the work of Buxtehude, a theme of four bars in the bass is used as an ostinato. Bach's theme is double this normal length, but its first four bars correspond to a passacaglia melody used by the French composer André Raison around 1700 (see *HMS*, VI, s. 2, b. 5, b). In this work, there are in all twenty-one statements of the ostinato melody, usually as cantus firmus in the bass but also in the uppermost part or else broken up into figuration. The character of the accompaniment changes from variation to variation. In the long fugue that follows, Bach makes use of a subject based on the first four bars of the passacaglia and employs in succession two countersubjects, the first of which is introduced at the outset; both countersubjects are submitted to variation. Thematically, then, the fugue is bound up with the passacaglia, a circumstance that sets this work off from the organ preludes and fugues and toccatas in which there seems to have been no attempt to use thematic material from the prelude in the fugue associated with it.

The prelude and fugue is exemplified in a different way in what is Bach's most influential set of compositions, the two volumes of *The Well-Tempered Clavier* (*Das wohltemperierte Clavier*, S. 846–93), containing two preludes and fugues in all the major and minor keys, making forty-eight in all (*BG*, XIV; also XXXVI and XLV).[1] The title *The Well-Tempered Clavier* does not appear on the original manuscript of the second book but is popularly used since the plan is the same as that of the first book, to which Bach did give this title. Furthermore, the second book contains works that Bach wrote much earlier but that he arranged and, in some cases, transposed so that they would accord with this special plan (see Dadelsen).

That *The Well-Tempered Clavier* is a didactic work is made clear from the title statement; it is intended not only to assist young people in learning music, but also for the diversion of those already accomplished in the art.[2] The designation "well-tempered" has to do with Bach's adoption of even temperament (in

---

[1] There are many detailed discussions of these compositions, many of which are to assist in performance. We can mention here a few: Riemann, Fuller-Maitland, Czaczkes, Brandts-Buys, Misch, and the controversial one of Rothschild.

[2] Here is the full title in the original: *Das wohltemperierte Clavier oder Praeludia und Fugen durch alle Töne und Semitonia sowohl tertiam majorem oder Ut re mi anlangend als durch tertiam minorem oder Re mi fa anlangend. Zum Nutzen und Gebrauch der Lehrbegiergen Musicalischen Jugend als auch deren in diesem Studio schon habil seyender besonderen Zeitvertrieb aufgesetzet und verfertiget von J. S. Bach.*

which the octave is divided into twelve equal parts or semitones) in place of the mean-tone system, which had been in use since the Renaissance and which worked out well enough as long as one did not exceed keys with signatures greater than two sharps or flats. The instrumental medium intended by Bach is not expressly stated beyond the designation "clavier," a term denoting keyboard instruments in general. There has been much discussion on this subject, some people supporting the harpsichord, others the clavichord, and still others the organ; others even venture the opinion that Bach would have used the piano had it been available. For Bach, however, the term "clavier" was sufficient—the pieces are simply for keyboard instruments; their intent, as has been seen, is primarily didactic, so that properly they may be realized on whatever instrument happens to be at hand, be it harpsichord, clavichord, or organ. In this spirit, then, there should be no objection to the use (hopefully with discretion) of the piano.

We have seen that the previous history of the prelude and fugue form lies primarily in organ music, an outgrowth of the Italian toccata. But the form as treated by Bach here differs from its counterpart in organ music in that the works are shorter and less elaborate. This is particularly true of the preludes, in which the large sectional form with great contrasts is largely abandoned. The fugues also are more concise.

In the preludes, the essential character of the genre is maintained. These are short, highly unified pieces; each has its own sharply drawn character, which is maintained throughout. The tendency is to operate with a short theme or motive —a phrase, a characteristic texture, rhythmic pattern, or type of figuration—that provides the basic thematic material of the piece and establishes its character at the outset. Often this thematic material will consist of figuration: scale patterns predominate in the Preludes in D (Part I) and F (Part II); arpeggio patterns in the Preludes in d and G (Part I); broken chords in the Preludes in F and B-flat (Part I) and d (Part II). Once established, the thematic pattern or motive is usually carried all the way through.

At the same time, there are preludes that fall into clearly defined sections; the one in E-flat (Part I) is, with its three sections and characteristic mixture of imitation and figuration, still closely related to the older toccata, if on a smaller scale. Others employ changes in tempo: those in c and e (Part I) and the one in C-sharp (Part II). Binary form (with double bar and repeat signs) appears once in Part I (b, the last prelude) but nine times in Part II (c, d-sharp, E, e, f, G, g-sharp, a, B-flat). In several preludes, the thematic material of the beginning reappears towards the end in its original key, thus having the effect of a recapitulation (Part I: c-sharp, D [in the subdominant], A; Part II: F, f, f-sharp, B-flat). And when, as in the Prelude in f (Part II), this comes together with the use of binary form and the double bar with repeat signs, one can speak, with Apel, of "rounded binary form," known as one of the types from which the sonata form emerged in the second half of the eighteenth century.

From time to time, we have had occasion to notice how forms and procedures of other types of instrumental music have had an important effect on keyboard music. Such an influence is evident also in the preludes of *The Well-Tempered Clavier* (and the fugues as well for that matter, but to a lesser extent); that is to say, the characteristic procedures and specific forms from other media can be observed here. A few examples will serve as illustrations. For instance, the *style brisé*, characteristic broken-chord patterns of lute music, is plain in the Preludes in C (Part I) and, to a lesser extent, E-flat (Part II). The important chamber-music medium of the trio sonata (two voices over a bass) may be observed in the Preludes in c-sharp, g-sharp, A, and B of Part I, and those in c-sharp, E, A, and b-flat of Part II. The violin-continuo sonata, with concertato relationship between the two parts, doubtless lies behind the Preludes in e and A-flat (complete with double-stops) of Part I and that in g-sharp of Part II. Orchestral in conception is the Prelude in D of Part II with its "trumpet tune." The arioso, associated with the *accompagnato* of the *opera seria*, is impressively present in at least three preludes: e-flat, e (first section only), b-flat (instrumental rather than vocal conception) of Part I. Yet another type is the pastoral (which often is related to the *siciliano* dance), seen in the Preludes in E (Part I) and c-sharp, E-flat (to some extent), and A (Part II). Specific dance types are suggested by other preludes: the allemande (Part I, f-sharp and B), corrente (Part II, E), gigue (Part I, F-sharp; Part II, B-flat, both in 12/16 time), and the saraband (Part I, e-flat, also, as above, an example of the arioso). The thematic material is not infrequently treated in imitation, as in the Preludes in E-flat, F-sharp, g-sharp, and A of Part I, the last featuring double (or invertible) counterpoint, or the Preludes in d-sharp, e, a (also with double counterpoint), and b of Part II, that in a being noteworthy for its intense chromaticism.

EXAMPLE 30

BACH: *Prelude* in A-flat (S. 862), from *The Well-Tempered Clavier*, Part I —beginning

Interesting and influential as the preludes themselves have been (their influence, as will be seen, was particularly marked in nineteenth-century music), it nonetheless is true that by and large the fugues have generally outweighed them in significance. Most of the fugues in *The Well-Tempered Clavier* are either three-voice (Part I has eleven and Part II, fifteen) or four-voice (Part I has ten and Part II, nine), but Part I contains one two-voice fugue (e) and two five-voice fugues (c-sharp and b-flat). In contrast to what is sometimes said, there is no one procedure or form that appears here beyond the rather general consideration that all are in one way or another examples of imitative counterpoint. At the same time, many of these fugues contain important episodes and other passages that are motivic or sequential rather than imitative (c, C-sharp, D, A in Part I; d, F-sharp, G, g, A-flat in Part II), and toccata-like passages at the very end are not uncommon. Again, generally in a fugue of *The Well-Tempered Clavier*, there will be found an alternation between straightforward presentations of the theme (subject) in each voice (the expositions) and passages that use either motives taken from the theme, its countersubject, or free material (the episodes). But one can also point to fugues that lack such episodes, like the Fugue in C (Part I).

In most cases, a fugue of *The Well-Tempered Clavier* will have a principal theme (the subject) and, along with it, a countersubject that is usually defined as the thematic material used in the first voice to accompany the entrance of the second voice with the answer; this countersubject often is important in the episodes. In both Fugues in C-sharp, two countersubjects are introduced. Then, there are instances of the double fugue and of the triple fugue, that is, where two or three different subjects are "exposed" independently of one another and then presented in contrapuntal combination (Part II, f-sharp and g-sharp). There are also instances of the opposite, as in the Fugue in g (Part I) in which the counter-subject is the inversion of the subject, so that the whole piece is rigorously mono-thematic. In most cases, the fugues of *The Well-Tempered Clavier* employ one subject and one countersubject.

There has been much discussion of the theory that the uniqueness of Bach's fugues lies in his ability to invent suitable subjects that in themselves are in-herently adaptable, idiomatic as it were, for use in fugues. While this may be seen in any of Bach's fugal compositions, its plainest manifestation is in *The Well-Tempered Clavier*. There are many elements involved: continuously driving rhythms, figuration patterns, sequential phrase structures, striking intervals in the subject, and so on. Some characteristic types of fugue subject, as they appear in *The Well-Tempered Clavier*, may be identified here. (The types are by no means necessarily mutually exclusive.) Noteworthy from the historical standpoint are the subjects in long, slow notes in the tradition of the ricercare (Part I: c-sharp, e-flat, f, f-sharp, and b-flat; Part II: E-flat, E, and b-flat). Themes related specifically to the old canzone are rare; an example is the Fugue in D (Part II). Generally, the rapid subjects consist of driving figuration, as was seen in several of the fugues for organ; in *The Well-Tempered Clavier*, we can point to the Fugues in E and G in Part I and c-sharp and G in Part II. Several of the fugues use a similar type of theme in which the melodic motion is continually around, above, and below a central tone, thus becoming in a way a stylized ornament (Part I: c, E-flat to some extent, F-sharp; Part II: c). In others, particular types of ornaments seem to lie behind the subjects, for instance, the slide or *Schleifer*, very stylized in the Fugue in D (Part I), or the *pathétique* appogiatura (known as the "sigh") in the Fugue in b (Part I). Apart from these, we find short subjects (A-flat in Part I; and C-sharp in Part II, the latter having only four notes) as well as long and elaborate subjects with a variety of rhythms and motives employed (Part I: G, B-flat, B; Part II: d, e, g). It is not uncommon for a fugue subject to be divided into two distinct parts, the one quite different from the other (Part I: D, E-flat, E, g, a; Part II: C). A noteworthy instance of this may be seen in the Fugue in g (Part II) in which, after detached statements of a motive employing an upward leap of a fourth and a descending one of a third, there comes a phrase featuring a note repeated no less than seven times. Several of the fugue subjects seem also to be somehow related to dances, for instance, the passepied (Part I: F) and the gigue (Part II: c-sharp and b, the last with octave leaps). Still other fugue subjects move in even notes (Part I: f, A-flat, A, b; Part II: B-flat).

In connection with the fugal working-out, it is interesting to note that the devices of learned counterpoint are by no means as prominent in *The Well-Tempered Clavier* as one is often led to believe. To be sure, stretto and inversion are employed with great frequency; as examples of stretto, we can mention the Fugues in C, c-sharp, d, e, e-flat, F, G, A, and a of Part I and those in C-sharp, D, d-sharp, E-flat, and b-flat of Part II; and examples of inversion are to be seen in the Fugues in d, e-flat, f-sharp, G and B in Part I, and in c, C-sharp, c-sharp, d, and b-flat in Part II. On the other hand, diminution appears not at all in Part I and only three times in Part II (C-sharp, E, and a; in the last, the second part of the subject is the diminution of the first), while augmentation appears but three times all told, in the Fugues in e-flat (Part I) and c and c-sharp (Part II) and retrograde only once altogether, in the Fugue in C-sharp (Part II). It may be noted that the most learned fugue, the one in C-sharp (Part II), which employs all the learned devices including retrograde motion, is also distinguished by the shortest subject; three other fugues in which learned aspects are prominent are those in e-flat (Part I) and c and E (Part II), two of which have subjects of the ricercare type. By contrast, the least learned fugues appear to be those in D and e (Part I), the first because of the nature of the subject is as motivic as it is imitative. The second, in e, (the only two-voice fugue in *The Well-Tempered Clavier*) even contains passages with parallel octaves.

It would appear, then, that, contrapuntal as these fugues are, their strictness—and, by extension, their learnedness—has been somewhat exaggerated. In fact, by and large these works, the preludes as well as the fugues, share in the central aim of Baroque music: the expression of the affections. This expression is inti-mately bound up with the keys, the meters, and the melodic types, as well as the various genres that are involved or suggested. While this representation of the affections cannot be demonstrated in all cases, there are a few pronounced examples that may be mentioned (see Besseler). The affection of joy seems clear in the Prelude and Fugue in G (Part I), while the works in g (the one in Part I, *HSM*, VI, s. 1, b. 6) in both parts seem to be *pathétique* compositions; a passionate character is clear in the Prelude in e (Part I), a solemn one in the Fugue in f-sharp (Part I), and a maestoso-like repose in the Fugue in E (Part II, a ricercare). All in all, this is a subject much in need of further study, the results of which should be both interesting and significant.

Much attention has been given to the question concerning the extent to which the paired preludes and fugues of *The Well-Tempered Clavier* are specifically related to one another (see Werker, whose methods are suspect; also Gerstenberg). Various answers have been given, some in the negative and others in the positive, largely depending on the methods and particular views of the writer and analyst. The conventional answer has always been that, with a few exceptions, Bach has not used the same thematic material in both the prelude and its companion fugue; the most often alleged exceptions are the Prelude and Fugue in B (Part I), but even this can be disputed since the characteristic downward leap of a fifth in the fugue is not found in the prelude, and the Prelude and Fugue in D (Part I), to which similar objections can be raised. At the same time, there is, again, room for further study.

Other didactic pieces of Bach are contained chiefly in little books that he prepared for his children: for Wilhelm Friedemann, a *Clavierbüchlein* in 1720–1721 (original at Yale University; see Plath) and for Anna Magdalena, two *Notenbücher* in 1722 and 1725. These contain short pieces of all sorts—preludes, contrapuntal works, dances, organ chorales, and so on. The *Clavierbüchlein* contains the well-known two- and three-part inventions (or *sinfonie* as the three-part inventions are called (S. 772–801; see David), which are short fugal compositions designed to teach a beginning player to present clearly two or three contrapuntal voices preparatory to undertaking larger and more elaborate compositions (*BG*, III); it also contains, among others, some preludes that also appear in *The Well-Tempered Clavier* and a set of little preludes (S. 924–32). In the two books for Anna Magdalena are found, among others, five of the French suites (see below). It might be mentioned that the *Orgelbüchlein* was also originally intended for Wilhelm Friedemann. There are also two other sets of little preludes for harpsichord (S. 933–8 and 939–43), also for teaching purposes (*BG*, XXXVI).

The large form of the fantasia (or prelude) and fugue also appears in Bach's harpsichord music. Here, the chief work is the famous Chromatic Fantasia and

Fugue in d (S. 903), composed between 1720 and 1730 (*BG*, XXXVI). The fantasia type is manifested here in all its glory. There are many sections involving sudden changes of tempo, key, and texture; noteworthy, especially in view of the subsequent history of the fantasia form, are the passages marked "arpeggio" and "recitativ," the latter term relating the fantasia to the *recitativo accompagnato* of the *opera seria*, as we observed earlier in connection with the Toccata in d for organ. The fugue, which is rather freely treated, has, as expected, a chromatic subject. Along with this work, there are several other fantasias and fugues composed for clavier as well as independent preludes and fantasias and independent fugues.

Related to this form are the toccatas for harpsichord of which there are seven (*BG*, III and XXXVI). These works resemble the toccatas for organ except that the individual sections grow so large that they stand almost as separate movements; this may be seen, for instance, in the Toccatas in D (S. 912), d (S. 913), and e (S. 914). In general, however, these toccatas are long, multisectional works (usually with three or four sections), opening in the traditional toccata style and ending with a long and elaborate fugue; some, like the Toccatas in f-sharp (S. 910) and c (S. 911), have several fugal sections. Dynamic indications and inversion of the fugue subjects are features of the Toccata in g (S. 915).

The largest group among Bach's secular keyboard works are the suites (see Fuller-Maitland), the most important of which are the *English Suites* (S. 806–11), *French Suites* (S. 812–17), and *Partitas* (S. 825–30); there are six of each. To these must be added the so-called *French Overture* in b (S. 831). While the *French Suites* and *English Suites* were composed in Cöthen, the others were composed in Leipzig and were published together as Part I of the *Clavier-Uebung*.

The earliest are the so-called *English Suites* and *French Suites*, which are as follows: *English Suites*: A, a, g, F, e, d; *French Suites*: d, c, b, E-flat, G, E (*BG*, XIII ii and XLV i). Here, the chronology is somewhat uncertain, but generally the *English Suites* are regarded as having been composed before the *French Suites* (see Fischer). The designations "French" and "English" usually associated with these works are not Bach's own and are, in fact, confusing and even misleading as far as the musical style is concerned. Both sets are "French" to the extent that the old dances—allemande, courante, saraband, and gigue, with various extra dances inserted between the saraband and gigue—are used; their order, as has been seen, is "German." Furthermore, the stylization of the dances, the degree of elaboration, and particularly the emphasis on contrapuntal writing goes far beyond what is to be found in French harpsichord suites of the time. With but a few exceptions, an external form is common to all these dances; they are in binary form with the double-bar near the middle, each part to be repeated. In general, the two parts parallel one another and present the same or similar material in much the same sequence. But they are distinguished by key; the first part moves from the tonic to the dominant or relative major and the second, with some excursions, moves back to the tonic.

In the allemandes, only the characteristic slow duple meter is taken over, while the characteristic rhythmic pattern is not present. Instead, the thematic material consists of a short motive frequently made up of figurational elements, scale runs, arpeggios, or standard ornamental turns, which are treated sequentially and contrapuntally and provide the basis for the composition. Frequently, consistent motion in sixteenth notes may be found. The dance has become, as it were, "generalized"; its specific features are lost as a result of an elaborate process of stylization. While this type of allemande may be found in any of the *French Suites* or *English Suites*, particularly clear examples are in the *French Suite* in c (where the disposition of the three voices suggests the trio sonata medium) and the English suite in A.

EXAMPLE 31

Bach: Dances from the harpsichord suites

A. Allemande from *French Suite* in c (S. 813)—beginning

B. Corrente from *French Suite* in c (S. 813)—beginning

C. Courante from *English Suite* in a (S. 807)—beginning

In the courantes (see Feldmann), Bach made a careful distinction between the French type (courante) and the Italian corrente, even preserving the difference in terminology; but later editions, including that of the *Bach-Gesellschaft*, have suppressed this, labeling them all courante. The corrente, found in four of the *French Suites* (c, E-flat, G, and E) but not in the *English Suites* is in quick triple time (3/4); it has no characteristic rhythmic patterns of its own, but rather makes use of motives made up of figurational elements (see especially that in the *French Suite* in E). On the other hand, the courante, found in the other suites, is a much more elaborate and refined affair, moving in compound meter (6/2 or 3/2) with constant oscillation between the pattern of two beats each divided by three and three beats each divided by two (see especially the courante in the English Suite in a).

The saraband, the dance in slow triple time, although stylized in the same way as the allemande, still presents characteristic rhythmic patterns of the dance in recognizable form; the process of stylization, in other words, had not progressed as far here as it had in the case of the allemande. Some of the rhythmic modifications used by Bach in the sarabands are shown in Example 32. In the *English Suites*, the saraband becomes an important, elaborate, and highly expressive slow movement (see particularly those in the *English Suites* in a and F or the very expressive one in g).

EXAMPLE 31—*continued*

While the gigue, like the courante, also exists in both French and Italian types, in these suites Bach uses only the more elaborate French gigue. The gigue retains the fast compound triple time (frequently dotted) and is treated in imitative counterpoint in two or three voices, often with the theme given in inversion after the double bar; this "standard" form may be seen in all the *French Suites* except the one in b and in all the *English Suites* except the one in a; both of these exceptions lack imitation. Noteworthy is the elaborate subject in the gigue of the French Suite in d and the chromatic gigues of English Suites in e and d.

Among the "optional" dances it may be noted that the minuet appears in the *French Suites* in d, c, b, and E but only in one *English Suite*, the one in F; the bourrée, a dance in sturdy square duple time, appears in the *French Suites* in G and E and the *English Suites* in A and a; and the gavotte, in moderate duple time, may be seen in the *French Suites* in E-flat, G, and E and in the *English Suites* in g and d. Other dances less frequently used are the anglaise (*French Suite* in b); the loure (*French Suite* in G); the polonaise (*French Suite* in E); the passepied (*English Suite* in e), here in the form of a rondeau with three episodes; and the air

EXAMPLE 32

Variants of the saraband rhythm in Bach

A. "Normal" saraband rhythm

B. English Suite in a and French Suite in d

C. English Suite in g

D. English Suite in d

E. French Suite in c

F. Partita in D

G. Partita in B-flat

(*French Suites* in c and E-flat). Doubles appear in only two of the *English Suites*, those in A and d, a courante and saraband respectively.

The *English Suites* are much larger compositions than the *French Suites*. Not only are the individual movements larger, but each of the suites has a prelude as the opening movement. Except for the *English Suite* in A (whose prelude is built on one motive and thus has something in common with the preludes of *The Well-Tempered Clavier*), all these introductory preludes have a similar scheme: a large sectional structure in which a fugal passage alternates with one or two episodes in a way that bears some resemblance to the ritornello form of the Allegro movement of an Italian orchestral concerto; the types of themes and figuration patterns employed frequently suggest Italian writing for strings, as, for instance, the prelude of the *English Suite* in F. The prelude of the *English Suite* in d has a slow section preceding the fast, indicative of the *concerto da chiesa*, since the typical dotted rhythms and mass chords of the French overture are absent. These movements are therefore not unrelated to the organ toccatas of the Arnstadt-Weimar period.

The partitas are also six in number: B-flat, c, a, D, G, and e (*BG*, III). They were composed later than the *French Suites* and *English Suites*. Here, the resemblance is rather to the *English Suites*, since the partitas also contain introductory pieces. The more traditional short prelude appears as the praeludium of the Partita in B-flat and in the fantasia of the Partita in a. The others bring a more elaborate type of composition. The overture of the Partita in D is a full French overture with concerto-like episodes in its brilliant fugue; the sinfonia of the Partita in C, in much the same style as the prelude to the English Suite in d, is related to the opening movement of a concerto or *sonata da chiesa*; and the brilliant toccata of the Partita in e has a slow part full of arpeggios, full chords, and scale figuration and a long, impressive, and solemn fugue after which the slow part returns.

Apart from these introductory pieces, the partitas as suites resemble Bach's previous compositions in the genre. The set order of dances is maintained, the chief exception being in the Partita in c which substitutes a capriccio for the gigue as the concluding movement. The allemande is highly stylized, as before; attention may be drawn to the long-phrased example in the Partita in D. The elegant French courante appears in the Partitas in c and D while the simpler corrente is used in the others. The saraband appears as a slow movement, all emphasis going to the uppermost voice. The simpler Italian giga appears in the Partita in B-flat (in duple time), the French gigue in the others, with inversions of the theme occurring in the Partitas in a and e. Of optional dances there are: the minuet in the Partitas in B-flat, D, and G; the rondeau in the Partita in c; the burlesca and scherzo in the Partita in a; the passepied in the Partita in G; the gavotte in the Partita in e; and the aria (or air) in the Partitas in D and e.

Rather different is the *Ouverture nach französischer Art* (S. 831), the so-called *French Overture* or Suite in b that appears in the *Clavier-Uebung* along with the partitas (*BG*, III). Here, as elsewhere, we may note particularly the adaptation of orchestral styles and types to the harpsichord, and this work stands closer to Bach's orchestral suites (or overtures) than it does to his other harpsichord suites. A large French overture stands at the beginning with the characteristic italianate "orchestral" episodes in its fugal section and is followed by a large number of dances; from the usual suite arrangement come the opening courante (it is the French variety that is employed here), a saraband, and a gigue; the highly stylized allemande, be it noted, is absent; between them come two gavottes, two passepieds, two bourrées, and, at the end, an echo. The constant indications calling for *piano* and *forte* (as in the overture, the second gavotte, the second bourrée, and especially, the concluding echo) not only underline the orchestral orientation of the work, but also require a large, two-manual harpsichord for proper performance; this is one of the few works of Bach which requires the employment of

EXAMPLE 33

BACH: *Echo*, from Suite in b (S. 831, the so-called *French Overture*)—beginning

such a large instrument. The movements themselves, as might be expected, are simpler than those found in Bach's other keyboard suites; the phrases used are shorter and balanced, the rhythms are less elaborate, there is less use of figuration, and the harmonies are less complex. Particularly noteworthy are the drone bass figures in the courante and the dense, chordal texture of the saraband.

Two other traditional types of harpsichord music that appear in Bach's work are the capriccio and the sonata. Of the capriccio, there are two examples, both composed in Arnstadt in 1704. One is an extended imitative work in E (S. 993) in the Italian manner, and the other is the famous *Capriccio sopra la lontananza del suo fratello dilittissimo* om B-flat (S. 992), composed in honor of Bach's brother's departure to fight in Sweden (*BG*, XXXVI). This last is a programmatic work in the same spirit as Kuhnau's *Biblical Sonatas*: an introductory slow movement, Arioso, for the friends who try to restrain him from the journey; a fugal representation of the causes that make him want to go; the lament of his friends, complete with chromatic basso ostinato; the parting; the short fanfare-like *Aria di postiglione* and, as finale, a *Fuga all'imitazione della cornetta in postiglione*. We have encountered several programmatic capriccios before, but none on the same scale as this. Of the five sonatas for clavier, four are of doubtful authenticity (one is a fragment and three are transcriptions, one of a sonata for unaccompanied violin by Bach himself, three of sonatas from Reincken's *Hortus musicus*), so that there is but one *bona fide* work of this kind, in D (S. 963), composed like the capriccios in Arnstadt in 1704 (*BG*, XXXVI). It consists of three large fast movements, the first in the Italian homophonic manner and the others fugal (the last explicitly imitating a hen); between them come slow transitional passages. Like sonatas by Kuhnau, the work is related to Italian chamber sonatas.

An important harpsichord composition by Bach for the large type of instrument is the popular *Concerto nach italienischem Gusto* in F (S. 971, the so-called *Italian Concerto*), which is also found in the second part of the *Clavier-Uebung* (*BG*, III). This work is deliberately in the style of an Italian concerto, specifically those of Vivaldi, as were the trio sonatas for organ, some of the toccatas, and the preludes to the English Suites, which we mentioned earlier. Thus the *Italian Concerto* is cast in three movements in the succession Fast—Slow—Fast. In the first movement, there are two themes corresponding, respectively, to those of the *ripieno* and the *soli* of a real concerto grosso; the same is true of the third movement. In these two movements, one can also note the frequent use of dynamic indications, *forte* and *piano*, which again correspond to the *ripieno* and *soli*. The slow movement, Andante, is in the character of an aria. Notable in this piece is the preponderance of two- and three-part writing, indicative of the use of a rather large instrument with several registers for best results. A number of arrangements for harpsichord of concerti grossi are of doubtful authenticity.

Another group of harpsichord works are the sets of variations of which there are at least two: the *Aria variata alla maniera italiana* in a (S. 989), composed at Weimar around 1709, with ten variations (*BG*, XXXVI) and the celebrated *Aria mit dreissig Veränderungen* (S. 988), the so-called *Goldberg Variations* (*BG*, III), published in 1742 as Part IV of the *Clavier-Uebung* (the work was composed for the harpsichordist Johann Gottlieb Goldberg who had been a pupil of Bach). Another set of variations, the *Sarabande con partite* in C (S. 990), is of doubtful authenticity.

The outstanding work here is the *Goldberg Variations* (see Müller-Blattau). The theme as also in early sets of variations, is called simply "aria"; it is a melody in the saraband rhythm, highly embellished in the French fashion and cast in rounded binary form ||: *a* :|| ||: *ba* :||. It is not, however, the melody of the aria that is the subject of the variations, but rather its bass, which remains constant through the variations and in which descending stepwise motion is an important element. This part appears as the bass in all the variations except the sixth and eighteenth in which it appears in the uppermost part. Frequently, it is embellished, but it is always present. For this reason, the *Goldberg Variations* is closely allied to the standard variation procedures of the Baroque period—the use of a basso ostinato or variations on a ground, for which there were a number of standard melodies. In this work, then, there are thirty variations on this melody, each different in character. The work as a whole is organized into two parts, the break coming at the fifteenth variation; and, suitably enough, to commence the second half, the sixteenth variation is a small French overture. At the very end, the aria is repeated in its original form.

In addition to the aspect of the variations on an ostinato, canon also plays an important role in the *Goldberg Variations*. Every third variation is a canon, but, in each, a different interval is used for the canonic imitation so that a full cycle of canons is the result; the third variation is a canon at the unison, the sixth a canon at the second, the ninth a canon at the third, the twelfth a canon at the fourth in contrary motion, and so on; the twenty-fourth is a canon at the octave, and, to conclude the cycle of canons, the twenty-seventh variation is a canon at the ninth. All these canonic variations involve three parts, the two canonic voices and a supporting bass; the only exception to this is the last of them, which is in two parts.

Furthermore, each variation is given a specific character all its own, and definite forms and types of Baroque music make their appearance. For instance, the tenth variation is a fughetta; the sixteenth, as already stated, is a French overture; variations five, eight, fourteen, sixteen, twenty-three, twenty-eight, and twenty-nine are virtuoso pieces using much figuration and requiring crossing of the hands (*Pièces croisées*); the seventh and twenty-fourth have a conventional *siciliano* rhythm; three of the variations are in the minor (*minore*)—the fifteenth, twenty-first, and twenty-fifth, the first two canonic and the third in the character of an *aria pathetica*; the last variation is a quodlibet combining two old and well-known German songs, *Ich bin so lang bei dir gewest* and *Kraut und Rüben*.

Early in the discussion of Bach's keyboard works, reference was made to the oscillation between the sacred and the secular that was so characteristic of his career. Along with this can be noted the free and full exploitation of stylistic elements from all countries, a circumstance that led Bukofzer to qualify Bach's art as the "fusion of national styles." In drawing together all such elements, Bach added something peculiarly his own, an intensification produced in large measure by the employment of a contrapuntal elaboration that far exceeded the capacities of his contemporaries. Interestingly enough, this tendency became most pronounced in Bach's latest works where he not only composed a large cycle of fugues on one theme and its variations (*The Art of Fugue*), but also occupied himself with what is commonly regarded the strictest of contrapuntal forms— canon (*The Musical Offering*).

There is a keyboard work from the late period that not only exemplifies this preoccupation, but also represents a sort of summation, a bringing together of two important facets of his art—the treatment of a chorale melody and canon. The work in question is the canonic variations on *Vom Himmel hoch, da komm' ich her* (S. 769) for two manuals and pedal (hence, organ or large harpsichord) which was composed and published in the late 1740's (*BG*, XL). Chorale variations (the chorale partita) had figured in Bach's output before, as has been pointed out. It is the employment of canon in this genre that represents the departure. In four of the five variations, the chorale melody is stated in cantus planus style in the pedals while the canon is between the two accompanying voices. (In variation three, the chorale melody itself is varied.) The interval of the canonic imitation changes with each variation: octave, fifth, seventh, and, in variation four, at the octave and in augmentation. The last variation is the most elaborate, for here the chorale melody itself is treated canonically and, what is more, by inversion (*al rovescio*, as Bach has it); it is repeated four times with the interval of the canonic imitation varied each time (sixth, third, second, and ninth), a most remarkable accomplishment.

By way of conclusion, it may be pointed out that Bach's influence on composers of the late eighteenth and nineteenth centuries was exercised through the very small number of his works that were available in printed form. Apart from a few works, the bulk of his organ and harpsichord music remained unknown until the appearance of the *Bach-Gesellschaft* edition in the second half of the nineteenth century. The most important exception was the first book of *The Well-Tempered Clavier*, which alone served to establish Bach as the model for fugue writing, the learned style as it was called—to the admiration, aspiration, and often despair of his successors.

CHAPTER FIVE

The Time of Change
(c. 1720–1790)

It is a commonplace that Bach be regarded as the culmination of Baroque music. But this readily acceptable[1] assertion becomes ironic with respect to Bach himself, whose work, as has been seen, received neither wide currency nor general acceptance in his day and indeed gave rise to his considerable difficulties with the authorities of the Leipzig Thomasschule, from the 1730's on. For decisive and far-reaching changes were taking place that were as profound as had ever occurred in any period in the history of music, changes that made Bach's music sound needlessly involved, erudite ("learned" was the qualification used at the time), and old-fashioned. Perhaps the crowning irony with respect to Bach himself was that his sons became important in the development of the new musical style, and one of them, Carl Philipp Emanuel Bach, even went to the point of calling his father (rather affectionately, one hopes) "The old wig."

It is always difficult to survey a period of historical change, and the one presented by the eighteenth century is particularly difficult in view of the many cross-currents, the lingering on of the old, the early appearance here and there of the new, and the many mixtures and combinations of the two, as well as the great mass of material that is involved. But, in spite of the immense amount of music that is available, it can still be said that there is not enough, for the work of most of these composers, particularly the sons of Bach as well as many of the Italian composers, is generally available to us only in the most haphazard way. Furthermore, this historical period, extending on into the early nineteenth century, is one on which much research is presently being undertaken. It would appear, then, that whatever statements are made here must not be regarded as in any sense final, and much remains to be done.

[1] The interpretation advanced by Besseler and his disciple Hoffmann-Erbrecht, stressing many "progressive" features in Bach's music, has not been generally accepted, although it does provide room for valuable discussion.

143

The change went beyond musical style; it affected all aspects of musical life. Stated in a most general way, it involved the decline of the Italian vocal art of Baroque music and the rise of a predominately instrumental art in which the lead was exercised by German musicians. But the new emphasis on instrumental music also appears in the work of Italian composers, several of whom exerted an influence on their German contemporaries. The new importance of instrumental music brought with it new genres of keyboard music as well; or, to put it another way, a new emphasis is given to certain older types so that they are, in effect, transformed into something wholly different and hence new. Perhaps most striking is the decline of the organ and of organ music and, at the other end of the century, the rise of a new musical instrument—the piano. This caused a shift in the repertory of keyboard music; the old types—the cantus firmus settings, the imitative contrapuntal works, the toccatas, and so forth—gave way, to be replaced by the single genre capable itself of great variety, the sonata.

Apart from repertory, the change affected the position of music and the musician in society. Hitherto, the main genre of secular music for a public audience was the opera. In the eighteenth century, through the Collegium Musicum in Leipzig and similar institutions elsewhere, public concerts featuring instrumental music became important. Related to this was a gain in the importance of the amateur musician, to whom composers began to address their efforts. Hence, music became a vehicle for creating entertainment, diversion, and pleasure. While the aim of music as the delectation of the senses was patent in the seventeenth century as well, in the eighteenth it went much farther, as a few representative publications will show. Johann Kellner's *Manipulus musices* of 1753–1756 is described as "a handful of pleasant amusement to pass the time away" (*eine Handvoll kurzweiler Zeitvertreib*), a sentiment that also figured in Valentin Rathgeber's collection, *Musikalischer Zeitvertreib* of 1750. Johann Christoph Graupner, in his *Partien* in 1733, claimed as his purpose the pleasure (*Vergnügen*) of the player and the fame of the composer, an intent somewhat more specialized than the more traditional end, for "the glorification of God and the edification of man." In this spirit comes a new genre of music, sonatas and other works intended specifically for women. We have, from around the middle of the century, Giuseppe Paganelli's *Divertissement de le beau sexe*, a collection of sonatinas; in 1749, Christoph Nichelmann, a pupil of J. S. Bach, issued a collection called *Brevi sonate da cembalo massime all'uso delle dame*; such works also appear in the work of Carl Philipp Emanuel Bach, as his sonatas *à l'usage des dames* of 1770. Easy sonatas intended as teaching pieces are also common.

This new environment for music, with strong domestic overtones, went hand in hand with the change in musical style. The public taste had to be satisfied; music had to be agreeable, easy, graceful, directly perceptible, tasteful, and enjoyable. In the parlance of the time, it had to be *galant*, whereas the older way, particularly its contrapuntal aspects, came to be called "learned" (see Bücken).

As the famous German theorist and writer on music Johann Mattheson puts it in his *Grosse General-Bass Schule* of 1731, one of the standard manuals on continuo playing, "as the end of the orator is to persuade his listeners, that of the musician is to please the multitude." Another contemporary theorist and critic, Johann Adolf Scheibe, in his *Critische Musikus* states, "the beauty and naturalness of this manner of writing [i.e., the *galant*] may really be said to exist when the melody is always clear, lively, flowing, and also witty [clever, *scharfsinnig*], when it makes free and natural use of all sorts of well-conceived embellishments, when it is free, easy [*ungezwungen*], and ever new" (see Bücken). Note here the emphasis placed on melody, which is to be cantabile, ingratiating, the accompaniment simple and unobtrusive. (This is, be it remembered, the age of the "Alberti" and the "Murky" basses [see Marco and Halski]). It was this aspect of the change in taste, the turn to simplicity, that particularly victimized J. S. Bach.

Reference may finally be made to a new aesthetic ideal that made itself felt with regard to music, an ideal that is closely connected to a purely instrumental kind of music existing apart from any text. In Baroque music, the ideal was for a musical work to express one affection all the way through—*d'un teneur*; the musical materials and procedures were selected in accordance with the emotional or affective character of the composition. While this was especially true of the operatic aria, it applied to other genres of composition as well: harpsichord suites, fugues, individual movements of sonatas, and so on. But, as the eighteenth century wore on, the ideal changed; it was felt that many different characteristics and emotions should be embodied in a single work (see Steglich). This new attitude is seen in an article in Marpurg's journal *Der kritische Musikus an der Spree* (1749): "We know how fast emotions change, since they themselves are nothing but motion and restlessness. . . . The composer then must in alternation play a hundred different roles, he must take on a thousand characters." This attitude brought with it a striking change in the conception of musical compositions. This is not to say that such contrasts are unknown in the music of the seventeenth and eighteenth centuries (many of Handel's arias and oratorio choruses, for example, represent contrasting affections), but they are by and large the exception. By the middle of the eighteenth century, however, the new ideal of emotional contrast in a musical work is rather the accepted one. Carl Philipp Emanuel Bach, for instance, was famous for the extraordinary variety of his keyboard playing—the wide range of emotional contrasts he could produce in one and the same work.

It is also true that this new aesthetic ideal, with its decisive influence on the procedures of musical composition, was equally decisive in the realm of musical instruments. For the constant changing of character, in which dynamics are important, required an instrumental medium capable of registering such changes easily and rapidly. While the harpsichord is capable of some dynamic variation (particularly with the aid of elaborate additions like the celebrated Venetian swell), this clearly is not one of the instrument's strong points; it is rather the piano that responds readily to such changes in dynamics, so that inevitably it came to be the instrument *par excellence* of the new music.

Our task is now to present in some detail the keyboard music of the time and to show the transformation that it underwent as a result of these sweeping changes in music generally. First, some attention must be paid to the last representatives of the old way in whose work, as it happens, traces of what was to come may be discerned. We will then turn to the rise and early development of the new, commencing with Italy and culminating in the work of Germany composers, since it is Germany that gradually, through the century, assumed stylistic leadership of the new music, a leadership that it continued to exercise until the end of the nineteenth century.

The greatest German contemporaries of Bach were the theorist Johann Mattheson (1681–1764), Georg Philipp Telemann (1681-1767), Johann Christoph Graupner (1683-1760), and Georg Friedrich Händel (known here in the anglicized version, George Frederick Handel, 1685–1759). Mattheson was a prominent theorist, critic, and writer on music who issued two sets of keyboard works in the old style: the *Harmonisches Denkmahl* of 1714, a set of twelve suites, and *Die wohlklingende Fingersprache* in two volumes, 1735 and 1737, containing twelve preludes and fugues of two and three subjects. Besides these, he wrote an early sonata and suite for two harpsichords in 1705 and a sonata for harpsichord in 1713. The others are among the foremost composers of their time. Although all composed keyboard music, this contribution does not loom particularly large, neither with respect to the output of each nor with respect to keyboard literature as a whole. Telemann's work in this field is little known; there are few editions and no readily available critical studies (see Schaefer-Schmuck). By and large, it seems oriented around the harpsichord suite, contained in some four publications the last of which bears the suggestive designation *Sonates pour clavessin en suites*, thus making explicit the association of the two genres. Related to the suites is Telemann's *Musique heroique*, a set of twelve marches for harpsichord published in 1730. There are also two sets of easy fugues that obviously were intended as teaching pieces and a set of thirty-six *Fantaisies* (three *douzaines*). In these fantasies, an element of the new style may be discerned, since they present none of the toccata-like grandeur we have seen in the fantasias of Bach; rather, they are smaller works that are italianate in their thematic types and figuration, each cast in two distinct parts with the *da capo* instruction at the end (although those of the second *douzaine* seem to have rather a French background). In several cases, two separate fantasies are connected to one another, whereby the second is intended as a middle section between two presentations of the first. Telemann also issued a set of chorales and variations in 1736.

The keyboard work of Handel, if somewhat better known than that of Telemann, also occupies a secondary position in the great composer's work (see

Seiffert, Abraham, and Dale). All of it was composed in England, and in it the principal genres of music for the keyboard instruments are represented. For organ, there are the fugues or voluntaries of 1735; for the harpsichord, there are two sets of lessons or suites, of 1720 and 1733, respectively; and there are a number of miscellaneous works, among them a few odd suites, many independent pieces and dances—especially in the Aylesford manuscripts—and, finally, a set of easy didactic fugues. The fugues or voluntaries (see Pauly) are, quite simply, monothematic imitative compositions in which readily recognizable subjects are combined with countermaterial. In the Voluntary in b, there are two counter-subjects. Stretto and inversion are employed here and there. All of the voluntaries have an adagio conclusion. The fifth of them, in a, also appears, with modifications, as the second chorus of the oratorio *Israel in Egypt*.

Although Handel composed a number of independent harpsichord pieces of all sorts (preludes, capriccios, fantasias, marches, hornpipes, chaconnes, and even a *Suite à deux clavecins*), his most important contribution clearly lies with the suites (see Kahle). The old "normal" dance forms, where they appear, are treated in a conventional way. The allemande is the most stylized of them all, working mostly with much figural melody in long phrases; the Italian type, the corrente, is employed rather than the French; the saraband appears as the slow movement, and here the composer often appears at his most characteristic. Especially well-known are the sarabands of the Suite in g (Set I, No. 7) and the Suite in d (Set II, No. 3), which has two doubles; the gigue appears usually as the Italian *giga*, although there are instances of the imitative French version both with and without the inversion of the subject in the second part (in Set I, Suites in e and f, Nos. 4 and 7; in Set II, Suites in B-flat and g, Nos. 5 and 8). In some cases, these gigues become extended pieces, as in the Suites in g and e (Set II, Nos. 1 and 4). The preludes likewise are treated in full accordance with the tradition of the genre. They are short and work with figuration. Scale-passage work supplies the thematic material for the preludes to the Suites in A (Set I, No. 1) and f-sharp (Set I, No. 6), arpeggios to the prelude to the Suite in d (Set I, No. 3), while arpeggios and scale runs are combined in the prelude to the Suite in A (Set I, No. 1); the prelude to the Suite in g (Set I, No. 7) is a French overture, which also appears as the overture to Handel's opera *Orestes*, while that of the Suite in f (Set I, No. 8) is an adagio suggestive of an allemande (*GMB*, 279).

An important role in these suites is played by dances in variation form. Not only do we find the standard forms—the passacaille (Suite in g, Set I, No. 7) and the chaconne (printed as the *Leçon* in G, No. 3)—but others that are less usual also make their appearance with doubles, so as to constitute extended movements, there is a minuet and three variations in the Suite in d (Set II, No. 2), a saraband and two variations in the Suite in d (Set II, No. 3), and three airs with five doubles in the Suites in d (Set I, No. 3), E (Set I, No. 5, known as *The Harmonious Blacksmith*), and the *Leçon* in B-flat (which Brahms used for his set of variations on a theme of Handel). The largest of these are two Chaconnes in G, both on eight-bar themes; one is in the third of the three *Leçons* (with twenty-one variations) and the even larger independent work, with sixty-two variations, stands as one of the most impressive accomplishments in Baroque keyboard music.

As it happens, however, the "normal" arrangement of the movements in a suite, as we have it from Froberger, Bach, and others, is found only in the second set of Handel's suites (1733), a collection that was issued by the London publisher Walsh without Handel's cooperation and consent; and even here, it appears in but a few of the suites, the others making departures from it. In the first set of suites (1720), Handel's own, so to speak, none has this "normal" order; and while some show but small departures from it, others present suggestive variations. These occur by way of substitutions for the "normal" members of the dance suite; not only do we find minuets, airs, gavottes, passacailles, and chaconnes (frequently with doubles, or variations), but we also find movements that are not dances at all, such as fugues, largos, and prestos. In the Suite in d (Set I, No. 3), the "normal" dances are preceded by a prelude and fugue, and a long italianate Presto serves as finale; in the Suite in f-sharp (Set I, No. 6) in four movements (Prelude, Largo, Fugue, and Gigue) and in the Suite in F (Set I, No. 2), the four movements are in the fashion of the *sonata da chiesa*.

Here the fugues are prominent, but only in Handel's first set of suites; and these reveal the driving rhythms and the violinistic type of figuration found in Italian instrumental music of the time. This is especially true of the Suite in e (Set I, No. 4) but may also be seen in the fugal movements of the Suites in F (Set I, No. 2) and d (Set I, No. 3); the fugues in the Suites in f-sharp (Set I, No. 6) and f (Set I, No. 8) operate with slower themes. All of these are three-voice compositions, and none maintains the fugal procedure strictly and continuously throughout. More interesting, however, are those movements designated simply by tempi, since they are taken over from the Italian instrumental ensemble music and, by and large, are new to the suite. The Suite in d (Set I, No. 3) presents such movements, as already stated; others are the Largo, second movement of the Suite in f-sharp (Set I, No. 6) and the Andante and Allegro, second and third movements of the Suite in g (Set I, No. 7). Such movements are lacking in the second set of suites.

Handel's harpsichord suites, then, illustrate well the difficulties of historical interpretation that abound in any consideration of eighteenth-century music. For in any period in which far-reaching changes are taking place, elements of old and new are apt to appear not only in the work of an individual composer, but even side by side in the same composition. In Handel's suites, we find that, along with the old dances long associated with the suite, there are a number of forms taken over from Italian orchestral and chamber music. This we have also seen in the *English Suites* and, to a lesser extent, in the partitas of Bach; but in

Bach it is restricted largely to the opening movements while in Handel these pieces are used far more freely and, in two instances, play a dominant role in the organization of the suite as a whole.

When we turn to the keyboard music of Graupner, the cantor in Darmstadt and the man who saw fit to reject the offer extended him by the authorities of the Leipzig Thomasschule in 1722, thus opening the way for the offer to be given to J. S. Bach, we find again that keyboard music takes a secondary position. Again, it is the harpsichord suite that is most important; organ music, as far as we know, is not present at all. There are by Graupner two sets of *Partien,* one published in 1718 and the other in 1733, of which only the first is extant. Another set of suites under the title *Monatliche Klavier-Früchte* after the fashion of his teacher, Kuhnau, appeared in 1722. Also reminiscent of Kuhnau is another manuscript collection, the *Leichte Clavier Uebungen* of around 1730; this collection is in four sections containing suites and, in Part IV, miscellaneous pieces, mostly minuets (see Hoffmann-Erbrecht). There are other scattered suites and individual pieces in manuscript, and it is estimated that there are around sixty suites in all, of which forty-three are extant, along with thirty-eight other pieces and two preludes and fugues. Graupner's harpsichord suites, in contrast to those of

EXAMPLE 34

Handel: Allegro, from Suite in g (Book I, No. 7)—beginning

Handel, employ the "normal" dances in the usual order but often substitute another dance (the rigaudon or chaconne) for the final gigue; the standard dances are apt to appear twice in one and the same suite, and many optional dances are inserted as well. Twelve of Graupner's suites contain preludes, which is what one would expect; among these are toccata-like figuration pieces, pieces in the style of a French overture, or, in a few cases, an arioso (as has been seen in Bach's *The Well-Tempered Clavier*). For the most part, Graupner's suites are simpler and smaller than those in Handel's first set; the allemandes are short and homophonic, the sarabands become like short instrumental arias, the gigues are generally Italian, while the courantes are either Italian or French, or, in some cases, a mixture of the two. Unity of key is maintained, but cyclic form is not present.

What is perhaps most striking in the work of these leading German composers of keyboard music in the early eighteenth century is the lack of organ music. It is only in the work of Handel that the organ is given any attention to speak of. This situation is symptomatic of the century as a whole. As far as Italy is concerned, we find the liturgical cantus firmus genres in the work of Azzolino Bernardino della Ciaja (1671–1755), who wrote, along with harpsichord works in a conservative vein, an organ Mass and a treatise on organ building, and Domenico Zipoli (1688–1726), whose *Sonata d'intavolatura* of 1716 contains in its second part versets, post-Communions, Offertories, and *Elevation* compositions as well as toccatas and canzones and whose *Third Collection of Toccatas, Voluntaries, and Fugues*, published in London around 1730, emphasizes the old genres of organ music. But, with these, we have mentioned the sole perpetuators of this tradition in Italy.

In French organ music of the eighteenth century, the change can clearly be seen (see Labat and Gardien). The old form of the organ Mass, its tradition extending back through Titelouze and the publications of Attaingnant, was cultivated only in the early part of the century; there are two such works by François Couperin (1668–1733), the great composer whose harpsichord works will be dealt with later on, written in the 1690's: a *Messe pour les paroisses* and a *Messe pour les convents*.[1] Here, some of the movements employ the Gregorian chant cantus firmus while others are totally independent works; and, as before, the cantus firmus is treated either in one voice or else is made the subject of fugal expositions. The movements corresponding to those of the Ordinary of the Mass are divided into sections called "couplets" (five for the Kyrie, nine for the Gloria, and two each for the Sanctus and Agnus dei; the Credo is not present). The canon appears in the Sanctus of the *Messe pour les paroisses*. The Elevations are in toccata

---

[1] Couperin's authorship has in the past been disputed but is now generally accepted. See Mellers; see also Tessier.

style but are short, while the Offertory, which appears only in the *Messe pour les paroisses*, is a large work in the same style. Registration indications are supplied in abundance and appear as a prominent element in the composition in those movements and couplets independent of the plainsong; for instance, in the *Messe pour les paroisses*, the third couplet of the Kyrie is a *Récit de cromhorne* and the fourth is a *Dialogue sur la trompette et le cromhorne*. Along with récits and dialogues are duos and trios. All in all, Couperin adhered in these works closely to the characteristics of the genre as it was treated in the seventeenth century.

The other old established liturgical cantus firmus form of organ music in France was the Magnificat, which we find in the work of Jean Alain Guilain (dates unknown) in his *Pièces d'orgue pour le Magnificat* published in 1706 and in the work of Jean François Dandrieu (1682–1738), in his *Pièces d'orgue*, the first book, published in 1739. Guilain's Magnificats are arranged by mode and consist of seven movements each, presumably to be performed in alternation with plainsong: a *Plein jeu*, a Trio, a Duo, a *Basse de trompette*, a *Récit*, a Dialogue, and a *Petit plein jeu*. The plainsong is not present at all. In Dandrieu's collection (see Brunold), we find Magnificats of six movements, again composed independently of the plainsong: *Plein jeu*, Duo, Trio, *Basse de trompette* (or some other), Flutes, and a Dialogue.

Related to these works, which in the absence of the plainsong have only their title to connect them with the liturgy at all, are suites of organ pieces. Such compositions are prominent in the work of the more influential French organ composers of the time: Louis Marchand (1669–1732), a famous teacher; Louis Nicolas Clérambault (1676–1749); and Pierre du Mage (1676–1751 [see Raugel]), who was a pupil of Marchand and Dandrieu. Clérambault's *Premier livre d'orgue* contains two suites of organ pieces, one in the first mode and the other in the second; each has seven movements of the same nature as those just noticed in the Magnificats. The *Livre d'orgue* of du Mage, published in 1708, contains one suite in eight movements (a second volume, published in 1712, is evidently no longer extant). The organ works of Marchand, who led a wandering life and was celebrated as an organ virtuoso, were not published until after his death; here, we meet with separate pieces in a style similar to the organ suites of Clérambault and du Mage. In all of these compositions, the emphasis goes to the coloristic possibilities of the instrument, while the more elaborate forms of musical construction, especially those related to counterpoint, were more and more neglected.

This attitude, which was in keeping with the new *goût* of the time, is expressed in the preface to Dandrieu's *Pièces d'orgue*, Book I, of 1739: "I have tried all the time to capture that noble and elegant simplicity which constitutes the proper character of the organ." Actually, Dandrieu's suites occupy a middle ground; as he says in the preface, "each suite begins with an offertory, after which come several separate pieces, and finishes with a Magnificat in the same key," so that elements of the old liturgically based suite were combined with the new. The mixture becomes particularly clear when we see that the Suites in G and A contain movements called "Muzette," an element from the secular harpsichord suite.

Much of the same may be seen in the continued popularity of the noels, sets of variations on Christmas songs for organ, and it is here that secular elements— that is to say, features associated rather with harpsichord music—come to play an important part. This had long been true in connection with the variation form, as in the German chorale partitas of the seventeenth century. The collection *Nouveau livre de Noëls pour l'orgue et le clavecin* by Louis-Claude Daquin (1694– 1772), published in 1757 as his op. 2, already gives a prominent place to the harpsichord in what normally had been regarded as a genre of organ music. While some of these noels by Daquin employ forms and procedures like those we have already seen, others present decidedly secular aspects; the first noel presents the theme, two doubles (variations), and a conclusion, while the third is described as a *noël en musette*. Dandrieu also made contributions to this genre between 1721 and 1733, some of which were taken over from the work of his uncle, Pierre Dandrieu (*c.* 1660–1733), which also involve the harpsichord. Readily available is a *Basse et dessus de trompète* by Dandrieu (*HMS*, VI, s. 2, b. 5). And, from later in the century, there is a publication by Claude Balbastre (1727–1799), *Recueil de Noëls formant quatre suites avec des variations pour le clavecin ou fortepiano* (the exact date is not known), in which not only is the organ completely done away with, but also the form *par excellence* of harpsichord music, the suite, is used in conjunction with the noel.

In German organ music, one must speak of a decline rather than of a change in orientation (see Fellerer and Kelletat). Here it is, by and large, composers of lesser importance who continued somehow or other in the old ways. The change can be well observed in the Protestant organ chorale, one of the most fundamental genres in German organ music of the seventeenth century. Among the contemporaries of J. S. Bach who carried on the old form was Johann Gottfried Walter (1684–1748), who was also widely known as a theorist and the writer of a comprehensive encyclopedia of music; his principal publications devoted to the chorale prelude (see Schmidt) were the *Musikalische Vorstellung zwey evangelischer Gesänge* of 1712, containing two chorale partitas, and the *Harmonisches Denck- und Danckmahl* of 1738, containing eight chorale preludes; many others existed in manuscripts. Others were Heinrich Nikolaus Gerber (1702–1775), Johann Schneider (1702–1787), Johann Peter Kellner (1705–1772), Gottfried August Homilius (1714–1785), Johann Friedrich Agricola (1720–1774), and Johann Gottlieb Goldberg (1727–1756), of whom all but Homilius (see Stegich) and Kellner actually were pupils of J.S. Bach at one time or another. (Goldberg was the recipient of the famous set of harpsichord variations named after him.) But, by the second half of the century, the old contrapuntal emphasis in the chorale prelude was lacking; the accompaniment became far simpler, more homophonic. This may be seen in the chorale preludes of one of Bach's sons, Johann Ernst Bach (1722–1777), who for a time was organist at Weimar, but more pronouncedly in the work of Johann Friedrich Doles (1715–1797), also a pupil of Bach (see Banning), who was completely representative of the new *galant* taste. He insisted that the old genres of church music be brought into accord with the times, that they be made simple and "easy to understand" (*leichtfässlich*); this attitude is clear from the title of his large publication of chorale preludes, which are there described as "singable and easy": *Singbare und leichte Choralvorspiele* (in five volumes, 1794–1797); these works remained in use until the end of the nineteenth century.

A similar decline occurs in the liturgical organ music of the Catholic Church in Germany and Austria, whose chief exponent was Gottlieb Muffat (1690–1770), the son of Georg Muffat; here, we find versets along with toccatas, ricercares, and canzones; his large publication of this kind is the *72 Versetl sampt zwölf Toccaten*, published in Vienna in 1726 (see Knöll). The large form of the toccata (or prelude and fugue) likewise experienced a decline. The genre appears in its old state in the work of men like Wilhelm Hieronymous Pachelbel (1685–1764), like Muffat the son of a famous father, particularly in his large *Musicalisches Vergnügen bestehend in einem Preludio, Fuga und Fantasia* published in Nürnberg in 1725, and in the work of two members of the Krebs family, Johann Tobias (1690–1762) and, particularly, Johann Ludwig (1713–1780) who is thought to have composed the eight Little Preludes and Fugues often attributed to J. S. Bach; both had been pupils of Bach. But, by the second half of the century, it was cultivated solely by teachers and theorists such as Johann Joseph Fux (1660–1741) and Johann Georg Albrechtsberger (1736–1809).

In Spain and Portugal, there was a distinct tendency to continue the cultivation of the old genres that elsewhere in Europe were on the decline. The liturgical organ verset can be seen in the work of composers like Josep Jiménez, Miguel Lopez, Juan Moreno y Polo, and Pedro Carrere Lanchares; Moreno y Polo, however, shows some influences from the Italian *galant*. The conservative fugue was emphasized in the work of Joaquin Martinez de Oxinga, Padre Antonio Soler (1729–1793), also prominent in the harpsichord sonata; José Lidón; and Juan Sesé, whose fugues, published in 1774, are intended for organ or piano (*para órgano o piano forte*). This area has been little investigated, and the best account is still that of Frotscher, which already is thirty years old.

In England, the situation in organ music was somewhat similar. The contrapuntal voluntary was important in the work of men like the printer Thomas Roseingrave (1690–1766), Maurice Greene (1695–1755), John Travers (*c.* 1703–1758), the instrument builder Jacob Kirkman, William Boyce (*c.* 1710–1779), John Simpson (d. 1749), and Charles John Stanley (1713–1786) whose *Voluntaries* (Op. 5, 6, and 7), which appeared in 1742, reveal italianate features.

The fugue was cultivated by among others, James Nares (1715–1783), the author of a treatise on organ playing; Philip Hart (d. 1749); Charles Burney (1726–1814), the famous writer on and historian of music whose work includes *Cornet Pieces* which appeared in 1751 and a set of preludes and fugues which were published in 1787; Benjamin Cooke (1734–1793); and Samuel Wesley (1766–1837). But, as elsewhere, the organ art is on the decline and everywhere there is less and less real organ music; rather, forms, styles, and procedures associated with other genres simply transferred to the organ. The many foreign-born composers active in England worked with the more "modern" genres connected with the harpsichord or the piano.

All in all, then, the old, long-established genres of organ music fell out of favor. The emphasis in repertory shifted to forms of secular music, especially the harpsichord suite and, ultimately, to the sonata. As it happens, the exact details of the emergence of the keyboard sonata and its relationships to the suite, the toccata, and other forms of music are yet to be fully uncovered, and this task constitutes one of the more interesting and important fields of historical research in music at the present time. But some sort of sketch must be attempted here, first by dealing with the suite in the eighteenth century then by attempting to trace the development of the "progressive" genre, the sonata.

In France, there was a large body of important harpsichord compositions that reflect by and large the old style. The publications of such works almost always bear the title *Pièces de clavecin*, and were supplied by, among others, Louis-Nicolas Clérambault, Louis-Antoine Dornel (c. 1685–1765) in 1731 (with a later collection called *Le tour de clavier sur tous les tons*, in 1745), Joseph Bodin de Boismortier (c. 1682–1765) in 1736, François Dagincourt (1684–1758) in 1733, Louis-Claude Daquin in 1735, and Jacques Duphly (1715–1789), whose four volumes appeared between 1744 and 1768. But the culmination of the art of the French harpsichord suite appears in the work of two composers: François Couperin and Jean Philippe Rameau (1683–1764), the latter also well known as a composer of operas and ballets and as a theorist of music.

Couperin (known as *Le grand*), a member of a large musical family, was active in Paris throughout his life, first as organist at St. Gervais and then as organist at the court of Louis XIV; he retired in 1723 and spent the last ten years of his life in seclusion (see Mellers, Reimann, Cauchie, Bouvet, Brunold, and Citron). Unlike many of his German contemporaries, keyboard music is dominant in his output, and here the emphasis is on the harpsichord suite. He wrote twenty-seven suites, which he called *ordres* instead of suites; they were issued in four volumes, each with the title *Pièces de clavecin*, in 1713, 1717, 1722, and 1730 respectively.[1] Couperin was also the author of a treatise on harpsichord playing, *L'art de toucher le clavecin*, in 1717, which contains eight preludes for harpsichord.

[1] See the convenient listing compiled by Mellers in *GD*, II, pp. 494–8, as well as Mellers' book.

As would be expected, dances form the basis of Couperin's suites. Dominant is binary form with the double bar, each half to be repeated. The general style of the dances is much as has been seen. The melody is in the uppermost voice, in which improvised embellishments are important, and there is simple accompaniment, and a light and transparent texture. In many cases, Couperin presented his dances in two versions, one plain and the other with the melody ornamented. Of the slower dances, the allemande and the saraband, Couperin recognized two kinds: for the allemande, *legère* and *grave*; for the saraband, *tendre* and *grave*, corresponding to the lighter and serious characters. The other dances, courante and gigue, are represented almost always by their French versions. Other dances appear in Couperin's *ordres*: the rigaudon, the passepied, and the gavotte. Variations (doubles) are not uncommon. A most prominent form is the rondeau usually with three or four episodes or couplets. The larger movements are in variation form, the chaconne or the passacaille, as *Les folies françoises ou les dominos* of the Suite in b (No. 13); these forms also appear without variation in conjunction with a rondeau in the refrain section, as can be seen in the Suite in C (No. 3) or the large *passacaille en rondeau* of the Suite in b (No. 8), one of Couperin's largest and most difficult works, in eight couplets. A French overture appears with the Suite in E-flat (No. 25); but the traditional preludes are not present in the *Pièces de clavecin*.

Along with these usual dances go others that bear characteristic titles. This can be seen in the early suites from examples like the allemande *l'auguste* of the Suite in g (No. 1), the saraband *La prude* of the Suite in d (No. 2), or the allemandes *La fleurie* and *La ténébreuse* of the Suites in g and c (No. 1 and No. 3, respectively [*GMB*, 264], and so on. But, in later suites, such characteristic titles replace the names of the dances, and it is not unusual for the pieces themselves to be completely independent of dance forms, as, for instance, the well-known *Soeur Monique* and *Le rossignol en amour* (*HAM*, II, 265). The rondeaux almost always have descriptive titles: *Les barricades misterieuses* and *Les moissoneurs* (Georgii, *Keyboard Music*, II, pp. 46–9 and 50–1), *La gazouillement* (Georgii, *400 Years*, p. 15), or *La distraite*. Symptomatic of the origins of harpsichord music is *La harpée* of the Suite in e (No. 21), qualified by Couperin as a *pièce dans le goût de la harp* (piece in the style, i.e., taste or fashion, of the harp). In the rondeau *La bandoline* of the Suite in A (No. 5), Couperin provided the performance instruction "the right hand legato and the left marcato" (*la main droite coulée et la gauche marquée*) to emphasize properly the character of the mandoline that the piece is to represent. Several pieces emphasize the crossing of hands (*pièces croisées*), apparently an important adjunct in keyboard virtuosity, and, among many examples, we can name here the two musettes of the Suite in a (No. 15), the rondeau *Le tic-toc-choc, ou les maillotins* of the Suite in f (F) (No. 18), and the *minuets croisées* of the Suite in D (No. 22).

The arrangement of these various dances and other pieces into suites is largely in the French rather than the German tradition. The unity of key, the old attribute of the suite, is maintained. Of the four books of suites published by Couperin, the first might be looked upon as the most "Germanic," in form at all events, since most of its *ordres* preserve in some measure the "normal" sequence of allemande, courante, saraband, and gigue. This arrangement is varied by the use of more than one courante and by the free proliferation of dances added after the gigue; the Suites in g and d of the first volume contain eighteen and twenty-three movements, respectively. In the subsequent volumes of Couperin's *Pièces de clavecin*, this freedom with respect to the traditional members of the suite becomes even greater, and it is not unusual to have none of these dances present at all. Instead, we find pieces with programmatic or characteristic titles, each representing a particular affection, that most often are almost stylized dances but are sometimes also completely independent of any dance types. Frequently, little sets of such characteristic pieces will form a small entity, a little cycle in itself, within the larger frame of an *ordre*, while, in a few cases, such a set of pieces will constitute the entire suite. As examples of these little programmatic sets, we can mention, in Couperin's first book, *Les pèlerins* consisting of *La marche*, *Le caristade*, and *Le remerciement*; *Les bacchanales* consisting of *Enjoümens bachiques*, *Tendresses bachique*, and *Fureurs bachiques*; or the miniature drama in five acts of Book II, *Les fastes de la grande et ancienne Mxnxstrxndxsx* (actually the *Menestrandes*, the title disguised by replacing all the vowels with the letter *x*), a satirical work depicting the banquet of the musician's guild (Georgii, *Keyboard Music*, II, pp. 34–9). All of the Suite in D (No. 10) is devoted to war: *La triomphante*; *Rondeau, bruit de guerre*; *Rondeau, allegresse des vainceurs*, and *Fanfare*, all much in the tradition of the *battaglia* as seen, for instance, in Kerll, Kuhnau, and others. It is clear, then, that there is no real "form" for the suite in the work of Couperin.

EXAMPLE 35

F. COUPERIN: *La harpée*, from Suite in e (No. 21)—beginning

It might also be mentioned that the allemande of the Suite in A (No. 9) is for two harpsichords but that the rest of the *ordre* is for only one. And the piece *La juillet* of the Suite in d (No. 14) is an ensemble work to be performed either by two harpsichords or by harpsichord with solo instruments. All other pieces are to be performed by harpsichord.

The suites by Couperin contain no preludes. But that preludes were regarded by him as proper members of the suite is evident from his treatise *L'art de toucher le clavecin*, which contains eight preludes in keys corresponding to those of the *ordres* in the first volume of his *Pièces de clavecin*. In these short pieces, each of which employs a short thematic motive or type of figuration, the rhythmic freedom characteristic of the genre is to be seen. In the treatise itself, Couperin stresses this feature, referring to the prelude as a "free" form especially in the matter of rhythm and emphasizing the role of imagination. On the basis of rhythmic freedom, Couperin refers to the prelude as prose while other "measured" music is equated with poetry.

The harpsichord music of Rameau (he wrote no organ works at all) again is devoted to the suite, and again the various volumes go under the general title *Pièces de clavecin*: there is Book I, published in 1706; a second volume, in 1724 (reissued in 1731); the set of *Nouvelles suites de clavecin* of around 1736; five pieces from his *Pièces de clavecin en concert* of 1741, which Rameau arranged for harpsichord (see Girdlestone and Klitenic), and *La dauphine* of 1747. The set of 1706 contains a Suite in a (also A) while that of 1724 (1731) has Suites in e (E), d (D), and the set of *circa* 1736 contains suites in A (a) and g (G), so that in all there are five suites by Rameau. In three, we find some elements of the "normal" arrangement of a suite along with a number of modifications that, as in Couperin's earlier suites, take the form of dances added after the usual concluding dance, the gigue (except in the second Suite in A, which ends with a long gavotte before which come the three "optional" dance movements). All three have the allemande followed by the courante, while the first in A and the one in e also contain gigues; the saraband appears in its "proper" position in the second Suite in A, while the first of the suites in A has a saraband and its double included among the dances following the gigue. The courantes and gigues are of the French variety. The first Suite in A is the only one of Rameau's suites to have a prelude.

The two remaining suites make considerable departures from this usual scheme. The first, in d and D from the set of 1724 (1731), consists of ten numbers, each with a title *à la Couperin*, and the same is true of that in G (g) of the *Nouvelles suites* except that it has nine movements. While some of the individual numbers in these suites can clearly be related to dances, there are others that equally clearly cannot, such as *La poule* and the well-known *L'enharmonique* of the Suite in G (g), the former of which is noteworthy for its use of dynamic markings (*forte* and *doux*), that, along with the themes of rapidly repeated notes, aid in the musical depiction of the barnyard, thus maintaining the old genre as we have seen it in, for instance, Poglietti. (*La poule* is printed in Georgii, *Keyboard Music*, II, pp. 60–3.) Several of these dances in Rameau's suites have become established in their own right as independent works so far as the repertory is concerned. There are the two already mentioned. Others are *Le rappel des oiseaux* of the Suite in e (E); from the Suite in d (D), which has none of the usual members of a suite, there is *L'entretien des muses* and the rondeau *Les cyclops*, which has two episodes and a long refrain; from the *Nouvelles suites*, the one in A has *Les trois mains*, a virtuoso example of hand crossing (*pièces croisées*), and the Suite in G (g) has *Les sauvages*, which Rameau also employed in his opera *Les Indes galants*.

Like Couperin, Rameau sought a larger form for use in his suites and to this end gave prominence to the rondeau, which appears not only in those pieces with descriptive titles that are somewhat distant from actual dances, but also usurps the normal form of individual dances themselves. In the first Suite in A of 1706, it appears with the courante, the *Vénitienne*, and the gavotte; in the set of 1724–1731, it also comes with the courante and in the two gigues, the musette, and in *La villageoise*. A peculiarity of Rameau's terminology is that the episodes or couplets are called "reprises" as also are the second parts of dances in the usual binary form. The other effort in the direction of a larger form for use in the harpsichord suite lies in the doubles or variations. Examples of this are the rigaudon of the Suite in e (E) of 1724–1731, *Les niais de Sologne* of the Suite in d (D) from the same collection, and, particularly, the concluding gavotte of the Suite in A (a) of around 1736 with six doubles, Rameau's largest venture into variation form (Georgii, *Keyboard Music*, II, pp. 53–7).

In comparison with Couperin, Rameau may be said in general to be more Baroque, hence, more conservative. The delicacy and refinement of Couperin, which we associate more with the *galant* taste of the time, are not prominent in Rameau. Rameau's rhythms and phrase structures are more regular, the accents sharper, the texture denser; Baroque driving rhythms exist in abundance. The pictorial touches in Rameau are more direct. In some respects, then, Couperin, although earlier than Rameau (even though the latter's first suite appeared some eleven years before the former's), is more "modern" in his adaptation to the *galant*, but in his hands it bears little relation to what we will see the *galant* to be in the hands of the Italian composers of the eighteenth century.

Another group of composers who emphasized the harpsichord suite lived and worked in Belgium (see Clercx): Gerhardus Havingha (1696–1753), Josse Boutmy (1697–1779), Joseph-Hector Fiocco (1703–1741), and Dieudonné Raick (1702–1764); but the most important among them was Jean-Baptiste Loeillet (1680–1730). A native of Ghent, he was also active in London where he came under the influence of Handel (see Priestman). His published keyboard works comprise two volumes of suites, both printed in London: *Lessons* of around 1710 and six *Suits of Lessons* of 1722 and 1725. Here, the "German" form with its "normal" succession of dances is to be found. The Italian form of the courante and gigue (although Loeillet uses the English term, "jigg") appear, along with the English minuet *Round-O* in the Suite in g, while the Suites in D and E-flat contain imitative gigues in the French fashion; the Suite in g is note-worthy for its highly figured saraband with extensive dynamic markings.

Of greater moment as far as the "progressive" music of the time was concerned were the developments that took place in Italy.[1] Here, as elsewhere, we find the same intermingling between old and new; but it is here that the sonata became established as an important genre of keyboard composition. As far as the work of the more conservative musicians is concerned, the harpsichord fugue was continued in the work of Giuseppe Benchini, Antonio Caldara (1670–1736) who was active in Venice and Vienna, and Andrea Basili (1720–1777). The decline of this genre by the end of the century is evident in the work of the eminent Neapolitan composer resident in Vienna, Nicolo Antonio Porpora (1686–1768), for a time the teacher of Haydn, whose fugues show an emphasis on free episodes and on virtuoso showmanship rather than on strict contrapuntal working out. The toccata appears in the work of Francesco Durante (1684–1755) in its smaller one-movement version (see Paribene), Leonardo Leo (1694–1744), and Domenico Zipoli, who also composed suites; the important toccatas of Alessandro Scarlatti have already been discussed. All these composers, be it emphasized, directed their main efforts towards the composition of opera, and works for keyboard instruments are distinctly secondary.

The word "sonata," as has been seen, was used for many things in the seventeenth century, in accordance with its literal meaning of something to be played, i.e., simply, an instrumental work. We find that, although this continued to be true in the eighteenth century, the term ultimately came to refer to a work of several movements (two to four being the most usual), related either by being in the same key or in related keys. The relation to other genres of musical composition, however, can frequently be noted. There are sonatas in the work of the conservative composers della Ciaja and Zipoli that are, for all intents and purposes, identical with toccatas, while fugal pieces for organ in one movement, called "sonatas," were composed by Giovanni Battista Martini (1706–1784). Since this use of the term "sonata" represents the older viewpoint, and certainly one not characteristic of the latter part of the eighteenth century, it will be well to deal with such works first before tracing the growth of what leads to the so-called "Classical" sonata in the work of Haydn, Mozart, Beethoven, and their contemporaries.

It is, perhaps, somewhat ironic that Italy's leading and most celebrated composer of harpsichord music should have worked well-nigh exclusively in

[1] See the controversial account of Torrefranca, as well as those of Eitner, Faisst, Hoffmann-Erbrecht, Klauwell, Michel, Refoulé, Shedlock, and Stone.

the realm of the one-movement sonata—Domenico Scarlatti (1685–1757), the son of Alessandro. Domenico was trained and worked in several Italian cities (Naples, Venice, and Rome) before he moved to Portugal in 1719 or 1720 where he was the *maestro di capella* to the court of João V in Lisbon; on the marriage of João's daughter to Fernando, heir to the throne of Spain, in 1729, Scarlatti was placed in her service and removed to Madrid where he spent the remainder of his life. During his period in Lisbon, he made occasional visits to Italy; it is not clear whether he ever was in England; his friendship with Handel and Roseingrave dates from his years in Rome.[1]

Apart from a few isolated fugues and dances, Scarlatti's important output in keyboard music consists wholly of sonatas. Authorities differ as to their exact number, but the latest count, that of Kirkpatrick, gives 555 as the total number. The earliest of them (thirty works) were published, apparently in London, in 1738 and 1739 under the title *Essercizi per gravicembalo*. This was followed in 1739 by Roseingrave's publication of thirty-two more under the title *Suite de pièces pour le clavecin*, in which the works are arranged as suites (such attempts are always the work of editors and publishers, never of Scarlatti himself). But the vast majority of his works are preserved in manuscript; thirteen volumes, copied for the use of the Princess Maria Barbara between 1752 and 1757, and there are two others made in 1742 and 1749. This large collection is now in Venice; another group of manuscript copies of Scarlatti's sonatas, based on this first set, is now in Parma, and two smaller collections are in Münster and Vienna; no Scarlatti holographs have come to light. Dating these sonatas is difficult, but Kirkpatrick believes that these works generally were composed close to the time they were written down in the manuscript volumes. It thus appears that Domenico's major work commenced when he was sixty-seven years old (1752), a most unusual circumstance.

Scarlatti employed the term "sonata" for these works with great consistency. The chief exception to this is in the *Essercizi* (exercises) of 1738, but even here the individual pieces are called "sonatas." Occasionally in the various manuscripts, other designations are used: "toccata" in the first of the volumes at Parma, and here and there names like "fugue," "pastorale," "aria," "capriccio," "minuet," "gavotte," or "gigue" may appear. It seems clear that, generally, "sonata" is the proper term for these compositions.

Scarlatti's sonatas are one-movement compositions (a few of his early works are sonatas in several movements), and almost all have the same over-all formal plan; they are in binary form, or *forma bipartita*, with the double bar near the

[1] The most comprehensive edition of Scarlatti's sonatas is that of Longo, but this is marred by numerous editorial emendations. More recent and reliable is the selection edited by Kirkpatrick. Since both Longo and Kirkpatrick have made bibliographical studies of Scarlatti, we will have to deal, for identification, with both "L" and "K" numbers; the latter represent the attempt to arrange the sonatas in chronological order. On Scarlatti generally, see Kirkpatrick; see also Benton, Bogianchino, Gerstenberg, Hopkinson (bibliographical), Keller, Longo, Newton, and Valabrega.

middle, each part to be repeated. It is within this simple but fundamental plan that Scarlatti was able to produce seemingly endless variety. Of some significance is the generally neglected fact that 388 of Scarlatti's sonatas are grouped in pairs, each of two in the same tonality, and twelve more appear as little groups of three sonatas, also each in the same tonality. This procedure commences with the manuscript volume copied in 1749 and is consistently carried on through the subsequent manuscript volumes; the arrangement of the sonatas in the Parma set (and in some cases also in the Münster and Vienna sets) corresponds to that in the Venice volumes. It thus appears that about three-quarters of Scarlatti's sonatas were not intended to be performed as separate works.

Most attempts to classify the varieties of form to be found in Scarlatti's sonatas take as their point of departure the relation to the fully developed sonata form of the late eighteenth century, with a full exposition, development, and recapitulation. Walter Gerstenberg, then, sees three main types. In the first, both parts are roughly equivalent in length, and the work as a whole is mono-thematic; in the second, several themes are presented in the first part, while in the second there is a sort of working-out or development of these but no full scale recapitulation; in the third is the full sonata form. Rita Benton has given the works a similar classification. Kirkpatrick's system, on the other hand, studiously avoids any reference to the later sonata form and works with totally different terminology. In his parlance, a sonata is "symmetrical" if both parts are of about the same length and "assymetrical" if the second is longer, whereby the passage making the second part longer stands at its beginning and is termed "excursion"; a sonata is "closed" if both parts commence with the same thematic material and "open" if the second begins with something different (the "closed" type then has little or no excursion). An "open" sonata is "free" if its excursion employs much new thematic material and "concentrated" if its excursion operates entirely with themes already presented in the first part. Kirkpatrick's terminology has some similarities to that introduced by Gerstenberg. It seems evident that these are merely different ways of describing the same thing; but one must sympathize with Kirkpatrick for his efforts to make clear that there is no direct relation between these one-movement sonatas (whether in groups of two or three or not) and the later form of the piano sonata.

This becomes even clearer when individual works are examined, and one sees that in the multiplicity of themes introduced by Scarlatti during the course of a sonata, it is impossible often to decide which is principal and which subordinate, whether one takes key relationships or the importance of themes in the unfolding of the work as his point of departure. Accordingly, Kirkpatrick has developed his own system and terms to describe the Scarlatti sonatas, based on the view that the complementary relationship between the two halves of the *forma bipartita* is the most important formal factor in these works and that "the real life of a Scarlatti sonata resides in the central section of the first half and in the parallel section of the second." Therefore, "the meeting point in each half of the thematic material which is stated in parallel fashion at the ends of both halves with the establishment of the closing tonality" becomes the central part of a Scarlatti sonata, and to this Kirkpatrick gives the name "crux" (Kirkpatrick, pp. 254–5). The re-establishment of the tonic in the restatement of the same thematic material is what constitutes the "crux," and there are pre-crux, post-crux, opening, continuation, transition, closings, excursion, restatements, and the like.

That Scarlatti's sonatas have but the most superficial similarity to the later so-called Classical sonata is evident also from the types of themes that are used in them. These present a variety that is difficult to survey. Hoffmann-Erbrecht offers four large groups as the basis for such an attempt at a classification, restricted to those that appear at the openings of the sonatas: the continuously unfolding type using similar figurational or rhythmic patterns, often with much use of sequences (the German *Fortspinnungs*-type), of which he counts 275 instances; the use of themes whose component motives present great contrast, of which he counts ten examples; themes in paired complementary phrases of various kinds of which there are 130 cases; and, finally, a larger and rather ill-defined group in which there can be great variety, embracing echo-like repetitions, repetitions of phrases or bars, and variations of all sorts. These themes are likely to be of striking quality, and a number of them can be strung together one after the other with much repetition, either exact or sequential. Recurring rhythmic patterns are generally of great importance in the Scarlatti sonatas. The accompaniment to a theme is important, often so much so that it is inseparable from the theme itself; it is not simply neutral, merely providing harmonic support for the main voice, but rather the theme is conceived in polyphonic terms so that there is no separating a "theme" and its "accompaniment." This may be seen, for instance, in the Sonata in G (K. 105, L. 204) in fast triple time, whose first theme is dance-like; here, the accompaniment enters in the left hand one bar later with an imitation of the first bar of the theme but then goes on to present an important counterfigure which must be regarded as part and parcel of the theme. Another striking example is the opening of the cantabile Sonata in B-flat (K. 544, L. 497). Furthermore, within a section, greatly contrasting themes may be presented, as, for instance, in the Sonatas in D (K. 29, L. 461; K. 119, L. 415; K. 140, L. 107; K. 490, L. 206). In the Sonata in G (K. 235, L. 154) and two in B-flat (K. 202, L. 498; K. 273, L. 398), the "excursion" (the section immediately following the double bar) takes the form of a pastorale (the Sonata in B-flat, K. 202, L. 498, is in *HMS*, VI, s. 2, b. 2); while in the Sonata in e (K. 394, L. 275), the excursion commences with sudden cadenza-like passage using arpeggio figuration.

What has made Scarlatti's sonatas so important is the highly idiomatic treatment of the harpsichord, which often requires a considerable degree of skill from the performer. Here again, figuration patterns are fundamental in the constitution of the various themes. Wide leaps, rapidly repeated notes (in which the performer is to change fingers on the same note, *mutandi i detti*)—as in the Sonata in D (K. 96, L. 465)—arpeggios, brilliant figuration patterns, and so on, all contribute. Rapid trills (tremolo) often appear, as in the Sonatas in D (the one just mentioned and K. 119, L. 415), the latter containing a long trill in an inner part. Glissandi also appear; the minuet-sonata in F (K. 379, L. 73) contains an ornamental scale run, ascending, marked *con dedo solo* (with one finger). Many of these features appear in the Sonata in a (K. 175, L. 429 [*HAM*, II, 274]). Prominent is hand crossing, which has also been seen in French harpsichord music; it is particularly emphasized in Scarlatti's Sonatas in B-flat (K. 57, L. 38), D (K. 96, L. 465), and, especially, d (K. 120, L. 215).

An important aspect is that of tone color. We have already referred to the ambivalent position of the keyboard instruments relative to other families of musical instruments and have called attention to their ability to represent or suggest other instruments or groups of instruments. Even the keyboard music of Bach reveals many such relationships, as has been shown. Kirkpatrick attempts to bring this out in regard to Scarlatti's sonatas, on an admittedly rather subjective

EXAMPLE 36

D. Scarlatti: *Sonata* in D (K. 96, L. 465)—excerpt

basis; but there is much in it, and a few instances may be indicated here. Especially noteworthy are the many passages where Scarlatti evidently wished to suggest the violent and often passionate strumming of the Spanish guitar. This is done either by insistently rapidly repeated chords, often with dissonant appoggiaturas played on the beat (*acciaccature*) which imply an almost percussive touch, or by a rapidly repeated pattern of figuration in the bass; the former produces a most peculiar effect on the harpsichord, and such passages are to be found in, for example, the Sonatas in C (K. 309, L. 454) and e (K. 394, L. 275), which have unusual harmonic progressions; e (K. 402, L. 427) and D (K. 490, L. 206), which have dotted rhythms; and F (K. 518, L. 116). The latter is found in the Sonatas in C (K. 513, L.S. 3), a pastorale with guitar effects in the contrasting section, or in what seems like an Alberti bass (used rarely by Scarlatti) in the Sonata in d (K. 517, L. 266), or possibly in the Sonata in B-flat (K. 545, L. 500). Examples of each could readily be multiplied. Other imitative effects are less unusual for keyboard instruments. Trumpet or horn themes, triadic, dotted, and fanfare-like, exist in abundance; here, not surprisingly, the key of D is prominent, as in at least two sonatas (K. 96, L. 465; K. 119. L. 415); other sonatas to be

EXAMPLE 37

D. SCARLATTI: *Sonata* in d (K. 517, L. 266)—excerpt

listed here are two in C (K. 406, L. 5; K. 420, L.S. 2). A tympani-like figure in the bass characterizes the Sonatas in E (K. 46, L. 25), d (K. 120, L. 215), and G (K. 470, L. 304), while the *unisono* opening of a string orchestra work or aria is strongly suggested in the Sonata in c (K. 37, L. 406), as Kirkpatrick points out, and the violinistic figuration of a concerto is to be found in two Sonatas in G (K. 260, L. 124; K. 325, L. 37).

Along with this, it may be pointed out that many of the Scarlatti sonatas are related to other genres of musical composition. One of the most famous among them is a fugue, the Sonata in g (K. 30, L. 499), the so-called *Cat's Fugue*, named for its irrationally leaping principle theme; this appeared as the last of the *Esserciʒi* (Georgii, *Keyboard Music*, II, pp. 23–6) and is a very free fugue indeed. Many other sonatas, as already suggested, contain themes involved to some extent with fugal imitation. The minuet is explicit in the Sonatas in D (K. 282, L. 484) and G (K. 471, L. 82), while the gigue lies back of the Sonata in a (K. 54, L. 241). Another large group of Scarlatti's sonatas are cantabile, thus partaking of an important aesthetic requirement of the period, sometimes conceived largely in vocal terms but often a purely instrumental conception. In a number of the sonatas, a heightening of expression is achieved by the appearance of free passages in a cadenza-like style; examples would be the Sonatas in c (K. 116, L. 452), D (K. 119, L. 415), e (K. 394, L. 275), and the cantabile Sonata in B-flat (K. 594, L. 497) in which these passages are marked *arbitre* (free). Theme-and-variations form appears only once, in the Sonata in a (K. 61, L. 136), an early work.

Kirkpatrick has been able to establish in a general way a stylistic development in Scarlatti's sonatas. The sixty-two works of the *Esserciʒi* and Roseingrave's collection of 1738 and 1739 reveal the essential features of what the Scarlatti sonata will be like, except for the pronounced virtuoso and imaginative use of the harpsichord; in these works, the "closed" form predominates (for an example, see the Sonata in c, K. 11, L. 352, in *MPM*, 42). The virtuoso element is developed in the next group, consisting of works found in the manuscript volumes of 1742 and 1749, representing what Kirkpatrick calls the "flamboyant" period; it is here that the idea of grouping the sonatas in pairs makes its appearance and here also that the so-called "open" form and the interest in the "excursion" may be seen. In the next period (Kirkpatrick's "middle" period), comprising works found in the manuscript volumes of 1752 and 1753, there is a noticeable increase in the use of lyrical themes. And this interest is continued in the later works in which the virtuoso impulse dies down and the phrases in the themes become longer. Also, in this latest group, the keyboard range exploited by Scarlatti becomes greater.

In the preface to the *Esserciʒi* of 1738, Scarlatti wrote, "Do not expect any profound learning, but rather an ingenious jesting with art, to accommodate you to the mastery of the harpsichord." Here we see something characteristic of the new *galant* taste—the emphasis on entertainment and diversion coupled with a didactic aim—so that in Scarlatti the sonata becomes, in its earliest appearance at least, associated with the etude or teaching piece (*Handstück* in the German parlance of the later eighteenth century). But more striking is the "ingenious jesting with art," an aim that results in all the capricious elements that have been under discussion—"the original and happy freaks," as Burney called them, that come about from the unusual themes, harmonies, and textures, all bound up with the experimentation with the harpsichord itself and its possibilities for coloristic effects. The combination makes Scarlatti's sonatas unique not only with respect to the eighteenth century, but for the general repertory of keyboard music as well.

Since the one-movement form is not characteristic of the keyboard sonata of the eighteenth century, Scarlatti is not to be regarded as typical in this respect. The multimovement sonata form became the rule; but it was not much of a rule, since the varieties are many. We will find sonatas in four or five movements, others in three, still others in two; and, towards the end of the century, we even find the one-movement scheme in the work of Domenico Cimarosa (1749–1801), who is best known for his *opere buffe*. This period is the one in which the difficulties are multiplied; there is the inability to date many of the works, the lack both of adequate bibiliographical material, and, more especially, of comprehensive and reliable editions of the music—all of which makes the period virtually impossible to survey at the present time in a form comparable to what is hoped will be found to prevail in the rest of this book. Nevertheless, some sort of an attempt must be made; but what is presented here must be regarded as no more than that.

Typical of the unusual forms that are to be found in the keyboard music called sonatas are those of the well-known Neapolitan opera composer Francesco Durante, published around 1732 as *Sonate per cembalo divise in studii e divertimenti*, in which old and new are combined in an unusual way (see Paribene). These sonatas are two-movement works, each consisting of a *studio* and a *divertimento*; the former are conservative works in imitative counterpoint (two are strict enough throughout to merit the designation "fugue," and one other is canonic), while the latter are short and fast virtuoso pieces in two-part form with the double bar (but repeat for the first part only). Here it is not the form that is characteristic of what the genre is to become, but rather the title *sonate per cembalo*, which, as Hoffmann-Erbrecht points out, was used many times in the remainder of the century. Durante also composed several short toccatas in the one-movement form, as already noted.

We have seen that the keyboard sonata is closely related to the Italian chamber music of the seventeenth and early eighteenth centuries in its two genres *sonata da chiesa* (the sonata) and the *sonata da camera* (the suite or partita). We saw this in some of the harpsichord suites of Handel, and it can be seen from time to time in the work of Italian composers of harpsichord music of the eighteenth century. It is especially clear in the few sonatas by Ludovico Giustini, of whom little is known. Nonetheless, Giustini had the distinction of composing the earliest known music specifically for Cristofori's new instrument, the piano, published as his Op. 1 in 1732, *Sonata da cimbalo di piano e forte detto volgarmente di martellatti* (see Harding). Despite this prominence, these are modest works by a man who evidently was an amateur composer of no great merit. The suite element is strong in these works, but the "usual" order is not respected; of the twelve works, eight are in four movements and four are in five movements, some with names of dances as titles and others with tempo designations. From the *sonata da chiesa* comes the fast fugal second movement, but the fugal approach lapses into homophony as the movement progresses. Dynamic markings abound, as would be expected in this context, the work being what it is; but, as Hoffmann-Erbrecht points out, such dynamic indications operate with a simple change between *piano* and *forte* (a few places have three degrees—*forte*, *piano*, and *pianissimo*), and, since no use is made of a crescendo, there is nothing that could not be adequately rendered on one of the larger harpsichords of the time.

The *sonata da chiesa* provided the basis for the sonatas of Benedetto Marcello (1686–1739) who, apart from being a composer, was also a poet and lawyer, and whose most famous work was a satirical critique of opera, the *Teatro alla modo* (from 1721). According to Newman, Marcello's sonatas for harpsichord number approximately twenty and existed during his lifetime only in manuscript. Of the twelve in the Paris manuscript, eight show the four-movement scheme of the church sonata while three have three movements and one has five. There is only one movement connected with the *da camera* sonata, a minuet. Binary form, with the double bar, appears in most of the movements. An unusual feature is the employment of cyclic form, an obvious and explicit use of the same thematic material at the beginnings of movements in the same sonata.

Particularly varied is the sonata output of Giovanni Battista Martini of Bologna, the famous composer, theorist, and historian of music universally known as Padre Martini. He published two collections of keyboard sonatas: the *Sonate d'intavolatura per l'organo e'l cembalo* in 1742 and the *Sonate per l'organo e il cembalo* in 1747. The earlier set contains works closely related to the chamber and church sonatas, elements from the two being here presented in combination, the key for each work remains the same throughout, and a sequence of five movements is used, namely, prelude, fugue, slow movement, dance movement, and a set of variations (called "aria"). The preludes appear both in the simple form, using a single motive all the way through, and in the more elaborate sectional form of the French overture, which Bach also used in some of his English Suites and Partitas; the fugues use typical themes of the types handed down from the seventeenth century and display considerable contrapuntal ability, which shows itself in part through the use of the devices of the learned style. As it happens, contrapuntal elements appear in all movements, as might be expected considering Martini's background. The collection of 1747, on the other hand, shows the use of what we might regard as the more "modern" type of the keyboard sonata: the three-movement scheme (Fast—Slow—Fast), which evidently is to be connected with the Italian operatic overture, the sinfonia. This, however, holds only for the harpsichord sonatas; those for organ consist of two movements in the sequence Slow—Fast. Martini also composed liturgical sonatas for organ in one movement. A similar mixture of the two sonata types may be seen in the nine sonatas of Giovanni Battista Pescetti (*c.* 1704–1766), of which six were published in London in 1739 and in which, again, fugal movements are important.

Another mixture of the two may be seen in the work of the Venetian Giovanni Benedetto Platti (*c.* 1700–1762) who worked in Bamberg and later in Würzburg (Hoffmann-Erbrecht assumes the existence of two composers, father and son). Some eighteen harpsichord sonatas appeared in 1742 and 1746 (see the older and rather controversial account of Torrefranca along with the more recent one of Hoffmann-Erbrecht). While these sonatas clearly show the influence of the old *sonata da chiesa*, one work plainly is a *sonata da camera* in four movements—a prelude, a saraband, a minuet, and a concluding gigue. Typical is the *galant* finale of the Sonata in C (op. 1 ii [see *HAM*, II, 284]), with its opening themes

EXAMPLE 38

PLATTI: *Sonata* in C—beginning

descending scale-wise *all' unisono* and the short triadic motivic theme that follows, both of which are related to the thematic types of the *opera buffa*. Representative of the conservative type is the Sonata in D (op. 1 i) in four movements— Adagio, Allegro, Largo, and Presto (Newman, 2, pp. 36–41). On the other hand the later set (1746) shows the mixture of the two; a few works show the three movement scheme (Fast—Slow—Fast), while others cling to the old. Stylized dances are important, the saraband and siciliano types appearing as slow movements, the gigue type often providing the basis for the finales. In the first movements, something like the later so-called "sonata form" may be seen; the recapitulation is usually clear, but the development is both short and free. These works are also distinguished by a certain elaboration in the harmonic progression.

Sonatas in two movements appear, apart from Martini, in the work of Domenico Paradisi (1707–1791), often known under the apparently Germanized form, Paradies) and Domenico Alberti (*c.* 1710–*c.* 1739), both of whom were widely regarded as virtuoso performers and who were active in London. Alberti, for whom the "Alberti bass" was named, had a particular reputation in England as a great innovator in harpsichord music, as is seen from some remarks of Burney. His sonatas existed only in manuscript during his lifetime; the first published collection containing eight of them appeared in 1748 (see Wörmann). The exact number of sonatas he wrote is uncertain, but it is estimated that there were at least fourteen complete works in this genre. Here, the two-movement scheme is standard. Most have two fast movements, the first in duple time and the second in triple (usually a dance—a minuet or gigue); a few present the reverse arrangement. The two-part form is present but is kept uniform in character throughout. Typical of Alberti is the Sonata in G (op. 1 viii [see Newman, 3, pp. 42–7]) in two movements, showing the characteristically *italianate galant* style, the simple figuration types that form the melody, the homophonic texture, and the stereotyped patterns in the accompaniment. By and large, Alberti is to be regarded as an amateur in composition whose importance has been exaggerated by his association with the bass accompaniment pattern that bears his name (see Marco).

Paradisi is known for the collection of sonatas that appeared in London in 1754 containing twelve works (there are several later editions as well as manuscript copies). It appears that, like Alberti, Paradisi usually cast his sonatas in two movements, but the sequence varies; some have two fast movements, others a slow movement followed by a fast one, and others the reverse. In the fast movements, the relation to the old binary form of the suite dance seems clear enough, but it has been elaborated by Paradisi into something approaching the later so-called "sonata form" in these fast movements that stand first. This is evident from the first part of such movements (corresponding to the exposition) in the variety of the themes employed and the attempt to establish contrasting characters; often, after the double bar, a recapitulation of some sort may be found.

The idea of thematic contrast in a keyboard sonata is, according to Hoffmann-Erbrecht, taken over from the Italian operatic sinfonia, where it had been a practice of long standing; another suggestion would be to associate it with the concerto grosso, in which often the theme of the solo group would contrast with that used for the orchestra. In the fast finales, however, uniformity of character prevails. From later in the century, we also find two-movement sonatas by the abbot Lorenzo de Rossi (1720–1794), Antonio Sacchini (1730–1786), and Luigi Cherubini (1760–1842).

Sonatas in two and three movements dominate the large output of the well-known Venetian composer Baldassare Galuppi (1706–1785), called *Il Buranello*, who spent the last years of his life working in St. Petersburg (see Raabe). The total number of Galuppi's sonatas is now estimated at ninety, most of them existing only in manuscript during his lifetime (two sets of six each were printed in London by Walsh in 1756 and 1759, respectively). While the schemes used in these works are too varied to permit of any generalization (there are about as many in two movements as in three, and other sonatas are in one, four, and five movements), all of the sonatas printed in the eighteenth century show the three-movement form, an opening cantabile followed by two fast movements with the gigue type prominent among the finales. Although essentially *galant*, Galuppi's sonatas are characterized by a certain economy in the themes used with an emphasis on motivic development, as well as by a tendency towards the virtuoso treatment of the instrument; both these qualities set his works off somewhat from that of his contemporaries. Much the same situation exists in the sonatas of Ferdinando Turini (*c.* 1749–*c.* 1817).

Finally, there is a group of composers whose sonatas are cast in the three-movement form, usually in the sequence Fast—Slow—Fast, which undoubtedly comes from the sinfonia. Among these are the famous Milanese composer Giovanni Battista Sammartini (*c.* 1700–1775), the teacher of Gluck and Johann Christian Bach, and the traveled Giovanni Maria (or Marco) Placido Rutini (1723–1797), whose journeys took him to Europe and as far as Russia and who, like so many others, devoted himself chiefly to the composition of operas. The *galant* style, in all its elegant simplicity, its sweet and singing melodies (*suavitas* and *cantabilitas*), and the prevailingly homophonic texture is particularly evident in the sonatas of Sammartini, in which the finale usually is a minuet. Much the same goes for the sonatas of Rutini, the total number of which has been set at sixty. Accessible is the finale of a Sonata in E-flat (op. 6 vi [*HAM*, II, 302]) that shows the many typical features: the stereotyped Alberti bass, the melody with its simple scale-wise motion, the *forma bipartita* (which Kirkpatrick would call "closed"), and the gigue-like rhythm often found in the finales, a holdover from the old suite. To this group of composers we may add Giuseppe Paganelli (1710–*c.* 1762) of Padua, who was active mainly in Germany and who issued slight and pleasing little sonatas or sonatinas in two and three movements in his

Divertissement de le beau sexe around 1757; many of these sonatina movements appear in altered form in his other publication of keyboard music, the thirty *Arias pro organo et cembalo*, of 1756 (see Schenk).

There are other Italian composers of keyboard music in the eighteenth century, mainly of sonatas, whose exact output has yet to be established and whose significance is at present not clear or whose work, insofar as it is presently known, seems of minor importance. Among these, we can simply list Antonio Ferradini (*c.* 1718–1779), Giuseppe Ferdinando Bertoni (1725–1813), Giuseppe Sarti (1729–1802), the composer of popular operas satirized by Mozart in the last scene of *Don Giovanni*, and Giovanni Maria Grazioli (1746–*c.* 1802).

There seems little doubt about the decisive role of these Italian composers in the development of the sonata as the principal new genre of harpsichord music and of the various forms and ways of writing that go along with it. The influence of Italian musicians, in harpsichord music as in opera, was felt all over Europe; it was sometimes accepted with unqualified enthusiasm, at other times rejected with great vehemence, and occasionally provoking spirited controversies. This last was generally true in France where the merits of French music as opposed to those of Italian music were often the subject of heated debate. This situation is reflected in Couperin's "conciliatory" work, *Les goûts reunis* of 1724; and, in 1739, Jean Guilain published a similarly intentioned work called *Pièces de clavecin d'un goût nouveau* in which the "new taste" is plainly the Italian style. Nevertheless, it was not in France that the new Italian style had its most far-reaching effects; this took place in Germany. But before we attempt to survey this important subject, let us devote some attention to the situation of keyboard music in other countries—Spain, Portugal, and England—where, again, the Italian influence is of some importance.

In the harpsichord music of Spain and Portugal, this influence was especially colored by the example of Domenico Scarlatti, as is clear from the work of such leading composers as the Lisbon organist José Antonio Carlos de Seixas (1704–1742), the harpsichordist of the Escorial palace in Madrid, Padre Antonio Soler and Manual Blasco de Nebra (*c.* 1750–1784), who published a set of sonatas in Seville around 1780. Seixas' varied output (see Kastner) comprises sonatas, toccatas, minuets, fugues, and even works specifically for the clavichord; his toccatas are similar in size and form to the sonatas of Scarlatti, and his sonatas are varied, some in one movement, others in two, three, four, or five. In recent years, the sonatas of Soler have become well known. In all, there are roughly between one hundred and two hundred of them preserved in manuscript, as well as a group published in 1796 in London. Here, the Scarlatti type of sonata serves as the model: the one-movement form cast in the *forma bipartita* (but sometimes arranged in groups of two, three, or four), the prevalence of fast tempi, the exploitation of the harpsichord sound for special effects, and so forth. Soler is also the author of a treatise on harmony, *Llave de la modulación y antigüedades de la música*, published in 1762 in Madrid. On the other hand, the sonatas of Blasco de Nebra adopt the modern conventionally *galant* form that dominated the scene of Italian keyboard music of the time; he used the two-movement scheme, simple melodies, and simple stereotyped accompaniment patterns (the Alberti and the Murky basses), as is seen from his Sonata in c (op. 1 [printed in Newman, 7, pp. 68–74; the second movement is in *HAM*, II, 308]). Other composers of lesser significance include Rafael Anglés (*c.* 1731–1816), Narciso Casanovas (1747–1799), and Felipe Rodríguez (1759–1814).

In England, the modern genres associated with the harpsichord and the piano lead the way. Here foreign-born composers dominate the scene, as was the case in English instrument building of the time; the work of Scarlatti and Alberti, for example, enjoyed a particular reputation. An important Italian virtuoso player and composer active in London was Felice de Giardini (1716–1796); another was Muzio Clementi, who will be discussed later. In addition to Italians were many Germans; apart from the well-known Johann Christian Bach, we can mention men like Ignaz Pleyel (1757–1831) and the virtuoso Daniel Steibelt (1765–1823), as well as others whose work belongs to the nineteenth century; there was the Dutchman, Pieter Hellendaal (1721–1799). Among the native English composers are Charles Avison (1709–1770), James Nares (1715–1783), Thomas Augustine Arne (1710–1778), and Charles Burney (1726–1814). Arne's set of eight *Sonatas or Lessons* for the harpsichord of around 1756 may be regarded as the first works explicitly called sonatas published in England. According to Newman, they are mostly two-movement works, but there are works in one movement (in theme and variations form) and in four; the style is italianate. The work serves as yet another indication of the close relation that was often felt between the sonata and the suite. Both genres appear in the work of Burney, a set of suites in 1761 and a set of sonatas in 1766; in the early nineteenth century, he published independent rondos, perhaps under the influence of C. P. E. Bach. Burney also published duet sonatas for piano or harpsichord. Another English composer of lesser stature was James Hook (1746–1827).

But the most important reaction to the Italian keyboard style took place in Germany (see Faisst, Stilz, Lange, and Hoffmann-Erbrecht). It was here that elements of the new were taken, altered, and combined with older ideals, ultimately leading to the establishment of the characteristic genres of instrumental music so familiar today. This most important development again is difficult to follow; while the starting and ending points are reasonably well known, the steps in between are as yet far from clear. It would seem that the best procedure would be to attempt to distinguish the older or more conservative works from those that involve the more "progressive" ideals from Italy.

As far as the older types are concerned, the tradition of the harpsichord toccata was continued in Austria by the Viennese organists Ferdinand Tobias

Richter (1649–1711), the successor to Poglietti; Gottlieb (or Theophilus) Muffat, the son of Georg Muffat; and the famous Salzburg musician Johann Ernst Eberlin (1702–1762). The fugue was continued by two pupils of J. S. Bach, the theorist Johann Philipp Kirnberger (1721–1783) and Johann Ludwig Krebs; it ultimately became a strictly didactic genre. Gottlieb Muffat not only continued to write fugues, but also perpetuated its older versions, the ricercare and the canzone. The didactic intent is clear from the work of a man like the Viennese theorist Johann Georg Albrechtsberger.

More important is the harpsichord suite. We have already seen important contributions in the work of Handel, Graupner, and Mattheson. Among other German composers who continued this genre are Ferdinand Tobias Richter (mentioned above), Henrich Nicolaus Gerber (1702–1775), a pupil of J. S. Bach, and, particularly, Gottlieb Muffat, whose set of suites was published in 1739 under the title *Componimenti musicali* (see Adler and Knöll). This set is characteristic of the suite of the time, particularly for how it fared in the hands of a composer whose sympathies by and large were conservative. The unity of tonality is maintained, and the four "normal" dances appear; four of the suites are in eight movements while two have ten. But the new cantabile style, with its bent towards simplicity, came to the fore, as seems clear in the slower of the old dances, the allemande and the saraband, the latter always having an obvious reprise in the section after the double bar, which Hoffmann-Erbrecht associates with the *da capo* aria. French and Italian elements appear side by side in the courantes and gigues, and in both—but especially noteworthy in in the gigues—homophony prevails. All of Muffat's suites are introduced by preludes that here assume sectional form and in which imitation is important. The prelude to the Suite in C (*GMB*, 292) is a French overture. Other movements, independent of the usual dances and associated rather with the sonata, also appear, such as the finale of the Suite in C (*HAM*, II, 280). Readily available is Muffat's Suite in d (Georgii, *Keyboard Music*, II, pp. 76–89).

The suite also occupies an important position in the work of Johann Peter Kellner (1705–1772) who lived and worked in Thuringia. From him, we have three publications: the *Certamen musicum* of 1739–1749, the *Manipulus Musices, oder eine Handvoll kurzweiliger Zeitvertreib vors Clavier* of 1753–1756, the first of which contains suites along with preludes and fugues, while the second contains four works called either "suites" or "sonatas"; and a set of three *Sonates pour le clavecin* of 1752. Here, we see that the new Italian genre of the sonata takes its place beside the older suite. In the *Certamen musicum*, we find suites that bear little relation to the established form of the genre, so completely has the idea of the sonata taken hold. Apart from the preludes and fugues, the allemande is the only standard element that appears in all the suites; the saraband is transformed into a simple slow movement in triple time; in all but one instance, a fast allegro in *forma bipartita* serves as the finale, replacing the gigue. In the *Manipulus musices*, on the other hand, the process is carried to the point where none of the characteristic suite dances appears at all. Kellner's sonatas stand in need of investigation. Two other composers who wrote sonatas in which the influence of the suite is clear were Anton Franz Maichelbeck (1702–1750) and Jacob Wilhelm Lustig (1706–1796).

Much the same situation exists in the work of Conrad Friedrich Hurlebusch (1695–1765), a German who became organist in Amsterdam and who published three collections containing suites and sonatas for harpsichord: the *Compositioni musicali* of around 1735 and two sets with the title *Sonate di cembalo*, both of which appeared in 1746 as op. 5 and 6, respectively (see Seiffert). Whereas, in the early set, there are five suites that are in the old tradition (along with some toccatas), in the later sets, with sonatas, we find elements of the suite (particularly the prominence of dance types and a varying number of movements) combined with other movements more related to the sonata. (Hurlebusch also composed for harpsichord or organ short settings of the Psalms, in 1746, as also had the Dutch composer Quirinus van Blankenburg [1654–*c*. 1740], along with harpsichord arrangements of arias from operas.)

Symbolic of this change in the suite is a new term that came into use during the eighteenth century—"divertimento," used for the "lighter" genres of music intended simply for entertainment and diversion. This end, to be sure, is frequently sought in the sonata literature of the time, and distinctions are not easy to establish. Generally, however, the divertimento is closely related to the suite; but we have seen it in connection with the sonata in the work of the Italian composer Durante, whose sonatas, however, must be looked upon as rather exceptional. Two German composers who use the term "divertimento" in connection with keyboard music are Johann Gottfried Krebs (1741–1814) and, especially, the Viennese Johann Christoph Wagenseil (1715–1777), a pupil of Fux and composer to the Hapsburg court from 1739. Wagenseil published six sets of harpsichord works called "divertimenti" or "sonatas" between 1753 and 1761 (see Hausswald). In these works, we find again that the old concept of the suite had been replaced by something closer to that of the sonata; these divertimenti usually are in three movements, two fast movements with a minuet in the middle. The *forma bipartita* appears in the fast movements, which usually operate with a number of very short thematic motives. Only a few of the old dances are retained: a gigue or poloccha, the minuets, and, in one, a prelude (for which Wagenseil uses the term *ricercata*). Besides the divertimenti, Wagenseil published earlier, in 1740, a set of *Parthias* (six suites in all); composed some thirty others that exist at present only in manuscript (five sets of six in the Dresden library); and composed a few sonatas all of which reveal the same essential traits.

We see, then, in Wagenseil as in Kellner, that the suite was giving way to the sonata. In the work of other composers, the suite is largely ignored, and full attention given to the sonata. There is an isolated but in many ways rather interesting sonata by Gottfried Heinrich Stöltzel (1690–1749), who led a wandering life, holding positions in Leipzig, Breslau, Prague, and Gotha, as well as spending a few years in Italy (see Schmidt-Weiss). In 1761, his *Enharmonische Klavier-Sonate* was posthumously published, a work that still shows a conservative orientation, consisting as it does of a prelude (in the familiar small form), a fugue that soon became largely homophonic), and a fast finale. The work is noteworthy for its use of enharmonic modulations that necessitate the use of even temperament. Stöltzel is also the author of a little Suite in g. Other conservative sonatas that show the influence of the suite, especially in the number of movements and prominence of dance forms, exist in the work of Johann Agrell (1701–1765), a Swedish musician active in Kassel and Nürnberg in the 1740's, whose four-movement Sonata in e is readily available (Newman, 5, pp. 56–63). Other sonata composers to be listed here are the Viennese Mathias Georg Monn (1717–1750), Friedrich Wilhelm Marpurg (1718–1795), Johann Friedrich Agricola (1720–1774), Johann Philip Kirnberger, Johann Nikolaus Tischer (1707–c.1784), Johann Ernst Bach (1722–1777), Franz Vollrath Buttstedt (1735–1814), and Johann Gottfried Krebs.

Among the composers who gave the new genre a more important place in their work were Johann Joseph Fux and the celebrated opera composer Johann Adolf Hasse (1699–1783). Fux, the Viennese theorist, composed four suites and seven sonatas; most of the sonatas are in the three-movement form that we might regard as the most "modern" scheme, in the sequence Fast—Slow—Fast. One, the Sonata in E, has two movements, an Andante and an Allegro, and another, the Sonata in a (v) has three movements but in the sequence Adagio—Allegro—Adagio. The style, however, is conservative; Baroque *Fortspinnung* themes predominate, and counterpoint is important. Fux wrote other works in the old vein: a Prelude and Fugue in g, the prelude being an arpeggio piece, and a chaconne with thirty-three variations on an eight-bar theme.

Johann Adolf Hasse was one of the great masters of the Italian *opera seria*, of which he composed fifty-six; he was active in Italy, where he was known and esteemed as *Il Sassone* (the Saxon), and in Dresden. His harpsichord music, interesting as it is, takes a secondary position in his work as a whole (see Hoffmann-Erbrecht). Among his harpsichord compositions are seventeen sonatas, one toccata, and two works simply called "pieces." Six of the sonatas were published in London in 1758, while another was included in 1770 in a set of six *Lessons for the Harpsichord* containing works by several composers. Although Hasse's sonatas are in two, three, and four movements, a large proportion of them (eight) are cast in the three-movement form with minuets as finales, and it seems as if this was his tendency in the later works. The style is largely homophonic, in all respects that of the Italian *galant*. The only noteworthy feature is length; these sonatas are of larger dimensions than was usual for the sonata of the time. All in all, however, these sonatas are interesting because they are so typically italianate—the work of a thoroughly Italianized German composer, a mixture that symbolizes the main elements that went together to make up the new instrumental style. It is possibly not without significance that the characteristic "modern" form of the keyboard sonata—in three movements and the sequence Fast—Slow—Fast, the typical binary form of the fast movements with the cantabile allegro themes and their simple accompaniments that are either purely homophonic or use stereotyped figuration patterns—appears around the middle of the century in the work of two italianate composers working in Germany, Platti and Hasse. Platti, for his part, made the Italian background of his sonatas explicit in the titles, which describe his work as being *sur le goût italien* (in the Italian taste).

Among the lesser German sonata composers of the latter half of the eighteenth century, we can list Georg Andreas Sorge (1703–1778); Christoph Schaffrath (1709–1763); Christoph Nichelmann (1717–1762), a pupil of J. S. Bach and a harpsichordist active in Berlin who published two sets of sonatas especially intended for women, both apparently in 1745; Leopold Mozart (1719–1787), the Salzburg violinist and father of Wolfgang Amadeus who composed sonatas that were in three movements in the Fast—Slow—Fast sequence and, were italianate in all respects; Friedrich Gottlob Fleischer (1722–1806); Georg Benda (1722–1795), active in Berlin, Gotha, and Hamburg and a supporter of progressive tendencies in dramatic music who composed a number of modest italianate works, sometimes using the minuet as finale (see Stilz) of which a Sonata in B-flat, the first in his collection of 1757, is easily available (Newman, 4, pp. 48–55; other selections in Georgii, *Keyboard Music*, III, pp. 89–93); Johann Georg Lang (1724–*c.* 1794); Georg Simon Löhlein (1725–1781); Johann Christoph Monn (1726–1782); Johann Friedrich Daube (*c.* 1733–1797); Ignaz von Beecke (1733–1803); Ernst Wilhelm Wolf (1735–1792), active in Weimar; Christian Friedrich Carl Fasch (1736–1800), a harpsichordist at the court of Frederick the Great who founded the famous Berlin *Singakademie*; Christian Gottlob Neefe (1736–1798), Beethoven's teacher who composed a large number of sonatas, some solo (of which as an example is a Sonata in c [Newman, 6, pp. 64–7] and others with violin accompaniment (a genre we will consider below); Friedrich Wilhelm Rust (1739–1796); and Johann Gottlieb Naumann (1741–1801) of Dresden. In all these, we can note, as so often before, that their keyboard pieces are by and large unimportant not only in comparison to their other works, which generally relate to dramatic music, but also simply in themselves; many are specifically aimed at the amateur, particularly the rather unkilled amateur, and are simple and pleasing in all respects.

More important is the work of the sons of Bach (see Reeser and Geiringer): Wilhelm Friedemann (1710–1784), Carl Philipp Emanuel (1714–1788), Johann Christoph Friedrich (1732–1795), and Johann Christian (1735–1782). Of these, Johann Christoph Friedrich (known as the "Bückeburg Bach") is the least important, in keyboard music as in all else. The simple *galant* style and the aim of diverting the amateur is all too clear and is made explicit by the titles of the anthologies in which his work appears: *Musikalisches Vielerley* or *Musikalische Nebenstunden* (*Musical Varieties* or *Musical Little Hours*). His sonatas, which he always qualifies as *leicht* (easy), appeared between 1785 and 1789; they are in three movements and fulfill their minor purpose very well (see Schünemann).

The most important among Bach's sons is Carl Philipp Emanuel who, trained by his father, was active in the court of Frederick the Great in Berlin between 1740 and 1767 (see Helm) and then took over the leadership of the famous *Collegium Musicum* in Hamburg as Telemann's successor. He was associated at one time or another with many leading musicians (Quantz, Graun, Telemann) and men from the world of literature of the time (Lessing, Klopstock, Gerstenberg, Claudius) and was generally regarded as one of Germany's first composers. He was the author of a celebrated treatise on keyboard playing, the *Versuch über die wahre Art das Klavier zu spielen* (*Essay on the True Art of Playing the Keyboard Instruments*), published in two volumes in 1753 and 1762.[1] His most important contributions to the literature of keyboard music are contained in the following publications: a set of six sonatas dedicated to Frederick the Great published in 1742 (the so-called *Prussian sonatas*, W. 48); a set of six sonatas dedicated to the Duke of Würtemberg published in 1744 (the so-called *Würtemberg Sonatas*, W. 49); a set of six sonatas with varied reprises (*Sonaten mit veränderten Reprisen* or *Amalian Sonatas*, W. 50) published in 1760 (later editions in 1785 and 1787); two sets of six sonatas each, published in 1761 (W. 51) and 1763 (W. 52); and the important six volumes of sonatas, rondos, and fantasias *Für Kenner und Liebhaber* (W. 55–9, 61) published in 1779 and 1787; to this must be added the six sonatas that appeared as a supplement to his treatise (the so-called *Probestücke*, W. 63). Numerous individual works appeared from time to time in anthologies. Estimates as to the total number of Bach's sonatas vary; while Canave lists 143, others indicate as many as 200. A large portion were published during Bach's lifetime. It appears that the bulk of them were composed during his years in the service of Frederick the Great; Canave assigns only thirty to his twenty-odd years in Hamburg, among them such sets of out-and-out *galant* works as the sonatas *À l'usage des dames* (W. 54) of 1773 along with the important sets *Für Kenner und Liebhaber*.

To place first things first, it may be emphasized that possibly the most striking thing about all this is that the old suite is generally neglected by C. P. E. Bach and that he worked primarily, as far as keyboard music is concerned, with the large form, the sonata; and it is the "modern" form of the sonata, as we have seen in

---

[1] English translation by Mitchell. There is no complete edition of C. P. E. Bach, but the more famous sonatas are available in reliable editions. Wotquenne has compiled a thematic catalogue, and his "W" numbers are used here; a comprehensive listing of his works is in *MGG*, I, cc. 930–5. Recent studies are by Canave, Clercx, Beurmann, Fischer, Müller, Jurisch and Wyler.

Hasse and Platti. But there is more; if in Hasse we noted some sort of effort to make the sonata a bigger and more important genre by casting individual works on a larger scale, this intent is also found in C. P. E. Bach but in a different way. This immediately is evident from the first *Prussian Sonata* in F; in its Andante, in f (the appassionata key), these are passages suggestive of the recitative style of the opera (which we have in the past seen in the toccata, for instance, in the work of J. S. Bach) and an elaborate indication of dynamics. Similar passages are to be found in the second work, a Sonata in B-flat, where the slow movement is an Adagio in g with room for a cadenza near the end; and in the first movement after the double bar comes a long passage that stylistically resembles the Baroque prelude. The adagio movement of the Sonata in A (vi) shows recitative-like passages and a cadenza. Much the same thing may be seen in the *Würtemberg Sonatas* where it appears in the first movements, as in the sonatas in a (i), A-flat (ii) with its tempo changes and explicit retardations, and b (vi); the relatively uneventful Sonata in e, which even so has much variety in its first movement, is readily available (Georgii, *Keyboard Music*, III, pp. 48–55.) Dynamic markings abound throughout the collection.

EXAMPLE 39

C. P. E. Bach: Adagio, from *Sonata* in B-flat (*Prussian Sonatas*, No. 2)— beginning

The sonata with varied reprise is a special type that appears first in 1760; but Beurmann points out that the type was continued by Bach only here and there. The variation of the reprise is not quite what one might expect. In the first place, it is found only in the outside Allegro movements; in the second, it does not in-involve the recapitulation, but rather all the repetitions in the movement. Such a movement is always in bipartite form, each half to be repeated; but, where normally the double bar with repeat signs would appear in these movements with varied reprises, the double bar is not used, and everything is written out in full so that the variations can be made. One would find, then, in such a movement, the exposition, the repeat of the exposition with variations, then (corresponding to the part of the movement that would come after the double bar) the "develop-ment" and the recapitulation, both of which are then repeated with variations. In the earlier works of this kind, the types of variations are simple enough— application of figuration, triplets, and scale runs to the melodies; but later this process of variation became more elaborate and more subtle and even, at times, allowed for the presentation of extensive cadenza-like passages.

Generally speaking, the sonatas found in the six collections *Für Kenner und Liebhaber* represent Bach's most ambitious work. It is obvious that his audience for these works did not consist largely of unskilled amateurs who sought enter-tainment and diversion; rather, his aim was towards those who have a certain amount of musical knowledge and sophistication, who are not merely amateurs and dilletantes but also connoisseurs; this much seems implied by the term *Kenner*. To restrict ourselves, first, to the sonatas, standard here, as before, is the three-movement scheme (Fast—Slow—Fast) with the slow movement usually in a contrasting but related key. Among the departures that can be connected with Bach's aim to increase the scope of the sonata, we can mention the following: occasional direct linking together of movements emphasizing their continuity and, by extension, the unity of the sonata as a whole (from Set I, Sonatas in F and b; Set II, Sonatas in G and F; Set III, Sonata in a; Set IV, Sonata in G; Set V, Sonata in e; Set VI, Sonata in D); an increase in the elaboration of the first movements, the employment of motivic themes that are used to construct a development, and, in most cases, a clear recapitulation; a continuation of the serious and expressive type of slow movement of which noteworthy examples would be the Cantabile e mesto of the Sonata in d, Set III (*HAM*, II, 297) and the Largo e sostenuto of the Sonata in G, Set IV; and the use of passages in fantasia style, with recitative-like passages, in both fast and slow movements. Particularly large-scaled works are the Sonatas in A and C of Set I, which deserve wider recognition than is now their due.

Turning to the other genres represented in these six sets *Für Kenner und Liebhaber*, we have the fantasias and the rondos. The former represent one of Bach's most characteristic contributions to the keyboard repertory. The aim of this genre is clearly explained by Bach in his treatise; the whole last chapter of the work is devoted to this subject. From this discussion, it is clear that the background of the fantasia lies in improvisation. Bach says, "A fantasia is said to be free when it is unmeasured and moves through more keys than is customary in other pieces which are composed or improvised in meter." There are, then, two important features—the unusual modulations and the freedom of meter. Further, he says, "A free fantasia consists of varied harmonic progressions which can be expressed in all manner of figuration and motives" (both quotations from Mitchell's translation, p. 430). Such a work is obviously related to the improvised prelude as we have seen it; and this relationship is explicitly acknowledged by Bach, except that a prelude is a piece "which prepares the listener for the content of the piece that follows . . . (and) is more restricted than the fantasia," the latter being completely independent. The rest of the account offers suggestions for suitable modulations in the improvising of such a free fantasia, in which it is emphasized that the fantasia must be oriented to a particular tonality in which it commences, to which it returns periodically, and in which it ends.

The fantasias in the *Für Kenner und Liebhaber* (Sets IV, V, and VI) obviously are related to this improvised free fantasia. All are sectional works in which much variety is presented; figuration is important, and there are many unmeasured sections (*senza misura*), candenza-like phrases ending in fermatas, sudden chromatic changes, and sudden changes of style and texture. Readily available is the Fantasia in E-flat from Set IV (Georgii, *Keyboard Music*, III, pp. 62–7). It is in three large parts, the first consisting solely of figuration (arpeggios being prominent) with a recitative passage in the middle; then there is a Poco adagio, a primarily chordal passage barred in the regular way but with unusual harmonies; and then there is an Allegro that brings back much of the material of the first part. The repetition of themes in different sections of a fantasia comes to be of greater importance in later volumes of the series *Für Kenner und Liebhaber*, as can be seen from the Fantasia in C of Set V (Georgii, *Keyboard Music*, III, pp. 72–9) in which several themes appear in alternation and in various keys; especially characteristic here are the very rapid changes in tempo, key, and rhythm that take place within the space of only a few bars: six bars of Andantino (bars 74–7) consisting of modulating arpeggiated chords, then seven bars of Allegretto (bars 80–7), a simple, accompanied melody (bars 95–106), then seven more of the Andantino (bars 88–94), twelve more of the Allegretto, and so on. This type of fantasia reappears in the work of the so-called "Classical" composers and leads to something quite different in the following century. Other readily accessible fantasias of Bach are the Fantasia in g that appeared in Haffner's publication, *Musikalisches Vielerley*, a shorter and less ambitious work which yet shows the main features of the genre (*HAM*, II, 296), and the Fantasia in c (W. 63 vi), which was included among the illustrative examples in Bach's treatise on keyboard playing (*HMS*, VII, s. 6, b. 5), a work whose expression is such that the poet Gerstenberg was moved to fit words to it.

This he did twice, once adapting a soliloquy of Hamlet, and the second time one of Socrates.

The remaining genre in the sets *Für Kenner und Liebhaber* is the rondo, which appears in all but Set I. Here, the basic scheme is that of the French rondeau, which originally was a dance in which the introductory section was repeated, and, between its repetitions, contrasting sections (episodes or couplets) appeared; there is no set number of couplets. Bach's rondo is in keeping with the general trend of his work, more elaborate; the dance elements are eliminated, a good deal of thematic variation is applied to the rondo section, and frequently free passages are found that suggest the influence of the free fantasia. The Rondos in B-flat and c from Books IV and V are readily available (Georgii, *Keyboard Music*, III, pp. 56–61 and 68–71).

Carl Philipp Emanuel Bach is associated with a peculiarly Germanic trend in the late eighteenth century known as *Empfindsamkeit*, a term difficult to translate but meaning roughly "sensibility" or "sensitivity" and implying "expression." This plays a most important role in Bach's fantasias and in the slow movements of the sonatas. Here we see clearly one of the central problems of the period—the expression of the affections by means of instrumental music; music is regarded as the language of the emotions (*die Sprache der Empfindung*). In the

EXAMPLE 40

C. P. E. BACH: *Fantasia* in E-flat (*Für Kenner und Liebhaber*, Book IV)— excerpt

rendition of this emotional style, Bach preferred that most "emotional" among the keyboard instruments, the clavichord, which, by virtue of this peculiarly Germanic movement, was able to maintain itself until the second decade of the nineteenth century in spite of the constant ascendance of the piano; but this was so only in Germany (see Auerbach). The role of emotional expression in Bach's music—and in his playing, in which the considerable place of improvisation is difficult now to assess—is well supported both in his own writings and in those of his contemporaries. Steglich has assembled a number of pertinent quotations, some of which may serve as illustrations here. Cramer, for instance, referred to "the endless nuances of shade and light" that were heard in Bach's playing, while Reichardt emphasized the extraordinary range of dynamics that Bach could elicit from his clavichord and added elsewhere that, when Bach played, "his whole soul is involved" and that he was the first to bring such complete expressive power to keyboard music; and Schubert stated, "When I wish to play a sonata by Bach, I must allow myself wholly to sink into the spirit of this great man, so that my own identity vanishes and becomes Bach's own idiom." It is all this, then, that has given Bach a critical position with respect to the development of the new instrumental music in general and that of keyboard music in particular. In his time, he was regarded as original, even as an original genius (*Originalgenie*), and, as we will see, his influence is difficult to overestimate.

Wilhelm Friedemann Bach (1710–1784), the oldest of J. S. Bach's sons, has been called the most gifted among them (see Falck). But in temperament he was restless, unable or unwilling to hold any one position for any length of time; this led to an erratic, wandering existence. He had, however, a great reputation as a performer and was especially known for the brilliance and originality of his improvisations. It must be assumed, then, that much of his keyboard music was never committed to paper and that what we have represents but a fraction of his actual work. We have nine sonatas (one was published in 1745) and ten fantasias, along with twelve fugues (published in 1778), a set of twelve polonaises composed around 1765 and arranged according to key, and a small number of chorale preludes for organ. The cultivation of the fugue, the chorale prelude, and the polonaise would tend to connect him with an older generation, but at the same time these polonaises are highly stylized, and the fugues, although strictly contrapuntal and often employing "expressive" chromatic harmonies, are on a much smaller scale than those of his father. An example of each is readily available (*HAM*, II, 288 and 289; one other may be seen in Georgii, *Keyboard Music*, III, pp. 44–7). The sonatas, and especially the fantasias, surely place him well in the forefront among his contemporaries, and the presence of both elements in the work of one man is by no means unique or even unusual for the eighteenth century. The sonatas show clearly his essentially progressive approach; the three-movement form used by his brother, C. P. E. Bach and also by Hasse and Platti appears along with the Italian cantabile melody and many of the expressive traits noted in the work of his brother. Much the same applies to the fantasias in which his bent for unusual effects reached its fullest expression.

If C. P. E. Bach and Wilhelm Friedemann Bach represent the more Germanic type of sonata in which expression is important, then the younger brother, Johann Christian Bach, represents the simple ingratiating and diverting type from the Italian *galant* at its finest (see Terry and Schöckel). Johann Christian learned the style at first hand from Sammartini in Milan (where he arrived in 1757) and practiced it in London, where he lived and worked from 1762 until his death. The bulk of his keyboard music is taken up by the sonatas, of which the main collections are the sets of six of op. 5 (*c.* 1768) and op. 17 (of 1779); later sets were issued in Paris and Amsterdam. All bear the qualification "for harpsichord or piano," an option that is to remain common until the early nineteenth century. Most of these are three-movement works, but a significant number of them have two movements; both schemes were common in the Italian keyboard music of the time, particularly in the work of those active in England, Alberti and Paradisi. Especially italianate are the first movements, which feature the cantabile (singing) allegro type of theme over a stereotyped accompaniment; many examples could be named, such as the Sonatas in E-flat, G, and A of op. 17. The first movement of the Sonata in G (op. 17 iv) shows all these features: a singing allegro theme over a simple homophonic accompaniment, with stereotyped bass patterns, simple harmonies, several themes in the first section, a short development or transition, and a somewhat abbreviated recapitulation (*HAM*, II, 303). Unusually large is the Sonata in D (op. 5 ii) that, through its full chords and tremolo passages, creates an orchestra-like effect. Similar works are by no means uncommon in the latter part of the eighteenth century and are usually associated with the key of D; with this go certain thematic types that seem related to those current in t he *opera buffa* overture; there are short phrases emphasizing trills or short scale runs played very fast, so that the motive might be called sheer ornamentation without melody. A work in which Johann Christian Bach approaches the *pathétique* is the Sonata in c (op. 17 ii [Georgii, *Keyboard Music*, III, pp. 80–8]), in which the most attention goes to E-flat where *galant* and *buffa* elements come to the fore, a combination common in the works of the period in the minor. Unlike C. P. E. Bach, who used the *forma bipartita* in his finales, Johann Christian has more variety—the minuet, the theme and variations, the rondeau—so that his repertory of forms for the finales is that of the "Classical" composers.

For the rest, Johann Christian's output for keyboard contains sonatas and works for four hands and for two harpsichords, a set of *Progressive Lessons*, works in which the old suite forms have been supplanted by those of the sonata. To these are added two genres that became characteristic of keyboard music— the set of variations on popular melodies and the arrangement of popular orchestral pieces for keyboard. Christian has a set of variations on *God Save the King* as well as collections of operatic overtures arranged for keyboard. These last two genres particularly have the dilettante musician in mind, and both became very numerous in the late eighteenth and nineteenth-centuries.

A composer who has only recently emerged as a figure of some significance in the history of German keyboard music of the eighteenth century is Johann Gottfried Müthel (1728–1788), another pupil of J. S. Bach who was also in contact with Telemann and particularly C. P. E. Bach (see Hoffmann-Erbrecht and Salmen). Again, the number of works that have come down are few, of which the

EXAMPLE 41

J. C. Bach: Allegro, from *Sonata* in D (op. 5 ii)—beginning

prime sources are the sets of sonatas and *ariosi* published in 1756 (the *ariosi* are sets of themes and variations). In all, there seem to be nine sonatas, a set of forty-one minuets, a set of etudes in manuscript, two sets of variations, and a handful of organ works, along with seven concertos and a piece for keyboard four hands. Here it is again the sonatas that draw the most attention; the three-movement scheme is standard, but the dimensions of the individual works are expanded so that each sonata is roughly double the length of the normal keyboard sonata of the time. The tendency towards expression that was noted in C. P. E. and Friedemann Bach may also be seen here: the highly characteristic, varied, and elaborately conceived themes full of dynamic contrasts, short rests, and sudden changes in style and register. The scores contain many dynamic markings and call expressly for crescendos. In short, what we have here seems to be music conceived by and large for the piano rather than the harpsichord or clavichord. The same features are to be found in Müthel's variations. Müthel's unusual qualities were noted by Charles Burney, who associated him with C. P. E. Bach but attributes many innovations to him: "I should not hesitate to rank them [his compositions] among the greatest productions of the present age" (*Present State of Music in Germany*, ed. by P. Scholes [London, 1958], II, p. 240). Müthel's individual and rather extreme form of expression sets him far apart from most of his contemporaries.

The influence of the new Italian instrumental music was far less in France than in Germany. The sonata generally was neglected in France. Around 1742, however, there was published a set of six sonatas for harpsichord by the famous violoncellist and composer Jean Barrière, all of which clearly reveal their background in the *sonata da chiesa*, as may be seen from his Sonata in b (Newman, 1, pp. 29–35). When the new type of sonata did make itself felt in France, it did so through German musicians active in Paris from around the middle of the century and afterwards, such as Johann Schobert (d. 1767) and Johann Gottfried Eckhard (1735–1809), both of whom were celebrated as virtuoso performers on the harpsichord. Both published a number of sonatas in the three-movement scheme. But while Schobert (see David and Turrentine) composed for the harpsichord, Eckhard (see Reeser), in several of his publications, particularly that of 1764, drew on the special qualities of the piano, and this set is specifically intended for the Stein piano, since it contains many markings necessarily conditioned by the piano: *rinforzando, mezzo voce, tenuto, legato*, and so forth. Other German musicians active in Paris were Nicolas Joseph Hüllmandel (1756–1823), who had to remove to England in 1790 as the result of his aristocratic associations, which at the time were unpopular, and Johann Friedrich Edelmann (1749–1794) from Strassburg, who was less fortunate than Hüllmandel since he fell victim to the guillotine but who was important in advancing the cause of the piano in France (see Benton).

A French composer of the time whose work well merits some revival is Claude Balbastre, a pupil of Rameau who was well known as a virtuoso performer. (His skill and fame as an organist attracted such attention that on two occasions the church authorities had to forbid him from playing during services.) Along with a number of organ compositions, Balbastre composed clavier works that are to be connected with the progressive tendencies represented by the German circle of composers just mentioned. His *Pièces de clavecin* of 1748 and 1759 show, in their three-movement format, a link to the modern sonata. Here, Balbastre distinguished between two styles: the *style intrigué*, corresponding to the learned style of polyphonic imitation, and the *style galant*, the new italianate manner. Balbastre also composed sets of variations, a set on the *Marseillaise*, and a number of noels, which have already been mentioned, as well as arrangements of popular operatic arias for keyboard. In his publications, Balbastre often made it clear that the piano could be used for the performance of his works; *pour le clavecin ou fortepiano* is the common direction, but the *Marseillaise* variations are expressly for the piano. Balbastre also was involved in efforts to alter the sound of the harpsichord to make it more competitive with the new piano by adding special attachments to it—the *jeu de buffle* and the *jeu de flûtes*.

A most important genre of the latter eighteenth century, which figures prominently in the work of these composers working in Paris, especially Schobert, Eckhard, and Edelmann, is the accompanied keyboard sonata (see Reeser). This is a genre that presents unusual features since it occupies an ambivalent position both with respect to keyboard music as with respect to chamber music. Basically, it is a keyboard sonata with the accompaniment of instruments, usually violin or flute, and sometimes with violoncello or occasionally with such other instruments as a pair of horns added. The keyboard instrument has the most importance, the accompanying instruments often simply doubling the upper or lower voice of the keyboard part so that in some cases they could be omitted without seriously deforming the work. Newman refers to earlier instances of this sort of thing, among which individual works of Bach (trio sonatas), Telemann, and Mattheson are prominent. A famous case is represented by Rameau's *Pièces en concert*. But the genre experienced a rush of popularity in the late eighteenth century; some of the works clearly are reductions of orchestral compositions, while others are originally for the medium, such as Schobert's *Sinfonies*.

As an example, a Sonata in E-flat by Schobert (from his op. 10 [Georgii, *Keyboard Music*, III, pp. 36–43]) may be examined. It was originally for keyboard with the accompaniment of a violin and the possible addition of two horns. Here, a quasi-orchestral quality is evident. In the first movement, the opening theme is motivic and appears in octaves; later, there comes a short phrased *galant* theme over a pedal point; and, still, later, there is a passage with tremoli in the upper treble accompanying a sequential bass figure moving in octaves. The slow movement is a Minuet, and an Allegro in binary form concludes the work. Another example, the first movement of a Sonata in E-flat for keyboard with violin accompaniment by Edelmann, is also at hand (*HAM*, II, 304).

Its optional instrumentation and the possibility of performance on the keyboard instrument alone (which could not be done in all cases) made this genre appealing to the class of amateur musicians to whom it doubtless was primarily directed. Apart from Schobert, Eckhard, Edelmann, and Hüllmandel, we find the genre in the work of de Mondonville, Guillemain, Gossec, Cramer, Clementi, even Haydn and Mozart, and down into the nineteenth century in Dussek, Hummel, and Czerny. But by the 1780's and 1790's, it had outlived its course and had been superseded on the one hand by the real sonata for violin and piano (early instances of which were often identified by the qualification *en duo, concertante,* or *obligé*) or, on the other, by the piano trio.

To draw this together, we have seen that, in the eighteenth century, important—even fundamental—changes in keyboard music took place. And these changes are at their most explicit when viewed in regard to repertory. Organ music experienced a most striking decline so that by the end of the century no important composers paid much attention to it. In harpsichord music, the older forms declined—the toccata, the fugue, the suite—while the sonata emerged as the principal new genre. Early in the century, the sonata appeared in a number of different forms, but, by the end, it had become virtually standardized. This development was carried on mainly in the hands of Italian composers, but the lead then passed to German musicians, and the sons of J. S. Bach are important. C. P. E. Bach and Wilhelm Friedemann Bach imparted a new seriousness of expression into the sonata and into keyboard music generally and were eagerly followed by Müthel. This search for expression caught on, and it was often connected not with the older harpsichord, but with the new instrument, the piano—the instrument most capable of representing the new type of dynamics that went hand in hand with the new expression (see Parrish and Hess). We have seen that, all through the second half of the eighteenth century, keyboard works were composed *pour le clavecin ou fortepiano* or *per il cembalo o forte piano;* but here and there, we find works intended specifically for the piano, commencing as early as 1732 with Giustini (an isolated instance) and including Müthel, Eckhardt, Balbastre, and Johann Christian Bach. The new style of "expressive" keyboard music had found its proper instrumental medium by the end of the century.

CHAPTER SIX

Haydn, Mozart, Beethoven, and Their Contemporaries

We have seen that the eighteenth century presents a varied and somewhat confusing picture of currents and countercurrents of musical forms, types, and styles. Essentially, it was a time of great change, the new replacing the old but with elements of the old not infrequently hanging on and, in turn, influencing the new. The change commenced in Italy, and the new taste or style, as is clear from many publications of the time, was that of the Italian *galant*. Many of the old types of keyboard music declined; the old harpsichord suite was replaced by the new sonata, and, more strikingly, the old tradition of organ music virtually dropped out and was not replaced by anything of comparable stature. But the old contrapuntal art continued its existence, sometimes in connection with sonatas and other works associated with the new style but more often in didactic works of various sorts. Generally speaking, the new leading type of keyboard music, the solo sonata for harpsichord, was developed in Italy. But it was carried on in Germany by Italians working there, such as Platti (and many Italian sonatas appeared in the anthologies of the Nürnberg publisher Haffner [see Hoffmann-Erbrecht]), as well as by native German composers among whom the sons of Bach occupied a leading position.

It has been said that to be a genius is the same as being the right man at the right place at the right time. In the musical scene presented by the mid-eighteenth century, this would involve a man who could take all the various traditions, the various forms and types, and, by a judicious combining of the many elements, selecting this and rejecting that, would be able to give a solid basis for the new instrumental music as the vehicle for serious musical expression. And fate indeed put such a man on the scene at this critical time—Franz Joseph Haydn (1732–1809).

Haydn's life story is too well known to require detailed retelling here: his engagement to the choir of St. Stephen's cathedral in Vienna, his years

189

of apprenticeship, the long years at the Esterhazy's, and his final years as an international celebrity and the concerts in Vienna and London. Of particular significance is the long association with the court of the Esterhazy family that commenced in 1761 and lasted until his death, although his services were not drawn upon in the years 1790 to 1795. After 1766, the Esterhazy family spent the long winters not in Vienna, but in their country residence, Esterhaza. As a result, Haydn was not in Vienna during those years, but out in the country; and he began to feel isolated, cut off from what was going on in that great musical center. At the same time, although his duties were great, he was in an excellent position to experiment since the performing groups—the instrumentalists, the singers, and the chorus—were all under his direct supervision and control. And he did indeed experiment; he was, as he put it, "forced to become original." The results of his experimentation involved basically the endowment of the *galant* forms of instrumental music with serious aspects.

It must be admitted that keyboard works play a relatively minor role in Haydn's total output and artistic development;[1] he concentrated rather on the string quartet and the symphony, although he did compose some notable operas and religious compositions of various sorts. Among the keyboard works, the solo piano sonatas, of which there are forty-nine, constitute the most important group, and our discussion will of necessity center around them. They can best be treated by various chronological periods in the composer's creative life, and although several such periodizations have been worked out and employed, here we can conveniently use three: the early period (1750–1767), a middle period (1768–1780), and a late phase (from 1780, but particularly after 1783).

Into the first group of sonatas, composed during Haydn's time in Vienna following his dismissal from St. Stephen's and then during the short period of employment at Lukavec, fall the first nineteen sonatas (see Larsen). These works present a uniform character for the most part. Basically, they are closely related to the suite or divertimento in its Viennese form; Sonatas Nos. 1 and 2 even bear the designation "partita." Most of them consist of three movements (Nos. 6 and 8 have four), all in the same key; one of these movements, generally the second or last, is a Minuet and Trio. The light divertimento (*galant*) character is plainly evident; these sonatas are small, simple, and unpretentious compositions, a kind of keyboard *Hausmusik*. The first and last movements show something of the sonata principle. They are cast in the so-called "rounded binary" form that derives from the suite dance—‖:*a*:‖ ‖:*ba*:‖—with a modulation to the dominant at the end of the first part and, after some excursions in the *b* part, a

---

[1] The bibliographical situation of Haydn still leaves much to be desired. But some improvements in this have been made, beginning with Larsen's detailed source study and continuing with the thematic catalogue by Hoboken and now the gradual appearance of a new collected edition under Larsen's editorship. As yet, there are no comprehensive studies of Haydn's keyboard works; articles are by Abert, Parrish, Radcliffe and Vignal. In the following discussion, the dates given are of composition.

return to the tonic key. There is no set number nor contrast of themes, nor is there any systematic development of themes; yet, the general outline of the form is the same as what later was to take on such paramount importance. The slow movements show the cantabile style—accompanied melody. The over-all simplicity may be seen in the simple figuration patterns frequently employed in the accompaniments; common here are the smooth broken triads of the so-called "Alberti bass." From this, it is clear that Haydn's piano sonatas have the same background as his symphonies and string quartets: the Viennese *galant* music of the time.

The next group of sonatas were composed in the years 1770–1780, a period in which Haydn engaged in much experimentation. The effects of his isolation, already mentioned, were beginning to tell on him, and we find him greatly stimulated by the highly expressive style employed by C. P. E. Bach, whose influence Haydn readily acknowledged (see Schmid). Haydn's experimentations were directed towards the establishment of a serious style for the new forms of instrumental music that hitherto had had only *galant* connotations. In the early stages of this preoccupation, we find Haydn producing some violently exaggerated works among, for instance, the quartets of op. 17 and op. 20, and the Symphonies in f (No. 35a or 49, *La Passione*) and in e (No. 44, *Trauersymphonie*), and others. One indication of this new passionate style is the use of minor keys.

In the Sonatas Nos. 20–39 we find works that reveal the same attitude. Among the works to be mentioned in this connection are the Sonatas in c (No. 20) of 1771, b (No. 32) of around 1775, e (No. 34) of 1778, and c-sharp (No. 36) of around 1780. Here, the passionate quality of the minor is fully exploited by Haydn; the external form remains the same as before, but the music itself strives for something more ambitious, extended, and incorporating a greater degree of intensity.

Most of the sonatas in the group, however, lack this violent passionate character associated particularly with the minor keys. Yet, while being essentially a continuation of Haydn's earlier kind of sonata, they do at the same time show unusual features. We note a preoccupation with the problem of the proper over all form for a piano sonata; in the Sonata in D (No. 24) of 1773, the Adagio goes without a break into the finale, while the Sonata in A (No. 30) eliminates the breaks between movements. Also to be remarked are the contrapuntal or learned traits in some of the minuets, for example, in the Sonata in E-flat (No. 25) of 1773, in which the minuet is canonic, and the Sonata in A (No. 26) of 1773, in which it is *al rovescio* (the second half is the retrograde version of the first).

As an example of the unusual combinations and varieties that appear in this group of sonatas, let us briefly consider one of them, the Sonata in c (No. 20) of 1771, a work which shows the connotations associated with the minor. It is in three movements—as indeed are the great majority of Haydn's piano sonatas—a

Moderato in 4/4 time, an Andante con moto in A-flat in 3/4 time, and a final Allegro, again in 3/4 time. The first and last movements are cast according to the sonata principle; the Andante is an aria-like piece in rounded binary form. It is the first movement that arouses the most interest and attention, for it is here that the characteristics given to the minor key are most evident. The principal theme is in two regular periods but is compounded of short motives and is rhythmically elaborate, with syncopations and unusual accentuations; also the theme itself, in thirds, is shifted from the right hand to the left, introducing a measure of contrapuntal interest. The bridge passage provides a sharp contrast and features extensive dynamic markings. There is a short candenza-like passage before the subordinate theme, which works with broken chords in dotted rhythmic patterns. The closing theme is in straight *galant* style, consisting of scale fragments over a rapid broken-chord accompaniment. Already we see the balance and contrast between the playing off against one another of different elements, themes with different associations, that is so characteristic of late eighteenth-century instrumental music. These elements are employed in the development section, which concentrates on the principal and closing themes and employs a great deal of figuration to reach a great crescendo before the section ends with a reference to the bridge theme. In the recapitulation, the principal theme and the bridge are shortened, but otherwise the recapitulation presents the exposition unchanged, even retaining the cadenza passage. The remaining movements are less problematical. The Andante consists of a cantabile melody over a slow, evenly moving bass; in the contrasting subordinate section, we find a long passage using expressive syncopations. The finale, again using the sonata principle, is in the character of a *perpetuum mobile*, the whole being pervaded by a single rhythmic pattern.

EXAMPLE 42

HAYDN: Allegro moderato, from *Sonata* in c (No. 20)—beginning

The third group of Haydn's piano sonatas embraces Nos. 40–52, written from 1780 to 1794 (see Strunk). The mature style, the Classical style, was established by Haydn in the string quartets of op. 33 (1783) and subsequently extended to other categories of musical composition, notably the symphony but also the piano sonata. In this Classical style, that intensely passionate and extreme kind of expression encountered in works of the previous group gives way to something more moderate in which a judicious balance between the various affections and the different styles, forms, and characters of the individual movements is sought.

Only a few of Haydn's piano sonatas reflect this. This is in part due to the fact that he composed no sonatas at all after 1794, but it is also due to the didactic quality of many sonatas, a quality that remained associated with the category from then on. Nevertheless, there are some outstanding works: the Sonata in E-flat (No. 49) of 1789–1790 composed for Marianne von Genzinger, with its strict thematic development in the first movement, and the Sonatas in D (No. 51) and E-flat (No. 52), all of which are in no way inferior to the best quartets and symphonies. (For the finale of the Sonata in D, see Georgii, *400 Years*, pp. 84–5.)

Particularly impressive is the last sonata, in E-flat (No. 52), a "big" work in three movements, which emphasizes virtuoso elements with something of the spirit that Beethoven was later to bring to the piano sonata. The first movement is an Allegro in sonata form, the second an Adagio in E (both the tempo designation and the key relationship are most unusual in Haydn), and the work concludes with a Presto, again in sonata form. It is the first movement that indicates the general "tone" of the work; the principal theme is chordal and in dotted rhythm, the figuration is rhythmically propelled, the full sound is achieved by using the extremes of the keyboard range, there are rapid scale passages in thirds, and there is broken-chord figuration. There is economy in the use of thematic material; the principal theme is used for the bridge passage and for the closing theme. Worthy of note is the passage immediately before the closing theme. There is a diminuendo with descending octaves in the bass and a hushed, repeated thirty-second note figuration over it; then, there is a sharp ascending scale run that leads to the closing theme (which is, as stated, the principal theme). Figuration is important in the development. The movement, as is customary with "big" movements, has a coda.

The Adagio, in three-part form, presents a simple theme in rounded binary form that is greatly embellished in typical *galant* fashion by many scale runs, grace notes, and rapidly repeated notes. Its unusual character emanates from the elaboration of the harmonies; the second part of the principal section ventures as far as G and C. The middle section of the movement, in e, has something of the air of a development, emphasizing figuration and seizing on the dotted rhythm of the principal section theme.

The last movement is a virtuoso piece. The theme itself outlines the tonic and dominant triads accompanied by a sustained pedal point in the bass, a combination suggesting folk dances with a drone bass (see also Haydn's Symphony No. 104 in D, the last movement). Then come fast sixteenth notes over a triadic "leaping" bass. The bridge is slower, a chromatically moving, syncopated line over a moving bass. Sudden full chords and much rhythmic drive highlight the movement, along with an impressive full stop and a dominant seventh chord, a brief Adagio in the style of a cadenza, following which comes the recapitulation.

This is clearly an important composition in which the essentials of the Classical style are realized; it is a serious work that emphasizes the principle of thematic development and exploits the possibilities of its medium. It is fully deserving of a place beside Haydn's late great symphonies and quartets. In short, we see that, through Haydn, the category of the piano sonata had been brought to a level where it may serve to provide the medium for serious works of musical art comparable to what was expected of symphonies and chamber music for strings; the *galant* character long associated with the category had been overcome.

Haydn's keyboard music includes a number of pieces in other genres. The other large form in which he worked is the theme and variations, represented by a

EXAMPLE 43

Haydn: Allegro, from *Sonata* in E-flat (No. 52)—beginning

number of works of which the most important are the two ariettes with variations in A and E-flat of 1771 and 1774, respectively, and a *Tema con variazioni* in C of 1790; but the outstanding work of this kind is the expressive set of Variations in f of 1793 in which the march-like theme is followed by a trio; after it come two variations on each and then a coda. Apart from some dances and smaller pieces, the only other significant piano works of Haydn are the Capriccio in G published in 1788 or 1789, based on a popular German song, and the Fantasia in C of 1789 with its tenuto effects in the bass. For piano duet, there are but three works, two partitas or divertimenti and a sonata.

When we turn to Wolfgang Amadeus Mozart (1756–1791), we find something different from Haydn, indeed in many respects the exact opposite. Where Haydn developed late, Mozart developed early; while Haydn's international reputation came about late in his life, Mozart became a celebrity as a child prodigy; and while Haydn's professional life was secure due to this tenure with the Esterhazy family, Mozart never had a satisfactory position, and his attempt to survive as a "freelance" artist was unsuccessful.

Alfred Einstein rightly emphasizes the wandering quality of the young Mozart's life; there were many concert tours undertaken at the instigation of his father, Leopold, himself a solid and well-known professional musician. At the age of seven, we find Mozart on a journey to Munich, Paris, and London (1762–1766); shortly thereafter, he went to Vienna (1767–1768); then there were two journeys to Italy (1769–1771 and 1771–1773); and, finally, he took his last journey to Munich, Augsburg, Mannheim, and ultimately to Paris at the age of nineteen (1777–1779), accompanied by his mother who died during the stay in Paris. Thereafter came the abhorrent duties at the Salzburg court and cathedral and the drastic decision of 1781 to break off altogether and remove to Vienna, the musical capital of the world—a move against the wishes of Leopold.

In Vienna Mozart made his ill-fated attempt to live from the fruits of his art —playing, composing, and teaching. For a while, indeed, it looked as if he might succeed, particularly in 1782 and 1783 when he gave several concerts, or academies, as they were called at the time. It must be said, however, that Mozart himself unavoidably was somewhat to blame for his lack of success and his hard lot, since he felt conscious of his own genius and incomparable superiority to most of his colleagues; and his attitude and conduct were such as to make relations with associates and potential employers difficult. Many references could be cited, of which only a few need be indicated here. A letter from Leopold (February 16, 1778) refers to his son's "bantering tone" and "undue familiarity," along with his tendency toward the disputatious. A letter from Melchoir Grimm, with whom Mozart was in contact while in Paris, to Leopold refers to Mozart as "too sincere, too little concerned with the means by which one may become successful" and states that he would be better off with half as much talent and twice as much tact. Mozart's own letters are full of highly incisive critical comments on other musicians, as doubtless was also his conversation. Some years later, Beethoven was able to get away with such behavior; but in this respect—as also in his musical composition—Mozart was ahead of his time, and he paid a heavy price. Thus his very genius brought about his extreme personal misfortunes and his ultimate downfall.

Although many of his contemporaries were well aware of his great qualities, some even going to the point of blocking his efforts to secure a regular appointment in Vienna, there was one who worked hard, if unsuccessfully, on his behalf—Haydn. In 1785, upon receipt of the six quartets that Mozart had dedicated to him, Haydn wrote to Leopold: "I tell you before God and as an honest man that your son is the greatest composer I know..." Two years later, he wrote to the directors of the Prague opera expressing his distress that Mozart had been unable to get a regular appointment and urging Prague to offer him one.

Whether Mozart received such an offer from Prague or elsewhere is not known; he certainly did not accept any, and he is known to have had a curious loyalty to Vienna. In any case, his last years were full of growing poverty, and from 1787 he complained of "melancholy attacks." It is this background that explains why the story surrounding the commission for and composition of the *Requiem* has provoked so much romantic legend. The irony is that, somewhat like Béla Bartók in our own time, shortly after his death he was accorded the wide-spread recognition that had so long been his due.

In spite of the fact that Mozart was an eminent pianist, works for piano solo do not assume anything like a central position in his total compositional *oeuvre*.[1] As concert pieces for piano, the concertos take the foremost position; the piano sonata was regarded either as a teaching piece written for pupils or as a piece of domestic music, *Hausmusik*, for entertainment at home, or was intended for use on the early concert tours; and the same applies to the sets of variations for piano and the other, shorter pieces. There are some exceptions, particularly among the piano sonatas, but these remain unusual compositions. In the piano sonatas, therefore, we only infrequently come across works on the same scale as those that we find in, for instance, the chamber music for strings, the piano concertos, the later operas, and the symphonies.

The twenty-one sonatas, which form the bulk of his contribution to the literature of solo piano music, fall into three chronological groups, as follows:

[1] Apart from the standard accounts of Abert and Einstein, see Dennerlein, who has attempted to revise the chronology of Mozart's piano works (see also Newman). The standard reference is Köchel's thematic catalogue, as revised by Einstein or in the new sixth edition; in this book, the Einstein numbers are given with Köchel's original numbers in brackets. Detailed stylistic discussions of individual works are by Wyzewa and St. Foix; a good survey of the piano music is by King; on the sonatas see Jöhde, Marks, and Merian; see also Badura-Skoda, Broder, Brunner, Gerstenberg, and Russell.

I. 1774–1775
  C (K. 189d [279])
  F (K. 189e [280])
  B-flat (K. 189f [281])
  E-flat (K. 189g [282])
  G (K. 189h [283])
  g (K. 189i [312]; first movement only; date uncertain
  D (K. 205b [284])

II. 1777–1778—Mannheim and Paris
  F (K. 547a, Anh. 135, Anh. 138a).
  C (K. 284b [309])
  D (K. 284c [311])
  a (K. 300d [310])
  C (K. 300h [330])
  A (K. 300i [331])
  F (K. 300k [332])
  B-flat (K. 315c [333])

III. 1780–1788—Vienna
  c (K. 457); published with the Fantasia in c (475), but the sonata itself may be
    earlier
  C (K. 545)
  B-flat (K. 570)
  D (K. 576)
  F (K. 533, 494)
  B-flat (K. 498a, Anh. 136); authenticity doubtful.

Surveying Mozart's sonatas as a whole, there is less of a "development" to be observed than as there was in the case of Haydn. With few exceptions, the "small" concept of the sonata is maintained all the way through; there are three movements of which either the middle or the last is a minuet, while the first movement reveals some application of the sonata principle. The general character, therefore, remains similar to Haydn's early sonatas, except that Mozart was more italianate and took over the *buffa* style of the sinfonia, while Haydn, as we have seen, remained true to the character of the Viennese diverti mento and suite. Mozart, unlike Haydn, made but few excursions into the more ambitious realm of passionate expression or the incorporation of virtuoso elements; rather, he remained true to the intimate and domestic type of sonata.

In the first group of sonatas, evidently planned as a set of six, composed in 1774 and 1775, we find the three-movement form. Typical is the Sonata in G (K. 189h [283]), with its initial Allegro in sonata form and a typical "singing Allegro" cantabile main theme, a simple Andante in G, and a *buffa* finale also in sonata form, with its free development section. Three works in the group show unusual traits. The Sonata in B-flat (K. 189f [281]) has a finale of surprising elaboration, incorporating unusual dynamic markings and quasi-improvisational

cadenza-like passages; the Sonata in E-flat (K. 189g [282]) has an unusual succession of movements—Adagio, then two minuets, of which the second is
intended as a trio, and a concluding Allegro in sonata form; and the first movement of the sonata in g (K. 189i [312]) has an unusually strong principal theme not
unrelated to other large works of Mozart in the same key. On a larger scale is the
Sonata in D (K. 205b [284]), the so-called *Dürnitz Sonata*, whose point of departure seems to come from orchestral music, particularly French. This is seen
most clearly in the first movement, which has a *unisono* opening theme, followed
by a sort of Mannheim crescendo; the slow movement is, most exceptionally, a
rondeau en polonaise, and the finale is a set of variations, both of which confirm the
relation to France.

In the next group of sonatas, those written in Mannheim and Paris in 1777
and 1778, the external form remains the same, and generally the *galant* character
is also maintained. This is especially true of the Sonatas in F (K. 300k [332]), see
Mason) and B-flat (K. 315c [333]); in the latter, the finale is cast in the so-called
hybrid sonata-rondo form, used so much by Haydn in his later works, in which
the second episode of the rondo is transformed into a development section. On a
larger scale than either of these is the Sonata in D (K. 284c [311]), which features
extensive thematic development in the first movement; the work as a whole
involves a "bigness" of conception that relates it to the serious symphonic
composition of the time. In this connection, the key, D, is not without signi-

EXAMPLE 44

Mozart: Allegro, from *Sonata* in D (K. 205b [284])—beginning

ficance, since it, as the key of trumpets of the time, is prominent in the more ambitious and elaborate symphonies of the period. Another large sonata in this group is the one in C (K. 284b [309]).

Two sonatas depart in different ways from what is usual in Mozart. One is the Sonata in a (K. 300d [310]), Mozart's first sonata in the minor; it is surprisingly powerful with its "tragic" principal theme in the first movement and dis-consolate theme in the rondo finale. The other is a most unusual and deservedly popular work, the Sonata in A (K. 300i [331]), which has its first movement in theme and variations form and the celebrated *Turkish Rondo* as the finale.

The last group of Mozart's piano sonatas reveal, as already indicated, a perpetuation of the same interpretation of the genre. Only one sonata breaks with the three-movement over-all structure, the Sonata in B-flat (K. 498a), and this is a work of doubtful authenticity. Typical in all respects is the famous Sonata in C (K. 545) in which the didactic intent is indicated by Mozart's own designation of the work as a "little sonata for beginners"; there is a "singing Allegro" of the main theme of the first movement over an Alberti bass, a cantabile slow move-ment, and the *galant* rondo. The larger "symphonic" type of sonata may be seen again in the Sonata in D (K. 576).

In this group of sonatas is a most unusual composition, one which requires special discussion—the Fantasia and Sonata in c (K. 475 and 457 respectively). Originally conceived as two independent works, Mozart combined them for publication in 1785, thus forming his largest composition for piano solo. The fantasia, which precedes the sonata, is a continuation of the old form from the Baroque period and has similar works by C. P. E. Bach as its most immediate predecessors. All the aspects associated by C. P. E. Bach with the form are pre-sent in the large composition, which fully exploits the *pathétique* character of c minor. The fantasia is divided into six sections that contrast sharply with one another in character. The first phrase, triadic and in octaves, is followed by a phrase consisting of two simple cadences; then, the triadic phrase is stated canta-bile over an Alberti bass, venturing later into passages involving considerable virtuosity—motivic work and fast figuration; a final section of the fantasia recalls the thematic material of the beginning.

The sonata itself is in three movements—an Allegro, an Adagio, and a concluding Allegro. The extreme expression of the fantasia is carried over into the sonata. There is a triadic principal theme in the first movement in octaves and *fortissimo* with an agitated figurative response, a chromatic bridge passage, a cantabile subordinate theme, and a climatic closing section, again emphasizing figuration. The Adagio is cantabile but contains sections featuring cadenza-like fantasia passages, abounding in scale runs and arpeggios. Last, there is a dis-consolate and highly irregular rondo that also has a fantasia section near the end. This clearly is Mozart's largest composition in the sonata genre; it is a most remarkable work and one that made a profound impression on Beethoven.

Outstanding in a different way is the late Sonata in B-flat (K. 570), composed in 1789 (and often regarded as a sonata for violin and piano, but the violin part is not by Mozart). This work may be viewed as the culmination and refinement of the more typical *galant* sonata usually associated with Mozart. It is cast in three movements: an Allegro in sonata form, an Adagio in E-flat, and a concluding Allegretto in an unusual sort of rondo form. There are several features to be noted. The first movement opens with a placidly lyric principal theme, then brings in the driving figuration of the transition and the secondary theme that is first stated in contrapuntal combination with the principal theme. The strict develop-

EXAMPLE 45

Mozart: Allegro, from *Sonata* in c (K. 457)—beginning

ment has sudden excursions into the minor and a remarkable succession of keys leading from D-flat to G. The Adagio has two alternating sections of contrasting character, both in rounded binary form; the first is a solemn melody presented in chords (something like what Beethoven was later to do in his "Lebewohl Sonata"), and the second is agitated, has a short, dotted figure in thirds over repeated notes, and octave leaps in the bass. The third movement is an unusual sort of rondo. The repetition of the first episode is suppressed, while the themes from both episodes dominate the long coda; the principal theme draws attention; it is a chromatic melody with syncopations that give it a "breathless" quality, presented over a broken-chord pattern in the bass.

Instead of the dramatic intensity of the Fantasia and Sonata in c (K. 457, K. 475), we find here a work still primarily oriented to the *galant* but bringing in a number of elaborations and making those sudden turns to the minor, to a more sombre expression. All in all, this sonata can take its place beside those other great late works of Mozart with which it has certain affinities: the Piano Concerto in B-flat (K. 595), the Clarinet Concerto (K. 622), and the Quintet for Clarinet and Strings (K. 581).

Another category of piano compositions cultivated by Mozart throughout his career was the theme and variations, of which there are some fifteen sets (see Mies and Fischer). The earliest date from his concert tour, made in 1766; then comes the group composed in Paris during his last tour in 1778, while others were composed in Salzburg and Vienna, the last of them dating from 1791, the final year of his life.

The themes used by Mozart for these variations are, with few exceptions, popular melodies of the time. Most come from arias, songs, choruses, and other numbers from operas or plays with music by prominent and popular composers of the time: Salieri, Grétry, Paisiello, Sarti, Gluck, and a song from Beaumarchais' *Le Barbier de Seville*; others come from less distinguished but perhaps even more popular works, such as the vaudeville by Dezède called *Julie* and the farce put on under the sponsorship of Emmanuel Schickaneder, *Der dumme Gärtner aus dem Gebirge, oder die zween Anton* with music by Benedikt Schack and Franz Gerl. Others come from songs, such as the famous *Ah vous dirais-je*, or from dances (minuets by Fischer and Duport).

Two of these appeared as improvisations in Mozart's concert held on March 23, 1782: the set of five variations on *Salve tu Domine* (K. 416 [398]), a chorus from Paisiello's *I filosofi immaginari*, and the set of ten on *Unser dummer Pöbel meint* (K. 455) from Gluck's *Der Pilger von Mekka* (originally called *Le rencontre imprévue*). With these works, then, Mozart was attempting to reach a large audience; and, in this, he did attain some success since many of the variations were published during his lifetime (in contrast to the piano sonatas and other works), a distinction not accorded to many of his other more ambitious and important compositions.

In keeping with this aim, Mozart made these works, for the most part, rather simple, affecting a "popular" character. The theme is first stated, and there then follows a series of variations, contrasting in character from one another, that embellish the theme in various ways without obscuring it. There are several standard types of variations found in these sets: those breaking the theme down into figuration, either sixteenth notes or triplets or broken octaves and sometimes involving considerable technical difficulties in execution; those treating the theme in dotted rhythms; those in the tradition of the French *pièces croisées*, keeping a figuration pattern in the middle with the right hand while the left leaps back and forth over it from treble to bass with short scale fragments or individual notes; and those accompanying the theme by a long trill. Most of the sets contain an "innocent" and highly embellished Adagio along with an expressive chromatic and frequently syncopated slowly moving *minore*. In the variations on *Je suis Lindor* (K. 299a [354]), there is a final variation presenting the theme as a minuet. Several of the sets have codas that recapitulate, at least in part, the theme in its original form: the variations on *Je suis Lindor*, *La belle française* (K. 300f [353]), *Lison dormait* (K. 315d [264]), *Unser dummer Pöbel meint*, the *Allegretto* (K. 500) and the minuet of Duport (K. 573). Unusual is the last set of variations, on *Ein Weib ist das herrlichste Ding* (K. 613). Here, in the original, the song had an instrumental introduction that Mozart kept intact, presenting it with some alteration before each variation; in the last variation, the order is reversed, and in the coda the two are combined contrapuntally.

Throughout, there is an effort to make the last variation a suitable finale. It is usually fast and brilliant, set off by being immediately preceded by an Adagio. In many of the late sets, however, it is distinguished even more by the incorporation of elements from the fantasia—arpeggios, "solos" after the fashion of the affective operatic recitative, and sudden changes of style, texture, and harmony. These features may be found at the end of the variations on *Je suis Lindor*, the Duport minuet, and *Ein Weib das ist das herrlichste Ding*. But there are others that even go to the extent of having passages marked "cadenza": the sets on *Lison dormait*, on Paisiello's *Salve tu Domine* and Gluck's *Unser dummer Pöbel meint*.

Such passages generally appear in the final variation of the set, thus making it more elaborate than the others; often, this last variation is divided into several distinct sections that contrast sharply with one another. The outstanding examples are in the Paisiello and Gluck variations just mentioned.

A remarkable group of Mozart's keyboard works, and one that is generally neglected, are the compositions written under the influence of Baroque music, particularly that of the keyboard works of Bach and Handel. Mozart came into contact with such works during the early years of his residence in Vienna when he frequented the salons held by Baron Gottfried van Swieten. These works, most of which date from 1782, comprise several large fantasias: one in d (K. 385g

[397]), another in c, originally written for piano and violin (385f [396]), and the large Fantasia and Fugue in C (K. 383a [394]). These works are in the tradition of German Baroque organ music. With the exception of the one in c, which shows something approaching sonata form, these fantasias are in sectional form, contrasting sharply with one another in texture, style, key, and thematic material; they show the features typical of the toccata style—arpeggios, full chords rapidly alternating with one another, sudden changes in harmony, and general style. The Fantasia in C (K. 383a [394]) concludes with an impressive three-voice fugue. Similar to these are later works composed for mechanical organ especially the Adagio and Allegro in f of 1790 (K. 594) and the Fantasia in f of 1791 (K. 608), both of which can be successfully performed on an organ. A number of independent fugues for piano or two pianos were also composed in 1782.

Also of considerable interest is Mozart's interpretation of the old Baroque keyboard (harpsichord) suite (K. 385i [399]), which also dates from 1782. It apparently was intended to be a full suite, but Mozart did not complete the work; what is extant is an overture, an allemande, a courante, and the beginning of a saraband. The Baroque unity of key, however, is not maintained; the overture moves from C to G, the allemande is in c, the courante in E-flat, and the saraband in G. Presumably, Mozart planned to lead the tonality back to the original C in the two (or more) following movements. The overture is very much in the style of the old French overture; full chords alternate with a charactristic vigorous rhythmic figure, and there are many sudden "affective" changes in harmony. This overture is followed by a rapid, fugal Allegro whose rapid subject emphasizes repeated notes and figuration; there is a countersubject and even stretto, the whole section being characterized by driving rhythms. Baroque traits are also present in the two dance movements. Missing, however, is the element of variation or cyclic form, that also characterized many Baroque keyboard suites (those called "partitas").

For the rest, Mozart's output of keyboard music contains many individual dances of various kinds and other miscellaneous pieces. His earliest works were minuets composed on the same bass, presumably under the guidance of his father. Outstanding among these miscellaneous works, however, is the Rondo in a of 1787 (K. 511). Here, the rondo form is maintained, except that the repetition of the first episode is missing. What is remarkable, however, is that this is no usual rondo; it is a melancholy Andante featuring an extremely expressive chromatic cantabile melody with a subtle alternation between major and minor, with episodes that provide some measure of contrast but not to the extent that the general character of the piece is ever lost sight of. Another expressive work is the Adagio in b (K. 540) of 1788 (Georgii, *400 Years*, pp. 86–9).

For piano duet, there are chiefly sonatas in which the influence of orchestral music is dominant. This is clear not only from the three-movement form (that of the operatic sinfonia), but more especially from the character of the themes, the use of dynamic contrasts, of tremolo figuration, of octave doubling, and so forth; the relation between the two parts is often concerto-like. While some of this may be seen in the very early Sonata in C (K. 19d) of 1765, which owes much to Johann Christian Bach who preceded Mozart in this form, it is wholly present in two works composed in Salzburg, the Sonata in D (K. 123a [381]) of 1772 and the Sonata in B-flat (K. 186c [358]) of 1774. The first of these commences with a strong D chord much like the *premier coup d'archet* so common in French orchestral music of the time and continues with a real Mannheim crescendo, while the Sonata in B-flat features a typically orchestral octave passage at its very beginning. Of the two other completed sonatas for piano duet, both composed in Vienna, the Sonata in F (K. 497) of 1786 (the largest of all Mozart's works in this genre) is a serious work pervaded with chromaticism; its first movement is preceded by a slow introduction. The other, in C (K. 521) of 1787, is completely *galant* and has much concerto-like writing. Another sonata, in G (K. 497a [357]), supposedly composed around this time, is incomplete and possibly spurious. There is also a theme and five variations for piano duet in G (K. 375a [448]) composed in Vienna in 1786 and much like the variations for piano solo. Finally, for two pianos, there is the large Sonata in D (K. 501) of 1781, another quasi-orchestral work in the spirit of a *buffa* sinfonia, and the Fugue in c (K. 426) of 1783, one of Mozart's "Baroque" compositions, complete with a chromatic subject featuring the downward leap of a seventh, a countersubject, inversion, stretto, and motivic breaking down of the subject.

We have seen that, in the latter half of the eighteenth century, keyboard music did not occupy anything like the major part of a composer's attention. This is quantitative as well as qualitative; that is to say, keyboard works not only occupied a small part of a composer's compositional work, but also are most often minor works, frequently in the conventional *galant* taste. An important case in point—and a highly pertinent one—is Mozart, who was celebrated in his day as a piano virtuoso; yet, he wrote relatively few major works for piano by itself, since, as has been pointed out, the concerto was the main vehicle for approaching the concert-going public. For this reason, particular importance must be attached to the varied career of Muzio Clementi (1752–1832) who was active not only as a pianist and composer, but also as theorist, impresario, conductor, music publisher, and instrument builder and who enjoyed a world-wide reputation. A famous event was his "contest" with Mozart at the Imperial Court in Vienna on December 24, 1781, which apparently showed the two to be more or less evenly matched, a circumstance that may help explain the critical abuse of Clementi observed in Mozart's letters.

The problems involved in any attempt to study Clementi are enormous, since there are no comprehensive thematic listings of his works, to say nothing of a collected edition, and his many compositions have come down in numerous publications, the same pieces not infrequently being assigned different opus numbers in different editions, some early works being published much later than their actual composition, while still other compositions are arrangements for piano of symphonies and concertos.[1] In spite of all this, it is clear that Clementi is a major figure in the history of piano music; most important are his piano sonatas, whose number Newman sets at seventy-nine; but there are many other works, particularly didactic in nature, of which the most famous are the *Gradus ad Parnassum* in four volumes that appeared between 1817 and 1824. (This should not be judged from the drastic abridgment of Tausig and von Bülow of 1865). There are also a large number of sonatinas. Of lesser significance are numerous small compositions of all sorts—dances, sets of variations on popular melodies, and so on. Among the dances are a group of *monferrinas*, Italian country dances from Piedmont, that enjoyed a certain vogue in early nineteenth-century England (see *HMS*, VIII, s. 5, b. 4).

Clementi composed sonatas beginning in the early 1770's and continued to do so throughout his career as a composer, except for a fifteen-year period between 1804 and 1820. In 1785, he began publishing sets of his own sonatas, commencing with a set of six (op. 13). Although two formal plans appear in these works, the old two-movement scheme and the newer three-movement scheme, it seems that the latter was regarded by him in later years as standard for the genre since in 1804, when the publication of his complete works was undertaken, he added a third movement to each of the two-movement works of op. 2. The four-movement plan seldom appears. But there is little of the old *galant* "little" sonata here; Clementi, like Müthel, C. P. E. Bach, Haydn, and Mozart in their later works, regarded the sonata as a large form capable of the most serious expression. The formal types common to late eighteenth-century instrumental music are fully exploited in Clementi's sonatas. The strong opening Allegro movement is in sonata form, and uses highly motivic themes not infrequently unified by the expedient of deriving the secondary thematic material from the principal theme; the slow movement is lyrical; and the brilliant finale is in sonata or rondo form. What distinguishes Clementi's sonatas, however, is the virtuoso employment of the piano coupled with the intense quality of the expression, two qualities associated particularly with Beethoven. Clementi's writing for the piano, in short, is "big"; the texture is thicker, the chords more sonorous, the quantity of sound considerably greater than can be found in the piano writing of Haydn, Mozart, or C. P. E. Bach.

Among individual sonatas that can be mentioned by way of illustration are two dramatically expressive works in minor keys, both of which are characterized

---

[1] Standard studies are by Unger and Paribene, more recently by Allorto; but see also Newman, who gives a comprehensive comparative chart of Clementi's sonatas and the various opus numbers used in the different editions and reference works; Newman's numbers will be used here; see also Barford and Stauch.

by slow introductions: the Sonatas in g (op. 34 ii), published around 1795, and b (op. 40 ii), published around 1801. The first is a particularly large composition, showing in its first movement the characteristically motivic principal theme, the relation between principal and subordinate themes, and the dynamic effects in the development; there is a cantabile slow movement and a finale in sonata form distinguished by the prominence of contrapuntal writing (Largo and Allegro in *HMS*, VIII, s. 5, b. 2). Still other sonatas that might be mentioned here are the Sonata in B-flat (op. 41 ii or 47 ii), the so-called *Magic Flute Sonata* since the main theme of its first movement is like that in the overture to Mozart's opera (this is the sonata played by Clementi during the famous contest with Mozart); the dramatic Sonata in f (op. 13 vi or 14 iii) published in 1785, with its suggestion, in the finale, of Beethoven's *Eroica-Prometheus* theme (see Ringer); and the large Sonata in d and D (op. 40 iii) published around 1801–1802, with the slow introduction to the first movement and the canonic second episode in the rondo. (Another example of canon in Clementi readily available is the Adagio of the late Sonata in A [op. 50 i] in the middle section [see Georgii, *400 Years*, pp. 81–3].) Another sonata that might be mentioned is the lyrical Sonata in f-sharp (op. 25 v or op. 26 ii), published around 1791, or the lone really programmatic Sonata in g (op. 50 iii), published in 1821 with the title *Didone abbandonata* and the description *scena tragica*, in which the virtuoso impulse is less prominent than in the usual Clementi sonata.

Three other composers who should be brought in here remained by and large true to the eighteenth-century conception of the piano sonata: the Viennese Carl Ditters von Dittersdorf (1739–1799) who wrote only two very *galant* piano sonatas (for his Sonata in A, see Newman, 8, pp. 75–89); the Bohemian Johann Baptist Wanhal (1739–1813) who also remained wholly in the *galant* vein (see Dewitz); Johann Friedrich Reichardt (1752–1814) of the Berlin School (see Dennerlein, Helm, and Stilz), who maintained in his earlier works the old idea of the unity of affection within a single movement, but whose later sonatas composed around 1809 show a preoccupation with thematic development and a more personal and intense kind of expression (see the Sonata in f; Newman, 11, pp. 124–39); and Joseph Wölfl (1773–1812), a virtuoso celebrated for his rivalry with Beethoven who composed a large number of sonatas (see Baum), the total being in the neighborhood of sixty, the majority of which are either typically small and *galant* or outspokenly virtuoso display pieces (for a more serious work, see the *Sonata precedée d'une introduction et fugue* in c, op. 9 [Newman, 9, pp. 90–113], a work that doubtless owes its inception in large measure to Mozart).

Ludwig van Beethoven (1770–1827) may well serve as an example of the new status attained by musicians at the close of the eighteenth century. Unlike Haydn, Beethoven was not attached to a court, except in his youth; like Mozart, he was a "free" artist, making his living from fees obtained from the giving of lessons and from the proceeds from public concerts, royalties from publishers, commissions for compositions and, finally, honorariums from the nobility. Beethoven, then, was able to succeed where a few short years before Mozart had failed, and in the same place, Vienna.

Beethoven was born in the North, in Bonn, in relatively poor circumstances. But his father was a singer in the employ of the local court, so Beethoven was in a musical environment from the very outset, and he gained considerable training and experience even in his youth. He went to Vienna in 1787 and had some lessons with Mozart, ultimately settling there five years later (1792). His gifts had long been recognized, although he was not regarded as a prodigy as Mozart had been. Upon his departure for Vienna in 1792, a friend of his, Count Waldstein, urged him to apply himself to composition in an extraordinarily acute assessment of the musical situation at that time: "Dear Beethoven! You are going to Vienna in fulfillment of your long-frustrated wishes. The Genius of Mozart is mourning the death of her pupil. She found a refuge but no occupation with the inexhaustible Haydn; through him she wishes to form a union with another. With the help of assiduous labor you shall receive Mozart's spirit from Haydn's hands."

Apart from his musical activities, Beethoven is remarkable for certain philosophical conceptions in which he believed, according to which he strove to live and work, and which he often attempted to manifest in his musical compositions. These ideas have their origin, for the most part, in the eighteenth-century enlightenment and show close relations to French thought. This Beethoven was exposed to during his years at Bonn where such influence was strong, particularly through his teacher Christian Gottlob Neefe, whose guidance was by no means restricted to music. The ideals that fired Beethoven's imagination were those that lay back of the French Revolution: *liberté, égalité, fraternité*. Along with them goes another idea that was almost a commonplace in eighteenth-century aesthetic thought: the moral value of an art work, the necessity that it purify and ennoble the audience, an idea related in some respects to Aristotle's theory of catharsis. Much of Beethoven's thought here was influenced by Schiller.

Beethoven's view of what an artist should be is implicit in a most unusual and revealing document, the *Heiligenstadt Testament* of 1802, that he wrote upon the realization that his deafness, which had been constantly increasing, would get worse and in fact was incurable. Here he took up the problem of what this deafness meant to him not only in terms of his work as a musician and composer, but in terms of his personal relationships as well. Up to this point, his inclinations had always been to conceal his growing deafness, an effort that had provoked many embarrassing situations; he often covered himself by withdrawing hastily in irritation. Often, he was in deep despair and contemplated suicide. Thus, he wrote this *Testament* to explain his state to his relatives and friends upon his death. Although he often contemplated suicide, he never took this fatal step;

"but little more and I would have put an end to my life—only art it was that held me back: ah! it seemed impossible to leave the world until I had produced all that I felt called upon to produce."

Much could be said in the interpretation of this document. The important point, however, is the reference to a calling: Beethoven's realization that he had been granted powers unlike those accorded to others; that he had been placed on the earth to exercise them, to compose; that this was, as it were, his mission; and that nothing, not even the severe infirmity of deafness, should cause him to waver in or cease from this endeavor. Thus he was clearly aware of his genius, his uniqueness as a human being; and this is what explains his unusual conduct, his treatment of the nobility and of his colleagues in the field of music. For Beethoven did not take much stock in the conventional ideas of what constituted aristocracy; he recognized an aristocracy of the intellect and of creative artists that set him apart from, if not above, all others.

Like Mozart, Beethoven was a pianist; but unlike Mozart—and Haydn too, for that matter—Beethoven put great emphasis on his works for piano solo, particularly the piano sonatas, so much so that the piano sonatas form perhaps the most important single category in all his musical composition. They stand in the center of his creative activity. Beethoven experimented with and worked out new ideas and methods at the piano and presented the results first in the piano sonata before extending them to other categories of composition. The truth of this will become more apparent as we discuss Beethoven's piano sonatas chronologically.

It has become conventional to divide Beethoven's work[1] into three chronological groups: the early works (up to 1802), the works of the middle period (1802–1815), and the works of the late period (1815–1822). The piano sonatas may then be grouped in this general framework as follows:

I. Early period
  A. Bonn (published 1783)
      Sonata in E-flat
      Sonata in f
      Sonata in D

  B. Vienna (1796–1799)
      Sonatas of op. 2: f, A, C (published 1796)
      Sonata in E-flat, op. 7 (published 1797)
      Sonatas of op. 10: c, F, D (published 1798)
      Sonata pathétique in c, op. 13 (published 1799)
      Sonatas of op. 14: E, G (published 1799)

[1] The standard biography remains that of Thayer, but the standard bibliographical reference is the thematic catalogue of Kinsky (completed by Halm). Of the new collected edition of Beethoven's works, the first volume to appear contains the variations for piano. On the conception of the sonata as a large form, see Misch; on the piano music in general, see Westerby; on the sonatas, see, among others, Blom, Prod'homme, and Rosenberg; on fugues, see Cockshoot; see also Weber and Löw; on Beethoven's relations to Mozart and C. P. E. Bach, see Oppel.

C. Vienna (1801–1802)
   Sonata in B-flat, op. 22 (published 1802)
   Sonata in A-flat, op. 26 (published 1802)
   Sonatas of op. 27: E-flat, c-sharp (published 1802)
   Sonata in D, op. 28 (published 1802)

II. The second period
   A. 1802–1809
      Sonatas of op. 31: G, d, E-flat (published 1803–1804)
      Sonata in C, op. 53 (published 1805)
      Sonata in F, op. 54 (published 1806)
      Sonata in f, op. 57 (published 1807)

   B. 1809–1815
      Sonata in F-sharp, op. 78 (published 1810)
      Sonata in G, op. 79 (published 1810)
      Sonata in E-flat, op. 81a (published 1811)
      Sonata in e, op. 90 (published 1815)

III. Last period
      Sonata in A, op. 101 (published 1817)
      Sonata in B-flat, op. 106 (published 1819)
      Sonata in E, op. 109 (published 1821)
      Sonata in A-flat, op. 110 (published 1822)
      Sonata in c, op. 111 (published around 1823).

There are also four easy sonatas, two from the Bonn period (in F and C) and the two of op. 49 (g and G), composed between 1795 and 1798 and published in 1805.

To be noted at once is the fact that while the sonatas are broadly distributed over Beethoven's whole career as a composer, there is a progressive decline in quantity over the years. If we consider only the larger works (excluding the "easy" sonatas), thirteen sonatas were written up to 1800, five in the single year 1801–1802, only ten between 1802 and 1815, but five between 1817 and 1823, and none thereafter in the remaining four years of his life. This distribution doubtless has something to do with Beethoven's employment of the piano sonatas as a sort of "proving ground"; namely, we find in the piano sonatas, especially those composed after 1801, considerable variety in the forms, procedures, and types employed by Beethoven, so much so that this variety becomes a main feature of these works taken as a whole. After having worked out or "tested," as it were, these ideas and procedures, Beethoven applied the harvest to other categories of composition, particularly the string quartet and the symphony.

The three early sonatas that Beethoven composed in Bonn at age eleven and dedicated to the Elector Maximilian Friedrich already promise much. All are in the three-movement form that was standard for the sonata in the eighteenth century. The Sonata in E-flat is a rather small composition, but in the first movement there is real motivic development of themes. More impressive is the Sonata in f, a real forerunner of the later so-called *Appassionata Sonata*, also, be it noted, in f (op. 57). In this early Sonata in f, we see the slow introduction to the first movement, full of sudden changes in dynamics and chromaticism, followed by an Allegro in sonata form with a theme composed of the f minor scale in driving sixteenth notes; the secondary theme, as indeed was often true in the sonatas in the minor by Haydn and Mozart, is more in the *galant* vein, while the last theme of the exposition returns to the "passionate" style of the outset. The development works with the principal theme but is dramatically interrupted in the middle with the appearance of a few bars from the slow introduction. While the Andante is lighter and greatly embellished after the fashion of the time, in the final Presto the dramatic and passionate character comes back. In associating this character with the minor mode, Beethoven followed the example of Haydn and of the late eighteenth century generally. The early Sonata in D is an even larger work, brilliant and virtuosic. What emerges from the consideration of these three

EXAMPLE 46

BEETHOVEN: First movement, from *Sonata* in f (*Bonn Sonata*, No. 2)— excerpts

A. Larghetto maestoso

B. Allegro assai

Bonn Sonatas or *Kurfürsten Sonatas* is that Beethoven was not content with the domestic or "intimate" type of sonata common at the time, but saw it as destined for bigger and more important things. In this, he may well have been following the example of Clementi.

It is the group of ten sonatas published in 1796–1799 that forms the bulk of Beethoven's early piano sonata composition. The direction taken by Beethoven here is the same as was indicated in the *Bonn Sonatas*; the piano sonata is regarded as a large form. Here, however, Beethoven went a step further and, half of the time, abandoned the three-movement form that had been standard for the genre; five of these ten sonatas are cast in four movements, a form used in very few eighteenth-century sonatas, but, rather, characteristic of the symphony and "serious" types of chamber music for strings alone—string quartets and quintets. One might assume that Beethoven had already decided to interpret the old didactic character of the sonata as preparation for composition in larger media, so that these sonatas can be regarded as the preparation for the string quartets of op. 18 and the first two symphonies. The symphonic character, for instance, is quite clear in the Sonata in D (op. 10 iii). It might be noted that the four-movement scheme in Beethoven gave way after the Sonata in D (op. 28) and never regained the importance it had achieved in these early works.

The first movements of these sonatas show the use of the sonata form throughout. They are "big" movements operating with motivic themes so characteristic of Beethoven. The slow movements are of the cantabile type, generally in simple three-part form (or five-part form, *A B A B* [or *C*] *A*). While most of these slow movements are on the "light" side, there are some notable exceptions: the three deeply expressive Largo movements in the Sonatas in A (op. 2 ii), E-flat (op. 7), and D (op. 10 iii). The dance movements, either minuets or scherzi (as in the Sonatas in C [op. 2 iii] and G [op. 14 ii]) and trios, remain formally the same as those found in Haydn, Mozart, and elsewhere; but here the *galant* and frequently *grazioso* character is lacking, and motivic themes are frequent. The Sonata in E-flat (op. 7) has a *minore* trio, using broken-chord figuration with crescendo and decrescendo.

Two of these sonatas may be singled out for more detailed consideration: the Sonata in C (op. 2 iii) and the *Sonata pathétique* in c (op. 13). The first of these shows the large four-movement scheme so prominent in this group of sonatas; there is an Allegro con brio in sonata form, an Adagio (E) in five-part form, a Scherzo with trio, and a concluding Assai allegro in rondo form. The first movement shows Beethoven's characteristic type of thematic materials in abundance. There are terse motives that often involve figuration and are sharply delineated rhythmically, readily identifiable, susceptible to repetition, development, variations, and combinations of various sorts, and often contrast sharply with one another. The subordinate theme here is cantabile and in g, and the close of the exposition features figuration. The recapitulation is varied by inserting into the closing section a fantasia-like passage something in the nature of a cadenza, after which the closing section resumes and the movement is brought to its brilliant conclusion. The Adagio, most exceptionally in the key of E (tertian relation to the over-all tonic of the work) has an alternation between a principal theme with a clearly organized phrase structure and a subordinate theme that is primarily harmonic in effect, with arpeggiated chords, octaves in the bass, and cantabile scale fragments up above. This subordinate passage occurs twice, considerably modified the second time; shortly before its second appearance, there is a sudden turn to C in the principal theme, thus re-asserting the main key of the sonata. The Scherzo emphasizes a strongly rhythmical motivic theme repeated insistently with many touches of contrapuntal work, and is far removed in character from the minuet, which was the origin of such a movement; the trio contrasts sharply, with its fast arpeggios accompanied by accented octaves in the bass. The concluding Assai allegro is a straightforward rondo: the principal theme uses rapidly moving staccato sixth chords, while the first episode consists of a cantabile line over a stereotyped broken-chord bass. The long second episode contains two contrasting elements that alternate with one another—a chordal passage and one with *grazioso* arpeggios. Figuration added to the final appearance of the main theme produces a suitably brilliant conclusion.

The *Sonata pathétique* in c (op. 13 of 1799) differs in that it embodies the expression of a particular affection. It is one of two sonatas to which Beethoven

EXAMPLE 47

Beethoven: Allegro con brio, from *Sonata* in C (op. 2 iii)—beginning

himself gave a descriptive title. (The other is the Sonata in E-flat, op. 81a, *Das Lebewohl.*) The key, c, had all through the eighteenth century been associated with the *pathétique*, an association it indeed often retained throughout the nineteenth century as well. The *Sonata pathétique* is in three movements: a Grave-allegro, an Adagio cantabile in A-flat, and a concluding rondo (Allegro).

The *pathétique* character is clear from the outset; there is a *grave* introduction with solemn heavy chords in dotted rhythm and then a cantabile line with ponderous chordal accompaniment. The Allegro part of the movement commences with an agitated principal theme: rapidly ascending chords, off-beat accentuations, and broken-octave accompaniment, to which the subordinate theme, staccato and with grace notes in a *grazioso* character, provides relief; but, with the closing theme, the rhythmically driven figuration returns. Then, before the development starts, the *grave* beginning of the introduction is repeated. The development itself is short, working mostly with the principal theme; the recapitulation is regular, and, in the coda, both the principal theme and the theme from the introduction are stated again.

The Adagio cantabile is an example of the large-scale serious lyric slow movement. The form is that of alternating sections which contrast with one another after the fashion of a rondo (A B A C A). The principal section is slow and even, the cantabile melody given out over an accompaniment of broken chords, while the first subordinate section also consists of such a cantabile line over an accompaniment of broken chords; but the second subordinate part brings a contrast with its agitated triplet accompaniment, a crescendo culminating in a *forte-piano*, staccato chords, and sudden changes of harmony.

The finale is, as stated, a Rondo. Along with the disconsolate principal theme (a character that the grace notes do nothing to alleviate) are two subordinate sections, both considerably longer than the principal theme; the first has figuration themes of eighth notes and triplets along with a chordal theme, while the second features an extended passage in two-voice writing and figuration. At the end is a coda that uses the theme of the principal section.

The last five sonatas of Beethoven's early group, those composed in 1801 and 1802, show the experimentation that was to be a chief characteristic of his treatment of the genre. The experimentation here involved the over-all organization, the gross anatomy, as it were, of the sonata—the relations between the various movements and the forms employed in them. Most experimental are the two sonatas of op. 27, in E-flat and c-sharp, each of which was specifically designated by Beethoven as *sonata quasi una fantasia*. The fantasia character was by no means entirely new to the piano sonata, as has been seen from the discussion of Haydn's, Mozart's, and even Beethoven's earlier works in this form. In these instances, however, the fantasia character takes the form either of passages in fantasia style inserted during the course of a movement, or of a fantasia movement that precedes the sonata as a whole; with Beethoven, on the other hand, we will see that the fantasia element affects the over-all disposition of the sonata itself.

In the Sonata in E-flat (op. 27 i), the fantasia is clearly seen in the first movement, which is divided into three parts: Andante—Allegro—Andante; let it be emphasized that there is nothing of the usual Allegro first movement in sonata form. Likewise, the first movement of the companion Sonata in c-sharp has nothing of the sonata form (this first movement being the one that has provided the sonata with the designation *Moonlight*, a name that did not come from Beethoven himself). This produces a new orientation in the over-all organization of these compositions; in both of them, the "biggest" movement is the finale, to which all preceding movements lead, a sonata-rondo in the E-flat Sonata and a dramatic movement in sonata form in the c-sharp Sonata. The Sonata in E-flat is noteworthy for two other features, both also related to the fantasia character. First, the movements are to be played without interruption; and, second, the theme of the slow movement, an Adagio, makes a brief appearance at the end of the finale, thus introducing the element of cyclic form.

The three other sonatas of the group, in B-flat (op. 22), A-flat (op. 26), and D (op. 28), are cast in the four-movement scheme already employed frequently by Beethoven in his piano sonatas. It seems evident that the Sonatas in B-flat and D are conservative works. The Sonata in D, which has close thematic relations to Clementi, is also one of the few Beethoven sonatas in which all movements are thematically related (see Misch). In the Sonata in A-flat, the place of the sonata form in the first movement is usurped by a movement in theme and variations form; and the same sonata has as slow movement, a *Marcia funebre sulla morte d'un Eroe*, marked Maestoso andante, a movement that foreshadows the slow movement of the famous *Sinfonia eroica*. While the Sonata in B-flat has a minuet (with trio in the minor), the sonatas in A-flat and D have scherzi.

Turning to the sonatas of Beethoven's second period, there is a group written prior to 1807 and another composed between 1808 and 1815. Even in the first of these groups, we can note that quantitatively the output of sonatas begins to fall off; there are the three sonatas of op. 31 in 1803–1804, but the next three come one a year during the period 1805–1807. Still, there is great variation between these sonatas, nowhere is there a fixed, formal scheme that is followed. While the old four-movement form appears here only once, in the Sonata in E-flat (op. 31 iii), the three-movement scheme is much in evidence, as in the sonatas in G (op. 31 i) and d (op. 31 ii). But even the three-movement plan is varied; in one case, in the Sonata in f (op. 57), the slow movement is linked to the finale, while in another, the Sonata in C (op. 53), it is called *introduzione* and performs thus in relation to the finale. Most unusual is the Sonata in F (op. 54), which is in two movements. Thus, the four-movement form, so prominent in Beethoven's early sonatas, was largely abandoned; he returned to it only once again in a piano sonata, the Sonata in B-flat (op. 106).

In the first movements of these sonatas, we find the presence of the sonata form along with all the dramatic and virtuoso characteristics usually associated with Beethoven's piano music. Noteworthy is the opening movement of the Sonata in f (op. 57), which dispenses with the double-bar and thus with the repetition of the exposition. The themes employed here are motivic, short, highly characteristic, and full of potentiality for development (see particularly the often quoted theme of the Sonata in E-flat [op. 31 iii]); they frequently consist of triads (especially the Sonata in f [op. 57]) or of figurative elements (particularly the brilliant "Waldstein" Sonata in C [op. 53]). Most unusual is the Sonata in F (op. 54), in which the opening movement is a minuet with aspects of the sonata form drawn in. The slow movements present little that is unusual. There is the Adagio of the Sonata in d (op. 31 ii), the theme and variations of the Sonata in f (op. 57), and the Andante grazioso of the Sonata in G (Op. 31 i); the slow movement of the Sonata in C (op. 53) serves as introduction to the last movement, as previously noted. The reduction in the number of movements found in all but one of these sonatas had drastic consequences for the minuet or scherzo movement, normally the third or second movement. In most of these sonatas, it is this movement that is cut out. We have already noted the use of the minuet in a first movement in the Sonata in F (op. 54). The situation in the only four-movement work in the group, the Sonata in E-flat (op. 31 iii), is by no means what would be expected: the scherzo, in 2/4 time, stands in second place, and as a slow movement, in third place, comes a cantabile minuet. In the finales, we find both sonata and rondo form, with the former predominating; there are three in sonata form—the Sonatas in E-flat (op. 31 iii), d (op. 31 ii), and f (op. 57)—while two have finales in rondo form—the Sonatas in G (op. 31 i) and C (op. 53). Exceptional again is the Allegretto finale of the two-movement lyrical Sonata in F (op. 54).

These works, along with a few other sonatas, such as the *Sonata pathétique* or the Sonata in c-sharp (op. 27 ii), are among the most popular compositions in this genre composed by Beethoven or anyone else for that matter. Here, there is a certain happy combination of qualities; these are large, outspokenly concert pieces in which Beethoven's particular motivic type of theme and thematic development appear with a virtuoso exploitation of the piano, and the combination is productive of most impressive effects. This particular combination, especially the exploitation of the full range of the piano's capabilities, appears to have only one real forerunner—Clementi. While it is not possible here to present a detailed discussion, a few aspects may be singled out as representative of the qualities that have given these works their unique position in the piano repertory.

The dramatic qualities are at their most impressive in the Sonatas in C (op. 53) and f (op. 57). The Sonata in C, known as the "Waldstein," is remarkable for the consistent thematic use of figuration and figurational elements. The principal theme of the first movement is little more than a very rapidly repeated chord in subdued dynamics, and then, on the repetition, the chord is simply broken up;

in this theme, therefore, the rhythmic motion is very great and the harmonic motion very slow. The subordinate theme is chordal and presents an effective contrast, but the figurational element returns in the closing theme, which consists of arpeggios. A most remarkable passage in this respect comes towards the end of the development section, as a transition to the recapitulation. This is a large crescendo in which all is figuration, the rhythmic motion is very fast (sixteenth notes for the most part), and again we note the static quality in the harmonic rhythm. The whole passage is merely a dominant triad; there is an ostinato-like repeated scale-wise descending motion through a fourth in the bass, ascending scale fragments rising with constantly increasing loudness until the culmination is reached, and an abrupt descending scale run that ushers in the recapitulation. Another crescendo passage may be seen in the statement of the main theme of the rondo movement, a triadic cantabile line over figured accompaniment that is repeated twice, each time louder and with greater amounts of figuration; the episodes of the rondo likewise show primarily the use of figuration. And, in the principal theme, we can again note that the harmonic rhythm is slow and the rhythmic motion, on the other hand, fast.

A highly dramatic character is also to be seen in the so-called *Appassionata Sonata*. This appears at once in the principal theme of the first movement. The theme is triadic and moves in a dotted rhythm, again in subdued dynamics, coming to a rest after a trill; the repetition of the short up-beat produces a sense of expectancy that is fulfilled with a sudden loud diminished seventh-chord

EXAMPLE 48

BEETHOVEN: *Sonata* in C (op. 53, *Waldstein Sonata*)—excerpts

A. Allegro con brio: principal theme—beginning

B. Allegro con brio: transition to recapitulation

C. Rondo—beginning

EXAMPLE 48—*continued*

arpeggio leading to a suspenseful half cadence, after which the theme is restated with sudden interjections of chords. While the subordinate theme seems to be in great contrast, with its broadly cantabile character, it actually shares two important features with the principal theme—the dotted rhythms and the triadic nature of the melody. We can note, too, the impressive motivic development and the recapitulation, in which the principal theme appears over a dramatic pedal point consisting of rapidly repeated sixteenth notes. Particularly dramatic is the finale of this sonata with its "whirlwind" principal theme consisting of very fast but soft scale runs in f minor that then become the accompaniment to a chordal theme moving in dotted rhythms.

   In the period between 1809 and 1814 Beethoven composed only four piano sonatas. Again, there is no over-all conformity to a basic scheme or plan, no

EXAMPLE 49

BEETHOVEN: Allegro assai, from *Sonata* in f (op. 57, *Appassionata Sonata*) —excerpts

A. Principal theme

B. Subordinate theme

fixed conception of what the form of a piano sonata is or should be. The two-movement form appears twice, in the Sonatas in F-sharp (op. 78) and e (op. 90); the others employ the three-movement scheme—the Sonatas in G (op. 79) and E-flat (op. 81a) known as *Das Lebewohl*, except that here, as in the earlier *Waldstein Sonata* (op. 53), the second movement serves as an introduction to the third. In general, it may be said that these sonatas are "smaller" than the group of sonatas that immediately precedes them, with the exception of the E-flat Sonata, *Das Lebewohl*.

Sonata form dominates in the first movements, but, again except for the Sonata in E-flat, they are not of the large dramatic kind full of extreme contrasts and embodying a high degree of virtuosity; their character rather is lyrical, as may be seen from the broad cantabile theme in the first movement of the Sonata in F-sharp (op. 78), in many respects so typical of Beethoven in the middle period, or the opening of the Sonata in e (op. 90). The first movement of the Sonata in e is a free sonata form in which the usual double bar is absent, while that of the Sonata in G (op. 79), marked Presto alla tedesca, is a short and simple movement somewhat in the character of a dance (a *Teutsche* or *Ländler*) in lilting triple time. Two sonatas of this group have slow introductions to the first movements: the Sonatas in F-sharp (op. 78), where it is very short, and E-flat (op. 81a).

Only two of the sonatas have slow movements, and both are cast in three-part form—an Andante in the Sonata in G (op. 79) and Andante espressivo in the Sonata in E-flat (op. 81a). Furthermore, these sonatas lack the minuet-scherzo movement altogether.

The finales do not present a uniform picture in regard to the forms employed for them. Rondo form is used in the Sonata in G (op. 79) and in the Sonata in e (op. 90); sonata form is used in the Sonata in E-flat (op. 81a), while the hybrid sonata-rondo structure so often employed by Haydn in his symphonies appears in the Sonata in F-sharp (op. 78). Most unusual is the slow "singable" (*singbar*) rondo with contrasting episodes in the Sonata in e (op. 90), a movement marked *teneramente*—the finale of a two-movement sonata.

The most conventional work in the group—the Sonata in E-flat (op. 81a)—is in some ways also the most unusual. Its three movements bear titles *Das Lebewohl* (*The Farewell*), *Die Abwesenheit* (*The Absence*), and *Das Wiedersehen* (*The Reunion*); hence, a series of definite characteristics or affections, a program, as it were, is set up. Concerning the French translation of the designation for the first movement, *Les Adieux*, by which the entire sonata is generally known, Beethoven, insisting on the German *Das Lebewohl*, stated that one says *Lebe wohl* to a single person but *adieu* to assemblies and whole towns; in character, therefore, the sonata is rather intimate.

The last piano sonatas composed by Beethoven—the five written between 1815 and 1823—again present much variety. New elements appear, and Beethoven himself was conscious that he was taking a new direction in his music that he declared had nothing at all to do with what he had previously composed—"It is somewhat better." Formally, there is little that arouses attention. The three-movement plan is dominant, in the Sonatas in A (op. 101), E (op. 109), and A-flat (op. 110); and two movements are used in the Sonata in c (op. 111). Noteworthy, however, is the reversion to the older four movements of his earlier sonatas in the large Sonata in B-flat (op. 106);[1] this formal plan had not been employed by Beethoven since 1803, in the Sonata in E-flat (op. 31 ii).

Two musical styles not associated with Beethoven's sonatas prior to these receive emphasis here, as in his late works generally—the fugue, on the one hand, and the theme and variations form, on the other. Both are treated by Beethoven in a highly original manner. The fugue appears in three ways: as a

[1] The term *Hammerklavier* that is associated with this work has no programmatic or expressive significance; it is simply the German word for pianoforte and was used by Beethoven in his later years instead of the current Italian designation *pianoforte* or *fortepiano*. It is noteworthy, however, that the earlier designation of the sonatas as playable on either harpsichord or piano (*pour le clavecin ou fortepiano*) here is modified to the exclusion of the harpsichord.

EXAMPLE 50

BEETHOVEN: Third movement (variations), from *Sonata* in E (op. 109)—excerpt (near end)

separate movement, a finale, as in the sonatas in B-flat (op. 106) and A-flat (op. 110); as the development section of a movement in sonata form, as in the finale of the Sonata in A (op. 101) and the first movement of the Sonata in B-flat (op. 106); or as part of a theme and variations movement. The most grandiose example of fugue in these piano sonatas is the great finale of the Sonata in B-flat (op. 106), marked *fuga a tre voci con alcune licenze*; among the fugal procedures are inversion and cancrizans, devices associated with learned counterpoint. Inversion is also featured in the fugue finale of the Sonata in A-flat (op. 110). Variation form appears twice in these sonatas, both times as finale, in the Sonatas in E (op. 109) with six variations and in c (op. 111) with four variations and an elaborate coda. In both, the themes are simple and short, cast in the usual binary form. Each commences quietly, the variations in turn bringing changes, progresses to a climactic point, and then subsides and ends with a reprise of the theme. In these climatic points, which are noteworthy for their lyricism, the piano writing is most unusual, involving small note values (thirty-second notes), much figuration especially in the accompaniment and the use of the extremes of the keyboard range.

As elsewhere in Beethoven's sonatas, we find that elements from the fantasia are present. This is especially true of the Sonatas in A (op. 101) and A-flat (op. 110). In the first of these, the theme of the first movement recurs immediately before the last movement, so that the fantasia character again brings with it the element of cyclic form; in the second, the A-flat sonata (op. 110), it is the Adagio movement whose theme is repeated, this time between the two sections of the

EXAMPLE 50—*continued*

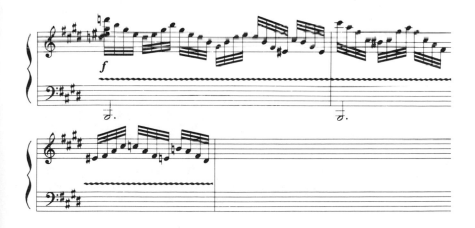

fugue finale, but other thematic correspondences have been found (see Knab). A similar procedure of repetition was noted earlier in the pronouncedly fantasia Sonata in E-flat (op. 27 i). Passages displaying the quasi-improvisational style associated with the fantasia are, first and foremost, the lengthy introduction to the fugue in the Sonata in B-flat (op. 106); the Adagio sections of the first movements of the Sonata in E (op. 109) and the Adagio movement of the Sonata in A-flat (op. 110); and, finally, the coda of the second movement of the Sonata in c (op. 111).

The old minuet or scherzo movement with trio almost disappears, appearing only in the Sonata in B-flat (op. 106). In its place, the other sonatas bring in different elements: a Marcia in the Sonata in A (op. 101) and a violent Molto allegro in the sonatas in E (op. 109) and A-flat (op. 110). Likewise, the slow movement is displaced in these late sonatas. It takes the form of long sets of variations or the fantasia-arioso of the Sonata in A-flat (op. 110), or the short Adagio of the Sonata in A (op. 101). The only "set" slow movement in the old sense is to be found in the Sonata in B-flat (op. 106), an Adagio sostenuto, appassionato e con molto sentimento.

EXAMPLE 51

BEETHOVEN: Largo (introduction to finale), from *Sonata* in B-flat (op. 106) —beginning

To be emphasized here is that this shifting around of the various movements and forms has a drastic effect on the one form long regarded and used as the mainstay, as it were, of the piano sonata—the sonata form. Although the traditional type of the big opening movement is maintained in the Sonatas in B-flat (op. 106) and c (op. 111), in the Sonata in A (op. 101) it comes not as the first movement, but as the finale, and in the Sonata in A-flat (op. 110), while it comes as the first movement, it is a very lyrical manifestation and has a very short development; and in the Sonata in E (op. 109) it does not appear at all. It has already been stated that two of these movements in sonata form employ fugue in their development sections, the Sonatas in A (op. 101) and B-flat (op. 106).

We have said that the piano sonata occupies a central position in Beethoven's work, a genre that drew his attention constantly and in which he worked out new interpretations and procedures that then were incorporated into other genres of musical composition. The "big" four-movement early sonatas paved the way for the string quartets of op. 18 and the first two symphonies; similarly, the sonatas of op. 31, 53, and 57 may be seen as the predecessors of the large string quartets of op. 59 and 74, the later piano trios, and the great symphonies and concertos of the middle period; while the last five sonatas take us directly into the world of the *Ninth Symphony* and the late string quartets.

The other large form of keyboard music cultivated by Beethoven was that of the theme and variations, of which there are twenty-one sets (see Müller-Blattau and Fischer). Two types can be distinguished. First there is the "popular" type, works related to Beethoven's public appearances as a pianist, in which melodies of popular songs and arias of the time are taken as the basis for the variations (works of Dittersdorf, Salieri, Paisiello, Righini, and Süssmayr, as well as *Rule Britannia* and *God Save the King*). These works represent the fruit of Beethoven's improvisations at concerts and in general are similar in character and intent to the variations of Mozart.

Then, there are the more ambitious and serious examples of the genre, works composed in the same spirit as the piano sonatas and other important instrumental compositions, that lack this popular orientation. These are the *Variations* (six) *on an Original Theme* in F (op. 34), *Variations* (fifteen) *with Fugue on a Theme from Prometheus* (op. 35)—both of which were composed in 1802 and published in 1803—the *Variations* (thirty-two) *on an Original Theme* in c (known as op. 191)—composed in 1806 and published without opus number in 1807—and, finally, the great set of *Variations* (thirty-three) *on a Waltz of Diabelli* in C (op. 120)—composed between 1819 and 1823 and published in 1823. Two of these sets of variations are based on themes original with Beethoven, one of these being a theme from one of his previous works, the ballet *Prometheus* (also used in the finale of the *Eroica Symphony*), so that only one is based on a theme from outside (so to speak), the *Diabelli Variations*.

In connection with the variations in F and E-flat (op. 34 and 35), Beethoven wrote his publishers Breitkopf & Härtel in October, 1802, that these works "have been worked out in an entirely new manner," something totally different from previous sets of variations, a "new idea," a "complete innovation" on his part. The works themselves certainly present unusual features. In the set of variations in F we find a constant changing of key throughout. The theme is in F, the first variation is in D, and there are successive variations in B-flat, G, E-flat, c, concluding again in F; hence, the progression of keys moves down the scale by thirds. The theme itself is a simple cantabile Adagio in small three-part form, and the

EXAMPLE 52

BEETHOVEN: Variations in E-flat (op. 35)—excerpts

A. Introduction—beginning

B. Theme—beginning

variations present the expected changes in character but here are quite pronounced; the fourth variation is a minuet, the fifth a march, and the sixth a
bright Allegretto with the theme in staccato octaves over a broken-chord
accompaniment. At the end stands a long and elaborate coda incorporating
fantasia elements, a recapitulation of the theme, and, finally, accompanying
motives from the theme with brilliant arpeggios and scale runs.

In the *Prometheus Variations* (op. 35), we can also note several original
elements. First, there is the relation to the old practice from the Baroque period of
variations on a basso ostinato, or ground; in an *introduzione*, the bass part of the
theme is stated first, and three variations on it follow, after which the theme
together with its bass appears. (This procedure is also followed in the *Sinfonia
eroica*, but it is not found in the ballet *Prometheus*.) Of the succeeding variations,
some employ the theme (melody), while others use only its bass. Second, we can
note that after an impressive *minore* variation and a Largo with fantasia passages,
there is a free fugue on the bass part of the theme (see Misch) after which a long
coda recapitulates the theme itself.

If the Variations in E-flat (op. 35) represent a rapprochement between the
usual practice of variation and the old practice of variations on a ground, the set
of Variations in c (known as op. 191) impressively revive this old practice with
all its original force and magnitude. Here, the theme is a real ground—a set of
harmonic progressions, eight bars in length in triple time—and are thus closely
related to the eighteenth-century types of chaconne and passacaglia.

EXAMPLE 53

BEETHOVEN: Variations in c (op. 191)—theme and first variation

continued

The last work in variation form to be considered here is the celebrated thirty-three *Variations on a Waltz of Diabelli*. The theme itself was composed by the music publisher Anton Diabelli of Vienna, who submitted it to fifty composers that they each might contribute a variation on it, all fifty then to be published together. Beethoven delayed, so his effort was not included; but, as it happens, his effort resulted in one of the largest sets of variations ever composed for keyboard. This, then, is the only one of Beethoven's major sets of variations for piano to use a theme by another composer, and, in fact, the theme—a simple waltz—is very much in the popular character generally associated with the theme and variations form.

In accordance with the usual interpretation of the genre, there is a considerable measure of contrast between the individual variations themselves. Reference can be made to the Marcia of the first variation; the *Serioso* of the sixth; the *Grave e maestoso*, in character much like the first part of a French overture, in the fourteenth; the one in which the waltz theme is converted also into a variation of

EXAMPLE 53—*continued*

Leporello's song at the beginning of *Don Giovanni* (the twenty-second); the fugetta (the twenty-fourth); and the Largo con espressione (the thirty-first). The thirty-second variation is a full fugue, and, at the very end, as if to recall the dance character of the original theme as well as the old *galant* associations of the genre, there is a highly stylized and very elaborate minuet.

What is important in these sets of themes and variations, however, is the general interpretation of the category, and it is here that the originality to which Beethoven himself refers (in connection with op. 34 and 35) doubtless really lies. In the hands of Beethoven's contemporaries and immediate predecessors (Mozart, for instance), this genre was regarded largely as a popular and *galant* form. And, while in many of Beethoven's sets as we have seen, this character was preserved, it is emphatically broken in these works, which become serious major compositions. This can certainly be regarded as an important innovation. And it is interesting to note that in three instances it goes hand in hand with a re-interpretation of the old idea of variations on a ground.

In Beethoven's compositions for keyboard, there are numerous miscellaneous shorter pieces—dances (minuets, Austrian *Ländler*, waltzes) and marches. Notable among these are the three sets of bagatelles or, as Beethoven also called them, *Kleinigkeiten* (little things), short and simple pieces, usually in three-part form. The main sets of these are op. 33, op. 119, and op. 126, published in 1803, 1823, and 1825, respectively (see Tyson); readily available are the Presto in B and the Allegretto in G (op. 126 iv and v [Georgii, *400 Years*, pp. 90–5]). Then there are other independent little pieces of all sorts, including the famous *Für Elise* in a of 1810 and the *Lustig–Traurig (Happy–Sad)* in C and c, composed in the late 1790's. Larger are the three rondos, all composed in the late 1790's. There are the two in C and G (op. 51); the well-known *Rondo a capriccio* in G (op. 129), subtitled *The Rage over the Lost Penny*, which was not published until 1828; and the Polonaise in C (op. 89), composed in 1814. All of these were designed as vehicles for virtuoso display. Of a different order are the few works that suggest the old Baroque tradition, albeit in highly modified form. Here are the two preludes in all the major keys (op. 39) of 1789 and published in 1803, each prelude modulating successively through the keys in accordance with the circle of fifths, and the independent and more conventional Prelude in f composed in Bonn. A large work is the Fantasia in B (op. 77) of 1809, which begins in g; it begins in the fashion of a late eighteenth-century fantasia, but then, at the Allegretto, goes over into variation form with a coda at the end. There is also an early two-voice fugue for organ composed in Bonn. Finally, for piano duet there is little—an early, highly *galant* two-movement Sonata in D (op. 6), two sets of variations, and a group of three marches (op. 45).

In conclusion, several general observations can be made on the subject of Beethoven's keyboard music. We have noted, for instance, the emphasis laid on the genre of the piano sonata itself. Formerly, the sonata was not regarded as an important large form of musical composition, but as something small, in the *galant* idiom and intended chiefly for use as teaching pieces. With Beethoven, they are still teaching pieces but in a different sense—for here it is, as it were, himself that he is teaching, employing the category of the piano sonata as a proving ground. This is to be explained not only by the fact that the piano was Beethoven's instrument, but also by the importance of keyboard improvisation at the time, a skill for which Beethoven was renowned. So we see that with Beethoven the piano sonata came into its own as the large form of keyboard music. And we have also noted that much the same thing took place in the theme and variations form, which had not been manifested on such a scale since the Baroque period. Finally, there are the shorter pieces in which Beethoven looked ahead to the music of the Romantics.

CHAPTER SEVEN

The Early Nineteenth Century

The nature of the change that Romanticism brought to music in the early nineteenth century has often been misunderstood and even exaggerated. For the most part, misconceptions seem to rest on an imperfect appreciation of the intents and accomplishments of Haydn and Mozart, so that the relation between the work of these musicians and that of Beethoven and Schubert is also often misconstrued. While it is not possible to explore this question fully in the present context, a few leading ideas must nevertheless be presented.

In the first place, it must be emphasized that the great change in musical style —one of the farthest-reaching and most thoroughgoing in the whole history of music—took place around 1750 (see Chapter Five). It was this change that put instrumental music in the forefront; from the modest genres of the *galant* emerged the string quartet, the symphony, the piano sonata, and the other leading forms of instrumental music that centered, to a large extent, around the newly worked out technique of thematic development. But the artist's intent went even beyond this; each of these large musical works was conceived as an entity, a totality that was also in a wholly individual way the expression of the artist. Hence, the idea that the musical work, in these large forms at all events, is the unique expression of the composer was clearly established in the mature works of Haydn and Mozart and therefore does not represent anything new in the work of subsequent composers.

The change that does take place in the early nineteenth century, and here is where piano music becomes important, has to do rather with repertory. The large Classical sonata, particularly as it appears in the mature work of Beethoven, is retained but modified, and the same may be said of the large version of the theme and variations; even the old prelude and fugue persists in some form or other throughout the nineteenth century. But, clearly, these large forms were no longer favored by composers; in their place came something new, a small form that was eagerly seized upon and made a typical Romantic genre of musical composition—the character piece.

One of the leading preoccupations of the Romantic literary movement, particularly in Germany, which goes back to the 1790's, had to do with music; music figures prominently in Romantic literary works by, for instance, Wackenroder, Novalis and, especially, E. T. A. Hoffmann, himself a composer of some stature. Part of this interest in music among literary men had to do with a subtle power that was attributed to music; that of being able to express the unspeakable, to express the subtlest and most powerful emotions of the human soul more directly and more accurately than any other artistic medium. Hence, it is not unnatural that along with this there arose a corresponding musical form, and this can best be called the "character piece" or "characteristic piece" (see Kahl). This is a small composition, usually in a simple form (the ternary scheme *ABA* is by far the most common) in which the middle section often forms a sharp contrast with the principal one. Pieces of this type were given a "programmatic" or emotional title, indicative of what they are to express or what their associations are. Music, then, became associated with the expression or characterization of extramusical ideas.

As has been seen, such descriptive compositions were not entirely new. Reference can be made to pieces of this kind in the English virginal music of the late sixteenth and early seventeenth centuries or, again, to the famous Biblical sonatas of Johann Kuhnau written in the late seventeenth century; and such indications abound in French harpsichord music of the seventeenth and eighteenth centuries as well. Towards the end of the eighteenth century, we begin to see keyboard pieces (the designation is *das charakteristische Klavierstück*) that represent, in more or less standard ways, a particular affection, in accordance with the procedures common in the opera of the time; among others, collections by G. C. Füger, Johann Karl Friedrich Rellstab (1759–1813), Carl Friedrich Zelter (1758–1832), and Johann Abraham Peter Schulz (1747–1800) may be mentioned. Characteristic and much earlier is Sperontes' collection of 1736, *Singender Muse an der Pleisse*, which consists of songs with keyboard accompaniment but with the express option of playing the keyboard accompaniment alone without the singing; in a most concrete sense, these are songs without words. Another small form in the keyboard music of the time was the so-called *Handstück*, a teaching (or study) piece frequently emphasizing virtuosity, which also attempted to express a particular affection or character. Such pieces are prominent in the work of Daniel Gottlob Türk (1756–1813), who published, along with eight sets of sonatas, many collections of these smaller works, twelve of which are included in his celebrated *Clavierschule* of 1789 (later editions, 1805 and 1806).

But the character piece did not become an important genre of musical composition, one capable of seizing the attention of the leading composers, until the early years of the nineteenth century. Beethoven, for one, has a few works of this kind, which he termed "bagatelles," or "trifles," but they are modest works, intended and recognized as such. It is not until the 1820's, in the works of Schubert, that we see a leading composer emphasizing the new category.

The change in attitude seems to stem from the work of several Bohemian composers (see Golos), Václav Jan Tomášek (1774–1850) and Jan Hugo Voříšek (1791–1825) particularly. Tomášek (see Thompson) composed such small-scale pieces beginning around 1810, calling them "eclogues," "rhapsodies," and "dithyrambs," the last somewhat larger than the others; the Eclogue in A-flat (op. 47 ii) is easily available (*HMS*, VIII, s. 4, b. 3). His pupil Voříšek, who was active in Vienna, used the designation "impromptu." In the often-quoted description of Riemann, in this genre music acquired a poetic meaning in which it was rather reflection that became the leading principle, aiming at a direct spontaneity of expression (or, at least, the appearance of such direct spontaneity). And this seems to be the meaning behind the designation "impromptu." Another composer important here is Heinrich Marschner (1795–1861), known chiefly for his contributions to Romantic opera but who also published two sets of impromptus (op. 22 and 23) and several sets simply called *Charakterstücke* (and who, interestingly enough, worked also with the *sonata quasi una fantasia*). In all of these character pieces, we find great simplicity of form, the simple ternary plan being found in most; lyricism comes to the fore, and the sound element of music becomes dominant. Other descriptive designations for pieces of this type that came into use in the nineteenth century are *Albumblatt* ("album leaf"), "fantasy" (or *Fantasiestück*), "nocturne" (or *Nachtstück*), "humoresque," "song without words," "intermezzo," "prelude," "scherzo," "caprice," or, simply, "lyric piece." One can also mention that, in regard to form, many of these works resemble individual movements of a sonata. Independent pieces in sonata form appear under various names. The nocturnes, intermezzi, and impromptus resemble slow movements, scherzos are like their counterparts in sonatas, and there are many independent pieces called rondos (see Tischler). This seems an indication that the small form was coming to the fore while the old large form of the sonata was being pushed into the background (on the sonata generally, see Egert and also Mayer). At the same time, however, it must be noted that there are instances of the reverse, namely, that certain features of the character piece appear in sonatas. By way of example, we can refer to the *Grande sonata charactéristique*, as composed by Eberl in f (op. 12) and Moscheles (op. 27), or a work like Moscheles' *Sonata mélancolique* in f-sharp (op. 49) of 1820–1821 (see Newman, 13, pp. 162–75); *pathétique* sonatas belong here as well and are by no means new, and, along with the famous work of Beethoven goes one by Ludwig Berger in the same key (revised version, op. 7, 1815). A Sonata in f by the German writer Ernst Theodor Amadeus Hoffmann

(1776–1822), composed apparently between 1804 and 1808 (see Newman, 10, pp. 114–23), in four movements which follow one another without pause, is also related to these characteristic sonatas.

A not unimportant but nonetheless secondary figure is Johann Wilhelm Hässler (1747–1822). Taught by Carl Phillip Emanuel Bach, Hässler worked first in Erfurt and then in St. Petersburg. His voluminous output includes a great many sonatas (several of which are associated with fantasias, caprices, and preludes), fantasias, a set of preludes (360 strong) in all the major and minor keys (op. 47, 1817), a set of *Etudes en quatre-vingt valses* (op. 29), a set of simple organ works (op. 48, 1789), and sets of variations. A group of his sonatas is large (*grandes sonates*, particularly op. 26), while others are small (*leichte Sonaten*) and often didactic (*sonatas instructives*). Hässler also has sonatas preceded by caprices or fantasias. But the characteristic is also there in his *Sonates expressives* (op. 16, 1803) and, more important, the set of *Pièces caractéristiques* (op. 27), all of which are based on the same theme. A popular bravura work by Hässler is the *Grande gigue* in d (op. 31 [see Georgii, *Keyboard Music*, III, pp. 94–103]).

With this as background, we can proceed to a consideration of the keyboard music of Franz Peter Schubert (1797–1828), who stands at the crossroads, so to speak. In his works we find not only the continuation of the old Classical large form of the sonata on a high level, but also much preoccupation with the new Romantic genre, the character piece, in which he reveals himself to be strongly influenced by Voříšek in particular. It is this situation that has made Schubert most difficult to classify and even to appreciate. It is rather ironic that of all the composers who may be associated with Viennese Classicism, Schubert is the only one who actually was a native-born Viennese, since Haydn, Mozart, and Beethoven all came from elsewhere; and yet Schubert's essential similarity to these composers is often questioned. Born in one of Vienna's suburbs, he entered the Chapel Royal in 1808 as a choir boy and prepared to follow in his father's footsteps and become a schoolmaster. In 1814, he did in fact take such a position but resigned it two years later, moved back into the city, and resolved to become a professional composer.

Schubert's fame, in large measure, rests on his songs, of which there are more than six hundred. Yet in the later years of his life, the output of songs fell off while he devoted himself more and more to the large forms of instrumental music. A letter of March 31, 1824, makes his attitude quite clear. He refers to the fact that, while he has been recently engaged in the composition of a few songs, he has concentrated on several string quartets and the octet; "in fact," he continues, "I intend to pave my way to grand symphony in this manner." But along with chamber music, there is an abundance of music for keyboard of all kinds. An important position here is taken by his extensive contributions to the new genre of piano music, the character piece (see Kahl). The most important of Schubert's collections are:[1]

Moments musicals (op. 94, D. 780, composed 1823–1828 and published 1828)
Impromptus (op. 90, D. 899, composed and published 1827)
Impromptus (op. 142, D. 935, composed 1827 and published 1838)
Klavierstücke (D. 946, composed 1828 and published 1868).

The smallest of these are the six *Moments musicals* (like Einstein, we retain Schubert's incorrect French), published in 1828 in two small volumes each containing three pieces, two individual numbers having already appeared under different titles: the Allegro moderato in f (iii) as *Air russe* in 1823 and the Allegretto in A-flat (vi) as *Plaintes d'un troubadour* in 1824. Here the main features of Schubert's character piece become clear. There are the simple repetitive formal schemes, namely, the three-part "song form" in the Moderato in C (i) with a transitional passage back to the restatement of the first section, of the Allegretto in A-flat (vi), where the middle part is labeled "trio"; and it appears with a coda in the Moderato in c-sharp (iv) or extended into a five-part plan with the subordinate passage appearing twice (varied the second time) in the popular Andantino in A-flat (ii); somewhat more elaborate, the well-known Allegro moderato in f (iii), the *Air russe*, has two subordinate passages with the principal passage appearing at the beginning and the end; most unusual, then, is the organization of the vigorous Allegro vivace in f (v) with its binary form, each part to be repeated.

Throughout there are many new touches that are particularly associated with the new genre, some of which are adopted from the work of Tomášek and Voříšek. We can point to the preoccupation with harmony and modulation, especially to be noted in the Moderato in c-sharp in which the subordinate passage stands in enharmonic relation to the principal part (c-sharp = D-flat); enharmonic changes also are prominent in the Allegro vivace in f (v), which is also distinguished by its insistent "square" rhythms characteristic of the *all'ongarese* (Hungarian idiom). Also, there is the rhythmically elaborate theme of the Moderato in C (i) with its triplet eighth notes alternating with dotted quarters and eighths. Or, finally, the highly lyrical Andantino in A-flat (ii) in which the placid, slow-moving chordal melody is contrasted with the gentle cantabile of the subordinate section (in f-sharp), which in turn is made impassioned with full *fortissimo* chords upon its return.

The impromptus present much the same sort of thing, but, generally speaking, on a somewhat larger scale. The first set of four (D. 899), published in 1827 as op. 90—comprising an Allegro molto moderato in C, an Allegro in E-flat, an

[1] Thematic catalogue, as well as a collection of documents on Schubert, by Deutsch, whose "D" numbers are assigned to Schubert's works in chronological order. The most comprehensive and sympathetic discussion of Schubert in general is by Einstein.

Andante in G-flat, and an Allegretto in A-flat—again reveals the use of simple external schemes. There is a three-part form in the Allegretto and, with a coda, in the Allegro and the Andante, elaborated to the five-part plan with a coda in the Allegro molto moderato; in the Allegro (ii) and the Allegretto (iv), there is great contrast between the two sections. Most elaborate are the first and last. The opening Allegro molto moderato features the lyric theme stated first as un-accompanied melody and then harmonized in "block" chords; it is then varied and used in the subordinate section to an arpeggiated triplet accompaniment, thus lending an over-all continuity to the work. The Allegretto, whose subordinate section is marked "trio," presents a principal section in several distinct parts. First, there is a descending scale figuration over a simple accompaniment that then provides the accompanying figure to a lilting dance-like melody in the left hand and then moves into an easy cantabile line with light arpeggiated triplet accompaniment; to all of this, the middle part, in c-sharp, agitated and marked *passionato*, comes as a strong contrast. Typically Schubertian, however, is the lyrical Andante in G-flat (the original publisher had it transposed to G); it is uniform in character throughout with a long cantabile line over a flowing arpeggio accompaniment with strikingly Romantic changes in harmony. Here, there is attained a new and characteristic sound quality or sonority, as it might be called nowadays, that is a most important formal element in the work. This pre-occupation with sound may be seen elsewhere in these impromptus, for example, in the first one, Allegro molto moderato in C, at the first return of the principal section, especially where the dynamic suddenly becomes *pianissimo* with the melody given out in the bass to the accompaniment of rapidly repeated octaves in the right hand; in this context, the shift from minor to major seems almost magical. Such an exploitation of pure sound, of harmonic and textural color, as it were, is something new, something typically Romantic.

The situation is more involved in the next set of impromptus (D. 935), published in 1838 as op. 142. Ostensibly, these four works were planned as a sequel to the previous impromptus, and Schubert's own manuscript certainly bears this out. But Robert Schumann, who reviewed them upon their publication, took them as forming a Sonata in f, and this view is ardently supported by Einstein. There are several reasons for such an interpretation. The most important aspects here are the disposition of the individual pieces, the formal types that appear, and their key relationships; there is an Allegro moderato in f, then an Allegretto in A-flat, an Andante in B-flat, and, concluding, an Allegro scherzando again in f. Such a plan is certainly not to be found in the earlier set of impromptus. But the musical forms themselves are unusual. The third piece is a theme and variations, a form not associated with the impromptu nor even, generally speaking, with the character piece; and the second piece is in three-part form with rounded binary form in each part, and the middle section is called "trio," to say nothing of its cantabile dance melody, so that it could easily be seen as a sort of minuet (Einstein describes it as being in the "saraband" rhythm—but it is certainly a highly Romantic kind of saraband); the last piece resembles the rather irregular rondo structure that often appears in Schubert's sonatas, as will be seen. The main problem in this interpretation, then, is the first movement, which does not resemble what is found in Schubert's sonata composition. The opening

EXAMPLE 54

SCHUBERT: Impromptu in G-flat (op. 90 iii, D. 899)—beginning

section with its abundance of themes and is modulation from f to A-flat would certainly qualify as an exposition of sorts, but it would be an exposition without the double bar, and there is no development; the development is, as Einstein says, "replaced" by a contrasting section, contrasting completely in style with no thematic connection to the exposition; furthermore, this middle passage returns *in toto* near the end, after which the principal theme is heard in abbreviated form. This first piece, then, differs radically from what Schubert was wont to employ in his piano sonatas, and, as will be seen, whatever original features Schubert brought to the sonata, he did not engage in formal innovations of this sort. All in all, then, the case for calling these four impromptus a sonata, while it has much to recommend it, cannot be regarded as conclusive.

At all events, these works show features similar to what we noticed in the previous set of impromptus. Here again it is the new sound that attracts attention, the great freedom in modulation, and the emphasis on harmonic surprise. A most characteristic example can be seen in the very first piece, in Einstein's "replaced" development; it is *pianissimo* but *appassionata* with gentle triadic sixteenth-note figuration in the middle, while above and below it come short, fragmentary phrases that often outline chords. Another characteristic passage appears in the Allegretto (ii), in the transition just before the reprise of the principal section, where the fragmentary arpeggio figures are used in a diminuendo to the accompaniment of a softly sustained diminished triad gradually moving from G-flat to the dominant, C.

Special comment is called for by the Andante and the concluding Allegro scherzando. The Andante, in B-flat, brings five variations and coda on a theme used on several other occasions by Schubert, best known as the *Rosamunde* theme (it is the second entr'acte), but also prominent in the String Quartet in a. In modified rounded binary form (the reprise is varied), simple in its regular phrase structure, it is given out over an easy regular accompaniment. While all the variations adhere to the rounded binary scheme, their character changes considerably: the figural first variation; the dance-like second and fifth (the fifth seems like an elaboration of the second); the third, in b-flat, with its lilting accompaniment; the Romantic sound of the fourth, in G-flat; and the short coda at the end. The concluding Allegro scherzando is a typical example of the *all'ongarese* in its principal section, which is in the minor; it is in fast triple meter with grace notes and has a leaping accompaniment and accents on weak beats, both of which at times suggest a change to duple time; in addition, there is use of parallel thirds, grace notes in the melody, and ornate scale figuration and trills that bring the passage to a close.

Schubert's other set of impromptus are the three *Klavierstücke* (D. 946). Although they were composed in 1828, Schubert decided to leave them unpublished, and they appeared (under the anonymous editorship of Brahms) only in 1868. Apparently, Schubert had planned another set of four impromptus, but these three are all that he was able to complete. They are an Allegro assai in e-flat (ending in E-flat), an Allegretto in E-flat, and an Allegro in C. These works are of lesser stature than the impromptus, a statement that is supported by Schubert's decision not to publish them. The formal plans used here are simple and regular: simple three-part form (with retransition passage) in the Allegro in C and simple five-part form with two episodes in the others, except that in the piece in e-flat the first episode is brought back at the end. In two of these works, individual sections are organized by rounded binary form: the second episode of the e-flat work and all parts of the Allegretto in E-flat (rather freely treated in the principal section). Einstein regards these *Klavierstücke* as rather typical and conventional examples of standard musical types. The first is *alla francese*, as is most clearly seen from the second episode, a romance with the melody given out in parallel sixth chords featuring grace-note scale figurations; the Allegretto in E-flat is *all'italiana* with its lilting melody (the meter is 6/8) in parallel thirds; the last is *all'ongarese* with its fast, sharply accented syncopations. Harmonic effects are to be found here as well but in less profusion than elsewhere in Schubert's character pieces. There is an enharmonic change in the first Allegretto leading into the second episode, and, especially, an episode in the Allegro in C (the third piece), with the simple chords in a rhythmic pattern. It may be conjectured that Schubert desired to try a simpler and more popular style for his impromptus but was dissatisfied with this particular result.

Along with these more important essays in the new Romantic genre of the character piece come many others of smaller stature: the *Albumblatt* (D. 844 of 1825), actually a waltz, along with a number of separate allegros, adagios, andantes, allegrettos (one in c [D. 915] in Georgii, *400 Years*, pp. 102–3), and scherzos.

But these character pieces do not tell the whole story of Schubert's keyboard compositions. Earlier in the discussion, reference was made to Schubert's expressed determination in 1824 and 1825 to cultivate the larger forms of instrumental music and the association of the three big string quartets with his desire to, as he put it, "pave the way to grand symphony." In this, it seems that the piano sonata also played an important part (for a general account, see Költzsch). This is borne out by the fact that, although the over-all form is retained in all its essentials, there is a good deal of experimentation to be found in the piano sonatas of Schubert, and there are even several fragmentary works—even movements—especially from the years 1818–1819. There are in all some twenty-one sonatas by Schubert, and these may be listed and grouped chronologically as follows (the asterisk is used to indicate incomplete compositions):

1815–1816:

*I	E	D. 157
*II	C	D. 279
III	E	D. 459 (published as *Fünf Klavierstücke*)

1817:

IV	a	D. 537 (published as op. 164)
V	A-flat	D. 557
VI	e	D. 566[1]
VII	E-flat	D. 568 (published as op. 122; first version in D-flat, D. 567)
*VIII	f-sharp	D. 570–571 (two Allegro fragments and a scherzo)
IX	B	D. 575 (published as op. 147)

1818–1819:

*X	C	D. 613 (first and last movements completed)
*XI	f	D. 625 (three movements)
*XII	c-sharp	D. 655 (sketch of first movement)
XIII	A	D. 664 (published as op. 120)

1823–1826:

XIV	a	D. 784 (published as op. 143)
*XV	C	D. 840 (*Reliquie*; last two movements incomplete)
XVI	a	D. 845 (published as op. 42)
XVII	D	D. 850 (published as op. 53)
XVIII	G	D. 894 (published as op. 78, *Fantasie-Sonate*)

1828:

XIX	c	D. 958 (published as op. posth.)
XX	A	D. 959 (published as op. posth.)
XXI	B-flat	D. 960 (published as op. posth.).

There are, then, two sonatas from 1815 and one from 1816, six from 1817, three from 1818, one in 1819, and one in 1823, three in 1825, and one in 1826, and, finally, three great sonatas in 1828. From the quantitative point of view, there are three high points: 1817, 1825, and 1828. It is significant that it was precisely around 1825 that Schubert expressed his determination to devote himself more and more to the large forms of instrumental music.

Although two remained incomplete, the early sonatas of 1815–1816 nonetheless provide an accurate indication of the type of piano sonata that was favored by Schubert. It seems, first, as if the four-movement scheme was planned from the outset. (The Sonata in E, No. 3, D. 459, is, most exceptionally, in five movements.) This scheme is generally standard with Schubert, in whose sonatas we do not find the great varieties in the arrangement, forms, and compositional procedures that existed in similar works of Beethoven. What is of most importance for Schubert, however, are the themes employed and the treatment of the sonata principle. In these early sonatas, Schubert's way of doing things is clear. The themes are lyrical, often appearing balanced in antecedent and consequent phrases; all interest goes to the theme itself as a melody rather than to its inherent susceptibility to thematic development. Indeed, the development sections are small,

[1] Published under the editorship of K. Dale (London, 1948).

and, instead of the motivic work that was so characteristic of Beethoven (to say nothing of Haydn), we find rather that Schubert took a phrase of his theme and used it as the basis for a sequential passage with modulations.[1] With this, we have touched on a fundamental element in Schubert's art: the prominence given to modulation, the free use of keys and slipping from one to another often in a most unexpected fashion, exploiting the "sound" aspect of music, the element of harmonic surprise. Another feature of Schubert's treatment of the sonata principle may be seen in the first movement of this early Sonata in C; the recapitulation enters in the subdominant rather than in the tonic.

The slow movements are cast in what are termed "song forms," in alternating sections, either three parts or five, with considerable contrast in some cases (see the Sonata in E, No. 1, D. 157); again, there is constant preoccupation with harmony. The minuets and trios present much that would be expected, except, again, the astonishing freedom in modulation (see, particularly, the Sonata in E, No. 1). The scherzo in the Sonata in E (No. 3, D. 459) is faster, exploits motivic themes and abounds in sudden changes in dynamics.

Another important general feature is the small scale and generally moderate character of these sonatas. This may be seen, for example, from the tempo designations assigned by Schubert: Allegro moderato, Allegro ma non troppo, or Andante (Adagio is most unusual). The moderate first movements require neither long, weighty Adagios nor brilliant finales. This aspect would associate the sonatas of Schubert more with the ideal of Mozart than with that of Beethoven.

The six sonatas of 1817 (see Brown) present us with Schubert's first group of complete works in this genre. (Only the Sonata in f-sharp, D. 570–1, is incomplete here.) They present, on a larger scale, essentially the same features observed in the earliest sonatas. This greater length and elaboration is evident in the Sonatas in a (op. 164, D. 537), E-flat (op. 122, D. 568), and B (op. 147, D. 575). As illustrations, we can point to the thematic variety in the first movements of these sonatas; particularly striking is the Sonata in a with its change of key, the lyrical thematic material of the principal theme, and the use of dance-like melodies along with appropriate accompanying figures (prominent in the Sonatas in a and E-flat). The Sonata in a, Schubert's first large work in the minor, is interesting for its exploitation of the tone possibilities of the piano: the full chords, widely spaced, of the principal theme in the first movement; the crescendo in the bridge with off-beat accentuations and incessantly driving rhythmic motives; the dramatic rest before the entrance of the subordinate theme (used again in the development); and the soft pedal point of the closing theme. Particularly striking is the treatment of the development sections, which still remain short. In the Sonatas in a and E-flat, the development does not work with themes from the exposition, but with new material, making only some reference to themes

---

[1] The exception here is the early Sonata in C (No. 2, D. 279), in which the principal theme of the first movement is motivic and highly rhythmic, features that are exploited in the development.

already introduced, again with great freedom in modulation; and the large Sonata in B, although it takes in its development the principal theme and uses it as a modulating sequence, shows Schubert's preoccupation with sound—the sudden modulation, enharmony, changes in key signature, and pronounced dynamic effects. In the slow movements we again find the song forms in three parts and five parts, minuets and trios as third movements (the Sonata in B has a scherzo), and an easy finale, generally in sonata form. (The Sonata in a has a simple rondo, the same episode appearing twice.)

In the next group of sonatas, we find uncertainty; the set form of the 1817 group does not appear, and instead we find evidence of experimentation. Although the Sonata in C (D. 613), of which two movements were completed, was apparently to be in the same style as the works of 1817, unusual aspects may be noted for the other sonatas. Two of the four works are in the minor, and both are incomplete. In these sonatas in the minor, we note, in the first movements, an emphasis on motivic themes and on a more extravagant and intense type of expression. This is particularly true of the opening theme of the Sonata in f (D. 625)—the key, be it noted, of Beethoven's *Appassionata*—with its wide leap and virtuoso figuration; another example is the motor rhythm generated at the beginning of the Sonata in c-sharp (D. 655), whose first movement exists only as a sketch; while the finale to the Sonata in f presents a principal theme that is pure figuration. In all this, we may see that Schubert was attempting to make his sonatas more in the spirit of Beethoven. But in spite of the preoccupation with motivic themes and their working out, Schubert still continued to exploit the resources of harmonic color, as is, again, particularly evident from the Sonata in f, both in the exposition and the development of the first movement, which contains a quick shift from the flat keys (D-flat and A-flat) to the sharp keys (C-sharp, A, D, G, and e) and enharmonically (G-sharp = A-flat) back to f where he commenced.

In view of this effort at heightening the expression of the piano sonata, Schubert's next work in the genre comes as something of a surprise. The popular Sonata in A (op. 120, No. 13, D. 664) returns with seeming unconcern to the 1817 type of sonata. It is on a small, intimate scale, in three movements; the lyrical impulse is dominant, the development short and modest (in spite of the octave runs) with but little thematic connection to the exposition; there is a simple three-part slow movement, and the "light" finale is in sonata form (with the recapitulation in the subdominant), interrupted by a subordinate theme consisting of scale figuration, octaves in the bass, and weighty chords.

But this work is symptomatic in some ways of what was to come in the next group of sonatas, composed in 1825 and 1826. These compositions take on particular importance in the work of Schubert as a whole, since we have now reached the period when Schubert, as has been seen, expressed his desire to emphasize the composition of large instrumental works. These sonatas are among his first successes in this endeavor in that three of them were published shortly after their completion and even received favorable notices in the press: the Sonatas in a (op. 42, D. 845, composed in 1825 and published in 1825 or 1826), D (op. 53, D. 850), composed in 1825 and published in 1826), and G (op. 78, D. 894, composed in 1826 and published in 1827 with the title *Fantasia, Andante, Menuetto,* and *Allegro*). The incomplete Sonata in C (D. 840) of 1825 has been sympathetically discussed by Truscott. Here, there is not so much that is different from the Sonatas of 1817. The four-movement form is established for good (except for the three-movement Sonata in a, op. 143, D. 784, composed in 1823). For the most part, these compositions are cast on a large scale, and major keys are predominant. We can note the new importance played by codas to movements in sonata form; and, possibly as a result of the motivic work in the sonatas of 1818–1819, we can see that here, unlike the sonatas of 1817, Schubert systematically worked in the developments with thematic material from the expositions. The slow movements, as before, reveal the song form with its alternating sections (except for the theme and variations in the Sonata in a, op. 42, D. 845); minuets appear in the sonatas in C (*Reliquie*, D. 840) and G (op. 78, D. 894) and scherzi in the sonatas in a (op. 42, D. 845) and D (op. 53, D. 850); and, as something of a departure, in the finales, we find established the rondo form with one episode, usually treated with a degree of freedom and with great contrast between the various thematic components.

Here again, the lyric impulse, coupled with an even more grandiose exploitation of the sound capabilities of the piano, is of the greatest importance. Good examples of both may be seen, for instance, in the first movements of the Sonatas in a (D. 845) and G (D. 894); in the former, it may be seen at the close of the exposition where the principal theme is stated in a resounding *fortissimo*, and in the register shifts of the same theme near the beginning of the development, and again in the impressive dynamic effect in the coda where the piano may be said to be conceived orchestrally; similar features abound in the Sonata in G, and one should note especially the development of the first movement with its large scale crescendo and the harpsichord-like *pianissimo* effect in the trio to the minuet; one can also note the striking sound quality in the second movement of the Sonata in a (D. 845), the third variation with the dotted rhythms, the wide octave leaps and change in registration, the chromaticism, and the sudden turn to *pianissimo*.

Of a somewhat different order is the ambitious Sonata in D (op. 53, D. 850). Here we see something not at all usual in Schubert: the treatment of the piano as a virtuoso instrument. This quality appears at once in the first movement in the sudden *fortissimo* opening, the loud repeated chords in fast tempo, and the triplet figuration; it is a primarily rhythmic impulse, and this element, while nowhere really lacking in the movement even in the more lyrical subordinate theme, really attains its culmination in the development. Such a large-scale first movement needs and gets a long and serious slow movement, marked Con moto, in A, and in five-part form; a particularly Romantic effect is achieved towards the close of the subordinate part with the gentle dissonance between the thirds of the right hand and the static minor seventh in the bass. The scherzo, too, is suitably vigorous with full chords in dotted rhythms and a *pianissimo* trio consisting entirely of repeated chords and unexpected changes in harmony. The finale presents,

EXAMPLE 55

SCHUBERT: Allegro vivace, from *Sonata* in D (op. 53, D. 850)—beginning

as is typical of Schubert, great variety. There is a "naïve" rondo theme that is varied each time it appears and harmonically simple; the figuration becomes more brilliant and excited in the first episode and again in the second episode, which is in itself a closed three-part form with a vigorous middle section of full chords and octave passages that make a strong contrast to the lyric first part. It is entirely possible that the bigness of conception and the virtuoso treatment of the instrument are related to the fact that Schubert composed the work for his friend Karl Maria Bocklet, a pianist of great skill, so that here the two elements complement one another.

The last three sonatas of Schubert were composed in the late summer of 1828. (The manuscript of the last of these is dated September 26, 1828.) As already stated, the four-movement form is found in all. The large first movement (Allegro or Moderato) is in sonata form, Andantes are in song form (five-part in the Sonata in c, three-part in the others), there are two scherzi and a minuet (again in the Sonata in c), and the typical Schubertian rondos as finales. While these works may be said to represent a culmination of Schubert's sonata composition, they also represent a combination of Schubert's two previous ways of dealing with the big first movement in sonata form. In the Sonatas in c and A, we find the characteristic wealth of greatly varied material presented in the expositions: the full chords, dotted rhythms, and figuration of the Sonata in c and the brilliant sonorous opening of the Sonata in A with its sustained chords against downward octave leaps in the bass along with the more lyrical or "naïve" subordinate themes. In the great Sonata in B-flat (D. 960) all is lyricism, both in the broadly cantabile main theme over a rich, full harmonic accompaniment, which appears as the high point of a crescendo in the bridge passage, and in the lighter subordinate theme that gradually is dissolved into light, *Ländler*-like triplet arpeggios at the close. But in the development sections, we find that, strictly speaking, themes from the exposition are not exploited; instead, new themes are introduced. This is perhaps most striking in the Sonatas in c and A whose principal themes certainly have the possibility of being broken down into component motives for development; but Schubert did not take advantage of this. Instead, we find characteristic accompaniment and rhythmic figures retained, which then leads to the presentation of new thematic material. The Sonata in B-flat, however, while it does employ its lyric principal theme in the development as the basis for a long modulating sequence, eventually also introduces a totally new theme that is worked to a grandiose climax after which the principal theme is brought in once again. In all these sonatas, as before, modulation plays an important part.

The slow movements, as before, take the song form and often are in no way different from character pieces. In their first sections, they present simple, often "innocent" melodies that could easily be taken from songs, with clear, balanced phrases over unobtrusive accompaniments. But in the contrasting sections, there is a good deal of variety with climaxes of great proportions being attained in the Sonatas in c and A (the rapid repeated chords in triplet rhythm in the former, the broken octaves in the latter). Especially noteworthy is the Andante (in c-sharp) of the "lyrical" Sonata in B-flat: the slow melody in thirds over the disconsolate broken accompaniment figure, the broad chordal lyricism (in A) of the second part, then the return with the accompaniment pattern varied ever so slightly and and the gentle change to the major near the end.

The third movements are light and dance-like, while the finales, in rondo form, have also not undergone any changes since the works of 1825 and 1826. The schemes employed in the finales of the Sonatas in A and B-flat are less regular than that used in the Sonata in a. But all have great variety and abundant opportunity for display and a carefully worked out "effective" finish.

Here we see, then, that Schubert had reached his own characteristic interpretation of the piano sonata, in which we find but little that has anything to do with the motivic development so prominent in the work of Haydn and Beethoven. Instead, we have an essentially lyrical interpretation of the form with all attention being lavished on the themes themselves and not on what can be constructed from their component elements. If the influence of Beethoven can be seen at all, it lies in the large dimensions and profound character of these sonatas. And while the large dimensions are easily observable, it is different with the profound character. For this profundity is not achieved by the employment of learned or difficult musical procedures, as in the past, but rather in the melodies themselves. Here again, there are examples in the work of Beethoven, particularly prominent in his later works but not entirely lacking even in his earlier compositions: the first movement of the Sonata in A-flat (op. 110), the slow movements in general and those of the late sonatas in particular (also, the Symphony No. 9), and the first movement to the so-called *Archduke Trio*. Schubert had taken this conception of music and made it the *sine qua non* of his art.

Much has been made of the song-like qualities of Schubert, both in his themes and slow movements as well as in other large instrumental compositions. This brings with it not just the melodies, but also that great accomplishment of Schubert's work with songs—the characteristic accompaniment that makes possible a musical interpretation of the poem being set. In this, we are close to the character piece. Einstein, for one, sees several movements from the piano sonatas as being related to or having "affinities with," as he puts it, individual songs, for instance, the relationships of the slow movements of the Sonata in A (D. 664) to *Der Unglückliche* (D. 713), of the Sonata in D (D. 850) to *Fülle der Liebe* (D. 854), and of the Sonata in A (D. 959) to *Pilgerweise, Ich bin ein Waller* (D. 789); while the finale of the same sonata is connected to *Im Frühling, Still sitz' ich* (D. 882), and the first movement of the last Sonata in B-flat is related to Mignon's song *So lasst mich scheinen*. While some of these may be speculative, they are inspired by the fact that song melodies are featured in several of Schubert's large instrumental works, usually in the form of theme and variations: *Die Forelle* (D. 550) in the Quintet in A for Piano, Violin, Viola, Violoncello, and Double Bass (D. 667); *Der Tod und das Mädchen* in the String Quartet in d (D. 810); and, similarly, the second entr'acte from the ballet *Rosamunde* in the String Quartet in a (op. 29 i, D. 804) and *Sei mir gegrüsst* in the Fantasia for Violin and Piano in C (op. 159, D. 934).

This is emphasized here because there is an example—possibly even more striking—of this in Schubert's music for piano solo, in one of his most elaborate and grandiose compositions, the Fantasia in C, called *Der Wanderer* (op. 15, D. 760) of 1822. Here, one line of the song with the same title (op. 4 i, D. 493) of 1816 (*Die Sonne dünkt mich hier so kalt*) supplies the theme from which is generated a large work of four closely connected movements to be played without pause: a brilliant opening Allegro, an Adagio (in E), a Presto (actually a scherzo with two trios), and a concluding Allegro with triumphant fugal beginning. Here, the slow movement is in the form of theme and variations, but elements of this melody dominate the thematic material of all movements of the work. Thus we have here the first large piano work by a major composer to be completely cast in cyclic form. Noteworthy is the absence here of sonata form and of thematic development; development is replaced by variation. Conceived on an orchestral scale with many tremolos, crescendos, broken octaves, full chords, and scale runs, this work has no real predecessor and but few successors. Significantly enough, it was arranged for piano and orchestra by a later composer who could well appreciate all these elements—Franz Liszt.[1]

In the keyboard music of Schubert, then, there is established a broad division of compositions into two main classes, the one representative of the old large form of keyboard music handed down from the work of Haydn, Mozart, and Beethoven and the other the new, small, essentially lyrical character piece that was to become of prime significance for Romantic music. There are, as has been noted, innumerable instances of the capability of the new to influence the old, in some respects even to cause important changes in the old, as well as, in the *Wanderer Fantasia*, an instance of the two traditions being fused into one large-scale work. But the two bodies of music, generally speaking, existed side by side throughout the nineteenth century, and a composer's relation to and treatment of them will prove to be a matter of cardinal significance in the judgment of his music.

Unlike Beethoven but somewhat like Mozart, Schubert wrote a number of pieces for piano duet. Most of these are clearly domestic, small, easy, and pleasing works for entertainment at home. Among these can be mentioned various kinds of dances, especially *Ländler* and *Deutsche Tänze* or marches (among them the famous *Marches militaires*, op. 51, D. 733, or around 1822 and published in 1827) or the two three-movement *Divertissements*, one *Hungarian* in g (D. 818), the other *French* in e (D. 823), as well as several overtures, some of which are

---

[1] There is also an unpublished Fantasia in c, composed probably around 1813 (D. 993).

arrangements of his own orchestral works. But there are also large compositions for the duet medium: variations, sonatas, and fantasias. Of the three sets of variations by Schubert (the set in B-flat with introduction [op. 82 ii, D. 603] is

EXAMPLE 56

SCHUBERT: Fantasia in C (*Der Wanderer*, op. 15, D. 760)—excerpts

A. Allegro con fuoco ma non troppo—beginning

B. Adagio—beginning

C. Presto—beginning

D. Allegro [fugato]—beginning

spurious), two are small and rather conventional (both are on French melodies),
but the other is a large effort; this is the *Variations* (eight) *on an Original Theme*

EXAMPLE 56—*continued*

in A-flat (op. 35, D. 813), composed in 1824 and published in 1825. The duet sonata, also cultivated by Mozart, appears twice: the early *galant* and rather virtuosic Sonata in B-flat (D. 617) and the large composition in C (op. 140, D. 812) of 1824 (published in 1838) in four movements, known as the *Grand Duo*. This work has been claimed to be a lost symphony by Schubert, the *Gmunden-Gastein Symphony* and has even been orchestrated, but Einstein refutes this claim by pointing to many specifically pianistic features in the writing that are not at all related to orchestral conceptions. But the claim, nonetheless, is an indication of the size of the work. As for the fantasia, which we have already encountered in Schubert's piano solo music, we find it for piano duet among his earliest compositions: the three-movement Fantasia in G (D. 1), his first known composition, and the four-movement Fantasia in g (D. 9); both works seem very much like sonatas. But the next work, a Fantasia in c (D. 48) also known as the *Grande Sonate*, reveals a relationship to Mozart's large quasi-Baroque piano fantasias with its toccata-like passages and concluding fugue with chromatic subject. (The fugue does not appear in the first version.) The third and last of Schubert's fantasias for piano duet is again one of his largest and most characteristic works: the Fantasia in f (op. 103, D. 940) composed in 1828 and published in 1829, in movements played without pause and with the cantabile principal theme of the first movement reappearing immediately before the finale. One other work to be mentioned is the long, passionate Allegro in a (D. 947), also composed in 1828, to which the publisher gave the title *Lebensstürme* (*Storms of Life*). This emphasis on piano duet seems to be something particularly Viennese; and while most of the pieces for this medium are small, there are nonetheless a few works of major significance.

Piano music is considerably less important in the work of Schubert's somewhat older contemporary, Karl Maria von Weber (1786–1826) whose career was also very different from Schubert's. For Weber was most known as a composer and conductor of opera, first in Prague and then in Dresden, which was his home from 1816. (His most successful work was *Der Freischütz*, 1820.) This activity was preceded by a period of wandering during which his skill as a pianist was his chief livelihood (see Georgii). It is concertizing that lies back of a large part of his music for piano, especially the many sets of themes and variations, many on themes taken from theatrical works of the time by Vogler, Méhul, and Bianchi or from current popular songs. Then there are the dances, among them early sets of allemandes and écossaises, the *Favorit-Walzer* for the Empress Marie-Louise of France, and then the larger works—the *Grande Polonaise* in E-flat (op. 21) of 1808 and the *Polacca Brilliante* in E (op. 72) of 1819, also called *L'hilarité*.

Related to the dances is an important composition, the celebrated *Aufforderung zum Tanz* in D-flat (*Invitation to the Dance*, op. 65) of 1819. This work is based on the waltz; it is cast in rondo form with an introduction and epilogue. Annotations given by Weber himself make it clear that the piece is programmatic: the introduction, the tentative approach to the lady, the invitation to dance, the acceptance, and so on. Here, we have what is generally regarded as the first of the concert waltzes, the first large programmatic or characteristic work based on the waltz. There are many to follow.

Weber also produced two works that, generally speaking, are related to the character piece: the *Momento capriccioso* in B-flat (op. 12) of 1808 and the *Rondo Brilliante* in E-flat (op. 62) of 1819, also called *La gaité*. In these, it is virtuosity that is paramount in the elegant "salon" melodies and the constant employment of scale figuration.

Along with these, Weber cultivated also the piano sonata, composing four: in C (op. 24; No. 1) of 1812, in A-flat (op. 39; No. 2) of 1816, in d (op. 49; No. 3) of 1816, and in e (op. 70; No. 4) of 1822. Most of these, it will be noted, are contemporaneous with the late sonatas of Beethoven, but they have virtually nothing in common with these works. Instead, Weber in effect maintained the old forms and connotations of the sonata, much as we saw in the work of Schubert, except that Weber did not expand the form to such an extent. Three of Weber's sonatas are in four movements. (The Sonata in d lacks the minuet and trio.) In the first movements, the sonata form is found; in the finales, rondo form; and, in the slow movements and minuets, the familiar ternary scheme is the one used (for the minuet of the Sonata in C, see Georgii, *400 Years*, pp. 96–101). In regard to form, then, these are conventional works. What attracts attention is the variety to be found in the individual movements, especially the stylistic contrasts of the various themes, the sudden changes, and the prominence of virtuoso elements. There is evidence that the Sonata in e was regarded by Weber as a programmatic work. The key of e minor had conventionally been associated with sadness (see Haydn's *Trauer Symphony*), but in this work it is carried further and linked by Weber himself with mental disturbance, depression, and death, capped by a tarantella finale.

While piano music is relatively unimportant in the work of Weber, it is much more significant in Felix Mendelssohn-Bartholdy (1809–1847). Unlike Schubert, Mendelssohn was in the forefront of European musical life for a number of years; he was universally known and admired as a composer, conductor, and pianist. Born of a wealthy family and living in Berlin, he received a broad humanistic education in which musical studies took an important place. He attended the famous *Singakademie* which at the time was still under the direction of Carl Friedrich Zelter, a conservative musician who admired and performed works of Bach and who also was a close friend of Goethe. In the years 1830–1833, Mendelssohn went on his grand tour, which took him to Italy, France, and England. Thereafter, he was active as music director in Düsseldorf on the Rhine, and, in 1835, he took over the directorship of the concerts at the Gewandhaus in Leipzig. Eight years later, he participated in the establishment of the Leipzig Conservatory of Music, the first such institution in Germany.

While keyboard music cannot be said to occupy the dominant position in Mendelssohn's musical work,[1] he did compose some of his most characteristic works for this medium. In one important respect, the repertory of his music for keyboard instruments parallels that of Schubert, that is, in the presence of works in the old large forms of instrumental music side by side with a large number of examples of the new character piece. And unlike the other major composers of his time, Mendelssohn composed some works for the organ, an instrument that, as has been seen, had fallen into neglect.

To commence with the large forms, Mendelssohn composed three piano sonatas: in g (op. 105) of 1821, E (op. 6) of 1826, and B-flat (op. 106) of 1827. (Only works with opus numbers 1–73 inclusive appeared during Mendelssohn's lifetime.) It will be noted that the sonatas are early works, the last one being composed when Mendelssohn was eighteen, and he did not continue work in the genre, but turned elsewhere. These works, therefore, are symptomatic of the general decline of the piano sonata that can be observed as the nineteenth century wore on. Some of this was noted in connection with the work of Schubert, and we will see that it obtains just as much in the work of the other important composers of keyboard music.

The earliest, the Sonata in g, is a minor work in all respects in which features of the old "little" or "easy" sonata are to be discerned; it is in three-movement form, the outer movements are in sonata form with double bar, and the middle is an Adagio cantabile in five parts with the same episode appearing twice. The other sonatas are more ambitious. The Sonata in E (op. 6), the only one that Mendelssohn himself published, has four movements to be played without pause; it shows the use of cyclic form (the recalling of the first movement near the end of the work). This work is unusual in that none of the movements is cast in sonata form; the first and last movements are in a sort of rondo form, the first employing one subordinate section and the last two. A minuet in the key of f-sharp is the second movement. Noteworthy is the slow (third) movement, which falls into several widely contrasting sections: an elaborate Adagio in the style of the fantasia or recitative and marked *senza tempo*, then an Andante in F-sharp of eight bars, an Allegretto con expressione in E, and finally a repetition of the recitative. It is evident that this work was influenced in several respects by the late sonatas of Beethoven; the cyclic form, the unusual succession of movements, and the thematic material of the first movement have led Georgii to state that the work is modeled specifically on Beethoven's Sonata in A (op. 101). At the same time, as Georgii notes, Beethoven's march is replaced by the minuet; and, further, the

---

[1] On Mendelssohn generally, see the new study by Werner; on the piano music generally, see Young and Tischler; on the organ music, see R. Werner.

fugal writing so important in the Beethoven sonata is not present in Mendelssohn. But the Beethoven influence in a more general way is confirmed by the recitative passages, which are found, as has been seen, in several of Beethoven's sonatas, among them those in d (op. 31 ii), B-flat (op. 106), and A-flat (op. 110).

The Sonata in B-flat (op. 106) of Mendelssohn also is a large work in four movements with cyclic form; but here we have sonata form as well, complete with double bar, in the first movement; there is, also, a typically Mendelssohnian scherzo in the tonic minor as second movement, a simple Andante quasi Allegretto in E (!) in three-part form, then a dramatic Allegro molto that forms an interlude leading to the finale, which is an Allegro moderato rondo with two episodes. Except for the presence of the interlude between the third and fourth movements, the formal plan of the work is not an unusual one.

Mendelssohn composed three sets of themes and variations: *Variations sérieuses* in d (op. 54) of 1841, Variations in E-flat (op. 82) of 1841, and Variations in B-flat (op. 83; also for piano duet, op. 83a). All are based on Mendelssohn's own themes. It is the *Variations sérieuses* that have found their way into the piano repertory. For here, there is nothing of the *galant* that we have so often seen in the theme and variations form (much of Mozart and Beethoven, some Schubert, all of Weber); rather, here the "seriousness" is evident at once from the theme itself—in the minor, sixteen bars long but in a free or irregular form, without the usual divisions or any internal repetitive structure, with many suspensions, and with much chromaticism. The seventeen variations, as expected, display a variety of different characters: staccato chords alternating between the hands (iii), a long crescendo with sudden changes of dynamics and register (vi), a chromatic fughetta (x), cantabile, the melody in even notes over smooth broken-chord figuration (xi), an Adagio in the parallel major (xiv), followed by an unusual variation that goes from *pianissimo* to *forte* and then diminuendo with tied chords in the right hand (xv), and at the end is a brilliant coda. (On nineteenth century variations generally, see Friedland.)

A final group of works by Mendelssohn related to the traditional large forms of piano music is formed by the fantasias. Here, there are two works: the *Fantasia on an Irish Song* (*The Last Rose of Summer*, op. 15) of 1827 and the large Fantasia in f-sharp (op. 28) of 1833. Then there is a set of three shorter pieces called "fantasias" or "capriccios" (op. 16) of 1829, but these belong rather to the character pieces. The first of the larger fantasias has several points of contact with other fantasias that have been discussed. It is based on a song (like Schubert's *Wanderer* Fantasia), and it also exhibits many striking changes of mood and character: a cadenza-like opening, the simple presentation of the song melody (Adagio in E), then a Presto agitato in e, sections with recitative-like melodies. All of this was commonplace in the fantasia of the late eighteenth and early nineteenth centuries.

The Fantasia in f-sharp (op. 28), on the other hand, is a much larger work.

Cast in three movements, all played without pause, its size is close to that of a sonata, as indeed are Schubert's *Wanderer* Fantasia and Schumann's later Fantasia in C (op. 17). This relationship is also evident from the fact that this work is also known as the *Sonata écossaise* (the *Scotch Sonata*), and, in general plan, it is not dissimilar to Beethoven's famous *Sonata quasi una fantasia* in c-sharp (op. 27 ii). First is an Andante in f-sharp in simple ternary form, then an Allegro con moto in A (actually a scherzo and trio but in duple rather than triple time), and third a typically brilliant finale in f-sharp, in sonata form complete with double bar and repeat of the exposition and characterized by 6/8 meter; there is a brief agitato passage that serves as a transition between the first and second movements.

Other works of Mendelssohn can be regarded as aspiring to the large form or, perhaps, as parts of projected piano sonatas. There is the Andante cantabile e presto agitato in B and b of 1838, which is a lyric slow movement followed by a brilliant rondo with one episode in the minor, or the two *Clavierstücke*, again an Andante cantabile followed by a Presto agitato (but here the keys are B-flat and g, respectively), the latter movement in sonata form with double bar and repeat signs. For piano duet, there is an Allegro brilliant in A (op. 92). But it is evident that the main interest in Mendelssohn's piano music is involved rather with his extensive contributions to the literature of the new Romantic character piece. Exclusive of the *Songs without Words*, Mendelssohn's principal character pieces are:

Capriccio in f-sharp (op. 5) of 1825

Characterstücke (op. 7) of 1827: *Sanft und mit Empfindung*, Andante in e; *Mit heftiger Bewegung*, Allegro vivace in b; *Kräftig und feurig*, Allegro vivace in D; *Schnell und beweglich*, Con moto in A; *Ernst und mit steigender Lebhaftigkeit* or *Fuga*, Sempre legato; *Sehnsüchtig*, Andante in e; *Leicht und luftig*, Presto in E

Rondo capriccioso (op. 14) of 1824

Fantasias or *Caprices* (op. 16) of 1829

Caprices (op. 33) of 1834

Capriccio in E (e) (op. 118) of 1837

Scherzo a capriccio or Presto scherzando in f-sharp.

The capriccio, which is so important here, was a genre of keyboard music without any distinctive forms or traits. Sometimes, it appeared to be something like the fantasia of the late eighteenth century—a sectional work displaying sudden changes of key, meter, and style—as can be seen in Clementi's caprices (op. 35). Or it would be associated either with the etude, as in Müller's caprices (op. 29) or with the popular potpourri, a medley of numbers from popular operas with variations and virtuoso cadenzas (see Engel's article in *MGG*). To the extent that the capriccio or the caprice was connected with virtuosity, there would also be a relation to the caprices of Paganini, as we will later see when the etudes of Schumann and Liszt are under consideration.

Mendelssohn's capriccio compositions do not present any distinctive features. The earliest of them, in f-sharp (op. 5), is a large work in three-part form with coda; each of the sections in turn forms a smaller three-part form in which the middle part is a sort of development, and the coda employs thematic material from the second large section. The piece is plainly intended as a brilliant show piece and contains figuration passages. Similar to this are the three capriccios (op. 33). Two of these, the first in a and the last in b-flat, have slow introductions that show a distinct similarity to the eighteenth-century fantasia; the main parts, both presto, resemble in general the first movements of piano sonatas, the Presto con fuoco in b-flat even employing the old double bar with repeat sign. Much the same thing is to be seen in the independent Capriccio in E and e (op. 118), which is cast in a rondo form.

These, then, are large works that have certain similarities not only with the late eighteenth-century fantasia, but also with the large movements of the piano sonata. The fantasias or caprices (op. 16), on the other hand, are smaller compositions; all are in three-part form and avoid the striking contrasts found in the larger fantasia. Particularly characteristic of Mendelssohn is the second, the scherzo, Presto in e, a typically Mendelssohnian scherzo; it is fast with evenly moving staccato chords embellished with grace notes in the upper register.

That the designation "capriccio" could be used as representing a particular character is clear from the Rondo capriccioso (op. 14), preceded by an Andante espressivo. The rondo itself with two episodes (the first is not recapitulated) again resembles Mendelssohn's typical scherzo style; it is light and fast, evenly moving and staccato, but with sharp accents on off-beats, very light texture, and much use of figuration. The same is true of the Scherzo a capriccio or Presto scherzando in f.

Then there are the *Characterstücke* (*Characteristic Pieces*, op. 7), the first set by a major composer specifically given this title. Although in many cases the external formal schemes are what would be expected—simple repetitive plans and rounded binary, ternary, or rondo form—these pieces are surprising for the prominence of archaic traits. The first, in e, is, in spite of the regular formal plan, much like a cantabile Bach prelude for harpsichord, with the incessant motivic use of a single figuration pattern (see Georgii, *400 Years*, pp. 108–9); and much the same can be said of the scherzo-like *Leicht und luftig* in E (vii). But even more to be noted is the emphasis on counterpoint. The *Kräftig und feurig* in D (iii) is a real fugue with a long subject in driving sixteenth-note figuration, not unlike the violinistic fugue subjects in Bach, which in the working out makes much use of stretto. But the most impressive example is the fifth piece, *Ernst und mit steigender Lebhaftigkeit*, also called *Fuga*, with a slow, triadic, ricercare-like subject and a fully-developed countersubject, the theme itself divided into several motives that are exploited separately in the working out; the standard fugal learned devices —diminution and augmentation—are both employed, and only at the very end is the strict fugal procedure relaxed. This work reveals a certain similarity with the Fugue in E in Part II of Bach's *Well-Tempered Clavier*.

These character pieces, then, present several features that are totally unexpected in such a context; and Mendelssohn's chief contributions to the genre of the character piece are to be found rather in the eight sets of his *Lieder ohne Worte* (*Songs without Words*), each containing six pieces (see Kahl and Tischler).

Set I (op. 19b) of 1829–1830: Andante con moto in E; Andante espressivo in a; Molto allegro e vivace in A; Moderato in A; Poco agitato in f-sharp; *Venetianisches Gondellied*, Andante sostenuto in g

Set II (op. 30) of 1833–1834: Andante espressivo in E-flat; Allegro di molto in b; Adagio non troppo in E; Agitato e con fuoco in b; Andante grazioso in D; *Venetianisches Gondellied*, Allegretto tranquillo in f-sharp

Set III (op. 38) of 1836–1837: Con moto in E-flat; Allegro non troppo in c; Presto e molto vivace in E; Andante in A; Agitato in a; *Duetto* in A-flat

Set IV (op. 53) of 1841: Andante con moto in A-flat; Allegro non troppo in E-flat; Presto agitato in g; Adagio in F; *Volkslied*, Allegro con fuoco in a; Molto allegro vivace in A

Set V (op. 62) of 1842–1844: Andante espressivo in G; Allegro con fuoco in B-flat; Andante maestoso in e; Allegro con anima in G; *Venetianisches Gondellied*, Andante con moto in a; Allegretto grazioso in A

Set VI (op. 67) of 1843–1845: Andante in E-flat; Allegro leggiero in f-sharp; Andante tranquillo in B-flat; Presto in C; Moderato in b; Allegretto non troppo in E

Set VII (op. 85) of 1834–1841: Andante espressivo in F; Allegro agitato in a; Presto in E-flat; Andante sostenuto in D; Allegretto in A; Allegretto con moto, sempre cantabile in B-flat

Set VIII (op. 102) of 1842–1845: Andante un poco agitato in e; Adagio in D; Presto in C; Un poco agitato ma andante in g; Allegro vivace in A; Andante in C.

The designation "songs without words" is apparently Mendelssohn's own. It appears in the correspondence with his sister Fanny, and an early manuscript sketch of a song without words uses the term *Lied* (song). The title of the original edition of the first set, published in London, was *Six Songs for the Pianoforte Alone*, and the French title of the same set was simply *Romances*. The idea is clear. A song without words is a short keyboard piece in the style of a song, hence a simple lyric work; the melody is in balanced phrases over an accompaniment that usually operates with the same pattern throughout. In most cases, the same thematic material is used for an entire piece, but, in a few, the element of contrast is sought.

A few connections between some of the *Lieder ohne Worte* and Mendelssohn's own songs have been noticed; the "evening song," *Auf den Flügeln des Gesangs*

(*On the Wings of Song*, op. 34 ii) is similar to the Adagio in F (*Lieder ohne Worte*, set IV, op. 53 iv), while the song *Herbstlied* (op. 63) originally had been intended as a song without words. It may also be noted that, in the *Lieder ohne Worte*, specific descriptive titles are usually avoided. Three pieces are called *Venetianisches Gondellied* (*Venetian Gondola Song*): the Andante sostenuto in g (op. 19b vi), the Allegretto tranquillo in f-sharp (op. 30 vi), and the Andante con moto in a (op. 62 v); and one other piece is called *Volkslied* (*Folk Song*, op. 53 v). Two other pieces have acquired titles: *Jägerlied* (*Hunting Song*, op. 19b iii) and *Spinnerlied* (*Spinning Song*, op. 67 iv). But, for the rest, no explicit title, character, or other affective quality is indicated.

A certain similarity has been established between these small pieces of Mendelssohn and a set by one of his teachers, Wilhelm Taubert's *An die Geliebte*, *Acht Minnelieder* (op. 16) of 1831, in which lines from poems of Goethe, Hauff, and others serve as titles and convey the idea of being songs for the piano (see the *Minnelied* [op. 70 xix] in Kahl, 15, pp. 46–7). Another possible influence on Mendelssohn may be found in the small etudes of Ludwig Berger (op. 12 of 1820 or op. 22 of around 1830). But another relationship is of even greater significance; to a large extent, the different types to be found in Mendelssohn's *Lieder ohne Worte* correspond to types of the polyphonic social song (the *geselliges Lied*) that was cultivated assiduously by Zelter, the director of the Berlin *Singakademie* and Mendelssohn's teacher. Three basic types have been distinguished in the *Lieder ohne Worte*: the solo song with piano accompaniment, the duet with piano accompaniment, and the more elaborate choral song for four voices without accompaniment. The first type, the solo song, is most common; it is a simple lyric melody in balanced phrases over an accompaniment. In the accompaniment, often a single pattern is maintained throughout, the use of arpeggios being common, along with simple chords (as in op. 30 vi). Examples of the duet with accompaniment are, first, the one piece actually called *Duetto*, in A-flat (op. 38 vi) in a lilting 6/8 with supporting bass and light, arpeggiated accompaniment, as well as the three *Venetianische Gondellieder* that have been mentioned, which have a melody in parallel thirds using much embellishment over simple accompaniments. Among other "duets" are the Moderato in b (op. 67 v) and the Allegro agitato in a (op. 85 ii), both in parallel tenths. The third type, the four-part choral song, embraces works with simple melodies presented chordally with an accompaniment. As examples we can mention the Allegretto in A (op. 85 v), the Adagio in d (op. 102 ii), and the Andante in C (op. 102 vi). An instrumental background is to be assumed for those songs without words that move in a rapid tempo and in which the thematic material is composed of different kinds of figuration; of many examples, we can point here to the Molto allegro e vivace in A (op. 19b iii), the Agitato e con fuoco in b (op. 30 iv), the long Agitato in a (op. 38 v). Needless to say, there are instances in which elements from two or more of these different types appear in one and the same piece.

There are also several independent small character pieces: the Scherzo in b, the *Gondellied*, Allegretto non troppo in A, and the *Albumblatt* in e (op. 117), all of which are related to the genre of songs without words (the last expressly so). There is also a *Perpetuum mobile*, Prestissimo in C (op. 119), the perpetual motion

EXAMPLE 57

MENDELSSOHN: *Venetianisches Gondellied* in f-sharp, from *Lieder ohne Worte* (op. 30 vi)—beginning

being manifested in the incessant sixteenth-note figuration, and, as teaching pieces, the *Kinderstücke* (*Childrens' Pieces*, op. 72) of 1842.

The impact of Baroque music on Mendelssohn, specifically the influence of Bach's *Well-Tempered Clavier*, has already been observed in the *Characterstücke* (op. 7). We know that Mendelssohn was much involved with the music of Bach, inspired in part doubtless by the example of Zelter, which led, among other things, to his revival performance of the *St. Matthew Passion* in 1829. Among the most important manifestations of this in his musical composition is the cultivation of the prelude and fugue, or of the prelude by itself, for piano as well as for organ. The works in this genre are:

> *Praeludien* (op. 104, Part I) of 1836: Allegro molto e vivace in B-flat; Allegro agitato in B; Allegro vivace in D
>
> *Preludes and Fugues* (op. 35) of 1837: Prelude, Allegro con fuoco and Fuge in e; Prelude, Allegretto and Fugue, Tranquillo e semper legato in D; Prelude, Prestissimo staccato and Fugue, Allegro con brio in b; Prelude, Con moto and Fugue, Con moto ma sostenuto in A-flat; Prelude, Andante lento and Fugue, Allegro con fuoco in f; Prelude, Maestoso andante and Fugue, Allegro con brio in B-flat
>
> Prelude, Allegro molto and Fugue, Allegro energico in e (for the album *Notre temps*, an anthology of Christmas pieces by leading composers, published in Mainz by Schott in 1842 or 1843).

In their uniform character, these preludes are modeled on those of Bach; they use the same thematic material, usually figuration, all the way through. This is especially true of the preludes (op. 104), in which figuration is important. While some of the preludes (op. 35) also operate primarily with figuration, others are cantabile and are based on a single melodic pattern. Examples of this last are the well-known Prelude in e (with the marcato melody in the middle accompanied above and below by consistent arpeggio figuration), the Prelude in A-flat (a duet over arpeggiated sixteenth-note accompaniment), and the Prelude in f (its cantabile line accompanied by full chords). The fugues likewise reveal an indebtedness to Bach; there is a canzone-like subject featured in the Fugue in f, while one resembling the old ricercare appears in the Fugue in A-flat, and driving figuration subjects are also used, as in the Fugues in b and B-flat. The subject of the Fugue in e (for *Notre temps*) is especially striking, beginning with the downward leap of a seventh and then ascending scalewise in dotted rhythm. Among the devices employed are breaking the subject down into its component motives and treating them separately and in stretto. Free, nonfugal, passages appear frequently. Noteworthy are the Fugues in A-flat and e (No. 1). The first (with ricercare-like subject) is a double fugue that presents both subjects in contrapuntal combination along with episodes not in fugal style at all. The other is a long and elaborate work in which the performer is required to make a long and gradual acceleration and accumulation employing the subject in inversion (so that a change in character accompanies the change in the form of the subject), culminating in a statement of what appears to be a chorale melody in full chords with full octave accompaniment (but the "chorale melody" is of Mendelssohn's own composition, with similarities to *Ein' feste Burg*); at the end, there is a return to the andante quality of the beginning. Here, we can see how the fugue has become adapted to the character piece, as indeed, in a somewhat different way, was also seen in the *Characterstücke* (op. 7).

There remain the didactic works for piano, the etudes, of which Mendelssohn in all composed four, all in 1836; there is the Etude in f (for the Moscheles-Fétis, *Méthode des méthodes*) and the three Etudes (op. 104, Part II): Presto in b-flat, Allegro con moto in F, and Allegro vivace in a. Each of these concentrates on the working out of a particular problem of pianistic execution: the accompanying of a marcato melody with arpeggio figuration (Etude in f), a study in arpeggios and chords (Allegro vivace in a), scales and arpeggios (Allegro con moto in F), and playing cantabile in the middle with octaves in the bass and brilliant arpeggios above, all *pianissimo* (Presto in b-flat). This working with a particular problem of execution brings about a certain thematic unity and uniformity of character, so that these etudes are not dissimilar to the preludes we have just examined. It will be seen that a close relationship between the two genres persists in nineteenth-century piano music, and we will be running into it constantly.

As the chief organ works of Mendelssohn (others are as yet unpublished), there are the three preludes and fugues (op. 37) composed between 1835 and 1837 and the six so-called "sonatas" for organ (op. 65) composed in 1844–1845. The preludes and fugues present essentially the same picture as did the preludes and fugues for piano (op. 35). With the sonatas for organ (see Hathaway, Mansfield, and Pearce), the situation is rather different. Here, one might assume that Mendelssohn was interested in composing for the organ in a large form that would be the equivalent of the piano sonata, the symphony, or other large forms of instrumental music. And, while these organ sonatas are generally in four movements (one, No. 3 in A, is in two, and No. 6 in d is in variation form), the schemes employed here have no connection with those used in the sonata or symphony. Rather, these organ sonatas are related to the voluntary, a type of concert music for church indigenous to England, which had, in the late seventeenth century, expanded into works in several contrasting sections. These organ sonatas of Mendelssohn were composed for an English publishing house. Other features of Baroque music are present here. There is the use of fugue (the finales of Sonatas No. 2 in c and No. 6 in d, as well as several individual sections of movements); the presence of the toccata style, with vigorous figuration passages and block chords (evident in the last movements of the Sonatas No. 1 in f and No. 5 in D); and the use of chorale melodies, in the first movements of the Sonata No. 1 in f, the large first movement of the Sonata No. 3 in A (*Aus tiefer*

Not)—here treated in cantus firmus fashion, with unusual figuration making striking use of the tritone, so that the movement actually is a chorale prelude—and the Sonata No. 6 in d (*Vater unser im Himmelreich*)—where the chorale is first stated simply and then appears in cantus firmus fashion in several sections in different meters and characters, ultimately serving to provide the motive for the concluding fugue. This last work, then, may be regarded as a revival of the old chorale partita of the seventeenth and eighteenth centuries. The beginning of the Sonata in D (No. 5) resembles a chorale, but evidently the melody was original with Mendelssohn. On the other hand, the Allegretto of the Sonata in B-flat (No. 4) is in effect a song without words, as can be seen in the cantabile melody, the constantly maintained figure in the accompaniment, and the even motion of the bass. So we see that much is brought together in these organ sonatas and that, generally speaking, they provide eloquent testimony to Mendelssohn's preoccupation with Baroque music. A truly symphonic style of organ composition came only in the latter part of the nineteenth century and in France.

Perhaps the most characteristically Romantic composer of the first half of the century was Robert Schumann (1810–1856), in whose hands the character piece came into its own replete with literary and other references and associations.[1] The background can be seen already from Schumann's father, who was engaged in the book publishing business and was also the author of successful novels somewhat in the fashion of Jean Paul. Schumann himself enjoyed the broad education provided by the German *Gymnasium*, during which time he and his friends organized a society for the study of German literature; Schumann's ambitions were literary as well as musical. The decision to study law at the University of Leipzig was on the basis of the uncertainties of the musical profession; but the law studies were soon abandoned. While at Leipzig, Schumann came under the influence of the renowned piano teacher Friedrich Wieck (1785–1873), whose daughter Clara (1819–1896) was to become his wife. Schumann had the ambition to become a virtuoso pianist; but a contraption that he designed to strengthen his fourth finger malfunctioned and crippled his right hand, so that thereafter he had to turn to other pursuits—composition, music criticism, and conducting. Much of his critical writing on music appeared in a journal that he founded in 1834, the *Neue Zeitschrift für Musik*; he also taught for a time at the Leipzig Conservatory, which had just been established, under the guidance of Mendelssohn. For a few years, Schumann served as the general music director in Düsseldorf on the Rhine (where Mendelssohn had also worked), but mental illness, which had been troubling him for years, grew worse, and led first to a suicide attempt and ultimately to his death.

[1] On Schumann generally, see the studies of Brion, Rehberg, and Abert, among others, and the collection of essays edited by Abraham; on the piano music generally, see Fuller-Maitland, Beaufils, Hohenemser, Hopf, and Gertler.

The preoccupation with literature and with music is one of Schumann's most important characteristics. While the various manifestations of this concern —which is of great importance for his keyboard works—will be dealt with as the occasion arises, there is one important aspect that has to do with his composition as well as his critical writing. In the pages of his reviews, Schumann emerges as the ardent supporter of the new serious forms of Romantic music and as the opponent of empty virtuoso bravura display. This is carried on in a sort of dialogue form, the participants in which are called the *Davidsbündler* (the companions of David), who set out to combat and defeat the musical Philistines of the time and to raise the art of music to the heights that it once had occupied (see especially Schumann's own account, written in 1854). The various members of his imaginary organization are Florestan, nervous, impetuous, passionate; Eusebius, reflective and dreamy; Raro, the wise one who draws the best from all different points of view. While these characters apparently correspond to different aspects of Schumann himself, others represent actual people: F. Meritis stands for Mendelssohn, Jeanquirit for Stephen Heller, Knif for Fink (a conservative editor and critic, whose name is spelled backwards), and Chiara, Chiarina, or Zilia (all three) for Clara. But, basically, all are imaginary, each representing part of Schumann's own character (see Jansen) and thus strikingly symptomatic of the mental illness from which he suffered. As we will see, both Florestan and Eusebius play a role in his musical compositions as well; the Sonata in f-sharp (op. 11) was attributed to them in its first edition, and as a group the *Davids-bündler* are associated with the *Davidsbündler* (op. 6) and *Carnaval* (op. 9). This manner of critical writing is characteristic of the time; the great German Romantic poet and writer (also musician and composer) Hoffmann had cast a whole series of short stories in a conversational frame (*Die Serapionsbrüder*), and Jean Paul, whose work had great impact on Schumann, often in his works employed twins, two paired characters whose qualities complemented one another (*Siebenkäs* and *Flegeljahre* particularly).

In Schumann, the character piece is the most important single genre of piano music. Although there are three sonatas and a few sets of etudes and variations (the two, as will be seen, being related to one another), it is clearly the character piece that received the most attention and in which we find his most representative works. The urge to compose in the large forms was not absent in Schumann, but it appears in a new guise—that of composing a cycle of character pieces conceived as an artistic entity, a suite; thus the character piece became the basis for a large form of piano music. The character pieces of Schumann are as follows (the dates of composition are given):

Papillons (op. 2) of 1830–1831
Intermezzi (op. 4) of 1832
Impromptus on a Theme of Clara Wieck (op. 5) of 1833

Davidsbündlertänze (in second edition, *Die Davidsbündler*), eighteen character pieces (op. 6) of 1837

Carnaval. Scènes mignonnes sur quatre notes (op. 9) of 1834–1835: *Préambule, Pierrot, Arlequin, Valse noble, Eusebius, Florestan, Coquette, Relique, Papillons, ASCH-SCHA, Lettres dansantes, Chiarina, Chopin, Estrella, Reconnaissance, Pantalon et Columbine, Valse allemande, Paganini, Intermezzo, Aveu, Promenade, Pause, Marche des "Davidsbündler" contre les Philistins*

Phantasiestücke (op. 12) of 1837: *Des Abends, Aufschwung, Warum, Grillen, In der Nacht, Fabel, Traumes-Wirren, Ende vom Liede*

Kinderscenen (op. 15) of 1838: *Von fremden Länden und Menschen, Kuriose Geschichte, Hasche-Mann, Bittendes Kind, Glückes genug, Wichtige Begebenheit, Träumerei, Am Kamin, Ritter vom Steckenpferd, Fast zu ernst, Fürchtenmachen, Kind im Einschlummern, Der Dichter spricht*

Kreisleriana (op. 16) of 1838: *Aeusserst bewegt* in d, *Sehr innig und nicht zu rasch* in B-flat, *Sehr aufgeregt* in g, *Sehr langsam* in B-flat, *Sehr lebhaft* in g, *Sehr langsam* in B-flat, *Sehr rasch* in c, *Schnell und spielend* in g

Arabeske (op. 18) of 1839

Blumenstück (op. 19) of 1839

Humoreske (op. 20) of 1839

Noveletten (op. 21) of 1838: *Markirt und kräftig* in d, *Aeusserst rasch und mit Bravour* in D, *Leicht und mit Humour* in D, *Ballmässig* in D, *Rauschend und festlich* in D, *Sehr lebhaft, mit vielem Humour* in A, *Aeusserst rasch* in E, *Sehr lebhaft* in c-sharp

Nachtstücke (op. 23) of 1839: *Mehr langsam, oft zurückhaltend* in C, *Markirt und lebhaft* in F, *Mit grosser Lebhaftigkeit* in D-flat, *Einfach* in F

Faschingsschwank aus Wien (op. 26) of 1839: Allegro in B-flat, Romanze in g, Scherzino in B-flat, Intermezzo in e-flat, Finale in B-flat

Romanzen (op. 28) of 1839: *Sehr markirt* in b-flat, *Einfach* in F-sharp, *Sehr markirt* in B

Waldscenen (op. 82) of 1848–1849: *Eintritt im Walde, Jäger auf der Lauer, Einsame Blumen, Verrufene Stelle, Freundliche Landschaft, Herberge, Vogel als Prophet, Jagdlied, Abschied*

Marches (op. 76) of 1849: *Mit grösster Energie* in E-flat, *Sehr kräftig* in G, *Lager-Scene* in B-flat, *Mit Kraft und Feuer* in E-flat

Bunte Blätter (op. 99) of 1836–1849: *Drei Stücklein, Albumblätter* (3), *Novelette, Präludium, Marsch, Abendmusik, Scherzo, Geschwindmarsch*

Phantasiestücke (op. 111) of 1851: *Sehr rasch, mit leidenschaftlichem Vortrag* in c, *Ziemlich langsam* in A-flat, *Kräftig und sehr markirt* in f

Albumblätter (op. 124) of 1832–1845: Impromptu, *Leides Ahnung, Scherzino, Walzer* in C, *Phantasietanz, Wiegenliedchen, Ländler, Lied ohne Ende,* Impromptu, *Walzer* in E-flat, Romanze, *Burla,* Larghetto in f, *Vision, Walzer* in A-flat, *Schlummerlied, Elfe, Botschaft, Phantasiestück,* Canon in D

Gesänge der Frühe (op. 133) of 1853: *Im ruhigen Tempo* in D, *Belebt, nicht zu rasch* in D, *Lebhaft* in A, *Bewegt* in f-sharp, *Im Anfang ruhiges, im Verlauf bewegtes Tempo* in D.

Many of these works correspond generally to what can be regarded as the "normal" types of the character piece: the intermezzo, impromptu (which here appear as variations), romances, fantasias (*Phantasiestücke*), nocturnes, arabesques, humoresques, album leaves, and even marches. Others are more specifically programmatic and more individualistic, and it is here that the extra-musical associations are of the greatest significance: *Papillons, Carnaval, Die Davidsbündler, Kinderscenen, Kreisleriana, Blumenstück, Noveletten, Faschings-schwank aus Wien, Gesänge der Frühe* (on Schumann and literature generally, see Schmitz). To Jean Paul, the famous and popular German novelist of the early nineteenth century, can be traced the term *Blumenstück*, associated with his novel *Siebenkäs*, and, perhaps, the *Papillons*, which are connected with the masked ball scene near the end of the novel *Flegeljahre* (see Kötz and Jacobs). Other points of contact can be established between Schumann and the Romantic writer and musician E. T. A. Hoffmann, to whose work the *Kreisleriana*, the *Phantasie-stücke*, and the *Nachtstücke* are related. A motto from Friedrich Hebbel prefaces *Verrufene Stelle* in the *Waldscenen*, and the collection as a whole is thought to have been inspired by Heinrich Laube's *Jagdbrevier*, a set of poems about the forest and hunting. The *Bilder aus Osten* (op. 66) for piano duet is expressly related by Schumann to Friedrich Rückert's *Makamen*, German versions of Persian epic poetry. The second of the *Noveletten* in Schumann's original draft was entitled *Sara꜀ene und Suleika*, thus associated with Goethe's *West-östlicher Divan*, a collection of poems closely related to Oriental (Persian) models. Finally there is the *Davisbund*, already mentioned, who are celebrated in the *Davids-bündlertän꜀e* (op. 6) and in *Carnaval* (op. 9); their relation to Hoffmann and Jean Paul has already been mentioned. It is clear, then, that a large and important part of Schumann's character pieces are connected with the German literature of the time.

Schumann's character pieces may—rather roughly—be grouped under several headings: the sets of short pieces (or miniatures), the larger works, and the sets or suites. To the first group belong *Papillons*, the *Davidsbündlertän꜀e*, the *Kinderscenen*, and the *Waldscenen*. The *Papillons* are actually dances, most of which are in triple time and related to the waltz. While the forms used are simple, there is no standard pattern; usually one finds three or four short sections frequently each to be repeated, and some sort of over-all repetitive design; some of the pieces have introductions and codas. Worthy of special mention are the piece in f-sharp (iii), with the canon in octaves reminiscent of Haydn's *Hexen* (*Witches*) *Minuet* (Quartet in d, op. 76 ii), and the finale, which introduces a popular German song of the seventeenth and eighteenth centuries, the *Grossvaterlied*, a tune Schumann later used in *Carnaval*. Also very short are the twelve impromptus (op. 5). These are based on a theme by Clara Wieck, taken from her *Romance varié* (op. 3) for piano. Here the principle of thematic variation is influenced by Beethoven's *Prometheus* or *Eroica* variations (op. 35), both the melody and its bass being used separately and in combination.

The other major set of miniatures is the *Davidsbündlertänze* (op. 6), eighteen in number (easily accessible in Apel, *Masters*, pp. 233–8). In these pieces, the inscriptions usually indicate the character to be expressed rather than merely the tempo: "lively," (i), "with humor" (iii), "impatiently" (iv), "like a ballade" (x), "simple" (xi), "as from the distance" (xvii); they thus depart from Schumann's practice in his earlier sets of character pieces. In the first edition, the individual pieces were signed with an "F" or an "E" designating "Florestan" or "Eusebius" as the alleged composer (in some cases both). Again in this set, we see a connection with dance types, along with the simplicity of formal organization that would be expected. Florestan's restlessness is seen in *Ungeduldig* (iv), ostensibly a *Ländler* but with a syncopated upper part using tied notes and with the accent constantly falling half a beat too late; while Eusebius' reflective and lyrical nature is exhibited in *Einfach* (v) and in the cantabile *Zart und singend* (xiv).

Two other sets of short pieces are the *Kinderscenen* (op. 15) and the *Waldscenen* (op. 82), both widely used as children's pieces (on the *Kinderscenen*, see Steglich). But here the qualification "for large and small children" (*für kleine und grosse Kinder*) used by Schumann in his pieces for piano duet (op. 85) seems equally appropriate, and these works frequently engage the attention of accomplished musicians. The key relationships are such that each set can be performed as a whole, thus making up a suite, although there is no other indication that such was Schumann's intent. The simple three-part scheme is the most usual, and a programmatic title elucidates the character of each piece. In the *Waldscenen* are some unusual pieces: *Verrufene Stelle* (iv), with a motto from Hebbel about the pale flowers in the shade surrounding the one that thrives since it feeds not from the sun but from human blood, all of which is depicted by staccato phrases and soft chords in dotted rhythms, and the well-known *Vogel als Prophet* (vii), *pianissimo* with piquant dissonances through the use of cross-relations, the fragmentary phrases rising and falling.

Two other sets of miniatures belong to the category of the album leaf: the fourteen *Bunte Blätter* (op. 99), which has been variously translated as "variegated leaves" and "promiscuous leaves" (the latter leaving something to be desired), and the twenty *Albumblätter* (op. 124). But unlike the *Kinderscenen* and *Waldscenen*, these sets are far from presenting a uniform and consistent character, since both include works written over a long period in Schumann's creative life, some of the *Albumblätter* going back as far as 1832.

Still another set, this one specifically intended for children, is the *Charakterstücke* (or *Album*) *für die Jugend* (op. 68) of 1848, which contains many well-known works, like the *Wilder Ritter* (*The Wild Horseman*) and *Fröhlicher Landmann* (*The Happy Farmer*), along with such more unusual pieces as two elaborations of chorale melodies, a little prelude and fugue, a folk-song setting (*Mai, lieber Mai*), and the more difficult *Knecht Rupprecht* (*Knight Ruppert*). The set is a remarkable instance of a composer working in a simple vein yet not losing any of his artistic individuality.

The sets of larger character pieces are the *Phantasiestücke* (op. 12 and 111) the *Kreisleriana* (op. 16), the *Noveletten* (op. 21), the *Nachtstücke* (op. 23), the *Romanzen* (op. 28), a set of highly stylized *Marches* (op. 76), and the late *Gesänge der Frühe* (op. 133). (The intermezzi, *Carnaval*, and the *Faschingsschwank aus Wien* are discussed below.) The best-known of these are the *Phantasiestücke* (op. 12) and the *Kreisleriana*, both related to E. T. A. Hoffmann, as noted. Although they are often played *in toto*, Schumann seems rather to have thought of them as groups of independent compositions, as is evident from the key relationships and the fact that all the pieces in each group are separate, there being no attacca indications anywhere. The most usual formal plan in these works is the ternary scheme, the middle section providing contrast of key, character, and thematic material; but since this middle section, apart from its key, often maintains features of the beginning, most of the pieces have a uniform character throughout. In *Kreisleriana*, the *Noveletten*, the *Nachtstücke*, and the *Romanzen*, the enlarged form with two contrasting sections assumes greater importance, and in the third of the *Romanzen* there are three such contrasting episodes. Where a subordinate section or episode is strongly contrasting in character, it is given the name "intermezzo" (op. 16 ii; op. 21 ii, iii; op. 28 iii); but, in the first and last of the *Noveletten* (op. 21 i and viii), they are called "trios."

The only group here in which individual pieces have descriptive titles is the *Phantasiestücke* (op. 12). Here the pieces vary widely. *Des Abends* (*Of the Evening*, i), is a quiet, lyrical nocturne, a melody moving in slow even notes over a gentle arpeggio accompaniment, uniform in character throughout; but *In der Nacht* (*In the Night*, v) is a strikingly passionate work (the key is f) with an irregular melody of fragmentary phrases over a furious accompaniment of arpeggios, an altogether different kind of nocturne. Much variety is found in *Aufschwung* (*Soaring*, ii), which has a loose rondo structure with two episodes in which the brilliant alternates with the lyrical. Also worthy of note are *Fabel* (*Fable*, vi), with its alternation between the lyrical and the capricious, and *Traumes-Wirren* (*Confusion of Dreams*, vii), as well as the sturdy concluding number, *Ende vom Liede* (*End of the Song*, viii).

Of the remaining sets, only *Kreisleriana* now appears comparable to the *Phantasiestücke*. Suggested by the figure of Kapellmeister Kreisler, a character in several works of E. T. A. Hoffman, the individual pieces are generally longer than those in the *Phantasiestücke*. Again, we find slow lyric pieces (ii, iv, vi) alternating with brilliant pieces abounding in figuration and dramatic effects (i and iv, in Georgii, *400 Years*, pp. 104–7). In the *Noveletten*, the influence of dances again appears. *Ballmässig* (*Like a Ball*, iv) in D is a waltz, *Rauschend und festlich* (*Rustling and Festive*, v) a sort of polonaise; typically Romantic in the *Noveletten* is the *Stimme aus der Ferne* (*Voice from the Distance*), the concluding piece (viii).

Then there are manifestations of the desire somehow to establish the character piece in an appropriate large form, possibly so that this genre could vie with the older sonata. Schumann did this in two ways: first, by composing larger character pieces and, second, by presenting a number of them in a unified set or cycle, thus producing a larger work. The first approach is evident in three lesser-known works composed in 1839: the *Arabeske* in C (op. 18), the *Blumenstück* in D-flat (op. 19), and *Humoreske* in B-flat (op. 20). In all, the general formal plan is that of the rondo, presented simply in the *Arabeske* but with many variations in *Blumenstück* and *Humoreske*. The elaborations in *Blumenstück* involve having an introductory passage before the ritornello (or refrain) section and having the various episodes themselves cast in small three-part form. This freedom of form is carried even further in *Humoreske*, a long sectional work with much variety and some sections repeated. Such an unusual work doubtless reflects the improvisational (inspirational?) origin of the work and its manifestation of Schumann's own personal emotions; this is made clear in the often-quoted letter to Clara of March 11, 1839: "I have been sitting the whole week at the pianoforte, composing and laughing and crying all at once; you will find all this beautifully depicted in my op. 20, the 'great Humoreske'..." (translation by Niecks).

Then there are two suites of character pieces, *Carnaval* (op. 9) and *Faschingsschwank aus Wien* (*Vienna Carnival Prank*, op. 26). Of the two, the *Carnaval* is more like a suite in the usual understanding of the term. It has a sub-title, *Scènes mignonnes sur quatre notes*; the term *scènes* suggests a background of the painting or drama. (Note that it is also used in the *Kinderscenen* and *Waldscenen* and in an early set of variations on a popular waltz by Schubert. It apparently was reserved for the very small pieces, the miniatures, as is also suggested by the qualification *mignonnes*.) In *Carnaval*, there are several factors that combine to produce an over-all unity. One of these is an extramusical association, which can be seen from *ASCH SCHA*, *Lettres dansantes* (x) in which letters of the alphabet are equated with their musical equivalents: "Asch" is the name of the city in which Ernestine von Fricken, a pupil of Friedrich Wieck, resided, and "Scha" is composed of those letters in Schumann's own name that are also the names of musical notes. The musical equivalents of *ASCH* and *SCHA* are various: A-flat, E, C, B (since in German, E-flat is *Es* and B natural is *H*) or A-flat, C, B (since A-flat is *As*); and, for SCHA, E-flat, C, B, A. These possibilities are given, without explanation, as *Sphinxes* (between viii and ix). Most numbers in *Carnaval* display these notes prominently in their thematic material, especially at the beginning, so that this is a most important factor in the over-all unity of the work. The opening *Préambule* and the concluding *Marche* likewise share thematic material; the *Marche* also employs the *Grossvaterlied* previously used in the finale of *Papillons*. Other factors promoting unity in *Carnaval* are: the frequent running together of individual numbers (as between *Florestan* [vi] and *Coquette* [vii] or, more extended between *Reconnaissance* [xiv], *Pantalon et Columbine* [xv], and *Valse allemande* [xvi]; an *attacca* indication (as between *Pause* [xx] and *Marche* [xxi]); the *Valse allemande* is followed by *Paganini*, called "intermezzo," after which the waltz is repeated *senza replica*; *Replique* (viii) is a short variation and development of part of the number that precedes it, *Coquette* (vii). All the way through, the principal key is A-flat, and keys closely related to it are most prominent—E-flat, B-flat, g, c, f, and D-flat—so that an over-all tonal unity is the result.

The individual numbers of *Carnaval* are short and are cast in forms that seem, for the most part, related to the dance, usually a small binary form with one or both parts repeated or a simple tenary scheme. All embody some definite character or characteristic. Particularly noteworthy is the striking musical manifestation of *Eusebius* (v), an Adagio with a melody meandering rhythmically in septuplets, quintuplets, and triplets over a slow chromatic accompaniment employing suspensions and not using the tonic in root position, creating thus an aura of dreaminess, immediately followed by *Florestan* (vi), a Passionato in which the melody rises impetuously over an assertive accompaniment of repeated cords and there are sudden and nervous changes and running-on into the next piece, *Coquette*. The other members of the *Davidsbündler* here in *Carnaval* are

EXAMPLE 58

SCHUMANN: *Carnaval* (op. 9)—excerpts

A. *Eusebius*—beginning

B. *Florestan*—beginning

Chiarina (xi), a passionate waltz representing Clara; *Estrella* (xiii) for Ernestine von Fricken, a lyrical and irregular waltz; and, of course, at the end, the *Marche des "Davidsbündler" contre les Philistins*. Chopin is represented by a short piece in typical nocturne style (xii), and Paganini (xvii) by a virtuoso intermezzo to the *Valse allemande* featuring fast staccato octave passages.

Carnaval, then, presents the combination in one variegated work of features found in other works that have been examined: the use of short dance types, as in *Papillons*; the employment of cyclic form with thematic variation, as had been used in a somewhat different way in the *Intermezzi* (op. 4); and the extensive

EXAMPLE 58—*continued*

extramusical associations, the letter–note relationships (used in the early *Abegg* variations and probably suggested by the custom of composing pieces of the name "Bach"). It is a work in which much that is characteristic of Schumann can be seen.

The *Faschingsschwank aus Wien* (op. 26) presents an altogether different situation. Here, there are but five sections or movements, each considerably larger than the individual numbers in *Carnaval*: an Allegro in B-flat, a Romanze in g, a Scherzino in B-flat, an Intermezzo in e-flat, and a finale, *Höchst lebhaft*, again in B-flat. Descriptive titles to the individual pieces are lacking. The first piece is in large sectional form and does not correspond to any recognized plan; rondo-like, it has five contrasting episodes in which some parody is found—the fourth is a variation of the *Marseillaise*, while the fifth is obviously related to the slow movement of Beethoven's Sonata in E-flat (op. 31 iii); the finale is a sonata form with coda. The second movement is lyrical with a florid melodic line, the fourth is an impassioned intermezzo in ternary form but uniform in character, and in the middle is the small scherzo without trio. In its key relationships and the features displayed in its movements, the *Faschingsschwank aus Wien* seems like a sonata (although the form of the first movement certainly would not fit the usual arrangement of a sonata) and, in an early version, was even called by Schumann *Grande romantique sonata*.

Although the character pieces take the first position among Schumann's keyboard works, the older forms—the sonata, the fantasia, and the theme and variations—are also represented. The sonata, as the largest, draws our attention first. Schumann completed three (again the dates of composition are given): in f-sharp (op. 11; No. 1) of 1833–1835; in g (op. 22; No. 2) of 1833–1838; in g (op. 14; No. 3, called *Concerto sans orchestre*) of 1835–1836 and revised in 1853. These are relatively early works; after 1838, Schumann did not compose in the genre except for the children's sonatas (op. 118) and the revisions of earlier works in 1853. But his path to the sonata was nonetheless a hesitant one, a circumstance to be attributed, in part, to this typically Romantic preference for the smaller genre of the character piece and, in part, to the general decline of the sonata that occurred during the nineteenth century. This reluctance shows itself in several ways. First, there are sketches of sonatas or of sonata movements: the first and last movements of a Sonata in A-flat of 1830, other movements belonging apparently to an unfinished Sonata in B-flat of 1832 on which he also worked in 1836, and an unfinished Sonata in f (which he went so far as to call No. 4) on which he worked from 1833 to 1837. Second, there are works planned or probably planned as sonatas but that appeared under different designations; the Sonata in f (op. 14) was originally a five-movement work, but, at the publisher's insistence, the two scherzo movements were eliminated so that it could appear as the *Concerto sans orchestre*; in his revision of 1853, Schumann restored the title "sonata" and with it one of the two scherzi; and, as we have seen, the *Faschingsschwank aus Wien* (op. 26) had been planned as the *Grande romantique sonata* in B-flat. Finally, the large Allegro in b (op. 8) might have also been the first movement of an intended sonata.

In all events, the three completed works called "sonata" are large works in four movements, fully in accordance with the conception of the genre as it had come down from the later works of Schubert: the large opening movements in sonata form, the equally large finales in rondo form, the scherzi, and the slow movements in three-part form (Sonatas in f-sharp and g) or theme and variations (Sonata in f). In the Sonata in f, the scherzo is the second movement and the slow movement comes third. The key relations also are conventional; all movements except one are in the same key—the slow movements of the Sonatas in f-sharp and g in the relative major and subdominant, respectively, the scherzo of the Sonata in f in a more removed key, D-flat. In the first movements, we find the sonata form with coda, and, in the Sonatas in f-sharp and g, we even find the double bar with repeat of the exposition. Noteworthy is the Sonata in f-sharp for the rhetorical introduction, the broad melody with sharply accentuated dotted rhythms over an arpeggiated accompaniment of fast triplets (recalled during the development), the dominance of the motivic principal theme all the way through the Allegro part of the movement, the enharmonic modulations, the striving for an orchestral quality, as evidenced by the tympani-like figure in the bass that precedes the statement of the principal theme, and the thick chordal texture that prevails. Thematic contrast appears in the first movements of the other two sonatas. As finales, we find the rondo form, as had often been true in the sonata since the work of Schubert. In the Sonatas in f and g, we find the sonata-rondo (the second episode becomes a development), while, in the Sonata in f-sharp, all episodes are contrasting. In all three works, these rondo finales are large, difficult movements, designed to provide brilliant and effective conclusions.

In between are the scherzi and slow movements. In the scherzi, again, the chief attributes of the type are maintained: the fast triple time, the "capricious" character, and the over-all three-part form with trio as the middle section. The scherzo of the Sonata in f-sharp has, however, two trios, of which the second is in striking contrast with the rest of the movement, with its pomposity, polonaise rhythm, and the fantasia-like passage (with quasi-oboe) near the end. Following the practice observed in certain of the character pieces (the *Noveletten* and the *Romanzen*), this episode is called "intermezzo." And the scherzo of the Sonata in f is basically a three-part form, but the trio (not so called by Schumann) employs the thematic material of the scherzo part of the movement.

Two of the slow movements are in no way different from character pieces, as indeed was also true of Schubert's slow movements; the Sonatas in f-sharp and g have slow movements in simple ternary form (that in the Sonata in g also has a coda). Interesting here is the movement in the Sonata in f-sharp which has the designation "Aria" and the direction *senza passione, ma espressivo*, a possibly rather fine distinction, highly Romantic in its vagueness. In the Sonata in f, the slow movement is a *quasi variationi*, four variations on a theme by the then Clara Wieck (see Fischer, *Variation*, 17, pp. 52–5).

The Andante of this movement appears in all movements of the sonata, which therefore is in cyclic form; in this, it has a similarity to Schubert's well-known *Wanderer* Fantasia. And, as in Schubert's works we saw instances of the influence from songs, so here in Schumann; in the Sonata in f-sharp, the second movement is taken from one of his songs, *An Anna*, part of which also provided the basis for the slow introduction to the first movement; again, the slow movement of the Sonata in g is rather freely related to a song, *Im Herbste*. (Both these songs, to poems of Kerner, are early pieces dating from 1827 and 1828.)

Along with the sonata, Schumann cultivated the fantasia. As has been seen, the fantasy piece (*Phantasiestück*) holds an important position in Schumann's character pieces. But the fantasia is something different, a large work in several movements on roughly the same scale as a sonata. Here again, Schubert's *Wanderer* Fantasia was doubtless of decisive influence. Schumann did not recognize any great distinction between fantasias of this type and piano sonatas, as is known from his famous review of the sonatas of Schubert: "So let them [composers] then write sonatas or fantasias (what's in a name?)." This large Fantasia in C (op. 17) of 1836, dedicated to Liszt, is in all respects an important contribution. Preceded by a four-line motto drawn from the great Romantic novelist and critic, Friedrich Schlegel ("Among all the sounds in the bright dream of earthly [life] there is emitted a soft tone for him who listens in secret")[1] are three large movements: *Durchaus fantastisch und leidenschaftlich vorzutragen* in c; a scherzo-like movement, *Mässig, durchaus energisch* in E-flat; and, as finale, a slow movement, *Langsam getragen, durchweg leise zu halten*, again in C. Originally, each movement had a title: *Ruinen* (*Ruins*), *Triumphbogen* (*Triumphal Arch*), and *Sternenkranz* (*Starry Ring*). The first movement can best be regarded as a free sonata form: it lacks the double bar, the "development" does not work with thematic material from the "exposition," and the "recapitulation" is abbreviated. The opening is arresting; the assertive melody is in octaves with dotted rhythm, and its accompaniment is in furious figuration maintained for most of the exposition. An important feature of the movement is thematic variation instead of thematic development; the principal theme is repeated in lyrical guise, a "bridge" theme is varied during the "development," in the section *Im Legenden-Ton* (*In the Character of a Legend*), and the subordinate theme itself is varied by the use of different accompaniments. The "scherzo" is clearly the largest of its kind in the work of Schumann. It is in a rondo-like form with two episodes, and the scherzo theme is varied slightly each time it appears. This theme is noteworthy for its pre-eminently "orchestral" quality—full chords ranging over a large extent of the keyboard—a quality that is intensified with each appearance. In the last move-

[1] *Durch alle Töne tönet / Im bunten Erdentraum / Ein leiser Ton gezogen / Für den, der heimlich lauschet.*

ment, we find a free form related to the ternary scheme. There are two contrasting sections each stated twice, and then elements of both are combined as a coda; each is in turn composed of several contrasting passages, so that, as a whole, the movement exhibits great variety; the climax takes place in the second section and is developed out of a lyrical line—again exploiting rhythmic irregularities in 12/8 meter, with stretto-like alterations between bass and treble, the activity increasing until the high point is reached with chords in dotted rhythm.

In contrast to this fantasia is an incomplete work of Schumann in which another meaning of the term is apparent: that of the fantasia as variations on a familiar melody. This work is the *Phantasie satyrique (nach Henri Herz)*, which he worked on in 1832. Since Herz was regarded by Schumann as the virtual embodiment of musical philistinism, this piece, had it been completed, would have afforded another instance of musical satire (a more famous one being Mozart's celebrated *Musikalischer Spass* for strings and horns). In any case, this connotation of the fantasia, that of variations on a theme, appears also in the work of Mendelssohn and, especially, Liszt.

Also related to the sonata, but in a different way, is the Toccata in C (op. 7) composed in 1832 (excerpt in Valentin, pp. 55–60). Apart from its emphasis on virtuosity, this work has no relation to the toccata, prelude, or fantasia of the eighteenth century at all. Rather, it is cast in a large and strict sonata form complete with the double bar and the repeat of the exposition. The principal theme consists of chordal figuration moving rapidly in syncopated rhythm with sixteenth notes prominent; the subordinate theme presents a short, cantabile phrase in dotted rhythm, but the sixteenth-note accompaniment is maintained. In the development, a new theme is introduced featuring rapid octaves, both repeated and in scale passages.

A final group of works in the large forms of "absolute" music is formed by the sets of themes and variations (see Schwarz). Here, there are certain works that overlap other genres. There are sets of character pieces (the *Impromptus*, op. 4, and *Carnaval*), sets of etudes (the one on a theme of Beethoven and the celebrated *Symphonic Etudes*) that are, in one way or another, themes and variations. As the out-and-out sets of themes and variations, we can list the following:

Theme on the Name Abegg with Variations (op. 1) of 1830
Andante (Mit Gott), Variations on an Original theme in G of 1831–1832
Sehnsuchtswalzervariationen of 1833 (also called *Scènes mignonnes* or *musicales sur un thème connu* or *Sur un thème connu de Fr. Schubert*, originally published as op. 10)
Variations sur un nocturne de Chopin of 1834
Variations in E-flat of 1854, incomplete.

Two of these are based on original themes—*Mit Gott* and *Abegg*; the latter is the name of a family Schumann knew, which produces a musical theme (A,

B-flat, E, G, G) in the same fashion as the *lettres dansantes* in *Carnaval*. The Schubert variations are on a well-known waltz, the so-called *Sehnsuchtswalzer* (*Waltz of Longing*), a piece with a varied history that had been attributed to Beethoven but was actually the second number of Schubert's op. 9 (D. 365), called *Trauer-Walzer* (*Waltz of Sadness*); the Chopin theme is the Nocturne in g (op. 15 iii). Of the three completed sets, the *Abegg Variations* is the most important. (The *Symphonic Etudes* are discussed below.) Its theme, the "Abegg" motto at the beginning, is a melody with simple chordal accompaniment unified by the use of a rhythmic pattern. In the first of the three variations, motives from the theme are employed; in the second, there is a basso parlando in syncopated rhythm; while, in the third, there is a rapid triplet figure; a sectional finale provides the conclusion.

We have seen in the work of Mozart, Beethoven, and especially Mendelssohn that the influence of Baroque music, particularly the fugue writing of Johann Sebastian Bach, continued to make its presence felt here and there during this historical period. This is true also of Schumann (see Dadelsen). There is a prelude in the *Bunte Blätter* (op. 99 x) and a canon as the last of the *Albumblätter* (op. 124); and, as already noted, there is a fughetta in the *Clavierstücke* (op. 32 iv); in addition, a prelude and fugue was composed in 1832, along with sketches for other fugal and canonic pieces, one of which evidently was intended as a finale for the impromptus (op. 5). Apart from these, there are the four fugues (op. 72) of 1845 and the seven *Stücke in Fughettenform* (*Pieces in the Form of Fughettas*, op. 126) of 1853. There are also works for the pedal piano, in which a separate piano action was provided to be played by the feet, thus making the piano similar to the organ and the large form of the harpsichord: the *Studien* (*Studies*, op. 56) and the *Skizzen* (*Sketches*, op. 58), both of 1845, of which the former reveal a strong influence from the music of Bach.

Schumann's largest work of this type, however, is the six *Fugues on the Name Bach* (op. 60), also of 1845, for pedal piano or organ. There is much besides the fugue subject itself that is inspired by Bach. These are large works in which, for the most part, the contrapuntal work is strictly carried out. The subjects used are in some respects of the same types as those employed by Bach; several resemble the old ricercare (i, iv, and vi), one seems like the old gigue (v), one is a long subject in two parts—the dotted terse statement of "Bach" followed by driving figuration (ii), while one more has a cantabile subject (iii). Learned devices make their appearance: augmentation, diminution, and even retrograde motion, the last actually labeled as such in the score (iv)—but it involves only the first notes ("Bach") and excludes the element of rhythm altogether. The last of the fugues, a true double fugue, includes the contrapuntal combination of the two subjects and is the largest work in the set.

The last group of Schumann's works for piano solo to be discussed consists of the etudes, which are as follows:

Studies after Caprices of Paganini (op. 3) of 1832

Exercise fantastique (originally op. 5, later dropped) of 1832

Concert Studies after Caprices of Paganini, Set II (op. 10) of 1833

Etudes in the Form of Free Variations on a Theme of Beethoven of 1833

Études en forme de variations (op. 13) of 1834, revised in 1852; originally called *Etudes in Orchestral Style* (or *Character*), attributed to Florestan and Eusebius but published as *Symphonic Etudes*.

Here we can take note of something that became important for the etude in the nineteenth century: Paganini, legendary master of the violin. Since the etude is intended chiefly as a means of improving playing technique and developing or showing off virtuoso mastery of the instrument, it is not at all unusual that the foremost virtuoso performer of the day should be associated with such compositions. Paganini's famous *Caprices for Unaccompanied Violin* (op. 1) of 1820 are used as the basis for countless sets of etudes for piano, here by Schumann (for op. 10 ii, see *HMS*, IX, s. 4, b. 3) but also, as will be seen, by two such opposite artistic temperaments as Liszt and Brahms as well as many others. The Beethoven theme is the Allegretto of the Symphony in A (op. 92; No. 7).

But the most important work in this genre by Schumann is the famous *Symphonic Etudes* in c-sharp (or D-flat, op. 13). In all, there are twelve etudes of which nine are variations of the theme that stands at the beginning (i, ii, iv, v, vi, vii, viii, x, xi). The theme, in binary form (a form that is maintained in most of the variations) is solemn, a slowly moving line accompanied by full chords. The etudes themselves differ widely in character; the first is staccato and quasi-contrapuntal, the second an impassioned lyrical line supported by a slow-moving bass part with rapidly moving chords in the middle, the third (not a variation) a Mendelssohnian piece with a cantabile line in the middle and rapid staccato passages above, the fourth a study in *sforzando* chord playing, the fifth a scherzando with chords in dotted rhythm, the sixth a bravura study with wide leaps for the left hand, the seventh a moto perpetuo with much figuration and accented chords, the eighth a marcato study featuring motives of scale segments in sharply dotted rhythms, the ninth (not a variation) another Mendelssohnian piece with very fast and light staccato chords, the tenth with full chords in the right hand against primarily scale figuration in the left, the eleventh another lyrical piece— a duet over an accompaniment characterized by much rhythmic motion and very slow and regular harmonic rhythm, and the finale employs a part only of the theme of the work as a whole, using it to develop a crescendo that works to a grand climax—here again Schumann's employment of full chords produces an orchestral effect. Near the end, a surprising turn to the major affords an effective climax and prepares the impressive conclusion to the work. All in all, this is one of Schumann's most effective and representative works.

Apart from the pieces for piano solo, there is a small body of works for piano duet and two pianos. For piano duet, there are the early polonaises of 1828 and the later *Bilder aus Osten* (*Pictures from the East*, op. 66), inspired by the *Makamen* of Friedrich Rückert; the *Klavierstücke für kleine und grosse Kinder* (*Piano Pieces for Small and Large Children*, op. 85); and two sets of dance pieces, *Ball-Scenen* (*Ball Scenes*, op. 109) and *Kinderball* (*Children's Ball*, op. 130). For two pianos, there is the major work, the Andante and Variations in B-flat (op. 46), a piece originally for two pianos, two violoncellos, and horn.

The last great composer of keyboard music to be considered here is Frédéric Chopin (1810–1849). Actually, one does not really need to speak of keyboard music here, since Chopin's work by and large is restricted to music for piano. Unlike Schumann and others, Chopin intended to be a musician from the beginning. His father, a school teacher to the nobility in Warsaw, saw to it that Chopin received the normal humanities course at the Lyceum before devoting himself exclusively to the study of music. From 1826 to 1829, Chopin went through the course at the Warsaw Conservatory, then under Joseph Elsner. Chopin was primarily a pianist and had some successful public appearances not only in and around Warsaw, but also, in 1829, in Vienna. Eventually, he left Warsaw to embark on a career as a virtuoso, but was severely disappointed on his second trip to Vienna in 1830–1831; his reception was considerably less favorable than it had been the previous year. In the late summer of 1831, he journeyed to Paris where he settled, helped by the auspicious success of his first concert there on February 26, 1832. But then his career turned, and he largely abandoned concertizing in favor of composing and teaching. All in all, he gave some thirty recitals, many of them before private aristocratic audiences. Apart from two visits to England and another to Germany, he spent the remainder of his life in Paris (apart from the unfortunate and well-known winter in Majorca).

In Paris, he was associated with the leading literary and artistic figures of the time. Among musicians, we find him on close terms with Liszt, Mendelssohn (who spent the years 1831–1832 in Paris), Hiller, Berlioz, Paganini, Rossini, and Bellini; he also was acquainted with Schumann; among literary men and painters, he knew de Musset, Balzac, Delacroix, Heine (who lived in Paris from 1834), the great Polish Romantic poet Adam Mickiewicz, and the novelist George Sand (Aurore Devanant), with whom he lived for some ten years, 1837–1847. Chopin thus was connected with the leading representatives of the most progressive aristic tendencies of his day.

More than any other leading composer, Chopin devoted himself to the piano to the virtual exclusion of all other media of music. Of symphonies, operas, and oratorios, he wrote none; chamber music is represented by a single piano trio; it was piano music, and here again chiefly the new genres connected with the character piece, to which he directed his attention. Along with the character pieces, there are etudes, other works related to various kinds of dances (mazurkas, polonaises, waltzes), and a few works of the older type of "absolute" music—three sonatas, two sets of variations, and a group of smaller works.[1]

Considered chronologically, we find among his earliest works polonaises, rondos, and other concert pieces, especially works for piano and orchestra, the nationalistic *Krakowiak* (op. 14, B. 29), and the variations on Mozart's *La ci darem le mano* (op. 2, B. 22) along with the first sonata, which he composed under Elsner's direction. The two piano concertos also date from around 1830. For the most part, then, these are works composed with an eye to the concert platform. But Chopin had begun other things even during these early years before leaving Warsaw—the etudes (op. 10, B. 42), the nocturnes (op. 9, B. 54 and op. 15, B. 55), and, during the disappointing second stay in Vienna, he commenced the Scherzo in b (op. 20, B. 65) and the Ballade in g (op. 23, B. 66). It is this direction that he was to follow henceforth, and works in either the older traditional genres or those particularly aimed at the concert stage remain relatively scarce in his work.

We have mentioned that the character piece was closely bound up with the Romantic ideal of the art work as the subjective emotional expression of its composer and that such a view gave rise to a glorification of inspiration as the source of all art; the extent to which this quality can be captured by the artist is the measure of the quality of his composition. It is likely that the term "impromptu" as the name for a musical work was employed with precisely this end in view. Several of Chopin's utterances are peculiarly representative of this attitude. In a letter of December 25, 1831, to a friend, he refers to his own personal internal conflicts: "In feeling I am always in a state of syncopation with everyone. . . . I am gay on the outside . . . but inside something gnaws at me . . ." (Murdoch's translation), a statement which could doubtless have been made just as well by Schumann. He often mentioned inspiration as the source of his musical compositions. To him, composition was something instinctive and natural. Chopin even went so far as to compare musical composition to childbirth.[2] Statements associating artistic creation with natural and instinctive creativity place Chopin squarely in the Romantic movement.

The character piece has been viewed here primarily as a small form that the Romantic musicians developed while generally turning away from the chief

[1] The bibliographical situation of Chopin has improved of late with the appearance of the new collected edition and, most recently, of the new thematic catalogue by Brown. The "B" numbers used in the chronological arrangement of Chopin's works in this catalogue are given here in the listings that follow, but, in the discussions, the more familiar opus numbers are used; however, one should keep in mind that op. 66–74 contain mostly early works. Standardard biographical studies of Chopin are by Niecks, Murdoch, Hedley, Rehberg, Egert, and Weinstock; analytical discussions are by Leichtentritt (comprehensive), Meister, and Abraham; see also Bronarski, Dunn, Holcman, and Ottich. A word of caution is in order concerning the "letters to Delphina Potocka" presented in 1945 by Paulina Czernicka (see the selections in translation in Mizwa), which are evidently forgeries, the work of Mrs. Czernicka herself (see Lissa).

[2] Wierczynski, pp. 197–8.

large form of piano music, the sonata. In the work of Schumann, as has been seen, the urge to compose in large forms had an effect on the character piece, either producing larger works or else causing a number of shorter pieces to be grouped together as a cycle or suite. Chopin, in his effort to create character pieces on a large scale, chose the former possibility. Examples of the older and small type of character piece are the impromptus, the nocturnes, and the preludes, as well as many individual works like the _Berceuse_ and the many stylized dances, the mazurkas, and the waltzes; and, on the other hand, examples of the large types of character pieces are the scherzi and the ballades as well as the polonaises.

The establishment of the scherzo as an independent type of composition apparently is related to the neglect of the sonata and to the practice, already noted, of putting out separate movements, which together would form a sonata, as individual compositions. The scherzo in the hands of Chopin became larger than it had been, but the form that he employed was clearly an outgrowth of the scherzo as a movement in a sonata. The scherzos of Chopin are four:

Scherzo in b (op. 20, B. 65), composed in 1831–1832 and published in 1832
Scherzo in b-flat (op. 31, B. 111), composed and published in 1837
Scherzo in c-sharp (op. 39, B. 125), composed in 1839 and published in 1840
Scherzo in E (op. 54, B. 148), composed in 1842 and published in 1843.

All have the same formal plan: the scherzo proper, a middle section called "trio," followed by the repeat of the scherzo. The Scherzo in c-sharp is in five-part form with two statements of the trio, a procedure for which there certainly was ample precedence. Two of the scherzos commence with impressive flourishes —those in b and c-sharp; and two have codas—those in c-sharp and E. As has been seen, the scherzo originally was no more than a fast minuet and hence could be expected to show the typical formal plan of a minuet—rounded binary form. And this is indeed to be seen here, although generally the double bars and repeat signs are not used. Nonetheless, the outlines of the rounded binary form are clear in the Scherzo in b, which uses the double bar at the end of the first part but has the subsequent repetitions written out in full, and in the Scherzo in E, in which everything is written out but in which the pattern ($AABABA$) is that of the rounded binary form. (There is also a short codetta.) With the other scherzos, this plan is less clear, but the repetitive scheme, at least, is present; here, several themes are stated, and then the whole section is repeated. The trios also show repetitive plans that would ally them with rounded binary form, and thus they too reveal their descendence from the scherzo as it existed in the piano sonata.

The main difference here is the size, for these works are on a larger scale than would occur in a sonata. Along with this goes an increase in the length and elaboration of all parts of the work. Since, as we saw, sonata form itself is related, in any case, to an expansion and elaboration of rounded binary form, it is not unusual that these scherzos of Chopin also show some similarity to sonata form. There is the employment of several themes of contrasting character, as is evident in the well-known Scherzo in b-flat. First, there is the upbeat triplet run in the bass that is repeated three times and followed by full chords in dotted rhythm; then, there is a brilliant descending figure accompanied by chords; then, a lyrical phrase accompanied by rapid broken-chord figuration, which rises, attains a climax, and passes to a section of "closing theme" character, figural runs, and chords; thereafter, the whole is repeated with variations and omissions. Here, we have something that is rather removed from the usual arrangement of a scherzo but whose relation to the genre can be seen. In the Scherzo in b, the second part of the scherzo section presents a development of themes stated in the first part, so that here the rapprochement to sonata form is made more explicit.

The trios too present a contrast to the scherzo parts. Generally, they are subdued, slower, lyrical, and uniform in character. The trio of the Scherzo in b is a simple setting of a popular Polish Christmas song *Lulajże Jezuniu*, the melody in the middle accompanied by simple chordal harmonies. Likewise uniform in character throughout is the trio of the Scherzo in c-sharp, in which the phrases of a chorale-like chordal theme are interspersed with a filigree of broken-chord figuration. In the Scherzo in E, the trio takes the form of a cantabile nocturne-like melody accompanied by sparse broken-chord patterns. Most elaborate is the trio of the Scherzo in b-flat, which, unlike the others, exhibits great variety. There is a simple melody using repeated notes and accompanied by chords and a more motivic section using figuration; as the trio proceeds, however, its character changes, and it draws in thematic material from the scherzo proper and becomes something like a development section.

More specifically Romantic are the four ballades:

Ballade in g (op. 23, B. 66), composed in 1831–1835 and published in 1836
Ballade in F (op. 38, B. 102), composed in 1838–1839 and published in 1840
Ballade in A-flat (op. 47, B. 136), composed in 1840–1841 and published in 1841
Ballade in f (op. 52, B. 146), composed in 1842 and published in 1843.

Here, Chopin brought to keyboard music something largely of his own devising, although, as we will see, certain hints had already existed. Again, the relationship to literature is of great importance. The ballad as a literary genre may be briefly described as a narrative of legendary or historical events; it frequently involves violence and the supernatural, generally has a tragic conclusion, is told in simple, "popular" verse, and is usually in a large number of short strophes. This genre enjoyed great favor in the late eighteenth and early nineteenth centuries; it was often associated with something handed down from the distant past, hence somehow a vestige of ancient bardic poetry, the northern counterpart to the chivalric epics of France. Leading poets of the time, particularly in Germany, were stimulated to write new ballads that, in form, corresponded to old folk poetry, and many composers set them to music; one musician, Johann Rudolf Zumsteeg (1760–1802), was especially prominent. All in all, then, the ballad contained many elements that would make it most appropriate for the attention of the Romantics, musicians as well as poets.

We have seen that, in the early stages of the development of the nineteenth-century character piece, an important part was played by the Bohemian composer Tomášek, whose work reveals several relations to that of Schubert. Along with smaller works called "eclogues," Tomášek composed larger pieces called "rhapsodies." In his autobiography, he stated, "I wanted to attempt to write pieces in which seriousness along with strength and energy are predominant. In this I approached primitive times with their rhapsodies, which struck through my soul like a magic blow: I saw and heard them declaiming long passages from Homer's *Iliad* and sending everyone into a state of enthusiasm."[1] Here, we have an attempt to compose a piece of music that would correspond to epic poetry, a rhapsody, or, by extension, to a ballad. And this seems to be what Chopin intended here. It has often been pointed out that Chopin was well acquainted with the great Polish poet Adam Mickiewicz, who lived in Paris in exile and who had made his reputation with his early ballads (1822). At the same time, we have seen intimations of this idea in the work of Schumann; one of the *Davids-bündlertänze* (op. 6 x) is entitled *Balladenmässig*, and, in the first movement of the large Fantasia in C (op. 17), a passage bears the qualification *Im Legenden-Ton* (*In the Style of a Legend*), hence, epic narrative. Thus, it must be emphasized that there is no evidence that any of Chopin's ballades correspond to particular literary works, whether by Mickiewicz or anyone else. It is simply that he envisioned a musical form that he saw as corresponding to the literary form of the ballad. Thus, any specific association of Chopin's ballades with poems of Mickiewicz has no basis.

Here, Chopin has no real predecessor. Tomášek's rhapsodies were all in simple three-part form. But Chopin conceived his ballades as larger and more elaborate compositions, which are in some respects outgrowths of this simple basic plan so common to the character piece. The Ballade in F is straightforward; the contrasting episode appears twice, and there are transitional passages along with a coda. The Ballade in A-flat contains one contrasting episode, but has a long and elaborate transitional passage leading up to the climactic restatement of the principal part. Most elaborate and irregular is the formal plan of the Ballade in f, which contains three separate episodes; the second is repeated near the end, and the third takes on something of the nature of a development. Finally, the Ballade in g, the earliest of the series, may be seen as a sort of sonata form, with introduction and coda and with the subordinate theme appearing first in the re-capitulation (a process that Chopin also used in his piano sonatas); the Ballade in A-flat has also been interpreted as a sort of free sonata form, although the "development" consists largely of free figuration and does not work with the

[1] Translated from a quotation given by W. Kahl, "Ballade," *MGG*, I (1949–1951), 1134.

EXAMPLE 59

CHOPIN: Ballade in A-flat (op. 47)—excerpts

A. Principal theme—beginning

B. Subordinate theme—beginning,

C. Transition to reprise—excerpt

continued

proper thematic material of the work until near its end. Thematic development may also be observed in the Ballade in F.

An important element in the ballades is the use of the same theme in varied form throughout. We have seen that this is an important device in Romantic music, especially since Schubert's *Wanderer Fantasia*. All Chopin's ballades show this to some extent. In the Ballade in g, it is the subordinate theme, first lyric and then transformed into something heroic; in the Ballade in F, the main theme is varied, particularly by its figural embellishment; and in the Ballade in f, it is the principal theme that serves as a sort of ritornello and is varied each time it appears.

EXAMPLE 59—*continued*

But the principle of cyclic form is carried farthest in the Ballade in A-flat where not only is the principal theme itself transformed from lyrical to heroic, but it also provides the material of the subordinate theme. This close relation between the two themes is plainly evident from the virtuoso transition section leading up to the climactic re-entrance of the principal theme, in which the subordinate theme is transformed to the principal theme right before one's ears.

It is possible that the use of thematic variation in the ballades can be related to the strophic form of the literary ballad, which, when set to music, would have —at least in the eighteenth and early nineteenth centuries—the same music for each strophe. For the rest, the ballades are brilliant and effective major pieces. Particularly effective is the "ballad tone" or "rhapsodic" opening in the Ballade in g, which seems to "set the stage" for a narrative of some moment. Sudden and effective contrasts are present in abundance; for instance, there is the crashing entrance of the subordinate theme of the Ballade in F after the gentle lilt of the simple siciliano-like main theme or the dramatic transformation of the lyric subordinate theme in the Ballade in g. An impressively rhetorical virtuoso display is at the end in the Ballade in f. Passages involving virtuoso figuration appear in each of the ballades, sometimes employing the theme of the work and other times independent of the thematic material of the composition (as is the case with much of the so-called "development" of the Ballade in A-flat).

Chopin's intent seems clear: the establishment of a large and difficult genre of the character piece taking its inspiration from the literary ballad, a kind of character piece that would be regarded as, in some way, the equivalent of the sonata.

But, quantitatively, the bulk of Chopin's work consists of the shorter type of character piece, and it is to these that we may now direct our attention. Among the most typical works of Chopin are the nocturnes; those published during his lifetime are as follows:

Larghetto in b-flat, Andante in E-flat, Allegretto in B (op. 9, B. 54), composed in 1830–1831 and published in 1833

Andante cantabile in F, Larghetto in F-sharp, Lento in g (op. 15, B. 55 and 79), composed in 1830–1833 and published in 1833

Larghetto in c-sharp, Lento sostenuto in D-flat (op. 27, B. 91 and 96), composed in 1835 and published in 1836

Andante sostenuto in B, Lento in A-flat (op. 32, B. 106), composed in 1836–1837 and published in 1837

Lento (or Andante sostenuto) in g, Andante (or Andantino) in G (op. 37, B. 119 and 127), composed in 1838–1839 and published in 1840

Lento in c, Andantino in f-sharp (op. 48, B. 142), composed and published in 1841

Andante in f, Lento sostenuto in E-flat (op. 55, B. 152), composed in 1843 and published in 1844

Andante in B, Lento in E (op. 62, B. 161), composed and published in 1846.

The posthumously published nocturnes are:

Andante in e (op. 72 i, B. 19), composed in 1827 and published in 1855
Lento con gran espressione in c-sharp (B. 49), composed in 1830 and published
    in 1875
Andante sostenuto in c (B. 108), composed in 1837 and published in 1938.

In the eighteenth century, the *notturno* (night piece) was a serenade for a group of instruments or a small orchestra (often of wind instruments) to be played out of doors. Such a serenade would normally consist of an opening Allegro, a slow movement, a concluding rondo, and several (usually two) minuets in between. Here, however, we have something rather different, and it can be said that Chopin was presenting a new genre of keyboard music; but this time, he had a predecessor. The Irish pianist and composer John Field (1782–1837), who had a great reputation in Europe (see Dessauer, Flood, Hibbard, Hopkinson, and Davies), published between 1815 and 1834 some twenty (the exact number is debated) works called "nocturnes" that are in three-part form with lyrical melodies, often greatly embellished and accompanied by standard types of broken-chord figuration patterns in the bass; generally, a uniform character is maintained throughout, but, in this, much depended on the performer's ability in cantabile playing and on the judicious and effective use of the pedal to produce the proper sound.[1]

Chopin took over this kind of piece but soon made it into something of greater artistic moment. The basic type remained the same: a simple lyrical melody over a simple patterned accompaniment, the melody often ornamented with grace notes, coloratura runs, and turns (*fioriture*), or it is presented in parallel thirds, sixths, or octaves (see particularly the Lento sostenuto in D-flat, op. 27 ii); generally, the melody is constructed in even periods of balanced phrases organized in accordance with a simple repetitive scheme. The small scale is confirmed by the tempo designations given by Chopin, as well as by the frequent appearance of *espressivo* and *dolce* or even *languido e rubato* (Lento in g, op. 15 iii). A few of the nocturnes of Chopin preserve the same character all the way through, thus adhering to the genre as established by Field, but most depart from this by the introduction of a contrasting middle section using new themes, different styles of writing, and a different key. The great majority of them, then, are in three-part form, in a few cases with coda or a transitional passage of some sort. Frequently, the middle section presents an impassioned climax that then subsides as the first part is recapitulated. Examples of this are to be seen in the Allegretto in B (op. 9 iii), the Larghetto in c-sharp (op. 27 i), the Lento in C (op. 48 i), the Lento in E (op. 62 ii), all of which are agitato in their middle sections; but the Lento in c (op. 48 i) uses the arpeggiated chordal figure of the contrasting middle section to accompany the repeat of the opening. The Andantino in c-sharp (op. 48 ii) has a

[1] For Field's Nocturne in B-flat (v), see Weinstock, pp. 232–4.

melody organized into long and irregular periods. Generally speaking, there is
much similarity among the nocturnes as a whole.

EXAMPLE 60

CHOPIN: Nocturne in D-flat (op. 27 ii)—beginning

Because of their simplicity and outspoken exploitation of sheer melodic lyricism, the claim has often been advanced that, in the nocturnes, Chopin deliberately adopted a vocal idiom, particularly the melodic style found in the arias of Bellini (see Abraham and Murdoch). The ornamentation especially would seem to confirm this. But there are objections to this, first on account of the earlier work of Field and second, because, as has been seen, Chopin commenced work on the nocturnes of op. 9 even while he was in Warsaw, before he became acquainted with Bellini. At the same time, there are surely similarities between the two. And this quality of simple lyricism has made the nocturnes the most characteristic and among the most popular of Chopin's works; we will be able to point out instances of what can be called "nocturne style" in other compositions of Chopin.

Another group of Chopin's smaller character pieces is formed by the impromptus.

Fantasie-Impromptu, Allegro agitato in c-sharp (op. 66, B. 87), composed in 1834 and published in 1855

Allegro assai, quasi presto in A-flat (op. 29, B. 110), composed and published in 1837

Andantino (or Allegretto) in F-sharp (op. 36, B. 129), composed in 1839 and published in 1840

Allegro vivace (or Tempo giusto) in G-flat (op. 51, B. 149), composed in 1842 and published in 1843.

With these works, we are dealing with a genre that had been extensively cultivated before Chopin. By and large, the main features are maintained by Chopin; again, we find the simple three-part formal plan, so important to the character piece generally, the middle section forming a contrast with the opening and close. The various sections can in turn be broken down into simple repetitive schemes, for instance, the *A A' B A C* plan for the first section of the Impromptus in A-flat and G-flat and the *A B A' C* of the corresponding section of the Impromptu in F-sharp; similar repetitive forms will be found in the contrasting middle portions as well. The principal thematic material is less melodic or cantabile than that found in the nocturnes and, instead, is based on figuration— triplets in the Impromptus in A-flat and G-flat and a complex two against three in the well-known *Fantasie-Impromptu* in c-sharp, actually four groups of six- teenths against two sextuplets of eighths. The exception is the Impromptu in F-sharp, whose "black-key" scheme is melodic but highly irregular in phrase structure with many chromatic *fioriture*. The middle sections are in contrast; they are generally lyrical with a simple melody and straightforward accompani- ment, of which a most popular example is in the famous *Fantasie-Impromptu* in c-sharp, which has been used as a popular song. Also noteworthy here is the long cantabile left-hand melody in e-flat in the Impromptu in G-flat and the impressive "martial" passage in the Impromptu in F-sharp. It will be seen, then, that the impromptus are more elaborate than the nocturnes; they are larger, the musical procedures used are more complex, and they are more demanding technically.

Among the other character pieces are a number of individually published works, the two best known of which are the Berceuse in D-flat (op. 57, B. 154), composed in 1843–1844 and published in 1845, and the Barcarolle in F-sharp (op. 60, B. 158), composed in 1845–1846 and published in 1846. The former is a most unusual work in that it is based on an ostinato harmonic progression one bar in length that is repeated over and over again through the entire composition, over which a lilting melody is continuously spun out with constant variations and elaboration; first in a single line, then in several, then with many figurations, rapid scale passages, scales in thirds, and all sorts of ornamental figures. More conventional is the Barcarolle with its ternary form and introduction and coda, the simple embellished melody in parallel thirds over a rhythmically constant accompaniment in the first section, while in the middle the same thematic material is given an entirely different accompaniment of chords leading up to the *fortissimo* restatement of the opening in full octaves. In principle, the piece is not unrelated to Mendelssohn's gondola songs but on a much larger scale.

Among the lesser-known character pieces of Chopin are the Bolero in a (op. 19, B. 81), the Tarentelle in A-flat (op. 43, B. 139), both designed as bravura pieces, a short *Feuille d'album* in E (B. 151) composed in 1843 but not published until 1927, a *Marche funèbre* in c (op. 72 ii, B. 20) used in modified form in the Sonata in b-flat (op. 33), and several other short works.

A most important group of Chopin's piano works is formed by the etudes (or studies) and the preludes, which are as follows:

Études
>   Twelve of op. 10 (B. 42, 57, 59, 67, 68, 74, 75), composed in 1829–1832 and published in 1833
>   Twelve of op. 25 (B. 78, 83, 97, 98, 99, 104), composed in 1832–1836 and published in 1837
>   Three *Nouvelles études* (B. 130), composed in 1839 for the Moscheles-Fétis *Méthode des méthodes* and published in 1840.

Preludes
>   Twenty-four of op. 28 (B. 100, 107, 123, 124), composed in 1836–1839 and published in 1839
>   Prelude in A-flat (B. 86), composed in 1834 for Pierre Wolff and published in 1918
>   Prelude in c-sharp (op. 45, B. 141), composed and published in 1841.

The etude, as is well known, is primarily a teaching piece, study, or exercise designed as a vehicle for the pianist either to improve or to exhibit his technical skill. Generally, an etude will concentrate on one technical problem of execution —a certain type of figuration, octave playing, arpeggios, staccato chords, scale passages, legato playing, and so forth. Therefore, a certain consistency is the result since the same type of thematic material, by and large, is maintained all the way through. It may be said that Chopin's etudes are virtuoso character pieces. Characteristic etudes were by no means unknown (see, for example, Moscheles' op. 95 and also Cramer), but Chopin's differ with their harmonic elaboration and the remarkable exploitation of the sound capabilities of the grand piano.

The prelude, on the other hand, achieves much the same result from a different point of departure. Here, the situation is as we saw it in Mendelssohn. The model is to be found in Bach; and we have seen that Bach's preludes (those in *The Well-Tempered Clavier*) also employ the same thematic material, usually based on figuration patterns, all the way through. The principal distinction between the two types of musical composition, the etude and the prelude, is that, in Chopin, the etudes are larger and the preludes smaller. We have abundant evidence of Chopin's great admiration for Bach, and it might be of significance that John Field, whose nocturnes were so important for Chopin's own, was especially famous for his performances of Bach. Following the example of Bach, the preludes of op. 28, each in a different key, are arranged in accordance with a simple plan, in pairs beginning with C, each prelude in the major followed by another in the relative minor and then descending a fifth, i.e., C–a, G–e, D–b, and so on. There is also a plan in the arrangement of keys in the etudes of op. 10, but one that is not strictly carried out. Again, the grouping is in pairs, and etude in the major following by one in the minor (again commencing with C), the next one in the major being a third higher (C–a, E–c-sharp, G-flat–e-flat); but the arrangement here breaks after the third pair, although the last two pairs consist of one in the major and one in the relative minor. There is no such arrangement in the etudes of op. 25.

Most of the etudes are based on the common three-part form often with coda. But, in most of them, there is no important element of contrast; the middle section usually employs the same thematic material as the beginning but is likely to modulate into distant keys, so that, when the theme is restated in its original key, one has the feeling of a recapitulation even though other variations often take place. Most of the etudes, then, are of a unified character throughout. The most obvious exceptions to this are the Lento in E (op. 10 iii), which in some respects is much like a nocturne and bears comparison with the nocturne in the same key (op. 62 ii); the Vivace in e (op. 25 v); and the Allegro con fuoco in b (op. 25 x).

The character of the etude is, as already indicated, bound up with the technical problem to which each is addressed. A few of these technical problems may be indicated here. (Some etudes appear under more than one heading.)

Arpeggio studies: Allegro in C (op. 10 i), Allegretto in E-flat (op. 10 xi), Molto allegro con fuoco in E-flat (op. 25 xii)

Scale passages: Presto in c-sharp (op. 10 iv), Allegro in F (op. 10 viii), Presto in f (op. 25 ii)

Chromatic scale passages: Allegro in a (op. 10 ii), Lento in c-sharp (op. 25 vii)

Double notes: Vivace in C (op. 10 vii)

Scales in thirds and sixths: Vivace in D-flat (op. 25 viii)

Leggiero chord playing: Vivace assai in A-flat (op. 10 x), Vivace in D-flat (op. 25 viii)

Chords accompanied by rapid figuration: Allegro con fuoco in c (op. 10 xii, the so-called *Revolutionary Etude*), Lento-Allegro in a (op. 25 xi, the so-called *Winter-Wind Etude*)

Syncopations and other rhythmic problems: Andantino in f and the Allegretto in A-flat of the *Nouvelles études* (i and iii, respectively)

Octave playing: Allegro con fuoco in b (op. 10 x)

Left-hand melody: Vivace in C (op. 10 vii), Vivace in e (op. 25 v) in the middle part, Lento in c-sharp (op. 25 vii)

Cantabile playing: Lento in E (op. 10 iii), Andante in e-flat (op. 10 vi), Allegretto in E-flat (op. 10 xi) combined with smooth playing of arpeggios, Allegro sostenuto in A-flat (op. 25 i, the so-called *Harp Etude*), Vivace in e (op. 25 v) in the middle part, Lento in c-sharp (op. 25 vii).

Smaller than, but in other respects similar to, the etudes are the preludes. Some of them are indeed small, several being less than twenty bars long; the Largo in E (op. 28 ix), the shortest, has but twelve bars; the Largo in c (op. 28 xx) has thirteen; and the Andantino in A (op. 28 vii) has a mere fifteen. By contrast, the longest of them, the Allegretto in A-flat (op. 28 xvii), is ninety bars in length. Many of the preludes are like the etudes in that a single motive provides all the thematic material. Often this will consist of rapid figuration, as can be seen in the Agitato in C (op. 28 i), the Molto agitato in f-sharp (op. 28 viii), the Molto allegro in c-sharp (op. 28 x), or the Allegro in e-flat (op. 28 xiv), to name only a few. Or it will be lyrical, a short melodic and rhythmic pattern that is repeated, varied, used in transposition or in a different range of the keyboard, and so on; as examples, we can mention the very short Largo in c (op. 28 xx), the Andantino in A (op. 28 vii), the Cantabile in B-flat (op. 28 xxi), or the Lento in F-sharp (op. xiii), the lyrical melody in chords over a steadily running broken-chord accompaniment; the single Prelude in c-sharp (op. 45) is also of this type. A few of the more lyrical preludes have contrasting middle sections and thus are similar to the nocturnes. This is true of the famous Sostenuto in D-flat (op. 28 xi), known as the *Raindrop Prelude*, in which the lyrical melody of the first part is given a contrast in the bass chords and crescendo in the middle section; only the eighth-note motion remains constant. There are two notable exploitations of contrasts in which melodic material is pitted against rapid figuration; there is a grazioso effect in the Vivace in G (op. 28 iii) with the melody stated in thirds and full chords and, dramatically, in the Allegro appassionata in d (op. 28 xxiv), a declamatory melody of wide leaps in dotted rhythm is punctuated with sudden furious scale runs, all of which is over an agitated accompaniment—a most impressive composition.

In the character pieces of Chopin, it is noteworthy that, unlike Schumann (and, as will be seen later, Liszt), literary associations are almost completely lacking. There is no trace of such connections in the impromptus, scherzi, nocturnes, or etudes; and it exists only in a general way in the ballades, as has been seen. Nor does there seem to be any connection between the preludes and literature, unless one views them as fragments and interprets them as the musical equivalent of the literary genre that was cultivated by many Romantic writers.

Turning to the larger, "absolute" works of Chopin, we find three sonatas and a fantasia.

Sonata in c (op. 4, B. 23), composed in 1828 and published in 1851
Sonata in b-flat (op. 35, B. 128), composed in 1837 and 1839 and published in 1840
Sonata in b (op. 58, B. 155), composed in 1844 and published in 1845
Fantasia in f (op. 49, B. 137), composed and published in 1841.

The piano sonatas represent Chopin's principal accomplishment in the older tradition of the large forms of piano music. In all essentials, the tradition is fully maintained; there is the big Allegro first movement in sonata form, the scherzo as second movement (a minuetto in the Sonata in c, op. 4), the slow movement, and the brilliant Allegro as finale, in two cases using rondo form (Sonatas in c and b). Also, the key relationships between the several movements are largely traditional. The minuetto of the Sonata in c is in the relative major, E-flat, and the trio is in e-flat; the scherzo of the Sonata in b-flat is in the subdominant minor, e-flat, and the subordinate passage is in G-flat; and the most distant relation, that of a tritone (E-flat), is to be seen in the scherzo of the Sonata in b, but here the trio is in b, thus reasserting the tonic of the work as a whole. In the slow movements, the Larghetto of the Sonata in c is in A-flat, the submediant major; the famous *Marche funèbre* of the Sonata in b-flat is in the tonic of the work, and its trio is in the relative major, D-flat; the Largo of the Sonata in b is in the parallel major, B, and its middle section is in the subdominant, E. Therefore, in the Sonata in c, only the first and last movements are in the tonic, while in the other two works, the slow movement also is in the main tonality; and regularly the scherzo (or minuet) is in a related key instead of the tonic. While these relationships are some-what unusual, they certainly are not to be looked upon as anything extraordinary.

In the treatment of the sonata form, we can note the presentation in all three works of the old scheme complete with double bar and repeat marks at the close of the exposition. In the exposition, several contrasting themes are presented; the first is the forceful and motivic type of theme (as is particularly to be seen in the Sonata in b-flat), and the second appears in the relative minor and is lyrical (chorale-like chords in the Sonata in b-flat, a nocturne-like, cantabile melody accompanied by slow and evenly moving arpeggios in the Sonata in b). In the early Sonata in c, the subordinate theme is derived from the principal theme. In all three works, it is the motivic principal theme that is exploited in the developments. (In the Sonata in b, use is also made of the subordinate theme, leading to a large and impressive climax.) Peculiar to Chopin is the individual treatment of the recapitulations; they commence not with the principal theme, but with the subordinate theme, the principal theme coming at the end. (In the Sonata in b-flat, it is used as the basis for the coda.) In the early Sonata in c, the recapitulation commences with the principal theme but in the "wrong" key of b-flat. It seems, then, that Chopin had accepted the traditional concept of sonata form.

The scherzo movements also employ the traditional scheme; the scherzos themselves are in expanded rounded binary form, and the trios are in simple, repetitive forms. While the minuetto of the early Sonata in c is a small piece in all respects, the scherzi of the other sonatas are large, although they do not approach the size of Chopin's independent scherzi. At the same time, there are similarities between the scherzi in the sonatas and the independent works. The scherzo of the Sonata in b-flat features elaborate virtuoso material, a fast motivic theme using staccato repeated chords that is offset by soft, chromatic octave passages in the bass, and the trio is in nocturne style; that of the Sonata in b presents a *leggiero* figuration theme, and in the trio, the lyrical melody is in a middle voice accompanied by chords with dissonant suspensions, an important feature.

Again, in the slow movements, we find conventional things. Three-part form is used in all. The Larghetto of the Sonata in c is unusual for the persistence of quintuple meter. Related to the nocturne is the Largo of the Sonata in b. But by far the most celebrated of these slow movements is the *Marche funèbre* of the Sonata in b-flat. Here, the ponderous march with its melody full of repeated notes in dotted rhythm accompanied by heavy chords and highlighted by the sudden turn to the relative major, is set off by the cantabile trio, also in D-flat. It must be noted that both sections of this movement are cast in the rounded binary form long associated with the march form.

In the finales, we meet with rondos in the Sonatas in c and b, the first having two episodes and the second a sonata-rondo in which the second episode is treated as a development. Against these stands the highly unconventional finale of the Sonata in b-flat, a movement that has aroused much comment and speculation. For here, instead of the large-scale movement in sonata or rondo form, we have a short piece (twenty-five bars) in uniform character throughout; there are extremely rapid chromatic scale passages, the two hands an octave apart throughout, to be played at whirlwind speed but *sotto voce e legato* right up to the end. This movement, then, is related rather to the prelude or etude, and Chopin's use of such a piece as a finale to a sonata represents something of a departure.

All in all, then, Chopin's sonatas stand squarely in the tradition of the genre as it had come down from the late eighteenth century and developed through the work of Beethoven, Schubert, and their contemporaries. The most unusual features are in the Sonata in b-flat with its *Marche funèbre* and the prelude-like finale. Much the same situation will be found in the other large work in one of the standard categories of piano composition, the Fantasia in f (op. 49), which ends in A-flat. We have seen instances of the fantasia being treated as a large form in three or four movements, *in toto* roughly equivalent to a sonata; and Schumann actually stated that there was no real difference between the two. This claim could certainly not be made for Chopin's fantasia, even though it clearly is a major work. It is cast in one long movement in loose sonata form with a short march serving as introduction and a coda at the end; the looseness has to do with the fact that the "development" does not develop themes of the exposition so much as restate them in various keys and arrangements, thus attaining a dramatic climax, and the recapitulation is prepared by a Lento sostenuto in B. This work, unlike other fantasias we have seen, does not make use of thematic variation.

The last important group of Chopin's piano works to be discussed are the dances: the waltzes, the mazurkas, and the polonaises. The waltz, the great international dance of the time will be dealt with first. The earliest are a few individual waltzes that were not published until long after Chopin's death: the Waltzes in A-flat, E, E-flat, and e (B. 21, 44, 46, 56). Then there are sets of earlier waltzes published posthumously in 1855.

> Lento in A-flat; Moderato in b (op. 69, B. 95 and 35), composed in 1829–1835
> Molto vivace in G-flat, Tempo guisto in f, Moderato in D-flat (op. 70, B. 92, 138 and 40), composed between 1829 and 1842.

But the main sets of waltzes, those published by Chopin himself, are:

> *Grande valse brilliante.* Vivo in E-flat (op. 18, B. 62), composed in 1831 and published in 1834
> *Grandes valses brilliantes.* Vivace in A-flat, Lento in a, Vivace in F (op. 34, B. 94, 64, and 118), composed respectively in 1835, 1831, and 1838 and published in 1838
> *Grande valse* in A-flat (op. 42, B. 131), composed and published in 1840
> *Valses.* Molto vivace in D-flat (known as the *Minute Waltz*), Tempo guisto in c-sharp, Moderato in A-flat (op. 64, B. 164), composed in 1846–1847 and published in 1847.

Up to now, we have seen the waltz in keyboard music first as a very short, modest piece, often with rustic overtones (as in the *Ländler*) and with its trio; later, it became an elegant type of dance cultivated in the refined circles of the aristocracy, in which context it could appear also as a bravura piece (see Weigel and Carner). This last is demonstrated by Weber's well-known *Aufforderung zum Tanze (Invitation to the Dance)*. It is this type of waltz that provides the basis for the waltzes of Chopin (see Koscewski). The earliest among them, however, are modest in all respects; they are simple and short with middle sections called "trios." The same is largely true of the waltzes published in 1855 as op. 69 and 70, especially the nocturne-like Lento in f (op. 69 i). But the really representative of Chopin's waltzes are those that he himself published. In these, as in Weber, the waltz appears as an elegant and brilliant piece.

There is no one formal scheme used in these waltzes. Generally speaking, they are in several sections of which the first is regarded as the waltz proper and is repeated near the end, while, in between, come a number of short and contrasting waltzes; this can be seen clearly in the *Grande valse brilliante* in E-flat (op. 18). Sometimes, a refrain is introduced, as in the *Grande valse* in A-flat (op. 42), in which there are three episodes. The principal section of this waltz is noteworthy for its cantabile theme in even notes and its smooth, chromatic, broken-chord accompaniment. Much shorter, and thus resembling rather the early waltzes, is the popular Waltz in D-flat (op. 64 i), the *Minute Waltz* in simple three-part form, the first with a theme in scale passages and the second lyrical. Frequently in the waltzes, there will be a ceremonial "martial" introduction, fanfare-like, as well as a coda featuring brilliant figuration, both of which are found in op. 18 and 34. The *Grande valse brilliante* in A-flat (op. 18) even uses the old rounded binary form in all of its sections. But not all Chopin's waltzes have this elegant brilliance; there is the Lento in a (op. 34 ii), the Moderato in b (op. 69 ii) and particularly the Tempo giusto in c-sharp (op. 64 ii), whose lyric principal section is not far removed from the world of the nocturne.

Far more individual, however, are those dances that relate to his native Poland. Of these there are two, one small and the other large: the mazurka and the polonaise. The mazurkas, of which there are sixty-two according to Brown, may be grouped as follows. First are the earliest, most of which, like the early waltzes, remained unpublished until long after Chopin's death. (But some appear in his published sets: op. 7 iv, op. 17 iv, op. 68 ii.)

Mazurka in D (B. 4), composed around 1820
Vivace in B-flat, Con anima in G (B. 16), composed in 1825 and published in 1926
Allegro non troppo in D, composed in 1829 (B. 31), revised in 1832 (B. 71), and
   published in 1872.

Then comes the main corpus of mazurkas, published by Chopin himself:

Mazurka in f-sharp, Mazurka in c-sharp, Vivace in E, Presto ma non troppo in e-
   flat (op. 6, B. 60), composed in 1830–1831 and published in 1832
Vivace in B-flat, Vivo ma non troppo in a, Presto ma non troppo in A-flat, Vivo in
   G (op. 7, B. 45 and 61), composed in 1830–1831 and published in 1832
Vivo e risoluto in B-flat, Lento ma non troppo in e, Legato assai in A-flat, Lento
   ma non troppo in a (op. 17, B. 77), composed in 1832–1833 and published in 1834
Lento in g, Allegro non troppo in C, Moderato con anima in A-flat, Moderato in
   b-flat (op. 24, B. 89), composed in 1834–1835 and published in 1836

Allegro non tanto in c, Allegretto in b, Allegro non troppo in D-flat, Allegretto in c-sharp (op. 30, B. 105), composed in 1836–1837 and published in 1838

Lento in g-sharp, Vivace in D, Semplice in C, Mesto in b (op. 33, B. 115), composed in 1837–1838 and published in 1838

Maestoso in c-sharp, Andantino in e, Animato in B, Allegretto in A-flat (op. 41, B. 122 and 126), composed in 1838–1839 and published in 1840

Vivace in G, Allegretto in A-flat, Moderato in c-sharp (op. 50, B. 145), composed in 1841–1842 and published in 1842

Allegro non tanto in B, Vivace in C, Moderato in c (op. 56, B. 153), composed in 1843 and published in 1844

Moderato in a, Allegretto in A-flat, Vivace in f-sharp (op. 59, B. 157), composed and published in 1845

Vivace in B, Lento in f, Allegretto in c-sharp (op. 63, B. m162), coposed in 1846 and published in 1847.

There are two sets published posthumously in 1855 combining early and later mazurkas:

Vivace in G, Cantabile in g, Allegretto in C, Moderato animato in a (op. 67, B. 93, 167, 163), composed between 1835 and 1846

Vivace in C, Lento in a, Allegro ma non troppo in F, Andantino in f (op. 68, B. 38, 18, 34, 168), composed between 1827 and 1849.

Finally, two independent mazurkas were composed in the early 1840's:

Mazurka à Emil Gaillard in a (B. 140)
Mazurka in a (B. 134) for *Notre temps* (published in 1842 or 1843).

Related to these is an early work, the *Rondo à la mazur* in F (op. 5, B. 15), composed in 1826 and published in 1828. (There are a few other shorter mazurkas; see Brown.)

Although mazurkas had been composed for piano by other composers as early as 1830 (Miaczynski's set of fifty-six, among others), those of Chopin are clearly the finest examples of the genre and, even in his own work, take a position second to none. It is difficult to make a general statement concerning the musical forms found here since a great many schemes are used, no one of which takes a preponderance over the others. While some of the earlier mazurkas show a simple repetitive scheme—the mazurka and its trio—others, like the Vivace in C, reveal a more complex organization. While a good many of the later works show the simple ternary scheme, there are many others that do not. In any case, a mazurka is a sectional work in which the repetition of individual section is an important element; usually, there are three or four different sections that contrast in key, thematic material, and character and that are repeated and alternated in various combinations.

To gain a better understanding of these little pieces, it is necessary to know something of the original Polish dance types that underlie them (see especially Egert). Actually, the mazurka (named for the Mazur people of Mazovia) is but one of several related dances whose general name is *oberek*, a term denoting "turning dances" for couples. Of these, there came to be three kinds, all in triple time: in *kujawiak*, the slow and serious dance (named for the Kujawy region); the *mazur*, in faster tempo; and the *obertas* (sometimes called *oberek*, so that the terminology is not always clear), the fastest. There is, in the *kujawiak*, a prevalence of the minor mode (often with raised fourth and lowered seventh), and the slow tempo allows a good deal of embellishment as well as much rubato. In the faster *mazur* and *obertas*, the embellishment is replaced by dotted rhythms and wide leaps. Rhythmic features, then, are these dotted rhythms, syncopations, and irregular accentuations (especially the ends of phrases, where the second or third beat is often given the accent); grace notes and ornamental runs and figures also are important. Mazurkas originally were sung to the accompaniment of the *dudy*, a wind instrument similar to the bagpipe (compare the German term *Dudelsack*), which produced a drone bass.

EXAMPLE 61

Chopin: *Mazurkas*—excerpts

A. Lento in a (op. 68 ii)—beginning (a *kujawiak*)

B. Presto ma non troppo in e-flat (op. 6 iv)—excerpt (an *obertas*)

continued

While the majority of the mazurkas of Chopin are of the moderate *mazur* type, there are examples of the slow *kujawiak*, such as the Lentos in e and a (op. 17 ii and iv), in g (op. 24 i), and in a (op. 68 ii), as well as of the faster *obertas*, such as the Presto in e-flat (op. 6 iv), the Presto in A-flat (op. 7 iv), or the Allegro ma non troppo in F (op. 68 iii). The drone bass also appears in Chopin's mazurkas, used generally in one part of the piece only; examples may be seen in the Mazurkas in c-sharp and E (op. 6 ii and iii), the Vivace in F (op. 7 i), the popular Vivo e risoluto in B-flat, the Lento ma non troppo in e and in a (op. 17 i, ii, iv), the Andantino in e (op. 41 ii), the Allegro non tanto in B (op. 56 i), and the Allegro ma non troppo in F (op. 68 ii), to name only some of the most obvious. The modal feeling also appears here and there; a particularly clear example of the Mixolydian mode (major scale with flat seventh) is the Vivo in G (op. 7 v) and of the Phrygian mode (minor scale with flat second) is the Maestoso in c-sharp (op. 41 i) or the Allegretto in A-flat (op. 41 iv) in the middle section (in c-sharp); particularly common and characteristic is the raised fourth usually associated with the Lydian mode, which can be seen, among others, in the Allegro non troppo in C (op. 24 ii), the Allegretto in A-flat (op. 41 iv) at the beginning, the Vivace in C (op. 56 ii), or in the minor, in the Lento in a (op. 68 ii) at the beginning. There are many other examples in the mazurkas as well as in other genres composed by Chopin.

EXAMPLE 61—*continued*

Here, we are dealing with stylized dances. The basic features of the dance have been taken and used singly or in combination, and other musical procedures have been drawn in. Along with the modal scales, the drone bass, and the characteristic rhythmic and melodic patterns of the dance, we find occasionally a certain contrapuntal elaboration, as in the Moderato in b-flat (op. 24 iv), the Moderato in c-sharp (op. 50 iii), the Moderato in c (op. 56 iii), and the Vivace in f-sharp (op. 59 iii), in which the counterpoint in the reprise borders on canonic imitation; or we find it in the extremely chromatic mazurkas, some of which can be regarded as examples of the *kujawiak*—the Lento ma non troppo in a (op. 17 iv) with its nocturne-like *fioriture*, the Moderato in b-flat (op. 24 iv) with its suspensions, the Moderato in a (op. 59 i), or the Andantino in f (op. 68 iv [Georgii, *400 Years*, p. 114]). Although most of the mazurkas are short and seemingly modest works, there are a few that are designed as larger efforts: the Moderato in b-flat (op. 24 iv), already mentioned for its use of counterpoint, chromaticism, and suspensions; the Mesto in b (op. 33 iv) with the great contrast between its various sections; the Moderato in c-sharp (op. 50 iii), in which the use of counterpoint has already been mentioned; the Allegro non tanto in B and the long Moderato in c (op. 56 i and iii). The mazurka, in being submitted to this high degree of stylization, comes close to the character piece.

One important feature of the mazurkas is their complete eschewal of bravura display, so important in much of Chopin's work. But this one element is re-asserted in Chopin's other body of dances native to Poland, the polonaises. Again there are early works:

> Allegro ma non troppo in g (B. 1), composed and published in 1817
> Vivo in B-flat (B. 3), composed in 1817 and published in 1934
> Animato in A-flat (B. 5), composed in 1821 and published in 1902
> Moderato in g-sharp (B. 6), composed in 1822 and published in 1864
> Allegro moderato in b-flat (B. 13), composed and published in 1826.

There is also a group of early polonaises that were not published until after Chopin's death:

> Allegro maestoso in d, Allegro ma non troppo in B-flat, Allegro moderato in f
>   (op. 71, B. 11, 24, 30), composed in 1825–1829 and published in 1855
> Polonaise in E-flat (B. 36), composed in 1829 and published in 1870.

Finally, there is the main corpus of the polonaises:

> Allegro appassionata in c-sharp, Maestoso in e-flat (op. 26, B. 90), composed in
>   1834–1835 and published in 1836
> Allegro con brio in A (called the *Polonaise militaire*), Allegro maestoso in c (op. 40,
>   B. 120, 121), composed in 1838–1839 and published in 1840

Polonaise in f-sharp (op. 44, B. 135), composed in 1840–1841 and published in 1841

Maestoso in A-flat (op. 53, B. 147), composed in 1842 and published in 1843

Polonaise-Fantaisie in A-flat (op. 61, B. 159), composed in 1845–1846 and published in 1846.

To these should be added the Andante spianato and *Grande polonaise* in g and E-flat (op. 22, B. 88); the polonaise was composed in 1830–1831, originally for piano and orchestra; the Andante spianato was added to the polonaise, which was arranged by Chopin as a piano solo, in 1834.

If the mazurkas are small and "intimate" pieces, the polonaises are precisely the opposite; they are large-scale, brilliant works designed for the concert hall. It is true that the early polonaises are still small works showing the simple repetitive schemes we have seen in dances, especially the rounded binary form, and they also have middle sections called "trios"; they even call for the repeat of the first section by the *da capo* designation. Noteworthy among these early polonaises is the Allegro moderato in b-flat (B. 13), which Chopin composed just before his departure from Warsaw in 1826; the polonaise proper is marked *dolente* and has it melody presented first in thirds and then in chords; but the trio has as its melody an aria, *Veni fra questa braccia* from Rossini's opera *La ga͂͂a ladra*, which had been introduced to Warsaw in 1825.

In the polonaises composed in Paris, the type is expanded greatly, and the virtuoso element comes to the fore. In the first two sets, op. 26 and 40, the ternary form is still basic, and the rounded binary form is still evident in the polonaises proper and in some of the middle sections; but the over-all dimensions have been increased. Popular in this group is the so-called *Military Polonaise* in A (op. 40 i).

The next two polonaises are highly stylized concert pieces, in f-sharp (op. 44) and A-flat (op. 53). The former is one of the most interesting among Chopin's larger works. After a short introduction of octave figures in the bass comes the polonaise proper, a vigorous theme with insistent accompaniment, both to the typical polonaise rhythm; to this come several episodes, the second being a *tempo di mazurka*, after which the introduction appears again to herald the final statement of the polonaise proper. Less elaborately organized is the popular Polonaise in A-flat (op. 53) with its brilliant introduction of chromatic runs in chords, the bravura polonaise theme in thirds and grace notes, the melody high and the accompaniment low so that the full range of the keyboard is exploited, and the two subordinate sections, of which the virtuoso emphasis is most obvious in the second with its ostinato octave figure in the bass and the dotted theme in chords above it progressing from *sotto voce* to a resplendent *fortissimo*; a meandering transitional passage, very chromatic, leads to the culminating statement of the polonaise theme.

A special case is represented by the Polonaise-Fantasie in A-flat (op. 61), an

unusual and ambitious work. The fantasia, as has been seen, was one of the
large forms of "absolute" music, and Chopin's other contribution can be
regarded as such. Since the polonaise was also being interpreted as a large form, it
was not unreasonable to attempt a combination of the two, and this is what is
represented here. In regard to formal plan, it is a most complicated work; basically,
it is a large ternary plan with introduction, coda, and an extensive transitional
passage before and after the subordinate section but with many changes of key,
short episodes and variations, and the use of themes from one section in another
(particularly the second transition).

Of other works there are not many: a few early rondos; the large Allegro de
concert in A (op. 46, B. 72), composed in 1840–1841 and published in 1841, an
out-and-out bravura display piece in the form of a rondo with two episodes, one
a variant of the rondo theme; and the simple *Écossaises* of 1826 (op. 72 iii, B. 12).
There are also a few sets of themes and variations, all on popular melodies of the
time—an operatic aria by Hérold (op. 12, B. 80), the German song *Steh' auf, steh'
auf, o du Schweitzerbub* (B. 14), the *Souvénir de Paganini* (B. 37), a set of variations
on *Le Carneval de Venise*, and a single variation on a march by Bellini for the

EXAMPLE 62

CHOPIN: Polonaise in f-sharp (op. 44), principal theme—beginning

collection *Hexameron* (B. 113). For two pianos, there is a Rondo in C (op. 73, B. 27) originally composed for piano solo.

Chopin's works are now a mainstay of the pianist's repertory. And since he, alone among the great composers of the nineteenth century, concentrated single mindedly on writing for the instrument, there is a certain justice in this. At the same time, his exploitation of the capacities of the piano involved him in much experimentation, using new harmonies and different ways of writing for the instrument, that aroused attention at the time, not all favorable. We have referred to the use of quintuple meter in the slow movement of the early Sonata in c (op. 4) and the elaborate rhythmic combination in the *Nouvelles études*. In regard to harmony (see Lissa), extreme dissonances may be found in such etudes as the Andante in e-flat (op. 10 vi), the Allegro in F, and Vivace in e (op. 25 iii and v), the last two of which have a bold use of the appoggiatura. The use of modal scales has already been mentioned. In 1834, Chopin was attacked by a prominent critic, Ludwig Rellstab (1799–1860), who, in reference to the mazurkas (op. 7), spoke of the "ear-splitting discords, forced transitions, harsh modulations, ugly distortions of melody and rhythm," their "odd originality," the use of "strange keys," "unnatural positions," and "perverse combinations." Of the nocturnes (op. 9), Rellstab said: "Where Field smiles, Chopin makes a grinning grimace; where Field cries, Chopin groans; where Field puts some seasoning into his food, Chopin empties a handful of cayenne pepper."[1] But it is precisely these qualities, the result of much experimentation, that have given Chopin's works the position they now enjoy.

[1] Quoted by Murdoch, pp. 155-6.

CHAPTER EIGHT

Liszt and Brahms
and Their Age

The study of Romantic keyboard music has shown that it was largely the outgrowth of the new art of instrumental music that developed in the latter half of the eighteenth century. We have seen that, although during the early nineteenth century the large forms of so-called "absolute music," meaning here primarily the sonata and the theme and variations, continued their existence, they experienced a certain decline in importance, and their place was usurped by new and more typically Romantic genres of composition, those with extramusical implications—the character piece in its various guises. But, as has also been seen, these two tendencies in the music of the nineteenth century were by no means mutually exclusive, and there was a good deal of interaction between the two.

An important element in the aesthetic view of the time had to do with the art work as the unique individual expression of the artist and, on a less lofty but more practical level, as the manifestation of his particular individual emotions. This view had a peculiar importance for keyboard music at this time, for it affected not only the composer (an effect that it shared with other branches of musical composition), but also the performer, and here we mean primarily the virtuoso pianist. This was intimately bound up, in the first place, with the increase in concert activity since the early eighteenth century. In the second place, it was closely connected with a view of art that arose in the eighteenth century but that occupied a position of prominence in Romanticism: if the realm of art is taken as supersensible or even divine, then the artist becomes a person set off from other men as one who has insights that they lack, as one in intimate contact with a higher realm of which they know nothing. It will easily be seen that such a view would have peculiar consequences when extended to the performer of music as well as to the composer. Often, the musician united both functions by serving as the performer of his own works. We can recall that C. P. E. Bach, Mozart,

Beethoven, and Clementi, to name only a few, were all known as the most prominent virtuoso pianists of their day; while Weber, Mendelssohn, Schumann, Chopin, and Field were also known as virtuosos of their instrument. Schubert seems to have been one of the very first composers of the first rank to compose a large body of important piano music without himself being a prominent performer on the instrument. But it became more and more usual, as the century wore on, to have virtuoso performers who were not identified particularly with or known for their musical composition, whose reputations and livelihoods depended on their skill as performing artists playing chiefly the music of other composers (see Schonberg). It was virtuosity that made such a career possible, a virtuosity that sometimes reached to such an extent that it came to be regarded as something awe inspiring, even supernatural or demonic, so that the performing artist was also able to participate in the advantages that came to the creative artist. Among these we can name pianists like Ignaz Pleyel; Joseph Gelinek (1758–1825); Johann Ladislaus Dussek (1760–1812); Daniel Steibelt, a rival of Beethoven (see Müller); Anton Eberl (1765–1807); August Eberhard Müller (1767–1817 [see Haupt]); Johann Baptist Cramer (1771–1858); Ludwig Berger (1777–1839), the teacher of Mendelssohn (see Siebenkäs); Johann Nepomuk Hummel (1778–1837); Ferdinand Ries (1784–1838); Johann Peter Pixis (1788–1874); Friedrich Kalkbrenner (1785–1849); Carl Czerny (1791–1857); Franz Hünten (1793–1878 [see Zöllner]); Ignaz Moscheles (1794–1870 [see Heussner]); Henri Herz (1803–1885); Sigismund Thalberg (1812–1871); Alexander Dreyschock (1818–1869); Hans von Bülow (1830–1894); Karl Tausig (1841–1871); and, as we shall see in some detail, Franz Liszt (1811–1886).

Of the many things that go hand in hand with this sudden development of pianistic virtuosity, a few may be mentioned here. We have, first, a new and important body of bravura piano music that aimed to exploit these new virtuoso capabilities, particularly to provide the performing artist with the opportunity to make a profound impression, a "hit," on the audience. We have already seen this to some extent in the etudes of Chopin, which are as much *bona fide* concert pieces as they are etudes for the development of piano technique. We also find the nineteenth-century popular equivalent of the old intavolatura, transcriptions for piano of popular compositions of the time that were originally for other media. Here, it was opera that was singled out for particular attention; on the one hand there are arrangements of individual numbers from a popular opera or variations on the theme of a popular aria or duet (as had already been current in the work of Mozart and Beethoven), and, on the other hand, there are larger works that successively present the "highlights" or themes of the most popular arias, duets, ensembles, choral numbers, ballet music, and the like, from an opera under the general title of "potpourri," "fantasia," "reminiscence," "paraphrase," or something similar. In both, the emphasis was on virtuosity, the creation of a piece guaranteed to make an impression on the audience. Such works exist in great abundance from the nineteenth century.

Another result of the preoccupation with and interest in pianistic virtuosity showed itself in increased attention to piano methods—instruction manuals and courses of study in piano playing, many of which commence at the most elementary level and continue up to a most advanced stage of piano technique. Works of this kind went back to the sixteenth century, but they became numerous in the eighteenth century, well-known examples being François Couperin's *L'art de toucher le clavecin* of 1717, Jean-Philippe Rameau's preface to his *Pièces de clavecin* of 1724, or, more important, Carl Philipp Emanuel Bach's *Versuch über die wahre Art das Klavier zu spielen* in two volumes, 1753 and 1762. With the coming of the nineteenth century, there were more and more such publications, many of them by prominent virtuosos; a few can be listed here: Dussek's *Instructions on the Art of Playing the Pianoforte* (London, 1796), Cramer's *Grosse praktische Pianoforte-Schule* (Leipzig, 1815), Hummel's *Ausführliche theoretisch-praktische Anweisung zum Pianofortespiel* (Vienna, 1828), Kalkbrenner's *Méthode pour apprendre le pianoforte à l'aide du guidemains* (Paris, 1830), and Czerny's famous op. 500, the *Vollständige theoretisch-praktische Pianoforteschule* (Vienna, c. 1830). Three important similar works from the middle of the century are Moscheles and Fétis' *Méthode des méthodes* (Paris, 1837), Sigmund Lebert and Ludwig Stark's *Grosse theoretisch-praktische Klavierschule* (Stuttgart, 1858), and Adolf Kullak's *Aesthetik des Klaverspiels* (Berlin, 1861). Along with such instruction works go countless collections of teaching pieces, etudes, and the like, such as Clementi's well-known *Gradus ad parnassum* (1817–1820) or the many works of Czerny and Cramer.[1]

There are, then, broadly speaking, three principal divisions in the repertory of piano music of the nineteenth century: the old genres of so-called "absolute music," the new genres associated with the character piece, and those connected with the new virtuosity and public display with the performer in the forefront. Naturally, there are many cases in which elements from one group appear in another or even instances where aspects from all three are combined. Generally, however, these three can be readily isolated and distinguished from one another. Out of these traditions emerged two great figures who overrode all their contemporaries in significance, each of whom can be regarded as a peculiarly characteristic representative of an important stream in nineteenth-century music—Franz Liszt and Johannes Brahms, the former with the emphasis on virtuosity and the most outspokenly Romantic genres of music composition and the latter embodying many of the so-called Classical ideals.

The piano stands at the center of the artistic accomplishment of Franz Liszt, even though he did make many important contributions to other branches of

[1] For an extensive bibliography of this little-surveyed area, see the list compiled by H. Haase.

musical composition. As with so many composers, the piano brought him into the world of music with his first public appearance in 1820 at the age of nine, and it remained his chief vehicle through the great impression he made on Czerny in Vienna (1821–1822) and through the time of his early years in Paris (beginning in 1823) and the concerts he gave there, elsewhere in France, and in England, all under the guidance and supervision of his father. His skill in playing the instrument attracted wide admiration and brought him into contact with leading writers and musicians living in Paris in these years—men like Chopin, Berlioz Paganini, Rossini, Fétis, Lamartine, and Victor Hugo, as well as George Sand and Daniel Stern (the Countess d'Agoult) with whom he formed a liaison that lasted some ten years. In 1839, he commenced his great period of concertizing, during which his tours took him to all of Europe—Hungary, London, Vienna, Germany, Spain, Portugal, Turkey, Russia, Moldavia, Poland, and Denmark; in 1847, he presented his last concert in Elizabetgrad and never again did he accept payment for any concerts that he gave. During these years his emphasis was, of course, on performance. But there came a striking and rather startling change: from 1849 to 1861, Liszt took over the direction of the musical activities at Weimar, in the company of the intellectual Princess Carolyn Sayn-Wittgenstein whom he met in 1847. Weimar's cultural past had attained almost legendary standing through the presence there of men like Goethe, Schiller, Wieland, and Herder, and Liszt doubtless had ideas of restoring some measure of this past glory. Here Liszt devoted himself to conducting, composition, writing, teaching, and the formation of the progressive "Neo-German" school of musical composition, in which he warmly supported and performed the work of Wagner. These were the years of his large-scale works for orchestra. After 1861, he lived in Rome in a sort of retirement, although after 1869 he was active for part of each year in Weimar and Budapest. He took minor orders in the Roman Catholic Church in 1865. He emerged to make a tour celebrating his seventy-fifth anniversary, and he died in Bayreuth in the summer of 1886.

Liszt had made his reputation chiefly as a pianist. In so doing, he identified himself with the Romantic cult of virtuosity to which we have already referred. Most important in this was the development and exploitation of an amazing technique that seemed to border on sorcery and the demonic, sure to have a drastic effect on an audience. Liszt deliberately followed the practice of Paganini, whose bearing in concerts was such as to excite the suggestion that he actually was in possession of demonic powers. The use of a black costume was of great value in fostering such an impression, along with haughty posturing, elaborate gesturing, and other mannerisms. In this connection, it can also be noted that Liszt was the first pianist to appear by himself, unassisted, for a whole concert; before him, it had been customary for the virtuoso pianist to give a program in association with other musicians, singers or players, often even with an orchestra since the mainstay of the virtuoso's repertory had always been the concerto. But Liszt appeared by himself and established the term "recital" in its modern meaning.

Liszt also developed a totally new style of playing the piano and of writing for the instrument as well. Instead of working largely with scale technique, which had been the stock-in-trade of Hummel and Czerny and their contemporaries, Liszt exploited the capabilities of the rapidly developing instrument in a new and totally unheard-of fashion. He employed rapid and coloristic changes of register, using full chords and octave passages in all ranges often with wide leaps, arpeggio-vibrato figurations, arpeggios over the full extent of the keyboard, scales in thirds and sixths, octaves, and even full chords, diatonic and chromatic; elaborate cadenzas and recitative-like passages; and often a melody in the middle range with a difficult figuration accompaniment ranging over the whole keyboard. Many reports from those who heard him perform, such as Schumann and Berlioz, testify to the enormous effect he produced on an audience.

From our survey of Liszt's life, it appears that four broad periods can be distinguished: a preparatory phase, the period of concertizing (1839–1847), the years at Weimar (1849–1861), and the period of semiretirement lasting until his death. In each of these, we find that the activity in which he was principally engaged exerted a determining influence on the kinds of musical compositions on which he worked. Frequently, this correspondence may be only a rough one, but, in a general way, it appears to hold good. During the 1830's and 1840's, his musical composition emphasized those genres most closely connected with concertizing—etudes, operatic potpourris, and other types in which virtuoso elements were primary; in the decade of the 1850's, he turned away from this and devoted himself first to the character piece and then to other large forms in which virtuosity for itself was of lesser significance; in his very last period, the virtuoso impulse died down, and we find a number of very simple and short works that harmonically are most unusual. In general, it will be seen that Liszt neglected many of the more traditional genres of keyboard composition, like the sonata and the theme and variations, although they are not totally absent.[1] In the discussion of Liszt's keyboard music, we can, therefore, turn first to the etudes and the *Hungarian Rhapsodies* and then to the character piece, after which we can survey his other works.

---

[1] The bibliographical situation of Liszt leaves something to be desired. The collected edition, while it does contain the keyboard works, remains incomplete, and there is also a need for a modern thematic catalogue. The most comprehensive listing of his works is in Raabe, most accessible in its revision by Searle in *GD*, V; the numbers assigned to individual works by Searle are given here for ease in identification. The situation is complicated by Liszt's habit of reworking the same piece and including different versions in various collections, sometimes retaining the title and sometimes using a different one. General works on Liszt are by Searle, Sitwell, Schering, and Engel; on the early piano works, see Kokai; on Liszt and Chopin, see Waters.

Liszt's principal collections of etudes are:

Études d'exécution transcendante[1] (139, composed in 1851 and published in 1852: Preludio in C, Molto vivace in a, *Paysage* in F, *Mazeppa* in d, *Feux-follets* in B-flat, *Vision* in g, *Eroica* in E-flat, *Wilde Jagd* in c, *Ricordanza* in A-flat, Allegro agitato molto in f, *Harmonies du soir* in D-flat, *Chasse-neige* in b-flat

Études d'exécution transcendante d'après Paganini (140), first version composed in 1838 and published 1840; second version (141), composed and published in 1851

Ab-Irato. Grande étude de perfectionnement[2] (143), composed and published in 1852

Études de concert (144), composed around 1848 and published in 1849: A capriccio in A-flat, A capriccio in f, Allegro affetuoso in D-flat[3]

Études de concert[4] (145), composed in 1862–1863 and published in 1863: *Waldes-rauschen* in D-flat, *Gnomenreigen* in f-sharp–F-sharp.

It is in these works that Liszt's virtuosity is displayed in all its extremes and varieties; the most difficult elements of his piano technique are contained in these etudes. That this was deliberate on his part is testified to by the appellation "trascendental"; their difficulty transcended all other etudes of the time. This designation is interesting in that it also appears in philosophical writings of the time.

Through the three versions of the *Transcendental Etudes*, we find several changes made by Liszt, all producing an increase in the degree of difficulty. This can easily be seen with reference to *Mazeppa*. In the first collection, it is mainly a study in thirds, but later the figuration becomes considerably more elaborate so that the work ultimately turns into a study involving the presentation of a slow-moving melody in octaves at the extremes of the keyboard accompanied by very rapid chordal figuration (often in thirds) up and down the whole expanse of the keyboard. (The thematic material in this etude reappears in Liszt's symphonic poem of the same title.) Another important element of change is that, in their final version as *Transcendental Etudes*, many of the compositions receive descriptive titles and thus draw close to the character piece. In the combination of the two, we can see a parallel to the etudes of Chopin.

In regard to form, these etudes are sectional, and generally we find a basic ternary plan with some variation. But the basic tenary plan is obscured by extensive use of thematic alteration, so that often the contrasting middle section

[1] This represents for the most part the third revision of etudes published in two earlier collections: the *Étude en douze exercises* (136), composed in 1826, and published around 1827 as op. 1, and the *Grandes études* (137), composed in 1837–1838 and published in 1839.

[2] This work is a revision of the *Morceau de salon: Étude de perfectionnement* (142), written for Moscheles and Fétis' *Méthode des méthodes* (1837); but Searle gives the date of composition as 1840.

[3] Published as *Caprices poetiques* in Paris the same year with titles: *Il lamento*, *La Leggierezza*, and *Un sospiro*.

[4] Originally composed for inclusion in the *Grosse theoretisch-praktische Klavierschule* (Stuttgart, 1858) by Lebert and Stark, a circumstance that causes a discrepancy in the dating of the compositions.

employs the same thematic material as the first and last parts. Typical is the scheme of *Wilde Jagd*: three themes are used of which the second and third (both containing a figure derived from the first) appear first lyrically and then transformed in a heroic or dramatic guise. The large Allegro agitato molto in f might best be regarded as a loose sonata structure: three themes are stated, developed (a procedure that involves modulating statements of the three themes), and, after a brilliant and highly rhetorical climax, recapitulated.

Among the more brilliant and technically demanding are *Mazeppa*; *Feux-follets* (*Fireflies*), an allegretto whose theme bears some resemblance to Bartók's String Quartet No. 4, in which harmonic color is important; *Eroica*, martial and with a slow, ponderous melody and much use of dotted figures in the melody and in the accompaniment, suggestive of a military *marche funèbre*; the *Wilde Jagd* (*Wild Hunt*) featuring complex cross-rhythms, octave passages, and scale runs, the whole resembling in some respects a ballade; and *Chasse-neige* (*Snow Storm*) with its lyrical beginning and its gradual crescendo and accumulation. Other brilliant etudes, which lack decriptive titles, are the Preludio in C, which resembles Chopin's first prelude in the same key; the Molto vivace in a; and, particularly, the impressive Allegro agitato molto in f (the appassionata key), which seems not unrelated to Chopin's etude in the same key (op. 10 ii). But not all of these etudes concentrate on technical brilliance and virtuoso display; there are notable works whose impulse is lyrical and that require a cantabile style from the performer, such as the *Paysage* (*Landscape*) with its siciliano-like pastoral rhythm, *Ricordanza* (*Remembrance*), and the *Harmonies du soir* (*Evening Harmonies*). A ceremonial aura is achieved in *Vision* with its crashing chords, the use of unusual progressions, and its magnificent climax near the end.

The *Transcendental Etudes* afford an opportunity to take note of a typical style often employed by Liszt, one to which some reference has already been made. This consists of a melody that might have cantabile elements in it moving in slow and frequently even notes and that is accompanied by extremely rapid virtuoso figuration. Almost all of the pieces in the *Transcendental Etudes* show this kind of writing, so that only a few instances need be singled out here. *Vision* opens with such a melody in heavy chords in the bass register accompanied by light arpeggio figures in the treble that ultimately move over the whole keyboard. The procedure also appears in the Allegro agitato molto in f, particularly in the middle section, or in *Harmonies du soir* or *Chasse-neige*. Another prominent feature is the cadenza, a long "solo" line featuring scale runs, arpeggios, or parallel chords moving rapidly up and down the keyboard. Such passages occur particularly in *Paysage*, *Feux-follets*, and the Allegro agitato molto in f. Again, related to this, are the rhetorically simple recitative-like passages, as in *Mazeppa* and *Ricordanza*.

It is significant that Liszt should have based another set of *Transcendental Etudes* on compositions of Paganini. For, as has been pointed out, Paganini stood out as one of the foremost virtuoso performers of his day and was in many respects the model used by Liszt for his career as a concert artist. Like the first collection of *Transcendental Etudes*, here, too, we have a prelude followed by a series of etudes, but here the etudes are based on Paganini's *Caprices for Unaccompanied Violin* (op. 1). Particularly well known are *La Campanella* (also the subject of an independent fantasia by Liszt [420], also in variation form), *La Chasse* (v), and the sixth etude, which is based on Paganini's twenty-fourth caprice, a work which in the original was treated in variation form, and the variation form is retained by Liszt; this theme was also employed by Brahms and Rachmaninoff. The Preludio, in g, is a difficult tremolo study (*HMS*, IX, s. 4, b. 3).

The association of the etude with the character piece appears in the remaining etudes of Liszt. *Ab-Irato* is to represent rage by the insistence on heavy, thick chords in rapid tempo in the extreme bass, along with being a study in the rapid

EXAMPLE 63

Liszt: *Vision*, from *Transcendental Etudes* (No. 6)—excerpt

execution of chords; and the two *Études de concert* (145), *Waldesrauschen* (*Forest Rustling*) and *Gnomenreigen* (*Gnomes' Dances*), are likewise pictorial. The remaining three *Études de concert* (144) have descriptive titles only in their French edition; one of these, called *Un Sospiro*, in D-flat, a study in cantabile playing with a short phrase in even notes repeated with many ornamental variations, has become very popular.

Another most important group of works that were composed for the most part during Liszt's period of extensive concertizing are the famous *Rhapsodies hongroises* (244). Of these, there are nineteen, the first fifteen of which were published by 1853 (the first had appeared as early as 1847), while the last four are later works dating from the 1880's. Here, the impulse towards virtuosity is combined with the use of Hungarian gypsy melodies, which Liszt took to be the authentic voice of the Hungarian people. What he actually heard and used was the salon music played in the cities, so that one cannot accord Liszt a place of honor in the development of ethnomusicology. But whatever the actual result, the intent is certainly clear, and Liszt's motivations, here as elsewhere, are commendable.

Liszt reported on the *Hungarian Rhapsodies* in his book, *Des Bohèmiens et de leur musique en Hongrie* (*The Gypsies and Their Music in Hungary*) of 1859. From this, it appears that he had made large collections of these "gypsy" melodies and regarded them as constituting a central portion of Hungarian culture; he saw them as parts of a larger totality, parts that, in their great variety of forms and types, could be viewed as corresponding to components of a great gypsy epic. It is this conception that lies behind the term "rhapsody": the epic quality imputed to the melodies and their texts. The *Hungarian Rhapsodies* were preceded by earlier versions (242) under the title *Magyar Dallok* (*Hungarian National Melodies*) in ten books, the last six of which bore the title *Magyar rhapsodiak* (*Hungarian Rhapsodies*), all published between 1840 and 1847.

Many features of Hungarian folk music are reflected in the *Hungarian Rhapsodies*. Three of these works have descriptive titles: *Héroide-Elégaique* (v), *Le Carnaval à Pesth* (ix), and *Marche de Rakoczi* (xv). Frequently, one can find the use of the so-called "gypsy scale," using the augmented fourth, the minor sixth, and the major seventh, thus producing the familiar augmented second between the second and third and sixth and seventh steps of the scale. In several of the rhapsodies, Liszt imitates on the piano the sound of the zimbalo, a dulcimer-like instrument used in Hungary, as is evidenced by those in a and c-sharp (xi and xii). Again, there is a characteristically Hungarian type of melody often used here: a phrase commences in very long, slow-moving notes, and then, suddenly, there appear rapid ornamental figures, the effect being "rhapsodic" and melancholy. As Liszt said, "to be played in the haughty and melancholy manner of the gypsies" (vii). Frequently the qualification *mesto* (sad), *con duolo*, or *malinconico* appears. The effect is more pronounced in the Rhapsody in c-sharp (viii), which dispenses altogether with a time signature in the beginning, thus adding the "rhapsodic" element of free rhythm. This same characteristic type of melody can be found in the Rhapsody in d (vii) and in the famous popular one in c-sharp (ii), while traces of it appear in most of them—in the many melodies using slow notes with sudden interjections in dotted rhythms, sharp chords in the accompaniment, unexpected violent scale runs, and so on. Added to these are the more typically Lisztian features—the recitative-like phrases and the highly embellished cadenzas.

Also related to Hungarian folk music is a form that often appears in these rhapsodies, the *cȝardas*, a gypsy dance in two parts. The slow first part employs the type of melody already described, and the second part is rapid; the two parts were called *Lassu* and *Friska* respectively, and these designations appear in the *Hungarian Rhapsodies*, notably in the famous one in c-sharp (ii). Yet another

EXAMPLE 64

LISZT: Rhapsody in c-sharp, from *Hungarian Rhapsodies* (No. 8)—beginning

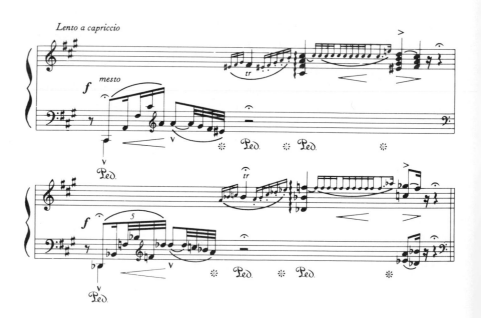

trait from Hungarian music is to present the melody in parallel thirds, as in the Rhapsody in c-sharp (i).

But the *Hungarian Rhapsodies* are also virtuoso show-pieces in all respects. The over-all form is usually loose and sectional with a great degree of contrast. The beginning is often slow, melancholy, and "rhapsodic"; contrasting parts follow—possibly a grazioso succeeded by a long impassioned recitative, a capriccioso, and then a grandiose virtuoso conclusion. The technical difficulties occasionally are great, and possibilities for showmanship exist in abundance; such features have doubtless contributed to the long-lasting popularity of these works. Here, we see the curious duality in Liszt's make-up: on the one hand the high-minded purpose, the lofty objectives, and, on the other, the intrusion of crasser elements aimed solely at popular acclaim, exploiting the grandiloquent gesture.

Similar to the *Hungarian Rhapsodies* is the *Rhapsodie espagnole: Folies d'Espagne et Jota aragonese* (254), composed around 1863 and published in 1867. Here, two Spanish melodies are accorded much the same treatment, but the first

EXAMPLE 64—*continued*

of them is the famous *La Follia* so often used as an ostinato in the seventeenth and eighteenth centuries, which lends a certain distinction to the work.

Turning to the character pieces of Liszt, the principal collections are:

Années de pèlerinage[1]

Première année: Suisse (160), composed in 1835–1851 and published in 1855: *Chapelle de Guillaume Tell, Au lac de Wallenstadt, Pastorale, Au bord d'une source, Orage, Vallée d'Obermann, Éclogue, Le mal du pays, Les cloches de Genève*

Deuxième année: Italie (161), composed in 1838–1849 and published in 1858): *Sposalizio, Il pensieroso, Canzonette del Salvator Rosa, Sonnetto 47 del Petrarca, Sonnetto 104 del Petrarca, Sonnetto 123 del Petrarca, Après une lecture de Dante: Fantasia quasi una sonata;* Supplement (162), composed in 1839 and published in 1861): *Venezia e Napoli—Gondoliera, Canzone, Tarantella*[2]

Troisième année (163), composed in 1867–1877 and published in 1883: *Angelus! Prière aux anges gardiens; Aux cyprès de la villa d'Este. Threnodie* (two compositions); *Les jeux d'eaux à la villa d'Este; Sunt lacrymae rerum: En mode hongrois; Marche funèbre. En memoire de Maximilien I, Empereur de Mexique† en 19e Juin 1–1867; Sursum corda*

Apparitions (155), composed in 1834 and published in 1835

Harmonies poétiques et religieuses (173), composed in 1845–1852 and published 1853: *Invocation, Ave Maria, Bénédiction de Dieu dans la solitude, Pensée des morts,*[3] *Pater noster, Hymne de l'enfant à son réveil, Funérailles, Miserere (d'après Palestrina), Andante lagrimoso, Cantique d'amour*

Ballades: in D-flat (170), composed in 1845–1848 and published in 1849; in b (171, composed in 1853 and published 1854)

Consolations (172), composed in 1849–1850 and published in 1850

Légendes (175), composed in 1863 and published in 1866: *St. François d'Assise. La prédication aux oiseaux, St. François de Paule marchant sur les flots*

Weihnachtsbaum. Arbre de Noël (186), composed in 1875–1876 and published in 1882: *Vieux Noël psallite, La nuit saint, Les bergers à la crèche, Adeste fidelis, Scherzoso, Carillon, Berceuse, Ancient Noël provençal, Cloches du soir, Jadis, Hongrois, À la manière polonaise*

Elegies: A-flat (196), composed in 1874 and published in 1875; A-flat (197), composed in 1877 and published in 1878

Magyar arcképek (*Pictures from Hungarian History*, 205), composed in 1885.

Along with these sets of pieces are a number of smaller individual compositions, of which the more important are:

---

[1] In part, the revision of pieces included in an earlier collection, the *Album d'un voyageur* (156), composed in 1835–1836 and published in 1842.

[2] The Petrarch sonnets originally were songs composed as early as 1838 (270); they were then arranged by Liszt himself for piano (158) and published in 1846. *Venezia e Napoli* likewise exists in part in an earlier version (159).

[3] An early version of this piece appeared as *Harmonies poétiques et religieuses* (154) in 1835.

Scherzo and March (177), composed in 1851 and published in 1854

Berceuse (174), first version composed in 1854 and published in 1862; second version composed in 1862 and published in 1865

Nuages gris (199), composed in 1881 and published in 1927

La lugubre gondola (200), first setting, composed in 1832 and published 1916; second setting, an arrangement of an earlier work for a solo string instrument and piano (134), the arrangement published 1886

Schlaflos! Frage und Antwort (203), composed in 1883 and published in 1927

Trauervorspiel und Trauermarsch (206), composed in 1885 and published in 1887

En rêve (207), composed in 1885 and published in 1888

Unstern, Sinistre, Disastro (208), composed *c.* 1886 and published in 1927.

With these works, we move into a realm that is of great importance for Liszt as a Romantic musician, and we meet with an aspect of his work that stands in great contrast to the musical *grand seigneur*, the towering virtuoso of the piano, the idol of European concert life. For Liszt, as has been indicated in the discussion of the *Hungarian Rhapsodies*, was in a way profoundly serious about his art, its meaning, and its general position in the culture of the time, as well as the position of musicians themselves in the society of the time. What was most important, however, was his belief in a cardinal aesthetic tenet of Romanticism the ability of music to express or suggest ideas, emotions, and impressions of various sorts—in short, its capability to give expression to extramusical subject matter. In this, it was chiefly the association between music and literature that drew Liszt's attention, and one of his central convictions had to do with, as he put it, "the renewal of music through its inner connection with poetry." Or, as he expressed it in the preface to his early collection, the *Album d'un voyager*, he was working with a rarefied art form, not for the many but for the few, in which the attempt is made to put into music the impressions of nature upon his soul, to express what he terms the "intrinsic and poetic meanings of things." And here, we can certainly see a contradition with the other Liszt, the great popular virtuoso pianist.

We find that Liszt frequently drew on the work of leading Romantic writers and poets for the subject matter of his character pieces, in which the world of nature is a common theme. Byron, the arch-Romanticist of English poetry, is represented with quotations from *Childe Harold's Pilgrimage*, and indeed the idea of a pilgrimage appears in Liszt's *Années de pèlerinage* (see Rüsch); the great French Romantic poet Lamartine provided the inspiration for the *Harmonies poétiques et religieuses* and the *Apparitions*; Victor Hugo provided the poem that Liszt "set" in his so-called *Dante Sonata*, the *Après une lecture de Dante. Fantasia quasi sonata*, as well as the epic *Mazeppa*; *Consolations* was the title of a collection of poems by the great critic Sainte-Beuve; the pastoral works, especially the *Vallée d'Obermann* and the *Mal du Pays*, are prefaced by excerpts from a most popular French novel, de Senancour's *Obermann*, written as early as 1804 but whose influence did not become important until it was reprinted in 1830. Inspired by German writers are *Au bord d'une source* (Schiller) and the *Mephisto-Waltz* (Lenau), actually the transcription of a work for orchestra. From earlier literature, we find sonnets of Petrarch (which originally had been composed by Liszt as songs) and Dante, who, as we have seen, Liszt has via Victor Hugo. From the fine arts, we find Liszt celebrating Raphael in *Sposalizio*, Michelangelo in *Il pensieroso*, and a song associated with Salvator Rosa. Stories related to two saints, Francis of Assisi and Francis of Padua, provide the background for the *Légendes*. Lesser known is the late nocturne *Schlaflos!* which is associated with a poem by Toni Raab. All in all, then, it appears from this assemblage of mainly literary sources used in his keyboard music that Liszt was earnest and very high-minded concerning his beliefs in the close connection between music and literature, poetry in particular.

In regard to the character pieces themselves, it will be seen that very often they fall under the regularly established types, even though the titles given them may be different. The tradition of Chopin is represented in the two ballades (for the one in D-flat, see *HMS*, IX, s. 3, b. 2), the Scherzo in B-flat, and the larger Scherzo in e and March in G. There are also several works with the title *Feuille d'album* (*Album Leaf*). But such designations are in the minority, and instead of appellations like "intermezzo," "song without words," "impromptu," and the like, we meet with more individualistic formulations; but even these often denote rather typical varieties of the character piece. A few important types may be given here; *Un soir dans les montagnes* (from the early *Album d'un voyager*) and the late pieces *Schlaflos!* and *En rêve* are nocturnes as is also, doubtless, the *Harmonies du soir* from the *Transcendental Études*. The first of these has as its middle section a thunderstorm that becomes a separate work in the *Années de pèlerinage*; a storm is also portrayed in the legend *St. François de Paule marchant sur les flots*. The singing of birds dominates *St. François d'Assise. Le Prédication aux oiseaux* in the *Légendes*. Less usual is the depiction of running water or the play of fountains in *Au bord d'une source* and *Les jeux d'eaux à la villa d'Este*, the latter being a brilliant allegretto with light arpeggio figures. Then there are pastoral compositions, such as the *Eclogue* and *Ranz des vaches*, from the early *Album d'un voyager*, or the *Pastorale* from the *Années de pèlerinage*. A larger number of compositions have to do with mourning and lamentation, especially among the later works. From the third part of the *Années de pèlerinage* are *Aux cyprès de la villa d'Este. Threnody* (which appears in two versions), *Sunt lacrymae rerum*, and *Marche funèbre*; and from the *Harmonies poétiques et religieuses* are the elaborate *Pensée des morts* and *Funérailles*, the latter with its heroic and military middle section indebted to Chopin's Polonaise in A-flat (op. 53); and the *Eroica* of the *Transcendental Etudes* could also be added. A final important group consists of works based on religious subjects, and while these appear in the early part of *Années de pèlerinage*, as the *Chapelle de Guillaume Tell* and *Les cloches de Genève*, they become far more important in the later collections: the third part of the *Années de pèlerinage*, with *Angelus! Prière aux anges gardiens* or, even more, the *Harmonies poétiques et religieuses*. Indeed, in this set, we find works like the *Ave Maria* and *Pater noster*, in which Liszt actually underlays the texts of Latin prayers, or the *Bénédiction de Dieu dans la solitude* or the *Miserere* (*d'après Palestrina*), the latter of which attempts to suggest the archaic but "pure" style of the sixteenth-century composer with simple chords in prevailingly diatonic harmonies and the absence of time signatures. In the *Pensée de morts*, Liszt draws on Psalm 129, *De profundis*, and again has the Latin words underlaid; by constantly repeated chords, the recitation of plainsong is suggested. Religious themes prevail, as seen in the two *Légendes*, while Christmas songs form the basis of much of the little-known collection *Weihnachtsbaum* (*Christmas Tree*), of which attention may be drawn to the setting of *Adeste fidelis* or the old Provençal Christmas song (Georgii, *400 Years*, pp. 120–1).

Virtuosity, which was so characteristic of the etudes and the *Hungarian Rhapsodies*, is less important in the character pieces. The most difficult among these works are to be found in the earlier sets of the *Années de pèlerinage*: the *Chapelle de Guillaume Tell* and *Orage* from *Suisse* and the large *Dante Sonata* from *Italie*. Virtuoso elements are largely lacking in the later sets of character pieces; especially simple are the six *Consolations*, in which lyricism is the main trait (see Kahl, 19b, p. 60). Lesser known are the late pieces composed by Liszt in his old age: *Nuages gris, Unstern, Schlaflos!* and *La lugubre gondola*, which are very short and very simple from the standpoint of pianistic technique, but from the standpoint of harmony, are very elaborate and experimental with an abundance of sudden, highly chromatic modulations; nonetheless, the relation to Mendelssohn's gondola song can be readily seen.

By far the biggest of Liszt's character pieces is the concluding number in *Italie*: the *Après une lecture de Dante*, called *Fantasia quasi sonata*, a designation that is the reverse of Beethoven's *sonata quasi una fantasia*. This work can best be characterized as a symphonic poem for piano. The usual features of the sonata are not present. It is a big virtuoso composition in a number of sections that follow one another in uninterrupted succession, all of which are related by the consistent use throughout of four themes and their variants. There is the slow introduction, Andante maestoso, with full octaves descending by tritones, followed by a Presto agitato assai (also designated "lamentoso") with rapidly moving broken octaves in sextuplets and a chromatic stepwise melodic line. Later, at the Andante quasi improvisato, the Presto theme is varied, as it is again in the Adagio; towards the end of the work, it is presented again in something more like its original form. Here, then, we have a large sectional work in cyclic form, which frequently contains passages whose difficulty is not less than that found in the *Transcendental Etudes*.

The other large-scale works for solo piano by Liszt are, externally at least, divorced from the character piece. The most important among them are:

Grosses Konzert-Solo (176), composed in 1849–1851 and published in 1851[1]
Sonata in b (178), composed in 1852–1853 and published in 1854
Weinen, Klagen, Sorgen, Zagen, Präludium nach Joh. Seb. Bach (179), composed in 1859 and published in 1863
Variationen über das Motiv von Bach. Basso continuo (ostinato?) *des ersten Satzes seiner Kantate Weinen, Klagen, Sorgen, Zagen, und des Crucifixus der H–molle Messe* (180), composed in 1862 and published in 1864.[2]

The *Konzert-Solo* and the sonata have much in common with the so-called *Dante Sonata* that concludes *Italie*. Both are sectional, use cyclic form, and afford much opportunity for virtuoso display. But far and away the most

---

[1] This work exists in two other versions: the *Grand solo de concert* for piano and orchestra (365), composed in 1850 and unpublished, and the *Concerto pathétique* for two pianos (258), composed in 1856 and published in 1866.

[2] This was subsequently arranged by Liszt for organ (673), composed in 1863 and published in 1865.

EXAMPLE 65

Liszt: *Sonata* in b—excerpts

A. Lento assai

B. Allegro energico

C. Grandioso

D. Andante sostenuto

A.

important of these is the Sonata in b, the only instance in which Liszt employed this designation pure and simple by itself. This work is cast in one long, continuous movement with several clearly definable sections that do not really correspond to the organization of a normal piano sonata. Again, there is cyclic form with extensive variation and transformation of four basic themes. (1) In the opening Lento assai section, the theme is constituted of staccato and separated

EXAMPLE 65—*continued*

B.

continued

chords and a bass line descending in a dotted rhythm (similar to Wagner's motive for Wotan's anger in his *Ring des Nibelungen*); this theme reappears in this form at the very end of the work and several times during its course. (2) What one might

EXAMPLE 65—*continued*

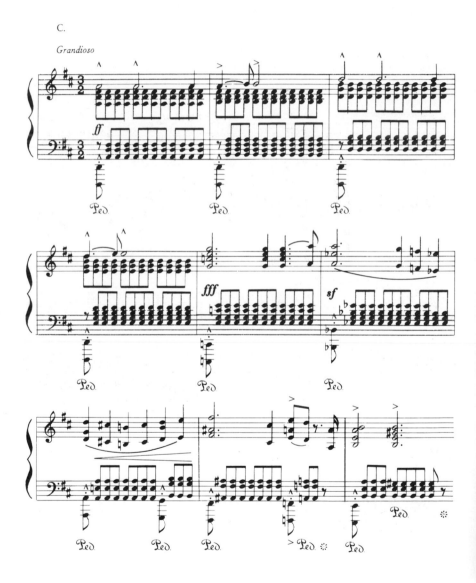

call the "principal" theme appears in the next section, Allegro energico, consisting of two motives, one employing wide leaps and slow dotted rhythms and
the other with strongly marked repeated notes preceded by an up-beat triplet
figure; these motives are used both singly and together, and are subjected to
many variations. The first of them appears in recitative guise over an arpeggio
accompaniment, and also as *Dolce con grazia*; the second motive appears in a
lyrical version, the up-beat eliminated and the note values augmented, *cantando
espressivo* and *dolcissimo*. The two remaining themes are of lesser import in the
plan of the work. (3) There is the grandioso theme, slow over ponderous, thick
repeated chords and (4) the Andante sostenuto, lyrical and used in combination
with the cantabile version of the second motive from the "principal" theme. In
its over-all organization, the sonata differs greatly from the normal sonata: there
are many sections contrasting in character, some of which recur. The work
begins solemnly with the impressive Lento assai, which also stands at the end;
the forceful Allegro energico, which presents the principal thematic material of
the work, comes next, and is not only repeated in similar form near the close, but

EXAMPLE 65—*continued*

D.

also appears during the course of the work as a three-voice fugue. Towards the end of the first Allegro energico, there are several rapid changes of tempo and character with much rapid octave work, which lead to a culmination immediately preceding the first presentation of the Grandioso. There are passages of great technical difficulty and climaxes of considerable proportions along with typically rhetorical passages, like the broad Grandioso and the recitative-like parts. In short, the Sonata in b is Liszt's largest work for piano solo and is at the same time a major contribution to the piano music of the nineteenth century. In its combination of cyclic form with thematic variation, the curious Lisztian rhetorical qualities, and enormous technical demands, it stands as an epoch-making work. The work is, all in all, typical of Romanticism, for although it has no literary program (as far as is known, at all events), it can clearly be regarded as a symphonic poem for piano; while it is called a "sonata," its formal principles are the same as those used by Liszt in his *bona fide* symphonic poems.

Two other large works by Liszt go back to the work of Bach. Both are based on the same melody, a chromatic ground bass used by Bach in the first movement of the cantata *Weinen, Klagen, Sorgen, Zagen* (Cantata No. 12), a movement which, with some changes, also appears as the Crucifixus of the Mass in b. While the first work, a prelude (in variation form) is relatively short, the second, also variations, is a major work. The variations are preceded by an introductory Andante and followed by recitative-like passages and then a coda in which the chorale *Was Gott tut das ist wohlgetan* appears with text underlayed. (This chorale also appears in Bach's cantata.) Liszt sets the darkness and lamentation of the ostinato against the affirmation of the chorale, so that typically Romantic features appear in a composition that takes its structural procedure from the Baroque period.

There is a large body of smaller works of various kinds for solo piano by Liszt. Among the original works are many dances: waltzes, mazurkas, galops, polkas, marches, and even Hungarian *c̜ardas*. These frequently appear with descriptive titles: *Valse di bravoura, Valse mélancolique, Caprices-valses, Maȥurka brilliant, Grand galopp chromatique.* Particularly noteworthy are the three *Valses oubliées (Forgotten Waltȥes,* 215), composed in 1881–1883 and published in 1881–1884; a fourth was made public in 1954. These are highly stylized waltzes with impassioned episodes in Liszt's grandiloquent manner and with harmonic, rhythmic, and coloristic effects in abundance. Especially interesting is the A-flat Waltz (ii), while the one in D-flat (iii) may be regarded almost as a crescendo study; best known is the one in d-sharp (i).

Liszt also was active as a transcriber of music, arranging the most popular works of the time in a most effective fashion for performance on the piano (see Friedheim). His settings (some two hundred in number) of the main numbers taken from operas of the time under the titles "reminiscences," "illustrations," "paraphrases," "transcriptions," or "fantasias," have already been mentioned as an important element in his repertoire during the years of concertizing. Reference can be made to only a few, merely by way of example. There are such works based on Meyerbeer's *Robert le diable* (413), composed in 1831 and published in 1841; *Le Prophète* (414), composed and published in 1849–1850; and *Les Huguenots* (412), composed in 1836 and published in 1837. And there are works based on Bellini's *I Puritani* (390), composed in 1836 and published in 1837; *Norma* (394), composed in 1841 and published in 1844; and *La Sonnanbula* (393), composed in 1839–1841 and published in 1842. There are also works based on Verdi's *Ernani* (432), composed in 1849–1859 and published in 1860 and *Rigoletto* (434), composed in 1859 and published in 1860, both published along with a version of the *Miserere* scene from *Il Trovatore* (433). The works of Wagner are abundantly represented, and apart from the *Phantasiestück* on themes from *Rienzi* (439), composed in 1859 and published in 1861, it is rather individual excerpts from his operas that Liszt arranged. There are several excerpts from *Tannhäuser* and *Lohengrin* and also an effective arrangement of the *Liebestod* from *Tristan und Isolde* (447), composed in 1867 and published in 1868, as well as individual numbers from *Die Meistersinger von Nürnberg*, *Rheingold*, and *Parsifal*. Also important is the potpourri from Mozart's *Don Giovanni* (418) composed in 1841 and published in 1843; the one on *Il Nozze di Figaro* (697) was left unfinished.

In addition to the transcriptions from operas, there are arrangements of instrumental works and songs. Prominent among the former are the *partitions de piano* of Beethoven's symphonies (464), six of Bach's preludes and fugues for organ (462), Berlioz's *Symphonie fantastique* (470), as well as Liszt's own *Totentanz* and the *Mephisto Waltz*. Among the songs arranged by Liszt are around fifty by Schubert (of which twelve each, from *Die Winterreise* [561] and *Schwanengesang* [560] stand out) along with songs of Beethoven, Schumann, Mendelssohn, Franz, and Chopin (*Chants polonaises*). Liszt also composed a number of songs himself and arranged many of them for piano solo, such as the Petrarch sonnets that found their way into *Italie*; in the case of the *Liebesträume* (541), the piano arrangements have become far better known than the songs from which they were arranged, as is especially true of the omnipresent *Liebestraum* in A-flat, an arrangement for piano of Liszt's setting of Uhland's poem *So lieb' so lang du lieben kannst* (298). In many cases, these transcriptions made by Liszt are eminently gratifying pieces and would serve to bring welcome variety to recital programs. Finally, it may be noted that Liszt was also active as an editor of music. He published his own editions of Beethoven's piano works, the selected piano works of Weber and Schubert, selected organ compositions of Bach, the etudes of Chopin, and exercises by Clementi.

There is a small body of music for piano duet and for two pianos by Liszt. Here, original compositions are in the minority and arrangements in the clear majority. Original works are, for piano duet, a polonaise and a set of variations on

Chopsticks (256) and, for two pianos, a large *Konzertstück* on themes from Mendelssohn's *Songs without Words* (257). Arrangements include Liszt's own symphonic poems (both for piano duet and two pianos), nocturnes of John Field for piano duet, Beethoven's *Ninth Symphony* (657), Schubert's *Wanderer Fantasia* (653), and Liszt's own *Dante Symphony* for two pianos (648), to name only the most important.

Likewise, there is a small body of organ music. There is the Fantasia and Fugue on the chorale *Ad nos, ad salutarem undam* (259), composed in 1850 and published in 1852, based on a chorus from Meyerbeer's *Le Prophète*, and a Prelude and Fugue on "Bach" (260), which exists in two versions, the first composed and published in 1855 and the second in 1870; the latter was also arranged as a piano solo. Both of these works have some relation to the Baroque toccata (prelude or fantasia) and fugue tradition, although the work based on Meyerbeer has many elements in common with Liszt's piano music: the emphasis on virtuosity, thematic variation, recitative-like passages, and colorful harmonies. On the other hand, Liszt took the organ, especially in later years, as a sort of mystical instrument and came to believe that church music should be "pure" and "serene"; in this, he was in part under the influence of the German Cecilian movement and the revival, usually with very romanticized organ accompaniments, of Gregorian chant. In this spirit, he composed a major work, the *Missa pro organo* (264), composed in 1879 and published in 1880, an organ Mass based on earlier vocal compositions, as well as a number of shorter pieces: *Pio X. Der Papsthymnus* (261), *Ora pro nobis*, *Litanei* (262), *Resignazione* (263), *Gebet* (265), *Requiem* (266), *Am Grabe Richard Wagners* (267), and two *Vortragsstücke* (268) —*Introitus* and *Trauerode*.

The piano, then, stands at the very heart of Liszt's life and work. By his technical mastery of this instrument, he became the most prominent musician in Europe; by the music he wrote for it, aside from the unabashedly display and etude-like compositions, he associated himself with the most progressive currents in musical composition of the time. Generally speaking, his uniqueness as a composer lies in his virtuoso interpretation of the romantic character piece, and this can be seen to particularly good advantage in the *Transcendental Etudes*.

The principal opposite number to Liszt in the field of keyboard music in the latter half of the nineteenth century was Johannes Brahms (1833–1897). The difference in their biographies is striking of itself. Brahms had none of the great "international" quality that was so characteristic of Liszt. Although, like Liszt, he was a pianist and even conductor by profession, Brahms was never in the public eye by such activities; indeed, when he made his Viennese debut as a pianist, he used his two piano quartets, a genre of composition that had never been associated with pianistic virtuosity. After holding several minor conducting posts in the provinces and in Vienna, in 1875 Brahms discovered that it would be possible for him to support himself adequately by composing, teaching, and giving occasional concerts, and thus be retired generally from public view.

In spite of this tendency towards withdrawal, Brahms almost inevitably—if against his will—came to be regarded as the head of the group of musicians opposed to the so-called "Neo-German" school, Liszt and Wagner. In 1853, Schumann, in a famous article, had hailed Brahms as a "young eagle . . . called forth to give us the ideal expression of the time." Later, in 1860, Brahms' name appeared among the signers of a manifesto directed against the Neo-German school, and, while this came out by accident, it certainly gave him a certain prominence among the opponents of Liszt and Wagner. Brahms was also closely connected with the critic and aesthetician Eduard Hanslick, the violinst Joseph Joachim, and the conductor Hans von Bülow.

Brahms' attitude is clearly to be discerned behind almost all of his music for keyboard, particularly in the large amount of music for piano. Here, he commenced, as did Schumann before him, with the old large forms, the sonata and the theme and variations; these were then abandoned for the various types of character pieces, but the large forms were cultivated in chamber and orchestral music. If we take up Brahms' works for piano by types—beginning with the sonatas, moving to the variations, and then coming to the character pieces—we also, generally speaking, follow his particular emphases in chronological order. Afterwards, we can look briefly at the smaller works for piano, the music for piano duet and two pianos, and then the small body of music for organ.[1]

Like Schumann, Brahms composed three piano sonatas (see Nagel):

Sonata in C (op. 1; No. 1), composed 1852–1853 and published in 1853
Sonata in f-sharp (op. 2; No. 2), composed in 1852 and published in 1853
Sonata in f (op. 5; No. 3), composed in 1853 and published in 1854.

All three were being composed at the same time (the one in f-sharp is the first one he completed) and were published the year of his first concert tour, on which he played with the violinist Remenyi and during the course of which he met some of the most important musicians of the time: Joachim, Liszt (then at Weimar), Wasiliewski, Hiller, Reinecke, and, especially, the Robert Schumann family. As might be expected, all three sonatas show similar features; the decisive influence seems to be that of Schumann and the decisive opposition is to Liszt. These are large, difficult, and, in some ways, rather extreme compositions, intended as major works from any standpoint. Suitably enough, the large four-movement scheme was used, as it had been by Schumann and Schubert (but not by Liszt); only the Sonata in f departs from this scheme but by expansion not contraction—

---

[1] Along with the collected edition, there is the recent thematic catalogue by Braunstein. Good general studies, among others, are by Kalbeck (standard), Geiringer, Murdoch, and Niemann.

322 A Short History of Keyboard Music

the addition of a fifth movement. There is the big opening Allegro in sonata form with coda, the lyrical slow movement, the scherzo, and the finale (rondo form in the Sonatas in C and f, sonata form in the Sonata in f-sharp). The Sonata in f belongs to the few sonatas that are in five movements: there is between the scherzo and finale a short slow movement called "Intermezzo—*Rückblick*," which is thematically related to the Andante movement of the work. In the Sonata in C, there is no pause between the scherzo and the finale.

The key relationships likewise are for the most part traditional, especially in the Sonata in f-sharp where the most unusual feature is that all movements are in the minor. In the other two sonatas, on the other hand, there is a carefully worked-out plan of tonalities involving the establishment of a second key that serves as tonal contrast with the tonic; in the Sonata in C, this key is e (subordinate theme of first movement, the scherzo, the theme of the rondo), and in the Sonata in f it is D-flat (development of first movement, Andante, trio, second episode of the rondo). This is important in the cyclic construction of these works, particularly the Sonata in f.

Turning first to the first movements as a group, we can note most of all the attempt to carry on the "Classical" tradition. The presence of exposition, development, and recapitulation sections is easily established, and the use of important codas testifies to the intent to create works of major proportions. Beyond this, Brahms returns to the old *forma bipartita* with the repeat of the exposition, at least in the Sonatas in C and f; the exposition in the Sonata in f-sharp, however, is not repeated. Squarely in the old tradition of the "Classical" sonata are the principal themes used by Brahms, which are typically "strong": the full chords in dotted rhythms of the Sonata in C, the brilliant fast staccato octave runs of the Sonata in f-sharp ranging over much of the keyboard, and the equally wide-ranging chordal theme of the Sonata in f, with its characteristic rhythmic figure ♩ ♩.♫ . Also present are bridge passages based on the principal theme, lyrical subordinate themes that provide suitable variety from the vigorous principal themes, and closing sections. The principal themes, which contain possibilities for motivic working out, are exploited in the development sections, which are sectional and often contain changes of key signature and work up to climaxes of considerable proportions. The recapitulations are shortened from the expositions (note the *fausse reprise* in the wrong key in the Sonata in f), and the codas provide suitably grand culminations, again exploiting the principal themes.

The slow movements (all Andantes) have much in common with the Romantic character piece. Particularly significant is the relation to lyric poetry that Brahms was at pains to make evident by, in one case, actually underlaying text words to the melody notes (Andante of the Sonata in C), and, in the Andante of the Sonata in f, he used as caption three lines from a love poem by Sternau.

Two of these Andantes are associated with poems and melodies from the German *Minnesinger* of the Middle Ages: the *Winterlied* of Count Kraft von Toggenburg (Sonata in f-sharp) and an anonymous poem (*Verstohlen geht der Monde auf*) in the Sonata in C; this last, however, is not a real *Minnelied*, but only an imitation written by Zuccalmaglio, whatever Brahms might have thought. (This song also appears in his *Deutsche Volkslieder* in an arrangement for chorus.)

Song forms certainly provide the basis for these Andantes. While the Andantes in the Sonatas in C and f-sharp may be said to be in variation form, this procedure can also be related to strophic song form. Each of these Andantes is in four sections, all based on the same melody; the third stanza, or variation, of the Andante in the Sonata in C is freer, turns to C, and presents the climax of the movement. The *Minnesinger* element in both is evident from the old "Barform" of the melodies (*A A B*), less clear in the Sonata in f-sharp but nonetheless present, as well as from the implied alternation between a soloist and choral refrain in the Andante of the Sonata in C. On the other hand, the Andante of the Sonata in f, associated with the Sternau poem, is more conventional in its formal plan; it is in three-part form with an important coda. Its main theme consists of a line moving in thirds in even quarter notes, first descending then ascending, the whole section being cast in binary form ||:a:|| ||:ba:||. The subordinate section, in D-flat, consists entirely of chords and is purely harmonic in its effect, while the coda, in the same key, presents a simple melody in sonorous chords over a dominant pedal point, a melody that is much like the *Watchman's Song* in Wagner's *Die Meistersinger von Nürnberg*; this brings the movement to its impressive climax after which the principal theme is suggested at the very end. This sonata, as already mentioned, has a second slow movement in small three-part form, presenting the main theme of the Andante but in the minor (b-flat) and in parallel thirds and accompanied by a tympani-like figure in the bass.

In the scherzi, we find the usual form with trios, rather short in the Sonata in f-sharp. The rhythms are vigorous and the chords full, sometimes loud and heavily accented (as in the Sonatas in C and f) and sometimes soft and staccato (as in the Sonata in f-sharp). This density of texture, using chords with doublings, is, as will be seen, a prime characteristic of Brahms. The most variety is present in the scherzo of the Sonata in f, which has first a wide-ranging theme in staccato octaves coupled with ornamental grace notes, all interspersed with short rests that create effective little syncopations. The trios form a contrast to the scherzi, again bringing the lyrical element to the forefront; there is an even, scale-wise cantabile melody in the Sonata in C, a *Ländler*-like passage with the melody in thirds, along with grace notes and short rests, in the Sonata in f-sharp, and a solid but lyric chordal passage in the Sonata in f.

For the finales, Brahms employs rondo form in the Sonatas in C and f (quite free in the latter) and sonata form with thematically related slow introduction in the Sonata in f-sharp, thus following in the tradition of Schubert and Schumann. These are large-scale movements with much contrast and variety that bring the sonatas to their impressive conclusions. The rondo form is treated rather freely by Brahms. In the Sonata in C, there are two episodes, of which the first is in three-part form with a coda; the second episode is clearly Scottish, its theme having been taken by Brahms from Schumann's song *Hochländers Abschied* (op. 25 xiii), the text of which is a translation of Burns' *My Heart's in the Highlands*. The rondo of the Sonata in f is regular until the second episode is introduced, but, from this point on, the normal scheme of the rondo is neglected as Brahms concentrates in a most unusual way on the development and variation of this theme, returning once—and briefly—to the principal theme of the rondo before the coda. We have already noted the rather free treatment of the rondo form in the sonatas of Schubert. In the rondo finales of Brahms, it is the principal theme that is "strong" and the episodes that are lyrical. In the sonata-form finale of the Sonata in f-sharp, we find a cantabile principal theme (with a written-in ritard playing an important part), a capricious *Ländler* with wide leaps, grace notes and, suspensions (presented with piquant cross-relations in the recapitulation); but the principal theme is made "big" in the development and in the coda.

An important question in regard to the piano sonata—and indeed to all large-scale compositions for instruments—has to do with the relationships between the several movements and how they all fit together to form a larger artistic entity. While there has been much speculation on this matter in the works of Haydn, Mozart, and Beethoven, as well as other composers, various methods having been employed and various answers given, the sonatas of Brahms provide an interesting and useful opportunity to reach some definite conclusions, since he was greatly occupied with this question of over-all unity, and this is manifest in his piano sonatas. Such elements of unity are present in the Sonata in C, especially between the principal themes of the first and last movements, on the one hand, and the second and third movements, on the other; but this work does not appear to be characterized by a thorough-going over-all cyclic organization. It is different with the Sonatas in f-sharp and f (see, especially, Georgii). The Sonata in f-sharp represents an extreme case, since one theme clearly underlies the whole composition, appearing in all movements, generally in various guises, and functions several times within a movement. In the Sonata in f, the thematic relation between the second and fourth movements is made abundantly clear by Brahms himself; but the cyclic relations in this work go much further than this, and one can point to the general correspondence among those passages in D-flat, which, as has been seen, is the important counter-tonality in the sonata: the development in the first movement, the coda to the Andante, and the important second episode of the rondo. Generally speaking, this use of cyclic form and the emphasis on thematic variation or transformation would associate Brahms more with the procedures of Liszt than is generally believed.

Characteristic features of Brahms' piano style also exist in abundance in the piano sonatas. Most common is Brahms' well-known density of texture through the constant use of full chords with many doublings. A most characteristic feature

EXAMPLE 66

BRAHMS: *Sonata* in f (op. 5)—excerpts

A. Allegro maestoso, principal theme

B. Allegro maestoso, D-flat section of development—beginning

C. Andante molto, coda—beginning

D. Finale, second episode—beginning

continued

is casting a melody in chords; often a melody is presented in thirds or sixths, as in the *Rückblick* of the Sonata in f, the main theme of the rondo in the Sonata in C, or the scherzo and trio of the Sonata in f-sharp; or the melody goes along with filled-in octave chords, as at the end of the Andante of the Sonata in f, the beginning of the second episode of the rondo in the same sonata, or the third movement of the Sonata in C; such instances can easily be multiplied. Similar impressive chordal passages may be seen at the outset of each of the sonatas, and the spreading of the themes over an extraordinarily wide range occurs in the Sonatas in f-sharp and f. In the Sonata in f-sharp, Brahms resorted to the unusual expedient of employing three staffs for the notation of certain passages in the second and fourth movements as an aid to making clear the various elements of which these passages are compounded. This density of texture is often bound up with what has been called an "orchestral" treatment of the piano; and while this may or may not be true, there are passages here and there that seem to emulate specifically orchestral effects. There is, for instance, the bass tremolo near the opening of the Sonata in f-sharp with the rising sequence in the right hand coupled with the crescendo; or, in the trio of the scherzo of the same sonata, there are in the bass "tympani" effects that also appear, as stated, in the *Rückblick* of the Sonata in f; and, in the first movement of the Sonata in C right

EXAMPLE 66—*continued*

at the end of the development, the left hand clearly suggests horns in stating the secondary theme.

    Another important facet of Brahms' style as evidenced in the sonatas has to do with rhythmic complexities and subtleties. The most common of these is the

EXAMPLE 66—*continued*

C.

D.

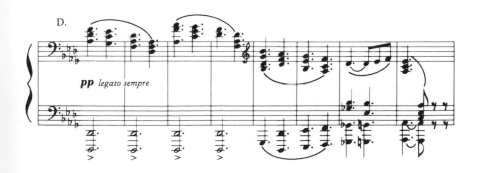

old hemiola, or two in one part against three in another, as can be seen in the Sonata in f at several points in the first movement as well as in the finale; in the last movement, we can also observe, in the important second episode, the use of three against four, so that here such subtleties in the treatment of rhythm are a means of thematic variation. Syncopations are not uncommon. More subtle, however, is the writing of accelerations and ritards right into the notation itself. There is an acceleration in the subordinate theme of the first movement of the Sonata in f; and, in the Sonata in f-sharp, for example, there is a ritard right at the end of the principal theme in the exposition of the first movement, the passages in thirds in which sixteenth notes give way to eighth-note triplets and finally to eighth notes, so that the direction calling for a ritard is reinforced by what is actually written into the score.

To summarize this discussion, it can be stated that Brahms' piano sonatas are fully in accord with the grand tradition of the genre established by Beethoven and continued by Schubert and Schumann, the tradition of the sonata as a large, difficult, involved, dramatic, and virtuoso composition. Much of this goes back specifically to Beethoven, and the resemblance in themes between Brahms' Sonata in C and Beethoven's late Sonata in B-flat (op. 106) is readily recognizable. The relation of keys between Brahms and Beethoven and Brahms and Schumann is also striking: f and f-sharp. But, in details, it would seem as if the influence of the later composers was the more important on the young Brahms. The slow introduction to the finale of Brahms' Sonata in f-sharp calls to mind the slow movement of Schumann's large Fantasia in C (op. 17); and one also recalls Brahms' free treatment of rondo form (also characteristic of Schubert), the close connection of the slow movements to song forms and thus to the character piece and the appearance here and there of *Ländler* themes. And, for all the opposition to Liszt, it is not amiss to point out that many passages in the Sonata in f-sharp seem closely connected to Liszt's piano style: the furious octaves in the first movements and such places in the Andante as the *espressivo* unaccompanied lines moving off in thirds and pausing on long fermatos, the grand climax marked *grandioso*, and the cadenza-like passages in the finale. What apparently belongs to Brahms' own particular way of doing things would then be the emphasis on cyclic form, making variations on a few themes prominent in all movements (another facet closely related to Liszt), the extreme density of texture, the strict treatment of sonata form and of thematic development, and the use of unusual metrical relationships.

The next group of Brahms' piano works are in theme and variations form (see Luithen), as follows:

Variations (sixteen) *on a Theme of Schumann* in f-sharp (op. 9), composed and published in 1854

Variations (seven) *on an Original Theme* in d, composed in 1860 and published in 1927

Variations (eleven) *on an Original Theme* in D (op. 21 i), composed in 1856 and
  published in 1861
Variations (thirteen) *on a Hungarian Song* in D (op. 21 ii), composed around 1853
  and published in 1861
Variations (twenty-five) *and Fugue on a Theme of Handel* in B-flat (op. 24), composed in 1861 and published in 1862
Studies (Variations) on a Theme of Paganini in a, composed around 1875 and
  published in 1879, Set I: fourteen variations (op. 35 i); Set II: fourteen
  variations (op. 35 ii).

To these, we may add a set of variations for piano duet (piano, four hands) on a
theme of Schumann (op. 23) and the famous set of variations for two pianos on a
theme of Haydn (op. 56b), which is best known in the version for orchestra.

The themes borrowed by Brahms here come chiefly from the work of other
prominent composers of his time. The op. 9 is from the *Albumblatt* in Schumann's
Bunte Blätter (op. 99 iv), the Paganini theme is taken from the celebrated twenty-
fourth Caprice for Unaccompanied Violin, and the Handel theme comes from the
first *Leçon* in B-flat for harpsichord. The prime characteristic of all these themes
taken over by Brahms is their brevity and simplicity; all operate with melodic
and rhythmic patterns. The Handel theme is cast in two-part form, each part to
be repeated; and the same is true of the Paganini theme; the Schumann theme is a
simple three-part form in prevailingly four-part harmony, in which the bass
serves as an important counter-voice to the melody. These qualities are also present in the other themes used by Brahms in these sets of variations. The original
theme (op. 21 i), heavily chordal but *espressivo* and *legato*, is again in two-part
form; while the Hungarian song (op. 21 ii), only eight bars in length, fast, and in
heavily accented chords, presents the striking time signature 3/4 C, designating
the alternation of bars in 3/4 with bars in 4/4, thus producing an unusual rhythm.

As for the variations themselves, they belong under the general heading of
the character variation. The harmonic basis of the theme normally is rather
closely followed (there are a few exceptions, as might be expected), and elements
of its thematic material are exploited as well, but the main element is the difference in character, or the effect, produced by the different variations. Various
textures are used as are new rhythmic patterns, new types of figuration, putting
the melody in a middle or bass voice, and so on. The exploitation of the theme in
the bass is prominent in the *Schumann Variations* (op. 9), and even the important
bass part of Schumann's theme is employed by Brahms. In the *Hungarian
Variations*, the alternation between 3/4 and 4/4 is maintained in most of the variations (ix–xiii inclusive use regular meter, either 2/4 or 6/8).

The character of the variations is frequently made clear in the designations
employed by the composer: the scherzo or scherzando, as in the *Schumann
Variations* (xii); the grazioso, as in the *Handel Variations* (xviii); the serious
largamente, as in the 1860 set for Clara Schumann (i), the Handel set (xiii), or

the various adagio variations. Each set of variations has either one variation or a group of variations in the minor; the Handel set has several in the minor (v, vi, and xiii; and xxi, the last, is in the relative minor). Contrapuntal elaboration is also an important part of Brahms' variation art and is given emphasis in the *Schumann Variations* where canon appears in one form or another, sometimes in contrary motion (viii, x, xiv, and xv); it is prominent also in the *Variations on an Original Theme* (op. 21 i, v), and, of course, there is the large fugue that ends the *Handel Variations*.

This last large set of variations can be regarded as the culmination of Brahms' efforts in this genre of composition. The theme itself—which Handel also used as the basis for five variations—is taken verbatim from Handel's suite; even Handel's marking, aria, is retained. Then come the variations, each of which has its own special individuality that results from the consistent use of a melodic or rhythmic motive or figure in each, e.g., the staccato 𝅘𝅥𝅮𝅘𝅥 (i), the chromatic triplets (ii), gentle chords (iii), fast octaves and leaps (iv), and so on. Attention should be drawn to some of the more unusual variations: the two-part canon, each voice given in octaves (vi), which suggests Bach's two-part Invention in

EXAMPLE 67

BRAHMS: *Variations on a Hungarian Song* in D (op. 21 ii)—theme

B-flat; the heavy chords, *sostenuto* and *fortissimo* and chromatic (ix); the ponderous largamente in b-flat with its appoggiaturas (xiii); and the musette-like piece with siciliano rhythm and mordents (xix). Then there is the fugue whose subject is plainly derived from Handel's theme, emphasizing sequential writing and driving sixteenth-note figuration. Although the learned devices are present (augmentation and inversion) as well as motivic treatment of the subject, this fugue makes several departures from "strict" form; the subject, as well as its contrapuntal accompaniment, is often given in parallel sixths or thirds, the contrapuntal elaboration often replaced by broken-chord figuration. Many of the same features can be seen in the last movement of Beethoven's Sonata in B-flat (op. 106)—even the key is the same. In any case, Brahms' intent is clear, and the movement, with its intermingling of fugal and developmental techniques, brings the work to an impressive conclusion.

A most interesting situation is presented in the *Paganini Variations*, to which Brahms gave the title *Studien* (studies or etudes). The etude character, which already belongs to Paganini's theme in its original context, is taken over into the theme and variations genre, so that the character of each variation is bound up with a specific technical problem of pianistic execution: passages in thirds and sixths; octave leaps and arpeggios, both loud and soft; rapid scales; difficult legato playing involving shift of fingers; and so on. In this, it may well be that Brahms was consciously following the lead of Schumann, who also published a set of *Études en forme de variations* (better known as the *Symphonic Etudes*).

After the completion of the three sonatas and the earlier among the sets of themes and variations, Brahms turned to the smaller forms of piano music, which he made over into something very much his own—the various types of the lyrical character piece. These works exist among his earlier compositions; then the category was dropped, only to emerge at the end as the most numerous among his late works. The character pieces of Brahms are as follows:

Scherzo in e-flat (op. 4), composed in 1851 and published in 1854

Ballades (op. 10), composed in 1854 and published in 1856: in d, D, b, and B

Klavierstücke (op. 76), composed around 1878 and published in 1879, Set I: Capriccio in f-sharp, Capriccio in b, Intermezzo in A-flat, Intermezzo in B-flat; Set II: Capriccio in c-sharp, Intermezzo in A, Intermezzo in a, Capriccio in C

Rhapsodies (op. 79), composed in 1879 and published in 1882: in b and g

Fantasias (op. 116), composed in 1891–1892 and published in 1892, Set I: Capriccio in d, Intermezzo in a, Capriccio in g; Set II: Intermezzo in E, Intermezzo in e, Intermezzo in E, Capriccio in d

Intermezzi (op. 117), composed and published in 1892: in E-flat, D-flat, and c-sharp

Klavierstücke (op. 118), composed and published in 1893: Intermezzo in C, Intermezzo in A, Ballade in g, Intermezzo in f, Romanze in F, Intermezzo in e-flat

Klavierstücke (op. 119), composed and published in 1893: Intermezzo in b, Intermezzo in e, Intermezzo in C, Rhapsody in E-flat.

The early Scherzo in e-flat (op. 4) is Brahms' largest character piece and is not unlike its counterparts in the three sonatas. Marked *Rasch und feurig* (fast and with fire, presumably Allegro con fuoco), it is cast in the large form with two contrasting trios; the theme itself, in fragmentary phrases, has a strong rhythmic propulsiveness that is offset by the lyricism of the two trios. The first of these trios has a number of directions to the performer that testify to the Romantic inclinations of the composer: *leggiero, scherzando, espressivo, piacevole, dolce, sostenuto poco*, and *teneramente*, all within the space of two pages. There is a dramatic transition that features an ostinato rhythmic pattern leading back to the scherzo and an impressive coda. On account of its very size and the varieties it contains, one cannot help thinking that the scherzo is related to a projected sonata.

With the ballades (op. 10), however, we reach the true realm of the Romantic character piece. Here, there are four compositions, three ballades and one (the third) called "intermezzo." The schemes employed resemble those common to the character piece: ternary form in the first ballade, in d, and in the intermezzo (with the first part repeated); two-part form with both sections repeated in the last ballade, in B; and a rather unusual and elaborate arrangement involving two subordinate sections, a principal part and a coda in the Ballade in D. But these works called "ballades" have no connection with the large-scale and virtuoso productions of Chopin, even though the ultimate inspiration in old epic and tragic poetry may well be the same. Brahms makes this inspiration abundantly clear in the first of the ballades (see *HMS*, IX, s. 3, b. 3), relating it expressly to the Scottish ballad *Edward*, which had been published by Herder in his famous collection of folk poetry. In the grim ballad, a mother questions her son concerning his blood-stained appearance and discovers he has murdered his father. The dialogue form is preserved in Brahms' ballade. There is the over-all ternary structure, all parts based on the same thematic material, but the opening betrays the dialogue form of the poem; the middle part evidently corresponds to the grisly revelation and the end to the son's voluntary exile. The strophic form of the ballade is suggested by the use of the same thematic material in all sections of the work. It has also been demonstrated that Brahms' theme fits perfectly with the poem as given by Herder (see Mies). This close link to the poem relates this *Edward* ballade to the slow movements of Brahms' piano sonatas. Links to literature are not so manifest in the remaining works of op. 10, nor is the idea of a ballade nearly as clear. While hints of this quality may be discerned in the intermezzo (in b and in three-part form with the first part repeated), the last ballade, Andante con moto in B, is extremely lyrical, a broad melody in long notes over a smooth and slow arpeggio accompaniment.

Except for his work with the theme and variations, Brahms abandoned composition of music for piano for some twenty years, then resumed it in the *Klavierstücke* (op. 76) and the two rhapsodies (op. 79), only to leave it again for twelve years, finally taking it up on a large scale in the four late collections containing thirty short character pieces. In spite of this second gap in the composition of character pieces, all these works present so many common features that it is possible to treat them as a group.

Looking over these collections of piano pieces, we can first note the titles used by Brahms, and it will be seen that, as far as the collections themselves are concerned, there is a tendency towards generalization. The early publication with title *Balladen* contains, as has been seen, one intermezzo; then, although there are rhapsodies (op. 79) and fantasias (op. 116), the tendency was towards the more neutral or general designation *Klavierstück* (piano piece), as in op. 76, 118, and 119, with but one set of intermezzi (op. 117); and even the designation "fantasia" of op. 116 does not seem to have any sort of programmatic or affective connotation. This is paralleled by the fact that the works of op. 118 originally were to have appeared under the name *Fantasias*, but Brahms later changed this to the more neutral designation *Klavierstücke*. As far as the individual titles are concerned, "intermezzo" leads with eighteen examples (op. 76: iii, iv, vi, vii; op. 116: ii, iv, v, vi; op. 117: all three; op. 118: i, ii, iv, vi; op. 119: i, ii, iii), and next is "capriccio" with seven (op. 76: i, ii, v, viii; op. 116: i, iii, vii); then there are three rhapsodies (op. 79: both; op. 119: iv), one ballade (op. 118: iii) and one romanze (op. 118: v). The difference seems to be one of size and scope, between larger and smaller works; the ballades and the rhapsodies are the larger works, the intermezzi and romanze the smaller, and the capriccio is somewhere in between. But even this distinction does not work in all cases, for there are several pieces called "intermezzo" that are sizeable works in their own right, such as those in A and e-flat (op. 118 ii and vi). Furthermore, in the designations for individual works, there again is the same tendency towards the neutral as was noted in the titles chosen for the collections themselves: the Intermezzo in E (op. 116 iv) originally was to have been called "nocturne," and the Rhapsody in b (op. 79 i) originally had been called "capriccio," so that a more neutral type of character piece is the result, most commonly called "intermezzo" by Brahms.

In general, the ballade and the rhapsodies retain their usual connotation as large dramatic works.[1] But these older genres are in the minority here, and the first place clearly goes to the intermezzo and the capriccio. The general nature and character of these genres may be indicated by citing a few of the markings used by Brahms, which here are particularly revealing. For the intermezzo we find over and over again such designations of moderation, sensitivity, and grace as Grazioso, anmutig ausdrucksvoll (grazioso, charming, and expressive) in the Intermezzo in A-flat (op. 76 iii); Con grazia ed intimissimo sentimento in the Intermezzo in e (op. 116 v); the simple Grazioso in the Intermezzo in B-flat (op. 76 iv); sanft bewegt (soft motion) in the Intermezzo in A (op. 76 vi);

---

[1] Not without interest is Chopin's distinction between a rhapsody and a ballade, as reported by his pupil Pozniak: In a rhapsody, a role is played by swords, but in a ballade by poison and daggers (quoted by Kahl, *MGG*, I (1951), 1135).

Moderato semplice in the Intermezzo in a (op. 76 vii), Andante teneramente in the Intermezzo in E (op. 116 vi). Thus, the more serious Largo e mesto of the Intermezzo in e-flat (op. 118 vi) or the Andantino un poco agitato of the Intermezzo in e (op. 119 ii) stand out as rather unusual. In the capriccios, on the other hand, things are more active, more vigorous; we find, along with the "grazioso" of the Capriccio in C (op. 76 viii), expressions like "energico" and "agitato," as in the Capriccios in d (op. 116 i and vii) and in c-sharp (op. 76 v). The same holds for the rhapsodies and the ballades.

We have observed that the character piece has often been closely bound up with literary works, and we have seen that this was the case in Brahms' early piano works—not only the ballades (op. 10), but also the sonatas. This tendency, a highly Romantic one, is not at all prominent in these late character pieces. But there are two notable exceptions to this general state of affairs: the Rhapsody in b (op. 79 i) has certain affinities to a Scottish ballad by Carl Loewe (*Archibald Douglas*), and the Intermezzo in E-flat (op. 117 i) is specifically related by Brahms to a Scottish lullaby that he found in Herder's collection of folk poetry, the same collection he had drawn upon for the *Edward* ballade in his op. 10. Beyond these, there are no relations or associations to literary works in these late piano works of Brahms, a circumstance that doubtless contributes to the more "general" and "neutral" tone that we have observed.

Formally, these compositions present much similarity. By far the most common is the old ternary scheme that had long been so important in the character piece. Here it often appears straight, and, of many examples, we can single out here the Intermezzo in A (op. 76 vi), the Capriccio in G (op. 116 iii), the Intermezzo in E (op. 116 vi), the large Intermezzo in e-flat (op. 118 vi), and the Romanze in F (op. 118 v). An example of a piece with the reprise varied is the Capriccio in c-sharp (op. 76 v); an example with a coda that makes use of thematic material already presented in the piece is the Capriccio in d (op. 116 vii) or the Rhapsody in E-flat (op. 119 iv). This formal type is occasionally expanded into a scheme of five or more parts similar in plan to a rondo. This occurs with one subordinate section that is heard twice in the Capriccio in c-sharp (op. 76 v) and the Intermezzo in f (op. 118 iv); two contrasting sections with coda appear in the Capriccio in b (op. 76 ii) and the Rhapsody in b (op. 79 i). But there are a few more unusual formal schemes used. There is a simple binary structure with coda in the short Intermezzo in C (op. 118 i). The old rounded binary form is used in the Intermezzi in a (op. 76 vii), with eight bars of introduction that are repeated at the end, and e (op. 116 v); and it can be noted that rounded binary form appears elsewhere in these works: in the principal section of the Intermezzo in A (op. 76 vi), in the middle sections of the Capriccio in d (op. 116 vii) and the Intermezzo in c-sharp (op. 117 iii) and, without repeat of the second part, in the Capriccio in g (op. 116 iii). A few pieces reveal a freer sectional organization that does not really correspond to any generally recognized scheme: the Capriccio in d (op. 116 i), the Intermezzo in E (op. 116 iv), and the Intermezzo in C (op. 119 iii). And while the capriccio and intermezzo might be regarded as very free treatments of rondo form and ternary form, the Intermezzo in C is in one continuous piece using the same thematic material throughout. Finally, we can note one lone instance of sonata form found in the Rhapsody in g (op. 79 ii).

If formally these character pieces reveal a general homogeneity, the same is true from the standpoint of musical style. Here, as elsewhere in the work of Brahms, one can note the lack of virtuoso display, of ornamentation for its own sake. In the early sonatas, particularly the one in f-sharp, this virtuoso quality is quite clear, but in these late character pieces it is wholly lacking. The density of texture, so common to Brahms, is here in abundance. The operation with full chords, often in close position with many doublings, is common—so much so that the relative sparseness found in parts of the Intermezzo in E (op. 116 iv) stands out as most exceptional. Again, we find that melodies themselves take chordal form and are stated in thirds, sixths, or with the octave, as in the middle part of the Capriccio in g (op. 116 iii) or the Intermezzi in E (op. 116 v), D-flat (op. 117 ii), or b-flat (op. 119 i). Closely related is the harmonic concept of melody in which the thematic material consists of arpeggiated chords often moving in thirds; of many instances, reference can be made again to the three intermezzi just mentioned or to the Capriccio in g (op. 116 iii). In several pieces, Brahms employs this dense chordal texture but puts the melody into an inner voice, as in the well-known *Scottish Lullaby* Intermezzo in E-flat (op. 117 i), or the Intermezzi in C (op. 119 iii) and E (op. 118 vi), the Romanze in F (op. 118 v), and the Intermezzo in c-sharp (op. 117 iii), where it is used as a means of variations. (This work is also noteworthy for the extreme range used in its subordinate section.)

This brings up the relationship between the main voice and the accompaniment. In many cases, this is a simple one. But there are instances of a more contrapuntal approach in which an important line is given in the accompaniment that calls for attention; a striking instance of this is in the Intermezzo in E (op. 116 vi), where one is not entirely certain which part is to be brought out. A most remarkable example is the Intermezzo in A (op. 118 ii), which displays several procedures taken over from counterpoint (see Georgii); there is inversion of the main theme, and, in the middle section, there is canon of a sort followed by double counterpoint (exchange of parts), both of which are most unusual in a character piece. Exchange of parts also appears in the Romanze in F (op. 118 v) and in the Intermezzo in a (op. 76 vii).

Another device used by Brahms to differentiate two elements in a particular passage is rhythmic elaboration. This has been observed in the piano sonatas, and it is also found here. Most common is the playing off of two against three: of a great many instances, we can mention here the Intermezzi in A (op. 76 vi), a (op. 116 ii), and f (op. 118 iv). Rhythmic elaboration in a melodic line may be seen in the Intermezzo in B-flat (op. 76 iv), with its dotted rhythmic patterns and syncopated accompaniment, all over a long, sustained subdominant pedal point in an inner part. Another syncopated melodic line may be seen in the Intermezzo in A-flat (op. 76 iii).

One important principle of Brahms' art is thematic variation, and we have observed this not only in the sets of themes and variations, but also in the piano sonatas. It is also important in the character pieces. A good illustration is the Rhapsody in b (op. 79 i) with two subordinate sections of which the second is clearly a transformation of the first. Frequently, we find that the subordinate and usually contrasting section is thematically related to or makes direct use of the principal theme. This may be seen in the Intermezzi in B-flat (op. 76 iv), D-flat (op. 117 ii), e-flat (op. 118 vi), e (op. 119 ii); the Capriccios in b (op. 76 ii) and g (op. 116 iii); and the Ballade in g (op. 118 iii).

In summarizing the character pieces of Brahms, there are several general remarks that can be made. It is clear, first, that here the character piece has become "generalized," made more neutral in tone, eschewing specific literary and other extramusical aspects for the most part at least. The use of the term "intermezzo" is symptomatic of this. It is also symptomatic of a second element, an avoidance of (or is it a withdrawal from?) all virtuoso elements, and, instead,

---

EXAMPLE 68

BRAHMS: Intermezzo in A (op. 118 ii)—excerpts

A. First part—beginning

B. First part—near end

C. Second part—beginning

A.

moderation is the predominant tone. The forms used are simple and the scale small, except for the rhapsodies, ballades, some of the capriccios, and a few intermezzi. But, along with this formal simplicity, there is an emphasis on strict compositional procedures, a high degree of rhythmic and harmonic elaboration, some attention to contrapuntal elements, and the extensive use of thematic variation. Thus, although the over-all frame may be small, there is much to be found in these character pieces. It may be pointed out that the use of strict musical forms is not unknown in the past history of the character piece; the work of Mendelssohn may serve as one important example. But all the same, it is as

EXAMPLE 68—*continued*

if Brahms were indeed looking backward, avoiding the brilliance that had been exploited by Liszt and going back to something more sober and strict. Perhaps the last of Brahms' character pieces is somehow symbolic of his attitude. The Rhapsody in E-flat (op. 119 iv) commences full of forthright assertion in strong E-flat only to close, after a grazioso middle section, in e-flat; instead of progressing from dark to light, as is common, Brahms does precisely the reverse.

This does not tell the whole story of Brahms' piano works, but it represents by far the major part of them. The other works deserve some mention and comment at the least. There are the "Neo-Classical" works, if the term be allowed to apply to a nineteenth-century composer—two gigues and two sarabandes of 1855 (not published until the twentieth century) in which one can note that the gigues, following the eighteenth-century practice, are fugal and employ inversion of the theme in the second part. Then there are the etudes (or studies) in two groups—six large works published in 1879 and the set of fifty-one published in 1893. While the latter are etudes (study pieces) in the usual sense, with emphasis on peculiarly Brahmsian aspects of pianistic technique, the former group is interesting because these etudes are reworkings of pieces by other prominent composers. In Chopin's Etude in f (op. 25 ii), the triplet scale runs become passages in thirds and sixths. Still other and rather unlikely material is provided in the sonatas and partitas for unaccompanied violin by Bach: the finale of the Sonata in g (S. 1001) gets another part written to it by Brahms, in one version with the original in the right hand and in the other with it in the left, while the chaconne from the Partita in d (S. 1004) is arranged as an etude for the left hand alone. Another etude is based on the Rondo in C of Weber. The left hand is emphasized in a separate arrangement of Schubert's Impromptu in E-flat (op. 90 ii, D. 899), where the fast triplet runs and other elements that formed Schubert's thematic material are all transposed down and assigned to the left hand. There is also an elaborate reworking, notated on three staffs, of the gavotte from Gluck's *Paride ed Elena*. Brahms also, in a similar vein, composed cadenzas to some prominent concertos of earlier masters: Bach's Concerto in d (S. 1052), Beethoven's Concertos in c (op. 37) and G (op. 58), and Mozart's Concertos in G (K. 453), d (K. 466), and c (K. 491). In the cadenza to Beethoven's Concerto in G, Brahms was able to employ the theme "Bach."

There is also a small body of music for piano duet and for two pianos, most of which exists also in other versions. The famous *Variations on a Theme of Haydn* (op. 56b) is best known in the version for orchestra, and the Sonata in f (op. 34b), also for two pianos, is best known as a piano quintet. Among the piano duets are the two sets of *Liebeslieder Waltzes* (op. 52a and op. 65a), both of which, in their original versions, are scored for a quartet of vocal soloists with accompaniment of two pianos; these pieces, let it be added, are in the old tradition of German *Tafelmusik* (table music) and the *geselliges Lied* (the social song). Also in a lighter vein are the *Waltzes* (op. 39) and the *Hungarian Dances* (four sets, two published in 1869 and two in 1880), both of which exist for piano duet and for piano solo. All of this leaves as the single original work of a serious nature the *Variations on a Theme of Schumann* in E-flat (op. 23) of 1863, a set of ten characteristic variations on a theme known as Schumann's *Letzter Gedanke* (*Last Thought*), a work that has much in common with Brahms' other works in variation form.

The last group of Brahms' keyboard works to be discussed is the organ music, which consists of forms handed down from the eighteenth century. There is a Fugue in a-flat published in 1864 and two Preludes and Fugues in a and g, which were not published until 1927; all these works composed in 1856 and 1857. There are also the chorale preludes, one with fugue on *O Traurigkeit, o Herzeleid* (composed also in 1857), and the collection of eleven chorale preludes (op. 122) completed in 1896 and published in 1902. All of this organ music, as might be expected, reveals the influence of the Baroque period, of Bach in particular. Apart from the repertory itself, one can refer to the sectional form of the preludes with the toccata-like passages and the fugue themes in which figuration is important, as in the long subject of the Fugue in a with its triplet passages and the toccata-like close and as in the very slow, ricercare-like Fugue in a-flat, which, in the exposition, has imitation by inversion. The same situation obtains also in the set of chorale preludes. Generally, the chorale melody appears as a cantus firmus in one voice, usually the uppermost part, sometimes plain and sometimes embellished

EXAMPLE 69

BRAHMS: Fugue in a for organ—beginning

(as in *Es ist ein Ros' entsprungen* or *Herzlich tut mich verlangen*, the first version). Even the old Baroque conventions regarding the affections are revived here, as can be seen from the first version of *O Welt ich muss dich lassen* in which sorrow is suggested by the "sobbing" appoggiaturas in the accompaniment and the use of chromaticism or, similarly, in *Herzliebster Jesu*, by the tritone leaps in the pedal and the inner parts; joy is represented in *Herzlich tut mich erfreuen* by the fast arpeggio figuration.

It is interesting to attempt a brief comparison between Brahms and Liszt, who may each be said to bring to a culmination one of the two principal tendencies in nineteenth-century keyboard music; but the differences are not always as obvious as one would think or perhaps like. While Liszt was universally known as the virtuoso pianist and was always in the center of musical life, Brahms made relatively few public appearances and led, on the whole, a retiring existence. Liszt concentrated on the new Romantic forms of musical composition and ignored the traditional genres; Brahms did precisely the reverse, deliberately working with the old genres—not only those handed down from the so-called "Classical" period, but even those from the early eighteenth century. This difference, and it is of basic importance, can be seen clearly in the kinds of sonatas the two men composed; while Brahms, by and large, adhered to the old prototype, Liszt converted the sonata into a large-scale symphonic poem for piano. It is true that both shared an interest in the music of Bach; but, while Liszt took his inspiration from Bach and then went about romanticizing it, Brahms made a conscientious and serious attempt to recreate the old genres in terms of contemporary musical practice, as is clear from the organ compositions. There is one other point of contact to mention here, a rather unexpected one— an interest in Paganini, which was of passing importance in the case of Brahms but nonetheless interesting; while Liszt drew on Paganini almost wholly for virtuoso display, Brahms took his famous melody and used it to fashion a large set of variations in the best tradition of the old absolute form.

CHAPTER NINE

The Later Nineteenth Century

Our discussion of keyboard music in the nineteenth century has up to now centered around the work of the major composers: Weber, Schubert, Mendelssohn, Schumann, Chopin, Liszt, and Brahms, whose importance is by no means limited to keyboard music. In short, most of the major composers up to, roughly, the end of the 1880's devoted considerable attention to piano music. But, in the second half of the century, the situation changes. If one can, for a moment, ignore Liszt and Brahms, one is struck by the fact that the central composers no longer cultivated keyboard music: the contributions of Wagner, Bruckner, Strauss, and Mahler are either completely nonexistent or else negligible in significance. In the work of Wagner the piano pieces are, with one exception, early works. His very first published work was a Sonata in B-flat (op. 1) of 1832, and there is an earlier Sonata in d; he made later attempts with the form, as is clear from an incomplete work in A and the Sonata in E-flat for Mathilde Wesendonck composed in 1853. There is also an early Fantasia in f-sharp of 1831; the second published work of Wagner was a Polonaise in D (op. 2) for piano duet also of 1832. Beyond these, there is a handful of character pieces, a *Lied ohne Worte*, three *Albumblätter*, and a waltz. Possibly of greater significance for Wagner's work as a whole is his arrangement for piano of Beethoven's *Ninth Symphony*, which he made in 1830. The neglect of keyboard music is seen also in the work of Bruckner and Strauss; this is rather surprising in the case of Bruckner, who was a noted organist renowned for his improvisations but who composed only a few contrapuntal works for organ and a few character pieces for piano, most of which are early. Early in his career, Strauss composed a number of piano works, sonatas, a fantasia, a set of variations, and character and other pieces, most of which he did not publish. (See his *Träumerei* in Kahl, 20, pp. 60–1). Mahler composed nothing for keyboard beyond the accompaniments to songs. The noted song composer Hugo Wolf left a few character pieces and unfinished sonatas, all early works.

There will, of course, here and there be seen exceptions to this state of affairs; Franck, Reger, and Grieg are, perhaps, the most prominent instances. But this does not alter the general picture; the attention of composers had shifted, and the piano no longer stood in general esteem as the great "universal" instrument. Composers who emphasized piano music in their work were, generally speaking, secondary figures who carried on in accordance with one or another of the traditions handed down from the first half of the century. It was orchestral music that held the lead and, as will be seen, exerted an important influence on the keyboard music of the time.

It is also clear that the initiative in the development of piano music—and most other genres as well—in the nineteenth century was in the hands of German composers; they, by and large, were the creators of the principal genres of piano music, and it is they who held up the example for the rest of Europe to follow. The situation, then, was similar to that prevailing in the fifteenth and sixteenth centuries, when it was Netherlands musicians who established the forms and techniques of musical composition, and in the seventeenth and early eighteenth centuries, when such leadership came from Italy. Now it is Germany that is in the foreground, and it was to Germany that musicians from other countries came for musical training. Our task is to survey the situation of keyboard music under this aspect, first by examining German keyboard music as it appears in the work of secondary composers and then to see the effects of this German art of keyboard music in the other countries of Europe, where it was always influential if not always wholeheartedly accepted (see Kretzschmar). In fact, in the reaction against German music in certain countries, we will find an important impetus to musical composition—one that has particular importance for the music of our own time.

We have seen that, in the course of the development of nineteenth-century piano music in Germany, the old "Classical" large forms—the sonata and the theme and variations—experienced a decline and were replaced by various types of character pieces as well as the outspokenly virtuoso show pieces and the lighter "salon" music. This emphasis seems related to the Biedermeier art of the time (see Funck). The examples of Mendelssohn, Schumann, Chopin, and Liszt show this conclusively, as has been seen, while Brahms' intense preoccupation with the older genres stands as plainly rather exceptional. As would be expected, the lesser composers were under the influence of the major figures, and it is revealing to consider them under this aspect.

The influence of Schumann was doubtless of the greatest importance. Even Brahms, as has been seen, came under his spell. A most comprehensive manifestation of Schumann's influence is to be seen in the work of Theodor Kirchner (1823–1903), born in Saxony, who had the honor of being the first student ever enrolled in the Leipzig Conservatory. His work for piano is completely dominated by the character piece in its simplest and smallest form—the miniature, a title he gave to a set of pieces (op. 62). Other titles are symptomatic of his dedication to the musical world of Schumann: *Phantasiestücke* (op. 14), *Neue Davidsbündler-tänze* (op. 17), *Florestan und Eusebius* (op. 53), and *Neue Kinderscenen* (op. 55); then, as homage to Mendelssohn, the other leading spirit in Leipzig of the time, there are *Lieder ohne Worte* (op. 13). Like Liszt, Kirchner arranged songs for piano solo—the works of Schumann and Brahms. He made no attempt to compose in the large forms; preludes and etudes there are, to be sure, but the largest form he attempted was the sonatina. Eveything is small, modest, simple, unassuming, and rather sweet.

A similar situation is to be seen in the work of Adolf Jensen (1837–1879) of Königsberg but active for many years in Russia, who studied with Liszt and Ehlert but, again, was chiefly under the influence of Schumann. Here, again, it is the smallest form of the character piece that dominates: there are *Fantasiestücke* (op. 7), *Impromptus* (op. 20), *Lieder und Tänze* (op. 33 [see Kahl, 17, p. 51]), *Nocturnes* (op. 38), and *Scènes carnavalesques* (op. 56), in which Schumann's world is clearly revealed. Jensen's best known and most representative work is *Erotikon* (op. 44), seven pieces with titles taken from ancient Greek poetry. But Jensen at times strove for other things. There is a Sonata in f-sharp (op. 25) and there is a Neo-Baroque work, the *Deutsche Suite* in b (op. 36), that consists of five

EXAMPLE 70

JENSEN: Romance in e (op. 33 vi)—beginning

movements in the old Classical succession (allemande, courante, saraband, gavotte, and gigue), which, as would be expected, are turned into Romantic character pieces. Jensen also composed a large body of music, again largely character pieces, for piano duet.

Also to be mentioned here are Clara Schumann's step-brother Woldemar Bargiel (1828–1897), Robert Volkmann (1815–1883), and the teacher and theorist Ludwig Thuille (1861–1907). Of the three, Bargiel is the most important. He was a friend of Brahms and Joachim and the editor of the first critical edition of the works of Chopin. In his musical composition, in which piano music forms the most important part, we again find the emphasis to be on small character pieces in Schumann's manner: the *Nachtstücke* (op. 3), the *Fantasiestücke* (op. 9 and 27), and the Impromptu in g (op. 45). But the larger forms are not lacking. There are three Fantasias in b (op. 5), in D (op. 12), and in C (op. 19); a Sonata in C (op. 34); and a Suite in g (op. 31), which consists of character pieces so arranged as to be comparable to a sonata, similar to Schumann's own *Faschingsschwank aus Wien*. Bargiel also composed large works for piano duet: a Suite in C (op. 7), a Sonata in G (op. 23), and a gigue. Volkmann, as is true of many of his contemporaries, appears at his best in the small character piece, of which there are a *Buch der Lieder* (op. 17) that has some relation to Mendelssohn and *Wanderskizzen* (*Sketches from Wandering*, op. 23). But, again, there are efforts in the larger forms: a Sonata (op. 12) and, like Brahms, *Variations on a Theme of Handel* (op. 26). Thuille is known especially for his activity as a teacher and theorist at the *Akademie* at Munich and contented himself with the composition of character pieces, of which his *Threnodie* is often heard.

Of somewhat greater standing was the Hungarian-born Stephen Heller (1813–1888), who spent much of his life in Paris where he was in contact with the leading composers of the time—Chopin, Berlioz, and Liszt. Like Chopin, he composed piano music to the virtual exclusion of all else. While there are some works in the large forms (four sonatas), most of his large output is given over to character pieces. Especially Schumannesque are the sets called *Im Walde* (op. 86), *Wanderstunden* (*Hours of Wandering*, op. 80 [see Kahl, 16a and 16b, pp. 48–50]), *Kinderscenen* (op. 124), and one connected with the work of the novelist Jean Paul, *Blumen- Frucht- und Dornenstücke*, *Nuits blanches* (op. 82), whom Schumann also celebrated. Along with these are scherzos, ballades, caprices, dances (waltzes, *Ländler*, tarantellas, and mazurkas), songs without words, preludes (op. 81, 117, 119, 150), and numerous etudes in which the influence of Chopin makes itself evident here and there.

Other composers to be mentioned are Adolf von Henselt (1814–1889), Cornelius Gurlitt (1820–1901), Rudolf Niemann (1838–1898), and Hans Huber (1852–1921). Here, again, the small form of the character piece is most prominent. Only the Swiss Huber made extensive excursions into the realm of the larger forms. Gurlitt is known especially for his novelty piece, a set of variations on

Ach, du lieber Augustin (op. 115), each variation in the style of a different composer; he also produced much children's music. Henselt has become noted for his etudes (op. 2).

A notable exception to this general trend is to be found in the work of the somewhat earlier Norbert Burgmüller (1810–1836), who showed great promise that his early demise did not permit him to fulfill (see Eckert). In contrast to most of the composers under consideration here, Burgmüller had a strong disposition to the larger forms, which sets him apart even from his contemporaries Mendelssohn and Schumann; there are a Sonata in f (op. 8), a Rhapsody in b (op. 13), and a Polonaise in F (op. 16).

The progressives of the time were the members of the so-called "Neo-German" school, adherents of Wagner and Liszt. For us, it is, of course, the influence of Liszt that is of the most importance. But, in the assessment of this, one must distinguish between Liszt's influence as a pianist and his influence as a composer. It is the latter that claims our attention here, and it is surprising that there were not more disciples to carry on in Liszt's type of composition. Actually, Liszt's example was more influential in orchestral music than in piano music. But we can point to the Sonata in b by Liszt's pupil Julius Reubke (1834–1858), which closely parallels the individual formal plan of Liszt's own sonata in the same key. Another composer of piano music who was associated with Liszt was Joseph Joachim Raff (1822–1882), also a pupil of Mendelssohn and a strong adherent of the "Neo-German" school, who issued polemical writings in support of Wagner; he also worked with Liszt on the orchestration of the symphonic poems. (The exact extent of his assistance is a matter of conjecture.) In his compositions, Raff gave quantitative emphasis to the character pieces, but there are also larger efforts: two sonatas (op. 14 and 168, respectively) and, especially, the four suites of which the one in d (op. 91) contains a gigue with variations involving a good deal of contrapuntal interest. Raff also wrote music for piano duet and for two pianos. Connected with this group was Hermann Götz (1840–1876) of Königsberg but active in Switzerland, who composed, along with operas in the Neo-German mold, piano pieces, many for piano duet.

Then there were a number of composers who stood in strong opposition to the Neo-German group and who were, as might be expected, associated with Brahms. Among these, we can refer to Heinrich von Herzogenberg (1843–1900) and Robert Fuchs (1847–1927), both of whom taught at the Vienna Conservatory of Music. Both cultivated principally the character pieces, but also made excursions into the world of larger forms. This is especially true of Fuchs (see Hagenbucher), who wrote three Sonatas in G-flat (op. 19), in g (op. 88), and in D-flat (op. 109) and two sets of variations in g (op. 13) and the *Fantasia quasi variazione* (op. 17). Fuchs also devoted much attention to the composition of pieces for children. In the work of Herzogenberg, we find, apart from character pieces, a number of variations and etudes as well as a number of works polemic

ghasel

for piano duet, with large sets of variations along with smaller pieces; there is also a set of Variations in D-flat (op. 13) for two pianos. To these composers, we may add Carl Reinecke (1824–1910), who composed a large body of music for piano in which Brahms' influence is clearly perceptible: variations on themes of Bach and Handel, a Ballade in A-flat (op. 20), some very easy sonatinas (op. 127a), and, as a curiosity, his *Studien und Metamorphosen* (*Studies and Metamorphoses*, op. 235) in which themes of Haydn, Mozart, and Beethoven are introduced and then subjected to extensive modification. Other composers to be named here are Julius Otto Grimm (1827–1903), Albert Dietrich (1829–1908) who was a close personal friend of Brahms, and Bernard Scholz (1835–1916).

Then there is Felix Draeseke (1835–1913) of Dresden who became a strong opponent of the Neo-German school and conducted a violent polemic against Strauss' opera *Salome* (see Rüder). Draeseke wrote a large *Sonata quasi fantasia* in c-sharp (op. 6) in cyclic form. Particularly noteworthy is his set of character pieces, *Fata Morgana, ein Ghaselenkranz* (op. 13), a cycle of pieces related to the ghasel, a Persian form of poetry that enjoyed a certain vogue in nineteenth-century Germany; in the ghasel, every second line ends with the same word, and this results, in Draeseke's musical equivalent, in a refrain structure. In his work, a strong tendency towards contrapuntal writing is quite clear.

Reference to composers whose sympathies were those of Brahms brings up an often neglected but most interesting subject: the influence of Baroque practices in nineteenth-century music. This is something that shows up again and again in the work of leading composers of the time; we have seen it, for instance, in Mozart, in Beethoven, in Mendelssohn, in Schumann, in Liszt, and in Brahms. And, if one takes the prelude, as it appeared in the nineteenth century, as a manifestation of this influence, then Chopin and several other lesser composers must be included as well. Most often, this influence stems directly and specifically from Bach; and, as is well known, it was in the last half of the nineteenth century that the first critical collected edition of Bach's works was undertaken (the *Bach-Gesellschaft*) with Brahms, characteristically, among the sponsors. Heinrich von Herzogenberg was a close friend of Philipp Spitta, the great biographer of Bach, and took part in the founding of the Bach-Verein in Leipzig. In his work, the contrapuntal element is strong; both Fuchs and Draeseke composed works with much use of counterpoint. Other German composers to be mentioned in this connection are Franz Lachner (1803–1890) of Munich, Friedrich Kiel (1821–1885) of Berlin, and August Halm (1869–1929). Lachner was associated with the revival of musical culture in Munich, but his influence declined after King Ludwig II of Bavaria fell in with Wagner. In the works of Kiel, there are found a set of gigues (op. 36) and a suite (op. 28). We might also include here the conservative teacher and theorist Simon Sechter (1788–1867). Individual works of this kind appear from time to time in the work of composers not generally associated with this movement; there is Jensen's *Deutsche Suite*, and we might mention here that the Norwegian Edvard Grieg, who is discussed later, contributed such a work, the *Holberg Suite*, which in its original version was for piano. Baroque forms, then, continue "below the surface," as it were, all through the nineteenth century, biding their time until circumstances brought them back into prominence, which took place in the twentieth century.

This leads us to a short consideration of a somewhat related subject, the fate of organ music in the nineteenth century (see Frotscher, Moser, and Schneider). We have seen that, since the eighteenth century, organ music everywhere had suffered a serious decline, as can most easily be seen from the fact that, since the time of Bach, the leading composers generally composed little or nothing for the instrument that had once occupied a central position in all musical activity. In nineteenth-century Germany, we have seen that, while contributions to organ music were made by Mendelssohn, Schumann, Liszt, and Brahms, such contributions were plainly in the minority as far as these composers' over-all work was concerned. It might be of interest to inquire into the reasons for this rather sudden and universal decline of an art that still, after all, continued to be cultivated in one way or another in countless churches all over Europe. But the fact must be recorded that this constant demand for organ music did not produce much of consequence in the way of new music for the instrument, at least not until the last decades of the century.

Most characteristic was the decisive effect on the repertory of organ music of the new musical proclivities of the nineteenth century. This had to do first and foremost with the genre of the organ chorale, the cantus firmus setting based on chorale melodies, which appeared mainly as chorale preludes. Here, the old genre received a new and completely different interpretation; whereas, earlier, the chorale prelude had been a contrapuntal elaboration based on a chorale melody, it now became an expression of the mood of the chorale text. This new attitude was clearly stated at the beginning of the century in a treatise on organ playing by Johann Christian Kittel (1732–1809), an almost exact contemporary of Haydn and a pupil of J. S. Bach (see Dreetz); in his *Der angehende praktische Organist* (3 vols., 1801–1808), we see that it was not the melody of the chorale that the organist was to employ, but rather it was the thoughts (emotions or sentiments) of the chorale that was to be sung that the organist must seek to express. This was to some extent true of the eighteenth-century chorale prelude, in which the composer expressed a particular affection in the contrapuntal accompaniment that he set to the chorale. But a further step was taken; the chorale melody became superfluous, so that the chorale prelude was converted into a Romantic character piece for organ. This gave rise to a new type, which Frotscher refers to generically as the "religious Adagio." Titles customary in Germany for such organ pieces were *Gebete* (*Prayers*), *Tröstung* (*Consolation*), *Stiller Friede* (*Quiet peace*), *Idylle*, and so on. Although the new religious Adagio became a genre of special importance, the old cantus firmus type of chorale prelude continued to lead a modest existence of some sort: the contrapuntal element was replaced by a homophonic context and the whole made much simpler and readily comprehensible to the congregation. This type is the so-called *gemeindemässige* (suitable to the congregation) type of chorale prelude, which is so prominent in the work of Johann Georg Herzog (1822–1909), who was also the author of a standard treatise on organ playing, the *Orgelschule* of 1867.

Other varieties of organ music have, in some respects at least, a closer correspondence with what had been common in the first half of the eighteenth century. These are related to the old toccata and appear sometimes as the prelude and fugue (in which the example of Bach's *Well-Tempered Clavier* was an important model, although not in itself specifically organ music); or else the genre was interpreted more freely as an outspoken concert piece, in which a virtuoso exploitation of playing technique and of the expanded, coloristic resources of the organ become important, in which case the term "fantasia" was often used. This gave rise to works for organ conceived on a symphonic scale, as would be appropriate considering the development of the organ as an instrument at this time. Such toccata-like works occasionally included settings of chorale melodies, in which case the term "chorale fantasia" was applied, but otherwise the large form is like that of the sonata for organ, examples of which we have already seen in the work of Mendelssohn. Other examples were composed by Reubke (a Sonata on the ninety-fourth Psalm) and Herzogenberg. In France, as will be seen later, there was even developed the genre of the symphony for organ solo.

As far as Germany is concerned, again certain regional groupings among the composers of organ music are useful in a survey such as this. An important group was in and around Berlin, related to the famous *Singakademie* of Zelter (where Mendelssohn was trained), where much attention was given to the music of Bach. There was Zelter's immediate successor August Wilhelm Bach (1796–1869) who was among Mendelssohn's teachers; Eduard Grell (1800–1886); Ferdinand Kiel who has already been mentioned as a composer of piano music; Carl Loewe (1796–1869), known rather for his songs; and Carl Friedrich Weitzmann (1808–1880), a friend of Liszt who wrote a history of keyboard (*Klavier*) music. Also active in the North Germany were several members of the Schneider family: Friedrich (1786–1853), Johann Gottlob (1789–1864), and, to a lesser extent, Johann Gottlieb (1797–1856). In the central part of Germany, particularly in Thuringia (see Wagner), the most important composers of organ music were Michael Gotthard Fischer (1733–1829), a pupil of Kittel; Johann Gottlob Töpfer (1791–1870); and August Gottfried Ritter (1811–1885) who cultivated all the genres of organ music and who also wrote an important history of organ music (the book that provided the basis for Frotscher's work). In Breslau, there was Adolf Friedrich Hesse (1809–1863) who maintained the old cantus firmus type of chorale prelude along with the new and less stringent religious Adagio; in Leipzig, there was especially Wilhelm Rust (1822–1892), the grandson of Friedrich Wilhelm Rust, for a time the cantor of the *Thomasschule* and one of the principal editors of the *Bach-Gesellschaft* edition of Bach's works; and, in Dresden, there was Gustav Adolf Merkel (1827–1885). Among the composers active in the central part of Germany we can mention Christian Heinrich Rinck (1770–1846 [see Donat]), who worked mainly in Giessen and Darmstadt, and who stressed cantus firmus forms in his compositon; and, finally, there was the theorist Simon Sechter, the Vienna court organist who worked particularly with the strict contrapuntal forms.

As is evident, organ music appears but seldom in the work of the best known composers; it is rarely totally absent, but its incidence is very small. There are, however, two prominent German composers of the late nineteenth century who not only gave organ music an important place in their musical composition but who cultivated it along with piano music as well as other types of musical composition. Both gave keyboard music such a prominent place in their total artistic achievement that they clearly stand out, apart from Brahms, as the most significant German composers of keyboard music of the time—Joseph Rheinberger (1839–1901) and Max Reger (1873–1916).

Rheinberger was born in the little principality of Lichtenstein but was active in Munich and, later, in Berlin. His bent towards organ music is indicative of a certain learned quality in his work for piano and an interest in the larger forms of the past. Character pieces, to be sure, appear in profusion; but they are, for the most part, early works. Then there are large works: the *Sinfonische Sonate* (*Symphonic Sonata*, op. 47), whose title is revealing; other Sonatas in D-flat (op. 99) and E-flat (op. 135); and the *Romantische Sonate* in f-sharp (op. 184), as well as the earlier fantasia (op. 23). But there are other works in which an even more conservative outlook is evident: toccatas (op. 12 and 104), pieces in fugue form (op. 39 and 68), preludes (op. 67), a prelude and fugue (op. 33), and pieces in canonic form (op. 180 [see Kahl, 18a and 18b, pp. 52–4]). Noteworthy in view of Chopin's close association of the etude and prelude is Rheinberger's set of twelve preludes in the form of etudes (op. 14) in which, again, an arrangement by keys is employed, but it is an unusual arrangement, symptomatic of the chromatic tendencies of the times: it is in groups of four and by the notes of the three possible diminished seventh chords (C, E-flat, F-sharp, A and F, A-flat, B, D and B-flat, D-flat, E, G). There is also an etude and fugato (op. 42). Like Brahms, Rheinberger wrote a set of variations (which he called *Studien*) on a theme of Handel (op. 45) and an improvisation on a theme from Mozart's *Zauberflöte* (op. 51). In line with this conservative inclination is Rheinberger's arrangement for two pianos of a selection from Bach's *Goldberg Variations*, the selection being made by Max Reger.

Of greater moment are Rheinberger's compositions for organ (see Grace and Molitor). Here, the character piece is not entirely lacking, as appears from the set of *Monologen* (op. 162) and *Meditationen* (op. 167), twelve each, or the *Stücke* (*Pieces*, op. 174); there are also trios (op. 49 and 189) in the spirit of Bach and a set of twenty-four *Fughetten* (op. 123); symptomatically, there is but one isolated chorale prelude. But far and away Rheinberger's most important contribution to the repertory of organ music are his concert works, the set of twenty sonatas for organ; his aim clearly was for a set of twenty-four, so that all the major and minor keys would be represented. Like the organ sonatas of Mendelssohn, there was here no attempt to transfer intact the piano sonata over to the organ or even to transplant the symphony over into organ music. The intent was rather to draw on the standard form of concert organ music—the toccata or the prelude and fugue—enlarging the form by the insertion of a slow movement in between; the result is a work that, in its over-all disposition, is not unlike Bach's large Toccata in C (S. 564). The difference, apart from obvious matters of style, lies in the thorough-going adoption of cyclic form, the same themes being used in more or less varied form throughout the work; this device, as we have seen, was extensively used by Liszt as well as Brahms (see Kremer). The first movements of these organ sonatas, usually called "prelude" or "fantasia," are generally fast and resemble the first movement of a sonata or symphony except that there is less emphasis on thematic development. Although the fugues are frequently strict with much resort to the devices of learned counterpoint, many have free episodes; the finale of the Sonata in D (op. 168; No. 15) is called "Ricercare." In the last three sonatas, fugal movements are lacking and, as finales, come movements in sonata or rondo form. The finale of the Sonata in e (op. 132; No. 8) is a passacaglia, that takes its place alongside other large examples of this genre. These organ sonatas, then, maintain many of the forms and procedures of Baroque music; but the slow movement, called "canzone," of the Sonata in E-flat (op. 101; No. 13) has nothing to do with the old contrapuntal form and is rather an accompanied melody more on the order of a song without words. Most unexpected is the slow movement of the Sonata in g (op. 193; No. 19), called *Provençalisch* and based on a monophonic *lai* by Machaut. Unlike Mendelssohn, Rheinberger nowhere in his sonatas for organ made use of chorale melodies, although the Sonata in a (op. 98; No. 4) is related to one of the psalm Tone recitation formulas of plainsong (the *tonus peregrinus*).

Max Reger stands out as, next to Brahms, the outstanding German keyboard composer of the late nineteenth century, a composer whose significance may well be greater than is generally appreciated in the United States.[1] Early in his career,

---

[1] The standard edition of his works is the *Sämtliche Werke*, planned to be in thirty-five volumes. There is a thematic catalogue of Reger by Stein. Important studies of his keyboard music are by Gatscher (fugues), Dejmenek (variation form), Wünsch (piano writing), Rahner (chorale preludes), and, Fischer and Kalkoff (general aspects of the organ music).

Reger was sympathetic to the Neo-German school but later he turned away and devoted himself, like Brahms, to absolute music, at the same time retaining certain practices associated with his earlier preference. Along with this goes his intense admiration for the music of the eighteenth century, an interest that doubtless was stimulated by his studies with Hugo Riemann, the famous historian of music, and with Karl Straube whose interest in the organ music of earlier times is well known.

Most of Reger's music for piano is devoted to the character piece, the model evidently being Schumann, although traces of Chopin, Liszt, and Brahms are by no means lacking. But it is the character piece in its small form that predominates. Particularly to be associated with Schumann are sets like *Lose Blätter* (*Loose Leaves*, op. 13) of 1894; *Aus der Jugendzeit* (*From Childhood*, op. 17), composed in 1895; *Humoresken* (op. 20), composed in 1898; *Fantasie-Stücke* (op. 26), composed in 1898; *Bunte Blätter* (op. 36) of 1899; *Intermezzi* (op. 45) of 1900; the *Episoden* (op. 115) of 1910; and pieces *Für kleine und grosse Leute* (*For Little and Big People*), an obvious variation of Schumann's phrase. Other smaller pieces of didactic intent are the *Kleine Vortragsstücke* (*Little Recital Pieces*, op. 44) and, particularly the large set in four parts called *Aus meinem Tagebuch* (*From My Diary*, op. 82), composed between 1904 and 1912. In a Brahmsian vein are the two sets of waltzes (op. 11) and the *Charakterstücke* (op. 32) of 1899, while Grieg seems to have provided the inspiration for the *Silhouetten* (*Silhouettes*, op. 53) and Chopin for the *Träume am Kamin* (*Dreams by the Hearth*, op. 143), composed in 1915, a set of twelve pieces, Reger's last work for piano (Molto adagio in A [iii] in Georgii, *400 Years*, pp. 130–1). Finally, there is a satirical contribution to the literature of popular salon music, a piece called *Ewig dein!* (*Eternally Yours!*, op. 17523), marked to be played *Noch schneller als möglich* (even faster than is possible), but with performance rights prohibited.

Reger did not take up the larger forms of piano music until rather late in his artistic career, and even then, he avoided the standard form of the piano sonata, which, as we have seen, was widely regarded as something old-fashioned; he composed in this vein only four sonatinas in e, D, F, and a (op. 89). He chose, rather, the other large form, the theme and variations, including the fugal finale that had become customary, and wrote two such large sets of variations for piano, the first being fourteen *Variations on a Theme of Bach* (op. 81) of 1904 and the second, twenty-four *Variations on a Theme of Telemann* (op. 134) of 1914, a late work. Baroque sources were used, as had been done by Brahms, but Reger surely avoided the obvious: the Bach theme is the oboe obbligato part to a duet in the cantata *Auf Christi Himmelfahrt allein* (S. 128), while the Telemann theme is the minuet of the first suite for oboes and strings in his *Musique de table*, Part III, of 1733. Both sets, especially the *Bach Variations*, are large and elaborate works that take their point of departure from Beethoven's famous *Diabelli Variations*. Reger's concept of a variation is much broader than the usual, say of Brahms; often, his procedure is to construct a sort of fantasia using motivic fragments of the theme, or he varies both the rhythm and the melodic intervals characteristic of the theme. Both sets, as has been indicated, culminate in large fugal pieces.

Similar large works appear also for two pianos, and, here again, the example of Brahms' *Variations on a Theme of Handel* was doubtless decisive; there are *Variations and Fugue on a Theme of Beethoven* (op. 86) of 1904 and on a theme of Mozart (op. 132a), which originally was written for orchestra. (An eighth variation was added by Reger to the version for two pianos.) The Beethoven theme is from the Bagatelle in B-flat (op. 119 xi), while the Mozart theme is from the Sonata in A (K. 300 i [331]), in which context it also serves as the theme for variations so that the situation here is analogous to that in Brahms' *Handel Variations* for piano. Reger's other large work for two pianos is in a Romantic-Baroque vein and bears a certain resemblance to his larger organ compositions, as will be seen—the Introduction, Passacaglia, and Fugue in b (op. 96) of 1906; but, again, a passacaglia is a variation form. For piano duet there are mainly smaller pieces, chiefly dances, in the spirit of Brahms, such as the *Waltz-Caprices* (op. 9) and the *Deutsche Tänze* (op. 10), but some few are character pieces, such as the *Pièces pittoresques* (op. 34) or the *Burlesken* (op. 58).

When we turn to the organ music, we meet with a rather different situation, one that is particularly interesting when held against the general condition of organ music at this time; for Reger, as might be expected, continued to respect many of the older forms of organ music, particularly the cantus firmus procedure and the prelude and fugue, while neglecting the nineteenth-century character piece for organ, the religious Adagio. There are, to be sure, many collections of organ pieces by Reger issued as *Stücke* (*Pieces*, op. 7, 59, 65, 69, 80, 129, 145), as well as the *Monologen* (*Monologues*, op. 63). But by no means all of these are character pieces in the sense of the religious Adagio. Many of them are rather in the older forms of organ music: the prelude, the fugue, the toccata, the fantasia, and the passacaglia (op. 63 vi). A striking example of this Neo-Baroque vein is a paired Toccata and Fugue in a (op. 80 xi and xii), both of which are closely patterned after the concertato style used in Bach's earlier work complete with virtuoso pedal passages. Baroque dance forms are also represented among these pieces for organ—the siciliano and the gigue (op. 47 ii and v). On the other hand, those pieces called "canzone," "canzonetta," or "capriccio" are not at all Baroque; they are not imitative, so that they, along with other pieces, have something in common with the organ character piece so common at the time.

In his organ music, Reger found his way to the large form earlier in his career and with greater frequency during the course of it than he did in his piano music. Here, it is the old Baroque toccata (or prelude and fugue) that provided the point of departure. In this spirit are several works called "fantasia and fugue": in c (op. 29), composed in 1899; one on "Bach" (op. 46) of 1900; another in d (op. 135b) of 1916; and the large *Symphonische Phantasie und Fuge* in d (op. 57) of 1901. Then, there are several pairs of preludes and fugues, especially the set of four in c-sharp, G, F, and e (op. 85), composed in 1904. Another large work is the Introduction, Passacaglia and Fugue in e (op. 127) of 1913. Reger's two sonatas for organ, in f-sharp (op. 33), composed in 1899, and in d (op. 60), composed in 1901, are related to this form and thus are similar in this respect to the sonatas of Rheinberger. Here again, Baroque organ music provides the basis. Both of Reger's sonatas have three movements; the Sonata in f-sharp contains a Fantasia, an Intermezzo, and, as finale, a Passacaglia; and in the Sonata in d, an Improvisation, an Invocation, and, as finale, an Introduction and Fugue. In Reger's fugue composition, the influence of Bach can be seen, most immediately in the types of themes that are employed; two of Bach's favorite types are prominent—the fast figurational kind, so prevalent in his works of the Weimar period, and the slow, frequently chromatic, ricercare type with all the learned elements included. Among Reger's other large works for organ are the two suites, one in e (op. 16), composed in 1894–1895 and dedicated to the descendants of Bach alive at that time, and the other in g (op. 92), composed in 1905; there is also the *Variations and Fugue on an Original Theme* in f-sharp (op. 73), composed in 1903. The suites again reveal essentially the same conception as the sonatas; the old forms of organ music provide the basis. The Suite in e even includes cantus firmus settings of chorale melodies.

   What is different in Reger's organ music, when compared, for instance, with that of Rheinberger, is the emphasis on the old cantus firmus procedure. While there are instances of the small and simple type of chorale prelude—such as in the fifty-two *Leicht ausführbare Vorspiele* (*Easily Playable Preludes*, op. 67), composed in 1902, or the *Kleine Choralvorspiele* (op. 135a), composed in 1914, which belong to the "congregational" (*gemeindemässige*) type mentioned earlier— Reger's emphasis went to the creation of large concert works using chorale melodies, which are called "chorale fantasias." Although such works are related to similar compositions of the Baroque period, they actually go much farther since elements from the prelude (or toccata) and fugue become important also. Here, there are seven large fantasias: *Ein' feste Burg* (op. 27) and *Freu' dich sehr o meine Seele* (op. 30), both composed in 1898; a set of two, *Wie schön leuchtet uns der Morgenstern* and *Straf mich nicht* (op. 40), composed in 1899; and another set, this of three, *Alle Menschen müssen sterben, Wachet auf, ruft uns die Stimme,* and *Halleluja! Gott zu loben* (op. 52), composed in 1900. In each, the setting of the chorale melody is preceded by a fantasia that is in what we have rather loosely been calling "toccata style"; in some cases, such as the three works of op. 52, a fugal movement is added as a finale, so that these three pieces resemble Reger's other large works for organ. Furthermore, Reger not only employed the same thematic material (often related to the chorale) throughout, but also attempted to give musical expression to the emotional content of the chorale, so that, in a way, the essential quality of the symphonic poem is combined with the cantus firmus setting while at the same time maintaining the other standard form of organ music, the toccata (or prelude) and fugue. What Reger has achieved here might be looked upon as a sort of *Gesamtkunstwerk* for the organ. This is especially clear in *Wie schön leuchtet uns der Morgenstern* (op. 40 i). Yet another similar work, already mentioned, is the *Variations and Fugue on an Original Theme* in f-sharp (op. 73) in which, likewise, the variations are preceded by an introduction in toccata style, so that, again, the over-all effect is not dissimilar to that of a chorale fantasia or organ sonata.

Many features common to nineteenth-century German music reach a sort of culmination in Reger's work. There are two particularly decisive aspects to be mentioned: the prevailing density of texture and the extreme use of chromaticism, the former of which we have seen in Brahms while the latter is rather associated with Liszt or, better, with Wagner. In Reger, there is great profusion of an emphasis on detail and, at the same time, a striving, in terms of sonority, for an orchestral or symphonic effect, especially in the larger concert works for organ. It is, by and large, a harmonic effect that is produced by Reger, and his harmonic vocabulary is elaborate indeed. It is perhaps such factors as these (a more detailed discussion has been given by Truscott) that has prevented the general acceptance of Reger's music, especially in the United States. At the same time, he must be regarded as the leading exponent of keyboard music in Germany at the end of the nineteenth century and possibly as the leading German composer of organ music since the death of Bach. At all events, he is a composer whose work deserves greater currency and recognition than it has as yet been given.

The relationship between France and other European countries in terms of music has always been most interesting. In the past, French musicians had waged a heated battle with Italian music and musicians; but, in the nineteenth century, the great musical rival had become Germany, and, even though Italian opera remained capable of stimulating controversy in France, it was clearly the new German instrumental music that got the most attention. In the field of keyboard music, this German influence was tempered by the work of Liszt and, especially, of Chopin. We will also find that a most important feature of keyboard music in France at this time was the prominence of organ music and that this interest in organ music even made itself felt in piano music.

In the tradition of Liszt was the obscure composer Charles Valentin Morhange, known as Alkan (1813–1888), who was active in Paris; he was a superb virtuoso of the piano who, at the same time, did not concertize extensively; and he was a friend of Liszt and the author of some of the most fabulously difficult works ever conceived for the piano for which Liszt's term "transcendental execution" would be entirely appropriate (see Bellamann, Bloch, and Searle). This virtuosity is employed by Alkan in the conventional types of music:

a *Grande sonata* (op. 33), *Morceaux dans le genre pathétique* (op. 16), *Esquisses* (*Sketches*, op. 61), *Toccatina* (op. 75), *Nocturnes* (op. 22 and 57), *Études* in the major keys (op. 35) and minor keys (op. 39), and a set of *Préludes* in all the keys (op. 31). A noteworthy forerunner of some twentieth-century endeavors is Alkan's etude *Chemin de fer* (op. 27), a graphic representation of a steam engine. And one cannot omit mention of Alkan's unique *Bambordo Carillon* for pedal piano with two players (four feet).

The two most important French composers of piano music (see Cortot) who devoted themselves, *à la* Chopin, to it to the exclusion of organ music were Charles Camille Saint-Saëns (1835–1921) and Gabriel Urbain Fauré (1845–1924). Both were organists by profession but, in their composition, neglected that instrument in favor of the piano. Saint-Saëns, a rather violent opponent of Liszt and Wagner, reveals nonetheless many traces of a profound Germanic orientation in his piano music, tempered by the influence of Chopin. In his large body of piano music, there is no attempt at all at the large form of the piano sonata; the sole work in anything approaching a large form is a Neo-Baroque suite in the old style (op. 90); there is also a set of fugues (op. 161), which, however, is a late work (1920). Otherwise, the usual types are present: bagatelles (op. 3); albumleaf (op. 72); three mazurkas, in g (op. 21), g (op. 24), and b (op. 66); waltzes; etudes (op. 52, 111, 152), as well as a set for the left hand alone (op. 135); and so forth. There are, for two pianos, a well-known set of *Variations on a Theme of Beethoven* (op. 35), along with a polonaise (op. 77) and a scherzo (op. 87), and, for piano duet, several sets of character pieces.

Fauré is much less involved with the specifically German tradition and followed more closely the example of Chopin (see Rostand). Along with an early set of *Romances sans paroles* (op. 17) of 1863 and a later set of *Pièces breves* (op. 84), there are barcarolles and nocturnes, thirteen of each; six impromptus; and four waltz-caprices. There is also a single mazurka and a set of nine preludes (op. 103). The large form of the character piece is represented by a single ballade (op. 19), which was later arranged by Fauré for piano and orchestra. For piano duet, there is a set of six pieces, *Dolly* (op. 56), and another set simply called *Pièces*. Fauré's music is completely idiomatic for the piano but, unlike that of Liszt, is subdued and delicate, on the one hand, and full of harmonic experimentation—a seeking out of new colors and sounds—on the other. In sharp contrast to Liszt is the complete absence of programmatic or pictorial associations or touches; and this absence is generally uncharacteristic of French keyboard music.

Of lesser importance as far as piano music is concerned are Emanuel Chabrier (1841–1894) and Ernest Chausson (1855–1899). Chabrier's most important work for piano is a set of *Pièces pittoresques* of 1880 (see Cortot and Roberts), while Chausson wrote a set of fantasies, a piece called *Paysage*, and another set called *Quelques danses*, three dances with a prologue, of which the pavane has become especially well known. Also to be mentioned is piano music composed by the leading French operatic composers of the time: Charles Gounod (1818–1893), Georges Bizet (1838–1875), Ambroise Thomas (1811–1896), and Jules Massenet (1842–1914). Of these, Gounod is the most important as a composer of piano music, with a surprisingly large output of small character pieces in a popular vein (waltzes, musettes, marches, pastorales, mediations, melodies, and the like). With this, we reach the area of popular salon music, well represented in the work of Benjamin Godard (1849–1895), Moritz Moszkowski (1854–1925), and Cécile Chaminade (1857–1944).

The most important French composer of the time, especially from the standpoint of keyboard music, was César Auguste Franck (1822–1890), a native of Liège who became a French citizen in 1873. Like Saint-Saëns and Fauré, he was by profession an organist and was for some time professor of organ at the Paris Conservatory. But, unlike them, he made important contributions to the repertory of organ music (see Haag and Grace) along with his piano music. Generally speaking, organ music appeared first in his artistic work. There is an early religious Adagio, actually an Andantino, of 1858 (the dates here are of composition), after which come the larger works: the set of three *Antiennes* (*Antiphons*) of 1859, the set of six large *Pièces pour grand orgue* (embracing op. 16 through 21) of 1860–1862, then three more *Pièces pour grande orgue* of 1878, and, finally, a late work, the three *Chorals* of 1890. In between, there appeared a number of pieces primarily for harmonium. The large form clearly stands in the center, a circumstance that sets Franck apart from many of his contemporaries. As expected, the old cantus firmus forms are not present; the *Antiennes*, as had long been customary, are freely composed pieces independent of any existing melody, and the same is true of the late *Chorals*.

The bulk of Franck's work for organ is related to concert music, of which the set of six *Pièces* represents his first effort. The individual works included are: a *Fantaisie* in C (op. 16), the *Grande pièce symphonique* in f-sharp (op. 17), a *Prélude, fugue et variation* in b (op. 18), a Pastorale in E (op. 19), a *Prière* in c-sharp (op. 20), and a *Final* in B-flat (op. 21). There is obviously no intent that these works form a larger entity in themselves; each is clearly planned as an independent composition. While the pastorale is related in some ways to the religious Adagio, the *Fantasie*, the *Prière*, and the *Final* are extended pieces in what approximates sonata form; the other works are related to the German organ sonatas and fantasias of the time, whose model is the large toccatas of Bach. Interesting in this connection is the *Grande pièce symphonique*. It is in three movements, the first not unrelated to sonata form, the second an Andante in three-part form (the middle part serving as scherzo), then there is a large finale in which all the previous themes are employed. Throughout, there is constant exploitation of the considerable tonal resources possessed by the organ of the time. As the French organ of the time vied with the orchestra and became more

and more symphonic, so the concert music composed for it went the same way;
and, as we will see, there actually appear works called "symphonies" for organ
alone. Here Franck's title is symptomatic. But there is counterpoint: canon in
the first movement and fugue in the finale. Also symphonic in style is the second
group of *Pièces*, consisting of a *Fantaisie* in A, the Cantabile in B, and, best
known, the *Pièce héroique* in b.

The three *Chorals* of 1890, in E, b, and a—Franck's last major work (see
Quittard)—are related to the German concert chorale-fantasia. The chief
difference is that Franck had composed his own chorale-like melodies for these
works, something not customary but at the same time by no means entirely
unknown in German organ music of the time, as has been seen, for instance, in
the organ sonatas of Mendelssohn. The melodies are chorale-like, diatonic, in
slow moving notes and symmetrical phrases, and with long pauses between the
phrases; in short, the melodies are handled much as the chorale melody was
handled by Bach in the large opening movements of many cantatas and in the

EXAMPLE 71

FRANCK: Choral in b for organ—beginning

continued

larger chorale preludes. But Franck went even further; the chorale melody then is used for variations, so that the old genre of the chorale partita is revived. The example set by Beethoven in the long slow movement of his Quartet in a (op. 132) was doubtless of some influence here. Thematic variation is used in two of the three *Chorals*. The one in E has three variations and a coda; the second, in b, presents its chorale as a passacaglia with variations, then brings in a lyric secondary theme, has a rhetorical fantasia-recitative passage in the middle after which the variations resume, and the two themes are finally presented in combination; the Choral in a is simply an extended presentation of the melody in large three-part form. In these works, then, the traditional form is considerably modified.

Turning to the piano music (see Cortot), we find that Franck composed a great many more works, most of which have gone entirely out of the repertory. This is especially true of the early piano works, those composed up to the year 1845, in which the conventional genres of the time appear to the exclusion of all else. There are fantasias (of the potpourri type) and variations on themes from

EXAMPLE 71—*continued*

popular operas, an eclogue (op. 3), a *Grande caprice* (op. 5), a ballade (op. 9), two *Grandes fantasies* (op. 12 and 19), and so on, along with similar works for piano duet. It has been said by d'Indy that, despite the various titles given these works by Franck, the same formal plan is found in all of them: a simple three-part form, the middle section fast, and the whole often preceded by a very slow introduction. All of this indicates an early and entirely conventional preoccupation with piano music. Thereupon, Franck abandoned the medium in favor of, so far as keyboard music is concerned, the organ; and when he returned to the composition of piano music, in the last six years of his life, the change could hardly have been more profound. Gone are the conventional and popular types of composition. It is as if Franck was struck not only by the general lack of pieces in large forms for piano, but also that he regarded the customary large forms of piano music—the sonata, the fantasia, the theme and variations—as somehow unsuited to his needs, for what he produced are two large works whose background clearly lies in the new "symphonic" organ works he had been composing (again the dates refer to composition): the *Prélude, chorale et fugue* in b of 1884, the *Prélude, aria et finale* of 1887, and a smaller work, the *Danse lent*, of 1885.

Both the large works have the proportions of a sonata, a genre with which, in other respects, they have little or nothing in common. The *Prélude, chorale et fugue* was originally thought of as a prelude and fugue in the tradition of Bach; then the slow movement was added. As with Franck's large symphonic organ works—and, for that matter, with his larger instrumental works generally—cyclic form is of great significance; the themes of the prelude and of the chorale are varied and brought together in the fugue. The prelude consists, to a large extent, of figuration and thus is clearly an offshoot of the old conception of the smaller form of the genre. Similar is the *Prélude, aria et finale* in which, following the eighteenth-century precedent, the aria is presented in variation; again, all themes of the work are employed in the finale, which here can be regarded as being in a sort of sonata form. Here is an unusual case: the large form of organ music determines that of piano music. The unifying device of cyclic form common in nineteenth-century French music was taken by Franck, on his own admission, specifically from the later works of Beethoven. Finally, it may be mentioned that the *Prélude, fugue et variation* (op. 18), originally an organ work included in the first set of *Pièces*, was arranged for piano solo by Franck in 1873.

Among Franck's younger contemporaries are Vincent d'Indy (1851–1931) and the Belgian Guillaume Lekeu (1870–1894), both of whom were his students, and Paul Dukas (1865–1935). Of the three, d'Indy is clearly the most important as a composer of keyboard music. Here, the Germanic influence is pronounced. Among the character pieces are the early *Romances sans paroles* (op. 1), a nocturne (op. 26), *Promenade* (op. 27), and *Schumanniana* (op. 30); in the spirit of Liszt, there are travel pieces: the *Poème des montagnes* (op. 15), *Helvetia* (op. 17), and

Tableaux de voyage (op. 33). For children, there are the three volumes of *Pièces pour les enfants de tous les âges* (op. 74) in the style of various composers, along with several other sets; there are also arrangements of French folk dances. A large work, somewhat in the spirit of Franck, is the Sonata in E (op. 63), by no means a "Classical" sonata. It is in three movements; the first is a theme and variations, the second a scherzo, then a finale in sonata form in which the theme of the first movement is prominent. Another large work is the *Fantaisie sur un vieil air de ronde française* (op. 99); an early and smaller essay is the *Petite sonate dans la forme classique* (op. 9), and another Neo-Classical work is the *Menuet sur le nom de Haydn* (op. 65). D'Indy also composed a handful of works for organ: a *Prélude et petite canon* (op. 38), a set of eight antiphons called *Vêpres et communes de martyrs* (op. 51), and a *Pièce* in e (op. 66).

Lekeu, a pupil of Franck and d'Indy (and, like Franck, a native of Belgium), died at the age of twenty-four. His few works for piano show much promise: a *Tempo di Mazurka* of 1885, a fugue in four parts of 1889, a Sonata in g of 1891, and a set of *Pièces* of 1891. As with so many of his French contemporaries, Lekeu was extraordinarily impressed by Wagner, especially *Tristan und Isolde*. Dukas, who has become known for his dramatic and orchestral works, composed a few interesting pieces in the large form for piano: a Sonata in e-flat of 1896 and *Variations, interlude et finale* of 1901, the latter based on a theme of Rameau; there is also a *Prélude élégiaque sur le nom de Haydn* and a character piece, *La plainte, au loin, du faune*, on the death of Debussy.

Since Franck must be regarded as the leading composer of the time, especially of instrumental music, the emphasis on organ music is most striking. But this cultivation of the organ is by no means limited to him. Indeed, France stands out as the one country in Europe which had an important school of organ composition. We have seen from the history of organ building that France was the leading country in this field in the nineteenth century, particularly as a result of the work of Cavaillé-Coll, in whose hands the organ became "symphonic." Along with organ building went a new literature of organ music that was also orchestral or symphonic in conception. In discussing Germany, we noted the cultivation of sonatas and chorale fantasias as the main large forms of organ music; in France, this was carried further, and we find works called, simply, "symphonies for organ." At the same time, those French works whose titles indicate them to be cantus firmus pieces—*Chorale, Antiennes*, and the like—turn out to be freely composed works. This has already been observed in the work of Franck.

Although there had been a number of French composers of organ music in the first half of the century—among them François Benoist (1794–1878), Louis Lambillotte (1796–1855), Théodore Nisard (1812–1888), Louis James Alfred Lefébure-Wely (1817–1869), and Théodore Dubois (1837–1924)—it is, apart from Franck, in the work of the Belgian organist Nicolas Jacques Lemmens (1823–1881), the French organists Leon Boëllmann (1862–1897), and, especially,

Alexandre Guilmant (1837–1911) that we see the appearance of the new symphonic style in organ composition. Lemmens had become known for a Lisztian
show-piece for organ, a fantasia in e, *L'Orage* (*The Storm*); Boëllmann wrote,
along with a number of small works of the religious Adagio kind published col-
lectively as *Heures mystiques*, two suites for organ (one a *suite gothique*) and a
Fantaisie dialoguée for organ and orchestra. It is this last medium that seems to
be significant here. It is a piece for organ and orchestra, of which Guilmant (see
Hull) composed a number; one of them, a Symphony in d (op. 42), also exists
as a sonata for organ alone, thus producing a real symphonic sonata for organ.
In addition, Guilmant composed six sonatas for organ: in D (op. 50), c (op. 56),
d (op. 61), C (op. 80), b (op. 86), and F (op. 89); one more, in A (op. 91), was
originally written for organ and orchestra. These sonatas are formally similar to
the works of Rheinberger and Reger. The point of departure is the large Baroque
toccata, the prelude and fugue with slow movement in between. But the older
traditional genres are by no means absent from Guilmant's work; there are cantus
firmus settings in his large two-volume set entitled *L'organiste liturgiste* and his
Noëls (4 vols., 1886), another genre of the French Baroque period. His *Offertoires*
are free concert pieces, also in the tradition of the French Baroque. There are
also numerous smaller independent pieces. Guilmant also served as editor of an
important pioneering collection of early French organ music, the *Archives des
maîtres d'orgue*.

Decisive for the development of the symphonic style in organ composition
is the work of Charles-Marie Widor (1845–1937), a student of Fétis, the scholar
and musical lexicographer, and of Lemmens. As organist at Brussels and later in
Paris, Widor was closely associated with the new large organs of Cavaillé-Coll;
he later became Franck's successor as professor of organ at the Paris Conservatory
(see Reynaud). In his work, the new genre of the symphony for organ is established; he composed some ten of these symphonies for organ. The first four
appeared together as op. 13, another group (Nos. 5–8) appeared as op. 42; after
these came two individually published works, the *Symphonie gothique* (op. 70)
in 1895 and the *Symphonie romane* (op. 73) in 1900; then there is a symphony for
orchestra and organ, the *Symphonie sacra* (op. 81). These difficult works are
"symphonic" by virtue of the way the full resources of the new kind of organ
are exploited rather than by the presence in them of the forms and procedures
associated with the orchestral symphony of the time. Since they are, for the
most part, in six or seven movements and employ the traditional forms of organ
music (toccatas, fugues, canons, passacaglias) to which are added others more
characteristic of the nineteenth century (marches, scherzos, and adagios), we
would be inclined to regard them as large suites rather than as symphonies. Seen
in this way, these organ symphonies of Widor represent yet another stage in a
French tradition of long standing, since the suite for organ goes back well into
the seventeenth century. Another typically French procedure that Widor

exploited as a means of unifying these symphonies is the device of cyclic form along with thematic variation. Widor thus established a type of organ music that found many successors in the twentieth century.

While Germany and France were clearly the leading European centers of keyboard music in the nineteenth century, it was especially the example set by German composers that was decisive. We must now turn our attention to the situation of keyboard music in other countries of Europe, a situation that was, to a large extent, determined by the acceptance of or reaction against the German type of music. The position of music often is related to political factors, and, in the latter nineteenth century, we witness a certain "emerging" of nations in Europe, mostly as the result of the gradual breaking up of the Hapsburg Empire in Austria. The component states, Bohemia and Hungary, began to develop strong nationalistic and patriotic sentiments, and the same is true of Italy; and, in Russia, there developed, in artistic questions at least, a movement highly critical of Western, specifically German, influences. Nationalism had an influence on music in many of these countries. Composers began to turn to their native lands for materials and inspiration. While this shows itself most clearly in operas and symphonic poems, other types of music were also greatly affected by it, for there are also native songs and dances and the characteristic sounds and styles of native musical instruments, all of which can be exploited in any sort of music. It was here that keyboard music came in; at the same time, it must be stated once again that, in the later nineteenth century, piano music seldom occupied a position of prominence; nationalistic organ music—probably on account of the specific associations that went along with the instrument and the music for it—was almost entirely lacking. We have already seen instances of musical nationalism in Liszt and, especially, Chopin, and some traces appear here and there in Brahms. But Chopin cultivated this nationalism from abroad, and the same is generally true of Liszt; but here we have to deal with composers living and working in their native countries on whose national musical resources they deliberately draw and whose national aspirations they wish to commemorate and augment (see Bücken).

The most important among these "national schools," as they are usually known, are those in Bohemia and Russia, with the latter being of particular significance for piano music; other such schools existed in Scandinavia and in Spain (the latter mainly in the early twentieth century and hence discussed in the next chapter). French music, as we have seen, does not reveal this sort of nationalistic preoccupation, nor does the music of England and Italy.

The earliest among the national schools is the Bohemian, the foremost representatives being Bedřich Smetana (1824–1884) and Antonín Dvořák (1841–1904), both of whom composed much piano music. Both cultivated the large forms common in the German repertory of the time. Smetana composed a Sonata in g cast in one long movement in 1846, a Sonata in e for two pianos, and a large *étude de concert* called *Na brehu morskem* (*By the Seashore*, op. 17); Dvořák (see Cohen and Sourek) wrote a set of Variations in A-flat (op. 36) and a Suite in A (known as the *American Suite*, op. 98). But the emphasis in their work goes, as would be expected, to the character piece. Here, Dvořák appears as the more conventional, Germanic, and hence international and less nationalistic— more an heir of Schumann and Brahms; in his works, the normal types are prominent: waltzes, mazurkas, impromptus, album leaves, humoresques (op. 101), even eclogues; best known is the set of *Poetische Stimmungsbilder* (*Poetic Mood Pictures*, op. 85). In Smetana's works, we find some of this as well: waltzes, bagatelles, impromptus, album leaves, and *morceaux caractéristiques*; but he gave much attention to the artistic elaboration of the national dance of his country, the polka, issuing three sets: *Polkas de salon* (op. 7), *Polkas poétiques* (op. 8), *Souvenirs de Bohème* (two sets, op. 12 and 13 [see Georgii, *400 Years*, pp. 115–16]), along with a late collection containing some polkas, *České tance* (*Czech Dances*). Here, the elements of the dance are taken and employed in artistic musical works, that is to say, they are stylized, as we have often observed in the history of dances, for keyboard instruments; generally speaking, it has been said that Smetana did for the polka what Chopin had done for the mazurka. At the same time, the nationalistic element is not wholly lacking in Dvořák; in his piano music, there are to be found examples of the *dumka*, both by itself (op. 35) and together with a *furiant* (op. 12). With the *dumka* we again meet with a type of narrative poetry, this one characterized by sudden changes from an elegaic mood to one of exuberance, while the furiant is a rapid and excited dance in triple time. (It also appears in Smetana's *Czech Dances*.) Dvořák's *eclogues* may be related to those of his predecessor Tomášek. Other nationalistic works by Dvořák are found among his pieces for piano duet: the *Slavonic Dances* (op. 41 and 72), *Legends* (op. 59), and *From the Bohemian Forest* (op. 68). Among other Bohemian composers of piano music of the time, Georgii lists Zdenko Fibich (1850–1900) who was an outspoken adherent of German Romantic music in all respects and who wrote a large number of character pieces (see Kahl, 24a and 24d, pp. 74–7), Eduard Napravnik (1839–1916) and Ottakar Nováček (1866–1900).

Of greater interest and significance for piano music was the musical situation in Russia (see Calvocoressi). Here, musical life had for years been in the hands of foreign musicians, first from Italy and then from Germany; in the eighteenth century, the important Italian harpsichordist Rutini spent time in Russia, and, later, the German composers Hässler, Henselt, and Jensen all were there, as was the Irish composer Field. But there occurred a sharp reaction to the foreign domination of Russian musical activity, a reaction doubtless stimulated to some extent by the Napoleonic wars. It appeared in the work of Glinka (1804–1857) and Dargomyzhkií (1813–1869), limited largely to opera. This reaction was consolidated and furthered by a group of five composers centered in St. Petersburg known variously as "the Five," or "the Mighty Handful." The guiding spirit was Mily Balakirev (1837–1910) and the others were César Cui (1835–1918), Alexander Borodin (1833–1887), Nicolas Rimskiï-Korsakov (1844–1908), and Modeste Musorgskiï (1839–1881). Interesting and characteristic is that most of them were amateurs in music who had received informal training from Balakirev, although some, like Rimskiï-Korsakov, eventually did undergo a formal course of musical studies. The element of musical amateurism worked both ways, most often with a negative effect, but positively in the case of Musorgskiï, the experimentor and innovator of the group.

Apart from Musorgskiï, piano music did not play an important part in the musical composition of this nationalistic group, and most of the piano works by members of the group are not representative of their nationalistic attitudes. Piano music is most emphasized by Balakirev, who was himself a pianist of some ability. His work shows some contact with the Western repertory: early character pieces (*Novellette*, *Phantasiestück*, *Tarantella*, *Berceuse*, *Capriccio*, *Humoresque*, *Nocturne*, *Gondellied*, and *Scherzo*), a Toccata in c-sharp, an impromptu on themes from two of Chopin's preludes, and mazurkas and waltzes, as well as a polka. The Sonata in b-flat, in four movements and using Russian folk songs as themes, is a late work (1905). Balakirev's most celebrated piece, a real virtuoso composition, is *Islamey*, composed in 1869; it is described as an "Oriental fantasy," built on Caucasian and Armenian melodies, three in all, and featuring a good deal of rhythmic drive. Otherwise, with the exception of Musorgskiï, the group produced but little piano music, and almost none of it in a nationalistic vein. Cui composed a suite (op. 21), a theme and variations (op. 61), and a number of character pieces in which the salon atmosphere is by no means lacking; Borodin also wrote a Little Suite in c-sharp (op. 7), *Variations on a Czech Theme* (unfinished), and character pieces (including polkas); and Rimskiï-Korsakov appears in a highly conservative light in which a few character pieces are balanced by a prelude and fugue on "Bach" and a set of six fugues (op. 17).

Far and away the most important and arresting member of the group is Musorgskiï, whose influence generally transcends the limits of mere musical nationalism. As with many of his colleagues, Musorgskiï was an amateur musician, his livelihood being secured through minor posts with the government. In his case, this allowed a direct approach to musical composition completely unencumbered with the large body of traditional procedures and produced unusual results. Musorgskiï's basic artistic credo was derived from nonmusical sources—the novelist Chernyshevsky, the psychologist Troitzky, and the German philosopher Feuerbach. As we can see from the incomplete biographical sketch that Musorgskiï prepared for Hugo Riemann's encyclopedic dictionary of music, his aim was for what he called "artistic truth": art is seen not as an end in itself, but as a means of communication; and since speech is controlled to a large extent by musical laws, music also contains in it elements of speech with which it shares the capability for expressing human emotions. The composer of music should aim at the communication of truth, that is to say, of true and genuine emotions, directed at the broad masses of the people and should avoid striving for mere beauty, for external finish and polish. Such an attitude would naturally set Musorgskiï far apart from the conventional salon and concert music of the time.

Piano music occupies an important place in his musical output, and it generally accords with his artistic beliefs. The large forms of so-called "absolute" music are largely lacking; there are some early sonatas (in E-flat and f-sharp) that have been lost, but an early Scherzo in c-sharp of 1858 has been preserved. The rest consists of character pieces: from 1859–1860, an *Impromptu passionée, Ein Kinderscherz (A Children's Prank)*, and an Introduction *in modo classico*; from 1865, the set of two pieces *From Memories of Childhood (Nurse and I—First Punishment: Nurse Shuts Me in a Room)*, *Duma* (a reverie), and *La Capricieuse*; from the 1870's, there are the *scherzino* called *The Seamstress* and his magnum opus of piano music, *Pictures at an Exhibition*, composed in 1874 but published only in 1886; and, from the 1880's, *On the Southern Shore of the Crimea* in two parts (*Gurzuf* and *Capriccio*) and three short character pieces, *Méditation* (an album leaf) and *Une larme*, both composed in 1880, and *Au village*, called *quasi fantasia* (see Georgii, *400 Years*, pp. 117–9). Musorgskiï also completed arrangements of movements from Beethoven string quartets for piano. For piano duet, there is an Allegro and Scherzo from an unfinished Sonata in C and several transcriptions from Balakirev, Berlioz, and others.

Most important is the set *Pictures at an Exhibition*, musical representations of drawings and paintings by Musorgskiï's friend Victor Hartmann. The whole question (which has been exhaustively discussed by Frankenstein) presents a most unusual instance of the connection between musical composition and art. The stimulus to Musorgskiï was a memorial exhibition of Hartmann's works in 1874 arranged by the critic Vassily Stassov, who played an important role in shaping the views of "the Five." It was Stassov who arranged for the publication of Musorgskiï's *Pictures at an Exhibition*, for which he provided descriptive comments (that have often been reproduced and drawn on without proper acknowledgment); Stassov also wrote a biography of Musorgskiï. Hartmann is not generally regarded as one of the outstanding Russian artists of the time, but his work had several aspects that attracted Musorgskiï's attention, particularly the emphasis on elaborately detailed ornamentation using folk and Oriental motives. Hartmann was known chiefly as an architect and as a designer of stage sets. (He prepared some for a revival of Glinka's opera *Russlan and Ludmilla*, an important nationalistic work, and for a ballet, *Trilbi*.)

Musorgskiï's *Pictures at an Exhibition*, then, is based on this memorial exhibition. It consists of a set of pieces representing individual paintings and drawings (most of which Frankenstein has been able to locate in Stassov's catalogue of the exhibition), which are preceded and connected by a *Promenade* representing the composer wandering through the gallery; the *Promenade* theme appears in certain of the pieces as well, so that the set is unified in musical terms. The various pieces are *Gnomus*, a gnome on awkward, deformed legs, a design by Hartmann for an elaborate toy nutcracker; *Il vecchio castello* (*The Old Castle*), a medieval castle and, in the foreground, a troubadour; *Tuileries*, the quarrelling of children at play in the famous Parisian gardens; *Bydlo*, the Polish ox-drawn cart on enormous wheels; *Ballet of the Chicks*, based on a series of sketches illustrating chicks in various roles and costumes, prepared by Hartmann for the ballet *Trilbi*; *Samuel Goldenberg and Schmuyle*, two Polish Jews, one rich and the other poor (the title is lacking in Lamm's collected edition of Musorgskii's works); *Limoges, the Market Place*, the "furious dispute" of French women (marginal notes on the manuscript by Musorgskii give the dialogue, which is more a conversation than a dispute); *Catacombae*, the artist viewing the catacombs by the light of a lantern; *Con mortuis in lingua mortua*, which has a marginal note by Musorgskii, "the creative spirit of the immortal Hartmann leads me toward the skulls and addresses them—a pale light radiates from the interior of the skulls"; *The Hut on Fowl's Legs*, a clock in the form of the witch Baba Yaga's hut, which is on fowl's legs (the drawing is a good example of Hartmann's detailed manner of ornamentation); *The Great Gate of Kiev*, a massive gate in the old Russian style, which again shows Hartmann's elaborate manner of ornamentation.

Musorgskii's pieces, then, are character pieces. But the titles and subjects represented are most unusual and are fully in accordance with his aim of depicting "truth" without any attempt at external polish. The over-all form is also that of the character piece, with three-part form (*A B A*) in the majority. What is new and different is Musorgskii's way of writing music, and his relative freedom from the traditional doctrines of music produces highly individual results. The *Promenade* illustrates this in several ways. There is the constant changing of meter (at the beginning, bars of 5/4 alternate with bars of 6/4), and the succession of harmonies is also not what would be prescribed in a harmony textbook, particularly in the avoidance of the dominant–tonic succession. The *Promenade* appears four times in varied forms as interludes, and the theme also appears in *Con mortuis in lingua mortua* and at the end of *The Great Gate of Kiev*. While *Il vecchio castello*, with its lyrical melody of a Slavic cast over a repeated pattern in the accompaniment, represents a type that is by no means new, in *Bydlo*, which is generally similar, the effect is made totally different by the heavy, "awkward" chords in the bass and the angular melody with its wide leaps and irregular accentuations; this is all brought, in the middle section, to a crescendo after which there is a gradual return to the quiet that prevailed at the beginning. The popular *Ballet of the Chicks* is another addition to the repertory of barnyard pieces, the noise of chicks being suggested by the treble register, rapid chords, and dissonant grace notes. But there are more unusual conceptions, such as, *Gnomus*, again with an irregular phrase structure in which the trill is used as an expressive device in the accompaniment; *Samuel Goldenberg and Schmuyle*, the rich Jew being represented by a long-phrased melody in octaves in the bass, all pompousness, while the poor Jew is in the treble with rapid staccato repeated notes, and their effective simultaneous statement at the end; and the *Hut on Fowl's Legs*, which is a virtuoso tour de force, practically an octave and chord study. There are two pieces in which tone color and changes in harmonies and in tessitura, in short, sonority, appears as the most important element: *Catacombae* with its long sustained chords and the concluding number, *The Great Gate of Kiev*, a study in sudden dynamic contrasts in which the themes seem to be folk songs. Near the end of this finale, there appears thematic material used by Musorgskii in the coronation scene of his opera *Boris Gudonov*.

The main question, the other side of Musorgskii's lack of formal training in music, arises from his ability to write for the piano. It has seemed to many that

---

EXAMPLE 72

Musorgskiĭ: *Pictures at an Exhibition*—excerpts

A. *Promenade*—beginning

B. *Bydlo*—beginning

continued

his conceptions suffer from the way he has put them down, as in *The Great Gate of Kiev* in which the total sound that one feels to be necessary and appropriate is simply not producible from what Musorgskii has written. This situation has given rise to many revised editions and different versions and arrangements of Musorgskii's works, and, ironically enough, *Pictures at an Exhibition* is better known in the orchestration by Ravel of 1922 than in its original version as a piano work. It appears, then, that a certain amount of judicious emendation is necessary to produce a satisfactory version, but one should take care that, in the process, Musorgskii's intentions are not totally violated. There is little doubt that, by and large, *Pictures at an Exhibition* stands among the few masterpieces for piano produced by any of the national schools and that it certainly represents the outstanding Russian piano work of the nineteenth century.

Although the nationalistic group "the Five" stood in the forefront of Russian musical life in the second half of the nineteenth century, there were other composers whose outlook was more conventional, closer to Western music, and in opposition to "the Five." This opposition was most pronounced in Anton Rubinstein (1829–1894), the great internationally known pianist, a one-time pupil of Liszt, who established the Conservatory at St. Petersburg in 1882. His large output of music for piano resembles that of many of the German composers discussed earlier in the chapter. An early nationalistic work is the *Fantasia*

EXAMPLE 72—*continued*

on Russian Themes (op. 2). Character pieces are the most numerous: caprices, serenades, romances, nocturnes, and the like, even including an essay in the larger form, a ballade (op. 93) based on a famous German narrative poem of the late eighteenth century, Bürger's *Leonore*. Along with these are the *Mélodies* (op. 3) in F and B (of which the first, needless to say, is very well known), two sets of etudes (op. 23 and 81), a set of preludes (op. 24), and preludes and fugues (op. 53). There are also many dances. Beyond these are suites of character pieces: *Kamennoy-Ostrov* (op. 10), *The Ball* (op. 14), *Soirées de St. Petersburg* (op. 44), and *Soirées musicales* (op. 109). The larger forms of so-called "absolute" music are also present. There are four Sonatas in E (op. 12), c (op. 20), F (op. 41), and a (op. 100) and a large set of Variations in G (op. 88). There are also several works for piano duet, a set of character pieces (op. 50), a set of stylized dances, *Bal costumé* (op. 103), and a Sonata in D (op. 89), along with a large Fantasia in F (op. 73) for two pianos. In his larger works, virtuosity is stressed, while the smaller works are easy and ingratiating in all respects and, in many cases, are examples of out-and-out salon music.

The leading Russian composer opposed to "the Five" was, of course, Petr Il'ich Chaikovskii (1840–1893, often spelled Tchaikovsky [see Dickinson]). Although there are nationalistic pieces in his work, he was oriented to the Western view, especially the German, in his activity as a composer, so that, generally speaking, piano music occupies a distinctly secondary position in his work, in no way comparable to what he did for opera or orchestra. There are two large Sonatas in c-sharp (op. 80) and G (op. 37) that have been studied by Frolowa, both in four movements; three sets of variations; an early work in a; the *Pieces on a Theme* (op. 21); and the Theme and Variations in F (op. 19 vi). The rest is given over to character pieces, in which, along with the usual types (*Scherzo à la Russe* and *Impromptu*, op. 1; *Waltz-caprice*, op. 4; Romance in f, op. 5; Capriccio in G-flat, op. 8; *Nocturne* and *Humoresque*, op. 10), there is *Dumka* (op. 59), similar to what we saw in the work of Dvořák, and his best-known work for piano, the suite *The Seasons* (op. 37b) of 1876; this latter is a set of twelve short pieces, one for each month, of which those of January (*At the Fireside*), April (*Snowdrops*), May (*Clear Nights*), June (*Barcarolle*), September (*Hunting Song*), and November (*Sleighbells*) are particularly engaging. There are also children's pieces. For piano duet, Chaikovskii published a set of fifty arrangements of Russian folk songs (1868–1869).

Two other Russian composers on the Western side are Anatolii Liadov (1855–1914) and Antonii Arenskii (1861–1906), both active in St. Petersburg. Both published a large amount of piano music in which the small forms dominate. In Liadov, particularly, the influence of Liszt and Chopin is easily discernible. Less usual in their work are Liadov's sets of preludes and mazurkas (op. 9–11) and the *Ballads from Days of Old* (Set I, op. 17; Sets II and III, op. 20–1) and Arenskii's *Sketches on Forgotten Rhythms Found in the Poetry of the Greeks*,

Romans, and Other Peoples (op. 28) and *Pieces in All Keys* (op. 36). Other composers to be named in this connection are Sergei Liapunov (1859–1924), Alexander Grechaninoff (1864–1956), Alexander Glazunov (1865–1936), and Rheinold Glière (1875–1956).

The third important national school is the Scandinavian, which has been exhaustively discussed by Niemann. Here, as might be anticipated, the German influence was particularly strong. Although Norway was the only Scandinavian country to produce a composer of real stature (in the nineteenth century), there was activity of various kinds in Denmark, Sweden, and Finland. In Denmark, the essentially Germanic orientation is clear from the work of Friedrich Kuhlau (1786–1832), who has become universally known for his short and simple sonatinas; Johan Peder Emilius Hartmann (1805–1900); and, especially, Niels Willem Gade (1817–1890), the close friend and colleague of Mendelssohn. Hartmann's work embraced character pieces and sonatas, there being two of the latter (op. 34 and op. 80); unlike many of his contemporaries, Hartmann also composed a number of organ works, including a large Fantasia in f (op. 20). Gade, on the other hand, remained completely under the influence of Mendelssohn and Schumann, as is seen immediately from his character pieces, among which are *Aquareller* (*Aquarelles*, op. 19 and 57), *Idyller* (op. 34), and *Fantasiestücke* (op. 41); there is also a Sonata in e (op. 28), originally written in 1839–1840 and revised in 1854, and a set of organ pieces (op. 22). Except for some arrangements of folk dances and a set of three character pieces for piano duet, *Norske Tonebilleder* (*Musical Pictures of the North*, op. 4), Gade did not engage in nationalistic music of the type we have been considering. He was noted as a teacher, two of his best-known pupils being August Winding (1835–1899) and Ludwig Schytte (1848–1909). The two Swedish composers to be mentioned here are Ludwig Norman (1831–1885) and Emil Sjögren (1853–1918).

The seat of Scandinavian nationalistic music in the nineteenth century clearly was Norway. While the German influence dominated the work of Ole Andreas Lindeman (1769–1859), primarily a composer of organ music, Halfdan Kjerulf (1815–1868), who, like Gade, studied with Mendelssohn and Schumann and thus was much in the German tradition, began to employ folk melodies in his works as early as 1824 and also made arrangements of folk songs and dances for piano, such as his twenty *Udvalgte norske Folkedanser* of 1861 and his *Norske Folkeviser* of 1867 (see Schjelderup-Ebbe). Another prolific composer of piano pieces was Agathe Backer-Grøndhal (1847–1907).

The dominant figure is, of course, Edvard Grieg (1843–1907). Again, we meet with the German orientation since Grieg, too, was trained at Leipzig and absorbed much of the Schumann-Mendelssohn influence; he also worked with Gade (see, generally, Dale). The large forms of absolute music are represented by an early work, a Sonata in e (op. 7) of 1865 (the dates are of composition) in four movements; in most respects, it is a typically Germanic production with big movements in sonata form at the beginning and end, an Andante in second place, and a minuet with trio in third. Another large work is the Ballade in g (op. 24) of 1875, perhaps Grieg's most satisfying venture into the large form, in which nationalistic elements come to the fore. The ballade, unlike ballades of Chopin and Brahms, is based on a Norwegian folk song, *E kann so mangen ein vakker sang*, on which it presents fourteen variations. The poem here is suggestive; as translated by Dale, it reads: "I know so many a pretty song / Of foreign parts far away-o, / But never once have I heard them sing / Of what we see every day-o. / And so I'm going to try my hand / And make a tune they'll understand / It's fine up here in our Northern land / Though Southern folks may not say so." Grieg's other large work is a suite for piano, *Fra Holbergs Tid* (*From Holberg's Time*, op. 40) in G, of 1884, which is better known in the orchestral version that Grieg made; this is a Neo-Classical work (Holberg was a famous eighteenth-century Norwegian dramatist) in five movements: Preludium, Saraband, Gavotte (with a musette as trio), Air (Andante religioso), and Rigaudon (with trio).

With the important exception of the Ballade in g and certain passages of the Sonata in e (the second movements and parts of the third), nationalistic elements are not important in Grieg's large works, but they do play an important role in his character pieces. Grieg's interest in Norwegian folk music apparently began rather suddenly as a result of his association with Rikard Nordraak (1842–1866) who, in the 1860's, composed music using native Norwegian melodies as themes. Grieg first did this in his set of *Humoresker* (*Humoresques*, op. 6, of 1865), which, despite their "Germanic" title, are little more than Norwegian dances for piano. Norwegian folk dances, which are so important in Grieg, are of three basic kinds: the *springdans*, in fast triple time, often a singing dance in which the melody is accompanied by a drone bass; the *halling*, a leaping dance in fast duple time native to the Halling Valley between Bergen and Oslo; and, of lesser importance, the *gangar*, a moderate "walking" dance in a steady and stately 6/8 with occasional shifting of accents to 3/4. In the *Humoresker*, there is some sign of the *springdans* in the waltz or in the last number, and the second is related to the *halling*. But folk dances become more pronounced in the *Albumblade* (*Album Leaves*, op. 28), composed between 1864 and 1876, again with a "Germanic" title; Grieg composed the *Albumblade* after his first contact with Nordraak to whom he dedicated this set. Each of the three dance types is found here. First, there is a *halling* with the characteristic triplets but elaborated by chromaticism in the harmony and syncopation in the accompaniment; then, there is a modified *gangar*, here in 3/4 time; and, finally, there is a *springdans*. The three types appear over and over in Grieg's piano music. After the *Albumblade*, however, the nationalistic aspect came out into the open with the appearance of the *Norske danser og viser* (*Norwegian Dances and Songs*, op. 17) of 1870, the *Folkeliusbilleder* (*Pictures from the Life of the People*, op. 19) of 1872, the set of two longer *Improvisata* on Norwegian folk melodies (op. 29) of 1878, the *Norske Fjeldmelodier* (*Norwegian Mountain Tunes*), and the *Norske Folkeviser* (*Norwegian Folk Melodies*, op. 66) of 1896, a set of nineteen melodies that Grieg himself collected and arranged for piano, employing extensive chromaticism in his harmonizations as was his wont in his later works (see Fischer).

A most interesting example of Grieg's preoccupation with folk music appeared near the end of his life, the *Slåtter* (op. 72) of 1902, a set of seventeen dances (see Horton). A *slåt* is any Norwegian dance played on a native instrument, in this case the highly characteristic *hardangerfelen* (Hardanger fiddle) with eight strings, four of which sound in sympathetic resonance. A Norwegian folklorist, Johan Halvorsen, fearful that this old art was dying out, collected a number of the melodies and adapted them for the modern violin; then, to give wider currency to this work, he persuaded Grieg to arrange them again for piano. This Grieg did, and the result was a skillful adaptation for piano of the characteristic texture and sonorities of the original. Readily available are a *halling* (*HMS*, IX, s. 4, b. 5) and a *springdans* (Georgii, *400 Years*, p. 122) from this set.

Grieg's remaining character pieces are generally more in the German tradition. Like so many of his contemporaries, Grieg emphasized the miniature, the very small type of character piece, as in the *Morceaux de piano* (op. 1) of 1862, the *Poetiske Tonebilleder* (*Poetic Tone Pictures*, op. 3) of 1863, the late *Stemninger* (*Moods*, op. 73) of 1906, and the three posthumous pieces. Grieg's largest collection of miniatures, however, is the ten sets of *Lyriske Stykker* (*Lyric Pieces*, op. 12, 38, 43, 47, 54, 57, 62, 65, 68, and 71), composed between 1867 and 1901, which, in a way, are his equivalent of Mendelssohn's *Lieder ohne Worte*. Here, although the formal plan is uniformly simple, the three-part scheme being in the vast majority, there is much variety. Along with some of the more usual kinds of character piece (album leaf, berceuse, elegy, papillon, melancholy, nocturne, cradle song, folk song, scherzo, and march), there are a number of little nationalistic pieces. Already, op. 12 contains a Norwegian melody; op. 38 and 47 both have a *halling* and a *springdans*, and a typical *gangar* appears in op. 54, to mention only a few. Especially popular is the *Wächterlied* (*Watchman's Song*, op. 12 iii) and effective is the *Klokkeklang* (*Bells Ringing*, op. 54 vi), in which fifths with thirds as appoggiaturas create a striking aural image.

A minor national school may be said to have existed in Poland in the nineteenth century in which, as far as piano music was concerned, the example of Chopin was decisive. The genres established by him are taken over in the work of Josef Nowakowski (1800–1865) who studied with Chopin, Ignaz Felix Dobryzynski (1807–1867), Stanislaus Moniouszko (1820–1872), Vladislav Zelenski (1837–1921), and Sigismund Noskowski (1846–1908). Of greater importance than these is Theodor Leschetizky (1830–1915) who distinguished himself as a teacher of pianists at the Vienna Conservatory.

In the rest of Europe, there does not seem to have been any attempt to establish a particularly nationalistic art of musical composition. In England, the leading native composers of piano music—since Elgar's works for piano are both few and modest—is an arch-disciple of Mendelssohn, Sir William Sterndale Bennett (1816–1875) who was born in Cambridge, studied in Leipzig, and later became director of the Royal Conservatory of Music. His piano music is fully in accordance with the tradition of Mendelssohn: a Sonata in f (op. 13), a programmatic sonata (op. 46) called *The Maid of Orleans*, a large Fantasia in A (op. 16), a set of variations, *Tema e variazioni* (op. 31), and, like Schumann, a toccata (op. 38). There are also a number of smaller works: a Capriccio in d (op. 2), *Musical Sketches* (op. 10), *Studies in Capriccio form* (op. 11), *Impromptus* (op. 12), *Romances* (op. 14), and the large set of sixty *Preludes and Lessons* (op. 33) containing works in all the keys. For piano duet, he wrote a set of character pieces, *Diversions* (op. 17), and, for organ, a Voluntary in a, a contrapuntal work. In English organ music of the time, the principal type, cultivated by a host of composers now almost totally forgotten, was the lyrical character piece, the religious Adagio. Other English composers of keyboard music to be named are Samuel Sebastian Wesley (1800–1876), C. Hubert H. Parry (1848–1918) and Charles Villiers Stanford (1852–1924).

In Italy, the German style of instrumental music never did succeed in becoming a really important branch of musical composition; the main interest, as before, was held by opera. The composers of keyboard music were in the minority, both in their working with the instrumental medium and in their being under German influence. There is Francesco Pollini (1763–1846), a pupil of Mozart whose *Esercizi in forma di toccate* appeared in 1820. The most important Italian composer of keyboard music is Giovanni Sgambati (1841–1914), a virtuoso pianist who studied for a time with Liszt and who taught piano at the conservatory at Bologna (the *Liceo musicale*). Sgambati composed a large number of piano pieces, mostly small: nocturnes (op. 3, 15, 24, and 26), *Fogli volanti* (op. 8), *Mélodies poétiques* (op. 29), *Pezzi* (op. 42), *Romanza senza parole*, and *Pièces lyriques*. A good many of his works are in the Neo-Baroque vein that has been mentioned: a Prelude and Fugue in E flat (op. 6); the *Pezzi* (op. 13), which consists of *Preludio, Vecchio Minuetto, Nenia*, and a concluding toccata; and the Gavotte in a-flat (op. 9). But his only larger work, the Suite (op. 16), consists of character pieces. Sgambati also wrote a set of lyrical religious Adagios for organ, the *Benedizione nuziale* (op. 23). Another prominent composer of piano music was Giuseppe Martucci (1856–1909), a virtuoso pianist who taught at Naples (see Fano); he was also an avowed supporter of the cause of German music in general and of Wagner in particular, and his works consist entirely of character pieces in which some of the Neo-Baroque is evident. The German influence also appears in Italy's leading composer of organ music, Marco Enrico Bossi (1861–1925), who taught organ at the Naples Conservatory and who also emphasized orchestra music in his work (see Paribene); along with sonatas (op. 60 and 71), he wrote a suite, *Res severa magnum gaudium* (op. 54), an *Étude symphonique* (op. 78), and a number of liturgical character pieces, all for organ.

From elsewhere in Europe, there are but few names to be mentioned. In Holland, the two most important composers of piano music were Julius Röntgen (1855–1932) who was born in Germany and became the director of the Amsterdam Conservatory, was a close friend of Brahms and of Grieg, and wrote a good deal of piano music in both large and small forms, and Gerard van Brucken-Fock (1859–1935), also trained in Germany (by Kiel and Bargiel), who wrote a large number of teaching pieces. From southeastern Europe, the piano was not used to any extent in Greece, while, in the Balkans, the relatively little activity worth noting was strongly under German influence; two Croatian composers listed by Georgii are Fortunatas Pintarić (1798–1867) and Ferdo Livadić (1798–1878), the former chiefly a composer of organ music.

The German tradition also had a dominant influence on the keyboard music of the United States in the eighteenth and nineteenth centuries.[1] From the eighteenth century, we can mention Alexander Reinagle (1756–1809), a native Englishman of Austrian parentage who came to New York in 1786 and later settled in Philadelphia where he was active as a teacher, impresario, pianist, and singer and where he established the New Theater (see Krohn). Among his keyboard works are a set of sonatas (unpublished) and a set of variations on several popular Scottish songs, which was published in London before his arrival in the United States and in Philadelphia after. Throughout the nineteenth century, there were a number of European musicians, particularly from Germany, active in the United States. Those most important for keyboard music were Rafael Joseffy (1853–1915), a pianist, teacher, and editor; Carl Baermann (1839–1913) who had previously studied under Lachner in Munich; Frederic Louis Ritter (1834–1891) who came from Alsace-Lorraine, lived in Cincinnati, and later taught for a time at Vassar College; and Richard Hoffmann (1831–1909) and Sebastian Bach Mills (1838–1898), both from England.

It was at this time customary for native Americans to obtain their musical education in Europe, especially in Germany. A number of American musicians studied with the most important German composers. Among the pianists and composers of piano music to be listed here are William Mason (1829–1908), the son of Lowell Mason, who studied with Moscheles and Liszt; John Knowles Paine (1839–1906) of Portland, Maine, who studied in Berlin (with Kotzschmar, not Kretschmar, as many references have it) and then taught music at Harvard University from 1862, where, in 1875, he became the first professor of music at an

---

[1] As yet, there are no comprehensive studies of this subject. A good recent survey of American music generally is by Chase; but earlier histories, such as that by Elson, should not be disregarded.

American university, a post he held until 1905, composing a few character pieces and also a few variations and fantasias for organ; Silas Gamaliel Pratt (1846–1916) who worked with Liszt and Dorn; Albert Ross Parsons (1847–1933) who studied in Berlin and Leipzig; William Hall Sherwood (1854–1911) who studied with Kullak as well as with Liszt; Edward Baxter Perry (1855–1924), a blind pianist who studied with Kullak, Clara Schumann, and Liszt, among others; Wilson George Smith (1855–1929), pupil of Kiel among others and composer of many popular character pieces; and Ethelbert Nevin (1862–1901) who studied in Berlin and, after a period of teaching in Boston, returned to France and Italy where he spent the remainder of his life, the composer of many popular or salon character pieces, among them *Water Scenes* (op. 13), of which *Narcissus* has become familiar.

With organists, the situation is much the same. There is Benjamin Johnson Lang (1837–1909) of Boston who studied in Berlin and also with Liszt; Dudley Buck (1839–1909) of Connecticut, trained in Leipzig and Dresden, who composed, among other things, two organ sonatas; George Elbridge Whiting (1840–1923), possibly the leading American organ composer of the time; Samuel Prowse Warren (1841–1915); William Wallace Gilchrist (1846–1916); Frederick Grant Gleason (1848–1903), a pupil of Buck, who also studied in Germany and lived in Chicago, the author of works for both organ and piano; George Chadwick (1854–1931) who trained with Jadassohn, Reinecke, and Rheinberger and was then active in Boston from 1880 as organist and later as organ professor at the New England Conservatory of Music; and Horatio Parker (1863–1919), like Chadwick a pupil of Rheinberger, who taught for a number of years at Yale University and who composed music for piano as well as for organ, mainly character pieces (and one piano sonata, in E-flat, op. 65). Henry Morton Dunham (1853–1929), on the other hand, received his training at the New England Conservatory where he subsequently taught for more than fifty years.

Easily the most colorful figure is Louis Moreau Gottschalk (1829–1869), born in New Orleans (see Loggins); unlike most of his colleagues, he went to France for his musical training, where he knew Berlioz, and returned to the United States in 1853 to take up a varied career as a pianist. His tours took him all over the country and even into Latin America; he spent time living in Cuba and died on a concert tour in Brazil. His life and many adventures are recorded in his autobiography, *Notes of a Pianist*, which was published in 1881. His works are exclusively of the popular show or salon piece type, among them a large *morceau de concert* consisting of variations on *America* (op. 41), an extremely *pathétique* funeral march (op. 61), and similar works like *The Last Hope, The Dying Poet, Morte,* and so on. Folk influences, Negro and Creole, appear here and there in his works, as in his *Caprice americaine* called *La Banjo* or *Bamboula*, along with a dash of Latin American flavoring, as in his *Souvenir de Porto Rico*, and *Ojos Criollos*.

By far the most important American composer of the time, of keyboard music as of anything else, was Edward MacDowell (1861–1908). Like many of his contemporaries, he was trained in Germany, under Ehlert and particularly Raff, and he even taught at the conservatory in Darmstadt before returning to the United States. In 1896, he became professor of music at Columbia University, where he remained until 1904, resigning in a controversy with the university's president, Nicolas Murray Butler; the principal chair in music at that institution is still called by his name. His lectures in music and music history, some of which have been made available, reveal the extent of his commitment to German musical Romanticism. In them, music is described as "a kind of soul language," "a language of the intangible"; "music is not an art but psychological utterance."

The bulk of his keyboard music—all of which is for the piano—consists, as would be expected, of character pieces, and again the titles are significant: *Forgotten Fairy Tales* (op. 4) of 1897 (here the dates are of publication); *Fancies* (op. 7) of 1898 (all published under the pseudonym of Edgar Thorn or Thorne); *Fantastic Pieces* (op. 17) of 1884; *Compositions* (op. 18) of 1884; *Forest Idylls* (op. 19) of 1884; *Idylls after Goethe* (op. 28) of 1887; *Poems after Heine* (op. 31) of 1887; *Little Poems* (op. 32) of 1894; *Les Orientals* (op. 37) of 1889; *Marionettes* (op. 38) of 1888; the familiar *Woodland Sketches* (op. 51) of 1896 containing *To a Wild Rose* and *To a Water Lily*; *Sea Pieces* (op. 55) of 1898; *Fireside Tales* (op. 61) of 1902; and *New England Idylls* (op. 62) of 1902. In the same vein are two sets of pieces for piano duet, *Pieces* (op. 20) of 1886 and *Moon Pictures* (*after H. C. Anderson*) (op. 21) of 1886. Along with these are other sets called *Pieces* or *Compositions*. Here, literary associations are important: Goethe and Heine, Hugo and Anderson, Shelley and Tennyson (in op. 32), and, from Americana, Br'er Rabbit (in the *Fireside Tales* and *Woodland Sketches*). At the same time, an element of musical nationalism appears here and there, as Indian and Negro melodies are occasionally employed. As had been usual with the character piece, simple three-part form is the most common, along with its extended five-part counterpart. MacDowell himself distinguished three varieties among his piano pieces: "quaint," the quiet lyrical pieces; "frisky," the lively spirited pieces; and "dramatic," the bigger pieces involving some degree of contrast. As will be seen, MacDowell was an admirer of Grieg, and many of his small character pieces resemble similar works by Grieg, especially those of the *Lyriske Stykker*. (Another American composer strongly influenced by Grieg was Wilson George Smith, who published a set of five pieces, *Homage à Grieg*.)

Later in his life, MacDowell took up the composition of piano sonatas, producing four large works all of which have descriptive titles: the *Sonata tragica* (op. 45) of 1893, the *Sonata eroica* (op. 50) of 1895, the *Norse Sonata* (op. 57) of 1900, and the *Keltic Sonata* (op. 59) of 1901. In these works, which have been discussed at some length by Gilman, we again meet with strong literary associations. The first commemorates the passing of MacDowell's teacher, Joachim

Raff, and its last movement is a lamentation, since the program of the work as a whole is, in MacDowell's words, "to heighten the darkness of tragedy by making it fall closely on the heels of triumph." Similar is the plan of the *Sonata eroica*, which is based on the King Arthur legends; the four movements represent, in turn, the coming of Arthur, a knight surrounded by elves (the scherzo), Guinevere (the slow movement), and the passing of Arthur. The two remaining sonatas strive again for an epic tone, both based on poetic fragments by MacDowell himself; the *Norse Sonata*, in three movements, has a motto describing the recounting of tales of heroic battles fought and won in bygone times around the fire of a great hall at night, while the *Keltic Sonata* is connected with the chronicles of the Gaels, the cycle of the Red Branch, and the characters Deidre, Nassi, and Cuchulling. Of this last work, MacDowell wrote that it is a "bardic rhapsody on the subject," and that, even though one might not know the literary background, one "will easily perceive from the music that something extremely unpleasant is happening." This northern inspiration immediately suggests Grieg, whom MacDowell greatly admired and to whom the last two sonatas are dedicated. All four are large compositions using cyclic form and bringing all the themes together in the finales.

Other works of MacDowell stand midway between the sets of character pieces and the large Romantic sonatas. Important here are the two *Modern Suites* (op. 10 and 14) of 1883. The qualification "modern" refers to the absence of the old dances common in the suite; the preludes and fugues are present, but the other movements are simply character pieces. The Neo-Baroque element, however, is present elsewhere in MacDowell's compositions; there is a Prelude and Fugue (op. 13) of 1883 and a later set of *Little Pieces on Sketches by Bach* of 1890. There are also etudes of considerable difficulty (op. 39 and, especially, op. 46).

It appears that MacDowell generally is to be looked upon not only as the leading American composer of the time, but also as the most representative of the situation of American composition of the time. Here, we meet with that peculiarly American phenomenon, the composer who is also a university (not a conservatory) professor, as was also the case with Ritter, Parker (even though Yale University had, and still has, a School of Music), and Paine. Thus, the problem of music in the essentially liberal arts type of education, so prominent at present, has roots going well back into the nineteenth century. The German influence in MacDowell is pronounced but tempered by an element of musical nationalism, both foreign (Nordic and ancient) and domestic. It was not until the twentieth century that composers in the United States sought to develop their own forms, procedures, and idioms in music.

CHAPTER TEN

Keyboard Music in the Twentieth Century in France and Germany

In looking back over the history of music, one is struck by the fact that each of the generally recognized historical periods was dominated or unified by composers from a particular country who provided the basic repertory, forms, and idiom or style. Thus, during the Middle Ages this leadership came from France (secular monophony, organum, conductus, the motet, isorhythm), even though Italy made an important contribution in the fourteenth century; during the Renaissance, it was the Netherlands that led the way (imitative counterpoint, the cyclic mass, the motet); and during the Baroque period, it was Italy (double chorus works, the continuo, the madrigal, the opera, and the like); and, from the eighteenth century, with the rise of instrumental music, it was German composers who dominated the scene. When we come to the twentieth century, however, the picture is by no means so clear; and, while certain conclusions have been drawn in the account that follows, it must be borne in mind that we are too close to the events for any conclusions to be accepted unconditionally. As we will see, the contemporary musical scene presents a good deal of variety, as indeed do all historical periods, but we do not have the benefit of the passing of time to place things in their true historical perspective. It is clear that a basic driving force in contemporary music is the reaction against German Romantic music; but this reaction takes different forms in different places. In some cases, the German tradition is completely rejected by composers who produce something as totally different as possible, while, in others, elements are taken from it and worked into something that, again, is completely different.

For our purposes, then, beyond this principal reaction, there is no central line that we are able to accept. Yet, several elements or trends in nineteenth-century music have proven productive of much that has taken place in the twentieth century. Most important is the development of nationalistic musical styles and, second, the undercurrent of interest in Baroque music that runs all

379

through the century. These, singly and in combination, play an important part in twentieth-century music. At the same time, there remains the German Romantic tradition in which many composers continue to work, sometimes introducing extensive modifications and new interpretations and sometimes not.

Before we can enter into this discussion, it is necessary once more to qualify the German Romantic tradition in music, since it plays such an important—if frequently negative—role in the history of twentieth-century music. We have seen how the so-called "Classical" tradition of instrumental music, as it had been established by Haydn, Mozart, and Beethoven, gave way in the nineteenth century to more Romantic manifestations favoring the smaller forms and intensely personal emotional expression in which extramusical qualities or subjects are expressed directly in a musical composition. Keyboard music, as has been seen, was in a decline in that the leading composers more and more neglected it, especially as the universal large forms—the symphonies of Bruckner and Mahler, the symphonic poems of Strauss, the Wagnerian music drama—came to dominate the scene. Brahms was an isolated if respected figure, and Liszt, who certainly enjoyed great respect in the new circles, was not followed in his devotion to keyboard music. The large musical art form had one important objective: to make an impression on the listeners, to stimulate their emotional response; it was big, it used large forces, it was expressive, and the composer was, to a large extent, governed by what would be necessary to be "effective." Piano music—apart from the brilliance of the virtuoso performer—could not compete with these large works. We have seen the old large form of the piano sonata decline in importance during the nineteeth century and this often altered its character by becoming a programmatic work (the sonata frequently became a symphonic poem for piano), while the quantitative emphasis went to the character piece in the smallest of its small forms, the miniature. The organ, however, did have the potential for competing with the large orchestral forces, and there was, as has been seen, a certain revival of interest in composing for the instrument, especially in France.

The question of the position of this essentially Germanic art of music in France is a most interesting one. There were, as is well known, many French elements taken up in this German art; and the operas of Wagner made a profound impression on French intellectual life, not only on a number of French musicians, but also on French writers, especially the so-called "Symbolist" poets (Baudelaire, Mallarmé, Verlaine, and Rimbaud). Yet, it was also in France that the first consequent reaction to the German Romantic art of music took place. This reaction took its point of departure from a manner of painting called "Impressionism" in which the emphasis went to color, shadings, and textures instead of clarity of design; in place of expression, there came suggestion. The aim was to suggest the shifting, transitory, ephemeral aspects of things. In music, the central figure was Claude Debussy and, along with him, Maurice Ravel and, to some extent, Erik Satie; in the work of all three, much that has become characteristic of twentieth-century music is clearly present.

Claude Debussy (1862–1918) led an outwardly uneventful life devoted to music, which was spent almost exclusively in and around Paris except for the few years when he was in Italy as the recipient of the Prix de Rome; he also visited Russia in the employ of Madame von Meck, who had befriended Chaikovskii; and he attended performances of Wagner's operas in Bayreuth. But in the main, he led a retiring life in Paris as a composer and music critic, making few public appearances and always in close association with literary people as well as other musicians.

It is noteworthy that, in his musical work,[1] the piano occupies a most prominent position, and the character piece is dominant; the older large forms, the sonata and the theme and variations, are totally absent, as is organ music. His early piano works include the two *Arabesques* of 1888, *Nocturne* and *Rêverie* of 1890, and a number of dances tinged here and there with national traits from Bohemia and Russia (the *Danse bohèmienne* and a *Ballade slave* of 1890 and the *Tarantelle styrienne* or *Danse* of 1890), which present nothing that would arouse attention. Then come two works in which Debussy revealed the direction that he was to follow—the *Suite bergamesque*, composed in 1890 but published in 1905, and the suite *Pour le piano*, composed between 1896 and 1901. The *Suite bergamesque* consists of four movements (*Prélude, Menuet, Clair de lune, Passepied*), two other pieces at one time planned for the suite being published separately (*Masques* and *L'isle joyeuse*). Here, there is something of a revival of the eighteenth-century suite, as can be seen from the minuet and passepied; but the prelude is clearly in Chopin's manner. The novelty here appears with the slow movement, the popular *Clair de lune* in D-flat, the first example of impressionistic piano music (see Georgii, *100 Years*, pp. 123–8). Here is an entirely new type of nocturne in which Debussy's new world of sound is plainly revealed: the "blurred" pedal effects, the employment of triads with added sixths, the rather undefined melody, and a roaming kind of phrase structure, that is meandering but sequential. The title of the piece is much in the Impressionistic tradition. In the next suite of piano pieces, *Pour le piano*, the Neo-Classical element is more pronounced. Here, all three movements show something of the eighteenth-century atmosphere (a prelude, a saraband, and a toccata); the prelude operates entirely with figuration but uses the whole-tone scale, the toccata is similar but more of a virtuoso piece (see Valentin, 23, pp. 65–7, an excerpt), and the saraband, which had been composed three years earlier, observes the old rounded binary form and the rhythmic pattern of the dance but employs also the new sounds

---

[1] There are a number of biographies, some of which deal with the piano music; on the piano music especially, see Cortot, Gatti, Perrachio, Schmitz, and Schulz; on his Impressionism generally, see Kölsch.

especially the parallel seventh chords (see Jakobik). What this means is that the supercharged emotional aura of the German music of the time was deliberately avoided and Debussy went back to the eighteenth century for his models—a more refined, delicate, and detached (aloof) art. This spirit, which came to be called "Neo-Classicism," became a prominent, perhaps even the central, trend in twentieth-century music.

The next few piano works of Debussy are more impressionistic, and the visual inspiration, related to impressionist painting, comes clearly to the forefront. There is the lesser piece *D'un cahier d'esquisses* (*From a Sketchbook*) of 1903, the collections of *Estampes* (*Prints*) of 1903, and the two sets of *Images* of 1905 and 1907. The three pieces in *Estampes* are quite characteristic. The first number *Pagodes*, was inspired to some extent by the Balinese *gamelan* (gong orchestra), which Debussy heard at the Paris International Exposition of 1899; it features the pentatonic scale and parallel chords using seconds and fourths that, in com-

EXAMPLE 73

DEBUSSY: *Pour le piano*—excerpts

A. Saraband—beginning

B. Toccate—beginning

A.　　*Avec une élégance grave et lente*

bination, create an exotic Oriental effect. The second piece, *Soirée dans Granade* (*Evening in Granada*) takes its inspiration from Spanish music; it is a nocturne using the characteristic *habañera* rhythm, again abounding in insinuating coloristic effects, especially imitating the guitar—the pedals and octaves high in the treble and *pianissimo* and deliberately disconnected changes. The last piece, *Jardins sous la pluie* (*Gardens in the Rain*), is another subject dear to the Impressionists in which, along with typical "watery" figuration, are two French nursery songs, *Do-do l'enfant du* and *Nous n'irons plus au bois*. This kind of piece, so prominent in the Impressionist repertory, clearly goes back to a work of Liszt, *Les jeux d'eau à la ville d'Este* from the third year of the *Années de pèlerinage*. Much the same holds for the *Images*. The "watery" *Reflêts dans l'eau* (*Reflections on the Water*, Set I i), again features arpeggios; there are bell-like effects in *Cloches à travers les feuilles* (*Bells Through the Leaves*, Set II i [*HMS*, X, s. 1, b. 1]), in which dissonance is used as tone color; there is also the nocturne, moon picture *Et la lune descend sur le temple qui fuit* (*And the Moon Descends over the Temple from the Past*, Set II ii), along with the more virtuoso, almost etude-like *Mouvement* (Set I iii), a moto perpetuo piece, and *Poissons d'or* (*Goldfish*, Set II iii), another Oriental inspiration, capricious and disconnected. The Neo-Classical element returns with *Hommage à Rameau* (Set I ii), actually a saraband that is simple in its essentially diatonic melodic line. Two larger works, published

EXAMPLE 73—*continued*

separately in 1904, are *Masques* and *L'isle joyeuse*, both originally planned as part of the *Suite bergamesque*. The former is related to the Italian *commedia dell'arte* and the latter to a painting of Watteau (*Embarquement pour Cythère*); both are large virtuoso works representing a sort of rapprochement between the large-scale German expressive manner and Debussy's more characteristic type of piece.

Roughly contemporary with these is the suite *Children's Corner* of 1906–1908 (all titles here were originally in English), written for the entertainment of Debussy's daughter but, like certain works of Schumann and others, for large as well as small children. It is not impossible that Debussy here was influenced by the example of Musorgskii, whose work he admired. Here, humor, a quality comparatively rare, especially in the music of the twentieth century, is prominent, first in the etude-like *Dr. Gradus ad Parnassum*, in which the Clementi kind of scale exercise is interrupted by Impressionistic episodes, and again in the *Golliwog's Cakewalk*, the popular concluding number of the suite; the latter piece draws its thematic material from American Negro minstrel show music, with a riff-like figure in the accompaniment, typical jazzy syncopated rhythms, and a touch of the blues here and there. Towards the end of the suite comes a satirical allusion to Wagner's *Tristan und Isolde*, marked "with great emotion." In between come *Jimbo's Lullaby*, for a toy elephant (Debussy must have meant Jumbo); *Serenade for the Doll*, capricious with rapid figuration and fourths; *The Snow is Dancing*; and the lyrical *The Little Shepherd* with its cantabile line, in which the augmented second is prominent, over a simple harmonic accompaniment.

Apart from a few isolated and relatively insignificant works, the remainder of Debussy's piano music is found in the two sets of preludes, twelve in each, of 1910 and 1914, and the two sets of etudes, six in each, of 1915. The preludes are characteristic pieces not principally different from those of the *Images* and *Estampes*, while the etudes are more particularly concerned with technical problems and less with manifesting some particular effect. Both genres, significantly enough, were prominent in the work of Chopin.

In the preludes, Debussy was at some pains to put the characteristic titles at the end of each piece rather than at the head; but, at the same time, these titles are most suggestive and very much in the Impressionistic manner, so that one is rather at a loss to evaluate his intentions. At all events, these preludes provide an excellent cross-section and summation of Debussy's pianistic art. There is the Impressionistic nocturne, with parallel chords and pedal effects, in *Les sons et les parfums tournent dans l'air du soir* (*Sounds and Perfumes Turn in the Evening Air*, Book I), an inscription from Baudelaire's *Harmonies du soir*; and, in *La terasse des audiences au clair de lune* (*Reception in the Moonlight*, Book II), a scene from India. Then, there are the striking aural images of winter, *Des pas sur le neige* (*Footsteps in the Snow*, Book I); of autumn, *Feuilles mortes* (*Dead Leaves*, Book II); and of fog, *Brouillards* (Book II). Two "water" pieces also appear, *Voiles*

(*Sails*, Book I) and *Ondine* (Book II). Light filigrees of arpeggiation with a touch of the capricious characterize *La danse de Puck* (Book I) and *Les fées sont d'exquisses danseuses* (*Fairies Are Most Exquisite Dancers*, Book II). Then, there are the bigger and more impressive pieces that require a good deal of virtuosity. From Book I, there is *Le vent dans la plaine* (*The Wind in the Plain*) and, particularly, the tumultuous *Ce qu'a vu le vent d'ouest* (*What the West Wind Saw*) with its striking coloristic use of dissonance; or, from Book II, there is *Les tierces alternées* (*Thirds in Alternation*) and *Feux d'artifice* (*Fireworks*), which, near the end, quotes *La Marseillaise*. Another larger work is *La cathédral engloutie* (*The Engulfed Cathedral*) of Book I, an impression of the cathedral of Ys rising from the depths of the sea, using murky, blurred, rising parallel fourth chords and the clangorous bell-like parallel chords. Also found in the *Préludes* is the exploitation of various nationalistic musical idioms, such as the Spanish in *La sérénade interrompue* (*The Interrupted Serenade*, Book I) and *La puerta del Vino* (Book II), complete with *habañera* rhythms and a lyrical *copla*; a suggestion of the Scottish in *La fille aux cheveux de lin* (*The Maid with the Flaxen Hair*, Book I), with its simple pentatonic melody, and the similar *Bruyères* (*Heaths*, Book II); American Negro music in *Minstrels* (Book I); and the Italian tarantella in *Les collines d'Anacapri* (Book I), a scene from Naples. Two ceremonial dances of antique inspiration, perhaps indebted to Satie, are *Danseuses de Delphes* (*Delphic Dancers*, Book I) and *Canope* (Book II), a Greek funeral urn. Finally, there are several humorous pieces in Book II—*General Lavine-eccentric*, the awkward clown of the *Folies-Bergère*, a disconnected dance; *Hommage à S. Pickwick, P. P. M. P. C.*, Dickens' character, replete with the impressive appearance of the British national anthem; and, to some extent, *Minstrels*, with the American minstrel show music.

The etudes eschew the expressive and impressionistic element and deal more "objectively" with technical problems. (Along with this, it is noteworthy that Debussy, in his later instrumental ensemble works, turned to the old and absolute genre of the sonata—the sole early work in this vein was a string quartet.) The first of the etudes, *Pour les cinq doigts d'après Monsieur Czerny*, clearly is a burlesque of the famous man's etude style, and, like the earlier *Dr. Gradus ad Parnassum* of the *Children's Corner*, is a humorous work. The others contain much that is useful and unusual. The first set contains a slow and prevailingly lyrical study in thirds and fourths, a Chopinesque exercise in sixths (somewhat like the middle part of the celebrated Etude in E, op. 10 iii), a waltz-like study in octaves, and a noteworthy etude *pour les huit doigts* featuring rapid scale patterns to be played without using the thumbs. In the second set, we find a fast exercise in chromatic scales in thirds, a delicate study in arpeggios, a barcarolle-like work with a cantabile heavily embellished with most unusual ornaments (*Pour les agréments*), and a virtuoso study in repeated notes that has some similarity to the earlier *Masques*; then, there are two pieces that exploit chordal passages and unusual sonorities of various kinds, *Pour les sonorites opposées* and the concluding *Pour les accords*.

　　While these works make up the bulk of Debussy's music for piano, there are two other sets to be mentioned, both written about the same time as the second book of preludes and the etudes: the six *Épigraphes antiques* for piano duet of 1914 and the set of three pieces *En blanc et noir* for two pianos of 1915. (There are several earlier works for both piano duet and two pianos.) The first of these, originally planned to go along with poems by Debussy's friend Pierre Louys (his *Chansons de Bilitis*), are short and simple pieces in the Impressionist vein. There is a rain picture (*Pour remercier la pluie au matin*) using the whole-tone scale, parallel fifths, and arpeggio figuration; an exotic piece with the customary augmented second prominent in its melodic line (*Pour L'Égyptienne*); the pentatonic lamentation (*Pour un tombeau sans nom*); and so forth. The other group, which Debussy originally planned to call *Caprices*, is longer and more varied; the most interesting piece is the second, *Lent, sombre*, a solemn dirge

EXAMPLE 74

Debussy: *Minstrels*, from *Préludes* (Book I, No. 12)—beginning

complete with a military episode using fanfare-like phrases and running bass figuration, for which the models clearly were Liszt's *Funérailles* (from the *Harmonies poétiques et religieuses*) and Chopin's famous Polonaise in A-flat (op. 53).

In the work of Debussy, then, we see a specific reaction against the prevailing German Romantic tradition. There was a definite assertion of peculiarly French conceptions, as represented, first, by the association with Impressionism and, second, by the seeking out of the spirit of eighteenth-century French harpsichord music. But other sources were exploited as well: the idiom of Spanish dances, the sounds of Oriental music, and the experimental, antitraditionalist attitude of the Russian nationalistic composers, Musorgskii in particular. This experimental attitude is perhaps the most important, for the ways in which it shows itself are many and varied: new and different scales are used, the old traditional functional harmonies are neglected, new combinations are devised, and so forth. The arch-Romantic work of passionate subjective expression, so typical of the German music of the time, was rejected; instead, the musical composition had become more objective, less personal, detached, and often much more modest.

Closely associated with Debussy was Maurice Ravel (1875–1937), born in the South of France, not far from the Spanish border but trained in Paris where he spent the greater part of his life. Like Debussy, he was a pianist, and, like him, he composed many important and representative works for this instrument; but works for solo piano (see Akeret and Sannemüller) cease after 1917, and he only returned to the instrument late in his career, writing two concertos (one for piano left hand) in 1931. Again, we must note the absence of organ music.

Ravel's piano music can be divided into two large groups, one Impressionistic and the other Neo-Classical, with the latter of greater significance than in the work of Debussy. Apart from the early unpublished *Sérénade grotesque* of 1893, the Neo-Classical element appears first in the famous *Pavane pour une infante défunte* (*Pavane for a Dead Princess*) of 1899. Then comes his first striking impressionistic work, *Jeux d'eau*, composed in 1901, which takes its place beside similar "water" pieces of Debussy; but it is interesting to note that Ravel's piece preceded those of Debussy and that all go back to the similarly entitled piece of Liszt. *Jeux d'eau* has in it many features characteristic of musical Impressionism: the simple ternary formal plan, the episodic character, the coloristic use of dissonance, here arpeggio figurations involving simultaneous seconds, the use of glissandi and chromatic scale runs, and irregularities in the rhythm, to name only some of the more important elements. This composition gained immediate acceptance and placed Ravel in the forefront among the progressive composers of the time.

The other Impressionistic works of Ravel for solo piano are contained in two sets of pieces, the five in *Miroirs* of 1905 and three in *Gaspard de la nuit* of 1908. The *Miroirs* are on the whole similar to Debussy's *Estampes* and *Images* (or the later preludes). This is most evident from the presence of the quiet mood piece abounding in unusual sonorities—chords and pedal effects—as in the vague and chromatic *Noctuelles* (*Night Moths*), the slow, fragmentary phrases interspersed with sudden outbursts of figuration in *Oiseaux tristes* (*Sad Birds*), or the lugubrious melody accompanied by bell-like chords in *La vallée des cloches*. (Compare with Debussy's *Cloches à travers les feuilles* from the *Images*, Book II.) On the other hand, there is the virtuoso etude *Une barque sur l'ocean*, in a basically slow tempo but employing rapid arpeggio figuration, as well as a Spanish piece, *Alborado del gracioso* (*The Morning Song of the Buffoon*) complete with *seguidilla* rhythm, the lyrical *copla*, and unexpected comic interruptions. (Compare Debussy's similar *La sérénade interrompue*, from the *Préludes*, Book I, which is later.) It might be mentioned that the Spanish idiom in Ravel had been foreshadowed in an earlier work, the *Habañera* for two pianos of 1895 (published as the second of two pieces under the title *Les sites auriculaires* in 1896).

But while *Miroirs* has many points of similarity to Debussy, the three pieces of *Gaspard de la nuit*, although still essentially Impressionistic, are much larger and more difficult than what is found in Debussy (except perhaps for *Masques* and *L'isle joyeuse*). The subject matter is taken from Louis Bertrand (1807–1842), a French Romantic poet in whose work the supernatural is important. The first of Ravel's pieces is *Ondine*, a sort of Lorelei who lures young men to drowning; in it, a typically Impressionistic "watery" figuration goes along with an enticing and innocent-sounding diatonic cantabile melodic line. (Debussy's suggestion of *Ondine* is in the *Préludes*, Book II.) Then comes the mournful *Le Gibet* (*The Gallows*) in which a slow melody, sometimes stated in parallel chords, is accompanied by an ostinato bell-like figure that tolls throughout with a pedal point that also is maintained all the way through. *Scarbo*, the last piece, is a depiction of a dwarf, an evil figure from the underworld; it is a virtuoso display piece, highly rhythmical and using short staccato motives and much figuration.

Turning to the Neo-Classical works, there is the *Pavane pour une infante défunte* of 1899, which has previously been mentioned; it is a stately dance in rondo form that uses many elements of the new manner—parallel chords that mitigate the customary harmonic progressions and the coloristic use of dissonance. This is, in fact, Ravel's first characteristic work. In 1905 came the second Neo-Classical effort, the Sonatina in f-sharp (a genre, be it noted, completely neglected by Debussy). This piece is clearly based on the eighteenth-century type of little or easy sonata; it uses the three-movement formal plan in the usual sequence, with sonata form in the outside movements while the slow movement is an up-dated minuet. The thematic material is predominantly lyrical with melodies of balanced phrase structure over an accompaniment that often is an Impressionistic version of the eighteenth-century accompaniment patterns. In the finale, the melody is cast in clear but irregular phrases and is accompanied, for the most part, by rapid figuration.

Ravel's principal Neo-Classical work, however, is his last composition for solo piano, *Le tombeau de Couperin* of 1917. Originally planned as a *suite française*, its succession of movements clearly associates it with the French harpsichord suite of the eighteenth century: prelude, fugue, rigaudon, minuet (with a musette as trio), and toccata. Beyond a certain similarity in harmonic idiom, the work shows little kinship with Impressionism: the individual movements are small in size, clear in form, simple in texture, and clear and balanced in their phrase structure. For the most part, these individual movements reflect the essential features of their eighteenth-century counterparts. The prelude and the concluding toccata emphasize figuration, the former in its lilting 6/8 meter and use of mordents, while the latter is a larger and more difficult piece with a repeated note pattern in the accompaniment using a pentatonic theme and attaining a climax. The lyrical fugue is quite correct, the Impressionist harmonies tending to obscure the movement of the individual lines. The forlane is also lyrical, in a dotted 6/8 rhythm with leaps in the melody, in simple three-part form with a modal flavor in the harmonies. The rigaudon is in bright and vigorous duple time and is essentially diatonic, although the middle part is chromatic. The slow, lyrical minuet, in which again the mordent is prominent, makes use of a pedal point and modal effects, with the musette using parallel chords as a trio. Here, then, we find little of the Impressionistic aura of vagueness and the suggestion of mood and atmosphere, nor do we find any of the virtuoso demands of *Gaspard de la nuit*. Yet, among the Neo-Classical works of Ravel—or the Impressionist group as a whole—*Le tombeau de Couperin* stands out as the finest single accomplishment.

Ravel also composed a number of other pieces for piano. There are the outspokenly lesser works, the minuet celebrating the centenary of Haydn's death; those pieces in the style of Borodin and Chabrier of 1913; and, from 1911, the collection of seven *Valses nobles et sentimentales*, in which the Viennese type is given an Impressionistic twist. (Ravel also composed in this vein for orchestra, as *La Valse* testifies.) The inspiration, as Ravel acknowledged, goes back to Schubert. Here, there are seven waltzes and an Impressionistic epilogue in which the themes of the previous waltzes are heard again. Apart from Schubert, there are also suggestions of Schumann, Brahms, and, especially, Chopin. In 1912, they were orchestrated to form the ballet *Adélaïd*. For the rest, there is a single publication for two pianos, the early *Les sites auriculaires* containing the symptomatic *Habañera* and *Entre cloches*, and two works for piano duet, *Ma mère l'Oye* (*Mother Goose*) of 1908 and a single work, *Frontispiece* of 1919. *Ma mère l'Oye*, later orchestrated to make a ballet, contains both Neo-Classical and Impressionistic elements (along with Oriental effects).

We have seen that, in this French reaction against German Romantic music and Wagner in particular, the Neo-Classical attitude was of considerable importance, since it meant that the composers specifically ignored their immediate musical heritage and sought inspiration and models from an earlier period in which the aim of personal and emotional expression was not central. In this, it seems that both Debussy and Ravel were indebted to a distinctly secondary composer who seems to have served as a sort of catalyst, a stimulator. This was Erik Satie (1866–1925), the son of a music publisher, a former café pianist, for a time a Rosicrucian, and always the arch-foe of German Romantic music (see Shattuck). His earliest keyboard music is characteristic of his bent as a composer: the sets of *Sarabandes* of 1887, *Gymnopédies* of 1888, and *Gnossiennes* of 1890, three in each. There is a suggestion of antiquity as well as of the Neo-Classical (see Danckert). In manner of composition, the three sets are similar. A simple, lyrical melodic line, clear and unproblematic in its phrase structure and with many repetitions, is presented over a deliberately simple chordal accompaniment with totally unusual harmonic progressions, often the result of modal organization. The over-all effect is frequently one of something vaguely liturgical; it all is simple, refined, detached, and aloof—all elements of the Neo-Classical orienta-

EXAMPLE 75

Satie: *Gymnopédies* (No. 2)—beginning

tion and all features that have become important for twentieth-century music. Let it be emphasized that Satie was the first of this group to compose sarabands. What is perhaps most striking in comparison with German Romantic music is the directionless quality; the pieces seem static, they lack a climax and central point, and they do not go anywhere—they simply *are*. The *Gnossiennes*, the most ornate of the three sets, have a distinctly Oriental cast about them by virtue of the augmented seconds, the florid ornamental phrases, and by a sort of free rhythm, since there are neither bar lines nor time signatures.

Subsequent works of Satie are similar, except that the element of satire, which had already appeared in the *Gnossiennes*, becomes more pronounced, even though restricted to the titles and markings. There are the three *Pièces froides* of 1897 and his longest work for piano, the "three" *Morceaux en forme de poire* for piano duet of 1903. (Debussy had told Satie that this work should have some definite form, and this was the answer; however, there are not three pieces, but seven.) Except for a Neo-Classical *Prélude en tapisserie* and *Passacaille* of 1906, Satie wrote nothing for piano between 1897 and 1912. After this came the humorous and satirical works: the *Préludes flasques*, the *Croquis et agaceries d'un gros bonhomme en bois* and *Chapitres tournés en tous sens*, all of 1913, and the *Heures séculaires et instantanées*, the *Valses d'un précieux dégouté*, and the *Sports et divertissements* of 1914, to name only some, in which are found performance directions like the well-known injunction to play "softly, like a nightingale with a toothache," which is aimed at the serious and often equally explicit directions in the German music of the nineteenth century. The styles of various celebrated and well-established composers are parodied here and there in these pieces: Chopin's funeral march (which Satie labels "Mazurka by Schubert") in the *Embryons desséchés* of 1913; Mozart, Chabrier, and Debussy in the *Croquis et agaceries* and the *Chapitres tournés*; and Gounod in the *Vieux sequins et vielles cuirasses* of 1914. In the *Sports et divertissements* of 1914, there is a satirical and dissonant treatment of a chorale-like melody, a slap at traditional instruction in part writing as well as at an important element in major French musical works of the nineteenth century, a movement that doubtless influenced Stravinsky in his *L'histoire du soldat*. Satie's last work of any significance for piano is the set of *Nocturnes* of 1919 in which the satire is restricted to the titles and the performance instructions, while the music is essentially similar to the other works except that the nocturnes are more pianistic, somewhat bigger, and use idiomatic figuration patterns.

Satie, then, was a stimulator, and the effects of his work are clearly to be seen in certain works of Debussy and Ravel, as has already been suggested. We have mentioned the Neo-Classical orientation. The satirical element in his views and in his music also appears in Debussy, as can be seen in the passing suggestion of Wagner in the *Golliwog's Cakewalk* of the *Children's Corner* and other humorous works. And who can say that the curious detached Grecian pieces in the *Préludes*,

Danseuses de Delphes and *Canopes* are not a sort of homage to Satie? As far as Ravel is concerned, it would seem that his early *Pavane pour une infante défunte* also owes something to the example of Satie, whose work he expressly admired.

Here, then, was the first breakthrough, as it were, of a new type of music, one that owed its inception to the desire to create music specifically different from the prevailing Germanic conception. Although the genre of the character piece was surely most prominent, it was handled in a very different fashion, and the standard and conventional types are lacking, except here and there in Debussy. The ideal of expression was replaced by suggestion; what had been dynamic and forthright now became veiled and aloof. Much of this had to do with the revival of eighteenth-century aesthetic ideals. An important component of the Romantic idiom had been the treatment of harmony—a rich, full, and highly chromatic manner—and this was seriously called into question in the work of this group. Here, it is Debussy that appears most important; in his work, one senses an atmosphere of experimentation, a trying-out of new sounds and procedures, an effort to be new and different.

The Impressionist way, with its component of Neo-Classicism, became of central importance for French music and, as will be seen, played a role of great significance in the general development of contemporary music. In one way or another it dominated the work and outlook of many composers, among the earlier of whom we can mentioned Albert Roussel (1869–1937), Florent Schmitt (1870–1958), and Déodat de Séverac (1873–1921), all three of whom wrote a good deal of piano music, mostly in the smaller forms. We can mention Roussel's early set *Des heures passant* (op. 1) of 1898, the *Conte à la poupée* of 1904, *Rustiques* (op. 5) of 1904–1906, and *L'accueil des muses* of 1920, a tombeau for Debussy; but, in his later work, the Neo-Classical element came to the fore, most impressively in the large Suite (op. 14) of 1909–1910 (in four movements: prelude, bourée, sicilienne, and rondo); a prelude and fugue (op. 46) of 1932–1934, which he called *Hommage à Bach*; and three pieces (op. 49) of 1933 the first of which is a toccata. Also somewhat in this vein is the Sonatina (op. 16) of 1912 and the *Petite canon perpetuel* of 1913. While Schmitt, for the most part, preferred the large forms (an influence from the German Romantic tradition that he doubtless had from his teacher d'Indy), in his piano music, it is the character piece that dominates. Of a great many, we can here single out especially the two volumes of *Musiques intimes* (op. 16 and 29), composed up to 1904, in which there is something of the German background; the purely Impressionistic *Ombres* (op. 64) of 1913–1917; and *Mirages* (op. 70) of 1920–1921. There are also two sets of preludes, of which the second (op. 5) is called *Soirs*; and, like Roussel, he wrote a tombeau for Debussy. Later in his career, he made the turn to the larger form but explicitly avoided the sonata, calling the work, somewhat ambiguously, *Suite sans esprit de suite* (op. 89), of 1938, and followed it with another set of four pieces composed in 1945, *Clavecin obtemperant* (op. 107). Séverac worked almost wholly in the realm of the character piece, as in his early suite *Le chante de la terre*, subtitled *Poème georgique*, of 1900; or *En Languedoc* of 1904; or *La nymphe émue ou le faune indiscret* of 1909. There is also a suite for piano duet, *Le soldat de plomb* of 1905. Prominent in his work is the *étude pittoresque*, the pictorial etude, that is not far removed from the characteristic etude of the nineteenth century, of which the *Baigneuses au soleil* of 1908 and the set *Cerdaña* of 1910 are worthy of mention. Yet, the large form is not totally lacking: there is a Sonata for Piano in b-flat and two Suites for Organ in E and d, as well as a number of shorter pieces.

Shortly after World War I, there set about in France a strong reaction against the delicacy and refinements of Impressionism. As far as music went, an important spokesman was Jean Cocteau (1891–1962), a poet, novelist, and dramatist who generally represented avant-garde tendencies in the artistic world of the time. In music, he was impressed with Satie, who had, in his words, dared to do the bravest thing: to be simple. Like Satie, Cocteau was opposed to the German Romantic tradition and to the refinements of Impressionism. Music should be simple and clear, and melody should emerge as the central formal element; the composer should seek his inspiration not from idealistic and romanticized regions, but from the world around him—from the music hall (and Satie had been a music-hall pianist), the circus, popular songs, even jazz, and so on. Some of this can be found in Debussy and Ravel, but the total effect and the new emphasis led to something rather different. The group of composers associated with Cocteau, whose works were in accordance with his ideas and were played on the same programs, were heralded in a newspaper article by the critic Henri Collet as "the Six," in an obvious analogy to "the Five" of nineteenth-century Russia (for more details, see Rásín), and the following year there appeared an album of piano pieces, one by each member of the group: Louis Durey (1888–), Arthur Honegger (1892–1955), Darius Milhaud (1892–), Germaine Tailleferre (1892–), Georges Auric (1899–), and Francis Poulenc (1899–1963). Just how much they really had in common, beyond the association with Cocteau and their own friendship, has been disputed, with Milhaud himself disclaiming much in the way of a common intent among the members of the group. In any case, neither Durey nor Tailleferre continued to make much of a reputation for themselves as composers, while Auric devoted himself to the composition of film scores; the other three, however, have emerged as important composers.

Perhaps most distinctively new and different and most in accord with the ideals of Cocteau is Darius Milhaud, who has composed a large amount of music, including much keyboard music, in large as well as small forms (see his auto-biography). But it is significant that a good many of his piano pieces also exist in orchestral versions, which would indicate that often his convictions concerning the piano as the proper medium for these works are not strong. In any case, there is nothing of Impressionism here. The forms are small, sharp, and clear; the textures simple; the melodies distinctly phrased; the harmonies extremely dissonant, often polytonal; and the rhythmic element always strong. Especially characteristic are the South American compositions (Spanish rhythms, be it remembered, also appear in Debussy and Ravel): the *Saudades do Brasil* (op. 67) in two books of 1920–1921, souvenir of his sojourn in that country, in which typical Latin dances are present in striking polytonal forms; the later *L'automne* (op. 116) of 1932, a suite of three pieces in recollection of a trip to Madrid; or the jazz works, three *Rag-caprices* (op. 78) of 1922, which exist also in a version for small orchestra. Among other sets of pieces are the four *Romances sans paroles* (op. 129) of 1933; the lively *Tour de l'exposition* of 1933 (revised in 1937); the five pieces of *Une journée* (op. 269) of 1946, representing various times of day; *Jeu* (op. 302) of 1950; and *Le candelabre à sept branches* (op. 315) of 1951, seven pieces corresponding to seven festivals of the Jewish year. With one exception,

EXAMPLE 76

MILHAUD: *Sumaré*, from *Saudades do Brasil* (No. 9)—beginning

the works in the larger, "absolute" forms appear early, but, even so, they are not really large. There is a suite (op. 8) of 1913 and a sonata (op. 33) of 1916, the latter an eighteenth-century kind of sonata, as is the much later second sonata (op. 293) of 1949; also early is a set of variations on a theme of Cliquet (op. 23) of 1915. Along with the children's pieces (op. 222) of 1941, Milhaud has composed music for two pianos, particularly the suite *Scaramouche* (op. 165a) of 1937, later arranged for saxophone and orchestra, which shows the bent towards elegance and satire, concluding with a Brazilian dance; another large work for this medium is *Kentuckiana* (op. 287) of 1948, using some twenty Kentucky folk songs, a piece that was orchestrated on commission from the Louisville Orchestra; there is even a set of six pieces for four pianos, *Paris* (op. 284) of 1948. Finally, there is a handful of organ works, a sonata (op. 112) of 1931, a pastorale (op. 229) of 1941, and a group of nine preludes (op. 231) of 1942.

Arthur Honegger, a close friend of Milhaud, was a Swiss who studied in France where he spent most of his life, finally teaching at the famous *École normale de musique*. Although associated with "the Six," he was not sympathetic, retaining instead his disposition towards the German Romantic tradition from which they had so avidly emancipated themselves. But, although this is so, Honegger's harmonic idiom is in full accord with that of his erstwhile colleagues. His emphasis on the larger forms is not really reflected in his piano music: there is only the early *Toccata et variations* of 1916 and the *Prélude, arioso et fughetta sur le nom de Bach* of 1932, which, despite its Franckian title, is a relatively small work based strictly on the four notes corresponding to the letters in Bach's name. On the other hand, his *Fugue et chorale* for organ of 1917 is closely related to the French symphonic organ manner of the nineteenth century. For the rest, there are pieces of various kinds: a set of three of 1915–1919; the *Pièces brèves* of 1919–1920; four miniatures in *Le cahier romande* of 1921–1923; the pictorial *Scenic Railway* of 1931, a small pianistic counterpart to his more famous orchestral *Pacific 231*; two *Esquisses* of 1941 written in a new manner of notation; and a *Souvenir de Chopin* of 1947. There are two extended works for two pianos, a partita of 1930 and a suite of 1948.

The piano is more important in the work of Poulenc, who remains more in the tradition of nineteenth-century French piano music in which, as has been seen, the elegant salon piece was important; and, by and large, it can be maintained that most of Poulenc's piano music is of this kind. We can note the almost complete avoidance of the larger forms in favor of the character piece, of which the more conventional types are represented in the three *Mouvements perpetuels* of 1918, the three *Pièces* of 1928, the seven nocturnes of 1929–1935, the *Feuillets d'album* of 1933, the *Mélancholie* of 1940, along with several intermezzi and waltzes. Of somewhat greater importance is the suite *Napoli* of 1922–1925 in three movements (pastorale, nocturne, and *Caprice italien*) the last of which uses popular Neapolitan song melodies and attains a brilliant conclusion. Also important is the cycle *Les soirées de Nazelles* of 1936 in which a theme and eight variations is preceded by a preamble and followed by a cadenza and finale; each of the variations is a musical portrait of one of Poulenc's friends, a situation that calls to mind Elgar's *Enigma Variations* for orchestra. Poulenc's principal Neo-Classical work is the *Suite française d'après Claude Gervaise* of 1935, which recreates something of Renaissance music; it is purely diatonic and uses modal scales, each dance short, simple, and clear. Other pieces show the same bent here and there, as in the toccata in the pieces of 1928, the *Feuillets d'album*, which contains an ariette and a gigue, or the children's piece *Bourée au pavillon d'Auvergne* of 1937. Poulenc composed his sole piano work in an established large form in 1919, a sonata for piano duet, but it is, like his other piano music, light and pleasing with a touch of humor, and its three movements (prelude, rustique, and finale) avoid the forms usually associated with the sonata.

The light salon style of Poulenc appears in other French piano music of the twentieth century and often draws in Impressionistic and Neo-Classical elements. Two composers to be mentioned are Jacques Ibert (1890–) and Jean Françaix (1912–), both of whom work with small forms and strive to be simple yet witty and elegant, as also did, to some extent, Satie and the members of "the Six." The result is what may be described as a twentieth-century counterpart to the eighteenth-century *galant* style, which frequently was surely quite deliberate and which has become an important category in twentieth-century music. Of the two composers, Ibert has composed the most for piano, ranging from early Impressionistic works, like *Le vent dans les ruines* and *Matin sur l'eau*, to his main efforts: *Histoires*, a set of ten short pictorial pieces; the Impressionistic set *Les rencontres*, a *petite suite en forme de ballet*; and the later *Petite suite en quinze images*. Ibert also wrote a *Toccata sur le nom de Roussel* for piano and, for organ, a chorale and a set of three pieces. Françaix is essentially similar, emphasizing, after his earlier scherzo of 1932, dance-like pieces arranged in suites; there is a set of five *Portraits de jeune filles* of 1936, here coupled with musical portraiture (as had also been done by Poulenc and, in a way, had been prominent in French harpsichord music of the eighteenth century), and *Éloge de la danse* of 1947, musical represenations of six epigraphs of Paul Valéry. For two pianos, there is the set of eight *Danses exotiques* of 1958.

This elegance and objectivity in music does not tell the whole story of twentieth-century French music. There are two other directions, both of which affirm music as an intensely serious and deeply expressive art and thus accord somewhat with the German Romantic tradition. One of these is the direct continuation of the nineteenth-century French school of symphonic organ music, the other the *Jeune France* group of the 1930's; both come together in the person of Olivier Messiaen, who, since World War II, has emerged as one of the leaders in the new serial type of music.

The school of organ music (see Dufourcq) is the direct offshoot of the work of Franck, Guilmant, and Widor (who lived on until 1937), its most prominent members being Charles Tournemire (1870–1939), Marcel Dupré (1886–), Louis Vierne (1870–1937), Maurice Duruflé (1902–), Jean Langlais (1907–), Gaston Litaize (1909–), and Jehan Alain (1911–1940), as well as Messiaen, whose work will be discussed later. Dupré and Vierne, both eminent organ virtuosos, continued the genre of the organ symphony as it had been established by Widor. Dupré (see Delestre) has two works, the *Symphonie-passion* (op. 23) of 1924 on a plainsong theme and the Symphony in c-sharp (op. 26) of 1929, along with two suites, the *Suite bretonne* (op. 21) of 1924 and a later suite (op. 39) of 1944. Vierne (see Gavoty) has no less than six symphonies (op. 14 of 1899, op. 20 of 1903, op. 28 of 1912, op. 32 of 1914, op. 47 of 1925, and op. 59 of 1930), along with four suites, each in six movements, which comprise the *Pièces de fantaisie* (op. 51–54) of 1926–1927. Generally, however, Dupré is a much more comprehensive composer of organ music. He gives prominence to older categories, as in the two sets of three preludes and fugues, those in B, f, and g (op. 7) of 1912 and those in e, A-flat, and C (op. 36) of 1938, and a set of twenty-four inventions (op. 50) of 1956. Then, there are a number of cantus firmus works: fifteen versets (op. 18) of 1919, *Variations sur un vieux Noël* (op. 20) of 1922 (another Baroque form), two large collections of chorale preludes (seventy-nine works in each), *Chorals* (op. 28) of 1931, *Le tombeau de Titelouze* (op. 38) of 1942–1943, *Paraphrase sur le Te deum* (op. 43), *Miserere mei* (op. 46), and a setting of Psalm 18 (op. 47). Related to these are liturgical works not based on borrowed melodies, including three small *Élévations* (op. 32) and three *Offrands à la Vierge* (op. 40) of 1944. His work also includes a number of sets of organ pieces of various kinds: a scherzo (op. 16) of 1919, *Cortège et litanie* (op. 19) of 1921, *Lamento* (op. 24) of 1926, seven *Pièces* (op. 27) of 1931, *Le chemin de la croix* (op. 29) of 1931–1932, *Angelus* (op. 34 i), *Évocation* (op. 37) of 1941, two *Esquisses* (op. 41) of 1945, and the large-scale *Vision* (op. 44) of 1947. Dupré has also composed, for piano, preludes, a set of pieces, and a set of variations.

Langlais, a pupil of Dupré who also studied with Dukas, has emphasized the organ piece, of which his early set of three *Poèmes évangeliques* of 1932 has become popular. His other works include two sets, one of twenty-four pieces written between 1937 and 1939 and the other of nine pieces of 1942–1943; the *Légende de St. Nicholas* of 1937; *Fête* of 1946; and *Hommage à Frescobaldi* of 1951. More liturgical are the three *Paraphrases grégoriennes* of 1933–1934, the *Offertoires pour tous temps* of 1943, and the *Incantation pour une jour sainte* of 1949. The large form is represented by a large and difficult symphony of 1941–1942 and three easier suites, the *Brève* and *Médiévale* of 1947 and the *Française* of 1948. There are also a few piano pieces, including a prelude and fugue and two suites, one for harpsichord and the other for piano duet.

Duruflé and Roger-Ducasse are of secondary importance here. Duruflé has but a handful of organ pieces to his credit, a scherzo (op. 2) of 1926; a *Prelude, adagio et chorale varié sur le theme du Veni creator spiritus* (op. 4) of 1929, a large work in the tradition of Franck; a suite (op. 5) of 1930 in three movements (prelude, sicilienne, and toccata); and a *Prélude et fugue sur le nom d'Alain* (op. 7) of 1943, in memory of his colleague who was killed in the early years of the Second World War. Roger-Ducasse, on the other hand, has but one organ piece, the early *Pastorale* of 1909.

In the work of these composers, the essential tradition of the French symphonic organ school is maintained: the emphasis on organ tone color, the impressive use of the full tonal resources of the instrument, and the large forms. However, the harmonic idiom has been expanded somewhat, even though it remains firmly rooted in the system of tonal functions. But this is not entirely true in the work of Jehan Alain, who is surely the most progressive member of the group, apart from Messiaen. Many of Alain's organ compositions may be seen as the outgrowth of the older religious Adagio but strongly influenced by Impressionistic elements, as in *Le jardin suspendu, Litanies, Aria,* and *Intermezzo;* while the suite of 1936, in three movements (introduction and variations, scherzo, and choral) would be associated rather with the larger works of the French organ school. Somewhat in the same vein are a prelude and fugue, a set of two *Fantasies* of 1939, and the *Ballade en mode phrygien.* Beyond these are two sets of variations, one on the plainsong *Lucis creator* and the other on a theme of the sixteenth-century composer of chansons, Jannequin. While this last is indicative of a Neo-Classical attitude, it also points to something else—a secular inspiration, something not characteristic of organ music since the Baroque period. Already, the character pieces show this; and Alain also composed two *Préludes profanes* and even dances for organ, the *Danses à Agni Yavishta* (from the Sanskrit) and a later large set of three *Danses* of 1937–1938, which is one of his major works. Here, the dance is not only highly stylized, but also is the means for the expression of an extramusical meaning—the joys and sorrows of life, the struggle and ultimate triumph over death. There are three dances—*Joies, Deuils,* and *Luttes*—all joined in a large cyclic work, since the themes of the first two movements provide the basis for the last. While the first movement is in a rather free sonata form, the *Deuils,* subtitled "dance in honor of the memory of a hero," is a passacaglia with thirty statements of the cantus firmus and, at the very end, a monophonic Oriental melody of lamentation; the last movement features sonorous chords. In its use of complex rhythms and curious kinds of tone color, especially in conjunction with certain dissonances and types of figuration, the *Danses* at times anticipates effects that have appeared in the music of the late 1950's and early 1960's; but, at the same time, the last movement culminates in chord progressions that, by and large, are not unconventional.

To the extent that it considered music as capable of serious and emotional expression and placed emphasis on composition in the large forms, the French organ school stands in some contrast to the ideals and principles of "the Six." But there are other composers and groups who opposed the *galant* tenor represented by "the Six." One of these groups consists of musicians who have become known largely as teachers and whose composition is on the conservative side but who have, through their teaching, become influential: Gabriel Pierné (1863–1937), a famous organist and conductor who wrote a number of piano and organ pieces but who ceased composition after 1920; Charles Koechlin (1867–1951), an ardent supporter of contemporary music who himself composed a great deal in all possible styles and media, even experimenting with Schönberg's dodecaphonic serialism; the eminent teacher Nadia Boulanger (1887–), whose influence is still most lively; and the pianist Robert Casadesus (1899–). Another group, of greater importance, emerges as being explicitly in opposition to the *galant* ideals, the so-called *Jeune France*, who will be discussed later. One other composer to be mentioned here is Henri Dutillieux (1916–) who began working in the fashion of the Impressionists but whose later work has been with the larger forms and includes much contrapuntal writing, as his large sonata of 1948 in four movements eloquently demonstrates.

There can be no question that the dominant attitudes and aims of contemporary music developed in France, first among the Impressionists and then in and around "the Six," which includes Cocteau and Satie; an important element was the opposition to the tradition of German Romantic music. It thus becomes of great interest to see the course of German keyboard music in the twentieth century, which, generally speaking, involves modifications of this older tradition in the face of the new aesthetic ideals that grew up in France.

The basic source of twentieth-century German keyboard music must be seen in the work of Brahms and Reger, who, despite a number of important differences, have one cardinal aspect in common: the emphasis on absolute or abstract music. Let it be emphasized that French Impressionism never became strong in Germany, and there are no German composers of any stature who can be regarded as Impressionists. It has already been seen that the Neo-German School (Liszt and Wagner) of the nineteenth century did establish an important tradition in keyboard music. In Reger, on the other hand, the emphasis on absolute or Classical types brings with it a certain Neo-Classicism (as has also been observed in the work of Brahms), which lies just below the surface in the work of a good many German composers of the nineteenth century. But, in Reger, this element comes clearly out into the open and leads him to large-scale pieces of organ music for the like of which one must almost go back to Bach.

Among the older representatives of German keyboard music of the twentieth century, we can include the eminent theorist and teacher Heinrich Lemacher (1891–); three men associated with the conservative and Romantically inclined

Munich School, Hans Pfitzner (1869–1949), August Reuss (1871–1935), and Joseph Haas (1879–); Armin Knab (1881–1951); Walther Braunfels (1882–1954); and Hermann Grabner (1886–). Lemacher wrote a number of children's pieces and has been a most influential teacher, and Braunfels, a pupil of Leschetizky and Thuille, is known for his set of scherzi for two pianos (op. 9). While Pfitzner is known primarily as a composer of operas (and, incidentally, as an ardent opponent of innovations in music, as is clear from the lively controversy he carried on against Busoni), he composed some piano pieces late in his career—a set of pieces (op. 47) and etudes (op. 51) in 1943. More important is the work of Haas and Knab. Haas, in particular, is much like a German *Kleinmeister* (composer of secondary importance) from the late nineteenth century in his extensive cultivation of piano music (see Laux), especially the miniature character piece, of which he published numerous sets including even suites of character pieces somewhat in the vein of Schumann, the *Deutsche Reigen und Romanzen* (op. 51) of 1919 and *Schwänke und Idyllen* (op. 55) of 1921. Consequently and characteristically, he neglected the larger forms (see his *Mummenschanz*, op. 34 ii [Kahl, 21, pp. 62–5]), although there are three sonatas and a set of variations on an original theme, the *Eulenspiegeleien* (op. 39) of 1912. Haas also composed a few works for organ—a Sonata in c (op. 12) of 1907, several suites, and a set of variations, as well as chorale preludes—but there is nothing comparable to the accomplishment of his teacher, Reger. Haas' music is distinguished by its lyricism and the use of imitative counterpoint, both features that derive from Reger. The same elements dominate the much smaller output of Knab, whose conservative bent is revealed in works like his set of eight *Klavierchoräle* (*Chorales for Piano*) of 1933–1934 (of which he later arranged four for organ) and the two suites, one in G for harpsichord or piano of 1937 and the other with the title *Aus alten Märchen* (*From Old Fairy Tales*) of around 1939, and the *Polyphone Studie* in 1942. There are also, in Schubert's vein, two sets of Austrian country dances, the *Ländliche Tänze* of 1927 and the *Lindegger Ländler* of 1935. The large form is represented in his work by the Sonata in E of 1928. Grabner has composed mostly for organ and much in the same vein as Reger, as in his partita on the chorale *Erhalt' uns Herr bei deinem Wort* and the *Orgelchoralbuch*, a collection of organ chorales.

Later composers of similar sentiments are Werner Egk (1901–), Gerhard Frommel (1906–), and Kurt Hessenberg (1908–). Of the three, Egk is at once the best known and least active as a composer of keyboard music, his chief effort being a sonata of 1948. Character pieces dominate the output of Frommel and Hessenberg, the former also with six sonatas to his credit, while the latter has composed inventions (op. 1) of 1930 and preludes for clavichord or piano (op. 35) of 1945, along with a number of organ works.

This essentially conservative attitude, the outgrowth of the nineteenth-century tradition, surely provides the basis for much twentieth-century keyboard music in Germany. But frequently modifications of one kind or another take place, sometimes on the model of Debussy's experimentations or under the influence of later French composers, especially the Neo-Classical element, which, as has been pointed out, is by no means entirely lacking in nineteenth-century German music. In contemporary German keyboard music, this shows itself primarily in a fundamentally linear conception of music, a concentration on imitative counterpoint, and experimentation with different organizations of rhythm, and in a certain sort of objectivity in the musical composition, an impersonal quality, and a preference for the more neutral genres of musical composition.[1] Some of this is clear from the work of Reger, but much is new and different as far as German music is concerned. The three most important German composers to be taken up here are Paul Hindemith (1895–1963), Boris Blacher (1903–), and Wolfgang Fortner (1907–).

Of the three, Hindemith doubtless is by far the most important; he was a theorist, teacher, and performer, as well as one of the foremost composers of his time. Like other twentieth-century composers, he evolved an individual system of relating musical notes that is of basic importance for his composition; this is explained in his instruction manual, *The Craft of Musical Composition.* It is a tonal but fully chromatic system, in which the various notes are related to the tonic by their position in its overtone series. Taking C as the tonic, the following would result: C, G, F, A, E, E-flat, D, B-flat, B, and F-sharp. Similarly, all the intervals are arranged from simplest to complex, moving from the consonant to the most dissonant: octave, perfect fifth, perfect fourth, major third, minor sixth, minor third, major sixth, major second, minor seventh, minor second, major seventh, and tritone. Polytonal combinations are also possible.

Although not professionally a keyboard player, Hindemith has composed a number of works for the medium, most for piano but some for organ. Characteristically enough, the character piece is not dominant, since, apart from three sets of children's pieces—the *Reihe kleiner Stücke* (op. 37 ii) and the *Kleine Klaviermusik* (the fourth part of the *Sing- und Spielmusik für Liebhaber und Musikfreunde*)—there are but two sets, both of them early. There is a set of fifteen pieces, *In einer Nacht* (op. 15) of 1921, and the eight *Tanzstücke* (op. 19) of 1928; there is also a set of rather difficult etudes, the *Uebung in drei Stücke* (op. 37 i), in the first of which jazz elements are to be found. Otherwise, it is to the large form that Hindemith turned. First, there is the *Suite 1922* (op. 26) consisting of five movements (*Marsch, Schimmy, Nachtstück, Boston,* and *Ragtime*), with some of the spirit of "the Six," in which the old dances of the suite are replaced by types of contemporary popular music with a nocturne in place of the aria.

---

[1] On the keyboard fugue in the twentieth century, see Unger. On the keyboard variation, see Albrecht. On the German organ sonata, see Stockmeier. On the German piano sonata, see Schulter-Bernet.

After the suite come the piano sonatas. Apart from the early sonata (op. 17) of 1917, there are the three well-known works of 1936. Here, we meet with the conception of the sonata as a large form (excepting the second of the three, which is more in the nature of a sonatina). The first of the three has five movements, the third, four. The first also has a literary inspiration, the poem *Der Main* by the prominent Romantic poet Friedrich Hölderlin, so that, in connection with the large form, the sonata appears to have several relationships to the nineteenth-century tradition. Hindemith even employs formal plans characteristic of the nineteenth-century sonata. A three-part division of the first movement on the order of the old sonata form is common, as is the three-part form of the slow movements and scherzi, and there is a rondo scheme in the finales. But, here the resemblance ends, for Hindemith's basic conception of music and of how it should be organized is something very different indeed. Here, the model is basically eighteenth-century music, Neo-Classical or, more accurately, Neo-Baroque. The individual movements tend towards homogeneity of character, thematic material, types of figuration, and rhythmic patterns, so that one might almost see a sort of revival of the Baroque *style d'un teneur*, the unity of affection, within a movement or large sections of a movement. The melodic principle is *Fortspinnung*, in which a characteristic motive is used in combinations, sequential passages, to produce a long, inherently endless, melodic line; this not infrequently has led him to abandon time signatures and have bars of different lengths but always keeping the same pulse unit, as in the first movement of the first sonata of 1936 (see Georgii, *400 Years*, pp. 132–8). Furthermore, Hindemith's conception is essentially linear, contrapuntal, even to the point of presenting several keys simultaneously in linear superposition. This can be seen everywhere in the three sonatas but is particularly clear in all movements of the third sonata. The first movement is a sort of siciliano; the second movement (corresponding to the scherzo) has an insistently repeated, terse thematic figure; there is a lyrical slow movement with a fugal middle section (a real Baroque figuration type fugue subject); and, as finale, there is an impressive double fugue with second subject from the middle part of the third movement. Then there are the impressively sonorous chordal passages that appear in all the sonatas. In these works, then, the preoccupation with continuity and similarity virtually precludes any individual personal emotional expression, and there is no attempt to stress the individual or the unique, as had been true of nineteenth century Romantic art; Hindemith seeks to be aloof and distant, presenting a well-made artistic product in which the high level of craftsmanship is plainly evident. This idea, so important in contemporary art, certainly marks a return to the aesthetic ideals of the earlier eighteenth century.

Hindemith's other main composition for piano, the *Ludus tonalis* of 1943, represents much the same thing, only more explicitly since it has a direct relation to two works of Bach, *The Well-Tempered Clavier* and, to a lesser extent, *The*

Art of the Fugue; it consists of twelve fugues, one in each tonality, with eleven interludes, a prelude, and a postlude. (The relationship with Bach has been discussed thoroughly by Tischler.) It is evident that Hindemith has conceived the *Ludus tonalis* as a large cyclical entity. In the first place, as in *The Well-Tempered Clavier*, there is a plan in the arrangements of the tonalities, but Hindemith's is much different since it is based on his own ranking of tonalities as given in his instruction manual, which has already been explained; the interludes serve to modulate from one tonality to the next. In the second place, the postlude is what one might call, in current terminology, the totalitarian retrograde inversion of the prelude in that all aspects are inverted and in reverse (crab), not only the individual parts, but also the vertical disposition of the parts. Finally, there is careful attention to contrast and balance in the tempi and characters of the various numbers as they succeed one another, so that, all in all, the work is clearly planned as an entity.

The fugues are all in three voices and much in the Bach manner and spirit, as is revealed from the themes used and in the continuous consistency that is achieved; but the counterpoint throughout is dissonant. Typical is the Fugue

EXAMPLE 77

Hindemith: *Mässig schnell*, from *Sonata* No. 3—fugue subject

in D (viii [see *HMS*, XI, s. 3, b. 6]). Unlike *The Well-Tempered Clavier*, these fugues frequently employ the devices of learned counterpoint; there is a triple fugue in ricercare style (i), a rapid double fugue (iv), a serious mirror fugue (iii), a fugue with inversion (x), one with retrograde and retrograde inversion (ix), and a lyrical canon (xi). This emphasis on learned devices connects the *Ludus tonalis* equally with Bach's *Art of the Fugue*. In the interludes, as in Bach's preludes, we find pieces in different characteristic styles, some related to Baroque types and others not but all Baroque in that, once the particular character is established, it is maintained throughout the piece. For instance, there is the small toccata or prelude type using figuration (iv and viii), a march (vi), a pastorale (ii), a waltz (xi), the lyric piece (ix), and so forth. The prelude is larger and sectional, corresponding to the bigger toccata or fantasia type, in three parts; the first is in typical toccata style, then an arioso, and finally a rapid conclusion based on an ostinato. And the postlude, as stated, is the retrograde inversion of the prelude.

Hindemith also has composed for piano duet and has treated this medium in accordance with the old Viennese tradition. Not only is the waltz, a kind of domestic music, represented, but the medium is also held capable of presenting larger works, as the sonata of 1938 eloquently demonstrates; both are also to be found in Schubert (although there the sonata is represented by large works called "fantasias"). The sonata of 1942 for two pianos is another large composition in four movements, not dissimilar to the bigger of the piano sonatas, with two contrapuntal movements, a slow canon, and an impressive fugal finale. Then, for player piano, there is a toccata (op. 40) of 1926.

Hindemith's other important contribution to keyboard music consists of the three sonatas for organ, two composed in 1937 and the third in 1940. We have seen that, in the nineteenth century, the sonata for organ was closely related to the Baroque toccata (with fugue) and hence, in a way, was already Neo-Classical. But Hindemith's organ sonatas depart from this tradition in most respects. The two earlier among them are in four and three movements respectively and have the same characteristics as are found in the piano works. The first sonata (the largest of the three) includes a piece in trio sonata style as the slow movement, while the first and last movements are prevailingly lyric. The second sonata has a lively opening movement with much repetition of figuration patterns, a pastorale as slow movement, and a canzone-like fugue as finale. The third is rather different in that its three movements each are based on old German folk songs, treated in accordance with the old cantus firmus procedure: *Ach Gott, wem sollt ich's klagen* in the first movement, *Wach auf mein Hort* as the slow movement, and, as finale, *So wünsch' ich ihr*. In the last movement, the figuration is virtuoso in nature, on the order of what one might find in a Baroque toccata. This third sonata, in its employment of folk songs as cantus firmus melodies, is like several of Hindemith's orchestral compositions, especially *Der Schwanendreher*, a concerto for viola and small orchestra, as well as the well-known symphony, *Mathis der*

Maler. Here Hindemith revives most impressively a type of musical composition that goes back to the Middle Ages.

Like Hindemith, Boris Blacher, associated with the Berlin School (he still teaches composition there), has worked primarily with the conventional types of so-called "absolute" music, and with an intellectual-objective bias, incorporating elements derived from Baroque music (see Stuckenschmidt). Unlike Hindemith, he has restricted himself, so far as keyboard music is concerned, to the piano. There are two sonatinas (op. 14) of 1941, a set of three pieces (op. 21) of 1947, the set of seven *Ornamente* (op. 38) of 1950, and a sonata (op. 39) of 1951 (but, in comparison with Hindemith, this sonata is a small piece). Also like Hindemith, Blacher has formulated a theoretical basis for his manner of composition, but one that involves the rhythmic organization of a musical work rather than the relationships between the notes of the scale. This is used by him in the *Ornamente*, which has the subtitle "seven studies in variable meters," and also in the sonata. What this amounts to is an arbitrary succession of bars of different lengths all with the same beat unit, a succession or pattern that is then repeated over and over again, in ostinato fashion, throughout the piece. In the first of the *Ornamente*, the pattern of time signatures in the successive bars is 2/8, 3/8, 4/8, 5/8, 6/8, 7/8, 8/8, 9/8 and then, in order, back to 2/8; in the second, it runs from 3/8 to 9/8 and back; in other cases, the pattern is less regular, as in the third where it is 2/8 to 4/8, 3/8 to 5/8, 6/8 to 8/8 and then back; and even more complex combinations appear in the later *Ornamente* and the sonata. This rhythmic principle thus provides the basic organization of the composition, establishing a pattern that remains unchanged throughout the work, one that also controls the melodic phrases and phrase structure. In his prevailing use of lean texture and dissonance, Blacher achieves a characteristic dryness or, to use the language of contemporary jazz, "coolness," a quality also of great importance in contemporary music.

Wolfgang Fortner has revealed many influences, among which the French Neo-Classical and the German Neo-Baroque have been most pronounced. He has composed for organ a Toccata and Fugue of 1930 (see the excerpt in Valentin, 24, pp. 68–71) and a *Preaembel und Fugue* of 1935; for piano he has a sonatina and a rondo on Swabian folk dances, both of 1936, a *Kammermusik* of 1944, and a group of seven elegies of 1950. Like Reger, his basic inclination is towards contrapuntal writing, except that he employs it in a totally chromatic and dissonant context. In his later work (since 1948) he has taken over some elements of Schönberg's dodecaphonic serialism, to be discussed shortly.

There are many other composers who can be mentioned as belonging in a general way to the stylistic direction under consideration here. Among the older representatives we can mention Philipp Jarnach (1892–); then, somewhat younger, are Hermann Reutter (1900–), Wilhelm Maler (1902–), Günter Raphael (1903–1960), Helmut Degen (1911–), and two pupils of Hindemith, Konrad

Friedrich Noetel (1903–1947) and Siegfried Borris (1906–). In all, we find the traditional types of piano music subjected to new modes of musical organization in which the principle of dissonant but tonally oriented counterpoint appears as the most important. It is worthy of note that several of these composers have pursued studies in music history and theory; this has been done by Hindemith himself, as well as by Maler, Degen, and Borris. There appears, perhaps, to be some relation between studies in music history and the revival of contrapuntal writing, albeit under different harmonic assumptions. The old character piece dominates the work of Jarnach (although there is also an unusually elaborate sonatina, op. 18, and a suite), while Degen's work appears evenly divided between early character pieces and later sonatas (a set of four appeared in 1949), as does the comprehensive keyboard output of Raphael. On the other hand, Reutter, who was schooled in the conservative Munich School, developed later in his career strongly Neo-Classical tendencies, and his piano music emphasizes Baroque forms: a Chaconne and Fugue in c-sharp (op. 4), a *Fantasie apol-calyptica* (op. 7), *Variations on a Chorale of Bach* (op. 15), and an unusual cyclic work, *Die Passion in neun Inventionen* (*The Passion in Nine Inventions*, op. 25) of 1930; there is also a set of pieces (op. 28) and the *Dance Suite* (op. 32); for two pianos, he wrote the striking *Antagonismus* (*Antagonism*, op. 1) and another group simply entitled *Musik* (op. 42). Much the same is true of Wilhelm Maler, who composed six sonatas between 1937 and 1946, and a suite, *Der Mayen*, in 1942, using a lyrical kind of dissonant counterpoint. Hindemith's pupils follow the lead of their teacher in giving prominence in their work to the larger forms of keyboard music.

Two important composers are Rudolf Wagner-Regeny (1903–) and Gottfried von Einem (1918–). Both have, from time to time, used various principles of organizing music. This holds especially for Wagner-Regeny who has experimented with Schönberg's tone rows and with Blacher's variable meters, even in one and the same work, in which, therefore, the serial principle underlies the two main elements of the composition. Of late, since Wagner-Regeny lives and works in East Germany, his works reflect the ideals of "Socialist Realism." Einem, whose work reveals here and there many influences (jazz, the Neo-Classical, and the harmonically updated Romantic expressiveness), has written much less for piano—a set of four pieces (op. 3) and two sonatinas (op. 7).

There is another important element in the work of this group of composers, the idea of music intended for use by particular persons in particular situations. In Hindemith's parlance, the word is *Gebrauchsmusik* (useful music, or music for use). Basically, what is meant are compositions in the composer's individual techniques and manner that avoid great technical difficulties of performance and execution; another term used in Germany for this is *Spielmusik* (music for playing), intended usually for the enjoyment and often the instruction of the young. Hindemith has composed piano pieces of this kind, as his *Kleine Klaviermusik*, a set of twelve little pieces each using five notes, demonstrates. While Fortner and Blacher have not engaged in this, there are notable contributions by Maler, Borris, and Degen. Perhaps the most notable figure to be mentioned is Carl Orff, whose comprehensive work does not include keyboard music. Another would be Paul Höffer (1895–1949), best known for his set of one hundred *Spielstücke* based on German folk songs.

It has been seen that many features of Baroque music are revived in the work of this group of composers. And it is by no means surprising that, along with this, should go a certain cultivation of organ music; the work of the influential Grabner and Hindemith has already been mentioned. Among the composers important here are Heinrich Kaminski (1886–1946), Johann Nepomuk David (1895–), Ernst Pepping (1901–), Hermann Schroeder (1904–), Kurt Thomas (1901–), Hugo Distler (1908–1942), and Siegfried Reda (1916–). For the most part, the older genres of organ music are here revived along with the procedure of contrapuntal imitation. Kaminski has a Regerian toccata on the chorale *Wie schön leuchtet der Morgenstern* of 1923, a sonata based on chorale melodies of 1926, four chorale preludes—three of 1928 and a later one composed in 1940—and a toccata and fugue of 1939; even his piano music is in Baroque forms and stresses contrapuntal writing. The same applies to Pepping, who has emphasized forms related to the chorale, the large form of the chorale partita (*Wie schön leuchtet der Morgenstern* and *Wer nur den lieben Gott lässt walten*); a large set of chorale preludes, the *Grosses Orgelbuch* of 1941; and a piece in the vein of Reger's chorale-fantasia, the toccata and fugue on *Mitten im Leben* of 1942. In his piano music, Pepping has emphasized the large form, with four sonatas (see Hamm), two sets of variations, and a group of three fugues on "Bach"; but there is also the large *Tanzweisen und Rundgesänge* (*Dances and Rounds*). David's work emphasizes contrapuntal genres: two ricercares, one in c of 1925 and another, in five voices, of 1937; a Chaconne in a of 1927; a Passamezzo and Fugue in g of 1928; several toccatas (and preludes) and fugues, and, more unusual, a fantasia of 1929 on *L'Homme armé*, the popular melody often used as cantus firmus in cyclic Masses of the Renaissance. Then, there are two hymn settings of 1928; his largest single collection, however, is the *Choralwerk*, in twelve parts composed over a period of twenty years (1932–1952), containing preludes, partitas, fantasias, and so on, all based on chorale melodies. Again, in Schroeder's work, we find the Baroque forms for organ: a toccata, a fantasy, and a prelude and fugue on the choral *Christ lag in Todesbanden*, all of 1930, and then a Sonata in b, composed in 1956.

On the other hand, one of the best-known figures in contemporary German organ music had little to do with the prevailing trend towards the Neo-Baroque—Sigfried Karg-Elert (1877–1933). In some respects a follower of Reger, Reinecke, and Jadassohn, Karg-Elert was nonetheless strongly attached to the traditions of the nineteenth century but was also influenced by French Impressionism (see

Sceats), so that, along with settings based on chorale melodies (particularly the *Choral Improvisations*, op. 65, and the *Symphonische Choräle*, op. 87), there are numerous character pieces in the vein of the old religious Adagio, such as the *Impressionen* (op. 72), *Pastels* (op. 92), *Pastels from Lake Constance* (op. 96), and *Cathedral Windows* (op. 106), which use plainsong themes. Many of these pieces, to be sure, are equally intended to be played on the harmonium, an instrument on which Karg-Elert was a virtuoso performer.

In Austria, there were a number of composers who, one way or another, continued the Romantic expressive tradition from the nineteenth century. The most important among them are Franz Schmidt (1874–1939), Joseph Marx (1882–), Hans Gál (1890–), and Franz Schreker (1878–1934). While Schreker was generally the most influential, he did not compose keyboard music. Marx, on the other hand, has described himself openly as a "Romantic Realist" and composed typically Romantic character pieces in 1916; much the same applies to Gál. Schmidt, a pupil of Bruckner, has worked largely with organ music in the old forms, treated rather conservatively (chorale preludes, chaconnes, preludes, and fugues), including a large set of *Variations and Fugue on an Original Theme* (for which he made three versions), and a Toccata in d for harpsichord or piano of 1938.

But, at the same time in Vienna, there were far-reaching innovations taking place. Again it was the essential constitution of music as such that was called into question; but, unlike French musical Impressionism, these experiments were looked upon by their authors as evolutionary, as the direct outgrowth of the nineteenth century tradition of musical composition. The principal figure here is Arnold Schönberg (1874–1951); his two pupils, friends, and colleagues, Alban Berg (1885–1935) and Anton Webern (1883–1945), although of general importance, did not compose much keyboard music. All three, but particularly Schönberg, have exerted such a profound influence that they have been called "the Second Viennese Classical School," to parallel the earlier trinity of Haydn, Mozart, and Beethoven. Webern's music, neglected for years, has been taken as the point of departure for much of the music composed since the end of World War II.

There can be no doubt that the central figure (especially as far as the particular case of keyboard music is concerned) is Arnold Schönberg, who must be regarded as one of the most decisive influences on contemporary music. The outward events of his life apparently had but little effect on his music. He was largely self-taught in Vienna, and, after a few years in Berlin as a theater conductor, he returned to teach composition, first in Vienna and then in Berlin from 1925 as the successor to Busoni; after 1933, he taught in Paris and then in the United States, first at the University of Southern California and then at the University of California at Los Angeles. He was not a concert performer and was not particularly a pianist. While in quantitative terms, piano works do not form a major portion of his output as a composer, nonetheless they occupy what might be termed a strategic position in his works in that they employ new procedures for the first time that were then extended to other varieties of musical composition. Here, it is the works for piano solo that assume the greatest importance: the three *Klavierstücke* (op. 11) of 1908, the six *Kleine Klavierstücke* (op. 19) of 1911, the five *Klavierstücke* (op. 23) of 1923, and two more *Klavierstücke* (op. 33a and 33b) of 1929 and 1932, the second of which was composed in the United States. Added to these is a single work for organ, the *Variations on a Recitative* (op. 40) of 1940.

By means of the piano works (see also the discussions by Steuermann, Tuttle, Friedberg, and Leibowitz), it is possible to trace the most important stages of Schönberg's evolution as a composer, in which the technical elements of the German Romantic tradition are subjected to a radical revision. It is clear that Schönberg accepted the dominant genre of piano music of this tradition, the character piece; there is but one exception to this, a suite, which represents an isolated instance of Neo-Classicism in his work. Schönberg's early compositions are very much in the Wagner-Mahler vein, especially the massive *Gurrelieder* of 1901, which employs, in addition to large orchestral and vocal forces, the full-blown chromatic idiom of Wagner. Schönberg then began to teach composition in Vienna and to reflect on the conventions of this type of writing with its constant chromaticism and its incessant modulations, which, in his view, undermined the overall tonal unity of a large musical work. From this, he moved to the notion of doing away altogether with the idea of key, of tonality (as he called it, "the suspension of the tonal system") and using constantly "the total resources of chromaticism." Along with this, he called into question traditional views of consonance and dissonance, which are purely relative concepts, and began "the emancipation of the dissonance"; instead of building chords in thirds, he often built them in fourths, as Debussy had also done, and, like Debussy, he used at times the whole-tone scale, which, along with its pronounced coloristic effect, also has the effect of negating the sense of tonality.

Among the earliest works in which this new development may be seen are the three *Klavierstücke* (op. 11). Clearly, they are related to the Romantic character piece and in many respects are not dissimilar to piano pieces of Brahms: the denseness of the textures, the phrases often presented in chords, the lyricism of the thematic material, the contrapuntal detail in the accompaniment, and the types of figuration. But dissonance has indeed been emancipated, and a completely new sound has been achieved. The largest and most Brahmsian of the three is the second piece, which follows a plan not uncommon in the Romantic character piece; there is a lyrical beginning that works up to a passionate climax and then falls off with a restatement of the opening thematic material near the end. With the third piece, Schönberg becomes more individual in that, along with the abandonment of tonal functions, he also abandons, to a large extent, themes, so that the piece, in addition to being atonal, has been described as "athematic" or "theme-less." The second and third pieces exhibit an unusually wide range of dynamics.

In the second group of piano pieces (op. 19), much of the same can be be observed, except that several common features of the character piece have been abandoned: thematic repetition, the use of melodic sequences, and the old set, formal plans. Here, the pieces are extremely short, to the point of being musical aphorisms, so that they can be seen as a reaction against the "long style" of the late nineteenth century. Nonetheless, definite types of piano writing are clearly present. The first piece is rather Impressionistic, with the use of a pedal point as a coloristic device, while bell-like chords appear as an important element in the last piece; a concertato effect of opposing chords is prominent in the third piece, while the fourth, extremely short, abounds in a new kind of purely virtuoso figuration; the fifth is purely cantabile, while the second works chiefly with chords.

Schönberg evidently felt that, although his abandonment of the traditional harmonic system of tonal functions was necessary, it created a void: some other means of establishing order controlling the succession and relationship among musical tones had to be found to replace the old functions of tonality. This attitude may help to explain the extreme brevity of the six pieces (op. 19), as well as of other works composed around the same time. In any case, Schönberg's output as a composer fell off markedly in the years 1915–1923, although he continued his activity as a teacher and theorist (the famous treatise on traditional harmony was written during these years), and he evidently was trying to work things out. Then there appeared the third set of piano pieces (op. 23), which generally seems similar to the two previous sets. Here again is the new sound, the abandonment of the old tonal functions; but many pianistic attributes of the old character piece are retained—the idiomatic types of accompaniment and em-bellishment, chordal passages, and so on. The first of the pieces has been described as a three-part invention, and the second is in small three-part form (see Georgii, *400 Years*, p. 134). But the last piece, a waltz, presents something new, a way of organizing musical tones that was to underlie almost all of Schönberg's subse-quent musical compositions; it is a dodecaphonic serial piece based on a series or tone row, the first work of its kind.

Although this is not the place to present a detailed explanation of serial composition, a brief description is surely in order. Schönberg's own discussion is the lecture, "Composition with Twelve Tones." This system is the outgrowth of his use of the total resources of chromaticism and the abandonment of tonality which, up to then, had served as the principal organizing factor in music. The new method of organization is based on the arbitrary arrangement of all tones of the chromatic scale, an arrangement designed specifically for the particular com-position. This is the series, or row, on which the work is based. Theoretically, each note of the row is to be sounded in order, and the restatements or repetitions of the row make up the elemental material of the piece; no note of the series is to be used a second time until all other notes of the series have been employed. In its original form, the series or row is called "prime." But variations are possible. The series can be transposed to any degree of the chromatic scale, its intervals may be inverted, or the series may be taken in retrograde motion or in the retrograde inversion. Furthermore, the series may be deployed either horizontally (melodically or contrapuntally) or vertically (harmonically). Still other variations can occur: for instance, the series can be segmented, divided into parts, one of which can be used, for example, to provide the raw material of the melody while the other provides the accompaniment. But there are many other possibilities. At least two things seem clear in regard to this new "method of composing with twelve tones." First, although it can be used harmonically, to control the notes in chords and chord progressions, it is primarily a polyphonic and linear device; second, since the series remains the same throughout a composition, even one in several movements, then the old principle of cyclic form with thematic variations is present.

EXAMPLE 78

SCHÖNBERG: *Walzer*, from *Klavierstücke* (op. 23 v)—beginning

A Short History of Keyboard Music

Once the new method had been devised and tried out in a small form, the waltz of op. 23, Schönberg employed it in larger forms. Significantly enough, in piano music, it was not the sonata that drew his attention but rather the suite, an earlier and perhaps smaller form. The suite is a genre associated, in part at least, with contrapuntal procedures, and consisting of a number of small pieces. Schönberg's suite (op. 25), along with the use of serial principle, is also Neo-Classical; its movements, all based on the same series, are all related to Baroque types (prelude, gavotte with a musette as trio, intermezzo, minuet and trio, and gigue). Here, the style is appropriately simple and leaner than in Schönberg's previous piano works, except for the intermezzo which is similar to his earlier character pieces. The prelude, as would be expected, employs largely figuration; the gavotte is contrapuntal and uses a balanced and symmetrical phrase structure, as does also the musette; the gigue is fast but, unlike its eighteenth-century counterpart, does not feature imitation; the lyrical minuet, on the other hand, is a canon with retrograde motion, and such canonic minuets were by no means unknown to the later eighteenth-century (especially Haydn).

The only other piano works of Schönberg are the two character pieces of op. 33, which, in spite of being strict serial compositions, show a return to the earlier kind of piece related to the work of Brahms, as is especially true of the first. It might be that there is some influence here from Schönberg's close friend and disciple Alban Berg, who sought to apply elements of the new methods of organizing tonal relationships to the large and traditional categories of German Romantic music.

Schönberg wrote only one other work for a solo keyboard instrument, the *Variations on a Recitative* for organ (op. 40) of 1940. In some of his later works, he abandoned the principle of serial composition and made a return to an essentially tonal orientation but colored, as always, with much chromaticism. The *Variations on a Recitative* are an example of this, composed in a very free kind of d. The recitative, then, is the theme, after which come ten variations, a cadenza, a fugue, and a coda. The idea of using a recitative for a theme in such a work is most unusual, since, by its very nature, a recitative is in a free form not following any strict formal plan; and whenever it has appeared in keyboard music, as in the toccata and fantasia of the late eighteenth century or Beethoven's piano sonatas, it has served the purpose of enhancing emotional expression. Schönberg's recitative reveals itself upon inspection to be unified by the use of a few characteristic motives, and it is these that are seized upon in the variations that follow. The fugue, since Beethoven a standard number at the close of a set of variations, employs imitation by contrary motion.

It thus appears that Schönberg's piano pieces reflect the various aspects of his development as a composer. What is perhaps most noteworthy is the attitude towards the repertory of keyboard music that had been handed down. The large form of the sonata is completely neglected in favor of the suite as the only large work of piano music; but the chief type of nineteenth-century piano music, the Romantic character piece, is retained as the vehicle for a complete re-organization of the principles of controlling musical tones.

In the work of Schönberg's two closest friends and disciples, Alban Berg and Anton Webern, the problem of old and new becomes especially clear: as Leibowitz has it, while Berg applied the basic elements of Schönberg's work to large expressive types in the Romantic tradition, Webern used them in a completely new and different type of music. Both published but one work for piano. Berg has a sonata (op. 1) of 1906–1908 (revised in 1920), written while he was still under Schönberg's tutelage (there is an earlier theme with twelve variations and finale of 1907, of which Redlich has reproduced Berg's manuscript of the variations); and Webern has a set of variations (op. 27) of 1936. Berg's sonata, which is contemporary with Schönberg's piano pieces (op. 11), is actually a single sonata movement that he finally decided to let stand by itself (he originally planned a three-movement work); it is in sonata form, containing all the elements one would normally expect. But the principle of thematic variation is prominent, and all the themes of the work are derived from what is presented in the first few bars. As with Schönberg's works of the same period, the "total resources of chromaticism" are freely and perpetually employed, although the basic tonality of b is evident. This is a highly expressive work. The phrase structure is clear, melodic sequences are used extensively, and the piece has an expressive ebb and flow much like that found in Wagner or Franck, so that the sonata is more closely related to nineteenth-century conventions than the later works of Schönberg. With Webern's variations, composed much later, we are in a completely different musical realm. The work is divided into three movements, but the whole is based on a single series, so that in over-all form one is reminded more of the sonatina than of variations; but the musical materials and procedures are not what one would associate with either of these genres. The work has been extensively discussed by Leibowitz and Klammer. (The latter restricts his account to the last movement.) The general effect is characteristic of Webern's style, in which extreme brevity (possibly derived from Schönberg's piano pieces, op. 19), sparseness of texture, and the absence of melodic phrases in the usual sense, are most important; here, it is the quality of particular intervals treated individually or even of isolated tones distributed over a wide range of the keyboard that come to the foreground. The usual conception of music, the organizing power of melodic phrases, a dynamic rising and falling, are completely absent; instead, there is a curiously static, suspended, and detached quality, something that we have noted here and there in French Neo-Classicism but never quite the same as appears here. Related to this static effect is a device most important in Webern that is employed constantly in the variations—the mirror canon. Each subsection is so disposed that the latter half is in all respects the mirror image (*Spiegelbild*) of the first, so that the older dynamic element is necessarily gone; the music quite literally "goes" nowhere—it simply is. Much of Webern's music is distinguished by a peculiar fastidiousness in the treatment of tone color, and, in his ensemble works, most unusual combinations are likely to appear. In his later work, there are only two compositions that use a "normal" medium: the variations for piano and the string quartet (op. 28). It is almost as if Webern sought here to purify his music by eliminating the "coloristic" element by the employment of an established and neutral instrumental medium for some of his strictest and most rarefied works.

Roughly contemporary with Schönberg's innovations were the experimentations of Joseph Matthias Hauer (1883–1959), who developed a system of arranging musical notes in set sequences or patterns ("tropes," as he called them), which in some ways resembles the method of Schönberg. But the effect of Hauer's work is completely different from Schönberg's, since the conventional harmonic functions are maintained. For piano, he wrote a number of character pieces and etudes in a manner not dissimilar from the nineteenth-century tradition.

Other German and Austrian composers who have taken up the Schönberg method of composing and have given some attention to keyboard music include the pianist Arthur Schnabel (1882–1951), Egon Wellesz (1885–), Paul Pisk (1893–), Ernst Krenek (1900–), Hans Erich Apostel (1901–), Hanns Jelinek (1901–), Lepold Spinner (1906–), and Hans Werner Henze (1926–). Of these, the most important and productive is Krenek, whose works show here and there traces of all main trends in contemporary music; but, since 1939, he has used the serial method to the exclusion of all others and, in his recent work, has demonstrated an interest in electronic music. Krenek has composed a good deal for keyboard instruments: apart from a single sonata for organ (op. 92 i), it is all for piano. There are six large sonatas, a set of sonatinas, a number of suites of various kinds, sets of character pieces, and variations.

It appears, then, that, generally speaking, a number of fundamental elements of nineteenth-century music were called into question and frequently rejected right from the very beginnings of the twentieth century, in France by the work of Debussy, Ravel, and Satie and in Vienna by the work of Schönberg and his associates. But in France, as well as in Germany and Austria, there were many composers who worked largely in the nineteenth century tradition, and there were still others who retained elements of it but who made certain changes, either of a technical nature or in relation to repertory. It is worth emphasizing that, even in the most "progressive" work of Schönberg and his associates, the actual repertory of keyboard music is not affected. The composers do not invent new formal types to go along with their new musical idiom; rather, they work with genres that have come down from the past.

CHAPTER ELEVEN

Keyboard Music of the Twentieth Century in the Other Countries of Europe and in the New World

U p to now, in the consideration of keyboard music in the twentieth century, we have limited ourselves to the countries that led in the development of nineteenth-century music and have seen the changes that took place with respect to this tradition. There is, however, another most important source of twentieth-century music, one that often stands in close relationship to the two that have been discussed and, yet, in other ways, is the direct outgrowth of the nineteenth century. This is nationalistic music. We have seen how, in the nineteenth century, the national schools grew up in various European countries—especially Bohemia, Russia, and Scandinavia—frequently rejecting the standard German forms and instead consciously drawing upon the idioms of their own native music; and, often, these folk themes would be used in connection with a large-scale instrumental composition. The continuation of these and other national schools has formed an important element in twentieth-century music and from them have emerged some of the greatest twentieth-century composers.

Perhaps the most important national school for twentieth-century keyboard music came out of Hungary. In the nineteenth century, Hungarian folk music, of one sort or another, had been exploited by Liszt as well as in a large number of so-called Hungarian dances by various composers, Brahms among them (Russia was important in other music). But Hungary did not produce any composer of real stature who was essentially involved with the national music of the country. Most Hungarian composers were trained in Germany and remained true to the ideals of the grand tradition; among these we can mention Istvan Thomán (1862–1940), Theodor Szántó (1877–1934), Albert Siklós (1878–1942), and Ernst (originally Erno) von Dohnányi (1877–1960), all of whom composed many

415

piano works, some tinged with Hungarian national features but most in the manner of Brahms and Reger. Szántó attracts some special interest for his *Essays and Studies* based on Japanese music, composed for piano between 1918 and 1922.

Nonetheless, out of this emerged one of the most powerful musical talents of the twentieth century, Béla Bartók (1881–1945), who devoted himself not only to the piano and composition, but also to the systematic and scientific study of Hungarian (and other) folk music (see Stevens). In this, Bartók is something like Liszt; he was a virtuoso pianist himself, and piano music is basic to his composition, a statement that can be made of few others among the outstanding contemporary composers. Indeed, it has been demonstrated by Moreux and Null that essentially pianistic procedures underlie much of his work in other media. It is also noteworthy that his composition for piano solo (exclusive of the concertos) ceased after 1926.

Bartók was trained at the Conservatory in Budapest, and his earlier compositions reveal the customary orientation towards the German Romantic tradition; among the unpublished early piano pieces are a sonata and a few character pieces, especially the set of four composed in 1903. In 1905, he commenced his work with Zoltán Kodály on Hungarian folk music, which began with field trips to various parts of the country collecting native tunes, work that was carried out in the summers; he also went on similar expeditions to neighboring countries, even going as far afield as Africa. From 1907, he was professor of piano at the Budapest Conservatory (he never taught composition); from 1912, he largely abandoned his work as a concert pianist and devoted himself to teaching, composition, and the study of Hungarian folk music, although, in 1937, he presented some recitals of early keyboard music. In 1934, he abandoned teaching and gave himself wholly—apart from composition—to researches in folk music. In 1940, he was forced to leave Hungary; he came to the United States, and, apart from some work in folk music at Columbia University, spent his last years in New York in poverty. As with Schubert, it was shortly after his death that interest in his work grew, and his true stature became apparent.

What is perhaps most noteworthy is the all-pervading influence of Hungarian folk music on his musical composition, even and most particularly on his organization of musical materials. Not only are there simple transcriptions and arrangements of folk songs and dances for the piano, but the very thematic stuff and way of writing in his larger works is permeated with the idiom, the melodic types, phrase patterns, rhythms, and instrumental color of Hungarian native music (see Weissman).

The direct transcriptions and arrangements for piano are for the most part simple and unassuming pieces of small proportions. Here, the composer stands back and presents the folk tunes direct and unadorned. The most important among these are the six *Rumanian Folk Dances* (op. 8a) of 1908–1909, the fifteen *Hungarian Peasant Songs* of 1914–1917, and the two sets of *Rumanian Christmas Songs* of 1915. The *Hungarian Peasant Songs* go back to melodies collected by Bartók on his field trips, and several of them reveal features that became important in his later and larger works. There is the slow, declamatory type (the so-called "parlando-rubato" type) and the rapid, dance type using ostinato rhythmic figures (the so-called "tempo giusto" type), both of which may also present a drone bass and driving insistent rhythms, as is particularly seen in the last work of the set. The central piece, however, is the *Ballad*, much longer than the others and in theme and variations form. We have already discussed various kinds of ballads for piano and pieces of other sorts related to narrative or epic poetry in the work of Liszt and Chopin and have seen that the strophic form of poetry frequently produces a sort of variation in its purely musical equivalent, as is also true here.

Two other sets of Bartók's arrangements of folk music are more elaborate in that the folk melodies are used to form larger musical entities: the three *Rondos on Hungarian Folk Tunes* of 1916 and 1927 and the seven *Improvisations on Hungarian Peasant Songs* (op. 20) of 1920. The first of the rondos is in straight-forward rondo form with two episodes that are simple and lyrical; the other two were composed ten years later and are much more "uncompromising" in their complexity of texture, use of dissonance, and driving rhythms. The improvisations (note the use of Grieg's title) again are not simple settings, but real artistic works based on folk melodies, and many features of Bartók's advanced style may be seen in them. In the slow, lyrical piece with modal harmonies, there is the prominent melodic use of the tritone, once as the interval of canonic imitation; polytonality is also employed; in the fast, vigorous dance type, there are ostinato figures and highly percussive chords, with second chords played *forte* on the extreme upper or lower register of the piano. (See the selections in *HMS*, X, s. 3, b. 3.)

In Bartók's character pieces—which, for the most part, appear as sets or even as suites—we find that the old form has been infused with a totally new sound, much as is true, in widely differing ways, in the work of Debussy and Schönberg. In the early pieces of 1903, we still find the German Romantic tradition dominant, especially as it appeared in the work of Liszt. This remains true of the two *Elegies* (op. 8b) of 1908–1909, a type we have also encountered in the work of Liszt. These are large and rather rhetorical pieces with expressive unaccompanied recitative-like phrases, even allowing for improvisation by the player, and loud, dissonant chords and coloristic pedal effects. The second elegy shows Bartók's characteristic economy of thematic material, based as it is on a five-note motive. Similar but shorter are the four *Nenies*, or *Dirges*, of 1910. In the three *Burlesques* (op. 8c) of 1908–1911, Bartók's use of Hungarian peasant melodies makes its full appearance in the polytonality of *Quarrel* and the orna-mental lyric of the *Molto vivo*. In the *Sketches* (op. 9), a set of seven small character pieces, the folk elements are even more explicit; there is a *Rumanian Folk Song* and a piece *In Wallachian Style*, while the *Lento*, with its ornate, rhapsodic melodic line, and the concluding two-voice *Poco lento* are related also to the declamatory type of folk melody. The first piece of the set, *Portrait of a Girl*, has some affinity with Debussy's *La fille aux cheveux de lin* from Book I of the *Préludes*. Then comes an explosive work that is symptomatic—indeed, almost programmatic—of much of Bartók's future work, a sudden violent breakthrough, the famous *Allegro barbaro* of 1911. It is a frenetic dance featuring driving rhythms, insistent ostinato patterns, and sharp, percussive, dissonant chords; the melodic structure, the short balanced phrases, and the use of the tritone point to the folk background of the work. There is indeed something primitive and elemental about this work, and it represents a type that Bartók was to use frequently in his composition. (It might be mentioned that the French virtuoso pianist Alkan has a similar work, composed around 1850; see Sietz.)

The two remaining sets of character pieces are designed to be performed as entities: a Suite (op. 14) of 1916 and the group of pieces *Out of Doors* of 1926.

EXAMPLE 79

BARTÓK: *Allegro barbaro*—beginning

In the suite, the folk elements are prominent, as in the opening Allegretto in simple three-part form or the fast second and third pieces that feature dyads and rapid, irregular ostinato patterns, while the last piece, Sostenuto, is intensely lyric and dissonant, in some respects an Impressionistic work. *Out of Doors* is an example of Bartók at his most fully developed and uncompromising stage. Loud, fast, and percussive are the opening and closing numbers, *With Drums and Pipes* and *The Chase*; the *Barcarolle* (ii) has a folk-like melody over an arpeggiated accompaniment but is sparse in texture, an up-dated gondola song; *Musettes* is an example of Bartók's bagpipe music, with long, held chords and a drone effect. Perhaps the most notable piece here is the fourth, *Musiques nocturnes* (*Music of the Night*), a Lento; this is not the usual kind of nocturne, but rather a musical representation of the sounds of a night in the Hungarian countryside; it is a study in sonorities, with a slow, steady, throbbing arpeggiated chord in the accompaniment, isolated notes, chords, short scale runs, and so on, occurring seemingly at random, and then a mournful folk-like melody in two voices three octaves apart. This is the first appearance in Bartók's music of a musical type that was to figure prominently in subsequent compositions: the *Music for Strings, Percussion, and Celesta*, the Fourth and Fifth String Quartets, and the Third Piano Concerto.

Of the old genres of so-called "absolute" music, Bartók wrote for piano only two works, the *Sonatina Based on Transylvanian Folk Tunes* of 1915 and a Sonata of 1926. But the sonatina, since it is made up of three character pieces, does not greatly resemble what one usually thinks of as a sonatina. While the first movement, *Bagpipes*, is another example of this genre in Bartók's work, the *Bear Dance* is short and simple and not at all as violent as one might expect, and the *Finale* is a typical Hungarian fast dance that shows the parallel phrase structure in the melody and much use of figuration. The sonata, on the other hand, is a large composition, the only one among the piano works that can rank with Bartók's major works in other media, as the string quartets, with which it has much in common. For here, alone among the piano works, we can see how the traditional forms and formal plan of the sonata are re-interpreted with elements from Hungarian folk music, which affects not only the thematic material, but also the very way of writing for the piano, the conception of the instrument as a musical medium. There are three movements: the first is an Allegro moderato in sonata form, then a Sostenuto e pesante in simple three-part form, and finally an Allegro molto in rondo form with thematic variation. The first movement immediately establishes the tone of the piece. There are the steady pounding chords in the bass, the motivic theme with its repeated notes and its upbeat character treated contrapuntally, the irregular accentuations, the continuous unfolding of the thematic material, all percussive and all very dissonant; in the development, the principal theme is presented in variation, and downwardly arpeggiated "strumming" chords produce a new kind of sound; the recapitulation commences in the "wrong" key, and there is a short coda. The slow movement is a dirge. There is a slow-moving and dense series of chords against which is a melody of long repeated notes; the harmonies involve polytonality. The finale is a fast dance, again displaying irregular and driving rhythm with tone clusters used percussively. In this work, there are no real folk melodies used: it is simply that the folk idiom has been so completely absorbed by the composer that it permeates the whole work. A striking new way of making the piano sound is one of the results of this. Yet, along with it goes a concern for musical structure and extreme economy of means, so that the composer works with a few basic raw materials—themes, very motivic in nature, that are varied and combined to produce the larger artistic entity—in a manner not essentially different from that of Haydn or Beethoven. All in all, this sonata, which unfortunately has been unduly neglected, must rank as one of the major works of contemporary piano music.

A final and very important group among Bartók's piano compositions are pieces for teaching purposes. Typical of his big virtuoso manner are the studies of 1918, the direct descendant of the nineteenth-century concert etude. More unusual is the large body of music for children. Here, while pianistic technique is simplified, none of the compositional approach is sacrificed; that is to say, the features that characterize Bartók's larger works also are found in the children's pieces, which makes them an excellent introduction to contemporary music, in addition to their value as a means of developing facility in playing the piano. Bartók's pieces of this kind are the ten *Easy Pieces* of 1908; the four volumes *For Children* of 1908 and 1909, which contain in all eighty-five pieces; and *The First Term at the Piano* of 1911, with eighteen pieces; and the nine *Little Piano Pieces* of 1926. The *Easy Pieces*, ten small works preceded by an introductory dedication, reveal the essential features of Bartók's conception of teaching pieces. They are miniatures in the nineteenth-century sense but use elements from Hungarian peasant music, as in the *Peasant Song*, the *Slovakian Boy's Dance*, the two folk songs, and, particularly, the *Bear Dance*, which, on a smaller scale, is the typical fast, frenetic dance with the simple melody in chords, the strong rhythmic element with rapidly repeated notes, and the percussive treatment of the instrument. Related rather to Impressionism is *Dawn*, while *Etude* is an outspoken— and perhaps also satirical—finger exercise of scale segments with an insistent accompaniment. *For Children* consists entirely of pieces based on folk music, Hungarian in the first volume and Slovakian in the second. Noteworthy in the first volume is the dissonantly harmonized chorale, which immediately suggests both Satie and Stravinsky. The *Little Piano Pieces*, although contemporary with Bartók's large works for piano—the sonata and *Out of Doors*—are still simple children's pieces, with a touch of the Neo-Classical idiom about them. The first four, called *Dialogues*, are short, two-voice, imitative compositions; then comes a minuet, an air, a march (called *delle bestie*), *Tambourine*, and, last, *Preludio all'ungherese.* All these dances have been strongly "Hungarianized" by the use of percussive harmonic sounds, irregular rhythms, the prominence of the tritone, and contrapuntal passages.

But Bartók's most comprehensive work of this kind is the *Mikrokosmos,* a complete progressive course in piano technique consisting of 153 pieces in six books, written from 1926 to 1937, ranging from extremely simple one- and two-voice pieces in the early books to very difficult works in the last few books (see Engelmann, Uhde, and Bernary). In its all-inclusiveness, virtually all of Bartók's devices and ways of writing may be found, so that the *Mikrokosmos,* more than the other teaching pieces, may be looked upon as a compendium of Bartók's music as well as of many devices that have become the common property of contemporary music. The following may be cited as illustrations of this comprehensiveness. As instances of the use of unusual scales, there is: among the modes, the Dorian (xxv and xxxii), the Phrygian (xxxiv), the Lydian (xxxvii and lv, to name only the most obvious), the Mixolydian (xlviii); of others, the pentatonic (lxi and lxxviii), the whole-tone (cxxxvi), and what Bartók describes simply as "Oriental" (lviii). Of new practices in harmony, there are many examples of polytonality, such as *Melody Against Double Notes* (lxx), *Two Major Pentachords* (lxxxvi), *Playsong* (two pentatonic scales, cv), *Clashing Sounds* (cx), *Boating* (cxxv), and the pictorial *From the Diary of a Fly* (cxlii); harmonics are exploited in *Harmonics* (cii), and tone clusters dominate *Melody in the Mist* (cvii); constant modulation is the subject of *Through the Keys* (civ), and a number of pieces involve the opposition between major and minor scales in the same tonality (lix, ciii–cxxxii, cxl, cxlii, cxliv, cxlvi). Bartók's manner of handling contrapuntal elements can be seen from a number of pieces: imitation (xxii, xxiii, xxix, xxx), canon (xxv, xxviii), and the dance canon (xxxi); then there is the more elaborate *Subject and Reflection* (cxli) and *Chromatic Invention* (cxlv) in two parts to be played separately or together on two pianos. Complex rhythmic procedures are to be seen in *The Scherzo* (lxxxii) and *Change of Time* (cxxvi), both of which feature constant change of time signature; *Syncopation* (cxxxiii); *Free Variations* (cxl), and the *Bulgarian Dances* (see below). There are also many pieces in one or another of the national styles. Hungarian (xlii, lxviii for two pianos, lxxiv), Yugoslavian (xl), Transylvanian (liii), Russian (xc), and even Balinese (cix), the last with an eye on Debussy's *Pagodes.* A large and important group here are the dances in Bulgarian rhythm, which is an irregular alternation between rapid duple and triple, expressed in time signatures like $\frac{423}{8}$, $\frac{223}{8}$, $\frac{323}{8}$, $\frac{332}{8}$; these rank among the most brilliant and difficult pieces in the entire work.

Naturally, such an enumeration of isolated elements and procedures serves largely as a catalogue of much that can be found in the *Mikrokosmos* without affording any sort of indication as to the extraordinary combinations, the new and characteristic sonorities, that often result. It can well be maintained that this work is the greatest single achievement in the realm of progressive piano courses, particularly distinguished in the easy pieces for beginners.

Bartók's general approach to musical composition has several similarities with that of Debussy and Ravel. The accepted means of organizing musical sounds has been questioned, and new procedures are sought with models taken from various sources. In Debussy and Ravel, the models were exotic (Oriental music) or from popular music of different kinds, while Bartók drew on the native peasant music of his own region. All three worked mainly with the character piece handed down from the nineteenth century, to the relative neglect of the larger forms of piano music. All three have much of the Neo-Classical about them, although, in Bartók, it appears in a different manner since the old forms connected with the eighteenth-century harpsichord suite are not very prominent (they appear only in the *Little Pieces* of 1926); but there is the emphasis on imitative counterpoint and the driving, consistent rhythms. At the same time, in Debussy, Ravel, and Satie there is an "objective" and static kind of music, whereas, in Bartók, the organizing force of tonality and of driving rhythmic arrangements is much stronger. In the parlance of jazz, while the Impressionist ideal is "cool," Bartók is almost entirely "hot." It is also clear that there is a principal difference between Bartók and the Impressionists, on the one hand, and Schönberg and his colleagues, on the other; while Schönberg may in many ways be looked upon as carrying logically to a final point basic harmonic conceptions of traditional music, Bartók and the Impressionists take a completely different point of departure by drawing on foreign conceptions in the light of which they carry out far-reaching new ways of organizing music.

Bartók clearly is the most important figure in Hungarian music, and probably the oustanding representative of a specific nationalist style in all of twentieth-century music. This is in some measure to be attributed to his studies in folk music, something most unusual to find among the preoccupations of a pianist and composer. But the similar combination of talents and interests that we find in his colleague Zoltán Kodály (1882–) did not produce results of nearly the same artistic quality. It was actually Kodály who interested Bartók in the study of folk music; and, unlike Bartók, Kodály actually earned a Ph.D. in the subject, with a dissertation on strophic forms in Hungarian folk music (1906). But Kodály, who was also trained in Budapest, spent a period in Paris where he studied with Widor and came under a certain French influence, especially of the Impressionists, and this tempers the strength of native Hungarian elements in his musical composition. Also unlike Bartók, Kodály has composed relatively little for piano, giving emphasis instead to choral music. But, in that little, it is the character piece that is dominant, and the Impressionistic basis is clear from the early *Méditations* of 1907, the nine pieces (op. 3) of 1909–1910, and the *Zungara-*

muzsika (Gypsy Music, op. 11), seven pieces composed in 1910 and 1918. Kodály also wrote some organ music—a prelude to *Pange lingua* and an organ Mass of 1942 that he subsequently arranged for chorus and orchestra.

Other Hungarian composers of lesser significance are Tibor Harsányi (1898–1954), Jenö Takács (1902–), Miklos Rosza (1907–), and Matyas Seiber (1905–1963). No one of them remained in Hungary. Harsányi settled in France, and in his work there appear many elements of French music (Impressionism, Neo-Classicism, and jazz); Takács has lived in Egypt, the Philippines, and the United States; Rosza, who has composed pieces much in the nineteenth-century tradition—a set of variations, a sonata (op. 21), and character pieces, especially *Kaleidoscope*—has for some years been in Hollywood, California; Seiber, who lived in England, has, like Harsányi, drawn on many different elements of contemporary music, the Magyar (like Bartók), the Neo-Classical, jazz, and even Schönberg's dodecaphonic serialism.

The leading national school of Europe in the nineteenth century, the Bohemian or Czechoslovakian, continued its existence in the twentieth century represented by composers such as Karel Strecker (1861–1918), Viteslav Novak (1870–1949), Joseph Suk (1874–1935), Josef Jiránek (1855–1940), and Rudolf Karel (1880–1945). The example of Dvořák loomed very large, especially in the work of Novak who was his pupil and Suk who was his step-son. Although Suk stressed Romantic and nationalistic character pieces, Novak's output in piano music is comprehensive and, in range, much like that of a nineteenth-century composer in the German tradition. There is a large programmatic *Sonata eroica* (op. 24) of 1900, six sonatinas and a set of variations on a theme of Schumann of 1893, and a number of suites; and there are character pieces, both large, like the ballade *Manfred* after Byron (op. 2) of 1893, and small, like the *Bagatelles* (op. 5) of 1899, the *Barcarolles* (op. 10) of 1896, the *Souvenirs* (op. 6) of 1894, and the *Éclogues* (op. 11) of 1896, a genre long associated with Bohemian music (Tomášek and Dvořák), as well as *Twilight* (op. 13) of 1896 and the cyclical suite *Songs of Winter Nights* (op. 30) of 1903; there are also arrangements of folk dances and children's pieces, in *Youth* (op. 55) of 1921; finally, there is a single late set of organ pieces, *Triptych* (op. 70) of 1941, arranged the following year for orchestra.

Three of the most important among recent Czech composers are Leos Janáčck (1854–1928), Bohuslav Martinů (1890–1959), and Alois Hába (1893–). The situation of Janáček is most unusual in that he passed many years in quiet and retiring work suddenly to burst on the scene via the opera in 1916, and, almost overnight, he became the country's leading composer. Like the Impressionists, Bartók, and Schönberg, he proposed new ways of organizing music, which he expressed in two treatises, one on the composition of chords and their progressions and the other a complete treatise on harmony. Although remaining essentially within the chromatic but still tonal late nineteenth-century harmonic idiom, Janáček introduced a few novel features. He believed that the progression from key to key was dependent on the speed and rhythm of a piece and the consequent ability of the ear to perceive the changes. Tonality in his work became "fluid," as he put it, avoiding the conventional cadences; in his later work, he even abandoned key signatures. In a piece, he would work with a few basic motives that, by a process of continuous variation, provided the thematic material of the whole work. Janáček wrote only a little piano music: an early set of variations; three sets of character pieces—*Hudba ke krouženi kužely* (*Music for Swinging Indian Clubs*) of 1895, *Po zarostlém chodničke* (*By the Overgrown Tracks*) in two sets of 1902 and 1908, and *V mlhach* (*In the Mist*) of 1912; and a programmatic sonata called *I. X. 1905* and *Z ulice* of 1924 in two movements, *Předtucha* (*Foreboding*) and *Smrt* (*Death*), two earlier sonatas having been lost. There is also a set of dances and two large concert works for organ of 1894.

In some contrast is Bohuslav Martinů, a pupil of Suk, who has lived and worked in Paris where he was influenced by Roussel, in the United States, and in Prague. His large output includes much piano music in which it is largely French conceptions that dominate over those of his native folk music. This is evident from his strong bent towards the Neo-Classical, as in the preludes for piano of 1930 and for harpsichord of 1935, along with *Les Ritournelles* of 1933 and *Fantaisie et rondo* of 1940. Even the dances show this French background, as in the *Esquisses de danse* of 1932 and the *Mazurka* of 1940, although there are the earlier *Danses tscheques* of 1925 and the *Études et polkas*, in three sets, of 1944.

Hába, a pupil of Novak and Schreker, has become known for his work with quarter-tone music, for which he designed a special piano. His keyboard works, which form an important part of his output, are in two groups, those in the semitone system (normal scale system) and those in the quarter-tone system. The genres represented in the form are varied. There is a fugue suite, variations on a canon of Schumann, several character pieces, a sonata, and a *Toccata quasi una fantasia*; in the quarter-tone system, there are mainly two kinds, suites and fantasias, and one sonata. For a specially constructed harmonium, there is a set of pieces in the sixth-tone system; and there are also two organ compositions. In any case, Hába does not represent any movement of significant proportions in Czechoslovakian music.

The Russian national school, like the Hungarian, has lived on to become one of the most important in contemporary music (see, generally, Laux). As we have seen, there were two principal elements in Russian musical life of the nineteenth century: the intensely nationalistic anti-Western group headed by "the Five" and those composers who preferred to work in the Western or rather, Germanic, tradition. This latter group was plainly in the majority, and among the composers to be listed here are Vassilii Il'ich Safanov (1852–1918), Sergei Taneyev (1850–1918), Vladimir Rebikov (1866–1920), and Vassilii Sapelnikov (1868–

1941). While Safanov and Rebikov studied in Germany (Safanov with Leschetizky in Vienna), Sapelnikov spent much of his life there; Taneyev and Rebikov were trained in Russia under Rubinstein and Chaikovskiĭ. Among these, only Rebikov made extensive contributions to piano music and this largely in the area of the character piece; in his works after 1900, there is a tendency towards experimentation, somewhat in the manner of Debussy, and we find coloristic use of dissonances, the use of the whole-tone scale and chords built in fourths, and so on. Striking are those pieces with psychological overtones, as in his op. 22, 24, and 25, a quality also found in Musorgskiĭ before him.

Two leading contemporaries of these composers are Alexander Skriabin (1872–1915) and Sergei Rachmaninoff (1873–1943), both of whom were closely related to Western music. Both made reputations first and foremost as pianists. Skriabin, however, is notable as an innovator in Russian music in the first decades of the twentieth century not only for his rapprochement with procedures of French Impressionism, but also for his preoccupation with theosophy, an Oriental occult religion that envisions man as ascending through several reincarnations towards ever higher spiritual spheres, with art the ideal reflection of this ascent. The result was his effort towards the achievement of a universal art work in which, among much else, the Impressionist notion of synesthesia, the correspondence between colors and musical tones, makes its appearance. His theosophical ideas led him to work out a mystic chord that supposedly was related to these higher levels of spiritual existence. The chord, however, was developed from wholly rationalistic principles: it consists of the upper partials of the note C, which are disposed in fifths, resulting in the chord C—F-sharp—B-flat—E—A—D. (The twelfth and fifteenth partials, G and B, are omitted.) Along with this, in later works, he developed a duodecuple scale, actually the full twelve-tone chromatic scale with all notes a semitone apart, but, except for the tonic, all notes have the same significance.

In his earlier compositions, Skriabin (see Montagu-Nathan and Hull) was greatly under the influence of Chopin from whom he took the genre of the prelude, which appears most importantly among his character pieces; but there are also polonaises, mazurkas (op. 3, 25, 40), impromptus (op. 10, 12, 14), nocturnes (op. 5), and etudes (op. 8, 42, 65). Later, he developed a large form of character piece, the poem, many of which have such characteristic titles as the *Tragic Poem* (op. 34), the *Satanic Poem* (op. 36), or the well-known *Poème vers la flamme* (op. 72), a theosophically inspired work; but others lack these titles. Typical is the poem *Étrangeté* (op. 63 ii) built on fourth chords (*HMS*, X, s. 1, b. 5). The preludes afford a notable opportunity for tracing Skriabin's stylistic development, since the series begins early in his career and continues right up to the end. They commence with a set of twenty-four (op. 11) that resemble those of Chopin, but, in the later preludes, Skriabin became more experimental (see Dickenmann), the harmonies rather adventurous (many of these late preludes lack key signatures), and those of op. 48, 67, and 74 contain some remarkable compositions. (For the Prelude in C, op. 48 ii, see *HMS*, X, s. 1, b. 4.) But this also holds for the piano pieces. (See the *Danse languide* in G, op. 51 iv, in Georgii, *400 Years*, p. 129). Skriabin also wrote a notable prelude and nocturne for left hand alone (op. 9).

Skriabin's work in the large form of piano music is seen in the ten sonatas: f (op. 6) of 1832; g-sharp (op. 19) of 1892–1897, called *Sonata-fantasia*; f-sharp (op. 23) of 1897, called *État d'âme (State of Soul)*; F-sharp (op. 30) of 1903; F-sharp (op. 53) of 1908; G (op. 62) of 1911–1912; F-sharp (op. 64) of 1911, called *The White Mass*; A (op. 66) of 1913; F (op. 68) of 1913, called *The Black Mass*; and C (op. 70) of 1913. All of these are Romantic, programmatic sonatas, related to theosophy, as can be seen from the Sonata in f-sharp (op. 23). First, the soul is cast into a sea of strife; second, the soul flounders in its own motion; third, there is illusory and transient rest; fourth, there is the ecstasy of the struggle. Another example is the Sonata in F-sharp (op. 53) with its motto, "I call you to life / O mysterious forces / Submerged in depths obscure / O thou creative spirit, / Timid embryons of life / To you I now bring courage" (see Hull). The manifestation of the mode of ecstasy is perhaps Skriabin's central aim, one that, apart from the religious aspects, is by no means unknown to the German tradition of Romantic music. Here, it is accomplished in large-scale compositions, the earlier of which are conventionally divided into several movements but the later of which are long sectional works. Frequently, individual themes stand for elements of the program, and the sonata becomes a large cyclic work that is nothing else but a symphonic poem for piano, again something not unknown to Western Romantic music. Along with the rhetorical-ecstatic element goes a concentration on technical display and the employment of lavish harmonies. The combination makes these sonatas highly individual and, in some ways, rather extreme compositions.

In contrast to Skriabin, Rachmaninoff remained throughout his life and in all respects a Romantic composer, never departing from the German tradition handed down from the nineteenth-century; the influence of Chaikovskii particularly, but also that of Liszt and Chopin, dominated his entire work as a composer. The character piece is most numerous in his work. There are five (op. 3) of 1892, seven (op. 10) of 1894, six *Moments musicaux* (op. 16) of 1896, two sets of preludes, ten (op. 23) of 1903–1904 and thirteen (op. 32) of 1910. (The popular Prelude in c-sharp is among the piano pieces, op. 3 ii.) Emphasizing virtuosity are characteristic etudes, called *Études-tableaux*, in two sets, six (op. 33) of 1911 and nine (op. 39) of 1916–1917. As for the large forms of piano music, again Rachmaninoff remained Romantic. There are two sets of themes and variations, one on a theme of Chopin (op. 22)—the theme being the Prelude in C (op. 28 xx)—and the other, a much later work, on a theme of Corelli (op. 42), the famous *Folia* theme; there are also two piano sonatas, in d (op. 28) of 1907 and b-flat (op. 36) of 1913. Other large works are the two suites for two pianos, the first, called *Fantasy* (op. 5) of 1893 and the second (op. 17) of 1901. There is also a set of six piano duets (op. 11) of 1894 consisting of smaller pieces.

Decisive for the history of Russian music was, of course, the revolution of 1917. Naturally, many of the wealthier Russian composers fled to live elsewhere; for those that remained or returned in later years, their artistic production had to submit to standards established by the government. Rachmaninoff was one of those who never returned to Russia after the revolution. Others who left the country include Nikolai Medtner (1880–1951), Isaay Dobrowen (1894–1953), and the two Cherepnin brothers, Nikolai (1873–1945) and Alexander (1899–). All of them made contributions to piano music; Medtner and Dobrowen have written sonatas and character pieces (Medtner composed some twelve sonatas, much in the nineteenth-century manner; for an account of the one in g, op. 22, see Truscott; see also Gerstlé), while Alexander Cherepnin, apart from these conventional genres, has also worked with folk music from his native province of Georgia.

By all odds, the outstanding among the expatriate Russian composers is Igor Stravinsky (1882–), whose works have had a profound effect on all contemporary music. His innovations commenced with the three celebrated ballets for the *Ballet Russe* in Paris (under the artistic direction of Serge Diaghilev) and have continued ever since. In the 1920's, he took up the French Neo-Classical style, and, of late, he has adopted the serial methods of Schönberg and his successors; but all have been shaped and stamped with his own individuality. By and large, Stravinsky has neglected the keyboard medium; although a concert pianist himself, he has composed but a handful of works for the instrument and nothing at all for the organ. As small works for piano solo, we can record only the early set of four *Studies* of 1908; the *Etude* for player piano of 1917; the *Piano Rag Music* of 1917, an exercise in the jazz idiom that was so common in France at the time; and the *Tango* of 1940, which was later orchestrated. As for larger works, there are two strongly Neo-Classical works from the 1920's, the sonata of 1924 (there is a much earlier sonata of 1903–1904) and the Serenade in A of 1925, the latter composed on commission from a recording company, the stipulation being that each movement fit on a single side of a twelve-inch disc. Both works indeed go back to eighteenth-century models, the sonata a small and objective work and the serenade rather freely related to the old divertimento. The sonata, in three movements in the old succession (Fast—Slow, marked "Adagietto"—Fast), employs the usual forms for the individual movements: a small sonata form with an insignificant development (what is often called sonatina form); as slow movement, a florid melody in simple ternary form, much like the old *da capo* aria; and a driving, toccata-like finale in rondo form (with two episodes each stated but once). All in all, it is a very *sec* (dry) composition featuring the continuously driving rhythms and figuration patterns so characteristic of Baroque music; even at the beginning of the first movement, the principal theme appears in thirds over the dissonant, rapidly moving figuration of the accompaniment. The Serenade in A reveals similar features, but its succession of movements and forms does not follow any particular model: a ceremonial *Hymne*, a *Romanza*, a *Rondoletta*, and a quiet *Cadenza finale*. For all their dryness and impersonal quality, these works are fully worthy of Stravinsky and completely representative of an important part of his work, so that, along with their purely musical merits, they surely deserve to be played more frequently than is presently the case.

Stravinsky has also composed music for piano duet and two pianos. For the former, there are easy pieces, a set of three written in 1915 and another set of five

EXAMPLE 80

STRAVINSKY: First movement, from *Sonata*—beginning

dating from 1917 that contains certain characteristic types (polka, march, waltz, *española*, *napolitana*, and *galop*, among others). Here, one part has been kept easy (for the pupil), while the other provides a good deal of rhythmic elaboration. For two pianos, there are the *Concerto per due pianoforte soli* of 1935 and a sonata of 1943–1944. The latter, in style not dissimilar to the earlier Serenade in A, consists of three movements, a Moderato, a theme with four variations, and a concluding Allegretto; it is on a small scale, Neo-Classical, and in what Stravinsky himself, in his *Dialogues and a Diary*, has described as a "linear contrapuntal style." The concerto, on the other hand, takes its place among his largest instrumental compositions. It is, as he says, a "large-scale symphonic piece . . . of orchestral volumes and proportions," which he composed to serve as a "vehicle for concert tours in orchestra-less cities," played by himself and his son Soulima. It is, as he also says, the "favorite child among my purely instrumental pieces." Indeed, the concerto is of the same family as the large instrumental works of the 1930's and 1940's, resembling especially the *Symphony in Three Movements*. Its four movements are a vigorous percussive Con moto that is sectional in a sort of sonata form, a lyrical *Notturno* of the *romanza* type, a theme and four variations, which is followed without pause by a short prelude and an elaborate fugue. Again, the driving rhythmic figuration of Baroque music is prominent, along with the sharply delineated motivic themes; this quality comes to the fore in the fugue, with an insistent, rapidly repeated note figure as the countersubject; the fugue also features inversion. Without a doubt, this concerto is Stravinsky's *magnum opus* of keyboard music.

The composers who have lived in the Soviet Union have had to contend with and conform to the artistic regulation of the Communist Party, which, on several occasions, has affirmed the aesthetics of art for the people, or "Socialist Realism"; this, by and large, means that the manner of Chaikovskii and of "the Five" is to be taken as the model and that Western influences, especially the innovations of the early decades of the twentieth century, are to be shunned as "formalistic" and "decadent." Among a great many composers we may mention, apart from Prokofiev and Shostakovich, are Nikolai Miaskovskii (1881–1950, Samuel Feinberg (1890–), Dimitri Kabalevskii (1904–), and Aram Khachaturian (1904–). Miaskovskii, an astonishingly productive composer with a number of sonatas and character pieces in an outspokenly nineteenth-century Romantic manner, was among the most wholehearted supporters of Soviet official music. Feinberg is more progressive showing some relation to the work of Skriabin and concentrating on the piano sonata. Nationalistic elements are stressed in the work of Kabalevskii and Khachaturian (the latter's toccata being a notable piece in a sort of Neo-Baroque manner).

Perhaps the outstanding among Soviet composers is Sergei Prokofiev (1891–1953). Unlike many of his colleagues, Prokofiev spent a good deal of his life abroad, first in the United States and then in Paris in the years after the First

World War, where he aroused attention as a virtuoso pianist and as a progressive and daring composer greatly under the influence of developments taking place in France at that time (see Nestyev). When he returned to the Soviet Union in 1933, it was by free choice; and, perhaps because of the many influences to which he had been exposed, his music frequently prompted severe criticism from the authorities.

In an autobiographical sketch, Prokofiev once itemized the five principal elements in his musical composition: (1) the Classical, related specifically to Beethoven's piano sonatas; (2) the search for innovation, seeking a new harmonic idiom for strong emotional expression; (3) the toccata or motor element, the use of insistently repeated rhythmic patterns; (4) the lyrical; (5) the satirical or grotesque, which he preferred to qualify as "scherzo-ness, jest, laughter, mockery." His statements on aesthetic matters, given in newspaper interviews, invariably emphasize his striving for simple melodic expression ("All my work is founded on melodies") and for the proper subordinate position of dissonance within an essentially tonal orientation. Yet, his interest in innovation led him to employ not only dissonance in the creation of most unusual harmonies, usually coupled with intensely lyrical melodies, but also to treat the piano as a percussive instrument; the combination of these with the toccata style is one of his most characteristic ways of writing.

All of this appears in rather conventional types of piano music (he did not compose for organ) handed down from the nineteenth century. Most prominent are the character pieces, issued both individually and in sets. The first three groups—a set of four pieces (op. 3) of 1907–1908 (dates refer to composition), another set of four (op. 4) of 1910–1912, and a set of ten (op. 12) of 1906–1913—already contain works that indicate the composer's particular bent. Especially characteristic is the well-known *Suggestion diabolique* (op. 4 iv), an extended virtuoso piece featuring the coloristic use of dissonance, the percussive treatment of the piano, the insistently repetitive mechanical rhythms and some of the grotesque quality. But other works of the set display here and there similar features, for example, *Élan* (ii) and the rapid ostinato pattern in *Désespoir* (iii), while lyricism prevails in *Reminiscence* (i). In the other sets, the Classical (perhaps one should say rather "Neo-Classical") element is to be seen, particularly in op. 12, which contains a gavotte (ii), a rigaudon (iii), and an allemande (viii). The two elements appear constantly in the remainder of the composer's piano pieces. The former is particularly striking in the set of five *Sarcasms* (op. 17) of 1912–1914, while the lyrical impulse dominates in the rest: the miniatures called *Visions fugitives* (op. 22) of 1915–1917, the two larger pieces of *Choses en soi* (*Things in Themselves*, op. 45) of 1928, and the three *Pensées* (op. 62) of 1933–1934. The Neo-Classical appears in the set of four pieces (op. 32) of 1918—a dance, a minuet, a gavotte, and a waltz—and in *Sonatine pastorale* (op. 59 iii) of 1934; there are other eighteenth-century type dances as well.

Among the other piano pieces, we must emphasize the early large composition with what, for Prokofiev, is a most symptomatic title: the Toccata (op. 11) of 1912, which goes back quite explicitly to the similar work of Schumann; it is a large, virtuoso, perpetual-motion piece with much figuration. Then there are the virtuoso etudes, the four etudes (op. 2) of 1909, and other easy teaching pieces; the four *Contes de la vieille grand-mère* (*Tales of My Grandmother*, op. 31) of 1918, composed in New York; and the *Musique des Enfants* (op. 65) of 1935, twelve short and simple pieces. Other piano pieces are transcriptions of orchestral works and other pieces: a set of six (op. 52) of 1930–1931 from the ballet *Romeo and Juliet* (op. 75) of 1937, the gavotte from the incidental music to *Hamlet* (op. 77b) of 1938, three pieces from the ballet *Cinderella* (op. 95) of 1942, and another set of waltzes (op. 96) of 1943, one from *War and Peace* and the others from *Lermontov*.

Prokofiev shared the Russian interest in the large form of piano music, the piano sonata, composing ten works in this genre (the last of which remained unfinished), covering his entire career as a composer. Most of them not only adhere to the usual three- or four-movement plan (although two among the earlier works are in a single extended but sectional movement), but also employ the standard formal plans associated with the sonata—the sonata form with thematic contrast and development, simple ternary form in the slow movements, and, in several cases, rondo form in the finales. Thus, while the harmonic vocabulary and the sonorous treatment of the piano may be new and characteristic of Prokofiev, the conception of the sonata as a large and expressive work using certain conventional musical forms and procedures represents the direct continuation of the nineteenth-century sonata.

The first two sonatas, in f (op. 1) of 1907–1909 and d (op. 14) of 1912, were composed while Prokofiev was still a student of Glazunov in St. Petersburg. The first is in one long movement; it is very romantic and rather derivative. The other in four movements, is roughly contemporary with the symptomatic *Suggestion diabolique* and Toccata; it reveals much of Prokofiev's mature style: the lyrical first movement in sonata form, the "mechanical" tarantella finale, the grotesque scherzo (the second movement), and the Romantic, almost popular Andante (the third movement). The next three sonatas were composed while Prokofiev was abroad; the third, in a (op. 28), and the fourth, in c (op. 29), were written in 1917 (but begun some ten years earlier), and the fifth, in C (op. 38), was written six years later, in 1923. While the Sonata in a, in one long movement, is a big display piece (and the most popular among Prokofiev's sonatas), the others emphasize lyricism (except for the grotesque dance, Andante, of the Sonata in C). There is then a long pause in Prokofiev's composition of piano sonatas, after which come three of his most important works in rapid succession during 1939–1944, the so-called *War Sonatas*: the sixth is in A (op. 82), the seventh in B-flat (op. 83), and the eighth is also in B-flat (op. 84). These are all big works in three movements, except for op. 84, which has four. Representative is op. 83, which, in its first movement, has a sonata form with great contrast between the themes and features the percussive treatment of the piano, with harsh tone clusters and repeated martial rhythmic patterns; there is a lyrical slow movement, again in three-part form, whose principal melody is sentimental, almost popular, but with ringing dissonant chords in the middle section; the finale presents Prokofiev's toccata type, a perpetual motion consistently in 7/8 meter with a driving ostinato pattern that, near the end, reaches a climax of great proportions. In contrast, the next Sonata in B-flat is to a large extent lyrical, as is the last completed sonata, the ninth in C (op. 103) of 1947; a tenth was left unfinished (op. 137), and still another was planned (op. 138).

EXAMPLE 81

PROKOFIEV: *Sonata* in B-flat (op. 83; No. 7)—excerpts

A. Allegro inquieto—excerpt

B. Precipitato—beginning

This concentration on the piano sonata seems something peculiarly Russian, since it does not appear, generally, in the work of composers in other countries; indeed, there is no other composer of major standing who gave to the sonata anything like the prominence accorded it by Prokofiev. We have noted that, even as the nineteenth century wore on, the genre declined in importance and that new sonatas frequently took very different forms. In the twentieth century, the sonata, with some exceptions, appears as a smaller work going back either to the Baroque or the late eighteenth-century divertimento (or sonatina) for its point of departure; the principal exceptions are Bartók's lone sonata, which makes extensive use of elements from Hungarian folk music, and Hindemith's larger sonatas (the first and the third of the group published in 1936). Prokofiev stands out, then, not only in his preoccupation with the genre, but also in his taking it as a large expressive form that he then submitted to his own individual idiom without, however, significantly altering either the forms or the intent of the genre.

The other Soviet composer to achieve wide and abiding international recognition has been Dimitri Shostakovich (1906–), who, although best known for his symphonies, has also written a good deal of piano music. There are two sonatas: the first (op. 12) of 1926, is a large virtuoso, highly dissonant work in one long movement, and the second, in b (op. 64) of 1943, is much more moderate, in three movements with a set of variations as finale. Among the pieces, most important are two sets of preludes, a set of eight (op. 2) of 1919–1920 and another of twenty-four (op. 34) of 1932–1933. For these, the model was plainly the preludes of Chopin; this is conclusively seen from op. 34, which presents the same sequence of keys as does Chopin's op. 28. In a more Neo-Classical (or Neo-Baroque) vein is the set of twenty-four preludes and fugues (op. 87) of 1951, in which the connection with Bach is inescapable; these preludes, unlike those of Chopin, often assume specific forms (dances like the saraband and passacaglia, marches, scherzos, or small sets of variations), while the fugues often employ striking and characteristic subjects. More like the usual kind of character piece are the *Fantastic Dances* (op. 5) of 1922 and the ten *Aphorisms* (op. 13) of 1916–1927. There is also a group of six children's pieces, miniatures using a good deal of two-voice writing.

The only other national school of overriding importance to be discussed here is the one that grew up on the Iberian Peninsula (see Chase). Here, in place of the German Romantic tradition, the influence came largely from France. We have seen that elements and features from Spanish music appear now and again in the work of French composers, especially Debussy and Ravel; and it is, in fact, the example set by the French Impressionists that proved decisive for Spanish composers, many of whom either studied or lived mainly in France. Two Spanish musicians of particular importance are Isaac Albéniz (1860–1909) and Enrique Granados (1867–1916), both of whom owe their interest in their native music to their teacher Felipe Pedrell, also the teacher of Falla, who himself undertook many editions of Spanish music. Except for their work with Spanish music and their dedication to the piano, the two present a good deal of contrast. Albéniz was the extraordinary, precocious, and impetuous virtuoso of the piano who spent the early part of his life in restless wandering, going to South America and to the United States, after which he returned to Europe and engaged in concertizing, a pursuit that he gradually abandoned after 1883; from 1893, he lived in Paris. Granados, however, although an excellent pianist, had less of traveling and lived a quieter life, but died when a boat on which he was traveling was torpedoed.

During his career as a concert pianist, Albéniz composed a large amount of music for the piano, mostly of the showy salon variety expressly aimed at popular consumption, a kind that was popular in France at the time, among them the *Piezas caracteristicas* and the Neo-Baroque *Suites anciennes*; during this time, he also wrote five sonatas. It was later that he turned to the composition of serious works that exploit features of Spanish native music. These are, as is usual, dances and settings of songs, such as the *Suite española* with its eight dance movements, the *Danzas españolas*, and the *Cantos d'España*. But his major work of this kind is the set of character pieces *Iberia*; these were called "impressions" and were issued in four books between 1906 and 1909, each with three pieces, in which native Spanish dances are everywhere in evidence, even though subjected to a good deal of stylization. Chase has discussed this question in some detail. The most characteristic type of Spanish dance is in fast triple time with rapid subdivision of the second beat and the incessant repetition of the pattern, but the whole is interspersed with a lyrical—an originally sung—refrain, the *copla*. This basic type is seen in *Iberia* in *Evocation* (Part I), a fandango, and in *Rodeña* (Part II), another fandango with alternation between 3/4 and 6/8 and with the contrapuntal combination of the dance with its *copla* near the end. There are also *Malaga* and *Jerez* (both in Part IV), the first a *malagueña*, and *Eritaña* (Part IV), which is a *seguidilla*, but the *copla* is lacking. Examples of the *paso-doble*, a rapid dance in duple time also with *coplas*, are *Triaña* (Part II), perhaps the most played piece of the set, and *Lavapiés*. Several Andalusian dance types are exploited in *El Puerto* (Part I): the lamenting *polo*, the cantabile *bulerías*, and the rapid Gypsy *seguidilla* (called *seguirya gitana*). The *polo* also appears in *El Polo* (Part III), while the *bulerías* underlies *El Abaicín* (Part III), one of the finest pieces in the set. Especially striking is the representation of the religious procession with the march and the lyrical middle part, the *saeta* or "arrow of song," in *Fête-Dieu à Seville* (Part I). Throughout *Iberia*, the writing for piano is brilliant, suggesting at times the passionate art of Spanish guitar playing. Unusual touches are the use of modal scales (Hypodorian in *Jerez*, Lydian in *Almería*), and the use of dissonances (*El Puerto* and *Triaña*). In the same spirit is Albéniz' last and unfinished piano piece, *Navarra*, completed by the French composer de Séverac.

Granados' work, on the other hand, reveals a more consistent adherence to the ideals of his teacher Pedrell in the use of native Spanish materials in his musical composition. Although there are works like the *Allegro de concert*, the *Marche militaire*, and the *Valse de concert*, in the majority are pieces like the *Capricho español*, *Danzes españoles*, *Jota aragonese*, *Rapsodia aragonese*, and so on; even conventional types get a Spanish twist, as the Spanish waltz *Carezza*, or the mazurka *Elvira*; there is even a set of *Valses poéticas*. We have seen that, in the literature of the German character piece, the sketch or scene is a common type; and this is particularly true of Granados' work, for not only are there three *Escenas poéticas* and *Escenas romanticas*, but also his major work for piano is in some degree related—the suite *Goyescas* with its subtitle *Las majas enamoradas* (*The Majas in Love*) of 1911–1912, which takes its inspiration from etchings of the great Spanish artist, Francesco Goya (see Wilson and Livermore). The etchings represent various scenes from a continuous narrative, so that it was later possible for Granados to use the piano suite as the basis for an opera with the same title. Not only does the work have this continuity of subject matter, but also themes from the earlier pieces of the set reappear later, especially in the long dramatic *El amor y la muerte*, subtitled *Balada*, and in the last piece, *Epilogo*, subtitled *Serenata del espectro* (*Serenade of the Ghost*), so that an element of cyclic unity is present. In this, the *Goyescas* differs markedly from Albéniz' *Iberia*, and thus the work emerges as one of the few large nationalistic works in piano music, along with Musorgskii's *Pictures at an Exhibition* (both with their inspiration from art, be it noted). But it must also be said that, generally, these pieces have a strong dash of the French salon music and do not always rise to the occasion indicated by the programmatic titles.

Two other well-known Spanish composers are Manuel de Falla (1876–1946) and Joaquin Turina (1882–1949), both of whom spent time in France and were influenced by Impressionism. While both exploited Spanish color in their compositions, Turina concentrated the most on piano music, producing a number of sets of character pieces with a good deal of Spanish color; there are also sets of Spanish dances; and, as larger efforts, there is the early *Sonata romantique sur un thème espagnol* (op. 3) of 1909 and *Sanlucar de Barrameda* (op. 24) of 1922, subtitled *Sonata pintoresca*. The earlier sonata is a cyclic work, its three movements all based on the song *El vito*. A later and more comprehensive set of piano pieces is the *Ciclo pianistico*, which consists of a *Tocata y fuga* (op. 50), a partita (op. 57), *Pieza romantica* (op. 64), and *El castillo do Almodovar* (op. 65), all composed in the late 1920's and early 1930's. Falla, on the other hand, has written but little for the piano. There is a set of four *Pièces espagnoles* of 1908 (for the *Montañesa*, see *HMS*, X, s. 1, b. 3); the large and difficult *Fantasia betica* of 1919, which smacks, to some extent, of the primitive and hence is similar to Bartók's *Allegro barbaro* (and, as we will see later, to Villa-Lobos' *Rudapoema*); two pieces in memory of Debussy and Dukas, respectively; and *Pedrelliana*, in honor of his teacher. Ironically, his most popular piece for piano is a transcription from a ballet, the ubiquitous *Ritual Fire Dance* from *El amor brujo*.

Somewhat less conventional is the work of Federico Mompou (1893–), who seems in some respects to be a counterpart of Satie in seeking out his own wholly individual manner, which he calls *primitavista*. It includes, along with great simplicity, the studious avoidance of normal musical devices like regular meters, key signatures, and cadential progressions. In his many pieces, it is the miniature character piece arranged in suites that dominates, among which we can mention the six *Impressions intimes* of 1911–1914; more in accordance with the usual repertory are the three variations of 1920 and the Neo-Classical preludes, ten in all, composed between 1928 and 1944.

Other Iberian composers to be mentioned are the Spaniard Joaquin Nin (1879–1949), known chiefly for his editions of eighteenth-century Spanish keyboard music but who has composed a number of Spanish dances; the Portuguese José Vianna da Motta (1868–1948), a pupil and associate of Liszt (whose piano works he edited for the collected edition) and also a friend of Busoni, who incorporated Portuguese elements in his music, notably the Portuguese scenes (op. 9) and Portuguese rhapsodies (op. 10); and two other Portuguese musicians, Luiz de Freitas Branco (1890–) and Ruy Coelho (1891–), of whom the former is of some importance for keyboard music with a number of character pieces inspired in part by French Impressionism (especially the *Mirages* of 1911) and even some organ works, an aria and choral of 1912 along with a larger *Rapsodia sobre cantos populares portugueses* of 1935. Finally, there is a pupil of Falla, Ernesto Halffter (1905–), who has worked largely with the more usual types of Romantic piano music, showing an unusual devotion to the sonata.

Piano music in twentieth-century Poland, the only other European country that can claim a real national school, is wholly indebted to its leading figure of the nineteenth century, Chopin. Among the leading composers are Ignacy Jan Paderewski (1860–1941), the great pianist, editor, and statesman; Karel Szymanowski (1882–1937), and Alexandre Tansman (1897–). Two others, important mostly as teachers, were the two Scharwenka brothers, Philipp (1847–1917) and Xaver (1850–1924). Paderewski, who had studied with Leschetizky, wrote a large number of piano pieces, mostly in the smaller forms and all in a basically nineteenth-century manner, of which the minuet from the first book of his *Humoresques de concert* (op. 14) is very popular. The Chopin influence dominates the work of Szymanowski, a pupil of Noskowski. There are nine preludes (op. 1) of 1900; two sets of Mazurkas (op. 50 and 62) of 1924–1926 and 1934, respectively; and two groups of character pieces, *Métopes* (op. 29) of 1915 and *Masques* (op. 34) of 1917; there is also a group of four studies (op. 4) of 1902. As for the larger forms, there are three sonatas, in c (op. 8) of 1904, in a (op. 21) of 1910, and the third (op. 36) of 1917; an early set of Variations in b-flat (op. 3) of 1901; and a Fantasia in f (op. 14) of 1909.

Tansman, like Chopin before him, has lived most of his life in Paris, and, although the influence of his great predecessor was strong in his earlier works, he subsequently came under the influence of Impressionism and then under that of Neo-Classicism. This is clearly reflected in his piano music. The example of Chopin is to be seen in his concentration on the character piece—preludes, two sets of mazurkas, and three large ballades; there is also *Novelettes* and *Impressions*, along with five sonatas and two suites. Impressionism appears in a work like *Lent* from the *Preludes* or in the *Impressions* of 1950; and Neo-Classicism appears in the *Suite dans le style ancien*, even with jazz elements, as in the three *Préludes en forme de blues*, the *Sonatine transatlantique*, or the big expressive sonata. More traditional are the two sets of teaching pieces, while in the *Novelettes*, pieces of moderate length and difficulty, many facets of his art are brought together.

A final national style to be reviewed is the Jewish, in which the central figure was Ernest Bloch (1880–1959), born in Switzerland, trained in Germany and France, and a long-time resident of the United States. His point of departure was French Impressionism, the harmonies and textures of which often appear in his works. While his most characteristic compositions are for orchestra, there are some piano works that are representative. Among the Impressionistic pieces can be listed the love-poem *In the Night* of 1922; *Nirvana* of 1923; the set of character pieces, the three *Poems of the Sea* of 1922–1924; the five *Sketches in Sepia* of 1923; and the five *Visions et prophécies* of 1940. Bloch is at his most characteristic when working with a large form of instrumental music, as can be seen in his single sonata for piano of 1935, a large cyclic work in three movements: there is a vigorous first movement in sonata form, a lyrical pastorale, and, as finale, a march. For organ, Bloch has written liturgical works for the synagogue, a set of five preludes and four wedding marches, both composed between 1946 and 1950. In the work of another leading Jewish composer, Paul Ben-Haim (1897–), Oriental elements are more pronounced, as in his nocturne (op. 20), the set of five pieces (op. 34). and the Sonatina in a (op. 38).

We have now to review the situation of keyboard music in those countries where a pronouncedly nationalistic style did not develop: Italy, England, The Netherlands, Scandinavia, Belgium, and Switzerland. Generally, the music in these countries was derivative, that is to say, closely related to and dependent on the music of either Germany or France. It will be seen that, in the twentieth century, generally speaking, the situation remains similar: again, the leadership comes from the same two countries, although France (and Austria) become more important.

In Italy during the nineteenth century, as has been seen, while the German Romantic tradition of instrumental music never took a firm hold on the musical life of the country, it nonetheless dominated what little instrumental music was composed by Italian composers. In the twentieth century, this situation continues (see Gatti), even though there is a strong flavor from France from Impressionism and Neo-Classicism. The most important composer to be discussed in this connection is Ferrucio Busoni (1866–1924), of German-Italian parentage and trained in Leipzig, who became a virtuoso pianist in the tradition of Liszt but who, after 1914, devoted himself more and more to musical composition. In his compositions for piano (he wrote little for organ), Busoni did not follow the German Romantic tradition at all. Most of his work all the way through his career as a composer took its point of departure from Baroque music, especially that of Bach. While it is true that this applies to certain works of Liszt and Reger, the striking emphasis is Busoni's own. He became involved with what he termed the "Young Classical" movement in which he emphasized the essentially absolute and objective nature of any musical composition and advocated a return to the ideals of Bach and of earlier Italian composers. His views are expressed in his *Entwurf einer neuen Aesthetik der Tonkunst* of 1907 (English edition, *Towards a New Esthetic of Music*, 1911). There are, however, among his earlier works, compositions like the *Racconti fantastici* (op.12) of 1878 (dates are of composition), three character pieces with literary associations à *la* Schumann and Liszt; the Sonata in a of 1883; the *Variations and Fugue on a Theme of Chopin* (op. 22) of 1884 (Chopin's Prelude in c, op. 28 xx); the set of twenty-four preludes (op. 37) of 1882; or the etudes (op. 16) of 1883, which he dedicated to Brahms. There are even later works like the *Elegies* of 1907; the Impressionistic *Nuit de Noël* of 1908; the *Indianisches Tagebuch* (*Indian Diary*, op. 47) of 1915, which has pieces based on American Indian themes; and the *Albumblätter* of 1917–1921, which even so are distinctly contrapuntal; and the famous fantasy on themes from Bizet's *Carmen* of 1920. Still, the Neo-Classical attitude shows itself even in his earliest works, the set of five pieces (op. 3) of 1877 (prelude, minuet, gavotte, etude, and gigue), and continues all the way through: the three *Pezzi nelle stile antico* (op. 10), the four *Danze antiche* (op. 11), and a gavotte (op. 25) all of 1880–1882; the *Kontrapunktisches Tanzstück* (*Contrapuntal Dance Piece*, op. 30) of 1890–1891 (revised in 1914); the *Fantasia in modo antico* (op. 33b iv), the *Macchiete mediovali*, and a prelude and fugue (op. 36) all of 1882; and a toccata of 1921 (in three sections—prelude, fantasia, and chaconne). The attitude is even extended to teaching pieces, as is demonstrated by the four parts of *An die Jugend* of 1909 and the first two parts of the virtuoso *Klavierübung* of 1918–1922.

The two major works in which Busoni reveals his Baroque and learned bent are the large *Fantasia contrapuntistica* of 1910–1912 (in four versions, including one for two pianos) and the two *Kontrapuntkstudien nach Bach* of 1917. The former is a most unusual work, a combination of several different musical forms. There is the chorale prelude on the hymn *Allein Gott in der Höh' sei Ehr'*, with much toccata-like figuration that alternatively suggests both the old toccata and the manner of Liszt; fugues on the subject of Bach's *Kunst der Fuge*; theme and variations with cadenza; and then a concluding section in which all themes used in the work are brought together in combination with the "Bach" theme. All in all, it is among the most ambitious works of its kind. Busoni made a simplified version of this work, published as a chorale prelude and fugue on a fragment of Bach in 1912. The *Kontrapunktstudien* are, first, a Fantasia and Fugue in a and, then, canonic variations and fugue on the theme of Bach's *Musical Offering*.

Among Busoni's other works are, first, those for which he has become best known, his transcriptions for piano of various works of Bach, among which are the more popular of the chorale preludes and preludes and fugues for the organ and the famous Chaconne in d that Bach wrote for unaccompanied violin. In these transcriptions, Busoni is once more wholly in the tradition established by Liszt. Busoni also prepared performing editions of many of Bach's keyboard works. For piano duet, there is a set of Finnish folk songs (op. 27) of 1889; and for two pianos, there is an improvisation on Bach's chorale *Wie weh ist mir* of 1916, a *Duettino concertante* on the last movement of Mozart's Piano Concerto in F (K. 459) of 1919, and an elaborate contrapuntal fantasia. For organ, there is but one early work, a prelude on a ground bass and a fugue on a chorale melody (op. 7) of 1881.

Other Italian composers of the later nineteenth and early twentieth centuries include Alessandro Longo (1864–1945), the editor of Scarlatti's harpsichord sonatas; Amilcare Zanella (1873–1949); and Ermanno Wolf-Ferrari (1876–1948). The German orientation is especially clear in the compositions of Zanella, who had been a student of Rheinberger, and, to a lesser extent, those of Longo. We might also note here that among the early works of the young Giacomo Puccini (1858–1924), who gained such fame as a composer of operas, is a set of character pieces for organ composed before 1880 in the manner of the German religious Adagio.

French influence, Impressionism and Neo-Classicism, is important in the work of Ottorino Respighi (1879–1936), Gian Francesco Malipiero (1882–), Alfredo Casella (1883–1947), Mario Castelnuovo-Tedesco (1895–), and Vittorio Rieti (1898–). Of these, Malipiero has composed the most for piano, mostly small character pieces of various kinds in which the harmonies are those of French Impressionism. Of note are the four *Preludi autonnali* of 1914, the three *Poemi Asolani* of 1916, the five pieces in *Barlumi* of 1917, the *Maschere che passano* and *Risonanze* of 1918, and, especially, the *Omaggio a Claude Debussy* of 1920 and *Il Tarlo* of 1922. Noteworthy are the three pieces in *Calvacate* of 1921, each representing a riding animal—*Somaro* (*Donkey*), *Camello* (*Camel*), and *Pestriero* (*Fast Horse*)—and the eight of *Hortus conclusus* of 1946. Among the larger works are the Impressionistic *Pasqua di risurrezione* of 1924, the Neo-Classical *Tre Preludi e una fuga* of 1926, the *Omaggio a Bach* of 1932, and a

Preludio e fuga of 1941. Gregorian chant is employed in his *Preludi, ritmi e canti gregoriani* of 1937. It might be added that Malipiero is the editor of the collected works of Monteverdi, another confirmation of the strong Neo-Baroque tendency that is revealed in many of his compositions.

Respighi composed but little for piano. There is a set of eight preludes based on Gregorian chants in 1921 (perhaps a model for the Malipiero works just mentioned) and a set of six children's pieces in 1926. On the other hand, both Casella and Rieti have composed a good deal for the piano, all under the influence of the French "the Six," with the contemporary *galant* idiom prominent. Again, it is character pieces and various eighteenth-century formal types that are dominant. Especially characteristic here are Casella's pavane (op. 1) of 1901, the variations on a chaconne (op. 3) of 1903, a toccata (op. 6) of 1904, and later works called "ricercares" and the larger *Sinfonia, ariosa e toccata* (op. 59) of 1936; Rieti has a *Sonata all'antica* for harpsichord. In 1939, Rieti went to the United States, as also did Castelnuovo-Tedesco, whose output of piano music also consists largely of character pieces.

Other Italian composers whose work is in the Impressionist vein are Domenico Alaleona (1881–1928) and Salvatore Musella (1896–), while the Neo-Classical tradition, with some nineteenth-century German Romanticism, appears in Riccardo Pick-Mangiagalli (1882–1949). The German background is also apparent in the character pieces of Ildebrando Pizzetti (1880–). The Schönberg school has its representatives in Goffredo Petrassi (1904-), and especially Luigi Dallapiccola (1904–), the latter having emerged as one of the most respected composers of our time (see the article by Nathan) with two important works for piano, the *Sonata canonica sui capricci di Paganini* in B-flat of 1942–1943 and the variations, *Quaderno musicale di Annalibera* (first version in 1952, second in 1953); there is also an early piece, *Inni (Hymns)* for two pianos, of 1935. Like Berg, Dallapiccola is especially concerned with the melodic and expressive potential of the series employed in any composition, and lyrical elements are uppermost in his work.

In England, the situation is, on the whole, similar. Again there was no native tradition of English instrumental music in the nineteenth century, and the gap was filled by German music and musicians, in which the influence of Mendelssohn was pronounced, so that the result was an essentially Germanic repertory colored here and there with themes and sounds of a peculiarly English flavor. Elgar, the leading British composer of the late nineteenth and early twentieth centuries, composed almost no keyboard music at all. Among the more important composers of keyboard music of this period, the late nineteenth and early twentieth centuries, we can mention Sir Alexander Campbell MacKenzie (1847–1935); Sir Granville Bantock (1868–1946), who worked with the small character piece, *Silhouettes and Miniatures* of 1912, and two sets of pieces based on poems by

Browning; John Ireland (1879–1962), whose character pieces frequently refer to celtic legends and rituals and have an aura of mysticism about them, as the *Decorations* of 1912–1913, the set of four preludes of 1914–1915, and the lone sonata with its subtitle *The Darkened Valley* of 1919, published in 1921; Frank Bridge (1879–1941), whose many character pieces are early compositions, but there is also a sonata and a few works for organ in the nineteenth-century fashion; Sir Arnold Bax (1883–1953), an outspoken Romanticist who wrote much piano music in both the large and small forms and in whose music Celtic elements appear along with others from Russian music; Sir Eugene Goossens (1893–1962); and the Australian, Arthur Benjamin (1893–). An interesting case is presented by Cyril Meir Scott (1879–), a poet as well as composer, who studied in Germany and who also became influenced by Oriental occult philosophy (theosophy), thus having some similarity with the Russian Skriabin. He expressed his views in several books, among them *Music, Its Secret Influence Through the Ages* of 1933 (second edition, 1952). Unlike Skriabin, Scott did not attempt to incorporate his beliefs into musical compositions but, instead, contented himself with pieces in the established forms, although he did adopt elements from French music: cyclic form, Impressionistic harmonies, and the abandonment of key and time signatures and/or regular barring. (See the close of his *Rainbow Trout* in Georgii *400 Years*, p. 134.) Two other composers who exploited and arranged English folk music in their piano composition are Gustav Holst (1874–1934) and the Australian Percy Aldridge Grainger (1882–1963).

Other British composers are more closely related to the innovations that were going on in France from the early years of the century. The only real English Impressionist composer is Frederick Delius (1862–1934), who studied in Germany and lived for some years in the southern United States and then in France; he wrote but little for the keyboard—a set of five pieces of 1921, a toccata, three preludes of 1923, a few dances, one of them for harpsichord. A strongly satirical composer in the spirit of Satie is Lord Berners (actually Gerald Hugh Tyrwhitt-Wilson, 1883–1950), a friend of Stravinsky. The satirical vein can be seen in his *Petites marches funèbres* of 1914, the *Fragments psychologiques* of 1915, and the *Valses bourgeoises* for piano duet of 1917, with the famous parody of waltzes by the various Strausses; on the other hand, the earlier *Le poisson d'or* of 1914 is pure Impressionism and a difficult piece at that. Straight Neo Classicism, not unrelated to "the Six," appears in the work of Sir Arthur Bliss (1891–) and, to some extent, in Michael Tippett (1905–) and Howard Ferguson (1908–), in whose work the large form of the sonata is by no means lacking. Tippett has a large and impressive *Fantasy Sonata* of 1948 (which he revised in 1954), while Ferguson has a long Sonata in f (op. 8) of 1938–1940 along with a set of bagatelles (op. 9) of 1944 and a long partita for two pianos (op. 5b) of 1935–1936. Finally, it is worth noting that the three major British composers of the twentieth century, Ralph Vaughan Williams (1872–1958), Sir

William Walton (1902–), and Benjamin Britten (1913–) have not given much attention to keyboard music. Walton has composed a set of piano duets for children, and Britten has written only the *Holiday Suite* for piano (op. 5) of 1934, several pieces for two pianos, and a prelude and fugue on a theme of Victoria for organ of 1947. Although Vaughan Williams composed the most keyboard music of the three, none of the large forms is represented in his work. Apart from a few contrapuntal exercises, there is the *Set of Six Short Pieces*, several independent character pieces, and the *Hymn Tune Prelude on Gibbons' Song 13* for organ; for two pianos, there is a single large work, the *Introduction and Fugue* of 1946, and, for organ, a group of three *Preludes on Welsh Hymn Tunes* of 1920. Then, there is Humphrey Searle (1915–), a composer and writer on music who, since 1946, has worked in the dodecaphonic serialism of Schönberg; his pieces are often Neo-Baroque in form: for piano, *Threnos and Toccata*, along with a sonata and a suite, and, for organ, *Toccata alla passacaglia*.

In Scandinavia, we find for the most part considerable dependence on German and French music, in which the traditions of nineteenth-century Germany are especially strong. Much in the vein of a Jensen or a Henselt in the cultivation of the lyrical character piece in its small form are composers like the Swedes Torsten Prete (1863–), Lennart Arvid Lundberg (1863–1931), and Hugo Alfvén (1872–); the Finn Erkki Gustaf Melartin (1875–1937); the Norwegian Halfdan Cleve (1879–) and two Danes, members of the Langgaard family, Siegfred (1852–1914) and Ruel Immanuel (1893–1952), his son. Lundberg shows some influence from French Impressionism. Other composers who also worked with the larger forms are especially the Norwegian Christian Sinding (1856–1941), whose *Rustle of Spring* (op. 32 iii) is universally known but who also wrote many other works for piano; the Norwegian Wilhelm Eugen Stenhammar (1871–1927), whose work shows the influence of Brahms; and the Finn Yrgö Kilpinen (1892–1959). Essentially the same orientation but with some flavoring of Scandinavian national music can be seen in the work of Olaf Wilhelm Peterson-Berger (1867–1942), who made use of Swedish folk songs (and who was also a strong partisan of Wagner, whose literary works he translated into Swedish); the Finn Selim Palmgren (1878–1951), who taught at the Eastman School of Music from 1923 to 1926; the Swede Kurt Atterberg (1887–), and the Norwegian Harald Saeverud (1897–), who, like Grieg, composed pieces called *Slåtter* adapting qualities of the Hardanger fiddle for the piano.

To this essentially conservative orientation in keyboard music we must also assign the most famous Scandinavian composer of the twentieth century, the Finn Jan Sibelius (1865–1957) in whose work piano music (see Blom) has a secondary significance compared to the symphonic compositions. There is in in Sibelius' work, to be sure, a substantial number of character pieces, some nationalistic, many of which are so light and simple as to be nothing more than salon pieces. The large form appears infrequently. The sole sonata is an early work in F (op. 13) composed in 1893. The only larger piano work to draw on the mythological background that provides the inspiration for many of the orchestral works (the Finnish epic, the *Kalevala*) is *Kyllikki* (op. 41) of 1904, a suite of three pieces depicting Lemminkäinen's courtship of Kyllikki. Another piano work of some interest is the set of three sonatinas (op. 67) of 1912, in f-sharp, E, and b-flat, respectively. For organ, there is but one work, a set of two pieces (op. 111) composed in 1926 as a memorial.

The situation is somewhat the same in the work of the greatest Danish composer of the time, Carl Nielsen (1865–1931), who, as a symphonist, did not give keyboard music a prominent place in his output. Unlike Sibelius, however, Nielsen, in his piano music, emphasized the larger genres, so that there is less discrepancy between these and his orchestral works than in the work of Sibelius. Among Nielsen's larger works for piano is the *Symfonisk Suite* (op. 8) composed between 1892 and 1894; a chaconne (op. 32) and a theme and variations (op. 40), both composed in 1916; and another suite (op. 45) composed between 1919 and 1920. In addition, there are sets of piano pieces, the *Klavierstykker* (op. 3 and op. 59), the *Humoreske-Bagateller* (op. 11), and a set of children's pieces (op. 53). For organ, Nielsen wrote two sets of preludes, the first (op. 51) consisting of small pieces, in addition to a large virtuoso work, *Commotio* (op. 58), composed near the end of his life, that is a modern interpretation of the old toccata.

Among the younger composers whose work shows the influence of new directions taken in twentieth-century music should be included the Dane Paul von Klenau (1883–1946), trained in Germany, whose early work is much in the late nineteenth-century manner but who later adopted certain aspects of Schönberg's serial method of composition (as can be seen in the two sets of preludes and fugues of 1939 and 1941); there is also the Swede Lars-Erik Larsson (1908–) who studied with Berg in Vienna, and the Danes Knudåge Riisager (1897–) and Karl-Birger Blomdahl (1916–), whose work has been influenced by Hindemith. Most important here is the Dane Niels Viggo Bentzon (1919–), who has embraced not only the serial principle but also much of the Neo-Classical. His piano music includes a toccata (op. 10) of 1941, a passacaglia (op. 31) of 1944, a partita (op. 38) of 1945, six sonatas, and a number of other works, all of which would entitle him to a position of pre-eminence among Scandinavian composers for the instrument.

A few composers working in other countries of Europe may be mentioned here. In Belgium, there were Désire Pasque (1867–1939), who was closely associated with French music, and Marcel Poot (1901–), who was interested in the ideals and aims of "the Six" and in whose work one finds humorous irony as well as jazz elements. Nearby, in The Netherlands, the German influence is more pronounced, as in the work of Dirk Schäfer (1873–1931), Bernard van den Sigtenhorst-Meijer (1888–1953), Willem Pijper (1894–1947), Henk Badings

(1907–), and Hans Henkemans (1913–). Here, the larger forms play a more important role, although the Neo-Classical element is also present. Of these, Pijper is the most significant composer of piano music (see Ringer), who has experimented with new scales, and has written pieces of extreme brevity, as in the early *Aphorisms* for piano of 1915.

The more important composers of keyboard music in Switzerland are Emile Jaques-Dalcroze (1865–1950), Othmar Schoeck (1886–1957), Willy Burkhard (1900–1955), Frank Martin (1890–), and Rolf Liebermann (1910–). While Jaques-Dalcroze is most famous for his eurhythmics, a system of music teaching, he wrote a large number of character pieces, also primarily for use in teaching. Both Schoeck and Burkhard belong to the conservative contrapuntal tradition that takes its point of departure from Reger, a tradition strong in nineteenth-century Germany, as has been seen. Burkhard especially has composed a good deal of keyboard music, for organ as well as piano. In his piano music, there is a preference for the abstract genres, as in his early fantasia, the two sonatinas (the second, a Christmas sonata), two sets of piano pieces, two sets of variations, and, among his last works, a set of six preludes; in the organ music, there is a fantasia on the chorale *Ein' feste Burg*, the *Choral-Tryptichon*, an early fantasia, a set of variations on a theme of the sixteenth- and seventeenth-century German composer Hassler, and a sonatina. More international is the work of Martin, who studied in France and in Italy and who, in his later work, has adopted elements from the manner of Schönberg; but there is relatively little for keyboard—an early fox trot for two pianos, a passacaglia for organ of 1944, and, for piano, the set of eight preludes of 1948 and *Clair de lune* of 1953. The best known of these are the preludes, which, in a general way, maintain the established features of the genre; they are small works in which the same character or mood is consistently maintained. The last two are larger sectional pieces, the last being a sort of rondo with "couplets"; the third, Tranquillo ma con moto, is clearly a nocturne, while the fifth, Vivace, is a virtuoso etude. Liebermann composed a sonata using dodecaphonic serialism in 1951.

In the twentieth-century, the United States came of age musically. We have seen that, in the nineteenth century, United States composers were strongly dominated by European traditions, particularly the German tradition of instrumental music. And while this influence continues in the twentieth century, other elements also make their appearance. In the first place, peculiarly French conceptions take on great significance; and then there is the conscious effort to develop a special American manner of writing music; finally, there were, as the result of political upheavals in Europe, a number of influential European composers who came to live and work in the United States. All of this has produced a situation that makes United States music in the twentieth century most difficult to survey.

At the beginning of the century, we have the remainder of the nineteenth-century practice—composers who lived and worked in the northeastern part of the country frequently teaching at colleges and universities in New England, a long-sanctioned environment; out of this environment have nonetheless emerged some of the outstanding and progressive voices in American music. We can mention, among the older composers who made some contributions to keyboard music, David Stanley Smith (1877–1949), Henry F. Gilbert (1868–1928), Frederick Converse (1871–1940), Edward Burlingame Hill (1872–), Daniel Gregory Mason (1873–1953), John Powell (1882–1963), Quincy Porter (1897–), and Richard Donovan (1891–). Here, generally, the Germanic character piece of the nineteenth century remains the most important genre of keyboard music. And the same is true of the composers who have given themselves over largely to organ music: Edgar Stillman Kelley (1857–1944), T. Tertius Noble (1867–1953), Seth Bingham (1882–), and Leo Sowerby (1895–).

Yet this New England academic environment played a role in the formation of one of the most unusual and characteristic figures in American music, Charles E. Ives (1874–1954) of Connecticut, a graduate of Yale and a pupil of Horatio Parker and Dudley Buck. (Besides the large work by the Cowells, see the informative article by Schrade.) Ives' work reflects the influence of his academically oriented teachers to no extent at all, for Ives, somewhat like the poet Whitman, was from the beginning an experimenter who took nothing for granted and respected no long-standing traditions concerning how music should be organized. In a way related to Cocteau and his associates, Ives was stimulated by what he heard around him: the off-key singing of hymns by a church choir, the sound of an out-of-tune organ, the clash of dissonance as two bands, each playing a different march in a different key, passed each other on Main Street during a parade, or the quarter-tone intonation of country fiddlers at square dances. Along with these, which often led to very dissonant and rhythmically irregular passages, appear other passages in his works whose manner of tonal and rhythmic organization is as conventional as a miniature of MacDowell.

Ives' work, from the first, aroused the opposition of his teachers, and he soon determined that he could not be a professional musician unless he was willing to abandon his ideals of what music should be; hence, he resolved to gain his livelihood in the insurance business. It was not until late in his life that his musical composition was recognized as a phenomenon in contemporary music; he received the Pulitzer Prize for music in 1947.

It happens that keyboard music is well represented in this work and that, in the keyboard music, one can observe the chief elements of his manner. There are two early pieces for organ, the *Variations on the National Hymn* (*My Country 'Tis of Thee*) of 1891, with polytonal additions in 1894, and the prelude *Adeste fidelis*, also of 1891; for piano, there are three sonatas, the first composed between 1902 and 1909 in seven movements of which but five are extant; the second, the celebrated *Concord Sonata*, composed between 1909 and 1915; and, as third, a smaller work, the *Three–Page Sonata* (it occupies three pages in Ives' original manuscript of 1905). Then there are a number of character pieces of various sorts, among them the *In the Inn* of 1904–1911, *Anti-Abolitionist Riots* and *Some South-Paw Pitching* of 1908 and the three *Protests*, apparently part of a longer theme and variations, of 1900–1914; *Twenty-Two* for Piano was composed in 1912 as one of a projected set of twenty-nine pieces but was not published until 1947. Ives composed but little after 1918; but among the later work is a set of three *Quarter Tone Pieces* for two pianos (tuned a quarter tone apart) of 1924.

The principal keyboard compositions are the two large sonatas. The first of these, of whose original seven movements only five presently exist, shows many of Ives' characteristic and novel effects: the use of popular songs, a parody of *How Dry I Am* and an ornamented version of *O Susannah*, the use of dance rhythms (rumba, Charleston, rag-time), second chords (dyads), and other dissonant harmonies. The second sonata, entitled *Concord, Mass., 1840–1860*, is equally large: it is in four movements that are, in order, *Emerson* (the fast opening movement), *Hawthorne* (the scherzo), *The Alcotts* (the slow movement), and *Thoreau* (the lyrical finale), thus associating Ives wholly with New England Transcendentalism of the nineteenth century. This work is accompanied by a brilliant exposition of Ives' thought—his views on what music expresses, the aims of composers, as well as his appreciation of the significance of Emerson, Hawthorne, the Alcotts, and Thoreau—the *Essays before a Sonata*, which first appeared in 1919. In a way, Ives justifies his association of music with philosophy —in this he is in the tradition of German Romantic instrumental music. But the proper expression of the idea requires him to seek out new ways of organizing music, drawing elements from here and there and using the most divergent styles and techniques, one right next to the other. From these essays, we see that Emerson, whom Ives calls "an invader of the unknown . . . America's greatest explorer of spiritual immensities," is celebrated by Ives for his role in revelation; in *Hawthorne*, it is not his fundamental preoccupation with guilt, but rather "some of his wilder, fantastical adventures in the half-childlike, half-fairylike phantastical realms"; *The Alcotts* is a souvenir of their home (Orchard House), where they dwelt in "conviction in the power of the common soul"; finally, *Thoreau* represents a day at Walden, spent in meditation, in solitary contemplation of nature, forsaking the normal, everyday pursuits of life. The *Concord Sonata*, then, is a large cyclic work based, as the Cowells maintain, on two central themes, the one "epic" and taken from the first movement of Beethoven's Fifth Symphony, the other "lyric"; both are used continually, often in varied form, throughout the composition. The Beethoven theme is related specifically by Ives, first, to Emerson and his groping for new revelations and, second, to the Alcotts, at whose house it was often played. But, since Emerson wrote both prose and verse, Ives distinguishes the two in his music by labeling parts of the movement either "prose" or "verse." The song *Loch Lomond* and the wedding march from Wagner's *Lohengrin* were also often heard at the Alcott's Orchard House; other recognizable thematic material is the minstrel show music and the march, both of which appear in *Hawthorne*. Just as Emerson constantly sought out the new, so did Ives, but in a purely musical manner; the *Concord Sonata* abounds in new and unusual procedures. Polytonality can be seen in *The Alcotts* and in *Emerson*; only a few parts of the various movements of the work contain regular time signatures (*Emerson* usually has none, but at times brings in 7/8, 8/8, 5/8, and 7/4), and, in *Hawthorne*, for long passages there are not even bar lines. Even more striking are the new sounds, mainly as the result of the unheard-of chord combinations; but even more remarkable is the use of harmonics in *Hawthorne*, in which a piece of wood is laid over a group of keys and silently depressed, so that the strings are free to vibrate when bass notes are played in the normal way. Again, just as Emerson, Hawthorne, and Thoreau often broke the bounds of what was generally and conventionally accepted, so Ives breaks the bounds of his medium and calls for other instruments, ostensibly on an *ad libitum* basis: a viola at the end of *Emerson* and a flute at the end of *Thoreau*. Expression plainly is the central aim, as Ives makes abundantly clear in the *Essays*, and this appears from the many performance directions in the score, which leave much up to the player, for example, the instruction that a certain passage is to be played as fast as possible.

Ives is surely a phenomenon. The oddities of musical style have no counterpart in the music of his time, and, as has been said, often appear right along with passages that accord with traditional harmonic practice. Since Ives worked in the insurance business, his musical compositions were, for most of his life, completely unknown; thus, although he anticipated by some years many of the musical procedures that made the names of a number of European composers, it was rather from Europe that these novelties came to the United States. But, while these innovations of European composers can always be related to the course of nineteenth-century music in one way or another, Ives' experimentations are the result, to some extent, of what he heard around him, but they result more from the desire to express in music things that hitherto had not been attempted.

Two other American composers have certain similarities with Ives, although without equalling his stature as a composer: Henry Cowell (1897–1965) and Carl Ruggles (1876–). Cowell is the more important here, since a good deal of his experimentation took place in piano music (see Weisgall). Here, it was the character piece, in the composition of which he explored new sound capacities of the piano, around 1911–1920: tone clusters; the use of the forearm on the keyboard, as in the *Tides of Manaunaun*, *Antinomy*, or *The Voice of Lir*; the use of dyads, as in *The Trumpet of Angus Og*; or strumming the string of the piano directly, as in *The Harp of Life*, *The Aeolian Harp* (in which a lyric melody on the keys is accompanied by glissandi on the strings), or *The Banshee* (in which the strings are plucked along with the glissandi). Melodies and harmonies of a folk-song character are common in these works, some of which are stylized country dances, as are *Exultation* and *Lilt of the Reel*. He even modified the sound of the piano by placing various objects on the strings—hammers, knives, coins, rubber bands, and so forth. While Cowell has long been a prominent composer, Ruggles has lived for many years a retiring life, almost unknown to the general world of music. Like Ives, he is a New Englander, and, like Ives, he has a lofty vision of the expressive power of music, and it was this that motivated his search for new ways of conceiving and organizing the materials of music. His two works for piano, both experimental, are the *Evocations* of 1937–1945 and the *Polyphonic Compositions* for three pianos of 1945.

As has been indicated, the chief impetus to musical composition in the United States stems not from any native tradition but from developments abroad. It was primarily French music and conceptions that were of decisive importance. Here, one can mention first Charles Tomlinson Griffes (1884–1920) who, although trained in Germany, composed very much in the manner of French Impressionism. This can be seen in his three well-known sets of character pieces, *Tone Pictures* (op. 5) of 1910–1912, *Fantasy Pieces* (op. 6) of 1912–1914, and *Roman Sketches* (op. 7) of 1915–1916, the first of which is the famous *The White Peacock*; later than these is a Sonata in F in manuscript, based on an Oriental scale, with an effect not unlike that of Skriabin. Another composer closely related to French music is Virgil Thomson (1896–), for many years a well-known music critic; in his work, the example of Satie and "the Six" proved significant. Along with the five inventions and children's pieces goes a large set of *Portraits*, forty pieces in five books that were composed between 1927 and 1940; other works for piano include four sonatas, an *Exotic Dance*, and ten studies; there are also organ pieces, where, along with an early fantasia of 1921, a passacaglia of 1922, and *Wedding Music* (two pieces, *To Come In* and *To Get Out*), are two cantus firmus compositions, the *Pastorale on a Christmas Plainsong* and the characteristic *Variations and Fugues on Gospel Hymns*. The French interest in Oriental music has also been reflected in the work of the Canadian composer Colin McPhee (1901–1964), whose *Balinese Ceremonial Music* for two pianos is suggestive of the *gamelan* (the Balinese gong orchestra).

Other composers of somewhat greater importance who are related to French music and ideas are Walter Piston (1894–), Arthur Berger (1912–), Vincent Persichetti (1915–), and Irving Fine (1915–1962). Piston, who is also an outgrowth of the American academic tradition, has written but little keyboard music; but what he has written shows his Neo-Classical associations clearly enough. Apart from an early sonata of 1926 (Piston did not take up music as a career until 1920) and a piece called *Improvisation* of 1943, there is a passacaglia of 1943, and, for organ, the *Chromatic Study on the Name BACH* of 1940, both genres taken over from Baroque music. Berger, like Piston, has composed but little for piano: a fantasy of 1940, a set of bagatelles, an independent rondo, a suite of 1946, and a partita of 1946, the last related to Stravinsky's manner as we have seen it in the Serenade in A. Persichetti, who was trained completely in the United States and who has written a good deal of keyboard music, mostly for piano, is much in what we have called the "contemporary *galant*" vein so prominent in France. He, too, emphasizes the "abstract" form of the sonata: there are fifteen in all for piano, of which the fourth is a substantial work, one is for two pianos, another is for harpsichord, and, in a Stravinskian vein, there is a concerto for two unaccompanied pianos. Strongly Neo-Classical is the sole piano work of Irving Fine, a suite called simply and characteristically *Music for Piano* of 1947, which also belongs to what we have been calling the "contemporary *galant*."

Much of the same spirit may be seen in Harold Shapero (1920–), who has written three piano sonatas, a set of variations, and another sonata for two pianos. A foreign-born composer of this persuasion is the Russian Alexei Haieff (1914–), also a pupil of Boulanger, who has composed in a Stravinskian vein a sonata for two pianos of 1945. We can also mention the piano pieces of Ellis Kohs (1916–), which include an extended toccata for piano or harpsichord based on the large Baroque form, *Variations on l'homme armé* (the popular song used in many cyclic Masses of the Renaissance and also used for an extended organ work by the German composer Johann Nepomuk David), and a group of ten inventions. Then there is Lou Harrison (1917–) who has written six sonatas, also for piano or harpsichord, in the style and spirit of Domenico Scarlatti. Finally, we can mention the harpsichordist and composer Daniel Pinkham (1923–).

The leading figure here—and one of the most important and influential American composers— is Aaron Copland (1900–). Unlike many of his colleagues Copland, being himself a pianist, has composed some of his most important works for the instrument (see Smith and Berger). In his earlier work, the French "contemporary *galant*" is evident, as in *The Cat and the Mouse* of 1920 (dates are of composition), also called *Scherzo humoristique*, or the two *Blues* of 1926 (included in the set of four that appeared in 1948), all three of which were written in Paris while he studied with Boulanger; the French organ style is evident in his symphony for organ of 1924, and, like Piston, he has a passacaglia for piano of 1921–1922. From the 1930's, Copland has deliberately composed in two separate veins: one is admittedly directed at the concert audience and the other is serious and makes no concessions to the large mass of the concert-going public. As far as keyboard music is concerned, the first is represented by the two children's pieces of 1939 and the *Danzon Cubana* for two pianos of 1942. The more significant works are in the other group and include, apart from the earlier passacaglia, the *Piano Variations* of 1930, the *Piano Sonata* of 1939–1941, and the *Piano Fantasy* of 1957. For organ, there is the *Episode* of 1940.

The three large piano compositions are the center of his keyboard music. The first really striking work, in which he reveals his own "style" in all essentials, is the *Piano Variations* (later arranged for orchestra), a theme, twenty variations, and a coda. What is important and individual is the aloof and objective atmosphere. Stimulating an emotional reaction or response from the listener is not the aim; the dynamic quality of the German Romantic tradition is not present; instead, the music is presented as something there, stable, detached, well made, and independent. This is the essential quality of Neo-Classical art and of much contemporary music. The basic motive of the *Piano Variations* consists of four notes, first presented in a declamatory fashion, monophonically, *marcato* and *fortissimo*, and well separated, then made the basis of all that follows. One of the principal devices used is that of octave transposition, which is also important in dodecaphonic music; and there is even some serial writing here. But it is the sound that is different. The old qualifications of homophonic and polyphonic do not really apply to the *Piano Variations*, since there is no melodic line or lines, no melody and accompaniment; rather, there are isolated notes and chords involving all ranges of the keyboard and exploitation of the overtones and the essential tone-quality of the grand piano. Copland often uses conventional

---

EXAMPLE 82

Copland: *Piano Variations*—excerpts

A. Theme—beginning

B. Variation One—beginning

C. Variation Four—beginning

chords, especially triads, but in completely new relationships, contexts, and progressions. Furthermore, although the large chord complexes are used, they are spaced; the instrument is allowed to "resonate" so that the full characteristics of the sound created have a chance to come across. All in all, there is a certain sparseness or leanness about the work that is characteristic of much contemporary music, especially that associated with the Neo-Classical.

The same features reappear in the *Piano Sonata* and the *Piano Fantasy*. The sonata has, apart from the three-movement scheme, little relation to previous sonatas; the formal plans of the movements are not those usually associated with the genre. Here, in the first movement, is a free sort of sonata form; the interval of the third is prominent, played in all ranges and in various combinations, so that it is sonority that is important. The second movement is fast with a chorale-like middle section, and the finale uses a folk-like theme not unlike those that

EXAMPLE 82—*continued*

Copland used in his ballets. The fantasy (see Berger) has no set formal plan (although, in the nineteenth century, it appeared either as a sonata or as an organ work in the manner of the Baroque toccata), but it shows the same concept of piano sound and preoccupation with thematic variation. (Here, while the theme is a ten-note series, the two other notes used in cadences, the work is not organized along serial principles.) The fantasy is also distinguished by the prominence of virtuoso elements.

In the work of other composers of this basic persuasion, the role of keyboard music is of lesser importance; that is to say, the keyboard music does not represent turning points in the composers' work, even though it may be fully representative of their conceptions of musical composition. One of the most serious and uncompromising of American composers has been Roger Sessions (1896–) who, unlike Copland and others, received his training in Italy and Germany. He has written in all a relatively small number of compositions. For keyboard, there are two sonatas, in 1930 and 1946, a march and a set of children's pieces of 1935, and a set of character pieces, *From My Diary*, of 1946; for organ, there are some chorales and chorale preludes. The sonatas typify his proclivity towards the large and abstract musical forms. They are big, complicated works in an individual manner that shuns any kind of external or superficial display or even any particular adaptation to the piano. Some of this is doubtless attributable to the influence of his teacher, Bloch. Bloch was also the teacher of Leon Kirchner (1919–), who also gives prominence to the large forms and whose work often has some of the rhapsodic and quasi-improvisational quality of Bloch. For piano, Kirchner's most important work is a sonata of 1948, a cyclic composition in three movements; there is also a more modest *Little Suite* of 1949 in something of a Neo-Classical vein (see Ringer). Finally, attention may be drawn to the sole piano work of Elliot Carter (1908–), a sonata in two large movements composed in 1945–1946. This work, greatly indebted to Copland for its sonorous conception of the piano (especially the exploitation of overtones), is somewhat more conventional in its formal plan. The first movement is in sonata form, in which two contrasting tempi are important. The last movement, somewhat less traditional, employs a chorale-like passage as a refrain element and features a brilliant Neo-Baroque fugue full of driving figuration; it is thus related to large forms of late nineteenth-century piano and organ music. (See the discussion by Goldman.)

The composers just discussed take their point of departure from French Neo-Classicism, which appears in many different and individual manners; they represent an important—possibly the most important—group among contemporary United States musicians. But there are others who are much more closely oriented to the Romantic-expressive tradition of nineteenth-century German instrumental music. In a sense, they accept the old aesthetic of the musical art work; they maintain the musical forms and the procedures, although their harmonic vocabulary is enlarged with many of the newer acquisitions. There are a large number of American composers who belong to this group, most of whom, however, have not given much emphasis to keyboard music. The earliest is the Russian-born Leo Ornstein (1893–), whose works created a sensation in the years between 1910 and 1930 but which have now passed out of view. Others would include George Antheil (1900–1959), who began adventurously; Paul Creston (1906–); Ross Lee Finney (1906–), who has experimented also with dodecaphonic serialism; the Austrian-born Ernst Toch (1887–), who has composed a large amount of piano music, chiefly character pieces; Norman dello Joio (1913; see Downes); and Peter Mennin (1923–), who also emphasizes the small forms, with a certain element of the Neo-Classical.

By all odds the most important composer of this persuasion—and, with Copland, doubtless the outstanding contemporary American composer of piano music—is Samuel Barber (1910–), whose work has been discussed most comprehensively by Broder. As is typical of other contemporary composers, his reputation in piano music is based on but two works (Copland's is based on three)—the set of four *Excursions* (op. 20) of 1944 (dates refer to composition) and the Sonata in e-flat (op. 26) of 1949. The *Excursions* are, as Barber himself puts it, "excursions in small classical forms into regional American idioms." The first comes from dance music, the boogie-woogie; the second, from jazz also, is a stylized blues (Copland has also composed such blues for piano); the third is a set of variations on an ornamented version of the cowboy song *The Streets of Laredo* (which Copland also used, in his ballet *Billy the Kid*); and the last is a vivid suggestion of a barn dance with the energetic country fiddler (previously much used, as has been seen, by Cowell). The sonata (see Tischler), commissioned by the League of Composers for its twenty-fifth anniversary, is a major work. In the traditional large form, its four movements are Allegro energico in sonata form, an Allegro vivace, an Adagio mesto, and, as finale, a brilliant fugue, Allegro con spirito. In the treatment of the forms, Barber remains strictly traditional. In the sonata form, there is abundant thematic contrast; the principal theme is strong and motivic, and the subordinate theme is lyrical and ornamented (in the development it becomes heroic). Both the scherzo and the Adagio mesto display the conventional three-part scheme and the character normally associated with such movements. The fugue, in three voices, has a long figurational subject (the countersubject is plainly derived from a stock jazz figure), and the working-out involves devices of learned counterpoint (augmentation, inversion, stretto, the motivic treatment of parts of the subject, and variation of the subject); the movement reaches a large climax followed by a cadenza. The key is e-flat, and the work is conventional in its treatment of tonality, although dissonant chromatic elements are present in abundance. (The slow movement contains some unsystematic dodecaphonic writing.) This is doubtless the outstanding work of its kind produced by an American composer. For organ,

Barber has written a set of variations on the Shaker melody *Wondrous Love* (op. 34) of 1959.

Another group of composers to be mentioned consists of composers who may be regarded as "nationalists" (and, in this respect, they are not unrelated to the Neo-Romantic group just discussed), preoccupied with the establishment of a native American music that is independent of European influences, drawing its inspiration and materials from native sources. We have already observed instances of this here and there: folk-songs, barn dances, and hymn tunes in Ives, Cowell, Copland, and Barber; jazz elements in Copland and Barber and so forth. As far as jazz itself is concerned, we must mention here the well-known set of three preludes by George Gershwin (1898–1937) composed in 1936, of which the second is a typical stylized blues; and, of course, jazz has appeared from time to time in the work of European composers beginning with Debussy, as has

EXAMPLE 83

Barber: *Sonata* in e-flat (op. 26)—excerpts

A. Allegro energico—beginning

B. Allegro con spirito—beginning

been pointed out. But this group of composers goes beyond this. Its members attempt to derive a set of basically American traits governing melodic style, the use of modal scales and their related harmonies, a linear sort of texture and freely changing meters; at the same time, they agree with the Neo-Classical group in their rejection of nineteenth-century forms and acceptance of those from the Baroque period. The outstanding exponent of this American nationalist manner is Roy Harris (1898–), whose work has had a profound impact. But, again, the impact has not been particularly on keyboard music, and, apart from an early sonata (op. 1) of 1928—which is most representative—and a toccata of 1949, his piano music is in the smaller forms: the *Little Suite* of 1948, the set called *Children at Play*, and pieces based on folk songs, such as the *Variations on an Irish Theme* of 1942 and the highly characteristic set of ten *American Ballads* of 1946, which are American equivalents of Bartók's folk-song arrangements. Another member of this group is Harris' pupil William Schuman (1910–), who for years was the director of the famous Juilliard School of Music in New York City and now heads the new Lincoln Center for the Performing Arts; he has but one keyboard work, the *Three Score Set* of 1943, a group of three character pieces.

EXAMPLE 83—*continued*

B

Essentially in the same vein are composers who at one time or another have been associated with the famous Eastman School of Music at the University of Rochester, which has established a small tradition of its own quite distinct from the older New England academic tradition to which reference has previously been made. The first director of the school, Howard Hanson (1896–), composed piano music only during his early career as a composer; his work is in the traditional types of character pieces (there is also a sonata), frequently with Nordic associations that would relate him to MacDowell. Other composers of this group have not written much for keyboard. Hunter Johnson (1906–) has a single sonata composed in 1933–1934 and revised twice in 1936 and 1947–1948; it is in three movements, is cyclic, and is an attempt to express the spirit of the American South. Burrill Phillips (1907–) has written piano music in the short forms, in which folk elements are combined with the Neo-Classical; his toccata of 1944 uses a boogie-woogie ostinato figure, the three divertimenti of 1945 contain a *Hommage to Monteverdi*, and among the three *Informalities* is a blues; there is also an earlier set of pieces, *Nine by Nine*, and a sonata for piano of 1947. Robert Ward (1917–) has composed a single piece for piano, *Lamentation* of 1949; Ulysses Kay (1917–) has composed a piano sonata and two *Meditations* for organ; and Gardner Read (1913–) has a single work for organ, a passacaglia and fugue of 1937 and *American Circle*, a piano work in the manner of a folk dance.

More prolific members of the group, as far as keyboard music is concerned, are David Diamond and Robert Palmer (both born in 1915). Whereas Palmer (see Austin) was trained entirely in the United States (apart from work at Eastman, he studied with Copland and Harris), Diamond also studied in France with Boulanger (and also with Sessions). Both show a preference for the larger and "abstract" forms. Diamond has a sonatina of 1935, a sonata of 1947, and a concerto for two pianos of 1941; Palmer has two large sonatas for piano solo, the first composed between 1938 and 1946 and the second between 1942 and 1948, and two others, one for two pianos of 1944 and the other for piano duet for 1952. Diamond also has a set of children's pieces and a long character piece, *The Tomb of Melville*, composed between 1944 and 1949, somewhat in the French tombeau tradition; Palmer has a set of three preludes of 1941 and a brilliant *Toccata ostinato* of 1945. One other composer, William Bergsma (1921–), has composed a number of piano pieces—the set of three *Fantasies* of 1943, and the *Tangents* of 1950, a cycle intended to be played as a single long work.

Finally, it may be mentioned that a number of contemporary American composers have worked with Schönberg's dodecaphonic serialism: Wallingford Riegger (1885–1961), George Perle (1915–), Milton Babbit (1916–), Ben Weber (1916–), and George Rochberg (1918–). Riegger, who did not write much for piano adopted a rather cavalier and distinctly American experimental attitude towards the serial method, using it selectively and with great freedom. Babbit has but one piano work, the three *Compositions* of 1947, which is strictly serial in all respects. Weber and Rochberg have emphasized the keyboard medium, Weber working in a Neo-Classical vein and Rochberg in large sonatas attempting—in the Berg tradition—to effect a rapprochement with the dynamic expressive ideal of nineteenth-century music. Perle's output comprises three suites, a set of preludes, and a sonata.

We see, then, that, while there has been much variety in contemporary American keyboard music, there are at the same time certain broad trends that correspond to trends that are observable elsewhere. There is the old Romantic tradition, largely Germanic in its background, and the new French manner with its stress on Neo-Classical elements and a certain objective quality; and then there are the "nationalists" who, in their conscious use of folk and folk-like melodies, frequently also use elements of either of the two other main directions. Dodecaphonic music did not become important in the United States until after World War II.

In South America (we include Mexico), we again find essentially the same picture: the overriding influence of European, especially French, music, and the attempt to adopt and derive some sort of individual form of expression. The number of South American composers to have attained any stature in the realm of contemporary music has up to now been small; there are three, however, who stand out as figures of considerable stature: Heitor Villa-Lobos (1887–1959) of Brazil, Carlos Chavez (1899–) of Mexico, and Alberto Ginastera (1916–) of Argentina. Villa-Lobos is, in many respects, wholly typical. He was curious about music, largely self-taught, susceptible to the native music of his country (making expeditions into the jungle to familiarize himself with the music of the primitive Indians), spent time in France, was under the influence of Neo-Classicism, and made the characteristic effort to fuse these elements into individual works of art. Among the outspokenly Neo-Classical works are the *Bachianas brasileiras* in which Brazilian and Bach-like elements are combined; the fourth, of 1930–1936, is for piano. Then there is the set of rather Impressionistic pieces, *Prole do bébé* (*The Baby's Family*), the *Suite floral*, the three *Maries*, and other sets of children's pieces. Nationalistic are the *Cielo brasileira* of 1936–1937, the *Saudades dos selvas*, and the *Carnaval des criancas brasileiras*. But by far the largest of his piano works is the grandiose quasi-improvisational *Rudepoema* (*Rude Poem*) of 1921–1926, a virtuoso conception in a number of extended and continuous sections that is evidently related to the rhapsodic–epic–ballade tradition in European piano music but in which aspects of Brazilian primitive music are effectively brought to expression.

Both Chavez and Ginastera have shown a strong impetus from the music of the United States along with their preoccupation with folk and Neo-Classical elements. Chavez has shown a preference for the established "abstract" genres of piano music. There are two early sonatas and a sonatina, a set of waltzes, a set of studies, *Cantos mexicanos* (a set of fugues), a set of seven pieces for piano (among them a blues), preludes (on the white keys, percussive), and a fugue. Ginastera, apart from his nationalistic pieces (the *Piezas* and *Malambo* of 1940, the *Danzas Argentinas* of 1937, and the early set of children's pieces) is especially known for the two books of *American Preludes*, six in each, of 1944; they are in various styles, some etude-like, others in some particular national idiom, and still others representing various composers. There is also a large sonata of 1952. This last work, in four movements, is, generally speaking, in the older Romantic, dynamic, expressive tradition of the sonata, although some of the thematic content is clearly nationalistic in its inspiration. The first movement is in sonata form with a declamative and rhetorical opening; then there is the scorrevole scherzo, the rhapsodic slow movement (both interior movements are in the usual three-part form), and the percussive, toccata-like, finale. In several places, the way of writing for the piano owes much to the example of Copland.

It appears, then, that, generally speaking, the dominant influence in contemporary music up to the Second World War came from France and that it was basically Neo-Classical in its attitude, which is to say that it ignored the central line of nineteenth-century German instrumental music and drew its aesthetic aims and musical forms and procedures from earlier periods, notably the eighteenth century. There was, however, in Austria, a school in which a new way of organizing music was developed, a system or method of composition, that may be regarded as the logical outgrowth of the nineteenth-century German manner: the dodecaphonic serialism of Arnold Schönberg, whose work—with that of his immediate disciples—has been discussed earlier. In the years following World War II, the music of Schönberg and, in particular, that of his pupil Webern (who, as has been seen, wrote but one composition for piano) has become more and more important, and more and more composers have come to adopt it in one way or another. These composers come from all countries, and some of them had previously been for years composing according to some other precept (such as Stravinsky), so that, in some ways, one can even refer to a new international style. Furthermore, as has been seen from the work of Schönberg himself, the new procedure is by no means incompatible with the conceptions of Neo-Classicism. (See the Suite for piano, op. 25.)

It is also true that, generally speaking again, the keyboard medium is not of central importance, and works for piano or organ are not abundant. This situation seems implicit from the example of Webern who sought to establish a melodic line produced by varieties of tone color (the *Klangfarbenmelodie*), for which obviously the piano, at least, would be unsuited but by no means the organ. This attitude has led to a search for new sounds to be exploited in musical composition, first in the concept of the "art of noises" of the Italian Luigi Russolo (1855–1947) of 1917 or the works of Edgar Varèse (1885–1965) or, more recently, in the employment of electronically generated tones. But, by and large, this has had but little effect on piano music. We have the novel effects of Henry Cowell, or the prepared piano of John Cage (see below), or the electronic instruments operated by keyboard, such as the Ondes Martinot. The newest music, then, is related to these new principles: the serial principle of organization and the employment of totally new media of musical sounds. The changes in some cases have been so far-reaching as to alter the very conception of what music actually is.

The newest development in music, although an outgrowth of Schönberg and especially Webern, oddly enough seems to appear first in France in the work of a group of composers who rebelled against the contemporary *galant* of "the Six" and who instead affirmed the essentially Romantic and expressive value of music, in short, seeking what they called a "rehumanization" of music. This group called itself *La jeune France* (the young France), and has as its members Olivier Messiaen (1908–), who was also one of the leading French composers of organ music; André Jolivet (1905–); Daniel-Lesure (1908–); and Yves Baudrier (1906–). Jolivet, interested in primitive forms of religion, has held that music has almost magical properties in tune with an all-powerful cosmic force and, hence, becomes almost incantation. For piano, he has composed only a few works: a set of three pieces, *Temps*, of 1930; a set of six *Mana* of 1935, an Oriental inspiration (the third number is called *La princesse de Bali*); an *Étude sur des modes antiques* of 1944; and a sonata in memory of Bartók of 1945; and, for two pianos, there is the *Hopi Snake Dance* of 1948. While Daniel-Lesure has a few piano pieces and a *Scène de la passion* for organ of 1931, Baudrier has emphasized other types of composition, particularly film music.

The leading figure is without any doubt Messiaen, who was trained under Dukas and Dupré at the Paris Conservatory and emerged as an ardent opponent of Neo-Classicism, insisting on the emotional power and appeal of music. Messiaen believes that there is a correspondence between musical sounds and religious elements, and in this he is similar to his colleague Jolivet and also to the earlier Russian Skriabin, the Englishman Scott, and possibly to an American like Ives or Ruggles. Messiaen's manner of writing music is most original and has been expounded by him at some length in two treatises, *Le technique de mon langage musicale* of 1944 (English edition, *The Technique of My Musical Language*, 1957) and the *Traite du rhythme* of 1954, both of which have been influential. Here, an essentially Romantic conception of music is clear enough; but the expressive power of music is to be heightened by various expansions in the idiom of the art from within and by the additions of new elements from without. Of particular interest are Messiaen's ideas on rhythm. Just as chromatic notes represent alterations of or additions to the diatonic scale, so he works with chromatic rhythms, which are in a similar relation to conventional metric relationships. New rhythmic patterns that he employs are taken from Hindu music. (Generally, they are identified and labeled in his compositions.) In many of his works, he operates with a series or row in Schönberg's sense, which affects not only pitches but also succession of rhythmic values (somewhat in the sense of the medieval *talea* or, more pertinently, of the Hindu *tala*). His vocabulary of scales includes not only the whole-tone scale so common in Debussy, but also Gregorian modes and even new divisions of the octave that he has worked out himself. Somewhat in the spirit of Cocteau, Messiaen is interested in natural sounds in his music, especially the musical representation of bird calls, as passages in several works and chapters in his treatise will readily demonstrate.

Messiaen's compositional work is extensive, and in it keyboard music for organ and piano (he is a well-known organist) is important. Generally, the works composed up to the Second World War are readily identifiable with traditional conceptions. For piano, there is *La dame de Shalott* of 1917, connected with Tennyson's poem; *La tristesse d'un grand ciel bleu* of 1925; the set of eight preludes of 1929; the jazzy *Fantaisie burlesque* of 1932; a memorial *Pièce pour le tombeau de Paul Dukas* of 1935; a rondeau of 1943; and the well-known set of twenty *Regards sur l'enfant Jésus* of 1944, in which his religious mysticism finds full expression. For organ, again the types that appear up through 1939 do not cause much amazement: an *Esquisse modale* of 1927; *Variations écossaises* of 1928; the popular *Le banque celeste* and *L'hôte aimable des âmes*, both of 1928; a *Diptyque* of 1930; another popular work, *L'Apparition de l'église éternelle* of 1932; a set of four pieces, *L'Ascension* of 1934 (which also exists in a version for orchestra); and a set of pieces, *La nativité du Seigneur* of 1935.

In the works composed after World War II, Messiaen reveals himself as among the most progressive composers of the time, at least from the standpoint of compositional techniques. The point of departure is Schönberg's dodecaphonic serialism; but Messiaen applies the serial principle to all aspects of the musical composition, so that, along with controlling the pitch content of the work, it also affects rhythmic values, dynamic levels, and types of attack. This has been called total serialism or, in Stravinsky's terminology, "totalitarian serialism"; and while we have seen something approaching it in the work of Boris Blacher and Rudolf Wagner-Regeny, here the idea is much more consequently carried out. It has become an important element in the most recent music. Along with it goes an entirely new conception of music, of musical sound (often employing electronically manipulated or generated tones), an unheard-of rhythmic complexity, a type of melodic and thematic conception that really has no precedent in Western music. The complexities, in fact, are such that no two performances could be the same, a situation that brings us to the concept of "random," "chance," or aleatoric music, in which the chance element in a performance becomes an important aspect, although one might hesitate to associate this notion with that of composition. At any rate, Messiaen's piano pieces that display such features are the four *Études de la rhythme*, comprising the *Modes de valeurs et d'intensité*, and the *Neumes rhythmiques*, both of 1949; the two sets of *Île de feu*, of 1950; then the long *Canteydjaya* of 1953; then two other pieces, *La rousselot effarvate* of 1958 and the *Catalogue d'oiseaux* of 1959. For organ, a medium that, in its vast possibilities for tone color, would seem not unsuited to a conception such as the *Klangfarbenmelodie*, there is the *Messe de la Pentecôte* of 1950 and *Le livre d'orgue* of 1951. The Mass is particularly interesting for us, since it is yet another example in the old genre of organ music. It is in five movements (*Entrée, Offertoire, Consecration, Communion,* and *Sortie*), each of which is prefaced by a quotation from the Bible. The largest of these is the *Offertoire*, a type that has enjoyed a long history in French organ music; here, it is a sectional piece with a refrain element. In the Mass, the chief features of Messiaen's manner are to be observed: the new world of sound in the new chord combination and the new kinds of tone color drawn from the organ, the use of Oriental and "chromatic" rhythms, and the serial principle of organization.

Other European composers to be mentioned here include Hermann Heiss (1897–), Knudåge Riisager, Jean-Louis Martinet (1912–), René Leibowitz (1913–), Alois Zimmermann (1918–), Bruno Maderna (1920–), Maurice Le Roux (1923–), Pierre Boulez (1925–), Karl-Heinz Stockhausen (1928–), Henri Posseur (1929–), and Bo Nilsson (1937–), to restrict ourselves to those who have composed piano music. Since the Second World War, the emphasis has been on musical composition with electronically generated tones, which either are real sounds from the natural world that are recorded and then modified electronically (*musique concrète*) or else purely electronic tones generated in an oscillator. In some cases, electronic sounds are combined with those of normal musical instruments. Some of these composers are older and have composed in a more conventional way for piano prior to the Second World War, even though their present preferences are somewhat more "advanced." Thus, Riisager wrote a sonata (op. 27) in 1931; Heiss, who worked with Schönberg and Hauer, has composed several pieces in the simple dodecaphonic principle of Schönberg, as indeed has Leibowitz.

By way of explanation, the *Klavierstück* (op. 12) of Stockhausen may be briefly described. The work, a piano piece ostensibly in the tradition of the Romantic character piece, is printed on a large sheet ($37'' \times 21''$) and consists of nineteen passages of varying lengths, textures, styles, and so forth. The composer has devised a scale of dynamic levels from *ppp* to *ff* and another scale of six possible tempi, from the slowest possible to the fastest possible, and has another scale of possible kinds of attack. In performance, the pianist begins with any of the nineteen passages, selecting any of the tempi, any of the dynamic levels, any kind of attack; when the end of the passage is reached, he moves on to any other one (at random), but, in performing this next passage, he must observe the performance directions relating to tempo, dynamic level, and kind of attack that appear at the end of the passage just completed, and so forth. There is, then, no sequence in which the passages are to be played, and hence there is no set length to the piece, which is to be regarded as having reached one of its possible conclusions when one passage has been played for the third time. Here, again, is the "random" or aleatoric element to which reference has already been made; it has been said, with some degree of justice, that every performance of the piece is a premiere. At one and the same time, then, the piece is highly, that is, totally, organized (serial in all respects) and yet free. Similar piano works by other members of the group are Nilsson's *Quantitäten* of 1958, Maderna's *Fantasia and Fugue on BACH* for two pianos of 1949, and especially the work of Boulez, who has several sonatas, three for piano solo of 1946, 1948 and 1957 and one for two pianos of 1946, and two extended sets of pieces, *Structures*, of 1955, which have some technical affinities with the larger works of Messiaen.

A number of composers in the United States have been working along the same lines. Perhaps the best known is John Cage (1912–), the only one to do much with the piano, who became known for his works for prepared piano; that is, the tone of the piano is modified by attaching and inserting into the action of the instrument various paper clips, erasers, keys, rubber bands, and so forth, which produces a startling modification of the piano sound (as had been done earlier by Cowell), making it sound, often, rather like an Oriental instrumental ensemble. Cage has been occupied with Oriental philosophy, as have other contemporary musicians, as has been seen. For this medium, he has composed a number of sonatas and interludes between 1946–1948. But recently he has embraced the electronic and aleatoric kind of music. Among other composers of this persuasion, we can name, along with Milton Babbitt, Mel Powell (1923–), David del Tredeci, and Charles Wuorinen.

It would appear, then, that the piano and organ—along with other standard musical instruments—are destined to be eclipsed should the electronic, serial, and aleatoric conceptions become dominant. But one can wonder if this is really destined to occur, for one important element of music has always been improvisation, and this has been particularly true of the keyboard medium. There is, to be sure, something of improvisation in aleatoric music, although of a new and rather restricted variety; but it does not seem as if the practice of improvisation will ever be important in the realm of serial music. The problem of complexity is not the only one, since it is known that, in the past, candidates for organ positions were expected to improvise strict three-voice fugues on subjects presented to them when they appeared for examination. The difference is that it is only the technique of imitation that is involved, whereas now it is not only the technique of the composition, but also the whole concept of how musical tones are to be organized in relation to one another that comes into play, and this creates what probably are insurmountable difficulties for improvisation. One hesitates to make predictions. But it seems reasonably safe to assume that the natural impulse towards improvisation will somehow re-assert itself.

Bibliography

This bibliography has been divided into two main parts. The first contains modern critical editions and facsimile reproductions of music and treatises important in the history of keyboard music, and the second presents the secondary literature. The first part, in turn, has been subdivided into two smaller sections: the first is devoted to anthologies, and the second lists editions of the works of individual composers, sources, and treatises. As a matter of policy, certain limitations have been observed to prevent the bibliography from becoming unduly large. The main consideration has been that only modern scholarly and critical publications have been included; works of a more or less popular intent have been disregarded.

In regard to music, only scholarly and critical editions are listed. Original first editions have been excluded as have smaller publications containing only a few pieces. Some exceptions have been made to this last in the case of important composers whose collected works have not been published and who would otherwise be unrepresented (such as Tunder and Lübeck). This policy also forces the exclusion of virtually all secondary composers of the nineteenth century and almost all composers of the twentieth century; it was felt that anyone seeking this music would have no difficulty locating it in publishers' or dealers' catalogues or in any of the larger music libraries, and, in any case, the problem of getting the critical and correct edition is not present here. Publications containing music edited primarily for performance have also largely been eliminated. The several standard sets containing national collections of music (the various *Denkmäler* or monuments) have not been listed as such, although individual volumes devoted to keyboard music contained in them have been included.

In regard to secondary literature, general historical and biographical works, including encyclopedias and dictionaries, have, with the exception of those concerned with keyboard music, been excluded. This principle is not easy to apply

463

and has sometimes been relaxed to permit the listing of a large work on a composer known particularly for his keyboard compositions or of a biographical work in which a composer's keyboard compositions receive special attention. An exception has also been made in the case of thematic catalogues, which are included since they are frequently mentioned in the text and furthermore are valuable references often neglected by all but the professional musical scholar. In cases where an author has published a number of articles that he subsequently incorporated into a book, the book is listed here instead of the articles (see, for instance, Newman). Generally, articles appearing in periodicals devoted to a particular composer (such as the *Bach-Jahrbuch* or the *Beethoven-Jahrbuch*) have not been included, since it is assumed that anyone conducting such a detailed investigation would look into such sets as a matter of course. An effort has been made to include important dissertations. Books and articles in languages less often read in the United States (such as Polish, Hungarian, Danish, Russian, and so forth) have generally been excluded. Shorter articles, contributions, notes, and reviews have in most instances also been excluded.

Comprehensive anthologies, sets, and standard works on keyboard music in general have throughout been designated by an asterisk (*).

This Bibliography was completed in August, 1964.

LIST OF ABBREVIATIONS

Acta	*Acta Musicologica*
AfMF	*Archiv für Musikforschung*
AfMW	*Archiv für Musikwissenschaft*
AM	*Annuario Musical*
CdMI	*I Classici della musica italiana* [d'Annunzio]
CEKM	*Corpus of Early Keyboard Music* [American Institute of Musicology]
CMI	*I Classici musicali italiana* [Fondazione Eugenio Bravi]
DDT	*Denkmäler deutscher Tonkunst. Folge I*
DJ	*Deutsches Jahrbuch für Musikwissenschaft*
DTB	*Denkmäler der Tonkunst in Bayern* [*Denkmäler deutscher Tonkunst, Folge II*]
DTOe	*Denkmäler der Tonkunst in Oesterreich*
EDM	*Das Erbe deutscher Musik*
Farrenc	Farrenc, *Le Trésor des pianistes*
Guilmant	Guilmant, *Archives des maîtres d'orgue des 16e–18e siècles*
JAMS	*Journal of the American Musicological Society*
JMP	*Jahrbuch der Musik Bibliothek Peters*
KJ	*Kirchenmusikalisches Jahrbuch*

MAB	*Musica antiqua Bohemica*
MB	*Musica Britannica*
MD	*Musica Disciplina*
MF	*Die Musikforschung*
MfM	*Monatshefte für Musikgeschichte*
MGG	*Die Musik in Geschichte und Gegenwart*
M & L	*Music and Letters*
MMA	*Mitteldeutsches Musik-Archiv*
MMB	*Monumenta Musica Belgicae*
MMN	*Monumenta Musica Neerlandica*
MMR	*Monthly Musical Record*
MQ	*Musical Quarterly*
MR	*Music Review*
NMA	*Nagels Musik Archiv*
PRMA	*Proceedings of the Royal Musical Association*
PSFM	*Publications de la société française de musicologie*
RBM	*Revue belge de musicologie*
RMI	*Rivista musicale italiana*
SIMG	*Sammelbände der Internationalen Musikgesellschaft*
SMW	*Studien zur Musikwissenschaft. Beihefte der Denkmäler der Tonkunst in Oesterreich*
Tagliapietra	Tagliapietra, *Antologia di musica antica e moderna per pianoforte*
Torchi	Torchi, *L'arte musicale in Italia*
TVNM	*Tijdschrift der Vereniging voor nederlandsche Muziekgeschiedenis*
VfMW	*Vierteljahrschrift für Muzikwissenschaft*
VNM	*Vereniging voor nederlandsche Muziekgeschiedenis*
ZfMW	*Zeitschrift für Musikwissenschaft*
ZIMG	*Zeitschrift der Internationalen Musikgesellschaft*

ANTHOLOGIES

Apel, Willi. *Keyboard Music of the Fourteenth and Fifteenth Centuries.* Vol. I of *CEKM.* 1963.

————. *Musik aus früher Zeit.* 2 vols. Mainz, 1934.

Arte antica e moderna: Scelta di composizioni per pianoforte. 21 vols. Milan, *c.* 1890–1910.

Benvenuti, Giacomo. *Cembalisti italiani del settecento: Diciotto sonate.* Milan, 1926.

Botsiber, Hugo. *Wiener Klavier- und Orgelwerke in der zweiten Hälfte des 17. Jahrhunderts.* Vol. XXVI of *DTOe.* Vienna, 1906.

*Corpus of Early Keyboard Music. Edited by Willi Apel. American Institute of Musicology. In progress.

Curtis, Alan. *Nederlandse Klaviermuziek uit de 16e en 17e eeuw.* Vol. III of *MMN.* Amsterdam, 1961.

Deutsche Klaviermusik aus dem Beginn des 18. Jahrhunderts. Vol. III of *NMA.* Hannover, 1927.

Esposito, Michele. *Early Italian Piano Music: A Collection of Pieces Written for the Harpsichord and Clavichord.* Boston, 1906.

**Farrenc, Aristide, and Farrenc, Louise. *Le Trésor des pianistes: Collection des œuvres choisies des maîtres de tous les pays et toutes les époques dépuis le 16e siècle jusqu'à la moitié du 19e.* 23 vols. Paris, 1861–1872.

Ferguson, Howard. *Style and Interpretation: An Anthology of Keyboard Music.* 4 vols. (2 vols. completed.) New York, 1964–.

Fischer, Hans, and Oberdörffer, Fritz. *Deutsche Klaviermusik des 17. und 18. Jahrhunderts.* 9 vols. Berlin, 1936. (2nd ed., 1960. English ed.: *German Keyboard Music of the Seventeenth and Eighteenth Centuries.* 9 vols. Berlin, 1960.)

Frotscher, Gotthold. *Orgelchoräle um Joh. Seb. Bach.* Series I, Vol. 9 of *EDM.* Braunschweig, 1937.

Fuller-Maitland, John Alexander. *Contemporaries of Purcell: Harpsichord Pieces.* 7 vols. London, 1921–1922.

Fuser, Ireneo. *Classici italiani dell'organo.* Padua, 1955.

Geiringer, Karl. *Music of the Bach Family: An Anthology.* Cambridge, 1955.

Georgii, Walther. *400 Jahre europäischer Klaviermusik.* Vol. I of *Das Musikwerk.* Cologne, 1951. (English ed. *400 Years of European Keyboard Music.* Vol. I of *Anthology of Music.* Cologne, 1959.)

————. *Musik aus alter Zeit: Meisterwerke für Klavier.* 3 vols. Cologne, 1960. (English ed., *Keyboard Music of the Baroque and Rococo.* 3 vols. Cologne, 1960.)

Gerdes, Gisela. *46 Choräle für Orgel von J. P. Sweelinck und seinen deutschen Schülern.* Vol. III of *Musikalische Denkmäler.* Mainz, 1957.

Glyn, Margaret. *Early English Organ Music (Sixteenth Century).* London, 1939.

466

*Guilmant, [Félix] Alexandre. *Archives des maîtres d'orgue des 16e–18e siècles.* Historical introductions by André Pirro. 10 vols. Paris, 1898–1907.

Halbig, Hermann. *Klaviertänze des 16. Jahrhunderts.* Berlin, 1928.
Howard, John Tasker. *A Program of Early American Piano Music.* New York, 1931.
Howell, Almonte C. *Five French Baroque Organ Masses.* Louisville, 1961.

Kastner, Santiago. *Clavistas Portuguezes.* 2 vols. Mainz, 1935–1950.
Keller, Hermann. *Achtzig Choralvorspiele des 17. und 18. Jahrhunderts.* Leipzig, 1937. (Reprint, 1951).
Klein, J. *The First Four Centuries of Organ Music.* 2 vols. New York, 1948.
Köhler, Louis. *Les maîtres du clavecin.* 2 vols. Braunschweig, 1860–1873.

Liber organi. Edited by Ernst Kaller. Mainz, in progress.

Malipiero, Gian Francesco. *Eighteenth Century Italian Keyboard Music.* Bryn Mawr, 1952.
Mitteldeutsches Musik–Archiv. Veröffentlichungen des Musikwissenschaftlichen Seminars der Friedrich–Schiller–Universität Jena. Reihe I: *Klaviermusik.* Leipzig, in progress.
Monumenta Musica Belgicae. Uitgegeven door de Vereniging voor Muziekgeschiedenis te Antwerpen. Berchem and Antwerp, in progress.
Moser, Hans Joachim. *Frühmeister der deutschen Orgelkunst.* Leipzig, 1930.

Newman, William S. *Thirteen Piano Sonatas of the Eighteenth and Nineteenth Centuries.* Chapel Hill, 1947.
Nin y Castellano, Joaquin. *Classiques espagnols du piano: Sonates anciennes d'auteurs espagnols.* 2 vols. Paris, 1925–1928.

Organum: Ausgewählte ältere vokale und instrumentale Meisterwerke. Edited by Max Seiffert. Reihe IV: *Orgelmusik,* 22 vols. Reihe V: *Klaviermusik,* 10 vols. Leipzig, 1925–1926.

Paoli, Domenico de. *Sonate italiane del secolo XVIII per cembalo o pianoforte.* London, 1939.
Pauer, Ernst, *Alte Meister: Sammlung wertvoller Klavierstücke des 17. und 18. Jahrhunderts.* 6 vols. Leipzig, 1868–1885.
————. *Old English Composers for the Virginals and Harpsichord.* London, n.d.
Pedrell, Felipe. *Antología de organistas clásicos españoles (siglos XVI, XVII y XVIII).* 2 vols. Madrid, 1908.

Raugel, Félix. *Les maîtres français de l'orgue aux XVIIe et XVIII siècles.* Paris, 1925.

Sachs, Curt. *The Evolution of Piano Music.* New York, 1944.
Schering, Arnold. *Alte Meister aus der Frühzeit des Orgelspiels: 12 Kompositionen für Orgel des 15. und 16. Jahrhunderts.* Leipzig, 1913.
Stevens, Denis. *Altenglische Orgelmusik.* Kassel, 1954.
Straube, Karl. *Alte Meister: Eine Sammlung deutscher Orgelkompositionen aus dem 17. und 18. Jahrhundert.* 3 vols. Leipzig, 1908.
————. *Choralvorspiele alter Meister.* Leipzig, 1907. Reprint, 1951.

*Tagliapietra, Gino. *Antologia di musica antica e moderna per pianoforte.* 18 vols. Milan, 1931–1933.
Torchi, Luigi. *L'arte musicale in Italia.* 7 vols. Milan and Rome, 1897–1907. (Vol. III contains keyboard music.)

West, John Ebenezer. *Old English Organ Music.* London, n.d.

INDIVIDUAL COMPOSERS, MANUSCRIPTS, AND TREATISES

Adlung, Jacob. *Musica mechanica organoedi.* Facsimile reprint. Edited by Christhard Mahrenholz. Kassel, 1931.
Annibale Padavano. *13 Ricercari.* Edited by N. Pierront and J. P. Hennebaine. Paris, 1934. See also Torchi, Vol. III.
Antegnati, Costanzo. *L'arte organica.* Modern ed. with German translation by P. Smets. Edited by Renato Lunelli. Mainz, 1938.
[Arnaut, Henricus.] *Instruments de musique du XVe siècle: Les traites de Henri Arnault de Zwolle et de divers anonymes.* Ms B. N. Latin 7295. Edited by G. LeCerf and E. R. Labande. Paris, 1932.
[Attaingnant, Pierre.] *Chansons und Tänze: Pariser Tabulaturdrucke für Tasteninstrumente aus dem Jahre 1530.* Edited by E. Bernoulli. 5 vols. Munich, 1914. (Also edited by F. Giesbert, *Pariser Tanzbuch aus dem Jahre 1530,* Mainz, 1950.)
――――. *Deux livres d'orgue . . . parus en 1531.* Edited by Yvonne Rokseth. Series I, No. 1 of PSFM. Paris, 1925.
――――. *Transcriptions of Chansons for Keyboard (1531).* Edited by A. Seay. Vol. XX of *Corpus mensurabilis musicae.* American Institute of Musicology. Rome, 1961.
――――. *Treize motets et une prélude pour orgue . . . parus en 1531.* Edited by Yvonne Rokseth. Series I, No. 5 of *PSFM.* Paris, 1930.

Bach, Carl Philipp Emanuel. *Klavierwerke: Die sechs Sammlungen von Sonaten, freien Fantasien und Rondos für Kenner und Liebhaber.* Edited by Carl Krebs. 6 vols. Leipzig, 1895. (Reprint, revised by Lothar Hoffmann-Erbrecht, Leipzig, 1953.
――――. *Preussische Sonaten.* Edited by Rudolf Steglich. Vols. VI and XV of *NMA.* Hannover, 1927–1928.
――――. *Versuch über die wahre Art das Klavier zu spielen.* Facsimile reprint, edited by Lothar Hoffmann-Erbrecht. Leipzig, 1957. (Modern ed., edited by Walther Niemann, Leipzig, 1906; 5th ed., 1925; English ed.: *Essay on the True Art of Playing Keyboard Instruments,* translated by William J. Mitchell, New York, 1949.)
――――. *Württembergische Sonaten.* Edited by Rudolf Steglich. Vols. XXI and XXII of *NMA.* Hannover, 1928.
Bach, Johann Christian. *10 Klavier–Sonaten.* Edited by Ludwig Landshoff. Leipzig, 1925.
Bach, Johann Christoph. *44 Choräle zum Präambulieren.* Edited by M. Fischer. Kassel, n.d.
Bach, Johann Christoph Friedrich. *Klaviersonaten.* Series III, No. 5 of *Veröffentlichungen des fürstlichen Instituts für musikwissenschaftliche Forschung Bückeburg.* Bückeburg, 1920. (Contains four sonatas.)

Bach, Johann Sebastian. *Clavier-Büchlein vor Wilhelm Friedemann Bach.* Facsimile reprint. Introduction by Ralph Kirkpatrick. New Haven, 1959.

―――. *Keyboard Practice, Consisting of an Aria with Thirty Variations* [*The Goldberg Variations*]. Edited by Ralph Kirkpatrick. New York, 1938.

―――. *Neue Ausgabe sämtlicher Werke.* Herausgegeben vom Johann-Sebastian-Bach-Institut Göttingen und vom Bach-Archiv Leipzig. 86 vols planned. Kassel, in progress.

―――. *Prelude and Fugue in B Minor* [*S. 544*]. Facsimile reproduction. Vol. IV of *The Harrow Replicas.* Cambridge, 1942.

―――. *Werke.* Herausgegeben von der *Bach-Gesellschaft.* 47 vols. Leipzig, 1851–1900 and 1926. (Reprint, 46 vols., Ann Arbor, 1947.)

Bach, Wilhelm Friedemann. *Complete Works for Organ.* Edited by E. Power Biggs. New York, 1947.

―――. *Fugen und Polonaisen für Pianoforte.* Edited by Walther Niemann. Leipzig, 1914.

―――. *Klaviersonaten.* Edited by Friedrich Blume. Vols. LXIII, LXXVIII, and CLVI of *NMA.* Hannover, 1930–1940.

Balakirev, Mily. *Complete Piano Works.* 2 vols. Moscow, 1951–1952.

Bédos de Celles, François. *L'art de facteur d'orgues.* Facsimile reprint. Edited by Christhard Mahrenholz. Kassel, 1934. (Earlier ed.: *Nouveau manuel complet de facteur d'orgues,* edited by P. M. Hamel, Paris, 1849; rev. ed., 1903.)

Beethoven, Ludwig van. *Klaviersonate in C-Dur op. 53* (*Waldsteinsonate*). Facsimile of Ms. Bonn, 1954.

―――. *Werke. Vollständige kritisch durchgesehene überall berechtigte Ausgabe.* 25 series, 33 vols. Leipzig, 1862–1890. (Reprint, Ann Arbor, 1949. Piano music in Series XVI, XVII, and XVIII.)

―――. *Werke.* Herausgegeben von Beethoven-Archiv Bonn unter Leitung von J. Schmidt-Görg. Munich, in progress.

Benda, Jirí Antonin. *Sonate 1–16, piano.* Edited by J. Racek. Revised by V. Sykora. Vol. XXIV of *MAB.* Prague, 1956.

―――. *Sonatine.* Vol. XXXVII of MAB, Prague, 1958.

Bermudo, Juan. *Declaración de instrumentos musicales.* Facsimile reprint. Edited by Santiago Kastner. Vol. I, No. 11 of *Documenta musicologica.* Kassel, 1957. (Music examples published separately as *Oeuvres d'orgue,* edited by P. Froidebise, Paris and Philadelphia, 1960.)

Blow, John. *Complete Organ Works.* Edited by W. Shaw. London and New York, 1958.

Böhm, Georg. *Klavier- und Orgelwerke.* Edited by J. and G. Wolgast. 2 vols. Leipzig, 1927–1932. (Reprints, Wiesbaden, 1952 and 1964.)

Boismortier, Joseph Bodin de. *Quatre suites de pièces de clavecin.* Edited by Erwin R. Jacobi. Munich and New York, 1960.

Boutmy, Josse. *Werken voor clavecimbal.* Edited by J. Watelet. Vol. V of *MMB.* Berchem and Antwerp, 1943.

Brahms, Johannes. *Sämtliche Werke. Ausgabe der Gesellschaft der Musikfreunde in Wien.* 26 vols. Leipzig, 1927–1928. (Reprint, Ann Arbor, 1949. Solo piano works in Vols. XIII, XIV and XV; piano duets and two-piano music in Vols. XII and XI; organ music in Vol. XVI.)

Bruhns, Nicolaus. *Gesammelte Werke.* Edited by Fritz Stein. 2 vols. Series II, Vols. 1 and 2 of *EDM.* Braunschweig, 1937–1939. (See also *Organum,* IV, 7 and 8.)

Bull, John. *Keyboard Music.* Edited by John Steele and Francis Cameron. Introduction by Thurston Dart. Vols. XIV and XIX of *MB.* London, 1960–1963.

[*Buxheim Organ Book.*] Facsimile reproduction. Edited by Bertha Anthonia Wallner. Series II, No. 1 of *Documenta musicologica*. Kassel, 1955. (Modern ed., edited by B. A. Wallner. Vols. XXXVII, XXXVIII, and XXXIX of *EDM*, Leipzig, 1958.)

Buxtehude, Dietrich. *Klaver Vaerker*. Edited by Emilius Bangert. Copenhagen and Leipzig, 1942. (2nd ed., 1944.)

———. *Orgelkompositionen*. Edited by J. Hedar. Copenhagen, 1952.

———. *Orgelkompositionen: Gesamtausgabe*. Edited by Philipp Spitta. 2 vols. Leipzig, 1876–1878. (Several later eds.: revised by Max Schneider, 1903–1904 and 1940; new ed. with preface by Walter Kraft, Wiesbaden, 1952.)

———. *Werke*. Herausgegeben von der Oberleitung der Glaubensgemeinde Ugrino. Edited by Wilibald Gurlitt. 7 vols. Ugrino, 1925–1937.

Byrd, William. *Collected Works*. Edited by Edmund H. Fellowes, 20 vols. London, 1937–1950. (Keyboard music in Vols. XVIII, XIX, and XX. Vols. I–XVII published as *Collected Vocal Works*.)

———. *Forty–Five Pieces for Keyboard Instruments*. Edited by Stephen D. Tuttle. Paris, 1939.

———. *My Ladye Nevells Booke*. Edited by Hilda Andrews. London, 1926.

Cabanilles, Johannis. *Musici organici: Opera omnia*. Edited by Higini Anglès. 4 vols. (in progress). Barcelona, Biblioteca de Catalunya. Sección de música. Public-caciones IV, VIII, XIII, XVII. Barcelona, 1927, 1935, 1936, 1956.

———. *Opera selecta pro organo*. Edited by Higini Anglès, C. Tournemire, and F. Peeters. 3 vols. Paris, 1948.

Cabezón, Antonio. *Claviermusik*. Edited by Santiago Kastner. London, 1951.

———. *Composiciónes*. Edited by F. Pedrell. Vols. III, IV, VII, and VIII of *Hispaniae schola musica sacra*. Barcelona, 1894–1898.

Cavazzoni, Girolamo. *Composizioni*. Edited by Giacomo Benvenuti. Vol. VI of *CdMI*. Milan, 1919. (See also Vol. III of Torchi.)

Cavazzoni, Marcantonio [da Bologna]. *Ricercari, motetti, canzoni*. (With works by Fogliano and Segni.) Edited by Giacomo Benvenuti. Vol. I of *CMI*. Milan, 1941. (Also edited by Knud Jeppesen, Vol. II of *Die italienische Orgelmusik am Anfang des Cinquento*, Copenhagen, 1943; 2nd ed., 1960. Also edited by O. Mischati, Mainz and New York, 1959.)

Chambonnières, Jacques. *Oeuvres complètes*. Edited by Paul Brunold and André Tessier. Paris, 1925. (Earlier ed., edited by H. Quittard, Paris, 1911.) See also Vol. II of Farrenc.

Chaumont, Lambert. *Livre d'orgue (1695)*. Edited by C. Hens & R. Bragard. Vol. A, No. 1 of *Monumenta Leodiensium Musicorum*. Liège, 1939. (Reprint, New York, 1950.)

Cherubini, Luigi. *Sei Sonate per cimbalo*. Edited by G. Buonamici. Florence, 1903.

Chopin, Frédéric. *Complete Works According to the Autographs and Original Editions*. (With critical commentary.) Edited by Ignace Paderewski. Warsaw, in progress. (A companion series of facsimile reproductions of Chopin's manuscripts has also commenced.)

———. *Werke*. 14 vols. and 3 supps. Leipzig, 1878–1880.

Cimarosa, Domenico. *Sonates*. Edited by Guido Pannain. Milan, 1915.

———. *32 Sonates*. Edited by Felice Boghen. 3 vols. Paris, 1925–1926.

Clementi, Muzio. *Sonate*. Edited by Guilio Cesare Paribene. Vol. VIII of *CdMI*. Milan, 1919. (Among other modern eds. of Clementi's sonatas are: F. Taylor, 4 vols., London, 1908 [32 sonatas]; G. Piccioli, 3 vols., Milan, 1949 [18 sonatas];

A. Ruthardt, Leipzig, *c.* 1905 [24 sonatas]; and H. Schmitt, 5 vols., Vienna, 1901 [32 sonatas]; see also Vol. XVI of Farrenc.)

Clérambault, Louis Nicolas. *Pièces de clavecin.* Edited by Paul Brunold. Paris, 1938.

————. *Premier livre d'orgue.* Vol. III of Guilmant.

Coelho, Manuel. *Flores de musica para o instrumento di tecla & arpa.* Edited by Santiago Kastner. Series A, Vols. 1 and 3 of *Portugaliae Musica.* Lisbon, 1959–1961.

Correa de Arauxo, Francisco. *Libro de tientos y discursos de musica practica y theorica de organo intitulado Facultad Organica.* Edited by Santiago Kastner. Vols. VI and XII of *Monumentos de la musica española.* Barcelona, in progress.

Couperin, François. *L'art de toucher le clavecin.* [German, French and English texts.] Leipzig, 1933.

————. *Oeuvres complètes.* Edited by Maurice Cauchie. 12 vols. Paris, 1932–1933. (Harpsichord music in Vols. II–V; organ music in Vol. VI.)

————. *Pièces de clavecin.* Ed. by Johannes Brahms and Friedrich Chrysander. 4 vols. London, 1889. (See also Vols. IV and V of Farrenc.)

————. *Pièces d'orgue consistantes en deux messes.* Edited by Paul Brunold. Monaco, 1949. (See also Vol. V of Guilmant.)

Couperin, Louis. *Oeuvres complètes.* Edited by Paul Brunold. Paris, 1936.

Croft, William. *Six Voluntaries.* Edited by K. Simpson. London, n.d.

Dagincourt, François. *Pièces pour orgue.* Edited by L. Pancl. Paris, 1934.

Dandrieu, Jean François. *Livre d'orgue.* Vol. VII of Guilmant.

D'Anglebert, Jean. *Pièces de clavecin.* Edited by M. Roesgen-Champion. Series I, No. 8 of *PSFM.* Paris, 1934. (See also Vol. III of Farrenc.)

Daquin, Louis Claude. *Livre de noëls.* Vol. III of Guilmant.

Della Ciaja, Azzolino Bernardino. *3 Sonate per il cembalo.* Edited by G. Buonamici. Florence, 1912.

The Dublin Virginal Manuscript. Edited by John Ward. Vol. III of *The Wellesley Edition.* Wellesley, 1954.

DuMage, Pierre. *Livre d'orgue.* Edited by Félix Raugel. Paris, 1952. (See also Vol. III of Guilmant.)

Durante, Francesco. *Studii, divertimenti e toccate.* Edited by A. Toni. Vol. XI of *CdMI.* Milan, 1920. (Also edited by Bernhard Paumgartner, Kassel, 1949; see also Vol. IX of Farrenc.)

————. *8 Toccate.* Edited by Guido Pannain. Milan, 1915.

Dvořák, Antonin. [*Works*] *Souborné vydáni.* Prague, 1955. (Piano music in Series V.)

Eckhard, Johann Gottfried. *Klavierwerke.* Edited by Eduard Reeser. Kassel, 1956.

Eijl, Anna Maria van. See Steenwick.

Erbach, Christian. *Werke für Orgel oder Klavier (Ausgewählte Werke I).* Edited by Erich von Werra. Vol. IV² of *DTB.* Leipzig, 1903. (With keyboard works of Hassler.)

Facoli, Marco. *Collected Works.* Edited by Willi Apel. Vol. II of *CEKM.* N.p., 1963.

[*Faenza Ms.*] *An Early Fifteenth Century Source of Keyboard Music.* The Codex Faenza, Biblioteca Communale 117. Facsimile reproduction. Edited by Armen Carapetyan. Vol. X of *Musicological Studies and Documents.* American Institute of Musicology. Rome, 1961. (Also *MD*, XIII [1959], 79–107; XIV [1960], 64–104; and XV [1961], 65–104.)

Fiocco, Joseph Hector. *Werken voor Clavicimbel*. Edited by Joseph Watelet. Vol. III of *MMB*. Berchem and Antwerp, 1936.

Fischer, Johann Kaspar Ferdinand. *Sämtliche Werke für Klavier und Orgel*. Edited by Erich von Werra. Leipzig, 1901.

The Fitzwilliam Virginal Book. Edited by John Alexander Fuller-Maitland and W. Barclay Squire. 2 vols. London, 1899. (Reprint, New York, 1949 and Ann Arbor, 1949.)

Frescobaldi, Girolamo. *Orgel- und Klavierwerke. Gesamtausgabe nach dem Urtext*. Edited by Pierre Pidoux. 5 vols. Kassel, 1949–1955. (See also Vols. V and VI of Tagliapietra; also *9 Toccate inedite*, edited by S. dalla Libera. Milan, 1962.)

Froberger, Johann Jakob. *Orgel- und Klavierwerke*. Edited by Guido Adler. Vols. VIII, XIII, and XXI of *DTOe*. Vienna, 1897, 1899 and 1903. (Reprint, Graz, 1960. See also Series IV, No. 11 of *Organum* and Vol. III of Farrenc.)

Fux, Johann Joseph. *Werke für Tasteninstrumente*. Edited by Erich Schenk. Vol. LXXV of *DTOe*. Vienna, 1947.

Gabrieli, Andrea. *Canzoni alla francese für Orgel oder Cembalo*. Edited by Pierre Pidoux. Kassel, 1953.

———. *Intonationen, für Orgel*. Edited by Pierre Pidoux. Kassel and New York, 1959.

———. *Ricercari für Orgel*. Edited by Pierre Pidoux. Kassel, 1952.

———. *3 Messe per organo*. Edited by S. dalla Libera. Milan, 1959.

Gabrieli, Giovanni. *Composizione per organo*. Edited by S. dalla Libera. Milan, 1957. (Also edited by G. S. Bedbrook, Kassel, 1957.)

———. *Opera omnia*. Edited by Denis Arnold. Vol. XX of *Corpus mensurabilis musicae*. American Institute of Musicology. Rome, in progress.

Galuppi, Baldassare. *Dodici sonate per il cembalo*. Edited by Giacomo Benvenuti. Bologna, 1920.

Gibbons, Orlando. *Complete Keyboard Works*. Edited by Margaret Glyn. 5 vols. London, 1922–1925. (More recent ed., edited by Gerald Hendrie, Vol. XX of *MB*, London, 1962.)

Gigault, Nicolas. *Livre de musique*. Vol. IV of Guilmant.

Giustini, Ludovico. *Twelve Piano–forte Sonatas*. Facsimile reprint. Edited by R. E. M. Harding. Cambridge, 1933.

Gottschalk, Louis Moreau. *Notes of a Pianist*. Edited by Jeanne Behrend. New York, 1964. (See also the excerpts, edited by John T. Howard, *MQ*, XVIII [1932], 106–118.)

Graupner, Johann Christoph. *Drei Partien*. Edited by Albert Küster. Wolfenbüttel, 1935.

———. *8 Partien*. Edited by Lothar Hoffmann-Erbrecht. Series I, No. 2 of *MMA*. Leipzig, 1954.

———. *Monatliche Klavier-Früchte*. Edited by Albert Küster. Wolfenbüttel and Berlin, 1928-1929.

Grazioli, Giovanni Battista. *Dodici sonate per cembalo*. Edited by Ruggiero Gerlin. Vol. XII of *CMI*. Milan, 1943.

Grigny, Nicolas de. *Premier livre d'orgue*. Vol. V of Guilmant.

Guilain, Jean Adam Guillaume. *Pièces d'orgue pour le magnificat*. Vol. VII of Guilmant.

Guillet, Charles. *Werken voor Orgel*. Edited by Joseph Watelet. Vol. IV of *MMB*. Berchem and Antwerp, 1938. (With works of Luython and Macque.)

Händel, Georg Friedrich. *Hällische Händel–Ausgabe. Im Auftrag der Georg Friedrich Händel–Gesellschaft*. Edited by Max Schneider and Rudolf Steglich. Kassel, in progress. (Keyboard music in Series IV.)

————. *Klavierwerke.* Edited Walter Serauky and Friedrich Glasenapp. 4 vols. Halle, 1949–1951.

————. *Pieces for Harpsichord . . . in the Aylesford Collection.* Edited by W. Barclay Squire and John Alexander Fuller-Maitland. 2 vols. London and Mainz, 1928.

————. *Werke. Ausgabe der deutschen Händelgesellschaft.* Edited by Friedrich Chrysander. 93 vols. and 6 supps. Leipzig, 1858–1894, 1902. (Keyboard works in vol. II, 1859.)

Hasse, Johann Adolf. *Claviersonaten.* Edited by Richard Engländer. Leipzig, 1930.

Hassler, Hans Leo. *Sämtliche Werke.* Edited by C. Crosby. *Veröffentlichungen der Gesellschaft für Bayerische Musikgeschichte.* Wiesbaden, since 1960.

————. *Werke für Orgel und Klavier.* Edited by Adolf Sandberger. Vol. IV^2 of *DTB.* Leipzig, 1903. (With keyboard works of Erbach.)

Havingha, Gerhardus. *Werken voor Clavecimbel.* Edited by Joseph Watelet. Vol. VII of *MMB.* Berchem and Antwerp, 1951.

Haydn, Franz Joseph. *Klaviersonate A-Dur [No. 26].* Facsimile reproduction. Edited by Jens Peter Larsen. Munich, 1928.

————. *Sämtliche Werke.* 11 vols. (Incomplete.) Leipzig, 1907–1933. (Piano sonatas in Series I.)

————. *Werke.* Herausgegeben vom Joseph-Haydn-Institut Köln. Edited by Jens Peter Larsen. Cologne, in progress.

Helmont, Charles Joseph van. *Werken voor Orgel en/of Clavicembel.* Edited by Joseph Watelet. Vol. VI of *MMB.* Berchem and Antwerp, 1948. (With works of Raick.)

Hurlebusch, Conrad Friedrich. *Compositioni musicali per il cembalo divise in due parte.* Edited by Max Seiffert. Vol. XXXII of *VNM.* Amsterdam and Leipzig, 1912.

Ileborgh, Adam. *Die Orgeltabulatur.* Facsimile reproduction. Edited by G. Most. Stendal, Altmärkische Museum, *Jahresausgabe,* VII (1954), 43–66. (Modern ed., edited by Willi Apel, Vol. I of *CEKM.*)

Jullien, Gilles. *Premier livre d'orgue.* Edited by Norbert Dufourcq. Series I, No. 13 of *PSFM.* Paris, 1952.

Kellner, Johann Peter. *Ausgewählte Klavierstücke.* Edited by C. Schröder. Leipzig, n.d.

Kerckhoven, Abraham van den. *Werken voor Orgel.* Edited by Joseph Watelet. Vol. II of *MMB.* Berchem and Antwerp, 1933.

Kerll, Johann Kaspar von. *Ausgewählte Werke.* Edited by Adolf Sandberger. Vol. II^2 of *DTB.* Leipzig, 1901. (Only one volume has appeared.)

————. *Modulatio organica.* Edited by R. Walther. Altötting, 1956.

————, *Stücke für Tasteninstrumente.* Edited by W. Hillemann. Vol. LXXXVII of *NMA.* Hannover, n.d.

Kindermann, Johann Erasmus. *Ausgewählte Werke.* Edited by Felix Schreiber and Bertha Anthonia Wallner. Vols. XXI and XXIV of *DTB.* Leipzig, 1913; Augsburg, 1924.

Krebs, Johann Ludwig. *Klavierübung.* Edited by Kurt Soldan. Leipzig, 1937.

————. *Orgelwerke.* Edited by C. Giessler. Magdeburg, 1847–1849. (Selections edited by W. Zöllner, Leipzig and New York, 1938.)

Krieger, Johann. *Gesammelte Werke für Klavier und Orgel.* Edited by Max Seiffert. Vol. XVIII of *DTB.* Leipzig, 1917. (See also Series IV, No. 17 of *Organum.*)

Kuhnau, Johann, *Klavierwerke.* Edited by Carl Päsler. Vol. IV of *DDT.* Leipzig, 1901.

————. *Six Biblical Sonatas.* Edited by Kurt Stone. New York, 1953. (Also edited by John S. Shedlock, London, 1905; see also Vol. III of Farrenc.)

LeBègue, Nicolas. *Oeuvres de clavecin.* Edited by Norbert Dufourcq. Paris, 1956.
———. *Oeuvres [organ].* Vol. IX of Guilmant.
Le Roux, Gaspard. *Pieces for Harpsichord.* Edited by Albert Fuller. New York, 1959.
Liadov, Anatoliĭ Konstantinovich. *Piano works.* Edited by K. N. Igumov. 2 vols. Moscow, 1947.
Liszt, Franz. *Liszt Society Publications.* 4 vols. London, 1952–1954.
———. *Musikalische Werke.* Herausgegeben von der Franz Liszt-Stiftung. 31 vols. (incomplete.) Leipzig, 1908–1933. (Piano music, edited by J. Motta da Viarra, in Part II.)
Locke, Matthew. *Keyboard Suites.* Edited by Thurston Dart. London, 1959.
———. *Organ Voluntaries.* Edited by Thurston Dart. London, 1957.
Loeillet, Jean Baptiste. *Werken voor Clavecimbel.* Edited by J. Watelet. Vol. I of *MMB.* Berchem and Antwerp, 1932.
Lübeck, Vincent. *4 Praeludien und Fugen.* Series IV, No. 9 of *Organum.* Leipzig, 1925.
Lublin, Johannes de. *Tablature of Keyboard Music.* Edited by John R. White. 6 vols. [of which one is complete]. Vol. VI of *CEKM.* Since 1964. (See also the selection of 36 dance compositions, Cracow, 1948.)
Lüneburger Orgeltabulatur KN 208a. Edited by Margarete Reimann. Vol. XXXVI of *EDM.* Frankfurt am Main, 1957.
Luython, Carolus. *Werken voor Orgel.* Edited by Joseph Watelet. Vol. IV of *MMB.* Berchem and Antwerp, 1938. (With works of Guillet and Macque.)

Macque, Giovanni. *Werken voor Orgel.* Edited by Joseph Watelet. Vol. IV of *MMB.* Berchem and Antwerp, 1938. (With works of Guillet and Luython.)
Marcello, Benedetto. *Composizioni per cembalo od organo.* Edited by G. Francesco Malipiero. Vol. XVII of *CdMI.* Milan, 1920. (With cantatas; see also Vol. XX of Farrenc and Vol. XI of Tagliapietra.)
Marchand, Louis. *Pièces choisies.* Vol. III of Guilmant.
Martini, Giovanni Battista. *Dodici sonate per cembalo od organo.* Edited by M. Vitali. Milan, n.d.
———. *Sonate.* Edited by D. Cipollini. Vol. XVIII of *CdMI.* Milan, 1920. (Also edited by Lothar Hoffmann-Erbrecht, Series I, No. 5 of *MMA.* Leipzig, 1955; see also Vol. IX of Farrenc.)
Mattheson, Johann. *Die wol-klingende Fingersprache.* Edited by Lothar Hoffmann-Erbrecht. Series I, No. 1 of *MMA.* Leipzig, 1954.
Mendelssohn-Bartholdy, Felix. *Werke.* Edited by Julius Rietz. 19 series, 36 vols. Leipzig, 1874–1877. (Piano music in Series XI; organ music in Series XIII.)
Mersenne, Marin. *Harmonie Universelle.* Facsimile reprint. 3 vols. Paris, 1963. (See also the English translation of the book on instruments by Roger E. Chapman, The Hague, 1958.)
Merula, Tarquinio. *Composizione per organo e cimbalo.* Edited by Alan Curtis. Vol. I, No. 1 of *Monumenti de musica italiani.* Brescia, 1961.
Merulo, Claudio. *Canzonen 1592 für Orgel und andere Tasteninstrumente.* Edited by Pierre Pidoux. Kassel, 1954.
———. *Toccate per organo.* Libro I. Edited by S. dalla Libera, Milan, 1959. (Earlier ed., edited by J. B. Labat, Paris, 1865.)
Mondonville, Jean-Joseph Cassanéa de. *Pièces de clavecin en sonates.* Edited by Marc Pincherle. Vol. I, No. 9 of *PSFM.* Paris, 1935.
Morley, Thomas. *Keyboard Works.* Edited by Thurston Dart. 2 vols. London, 1959.

Mozart, Leopold. *Ausgewählte Werke.* Edited by Max Seiffert. Vol. IX² of *DTB*. Leipzig, 1908.

Mozart, Wolfgang Amadeus. *Neue Ausgabe sämtlicher Werke.* In Verbindung mit den Mozartstädten Augsburg, Salzburg und Wien herausgegeben von der Internationalen Stiftung Mozarteum. Est. 170 vols. Kassel, in progress. (Piano music in Series IX.)

———. *Sonatas and Fantasias for Piano.* Edited by Nathan Broder. Bryn Mawr, 1956. (Rev. ed., 1960.)

———. *Werke.* 74 vols. Leipzig, 1877–1905. (Reprint, Ann Arbor, 1955. Piano solo music in Series XX and XXI; piano duets and two-piano music in Series XIX.)

Muffat, Georg. *Apparatus musico-organisticus.* Edited by R. Walter. Altötting, 1957. (Earlier ed. by S. de Lange, Leipzig, 1888.)

Muffat, Gottfried [Theophilius]. *Componimenti musicali.* Edited by Guido Adler. Vol. VII of *DTOe*. Vienna, 1896. (See also Vol. X of Farrenc.)

———. *12 Versetl sampt 72 Toccaten.* Edited by Guido Adler. Vol. LVIII of *DTOe*. Vienna, 1922. (Also edited by W. Uppmayer, Kassel, 1952.)

Mulliner Book, The. Edited by Denis Stevens. Vol. I of *MB*. London, 1951. (2nd ed., 1954.)

Murschhauser, Franz Xaver Anton. *Gesammelte Werke für Klavier und Orgel.* Edited by Max Seiffert. Vol. XVIII of *DTB*. Leipzig, 1917.

Musorgskiĭ, Modest Petrovich. *Sämtliche Werke.* Edited by Pavel Lamm. 8 vols. Vienna and Leipzig, 1928–1934. (Piano music in Vol. VIII.)

Müthel, Johann Gottfried. *Drei Sonaten.* Edited by Lothar Hoffmann-Erbrecht. Series 1, No. 6 of *MMA*. Leipzig, 1955. (See also Vol. CLXXVI of *NMA* (2 harpsichords).

———. *Zwei Ariosi mit zwölf Variationen.* Edited by Lothar Hoffmann-Erbrecht. Series 1, No. 7 of *MMA*. Leipzig, 1955.

Nivers, Guillaume-Gabriel. *Premier livre d'orgue, 1665.* Edited by Norbert Dufourcq. 2 vols. Paris, 1963.

———. *Troisième livre d'orgue.* Edited by Norbert Dufourcq. Vol. I, No. 14 of *PSFM*. Paris, 1958.

Noordt, Anthoni van. *Tabulatuur-Boek.* Edited by Max Seiffert. Vol. XIX of *VNM*. Leipzig, 1896. (Reprint, revised by P. Lagas, Amsterdam, 1957; selections edited by Pierre Pidoux, Kassel, 1955.)

Nordraak, Rikard. *Samlede Verker.* Edited by O. Anker and O. Gorvin. Oslo, 1942–1944.

Pachelbel, Johann. *Klavierwerke. Nebst beigefügten Stücken von W. H. Pachelbel.* Biographical introduction by Adolf Sandberger. Vol. II of *DTB*. Leipzig, 1901.

———. *94 Kompositionen: Fugen über das Magnificat für Orgel oder Klavier.* Edited by H. Botsiber & Max Schneider. Vol. XVI of *DTOe*. Vienna, 1901. (Reprint, Graz, 1959. See also the selection edited by Walter Emery, *Early Organ Music*, Vol. V, London, 1958; Series IV, No. 14 of *Organum*.)

———. *Orgelkompositionen. Nebst beigefügten Stücken von W. H. Pachelbel.* Vol. IV¹ of *DTB*. Leipzig, 1903. (See also Series IV, Nos. 12 and 13 of *Organum*.)

———. *Orgelwerke.* Edited by Karl Matthei. 4 vols. Kassel, 1931.

Paganelli, Guiseppe Antonio. *Sei Sonate per pianoforte.* Edited by Gino Tagliapietra. Milan, 1936.

Paisiello, Giacomo. *Sonate per cembalo e pianoforte.* Edited by C. Mola. Milan, 1941.

Paradisi, [Pietro] Domenico. *Sonate.* Edited by Dante Cipollini. Vol. XXII of *CdMI.*
    Milan, 1920. (Also edited by Giacomo Benvenuti, Milan, 1917; See also Vol. XIV
    of Farrenc.)
Parthenia. Facsimile reprint. Edited by Otto Erich Deutsch. Vol. III of *The Harrow
    Replicas.* Cambridge, 1942. (Modern eds. by Kurt Stone, New York, 1951, and
    Thurston Dart, London, 1960 [among others]; earlier ed., edited by Edward
    Francis Rimbault, London, 1847.)
Parthenia In-Violata or Mayden-Musicke. Facsimile reprint. Critical notes by Thurston
    Dart, R. Wolfe, and Sydney Beck. New York, 1961.
Pasquini, Bernardo. *Collected Works for Keyboard.* Edited by M. B. Haynes. Vol. V of
    CEKM. 1964. (See also the selections edited by John S. Shedlock, London, 1895;
    by Werner Danckert, Kassel, 1931; and the sonata for two harpsichords, edited by
    Felice Boghen, Paris, 1924; see also Vol. III of Torchi.)
[Paulirinus of Prague. *Tractatus de musica.*] Edited by Josef Reiss, in "Pauli Paulirini
    de Praga Tractatus de musica (etwa 1460)," *ZfMW,* VII (1924–1925), 259–64.
Paumann, Conrad. *Fundamentum organisandi.* (With the *Lochaimer Liederbuch.*)
    Facsimile reproduction. Edited by Konrad Ameln. Berlin, 1925. (Earlier ed.:
    Frank Arnold & Henry Bellamann, "Das Locheimer Liederbuch nebst der Ars
    organisandi von Conrad Paumann," *Jahrbücher fur musikalische Wissenschaft,*
    II (1867), 1–234; see also Vol. I of *CEKM.*)
Platti, Giovanni. *Zwölf Sonaten.* Edited by Lothar Hoffmann-Erbrecht. Series I, Nos. 3
    and 4 of *MMA.* Leipzig, 1954.
Poglietti, Alessandro. See Botsiber under "Anthologies."
———. *Zwölf Ricercare.* Edited by Friedrich Wilhelm Riedel. Series II, Nos. 5 and 6 of
    Die Orgel. Lippstadt, 1957.
Praetorius, Michel. *De Organographia: Syntagma musicum, II.* Facsimile reprint.
    Edited by Wilibald Gurlitt. Kassel, 1929. (Earlier reprint: Vol. XIII of *Publika-
    tionen älterer praktischer und theoretischer Musikwerke,* Berlin, 1885; English ed.,
    translated by H. Blumenfeld, n.p., 1949.)
Prokofiev, Sergei. *Piano Sonatas.* New York, 1957.
———. *[Works] Sobranie sochinenii.* Moscow, in progress. (Piano sonatas in Vol.
    II.)
Purcell, Henry. *Organ Works.* Edited by H. McClean. London, 1957.
———. *Suites, Lessons and Pieces for the Harpsichord.* Edited by W. Barclay Squire.
    4 vols. London, 1918.
———. *Works.* 32 vols. London, 1878–1962. (Keyboard music, edited by E. J. Hop-
    kins, in Vol. VI, 1895.)

Radino, Giovanni Maria. *Il primo libro d'intavolatura di balli d'arpicordo.* Facsimile
    reproduction and transcription. Edited by R. E. M. Harding. Cambridge,
    1949.
Raick, Dieudonné. *Werken voor Clavecimbel.* Edited by Joseph Watelet. Vol. VI of
    MMB. Berchem and Antwerp, 1948. (With works of Helmont.)
Raison, André. *Livre d'orgue.* Vol. II of Guilmant.
Rameau, Jean-Philippe. *Oeuvres complètes.* Edited by Camille Saint-Saëns. 18 vols.
    Paris, 1895–1924. (Keyboard music in Vols. I and II.)
———. *Pièces de clavecin.* Edited by Erwin R. Jacobi. Kassel and New York, 1958.
Rathgeber, Valentin. *Musicalischer Zeitvertrieb* [Selections]. Edited by Rudolf Steglich.
    Vol. CV of *NMA.* Hannover, 1933.
Redford, John. See Pfatteicher under "Secondary Literature."

Reger, Max. *Sämtliche Werke*. Unter Mitarbeit des Max-Reger-Instituts Bonn (Elsa-Reger-Stiftung). Wiesbaden, in progress. (Piano solo music in Vols. IX–XIII; piano duets in Vol. XIII; two-piano music in Vol. XIV; organ music in Vols. XV–XVIII.)

Reinagle, Alexander. *Four Piano Sonatas*. Edited by Fredrick Freedman. New York, 1964.

Richter, Ferdinand Tobias. See Botsiber under "Anthologies."

Rimskii-Korsakov, Nicolas. [*Works*] *Polnoe sobranie sochinenii*. Moscow, in progress. (Piano music in Vol. XLIXa.)

Roberday, François. *Fugues et caprices*. Vol. III of Guilmant.

Rodio, Rocco. *Cinque ricercate, una fantasia*. Edited by Santiago Kastner. Padua and New York, 1958.

Roseingrave, Thomas. *Compositions for Organ and Harpsichord*. Edited by Denis Stevens. Vol. II of *Penn State Music Series*. University Park, 1964.

Rossi, Michelangelo. *Compositizione per organo e cimbalo*. Ed. by A. Toni. Vol. XXVI of *CdMI*. Milan, 1920. (See also Vol. III of Torchi.)

Rutini, Giovanni Maria [Placido]. *Sonate per cimbalo*. Edited by F. Pratella. Vol. XXVII of *CdMI*. Milan, 1921.

Salvatore, Giovanni. *Collected Keyboard Works*. Ed. by Barton Hudson. Vol. III of *CEKM*. 1964.

Sancta Maria, Tomás de. *Libro llamado arte de tañer fantasia*. German translation by R. Boadella and E. Harich-Schneider. Leipzig, 1937.

Sandoni e Serini, Pier Giuseppe. *Sonate per cembalo*. Edited by F. Pratella. Vol. XXIX of *CdMI*. Milan, 1921.

Scarlatti, Alessandro. *Harpsichord and Organ Music*. Edited by John S. Shedlock. London, 1918.

——. *Primo e secundo libro di toccate*. Edited by Ruggiero Gerlin. Vol. XIII of *CMI*. Milan, 1943. (Also edited by R. Nardi, Kassel and Basel, 1948.)

Scarlatti, Domenico. *Compositizione*. Vol. XXXI of *CdMI*. Milan, 1919.

——. *5 Klaviersonaten*. Edited by Walter Gerstenberg. Vol. II of *Forschungsarbeiten des musikwissenschaftlichen Instituts der Universität München*. Regensburg, 1932.

——. *Opere complete per clavicombalo*. Edited by Alessandro Longo. 10 vols. and supp. Milan, 1907–1937. (See also Vols. VII and VIII of Farrenc.)

——. *Sixty Sonatas Edited in Chronological Order*. Edited by Ralph Kirkpatrick. 2 vols. New York, 1953.

——. [*150*] *Sonaten nach den Quellen*. Edited by Hermann Keller and W. Weissmann. 3 vols. Leipzig, 1957.

Scheidt, Samuel. *Ausgewählte Werke für Orgel und Klavier*. Edited by Hermann Keller. Leipzig and New York, 1939.

——. *Tabulatura nova*. Edited by Max Seiffert. Vol. I of DDT. Leipzig, 1892. (Reprint, revised by Hans Joachim Moser, Wiesbaden, 1958.)

——. *Werke*. Edited by G. Harms and Christhard Mahrenholz. 8 vols. Hamburg, 1923–1934.

Scherer, Sebastian Anton. *Oeuvres* [organ]. Vol. VIII of Guilmant.

Schlick, Arnolt. *Spiegel der Orgelmacher und Organisten*. Edited by Robert Eitner. *MfM*, I (1869), 77–114. (More recent ed., edited by P. Smets, Mainz, 1937; modern German version by Ernst Flade, Mainz, 1932; reprint, Kassel and Basel, 1951.)

————. *Tabulaturen etlicher Lobgesang und Lidlein uff die Orgel und Lauten*. Edited by
    G. Harms. Klecken, 1924. (2nd ed., Hamburg, 1957.)
————. *Hommage à l'Empereur Charles V*. Edited by Santiago Kastner. Barcelona,
    1954. (With five pieces by Sancta Maria and Cabezón.)
Schobert, Johann. *Ausgewählte Werke*. Edited by Hugo Riemann. Vol. XXXIX of
    DDT. Leipzig, 1909.
Schubert, Franz Peter. *Werke*. 40 vols. and 3 supps. Leipzig, 1888–1897.
Schumann, Robert Alexander. *Werke*. Edited by Clara Schumann. 34 vols. Leipzig,
    1886–1893.
Soler, Antonio. *Conciertos para dos instrumentos de tecla*. Edited by Santiago Kastner.
    2 vols. Barcelona, 1956–1957.
————. *Sonatas para instrumentos de tecla*. Edited by S. Rubio. 5 vols. Madrid, 1957.
    (Selection of 34 edited by Frederick Marvin, 3 vols., London, 1958–1959.)
Speuy, Hendrik. *Psalm Preludes*. Edited by Frits Noske. Amsterdam, 1963.
Steenwick, Gijsbert van (ed.) *Klavierboek Anna Maria van Eijl*. Edited by F. Noske.
    Vol. II of *MMN*. Amsterdam, 1959. (Earlier ed., edited by J. Röntgen, Vol.
    XXXVII of *VNM*, Amsterdam, 1920.)
Stölzel, Gottfried Heinrich. *Enharmonische Claviersonate*. Edited by E. W. Böhme.
    Vol. II of *Denkmäler thüringischer Musik*. Kassel, 1935.
Sweelinck, Jan Pieters. *Werken voor Orgel en Clavicimbal*. Edited by Max Seiffert.
    The Hague, 1894. (Reprint, Amsterdam, 1943. Selections edited by D. Hellmann,
    2 vols., New York, 1957.)

Tallis, Thomas. *Complete Keyboard Works*. Edited by Denis Stevens. London, 1953.
Telemann, Georg Philipp. *Fantasies pour le clavecin: Trois douzaines*. Edited by Max
    Seiffert. Vol. IV of *Veröffentlichungen der Musik–Bibliothek Paul Hirsch*. Breslau,
    1923.
————. *Musikalische Werke. Herausgegeben im Auftrag der Gesellschaft für Musik-
    forschung*. Kassel, in progress. (Organ music, edited by T. Fedke, in Vol. XIII,
    1960.)
Titelouze, Jean. *Oeuvres complètes*. Vol. I of Guilmant.
Tomkins, Thomas. *Keyboard Music*. Edited by Stephen D. Tuttle. Vol. V of *MB*.
    London, 1955.
Tunder, Franz. *Vier Praeludien*. Edited by Max Seiffert. Series IV, No. 6 of *Organum*.
    Leipzig, 1925.
Türk, Daniel Gottlob. *Klavierschule*. Facsimile reprint. Edited by Erwin R. Jacobi.
    Series I, No. 30 of *Documenta musicologica*. Kassel, 1959.
————. *Kleine Handstücke*. Edited by Cornelia Auerbach. Vol. XCIII of *NMA*.
    Hannover, 1933.
Turrini, Ferdinando. *Sonate per cembalo*. Edited by C. Pedron. Vol. XXXIII of *CdMI*.
    Milan, 1919.

Valente, Antonio. *43 Versi spirituali*. Edited by I. Fuser. Padua, 1958.
[Venegas de Henestrosa, Luis. *Libro de Cifra Nueva*.] Edited by Higini Anglés, in
    La música en la corte de Carlos V. Vol. II of *Monumentos de la música española*.
    Barcelona, 1944.
Virdung, Sebastian. *Musica getutscht*. Facsimile reprint. Edited by Leo Schrade. Kassel,
    1931. (New ed. in preparation; earlier facsimile reprint, Vol. XI of *Publikationen
    älterer praktischer und theoretischer Musikwerke*, Leipzig, 1882.)

Wagenseil, Georg Christoph. *Divertimenti [4] per cimbalo.* Edited by Friedrich Blume. Vol. XXXVI of *NMA.* Hannover, 1929.

Walther, Johann Gottfried. *Gesammelte Werke für Orgel.* Edited by Max Seiffert. Vols. XXVI and XXVII of *DDT.* Leipzig, 1906. (Reprint, revised by Hans Joachim Moser, Wiesbaden, 1959; see also Series IV, No. 15 of *Organum.*)

————. *Memorial Collection of Organ Preludes and Variations.* Edited by Walter E. Buszin for *Anthology of Sacred Music,* Vol. II: *Organ Music.* St. Louis, 1949.

Weber, Karl Maria von. *Compositionen. Erste rechtmässige Ausgabe.* Edited by H. W. Stolze. Wölfenbüttel, 1857. (Piano music in Vol. I; piano duets in Vol. II. The new ed. by Hans Joachim Moser lacks the piano compositions.)

Weckmann, Matthias. *Gesammelte Werke.* Edited by Gerhard Ilgner. Series II, No. 4 of EDM. Leipzig, 1942. (See also Series IV, No. 3 of *Organum.*)

Zachow, Friedrich Wilhelm. *Gesammelte Werke.* Edited by Max Seiffert. Vols. XXI and XXII of *DDT.* Leipzig, 1905. (Reprint, revised by Hans Joachim Moser, 1958.)

Zipoli, Domenico. *Sonate d'intavolatura per organo e cimbalo.* Edited by L. F. Tagliavini. 2 vols. Heidelberg, 1959. (Earlier ed., edited by A. Toni, Vol. XXXVI of *CdMI,* Milan, 1919; see also Vol. III of Torchi.)

Part Two: Secondary Literature

Abert, Hermann. "Joseph Haydn's Klavierwerke," *ZfMW,* II (1919–1920), 553–73; III (1920–1921), 535–52.

————. *Robert Schumann.* Berlin, 1903. (4th ed., 1920.)

————. *W. A. Mozart. Neubearbeitete und erweitete Ausgabe von Otto Jahns Mozart.* 2 vols. Leipzig, 1923–1924. (7th ed., 1955–1956.)

Abraham, Gerald. *Chopin's Musical Style.* London, 1939. (Reprint, 1960.)

————. "Handel's Clavier Music," *M & L,* XVI (1935), 278–85.

Adler, Guido. "I 'Componimenti musical per il cembalo' di Teofilo Muffat e il posto che essi occupano nella storia della 'Suite' per il pianoforte," *RMI,* III (1896), 1–35.

Akeret, Kurt. *Studien zum Klavierwerk von Maurice Ravel.* Zürich and Leipzig, 1941.

Albrecht, Adolf. "Die Klaviervariation im 20. Jahrhundert." Unpublished dissertation, Cologne, 1961.

Aldrich, Putnam. "Bach's Technique of Transcription and Improvised Ornamentation," *MQ,* XXXV (1949), 26–35.

————. "On the Interpretation of Bach's Trills," *MQ,* XLIX (1963), 289–310.

————. *Ornamentation in J. S. Bach's Organ Works.* New York, 1950.

*Alker, Hugo. *Literatur für alte Tasteninstrumente: Versuch einer Bibliographie für die Praxis.* Vol. IV of *Wiener Abhandlungen zur Musikwissenschaft und Instrumentenkunde.* Vienna, 1962.

Allorto, Riccardo. *Le sonate per pianoforte di Muzio Clementi: Studio critico e catalogo tematico.* Vol. XII of *Historiae musicae cultores Biblioteca.* Florence, 1959.

Altmann, Wilhelm. *Verzeichnis von Werken für Klavier vier- und sechshändig sowie für zwei und mehr Klaviere.* Leipzig, 1943.

Andrews, Hilda. "Elizabethan Keyboard Music," *MQ,* XVI (1930), 59–71.

Anglès, Higini. "Orgelmusik der Schola Hispanica vom 15.–17. Jahrhundert," in *Festschrift Peter Wagner zum 60. Geburtstag.* Leipzig, 1926, 11–26.

Apel, Willi. "Attaingnant: Quatorze gaillards," *MF,* XIV (1961), 361–70.

————. "The Early Development of the Organ Ricercare," *MD*, III (1949), 139–50.

————. "Early German Keyboard Music," *MQ*, XXIII (1937), 210–37.

————. "The Early History of the Organ," *Speculum*, XXIII (1948), 191–216.

————. "Early Spanish Music for Lute and Keyboard Instruments," *MQ*, XX (1934), 289–301.

*————. *Masters of the Keyboard*. Cambridge, 1947.

————. "Neapolitan Links between Cabezón and Frescobaldi," *MQ*, XXIV (1938), 419–37.

————. "Neuaufgefundene Clavierwerke von Scheidemann, Tunder, Froberger, Reincken und Buxtehude," *Acta*, XXXIV (1962), 65–7.

————. *The Notation of Polyphonic Music, 900–1600*. Vol. XXXVIII of *The Medieval Academy of American Publication*. Cambridge, 1942. (4th ed., revised with commentary, 1949; 5th ed., 1961.)

————. "Du nouveau sur la musique française pour orgue au XVIe siècle," *Revue musicale*, XVIII (1937), 96–108.

————. "Spanish Organ Music of the Early 17th Century," *JAMS*, XV (1962), 174–81.

————. "Die süditalienische Klavierschule des 17. Jahrhunderts," *Acta*, XXXIV (1962), 128–141. (See also Margarete Reimann, *Acta*, XXXV (1963), 114–24.)

————. "Die Tabulatur des Adam Ileborgh," *ZfMW*, XVI (1934), 193–212.

————. "Tänze und Arien für Klavier aus dem Jahre 1588," *AfMW*, XVII (1960), 51–60.

————, and Fischer, Kurt von. "Klaviermusik," *MGG*, VII (1958), 1129–75. Bibliography by W. Pfannkuch.

————, Riedel, Friedrich Wilhelm, and Laquer, Thomas-M. "Orgelmusik," *MGG*, X (1962), 331–85.

Arnold, Frank. *The Art of Accompaniment from a Thorough–Bass as Practised in the XVIIth and XVIIIth Centuries*. London, 1931.

Audsley, George Ashdowne. *The Organ of the Twentieth Century*. New York, 1919.

Auerbach, Cornelia. *Die deutsche Clavichordkunst des 18. Jahrhunderts*. Kassel, 1930.

Austin, William. "The Music of Robert Palmer," *MQ*, XLII (1956), 35–50.

Badura-Skoda, Paul, and Badura-Skoda, Eva. *Mozart-Interpretation*. Vienna, 1957. (English ed., *Interpreting Mozart at the Keyboard*, translated by L. Black, New York, 1962.)

Banning, Helmut, *J. F. Doles: Leben und Werke*. Vol. V of *Schriftenreihe des Staatlichen Instituts für deutsche Musikforschung*. Leipzig, 1939.

Barber, Elinor Louise. "Antonio de Cabezón's Cantus Firmus Compositions and Transcriptions." Unpublished dissertation, Michigan, 1960.

Barford, Philip, "Formalism in Clementi's Pianoforte Sonatas," *MMR*, LXXXII (1952), 205–8, 238–41.

Bauer, Elianne. "Die Klaviersuite Johann Jakob Frobergers." Unpublished dissertation, Saarbrücken, 1962.

Baum, Richard. *Joseph Wölfl (1773–1812): Leben, Klavierwerke, Klavierkammermusik und Klavierkonzerte*. Kassel, 1928.

Beaufils, Marcel. *La musique de piano de Robert Schumann*. Paris, 1951.

Bedbrook, Gerald Stares. "The Buxheim Keyboard Manuscript," *MR*, XIV (1953), 288–95.

*————. *Keyboard Music from the Middle Ages to the Beginnings of the Baroque*. London, 1949.

Beer, R. "Ornaments in Old Keyboard Music," *MR*, XIII (1952), 3–13.

Bellamann, Henry. "The Piano Works of C. V. Alkan," *MQ*, X (1924), 251–62.

Benton, Rita. "Form in the Sonatas of Domenico Scarlatti," *MR*, XIII (1952), 264–73.

———. "Jean-Frédéric Edelmann, a Musical Victim of the French Revolution," *MQ*, L (1964), 165–87.

———. "Nicolas-Joseph Hüllmandel: Quelques aspects de sa vie et de son oeuvre," *Revue de musicologie*, XLVII (1961), 177–94.

Berger, Arthur V. *Aaron Copland*. New York, 1953.

———. "Aaron Copland's Piano Fantasy," *Juilliard Review*, V, No. 1 (1957–1958), 13–27.

Bergmann, Walter. "Some Old and New Problems of Playing the Basso Continuo," *PRMA*, LXXXVII (1960–1961), 31–43.

Bernary, Peter. "Der zweistimmige Kontrapunkt in Bartók's *Mikrokosmos*," *AfMW*, XV (1958), 198–206.

Berner, Alfred. "Zum Klavierbau im 17. und 18. Jahrhundert," in *Kongressbericht Lüneburg 1950*. Kassel, n.d., pp. 239–43.

Bessaraboff, Nicholas. *Ancient European Musical Instruments*. Cambridge, 1941.

Besseler, Heinrich. "Bach als Wegbereiter," *AfMW*, XII (1955), 1–39.

———. "Charakterthema und Erlebnisform bei Bach," in *Kongressbericht Lüneburg 1950*. Kassel, n.d., pp. 7–32.

Beurmann, Erich Hermann. "Die Reprisensonaten Carl Philipp Emanuel Bachs," *AfMW*, XIII (1956), 168–79.

Bie, Oskar. *Das Klavier*. Berlin, 1921.

———. *Klavier, Orgel und Harmonium: Das Wesen der Tasteninstrumente*. Leipzig, 1910. (2nd ed., 1921.)

Bittermann, Helen Robbins. "The Organ in the Early Middle Ages," *Speculum*, IV (1929), 390–410.

Bloch, Joseph. *Charles-Valentin Alkan (1813-1888)*. N.p., 1941.

Blom, Eric. *Beethoven's Pianoforte Sonatas Discussed*. London, 1938.

———. *The Romance of the Piano*. London, 1928.

———. "[Sibelius] The Piano Music," in *Sibelius, a Symposium*. Edited by Gerald Abraham. New York, 1947; London, 1948, pp. 97–107.

Boalch, Donald Howard. *Makers of the Harpsichord and Clavichord to 1840*. London, 1956; New York, 1956.

Bodky, Erwin. *The Interpretation of Bach's Keyboard Works*. Cambridge, 1960.

———. *Der Vortrag alter Klaviermusik*. Berlin, 1932.

Bogianchino, Massimo. *L'arte clavecembalistica di Domenico Scarlatti*. Rome, 1956.

Book of the First International Musicological Congress Devoted to the Works of Frédéric Chopin, The. Edited by Zofia Lissa. Warsaw, 1963.

Bornefeld, Helmut. *Das Positiv*. Kassel, 1941. (2nd ed., 1947.)

Borrel, Eugène. *La sonate*. Paris, 1951.

Borren, Charles van den. *Les origines de la musique de clavier dans les Pays-bas nord et sud jusqu'à vers 1630*. Brussels, 1914.

———. *Les origines de la musique de clavier en Angleterre*. Brussels, 1912. (English ed.: *The Sources of Keyboard Music in England*, translated by J. E. Matthew, London, 1914.)

Bosquet, Émile. *La musique de clavier: Et par extension de luth*. Brussels, 1953.

———. "Origine et formation de la sonate allemande pour clavecin de 1698 à 1742," *Revue internationale de la musique*, I (1939), 853–62.

Bouvet, Charles. *Une dynastie de musiciens français: Les Couperins, organistes de l'église Saint-Gervaise.* Paris, 1919.

Brandts Buys, Hans. *Johann Sebastian Bach: 48 Praeludia.* Vol. XIII of *Componisten-Serien.* Haarlem, 1959.

———. *Het Wohltemperierte Klavier van J. S. Bach.* Arnheim, 1942. (2nd ed., 1944.)

Braunstein, Joseph. *Thematic Catalog of the Collected Works of Brahms.* Enlarged ed. New York, 1956.

Breig, Werner. "Die Orgelwerke von Heinrich Scheidemann." Unpublished dissertation, Erlangen, 1962.

———. "Der Umfang des choralgebundenen Orgelwerkes von Jan Pieterzoon Sweelinck," *AfMW,* XVII (1960), 258–76.

Brion, Marcel. *Schumann et l'âme romantique.* Paris, 1956. (English ed.: *Schumann and the Romantic Age,* translated by G. Saintsbury, London, 1956; New York, 1956.)

Broder, Nathan. "Mozart and the Clavier," *MQ,* XXVII (1941), 422–32.

———. *Samuel Barber.* New York, 1954.

Bronarski, Ludwik. *Études sur Chopin.* 2 vols. Lausanne, 1944–1946. (2nd ed., 1947.)

Brown, Maurice J. E. *Chopin: An Index to His Works in Chronological Order.* London, 1960.

———. "An Introduction to Schubert's Sonatas of 1817," *MR,* XII (1951), 35–44.

Bruggaier, Eduard. "Studien zur Geschichte des Orgelpedalspiels in Deutschland bis zur Zeit Johann Sebastian Bachs." Unpublished dissertation, Frankfurt am Main, 1960.

Bruinsma, Henry A. "The Organ Controversy in the Netherlands Reformation to 1600," *JAMS,* VII (1954), 205–12.

Brunner, Hans. *Das Klavierklangideal Mozarts und die Klaviere seiner Zeit.* Augsburg, 1933.

Brunold, Paul. *François Couperin.* Translated by J. B. Hanson. Monaco, 1949.

———. *Traité des signes et agréments employés par les clavecinistes françaises des XVIIe et XVIIIe siècles.* Lyon, 1925.

———. "Tres livres de Pièces de clavecin de Jean-François Dandrieu," *Revue de musicologie,* XVI (1932), 147–51.

Bücken, Ernst. "Der galante Stil, eine Skizze seiner Entwicklung," *ZfMW,* VI (1923–1924), 418–30.

———. *Die Musik der Nationen.* Leipzig, 1937.

Burns, Joseph A. "Antonio Valente, Neapolitan Keyboard Primitive," *JAMS,* XII (1959), 133–43.

———. "Early Neapolitan Keyboard Music from Valente to Frescobaldi." Unpublished dissertation, Harvard University, 1953.

Buszin, Walter E. "Buxtehude: On the Tercentenary of His Birth," *MQ,* XXIII (1937), 465–90.

Calvocoressi, Michael D., and Abraham, Gerald. *Masters of Russian Music.* London, 1936.

Canave, Paz Corazon G. *A Re–Evaluation of the Role Played by Carl Philipp Emanuel Bach in the Development of the Clavier Sonata.* Washington, D.C., 1956.

Caravaglios, Nino. "Una nuova 'Intavolatura di cimbalo' di Antonio Valente cieco," *RMI,* XXIII (1916), 491–508.

Carner, Mosco. *The Waltz.* New York, 1948.

Carpenter, Hoyle. "The Works of Antonio de Cabezón." Unpublished dissertation, Chicago, 1957.

Cauchie, Maurice. *Thematic Index of François Couperin*. Monaco, 1949.

Cavaillé-Coll, Cécile, and Cavaillé-Coll, Emmanuel. *Aristide Cavaillé-Coll: Ses origines, sa vie, ses oeuvres*. Paris, 1929.

Chase, Gilbert. *America's Music: From the Pilgrims to the Present*. New York, 1955.

————. *The Music of Spain*. New York, 1941. (Reprint, 1959.)

Chybinski, Adolf. "Polnische Musik und Musikkultur des 16. Jahrhunderts in ihren Beziehungen zu Deutschland," *SIMG*, XIII (1911–1912), 463–505.

Citron, Pierre. *Couperin*. Bourges, 1956.

Clercx, Suzanne. "Les clavecinistes Belge," *Revue musicale*, XX (1939), No. 192, 11–22.

————. "La forme du rondo chez Carl Philip Emanuel Bach," *Revue de musicologie*, XIX (1935), 148–66.

————. "Johann Kuhnau et la sonate," *Revue musicale*, XVI (1935), 89–110.

————. "Le toccate, principe du style symphonique," in *La musique instrumentale de la renaissance*. Edited by Jean Jacquot. Paris, 1955, pp. 313–26.

Closson, Ernest. *Histoire du piano*. Brussels, 1944. (English ed.: *History of the Piano*, translated by D. Ames, London, 1947.)

Cockshoot, John V. *The Fugue in Beethoven's Piano Music*. London, 1959.

Cohen, Harriet. "[Dvořák] The Piano Compositions," in *Antonin Dvořák: His Achievements*. Edited by V. Fisdel. London, 1942, pp. 127–32.

Cortot, Alfred. *La musique française de piano*. 2 vols. Paris, 1930–1932. (3rd ed., 1944; English ed.: *French Piano Music*, translated by H. Andrews, London, 1932.)

Cowell, Henry, and Cowell, Sidney. *Charles Ives and his Music*. New York, 1955.

Curtis, Alan. "Dutch Harpsichord Makers," *TVNM*, XIX (1960–1961), 44–66.

————. "Sweelinck's Keyboard Works: English Elements in Dutch Music of the Gouden Eeuw." Unpublished dissertation, Illinois, 1963.

Czaczkes, Ludwig. *Analyse des Wohltemperierten Klaviers: Form und Aufbau der Fuge bei Bach*. 2 vols. Vienna, 1956–1963.

Dadelsen, Georg von. "Originale Daten auf den Handschriften J. S. Bachs," in *Hans Albrecht in Memoriam*. Kassel, 1962, pp. 116–20.

————. "Robert Schumann und die Musik Bachs," *AfMW*, XIV (1957), 46–59.

Dale, Kathleen. "[Handel] The Keyboard Music," in *Handel*, a *Symposium*. Edited by Gerald Abraham. London, 1954, pp. 233–47.

*————. *Nineteenth Century Piano Music*. London, 1954.

Dale, William. *Tschudi, the Harpsichord Maker*. London, 1913.

Danckert, Werner. "Der Klassizismus Erik Saties und seine geistesgeschichtliche Stellung," *ZfMW*, XII (1929–1930), 105–14.

Dannreuther, Edward. *Musical Ornamentation*. London, 1893–1895.

Dart, Thurston. "Cavazzoni and Cabezón," *M & L*, XXXVI (1955), 2–6. (See also Santiago Kastner, *ibid.*, pp. 203–4.)

————. "A New Source of English Organ Music," *M & L*, XXXV (1954), 201–5.

————. "New Sources of Virginal Music," *M & L*, XXXV (1954), 93–106.

David, Hans Theodor. *Johann Schobert als Sonatenkomponist*. Kassel, 1928; Borna and Leipzig, 1928.

David, Johann Nepomuk. *Die dreistimmigen Inventionen von Bach*. Göttingen, 1959.

————. *Die zweistimmigen Inventionen von Bach*. Göttingen, 1957.

Davies, Hibberd Trevor, "The Slow Movements in the Sonatas of John Field," *MR*, XXII (1961), 89–93.

Deffner, Oskar. *Ueber die Entwicklung der Fantasie für Tasteninstrumente (bis J. P. Sweelinck)*. Kiel, 1928.

Degering, Hermann. *Die Orgel: Ihre Erfindung und ihre Geschichte bis zur Karolingerzeit*. Münster, 1905.

Dejmek, Gaston Roman. *Der Variationszyklus bei Max Reger*. Essen, 1930.

Delestre, R. *L'oeuvre de Marcel Dupré*. Paris, 1952.

Demuth, Norman. *French Piano Music. A Survey with Notes on Its Performance*. London, 1959.

Dennerlein, Hanns. *Johann Friedrich Reichardt und seine Klavierwerke*. Volume IV of *Universitas-Archiv*. Münster, 1930.

————. *Der unbekannte Mozart: Die Welt seiner Klavierwerke*. 2nd ed. Leipzig, 1955.

Dessauer, Heinrich. *John Field, sein Leben und seine Werke*. Langensalza, 1912.

Deutsch, Otto Erich. *Schubert, a Documentary Biography*. New York, 1947.

————. *Schubert: Thematic Catalogue of All His Works in Chronological Order*. With D. R. Wakeling. New York, 1950.

Dewitz, Margarethe von. *Jean Baptiste Vanhall: Leben und Klavierwerke*. Munich, 1933.

Dickenmann, Paul. *Die Entwicklung der Harmonik bei A. Skrjabin*. Vol. IV of *Berner Veröffentlichungen zur Musikforschung*. Bern and Leipzig, 1935.

Dickinson, A. E. F. "[Chaikovskii] The Piano Music," in *The Music of Tchaikovsky*. Edited by Gerald Abraham. London, 1946, pp. 114–23.

————. "English Virginal Music," *MR*, XVI (1955), 13–28.

Dietrich, Fritz. *Geschichte des deutschen Orgelchorals im 17. Jahrhundert*. Vol. I of *Heidelberger Studien zur Musikwissenschaft*. Kassel, 1932.

Dodge, A. *Pianos and Their Makers: A Comprehensive History of the Development of the Piano from the Harpsichord to the Concert Grand*. 2 vols. Coving, 1911–1913.

Donat, Friedrich Wilhelm. *Christian Heinrich Rinck und die Orgelmusik seiner Zeit*. Bad Oehnstein, 1933.

Donington, Robert. *The Instruments of Music*. London, 1949. (2nd ed., New York, 1951.)

————. *The Interpretation of Early Music*. New York, 1963.

————. *Tempo and Rhythm in Bach's Organ Music*. London, 1961.

Douglass, Robert S. "The Keyboard Ricercar in the Baroque Era." Unpublished dissertation, North Texas, 1963.

Downes, Edward. "The Music of Norman Dello Joio," *MQ*, XLVII (1962), pp. 149–72.

Downes, Ralph. "[Purcell] An Organist's View of the Organ Works," in *Henry Purcell, 1659–1695: Essays on his Music*. Edited by I. Holst. London and New York, 1959, pp. 67–73.

Doyle, John Godfrey. "The Piano Music of Louis Moreau Gottschalk (1829–1869)." Unpublished dissertation, New York University, 1960.

Dreetz, Albert. *Johann Christian Kittel: Der letzte Bach Schüler*. Berlin and Köpenick, 1932.

Dufourcq, Norbert. *Esquisse d'une histoire d'orgue en France*. Paris, 1935.

————. *Les grandes formes de la musique d'orgue*. Paris, 1937.

————. *La musique d'orgue française au XXe siècle*. Paris, 1939.

————. *La Musique d'orgue française de Jehan Titelouze à Jehan Alain*. Paris, 1941. (2nd ed., 1949.)

————. *Nicolas LeBègue (1631–1702)*. Paris, 1954.

———. "Recent Researches into French Organ Building from the 15th to the 17th Century," *Galpin Society Journal*, X (1957), 66–81.

Dunn, J. P. *Ornamentation in the Works of Chopin*. London, 1921.

Eberstaller, Oskar. *Orgeln und Orgelbauer in Oesterreich*. Vol. I of *Wiener musikwissenschaftliche Beiträge*. Graz and Cologne, 1955.

Eckert, Heinrich. *Norbert Burgmüller: Ein Beitrag zur Stil– und Geistesgeschichte der deutschen Romantik*. Vol. III of *Veröffentlichungen des musikwissenschaftlichen Instituts der Deutschen Universität Prag*. Augsburg, 1932.

Egert, Paul. *Friedrich Chopin*. Potsdam, 1936.

———. *Die Klaviersonate im Zeitalter der Romantik*. Berlin and Johannisthal, 1934. (Only the first of two projected volumes has appeared.)

Eggebrecht, Hans Heinrich. "Terminus 'ricercare,' " *AfMW*, IX (1952), 137–47.

Einstein, Alfred. *Mozart, His Character, His Work*. Translated by A. Mendel and N. Broder. New York, 1945.

———. *Schubert, a Musical Portrait*. New York, 1951.

Eitner, Robert. "Das Buxheimer Orgelbuch im Besitz der königlichen Hof- und Staatsbibliothek zu München," *Beihefte der MfM*, XX (1888), 1–112.

———. "Die Sonate: Vorstudien zur Entstehung der Form," *MfM*, XX (1888), 163–70, 179–85.

Elson, Louis C. *The History of American Music*. New York, 1904. (Revised by A. Elson, 1925.)

Emery, Walter. *Bach's Ornaments*. London, 1953.

———. "The London Autograph of 'The Forty-Eight,' " *M & L*, XXXIV (1953), 106–23.

———. *Notes on Bach's Organ Works*. London, 1957.

Emsheimer, Ernst. *Johann Ulrich Steigleder, sein Leben und seine Werke*. Kassel, 1928.

Engel, Hans. *Franz Liszt*. Potsdam, 1936.

Engelmann, Hans Ulrich. *Béla Bartók's Mikrokosmos: Versuch einer Typologie "neuerer Musik."* Vol. X of *Literaturhistorische-musikwissenschaftliche Abhandlungen*. Würzburg, 1953.

Epstein, E. *Der französische Einfluss auf die deutsche Klaviersuite im 17. Jahrhundert*. Berlin, 1940.

Ernst, Fritz. *Der Flügel Joh. Seb. Bachs: Ein Beitrag zur Geschichte des Instrumentenbaues im 18. Jahrhundert*. Frankfurt am Main and New York, 1955.

Eslava, H. *Museo orgánico español*. Madrid, n.d.

Faisst, Immanuel. "Beiträge zur Geschichte der Claviersonate von ihren ersten Auftreten bis auf C. P. Emanuel Bach," *Neues Beethoven-Jahrbuch*, I (1924), 7–85.

Falck, Martin. *Wilhelm Friedemann Bach: Sein Leben und seine Werke*. Leipzig, 1913. (2nd ed., 1919; reprint, Lindau, 1956.)

Fano, Fabio. *Giuseppe Martucci: Saggio biografico-critico*. Milan, 1950.

Farmer, Henry George. *The Organ of the Ancients from Eastern Sources (Hebrew, Syriac and Arabic)*. London, 1931.

Favre, Georges. *La musique française de piano avant 1830*. Paris, 1953.

Feldmann, Fritz. *Musik und Musikpflege in mittelalterlichen Schlesien*. Vol. XXXVIII of *Darstellungen und Quellen zur schlesischen Geschichte*. Breslau, 1938.

———. "Untersuchungen zur Courante als Tanz, insbesondere im Hinblick auf die Klaviersuiten-Couranten J. S. Bachs," *DJ*, VI (1961), 40–57.

Fellerer, Karl Gustav. *Beiträge zur Choralbegleitung und Choralverarbeitung in der Orgelmusik des ausgehenden 18. und beginnenden 19. Jahrhunderts.* Vol. VI of *Sammlung musikwissenschaftlicher Abhandlungen.* Strassburg, 1932.

———. *Orgel und Orgelmusik: Ihre Geschichte.* Augsburg, 1929.

———. *Studien zur Orgelmusik des ausgehenden 18. und beginnenden 19. Jahrhunderts: Ein Beitrag zur Geschichte der Orgelmusik.* Vol. III of *Münsterische Beiträge zur Musikwissenschaft.* Kassel, 1932.

———. "Zur Geschichte der Orgelmusik nach Bach," *KJ*, XXVII (1932), 135–145.

———. "Zür italienischen Orgelmusik des 17. und 18. Jahrhunderts," *JMP*, XLV (1938), 70–83.

Ferand, Ernst. *Die Improvisation in der Musik: Eine entwicklungsgeschichtliche und psychologische Untersuchung.* Zürich, 1938.

Fischer, Kurt von. "Bemerkungen zu Beethovens Variationswerken," in *Kongressbericht Basel 1949.* Kassel, n.d., pp. 111–13.

———. "Carl Philipp Emanuel Bachs Variationenwerken," *RBM*, VI (1952), 190–218.

———. "Chaconne und Passacaglia: ein Versuch," *RBM*, XII (1958), 19–34.

———. *Griegs Harmonik und die nordische Folklore.* Vol. XIII of *Berner Veröffentlichungen zur Musikforschung.* Bern and Leipzig, 1938.

———. "The Ms Paris, Bibliothèque nationale, nouvelle acquisition 6771," *MD*, XI (1957), 38–78.

———. "Mozarts Klaviervariationen," in *Hans Albrecht In Memoriam.* Kassel, 1962, pp. 168–73.

Fischer, Martin. *Die organistische Improvisation im 17. Jahrhundert: Dargestellt an der "Vierundvierzig Choräle zum Präambulieren" von Johann Christoph Bach.* Vol. V of *Königsberger Studien zur Musikwissenschaft.* Kassel, 1929.

Fischer, Wilhelm. *Ueber die Wiedergabe der Kompositionen von Max Reger.* Cologne, 1910.

———. "Zur Chronologie der Klaviersuiten J. S. Bachs," in *Bericht über den musikwissenschaftlichen Kongress in Basel.* Leipzig, 1925, pp. 127–30.

Flade, Ernst. "Literarische Zeugnisse zur Empfindung der *Farbe* und *Farbigkeit* der Orgel und beim Orgelspiel in Deutschland, *ca.* 1500–1620," *Acta*, XXVIII (1956), 176–206.

———. *Der Orgelbauer Gottfried Silbermann: Ein Beitrag zur Geschichte des deutschen Orgelbaus im Zeitalter Bachs.* Series V, Vol. 3 of *Veröffentlichung des fürstlichen Instituts für musikwissenschaftliche Forschung Bückeburg.* Leipzig, 1926.

Flood, W. H. Grattan. *John Field of Dublin, the Inventor of the Nocturne: A Brief Memoire.* Dublin, 1912.

Florand, François. *J. S. Bach: L'oeuvre d'orgue, suivi d'un essai sur l'expression musicale du sentiment religieux.* Paris, 1946.

Frankenstein, Alfred. "Victor Hartmann and Modeste Musorgsky," *MQ*, XXV (1939), 268–91.

Freundlich, Irwin. See Friskin.

Friedberg, Ruth. "The Solo Keyboard Works of Arnold Schönberg," *MR*, XXIII (1962), 39–50.

Friedheim, Phillip. "The Piano Transcriptions of Liszt," *Studies in Romanticism*, I (1962), 83–96.

Friedland, Martin. *Zeitstil und Persönlichkeitsstil in den Variationenwerken der musikalischen Romantik: Zur Geistesgeschichte und Schaffenspsychologie der Romantik.* Vol. XIV of *Sammlung musikwissenschaftlicher Einzeldarstellungen.* Leipzig, 1930.

*Friskin, James, and Freundlich, Irwin. *Music for the Piano: A Handbook of Concert and Teaching Material from 1580 to 1952.* Vol. V of *The Field of Music.* New York, 1954.

Frolowa, S. *Fortepiannye sonate P. I. Tschaiko.* Moscow, 1955.

Frotscher, Gotthold. *Deutsche Orgeldispositionen aus 5 Jahrhunderten.* Wolfenbüttel and Berlin, 1939.

*———. *Geschichte des Orgelspiels und der Orgelkomposition.* 2 vols. Berlin and Schöneberg, 1935–1936. (Reprint, Berlin, 1959.)

Fuhrmann, Franz. *Paul Hofhaymer.* Salzburg, 1959.

Fuller-Maitland, John Alexander. *The 48: Bach's Wohltemperierte Clavier.* 2 vols. London, 1925.

———. *The Keyboard Suites of J. S. Bach.* London, 1925.

———. *Schumann's Pianoforte Works.* London, 1927.

———. "The Toccatas of Bach," *SIMG,* XIV (1912–1913), 578–82. (Published separately, London, 1913.)

Funck, Heinz. "Musikalische Biedermeier," *Deutsche Vierteljahrschrift für Literaturwissenschaft und Geistesgeschichte,* XIV (1936), 398–412.

Galpin, Francis William. *A Textbook of European Musical Instruments.* London, 1937. (New ed., 1946.)

Ganz, Peter. "The Development of the Etude for Piano." Unpublished dissertation, Northwestern, 1960.

Ganzer, Karl, and Kusche, Ludwig. *Vierhändig.* Munich, 1937.

Gardien, Jacques. *L'orgue et organistes en Bourgogne et en Franche-Comté au 18e siècle.* Paris, 1943.

Gatscher, Emanuel. *Die Fugentechnik Max Regers in ihrer Entwicklung.* Stuttgart, 1925.

Gatti, Guido Maria. *Musicisti moderni d'Italia e di fuori.* Bologna, 1925.

———. "The Piano Music of Claude Debussy," *MQ,* VII (1921), 418–60.

Gavoty, Bernard. *La jeune école d'orgue française.* Paris, 1937.

———. *Louis Vierne, la vie et l'oeuvre.* Paris, 1943.

Geiringer, Karl. *The Bach Family: Seven Generations of Creative Genius.* New York, 1954.

———. *Brahms.* Vienna, 1934. (English ed., translated by H. B. Weiner and B. Miall, New York, 1936; 2nd ed., 1947; reprint, 1961.)

———. *Musical Instruments.* New York, 1945.

Georgii, Walther. *Karl Maria von Weber als Klavierkomponist.* Leipzig, 1914.

*———. *Klaviermusik.* Zürich and Berlin, 1941. (2nd ed., 1950; 3rd ed., 1956.)

Gerdes, Gisela. "Die Choralvariation J. P. Sweelincks und seine Schüler." Unpublished dissertation, Freiburg im Breisgau, 1956.

Gerstenberg, Walter. *Die Klavierkompositionen Domenico Scarlattis.* Vol. II of *Forschungsarbeiten des musikwissenschaftlichen Instituts der Universität Leipzig.* Regensburg, 1933.

———. "Ueber Mozarts Klaviersatz," *AfMW,* XVI (1959), 108–16.

———. "Zur Verbindung Präludium und Fuge bei Bach," *Kongressbericht Lüneburg 1950.* Kassel, n.d., pp. 126–9.

Gerstlé, Henry. "Piano Music of Nicholas Medtner," *MQ,* X (1924), 500–10.

Gertler, Wolfgang. *Robert Schumann in seinen frühen Klavierwerken.* Wolfenbüttel and Berlin, 1931.

Gillespie, John Edward. "The Harpsichord Works of Nicholas LeBègue." Unpublished dissertation, Southern California, 1951.

Girdlestone, Cuthbert. *Jean Philippe Rameau, his Life and Work.* London, 1957.
———. "Rameau's Self-Borrowings," *M & L*, XXXIX (1958), 52–6.
Glyn, Margaret. *About Elizabethan Virginal Music and Its Composers.* London, 1924. (Revised ed., 1934.)
Goehlinger, F. "Geschichte des Klavichords." Unpublished dissertation, Basel, 1910.
Göllner, Theodor. *Formen früher Mehrstimmigkeit in deutschen Handschriften des späten Mittelalters. Mit Veröffentlichung der Orgelspiellehre aus dem Codex lat. 7755 der Bayerischen Staatsbibliothek München.* Vol. VI of *Münchener Veröffentlichungen zur Musikgeschichte.* Tutzing, 1961.
Goldman, Richard Franko. "The Music of Elliot Carter," *MQ*, XLIII (1957), 151–70. (See also *MQ*, XXXVI [1951], 83–9.)
Golos, George S. "Some Slavic Precursors of Chopin," *MQ*, XLVI (1960), 437–47.
Gombosi, Otto. "About Organ Playing in the Divine Service circa 1500," in *Essays on Music in Honor of Archibald Thomson Davison.* Cambridge, 1957, pp. 51–68.
———. "Zur Vorgeschichte der Tokkate," *Acta*, VI (1934), 49–53.
Grace, Harvey. *French Organ Music, Past and Present.* New York, 1919.
———. *The Organ Works of Bach.* London, 1922.
———. *The Organ Works of César Franck.* London, 1948.
———. *The Organ Works of Rheinberger.* London, 1925.
Gray, Cecil. *The Forty-Eight Preludes and Fugues of Bach.* London, 1938.
Gress, Richard. *Die Entwicklung der Klaviervariation von A. Gabrieli bis zu J. S. Bach.* Vol. VI of *Veröffentlichungen des Musik–Instituts der Universität Tübingen.* Augsburg, 1929.
Gurlitt, Wilibald. "Die Wandlungen des Klangideals der Orgel im Lichte der Musikgeschichte," in *Bericht über die Freiburger Tagung für deutsche Orgelkunst.* Augsburg, 1926, pp. 27–42.

Haag, Herbert. *César Franck als Orgelkomponist.* Vol. IV of *Heidelberger Studien zur Musikwissenschaft.* Kassel, 1936.
Haase, H. "Klavierspiel," *MGG*, VII (1958), 1183–94.
Hagenbucher, F. "Die originalen Klavierwerke zu 2 und 4 Händen von Robert Fuchs." Unpublished dissertation, Vienna, 1940.
Halfpenny, Eric. "Shudi and the Venetian Swell," *M & L*, XXVII (1946), 180–4.
Halski, Czeslaw Raymond. "Murky: A Polish Musical Freak," *M & L*, XXXIX (1958), 35–7.
Hamburger, Poul. "Ein handschriftliches Klavierbuch aus der ersten Hälfte des 17. Jahrhunderts," *ZfMW*, XIII (1930–1931), 133–40.
Hamm, Walter. *Studien über Ernst Peppings drei Klaviersonaten 1937.* Vol. XII of *Literaturhistorische-musikwissenschaftliche Abhandlungen.* Würzburg, 1955.
Handschin, Jacques. "Das Pedalklavier," *ZfMW*, XVII (1935), 418–25.
Harding, Rosamonde E. M. "The Earliest Pianoforte Music," *M & L*, XIII (1932), 194–9.
———. *The Pianoforte: Its History to the Great Exhibition to 1851.* Cambridge, 1933.
Hardouin, P. "François Roberday (1624–1680)," *Revue de musicologie*, XLV (1960), 44–62.
Harich-Schneider, Eta. *The Harpsichord.* St. Louis, 1954.
———, and Boadella, Ricard. "Zum Klavierspiel bei Thomas de Santa Maria," *AfMF*, II (1937), 243–5.
Hartmann, Ludwig. *Das Harmonium.* Leipzig, 1913.

Hathaway, Joseph W. G. *Analysis of Mendelssohn's Organ Works: A Study of the Structural Features*. London, 1898.

Haupt, Günther. *August Eberhard Müllers Leben und Klavierwerke*. Leipzig, 1926.

Hausswald, Günter. "Der Divertimentobegriff bei Georg Christoph Wagenseil," *AfMW*, IX (1952), 45–50.

Haynes, Maurice Brooks. "The Keyboard Works of Bernardo Pasquini." Unpublished dissertation, Indiana, 1960.

Hedar, Joseph. *Dietrich Buxtehudes Orgelwerke*. Stockholm, 1951.

Hedley, Arthur. *Chopin*. London, 1947. (Reprint, 1962.)

Heimrich, Werner. "Die Orgel- und Cembalowerke Bernardo Pasquinis (1637–1710)." Unpublished dissertation, Berlin (Freie Universität), 1959.

Helm, Ernest Eugene. *Music at the Court of Frederick the Great*. Norman, 1960.

Hendrie, Gerald. "The Keyboard Music of Orlando Gibbons (1583–1625)," *PRMA*, LXXXIX (1962–1963), 1–15.

Hermann, Kurt. *Die Klaviermusik der letzten Jahre*. Leipzig and Zürich, 1934.

Hertz, Eva. *Johann Andreas Stein (1728–1792): Ein Beitrag zur Geschichte des Klavierbaues*. Wolfenbüttel and Berlin, 1937.

Hess, Albert G. "The Transition from Harpsichord to Piano," *Galpin Society Journal*, VI (1953), 75–94.

Heussner, Ingemar. "Ignaz Moscheles in seinen Klaviersonaten, Kammermusikwerken und Konzerten." Unpublished dissertation, Marburg, 1963.

Hibbard, Trevor Davies. "John Field's Rondeaux on 'Speed the Plow,'" *MR*, XXIV (1963), 139–46.

Hibberd, Lloyd. "The Early Keyboard Prelude." Unpublished dissertation, Harvard, 1940.

Hickmann, Hans. *Das Portativ: Ein Beitrag zur Geschichte der Kleinorgel*. Kassel, 1936.

*Hipkins, Alfred James. *A Description and History of the Pianoforte and of the Older Stringed Keyboard Instruments*. London and New York, 1896.

Hirt, Franz Joseph. *Meisterwerke des Klavierbaus*. Olton, 1955.

Hirtler, Franz. "Neuaufgefundene Orgelstücke von Johann Ulrich Steigleder und Johann Benn," *AfMF*, II (1937), 92–100.

Hoboken, Antony van. *Joseph Haydn: Thematisch–bibliographisches Verzeichnis*. Vol. I: *Instrumentalwerke*. Vol. II: In progress. Mainz, 1957–.

Hoffmann-Erbrecht, Lothar. *Deutsche und italienische Klaviermusik zur Bachzeit: Studien zur Thematik und Themenverarbeitung in der Zeit von 1720–1760*. Vol. I of *Jenaer Beiträge zur Musikforschung*. Leipzig, 1954.

——. "Johann Christoph Graupner als Klavierkomponist," *AfMW*, X (1953), 140–52.

——. "Johann Kaspar Ferdinand Fischer der Jüngere," *MF*, V (1952), 336–41.

——. "Der Nürnberger Musikverleger Johann Ulrich Haffner," *Acta*, XXVI (1954), 114–26; XXVII (1955), 141–2; additions, in part by William S. Newman, *Acta*, XXXIV (1962), 194–5.

——. "Sturm und Drang in der deutschen Klaviermusik von 1753–1763," *MF*, X (1957), 466–79.

Hofman, S. *L'oeuvre de clavecin de François Couperin: Étude stylistique*. Paris, 1961.

Hohenemser, Richard. "Formale Eigentümlichkeiten in Robert Schumanns Klaviermusik," in *Festschrift zum 50. Geburtstag Adolf Sandberger überreicht*. Munich, 1918, pp. 21–50.

Holcman, Jan. "The Labyrinth of Chopin Ornamentation," *Juilliard Review*, V, No. 2 (1958), 23–41.

Hopf, Helmut. "Stilistische Voraussetzungen der Klaviermusik Robert Schumanns." Unpublished dissertation, Göttingen, 1958.

Hopkinson, Cecil. *A Bibiliographical Catalogue of the Works of John Field.* London, 1961.

――――. "Eighteenth Century Editions of the Keyboard Compositions of Domenico Scarlatti," *Edinburgh Bibliographical Society Transactions* III, No. 1 (1948–1949), 47–71.

Horsley, Imogene. "The 16th-Century Variation: A New Historical Survey," *JAMS*, XII (1959), 118–32.

Horton, John. "Grieg's Slaatter for Piano," *M & L* XXVI (1945), 229–35.

Howell, Almonte C. "Cabezón : An Essay in Structural Analysis," *MQ*, L (1964), 18–30.

――――. "French Baroque Organ Music and the Eight Church Tones," *JAMS*, XI (1959), 106–18.

――――. "The French Organ Mass in the Sixteenth and Seventeenth Centuries." Unpublished dissertation, North Carolina, 1953.

Hudson, Barton, "A Portuguese Source of Seventeenth Century Iberian Keyboard Music." Unpublished dissertation, Indiana, 1961.

Hug, Manfred. "Johann Woltz und seine Orgeltabulatur." Unpublished dissertation, Tübingen, 1960.

Huggler, Hans Erwin. *J. S. Bachs Orgelbüchlein.* Bern, 1935. (Berlin dissertation, 1930.)

Hughes, John. "The Tientos, Fugas and Diferencias in Antonio de Cabezón's Obras de musica para tecla, harpa y vihuela." Unpublished dissertation, Florida State, 1961.

Hull, Arthur Eaglefield. *Bach's Organ Works.* London, 1929.

――――. *Handbook of the Pianoforte Works of Scriabin.* London, 1916.

Hünicken, Rolf. *Samuel Scheidt, ein althallischer Musikus: Sein Leben und Wirken.* Halle, 1934.

Husgen, R. *Der junge Max Reger und seine Orgelwerke.* Schramberg, 1935.

*Hutcheson, Ernest. *The Literature of the Piano.* New York, 1948. 3rd edition, revised by R. Ganz, 1964.

Hutchings, Arthur. "The English Concerto with or for Organ," *MQ*, XLVII (1961), 195–206.

――――. "[Mozart] The Keyboard Music," in *The Mozart Companion.* Edited by H. C. Robbins Landon and D. Mitchell. London. 1956, pp. 32–65.

Ilgner, Gerhard. *Matthias Weckmann: Sein Leben und sein Werk.* Vol. VI of *Kieler Beiträge zur Musikwissenschaft.* Wolfenbüttel, 1939.

Jachimecki, Zdislaw. "Eine polnische Orgeltabulatur aus dem Jahre 1548," *ZfMW*, II (1919–1920), 206–12.

Jacobik, Albert. *Die associative Harmonik in den Klavierwerken Debussys.* Würzburg, 1940.

Jacobs, Charles. *La interpretación de la música española del siglo XVI para instrumentos de teclado.* Vol. II of *Musica en Compostela.* Madrid, 1959.

Jacobs, Robert L. "Schumann and Jean Paul," *M & L*, XXX (1949), 250–8.

Jacquot, Jean. "Sur quelques formes de la musique de clavier élisabéthaine," in *La musique instrumentale de la Renaissance.* Edited by Jean Jacquot. Paris, 1955, pp. 241–58.

Jähns, Friedrich Wilhelm. *Carl Maria von Weber in seinen Werken: Chronologisch-thematisches Verzeichnis seiner sämtlichen Kompositionen.* Berlin, 1871.

James, Philip. *Early Keyboard Instruments.* London, 1930. (Reprint, 1962.)

Jansen, F. Gustav. *Die Davidsbündler: Aus Robert Schumanns Sturm und Drang Periode.* Leipzig, 1883.

Jeans, Susi. "The Pedal Clavichord and Other Practice Instruments of Organists," *PRMA*, LXXVII (1950–1951), 1–15.

Jeppesen, Knud. "Cavazzoni–Cabezón," *JAMS*, VIII (1955), 81–5. (See also Thurston Dart, *ibid.*, p. 148.)

———. "Eine frühe Orgelmesse aus Castell'Arquato," *AfMW*, XII (1955), 187–205.

———. *Die italienische Orgelmusik am Anfang des Cinquento.* 2 vols. Copenhagen, 1943. (2nd ed., 1960.)

Jöhde, Fritz. "Die Thematik der Klaviersonaten Mozarts," *Mozart-Jahrbuch*, II (1924), 7–53.

Jurisch, Hetta. "Principien der Dynamik im Klavierwerk Philipp Emanuel Bachs." Unpublished dissertation, Tübingen, 1959.

Kahl, Willi, "Frühe Lehrwerke für das Hammerklavier," *AfMW*, IX (1952), 231–45.

———. "Das lyrische Klavierstück Schuberts und seine Vorgänger bis 1810," *AfMW*, III (1921), 54–82, 99–122.

———. "Zu Mendelssohns Lieder ohne Worte," *ZfMW*, III (1920–1921), 459–69.

Kahle, Felix. *Georg Friedrich Händels Cembalosuiten.* Eisenach, 1928.

Kalbeck, Max. *Johannes Brahms.* 4 vols. Berlin, 1904–1914.

Kalkoff, Arthur. *Das Orgelschaffen Max Regers im Lichte der deutschen Orgeler-neuerungsbewegung.* Kassel and Basel, 1950.

Kastner, Santiago. *Antonio de Cabezón.* Barcelona, 1952.

———. *Carlos de Seixas.* Coimbra, 1947.

———. *Contribución al estudio de la música española y portuguesa.* Lisbon, 1941.

———. "Una intavolatura d'organo italiana del 1598," *Collectanea historiae musicae* II (1956), 237–43.

———. "Los manuscritos musicales ns 848 y 242 de la Biblioteca General de la Universidad de Coimbra," *AM*, V (1950), 78–96.

———. *Música hispanica. O estilo musical do Padre R. Coelho: A interpretação de música hispánia para tecla desde 1450 até 1650.* Lisbon, 1936.

———. "Parallels and Discrepancies between English and Spanish Keyboard Music of the 16th and 17th Centuries," *AM*, VII (1952), 77–115.

———. "Rapports entre Schlick et Cabezón," in *La musique instrumentale de la Renaissance.* Edited by Jean Jacquot. Paris, 1955, pp. 217–23.

———. "Relations entre la musique instrumentale française et espagnole au XVIe siècle," *AM*, X (1955), 84–108; XI (1956), 91–110.

———. "Tres libros desconocidos con música orgánica en las bibliotecas de Oporto y Braga," *AM*, I (1946), 143–51.

Kaufmann, W. *Beiträge zu einer Orgeltopographie Nordwestdeutschlands mit besonderer Berücksichtigung des Osnabrücker Landes.* Osnabrück, n.d.

Keller, Hans. *Reger und die Orgel.* Munich, 1923.

Keller, Hermann. *Domenico Scarlatti: Ein Meister des Klaviers.* Leipzig, 1957.

———. *Die Klavierwerke Bachs: Ein Beitrag zu ihrer Geschichte, Form, Deutung und Wiedergabe.* Leipzig, 1950.

———. *Die Orgelwerke Bachs: Ein Beitrag zu ihrer Geschichte, Form, Deutung und Wiedergabe.* Leipzig, 1948. (English ed., *The Organ Works of Bach*, translated by H. Hewitt, New York, 1964.)

Keller, Walter, "The Italian Organ Hymn from Cavazzoni to Aresti." Unpublished dissertation, Harvard, 1958.

Kelletat, Herbert. *Zur Geschichte der deutschen Orgelmusik in der Frühklassik.* Vol. XV [XVI] of *Königsberger Studien zur Musikwissenschaft.* Kassel, 1933.

Kendall, Raymond. "Notes on Arnold Schlick," *Acta,* XI (1939), 136–43.

*Kenyon, Max. *Harpsichord Music: A Survey of the Virginals, Spinet and Harpsichord.* London, 1949.

Kilian, Dietrich. "J. S. Bach, Präludium und Fuge, d moll, BWV 539," *MF,* XIV (1961), 323–8.

————. "Studie über Bachs Fantasie und Fuge c-moll (BWV 537)," in *Hans Albrecht In Memoriam.* Kassel, 1962, pp. 127–35.

King, A. Hyatt. "Mozart's Piano Music," *MR,* V (1944), 163–91.

*Kinkeldey, Otto. *Orgel und Klavier in der Musik des 16. Jahrhunderts.* Leipzig, 1910.

Kinsky, Georg. "Hanns Haiden, der Erfinder des Nürnbergischen Geigenwerks," *ZfMW,* VI (1923–1924), 193–214.

————. "Kurze Oktaven auf besaiteten Tasteninstrumente," *ZfMW,* II (1919–1920), 65–82.

————. *Das Werk Beethovens: Verzeichnis seiner sämtlich vollendeten Kompositionen.* With H. Halm. Munich, 1955.

Kirkpatrick, Ralph. *Domenico Scarlatti.* Princeton, 1953.

Kittler, Günther. *Geschichte des protestantischen Orgelchorales von den Anfängen bis zu den Lüneburger Tabulaturen.* Aeckermünde, 1931.

Klauwell, Otto. *Geschichte der Sonate.* Cologne and Leipzig, 1899.

Klitenic, Zelik. "The Clavecin Works of Jean-Philippe Rameau." Unpublished dissertation, Pennsylvania, 1955.

Klotz, Hans. "Bachs Orgeln und seine Orgelmusik," *MF,* II (1950), 189–203.

————. *Das Buch von der Orgel: Ueber Wesen und Aufbau des Orgelwerkes, Orgelpflege und Orgelspiel.* Kassel, 1938. (3rd ed., 1949; 6th ed., 1960.)

————. *Ueber die Orgelkunst der Gotik, der Renaissance und des Barocks: Die alten Registrierungs- und Dispositions-Grundlagen.* Kassel, 1931–1934.

Knab, Arnim. "Die Einheit der Beethovenschen Klaviersonate in As-Dur op. 110," *ZfMW,* I (1918–1919), 388–99.

Knöll, Heinrich Johann. "Die Klavier- und Orgelwerke von Theophil Muffat." Unpublished dissertation, Vienna, 1916.

Köchel, Ludwig von. *Chronologisch-thematisches Verzeichnis sämmtlicher Tonwerke Wolfgang Amadé Mozarts.* Leipzig, 1862. (3rd ed., revised by Alfred Einstein, 1937; reprint, 1947; 4th ed., 1958; 5th ed., 1962; 6th ed., revised by E. Reichert, F. Giegling, A. Weinmann, and G. Sievers, Wiesbaden, 1963.)

Kókai, Rudolf. *Franz Liszt in seinen frühen Klavierwerken.* Leipzig, 1933.

Kölsch, Hans Friedrich. *Der Impressionismus bei Debussy.* Düsseldorf, 1937.

Kölsch, Heinz. *Nicholas Bruhns.* Vol. VIII of *Schriften des Landesinstituts für Musikforschung Kiel.* Kassel and New York, 1958.

Költzsch, Hans. *Franz Schubert in seinen Klaviersonaten.* Vol. VII of *Sammlung musikwissenschaftlicher Einzeldarstellungen.* Leipzig, 1927.

Kooiker, Anthony. "Locke's Melothesia: Its Place in the History of Keyboard Music in Reformation England." Unpublished dissertation, Rochester, 1962.

Koscewski, Andrzej. "Das Walzerelement im Schaffen Chopins," *DJ,* V (1960), 58–66.

Kotterba, Karin. "Die Orgeltabulatur des Leonhard Kleber." Unpublished dissertation, Freiburg im Breisgau, 1958.

Kötz, Hans. *Der Einfluss Jean Pauls auf Robert Schumann.* Weimar, 1933.

Krebs, Carl. "Die besaiteten Klavierinstrumente bis zum Anfang des 17. Jahrhunderts," *VfMW,* VIII (1892), 91–126.

Krehbiel, Henry Edward. *The Pianoforte and Its Music.* New York, 1911.

Kremer, Rudolf. "The Organ Sonata Since 1845." Unpublished dissertation, Washington University (St. Louis), 1963.

Kretzschmar, Hermann. "Die Klaviermusik seit Robert Schumann," *Gesammelte Aufsätze,* I (Leipzig, 1910), 87–135.

Kreutz, Alfred. "Ornamentation in J. S. Bach's Keyboard Works," *Hinrichsen's Musical Yearbook,* VII (1952), 358–79.

Krey, Johannes. "Bachs Orgelmusik der Weimarer Periode." Unpublished dissertation, Jena, 1956.

Krohn, Ernst C. "Alexander Reinagle as Sonatist," *MQ,* XVIII (1932), 140–9.

Kunze, Stefan. *Die Instrumentalmusik Giovanni Gabrielis: Mit einem Notenanhang zum Teil erstmalig veröffentlichter Instrumentalkompositionen Gabrielis und seiner Zeitgenossen.* Vol. VIII of *Münchener Veröffentlichungen zur Musikwissenschaft.* Tutzing, 1964.

Kwasnik, Walter. *Die Orgel der Neuzeit.* Cologne, 1948.

Labat, Jean Baptiste. *Les organistes françaises au XVIIIe siècle.* Montaubon, 1872.

Lange, Martin. *Beiträge zur Entstehung der südwestdeutschen Klaviersonate im 18. Jahrhundert.* Berlin, 1930.

Larsen, Jens Peter. *Die Haydn-Ueberlieferung.* Copenhagen, 1939.

———. "Eine bisher unbeachtete Quelle zu Haydns frühen Klavierwerken," in *Festschrift Joseph Schmidt-Görg zum 60. Geburtstage.* Bonn, 1957, pp. 188–95.

Launay, Denise. "La fantaisie en France jusqu'au milieu de XVIIe siècle," in *La musique instrumentale de la Renaissance.* Edited by Jean Jacquot. Paris, 1955, pp. 327–38.

Laux, Karl. *Joseph Haas.* Mainz, 1931.

———. *Die Musik in Russland und in der Sowjetunion.* Berlin, 1958.

Leibowitz, René. *Schönberg et son école: l'étape contemporaine du langage musical.* Paris, 1947. (English ed., *Schoenberg and His School: The Contemporary Stage of the Language of Music,* translated by D. Newlin, New York, 1949.)

Leichtentritt, Hugo. *Analyse der Chopin'schen Klavierwerken.* Berlin, 1921–1922.

Lissa, Zofia. "Chopins Briefe an Delfina Potocka," *MF,* XV (1962), pp. 341–53.

———. "Die Chopinsche Harmonik aus der Perspektive der Klangtechnik des 20. Jahrhunderts," *DJ,* II (1957), 68–84; III (1958), 74–91.

———. "Ueber den nationalen Stil von F. Chopin. Kriterien und Wesensbestimmung," in *Bericht über den Internationalen Musikwissenschaftlichen Kongress Wien Mozartjahr 1956.* Graz and Cologne, 1958, pp. 355–64.

Lockwood, Albert Lewis. *Notes on the Literature of the Piano.* Ann Arbor, 1940.

Loesser, Arthur. *Men, Women and Pianos: A Social History.* New York, 1954.

Loggins, Vernon. *Where the World Ends: The Life of Louis Moreau Gottschalk.* Baton Rouge, 1958.

Longo, Alessandro. *Domenico Scarlatti e la sua figura nelle storia della musica.* Naples, 1913.

Lord, Robert Sutherland. "The Buxheimer Organ Book." Unpublished dissertation, Yale, 1960.

Lorenz, Helmut. "Die Klaviermusik Dietrich Buxtehudes," *AfMW,* XI (1954), 238–51.

Löw, Helmut. "Die Improvisation im Klavierwerk L. van Beethovens." Unpublished dissertation, Saarbrücken, 1962.

Löwenfeld, Hans Karl. *Leonhard Kleber und seine Orgeltabulatur als Beitrag zur Geschichte der Orgelmusik im beginnenden 16. Jahrhundert.* Berlin, 1897.

Lowinsky, Edward E. "English Organ Music of the Renaissance," *MQ,* XXXIX (1953), 373–95, 528–53.

Luithen, Viktor. "Studien zu Johannes Brahms Werken in Variationenform," *SMW,* XIV (1927), 286–320.

Lunelli, Renato. *L'arte organaria del rinascimento in Roma e gli organi di S. Pietro in Vaticano dalle origini a tutto il periodo Frescobaldiana.* Vol. X of *Historiae musicae cultores biblioteca.* Florence, 1958.

Machabey, Armand. *Gerolamo Frescobaldi Ferranensis.* Paris, 1952.

MacLean, Charles. "The Principle of the Hydraulic Organ," *SIMG,* VI (1904–1905), 183–236.

———. "Rubinstein as Composer for the Pianoforte," *PRMA,* XXXIX (1913), 129–51.

Mahrenholz, Christhard. *Die Berechnung der Orgelpfeifen-Mensuren vom Mittelalter bis zur Mitte des 19. Jahrhunderts.* Kassel, 1938.

———. *Die Orgelregister: Ihre Geschichte und ihr Bau.* Kassel, 1930.

———. *Samuel Scheidt, sein Leben und sein Werk.* Vol. II of *Sammlung musikwissenschaftlicher Einzeldarstellungen.* Leipzig, 1924.

Mansfield, Orlando A. "Some Characteristics of Mendelssohn's Organ Sonatas," *MQ,* III (1917), 562–76.

Marco, Guy A. "The Alberti Bass before Alberti," *MR,* XX (1959), 93–103.

Marcuse, Sibyl. "Transposing Keyboards on Extant Flemish Harpsichords," *MQ,* XXXVIII (1952), 414–25.

Marks, F. Helena. *The Sonata, Its Form and Meaning as Exemplified in the Piano Sonatas of Mozart.* London, 1921.

Mason, Wilton. "Melodic Unity in Mozart's Piano Sonata, K. 332," *MR,* XXII (1961), 28–33.

Mayer, O. "Die romantische Klaviersonate." Unpublished dissertation, Greifswald, 1929.

Meister, Edith. *Stilelemente und die geschichtliche Grundlage in Chopins Klavierwerke: Ein Beitrag zur musikalischen Romantik.* Hamburg, 1936.

Mellers, Wilfrid. *François Couperin and the French Classical Tradition.* London, 1950.

———. "John Bull and English Keyboard Music," *MQ,* XL (1954), 364–83, 548–71.

Mereaux, Amédée. *Les clavecinistes de 1637 à 1790.* Paris, 1867.

Merian, Wilhelm. "Drei Handschriften aus der Frühzeit des Klavierspiels," *AfMW,* II (1920), 22–47.

———. "Mozarts Klaviersonaten und die Sonatenform," in *Festschrift Karl Nef zum 60. Geburtstag.* Zürich, 1933, pp. 174–201.

———. *Die Tabulaturen des Organisten Hans Kotter: Ein Beitrag zur Musikgeschichte des beginnenden 16. Jahrhunderts.* Leipzig, 1916.

———. *Der Tanz in den deutschen Tabulaturbüchern.* Leipzig, 1927.

Meyer, Ernst Hermann. "Gerhard Disener," *ZfMW,* XVI (1934), 405–13.

Meyer, Hermann. *Karl Joseph Riepp, der Orgelbauer von Ottobeuern: Ein Beitrag zur Geschichte des Oberschwäbischen Orgelbaus im 18. Jahrhundert.* Kassel, 1939.

Michel, Henri. *La sonate pour clavier avant Beethoven.* Paris, 1908.

Mies, Paul. "Herders Edvard-Ballade bei Johannes Brahms," *ZfMW*, II (1919–1920), 225–32.

———. "W. A. Mozarts Variationenwerke und ihre Formungen," *AfMF*, II (1937), 466–95.

Miller, Hugh M. "The Earliest Keyboard Duets," *MQ*, XXIX (1943), 438–57.

———. "Fulgens praeclara: A Unique Keyboard Setting of a Plainsong Sequence," *JAMS*, II (1949), 97–101.

———. "John Bull's Organ Works," *M & L*, XXVIII (1947), 25–35.

———. "Sixteenth Century English Faburden Compositions for Keyboard," *MQ*, XXVI (1940), 50–64.

Misch, Ludwig. *Die Faktoren der Einheit in der Mehrsätzigkeit der Werke Beethovens: Versuch einer Theorie der Einheit des Werkstils.* Series IV, No. 3 of *Veröffentlichungen des Beethovenhauses in Bonn.* Munich and Duisberg, 1958.

———. "Fugue and Fugato in Beethoven's Variation Form," *MQ*, XLII (1956), 14–27.

———. "Zwei Fugen aus dem *Wohltemperierten Klavier* in neuer Beleuchtung," *MF*, V (1952), 179–90.

Mizwa, Stephen P. (ed.). *Frédéric Chopin, 1810–1849.* New York, 1949.

Moldenhauer, Hans. *Duo-Pianism: a Dissertation.* Chicago, 1951.

Molitor, Raphael. *Joseph Rheinberger und seine Kompositionen für die Orgel.* Leipzig, 1904.

Monroe, James F. "Italian Keyboard Music in the Interim between Frescobaldi and Pasquini." Unpublished dissertation, Michigan, 1959.

Montagu-Nathan, Montagu. *Handbook of the Pianoforte Works of Scriabin.* London, 1916. (Reprinted, 1922.)

Moreux, Serge. *Béla Bartók: Sa vie, ses oeuvres, son langage.* Paris, 1949.

Moser, Hans Joachim. "Hofhaimeriana," *ZfMW*, XV (1932–1933), 127.

———. *Orgelromantik: Ein Gang durch Orgelfragen von vorgestern und übermorgen.* Ludwigsburg, 1961.

———. *Paul Hofhaimer: Ein Lied- und Orgelmeister des deutschen Humanismus.* Stuttgart and Berlin, 1929.

———. "Ein Trienter Orgeltabulatur aus Hofhaimers Zeit," in *Studien zur Musikgeschichte: Festschrift für Guido Adler.* Vienna and Leipzig, 1930, pp. 84–6.

Müller, Gottfried. *Daniel Steibelt, sein Leben und seine Klavierwerke.* Vol. X of *Sammlung musikwissenschaftlicher Einzeldarstellungen.* Strassburg, 1933.

Müller, Werner. "Das Ausdrucksproblem in der Klaviermusik Carl Philipp Emanuel Bachs." Unpublished dissertation, Saarbrücken, 1959.

Müller-Blattau, Joseph. "Bachs *Goldberg-Variationen*," *AfMW*, XVI (1959), 207–19.

———. "Beethoven und die Variation," *Neues Beethoven-Jahrbuch*, V (1933), 101–36 (in abbreviated form, in *Beethoven-Zentenarfeier*, Vienna, 1927, pp. 55–7).

Murdoch, William. *Brahms: With an Analytical Study of the Complete Pianoforte Works.* London, 1933.

———. *Chopin: His Life.* New York, 1935.

Murphy, Richard. "Fantasia and Ricercare in the Sixteenth Century." Unpublished dissertation, Yale, 1954.

Mustel, Alphonse. *L'orgue expressif, ou l'harmonium.* 2 vols. Paris, 1903.

Nagel, Wilibald. *Die Klaviersonaten von Johannes Brahms.* Stuttgart, 1915.

Nef, Walter Robert. "Der St. Gallner Organist Fridolin Sicher und seine Orgeltabulatur," *Schweizerische Jahrbuch für Musikwissenschaft*, VII (1938), 12–143.

Nelson, Robert U. *The Technique of Variation: A Study of the Instrumental Variation from Antonio de Cabezón to Max Reger.* Vol. III of *University of California Publications in Music.* Berkeley and Los Angeles, 1948.

Nestyev, Israel. *Sergei Prokofiev.* Translated by R. Prokofieva. New York, 1946. (Another version, translated by F. Jonas, Stanford, 1960.)

Neudenberger, Lucia. *Die Variationstechnik der Virginalisten im Fitzwilliam Virginal Book.* Berlin, 1937.

Neupert, Hanns. *Das Cembalo: Eine geschichtliche und technische Betrachtung der Kielinstrumente.* Kassel, 1932. (3rd ed., 1956; English ed.: *Harpsichord Manual,* translated by F. E. Kirby, Kassel, 1960.)

———. *Das Klavichord.* Kassel, 1948.

———. *Vom Musikstab zum modernen Klavier.* 2nd ed. Bamberg, 1926.

Newman, William S. *The Sonata in the Baroque Era.* Chapel Hill, 1959.

———. *The Sonata in the Classic Era.* Chapel Hill, 1963.

Newton, Richard. "The English Cult of Domenico Scarlatti," *M & L,* XX (1939), 138–56.

Niecks, Friedrich. *Frédéric Chopin as a Man and Musician.* 2 vols. London, 1888.

Niemann, Walther. *Brahms.* Berlin, 1920 (Several later eds. English ed., translated by C. A. Phillips, New York, 1929.)

———. *Das Klavierbuch: Kurze Geschichte der Klaviermusik und ihre Meister.* Munich, 1907. (2nd ed., 1910; 11th ed., 1922.)

———. *Die nordische Klaviermusik.* Leipzig, 1918.

———. *Die Virginalmusik.* Leipzig, 1919.

Nolte, Ewald. "The Magnificat Fugues of Johann Pachelbel: Alternation or Intonation," *JAMS,* IX (1956), 19–24.

Nüll, Edwin von der. *Béla Bartók: Ein Beitrag zur Morphologie der neuen Musik.* Halle, 1930.

Oberdörffer, Fritz. "Ueber die Generalbassbegleitung zu Kammermusikwerken Bachs und des Spätbarocks," *MF,* X (1957), 61–74. (See also "Nachwort," *MF,* XI [1958], 79–82.)

Oppel, Reinhard. "Bachs D-Dur Präludium und Fuge für Orgel," *ZfMW,* II (1919–1920), 149–56.

———. "Ueber Beziehungen Beethovens zu Mozart und zu Ph. Em. Bach," *ZfMW,* V (1922–1923), 30–9.

Ottich, Maria. *Chopins Klavierornamentik.* Wolfenbüttel and Berlin, 1938.

Pannain, Guido. *Le origini e lo sviluppo dell'arte pianistica in Italia dal 1500 al 1730 circa.* Naples, 1917.

Paribene, Guilio Cesare. "Francesco Durante cembalista," *Il Pianoforte,* II (1921), 303–7.

———. *Muzio Clementi nella vita e nell'arte.* Milan, 1921.

———, Orsini, Luigi, and Bontempelli, Ettore. *M. E. Bossi, il compositore, l'organista, l'uomo.* Milan, 1934.

Parrish, Carl. "Criticisms of the Piano When It Was New," *MQ,* XXX (1944), 428–40.

———. "The Early Piano and Its Influence on Keyboard Technique and Composition in the Eighteenth Century." Unpublished dissertation, Harvard, 1939.

———. "Haydn and the Piano," *JAMS,* I, No. 3 (1948), 27–34.

Päsler, Carl. "Fundamentbuch von Hans von Constanz. Ein Beitrag zur Geschichte des Orgelspiels im 16. Jahrhundert," *VfMW*, V (1889), 1–192.

Paul, Oskar. *Geschichte des Claviers vom Ursprunge bis zum modernsten Form dieses Instruments.* Leipzig, 1868.

Pauly, Paul Gerhard. "Georg Friedrich Händels Klavierfugen: Ein Beitrag zur Geschichte der Fuge in der 1. Hälfte des 18. Jahrhunderts." Unpublished dissertation, Saarbrücken, 1961.

Pearce, Charles W. *Mendelssohn's Organ Sonatas.* London, 1902.

Perrachio, Luigi. *L'opera pianistica di Claude Debussy.* Milan, 1924.

Perrot, Jean. "Les origines de l'orgue carolingien," *Revue musicale* [Richard], No. 226 (1955), 7–15.

Pfatteicher, Carl. *John Redford, Organist and Almoner of St. Paul's Cathedral in the Time of Henry VIII: With Especial Reference to his Organ Composition.* Leipzig, 1934; Kassel, 1934.

Pietzsch, Gerhard. "Orgelbauer, Organisten und Orgelspiel in Deutschland bis zum Ende des 16. Jahrhunderts," *MF*, XI (1958), 160–8, 307–15, 455–61; XII (1959), 25–35, 152–61, 294–8.

———. "Orgelspiel und Orgelbauer in Speyer vor der Reformation," *AfMW*, XIV (1957), 201–20.

———. "Uebersehene Quellen zur mittelalterlichen Orgelgeschichte," *AM*, XII (1957), 83–96.

Pilkington, C. Vere. "A Collection of English 18th Century Harpsichord Music," *PRMA*, LXXXIII (1956–1957), 89–107.

Pirro, André. *Les clavecinistes.* Paris, 1924.

———. *Dietrich Buxtehude.* Paris, 1913.

———. *L'esthétique de J.-S. Bach.* Paris, 1907.

———. *L'orgue de J.-S. Bach.* Paris, 1897. (English ed., *Bach the Organist and His Works for Organ,* translated by W. Goodrich, London, 1902.)

Pirrotta, Nino. "[Faenza Ms.] Note sur un codice di antiche musiche per tastiera," *RMI*, LVI (1954), 333–9.

Plamenac, Dragan. "The Codex Faenza, Biblioteca comunale 117," *JAMS*, IV (1951), 179–201. (See also *JAMS*, XVII (1964), 78–81.)

———. "New Light on Codex Faenza 117," in *Kongressbericht Utrecht 1952.* Amsterdam, 1953, pp. 310–26.

Plath, Wolfgang. "Das Klavierbüchlein für Wilhelm Friedemann Bach." Unpublished dissertation, Tübingen, 1958.

Podolsky, Saul. "The Variation Canzona for Keyboard Instruments in Italy, Austria and Southern Germany in the Seventeenth Century." Unpublished dissertation, Boston, 1954.

Pols, André Marie. *De Ruckers en de Klavierbouw en Vlaaderen.* Antwerp, 1942.

Pontius, Josef. "Eine anonyme kurpfälzische Orgeltabulatur." Unpublished dissertation, Saarbrücken, 1960.

Priestman, Brian. "Catalogue thematique des oeuvres de Jean-Baptiste, John et Jacques Loeillet," *RBM*, VI (1952), 219–74.

———. "The Keyboard Works of John Loeillet," *MR*, XVI (1955), 89–95.

Prod'homme, Jacques Gabriel. *Les sonates pour piano de Beethoven (1782–1823): Histoire et critique.* Paris, 1937.

*Prosniz, Adolf. *Handbuch der Clavier-Literatur.* Vienna, 1887. (2nd ed., Leipzig and Vienna, 1908.)

Quittard, Henri. "Les chorales variés pour orgue de César Franck," *La Revue musi-cale*, XI (1911), 118–125.
———. *Les Couperins*. Paris, 1913.
Quoika, Rudolf. *Die altösterreichische Orgel der späten Gothik, der Renaissance und des Barocks*. Kassel, 1953.
———. "Der Orgelbauer Jacob Schedlich," *AfMW*, XVIII (1961), 141–54.
———. *Das Positiv in Geschichte und Gegenwart*. Kassel and Basel, 1957.

Raabe, Felix. *Galuppi als Instrumentalkomponist*. Frankfurt an der Oder, 1929.
Raabe, Peter. *Franz Liszt*. 2 vols. Stuttgart and Berlin, 1931.
Radcliffe, Philip. "The Piano Sonatas of Joseph Haydn," *MR*, VII (1946), 136–48.
Rahner, Hugo Ernst. *Max Regers Choralfantasien für Orgel: Eine Studie über Grund-lagen und Werden des Regerschen Orgelstils*. Vol. V. of *Heidelberger Studien zur Musikwissenschaft*. Kassel, 1936.
Rašín, Vera. "'Les Six' and Cocteau," *M & L*, XXXVIII (1957), 164–9.
Raugel, Félix. *Les Organistes*. Paris, 1923.
———. "L'organiste Pierre Du Mage (v. 1676–1751)," *Mélanges d'histoire et d'esthé-tique musicale offerts à Paul-Marie Masson*, II (1955), 125–32.
Redlich, Hans Ferdinand. *Alban Berg, the Man and his Music*. New York, 1957; London, 1957.
———. *Alban Berg: Versuch einer Würdigung*. Vienna, Zürich, and London, 1957.
———. "Girolamo Frescobaldi," *MR*, XIV (1953), 262–74.
Reeser, Eduard. "Johann Gottfried Eckhard, 1735–1809," *TVNM*, XVII (1954–1955), 89–127.
———. *De Klaviersonate met Vioolbegleiding in het Parijsche Muziekleben ten Tijde van Mozart*. Rotterdam, 1939.
———. *De Zonen van Bach*. Amsterdam, 1941. (English ed., *The Sons of Bach*, trans-lated by W. A. G. Doyle-Davidson, Stockholm, 1947.)
Refoulé, Robert. *La sonate pour piano*. Orleans, 1922.
Rehberg, Walther, and Rehberg, Paula. *Robert Schumann: Sein Leben und sein Werk*. Zürich, 1954.
Reichling, Alfred. "Ein bisher unbeachteter Kyriesatz nebst zugehörigen Praeambulum in *Buxheimer Orgelbuch*," *MF*, IX (1956), 443–6.
Reimann, Margarete. "Zur Deutung des Begriffs *fantasia*," *AfMW*, X (1953), 253–74.
———. "Zur Entwicklungsgeschichte des Double. Ein Beitrag zur Geschichte der Variation," *MF*, V (1952), 317–32; VI (1953), 97–111.
———. *Untersuchungen zur Formgeschichte der französischen Klaviersuite mit besonderer Berücksichtigung von Couperins Ordres*. Regensburg, 1941.
Reynaud, H. *L'oeuvre de Charles-Marie Widor*. Lyon, 1900.
Riedel, Friedrich Wilhelm. *Quellenkündliche Beiträge zur Geschichte der Musik für Tasteninstrumente in der 2. Hälfte des 17. Jahrhunderts*. Vol. X of *Schriften des Landesinstituts für Musikforschung Kiel*. Kassel, 1960.
———. "Eine unbekannte Quelle zu Johann Kaspar Kerlls Musik für Tasteninstru-mente," *MF*, XII (1960), 310–14.
Riemann, Hugo. *Katechismus der Fugen-Komposition*. 2nd ed. 2 vols. Leipzig, 1906-1907.
———. *Präludien und Studien*. 3 vols. Leipzig, 1895–1901.
Rietschel, Georg. *Die Aufgabe der Orgel im Gottesdienst bis in das 18. Jahrhundert*. Leipzig, 1892.
Rimbault, Edward Francis. *The Pianoforte. Its Origin, Progress and Construction*. London, 1860.

Ringer, Alexander L. "Clementi and the Eroica," *MQ*, XLVII (1961), 454–68.

———. "Leon Kirchner," *MQ*, XLIII (1957), 1–20.

———. "Willem Pijper and the 'Netherlands School' of the 20th Century," *MQ*, XLI (1955), 427–45.

*Ritter, August Gottfried. *Zur Geschichte des Orgelspiels, vornehmlich des Deutschen, im 14. bis zum Anfang des 19. Jahrhunderts.* 2 vols. Leipzig, 1884. (See also Frotscher.)

Roberts, W. Wright. "The Pianoforte Works of Chabrier," *M & L*, IV (1923), 132–43.

Roethlisberger, Edmond. *Le clavecin dans l'oeuvre de J.-S. Bach.* Geneva, 1921.

Rognoni, Luigi. *Espressionismo e dodecaphonia.* Turin, 1954.

Rokseth, Yvonne. *La musique d'orgue au XVe siècle et au début de XVI.* Paris, 1930.

Ronga, Luigi. *Girolamo Frescobaldi.* Turin, 1930.

Rosenberg, Richard. *Die Klaviersonaten Ludwig van Beethovens: Studien über Form und Vortrag.* Olton, 1957.

Rostand, Claude. *L'oeuvre de Fauré.* Paris, 1945.

Roth, Bärbel. "Zur Echtheitsfrage der Matthias Weckmann zugeschriebenen Klavierwerke ohne Cantus firmus," *Acta*, XXXVI (1964), 31–6.

Rothschild, Fritz. *A Handbook of the Performance of the 48 Preludes and Fugues of Bach According to the Rules of the Old Tradition.* 2 vols. London, 1955.

Rüder, E. *Felix Draeseke.* 2 vols. Dresden, 1932; Berlin, 1937.

Rumohr, Edith von. *Der Nürnbergische Tasteninstrumentstil im 17. Jahrhundert dargestellt an Arie, Variation und Suite.* Hermer, 1939.

Rüsch, Walter. *Franz Liszts Années de pèlerinage: Beiträge zur Geschichte seiner Persönlichkeit und seines Stiles.* Bellinzona, 1934.

Russell, John F. "Mozart and the Pianoforte," *MR*, I (1940), 226–44.

*Russell, Raymond. *The Harpsichord and Clavichord: An Introductory Study.* London, 1959.

———. "The Harpsichord Since 1800," *PRMA*, LXXXII (1955–1956), 61–74.

Ruthardt, Adolf. *Wegweiser durch die Klavierliteratur.* 10th ed. Leipzig and Zürich, 1925.

Rychnovsky, Ernst. *Smetana.* Stuttgart, 1924.

*Sachs, Curt. *The History of Musical Instruments.* New York, 1940.

———. *Das Klavier.* Vol. I of *Handbücher des Instrumentenmuseums der Staatlichen Hochschule für Musik.* Berlin, 1923.

*———. *Reallexikon der Musikinstrumente. Zugleich ein Polyglossar für das gesamte Instrumentengebiet.* Berlin, 1913. (Reprint, 1962.)

Salmen, Walther. "Johann Gottfried Müthel, der letzte Schüler Bachs," in *Festschrift Heinrich Besseler zum 60. Geburtstag.* Leipzig, 1961, pp. 351–9.

Salzer, Felix. "Ueber die Bedeutung der Ornamente in Philipp Emanuel Bachs Klavierwerken," *ZfMW*, XIII (1929–1930), 398–418.

Sandberger, Adolf. "Zur italienischen Klaviermusik des 17. und 18. Jahrhunderts," in *Ausgewählte Aufsätze zur Musikgeschichte*, I, Munich, 1921, 169–80; *JMP*, XXV (1918), 17–25.

Sannemüller, Gerd. "Das Klavierwerk von Maurice Ravel: Versuch einer stilistischer Grundlegung." Unpublished dissertation, Kiel, 1961.

Sartori, Claudio. "Organs, Organ Builders and Organists in Milan, 1450–1476. New and Unpublished Documents," *MQ*, XLIII (1957), 57–67.

Sceats, Godfrey. *The Organ Works of Karg-Elert.* Orphington, 1940. (Rev. ed., 1950.)

Schaefer-Schmuck, Käthe. *Georg Philipp Telemann als Klavierkomponist.* Borna and Leipzig, 1934.

Scheide, August. *Zur Geschichte des Choralvorspiels.* Hildinghausen, 1926.

Schenk, Erich. *Giuseppe Antonio Paganelli: Sein Leben und seine Werke.* Salzburg, 1928.

Schenker, Heinrich. *Ein Beitrag zur Ornamentik: Als Einführung zur Ph. E. Bachs Klavierwerken umfassend auch die Ornamentik Haydns, Mozarts und Beethoven* [etc.]. Vienna, 1903.

Schering, Arnold. "Carl Philipp Emanuel Bach und das redende Prinzip der Musik," *JMP,* XLV (1938), 13–29.

———. *Die niederländische Orgelmesse im Zeitalter des Josquin: Eine stilkritische Untersuchung.* Leipzig, 1912.

———. "Ueber Liszts Persönlichkeit und Kunst," *JMP,* XXXIII (1926), 31–44.

———. "Zur Alternatim-Orgelmesse," *ZfMW,* XVII (1935), 19–32.

Schierning, Lydia. *Die Ueberlieferung der deutschen Orgel- und Klaviermusik aus der 1. Hälfte des 17. Jahrhunderts: Eine quellenkündliche Studie.* Vol. XII of *Schriften des Landesinstituts für Musikforschung Kiel.* Kassel, 1961.

Schjelderup-Ebbe, Dag. "Modality in Halfdan Kjerulf's Music," *M & L,* XXXVIII (1957), 238–46.

Schlesinger, Kathleen, and Hurren, S. A. "Pianoforte," Vol. XVII of *Encyclopaedia Britannica.* Chicago, 1962, pp. 881–91.

Schlesinger, Thea. *John Baptist Cramer und seine Klaviersonaten.* Munich, 1928.

Schmid, Ernst Fritz. "Joseph Haydn und C. P. E. Bach," *ZfMW,* XIV (1931–1932), 299–312.

Schmidt, Jost Harro. "Johannes Buchner. Leben und Werke: Ein Beitrag zur Geschichte der liturgischen Orgelmusik des späten Mittelalters." Unpublished dissertation, Freiburg im Breisgau, 1957.

Schmidt, Warren Frederick. "The Organ Chorales of Johann Gottfried Walther (1684–1748)." Unpublished dissertation, Iowa, 1961.

Schmidt-Weiss, Wolfgang. *Gottfried Heinrich Stölzel als Instrumentalkomponist.* Vol. IV of *Schriftenreihe des musikwissenschaftlichen Seminars der Universität München.* Munich, 1938.

Schmieder, Wolfgang. *Thematisch–systematisches Verzeichnis der musikalischen Werke von Johann Sebastian Bach.* Leipzig, 1950.

Schmitz, Arnold. "Die ästhetischen Anschauungen Robert Schumanns in ihren Beziehungen zur deutschen Literatur," *ZfMW,* III (1920–1921), 111–18.

Schmitz, Elie Robert. *The Piano Works of Claude Debussy.* New York, 1950.

Schmitz, Eugen. *Klavier, Klaviermusik und Klavierspiel.* Leipzig, 1919.

Schneider, Martin. *Die Orgelspieltechnik des frühen 19. Jahrhunderts.* Vol. VI of *Kölner Beiträge zur Musikforschung.* Regensburg, 1940.

Schnoor, Hans. "Das *Buxheimer Orgelbuch,*" *ZfMW,* IV (1921–1922), 1–10.

Schöckel, Heinrich Peter. *Johann Christian Bach und die Instrumentalmusik seiner Zeit.* Wolfenbüttel, 1926.

Schonberg, Harold C. *The Great Pianists.* New York, 1963.

Schrade, Leo. *Die ältesten Denkmäler der Orgelmusik als Beitrag zu einer Geschichte der Tokkata.* Münster, 1928.

———. "Ein Beitrag zur Geschichte der Tokkata," *ZfMW,* VIII (1925–1926), 610–35.

———. "Charles E. Ives, 1874–1954," *Yale Review,* XLIV (1955), 535–45.

———. *Die handschriftliche Ueberlieferung der ältesten Instrumentalmusik.* Lahr, 1931.

————. "Die Messe in der Orgelmusik des 15. Jahrhunderts," *AfMF*, I (1936), 129–75.

————. "The Organ in the Mass of the 15th Century," *MQ*, XXVIII (1942), 329–36, 467–87.

Schrammek, Winifred. "Das deutsche Lied in den deutschen Orgeltabulaturen des 15. Jahrhunderts unter besonderer Berücksichtigung des *Buxheimer Orgelbuchs*." Unpublished dissertation, Jena, 1956.

Schuler, Manfred. "Das Orgeltabulaturbuch von Jakob Paix." Unpublished dissertation, Freiburg im Breisgau, 1958.

Schulter-Bernet, Dietrich. *Die deutsche Klaviersonate des 20. Jahrhunderts: Ein Formuntersuchung der deutschen Klaviersonaten der zwanziger Jahre.* Vol. XXIV of *Kölner Beiträge zur Musikforschung*. Regensburg, 1963.

Schulz, Heinz-Günther. *Musikalischer Impressionismus und impressionistischer Klavierstil: Ein Beitrag zur musikalischer Stilforschung.* Würzburg, 1938.

*Schünemann, Georg. *Geschichte der Klaviermusik*. Berlin, 1940.

————. "Johann Christoph Friedrich Bach," *Bach-Jahrbuch*, XI (1914), 45–165.

Schwarz, Werner. *Robert Schumann und die Variation: Mit besonderer Berücksichtigung der Klavierwerke.* Vol. XV of *Königsberger Studien zur Musikwissenschaft*. Kassel, 1932.

Schweitzer, Albert. *Deutsche und französische Orgelbaukunst und Orgelkunst.* Leipzig, 1906; also 1927. (Reprint, 1962.)

————. *J. S. Bach, le musicien-poète.* Leipzig, 1905. (German ed., 1908. English ed., *J. S. Bach*, translated by Ernest Newman, 2 vols., New York, 1911; reprint, 1963.)

Searle, Humphrey. *The Music of Liszt.* London, 1954.

————. "A Plea for Alkan," *M & L*, XVIII (1937), 276–9.

Seidler, K. "Untersuchungen zur Biographie und Klavierstil Johann Jakob Frobergers." Unpublished dissertation, Königsberg, 1930.

Seiffert, Max. "Antoni van Noordt," *TVNM*, V (1897), 85–99.

*————. *Geschichte der Klaviermusik*. Leipzig, 1899. (Only the first of the two planned volumes has appeared.)

————. "Joh. Pachelbels 'Musikalische Sterbensgedanken,'" *SIMG*, V (1903–1904), 476–88.

————. "J. P. Sweelinck und seine direkten deutschen Schüler," *VfMW*, VII (1891), 145–260.

————. "Konrad Friedrich Hurlebusch," *TVNM*, VII (1904), 264–77.

————. "Zu Händels Klavierwerken," *SIMG*, I (1899–1900), 131–41.

Selden-Göth, Gisela. *Ferrucio Busoni: Un profilo.* Vol. XX of *Historiae musicae cultores* Florence, 1964.

Shattuck, Roger. *The Banquet Years: The Arts in France, 1885–1918.* London, 1959. (Reprint, New York, 1961.)

Shedlock, John S. "The Harpsichord Music of Alessandro Scarlatti," *SIMG*, VI (1904–1905), 160–78, 418–22.

————. *The Pianoforte Sonata: Its Origin and Development.* London, 1895. (Reprint, New York, 1963.)

Shortridge, John D. *Italian Harpsichord-Building in the 16th and 17th Centuries.* Washington, D.C., 1960.

Siebenkäs, Dieter. *Ludwig Berger: Sein Leben und seine Werke.* Vol. IV of *Berliner Studien zur Musikwissenschaft*. Berlin, 1963.

Siebert, Frederick Mark. "Fifteenth Century Organ Settings of the Ordinarium Missae." Unpublished dissertation, Columbia, 1961.

————. "Mass Sections in the *Buxheim Organ Book:* A Few Points," *MQ*, L (1964), 353–66.

Sietz, Reinhold. "Ein Vorläufer von Bartók's *Allegro barbaro*," *MF*, V (1952), 370–2.

Sigtenhorst-Meyer, Bernard van den. *Jan P. Sweelinck en zijn instrumentale muziek.* The Hague, 1934. (2nd ed., 1946.)

Sitwell, Sachaverell. *Liszt.* London, 1934.

Slim, H. Colin. "Keyboard Music at Castell'Arquato by an Early Madrigalist," *JAMS*, XV (1962), 35–47.

————. "The Keyboard Ricercare and Fantasy in Italy, *c.* 1500–1550." Unpublished dissertation, Harvard, 1960.

Smith, Julia. *Aaron Copland.* New York, 1955.

Somer, Avo. "The Keyboard Music of Johann Jacob Froberger." Unpublished dissertation, Michigan, 1963.

Sourek, Ottokar. *Dvořáks Werke: Chronologisches und thematisches Verzeichnis.* Berlin, 1917.

Southern, Eileen. *The Buxheim Organ Book.* Vol. VI of the Institute of Medieval Music, *Musicological Studies.* Brooklyn, 1962. (See also her index in *Notes, XIX* [1961], 47–50.)

————. "Some Keyboard Basse Dances of the 15th Century," *Acta*, XXXV (1963), 114–24.

Speer, Klaus. "The Organ *Verso* in Iberian Music up to 1700," *JAMS*, XI (1958), 189–99.

Spitta, Philipp. *Johann Sebastian Bach.* 2 vols. Leipzig, 1873–1880. (3rd ed., 1921; rev. ed., 1935; English ed.: *Johann Sebastian Bach: His Work and Influence on the Music of Germany*, translated by C. Bell and John Alexander Fuller-Maitland, 3 vols., London, 1899; reprint, New York, 1951.)

Stahl, Wilhelm. *Franz Tunder und Dietrich Buxtehude: Ein biographischer Versuch.* Leipzig, 1926.

————. "Zur Biographie Johann Adam Reinkens," *AfMW*, III (1921), 232–6.

Stauch, Adolf. *Muzio Clementis Klaviersonaten im Verhältnis zu den Sonaten von Haydn, Mozart und Beethoven.* Bonn, 1930.

Steele, H. J. "English Organs and Organ Music from 1500 to 1650." Unpublished dissertation, Cambridge, 1959.

Steglich, Rudolf. "Karl Philipp Emanuel Bach und der Dresdener Kreuzkantor G. A. Homilius im Musikleben ihrer Zeit," *Bach-Jahrbuch*, XII (1915), 39–145.

————. *Robert Schumanns Kinderscenen.* Kassel and Basel, 1949.

Stein, Fritz. *Thematisches Verzeichnis der im Druck erschienenen Kompositionen von Max Reger.* Vol. I of *Veröffentlichungen der Reger Gesellschaft.* Leipzig, 1933.

Steuermann, Edward. "The Piano Music of Schönberg," in *Schönberg.* Edited by M. Armitage. New York, 1937, pp. 125–33.

Stevens, Denis. "Further Light on Fulgens praeclara," *JAMS*, IX (1956), 1–11.

————. *The Mulliner Book: A Commentary.* London, 1952.

————. "Pre-Reformation Organ Music in England," *PRMA*, LXXVII (1952), 1–10.

————. "Thomas Preston's Organ Mass," *M & L*, XXXIX (1958), 29–34.

————. "A Unique Tudor Organ Mass," *MD*, VI (1952), 167–75.

Stevens, Halsey. *The Life and Music of Béla Bartók.* New York, 1953.

Stevenson, Robert. *Juan Bermudo.* The Hague, 1960.

Stiehl, Carl. *Die Organisten an der St. Marienkirche und den Abendmusiken zu Lübeck.* Leipzig, 1886.

Stilz, Ernst. *Die Berliner Klaviersonate zur Zeit Friedrichs des Grossen.* Saarbrücken, 1930.

———. "Ueber harmonische Ausfüllung in der Klaviermusik des Rokoko," *ZfMW*, XIII (1930–1931), 11–20.

Stockmeier, Wolfgang. "Die deutsche Orgelsonate der Gegenwart." Unpublished dissertation, Cologne, 1958.

Stone, David. "The Italian Sonata for Harpsichord and Piano in the Eighteenth Century (1730–1790)." 3 vols. Unpublished dissertation, Harvard, 1952.

Strunk, Oliver. "Notes on a Haydn Autograph," *MQ*, XX (1934), 192–205.

Stuckenschmidt, H. H. "Synthesis and New Experiments: Four Contemporary German Composers," *MQ*, XXXVIII (1952), 353–68.

*Sumner, William Leslie. *The Organ: Its Evolution, Principles of Construction, and Use.* New York, 1952. (3rd ed., 1962.)

Sutherland, Gordon. "The Ricercari of Jacques Buus," *MQ*, XXXI (1945), 448–63.

Taylor, Stainton de Boufflers. *The Chorale-Preludes of J. S. Bach: A Handbook.* London, 1942.

Teichmüller, Robert, and Herrmann, Kurt. *Internationale moderne Klaviermusik: Ein Wegweiser und Berater.* Leipzig and Zürich, 1927.

Terry, Charles Sanford. *John Christian Bach.* London, 1929.

Tessier, André. "Les messes d'orgue de Couperin," *Revue musicale*, VI, No. 1 (1925), 37–48.

———. "L'oeuvre de clavecin de Nicolas LeBègue," *Revue de musicologie*, VII (1923), 106–12.

———. "Les Pièces de clavecin de Couperin," *Revue musicale*, VI, No. 7 (1925), 123–38.

———. *La vie musicale en France au siècle de Louis XIV: Nicolas LeBègue.* Paris, 1954.

Thompson, Verne W. "Johann Wenzel Tomaschek." Unpublished dissertation, Rochester, 1955.

Tischler, Hans. "Barber's Piano Sonata Opus 26," *M & L*, XXXIII (1952), 352–4.

———. "Hindemith's *Ludus tonalis* and Bach's *Well-Tempered Clavier*—A Comparison," *MR*, XX (1959), 217–27.

Tischler, Hans, and Tischler, Louise. "Mendelssohn's Songs without Words," *MQ*, XXXIII (1947), 1–16.

———. "Mendelssohn's Style," *MR*, VIII (1947), 256–73.

Torrefranca, Fausto. *Giovanni Benedetto Platti e la sonata moderna.* Vol. I of *Istituzioni e monumenti dell'arte musicale italiana, Nuova seria.* Milan, 1963.

———. *Le origini italiane del romanticismo musicali: I primitivi della sonate moderna.* Turin, 1930.

Trapp, Klaus. "Die Fuge in der deutschen Romantik von Schubert bis Reger." Unpublished dissertation, Frankfurt am Main, 1958.

Truscott, Harold. "Max Reger," *MR*, XVII (1956), 134–52.

———. "Medtner's Sonata in g op. 22," *MR*, XXII (1961), 112–23.

———. "Schubert's Unfinished Piano Sonata in C (1825)," *MR*, XVIII (1957), 114–37.

———. "The Two Versions of Schubert's op. 122," *MR*, XIV (1953), 89–106.

Tscheuchner, Eckart. "Die Neresheimer Orgeltabulaturen der fürstlich Thurn- und Taxisschen Hofbibliothek zu Regensburg." Unpublished dissertation, Erlangen, 1963.

Turrentine, Herbert C. "Johann Schobert and Clavier Music in France from 1700 to the Revolution." Unpublished dissertation, Iowa, 1962.
Tusler, Robert L. *The Organ Music of Jan Pieterʒoon Sweelinck.* 2 vols. No. I of *Utrechtse Bijdragen tot de Muʒiekwetenschap.* Bilthoven, 1958.
———. *The Style of Bach's Chorale-Preludes.* Vol. I, No. 2 of *University of California Publications in Music.* Berkeley, 1956.
Tuttle, Stephen D. "William Byrd: A Study of English Keyboard Music to 1623." Unpublished dissertation, Harvard, 1941.
Tuttle, T. Temple. "Schönberg's Compositions for Piano Solo," *MR,* XVIII (1957), 300–18.
Tyson, Alan. "The First Edition of Beethoven's op. 119 Bagatelles," *MQ,* XLIX (1963), 331–8.

Uhde, Jürgen. *Bartók's Mikrokosmos: Spielanweisungen und Erläuterungen.* Regensburg, 1954.
Unger, Max. *Muʒio Clementis Leben.* Langensalza, 1914.
Unger, Udo. *Die Klavierfuge im 20. Jahrhundert.* Vol. I of *Kölner Beiträge ʒu Musikforschung.* Regensburg, 1956.

Valabrega, Césare. *Il Clavecembalista Domenico Scarlatti: Il suo secolo, la sua vita.* Modena, 1937.
Valentin, Erich. *Die Entwicklung der Tokkata im 17. und 18. Jahrhundert (bis J. S. Bach).* Vol. XLV of *Universitas-Archiv.* Vol. VI of the *Musikwissenschaftliche Abteilung.* Münster, 1930.
Vente, Maarten A. *Die Brabanter Orgel: Zur Geschichte der Orgelkunst in Belgien und Holland im Zeitalter der Gothik und der Renaissance.* Amsterdam, 1958.
Vignal, Marc. "L'oeuvre par piano seul de Joseph Haydn," *Revue musicale, Carnet Critique* No. 249 (Paris, 1961).
Vogeleis, Martin. "Franz Xaver Murschhauser," *KJ,* XVI (1901), 1–15.

Wagner, Hans Joachim. *Die Orgelmusik in Thüringen in der Zeit ʒwischen 1830 und 1860: Ein Beitrag ʒur Geschichte der Orgelmusik im 19. Jahrhundert.* Berlin, 1937.
Waldschmidt, Carl. "Georg Boehm, His Life and Works." Unpublished dissertation, Northwestern, 1962.
Ward, John. "Borrowed Material in 16th-Century Instrumental Music," *JAMS,* V (1952), 88–98.
———. "The 'Dolfull Domps,'" *JAMS,* IV (1951), 111–21.
———. "The Editorial Methods of Venegas de Henestrosa," *MD,* VI (1952), 105–13.
———. "Les sources de la musique pour le clavier en Angleterre," in *La musique instrumentale de la Renaissance.* Edited by Jean Jacquot. Paris, 1955, pp. 225–36.
Wasielewski, Wilhelm Joseph von. *Geschichte der Instrumentalmusik im 16. Jahrhundert.* Berlin, 1878.
Waters, Edward N. "Chopin by Liszt," *MQ,* XLVII (1961), 170–94.
Weber, Friedrich. *Harmonischer Aufbau und Stimmführung in den Sonatensätʒen der Klaviersonaten Beethovens. Schriftenreihe des Musikwissenschaftlichen Seminars der Universität München.* Vol. VII of *Studien ʒur musikalischen Kultur- und Stilgeschichte.* Würzburg, 1940.
*Weigl, Bruno. *Handbuch der Orgelliteratur.* Leipzig, 1931.
Weinstock, Herbert. *Chopin: The Man and His Music.* New York, 1949.
Weisgall, Hugo. "The Music of Henry Cowell," *MQ,* XLV (1959), 484–507.

Weissman, John S. "La musique de piano de Bartók: L'évolution d'une écriture," *Revue de musique* [Richard], No. 224 (1955), 171–222.

*Weitzmann, Carl Friedrich. *Geschichte des Clavierspiels und der Clavierliteratur.* Stuttgart, 1863. (3rd ed., see Seiffert; English ed.: *A History of Pianoforte-Playing and Pianoforte Literature*, translated by T. Baker, New York, 1893.)

Werker, Wilhelm. *Studien über die Symmetrie im Bau der Fugen und motivische Zusammengehörigkeit der Präludien und Fugen des Wohltemperierten Klaviers.* Vol. III of *Abhandlungen des Sächsischen staatlichen Forschungsinstituts zu Leipzig. Forschungsinstitut für Musikwissenschaft.* Leipzig, 1922.

Werner, Eric. *Mendelssohn: A New Image of the Composer and His Age.* New York, 1963.

Werner, Rudolf. *Felix Mendelssohn als Kirchenmusiker.* 2 vols. No. II of *Veröffentlichungen der deutschen Musikgesellschaft. Ortsgruppe Frankfurt.* Frankfurt am Main, 1930.

Werra, Erich von. "Johann Buchner," *KJ*, X (1895), 88–92.

West, John E. "Old English Organ Music," *SIMG*, XII (1910–1911), 213–221.

Westerby, Herbert. *Beethoven and his Piano Works.* London, 1931.

———. *A History of Pianoforte Music.* London and New York, 1924.

———. *Liszt: Composer and His Piano Works.* London, 1936.

White, John R. "The Tablature of Johannes of Lublin," *MD*, XVII (1963), 137–62.

Wier, Albert E. *The Piano: Its History, Makers, Players and Music.* New York, 1941.

Wierczynski, Casimir. *The Life and Death of Chopin.* Translated by N. Guterman. New York, 1949; London, 1951.

Williams, Charles Francis Abdy. *The Story of Organ Music.* London and New York, 1905.

———. *The Story of the Organ.* London and New York, 1903.

Williams, Peter F. "J. S. Bach and English Organ Music," *M & L*, XLIV (1963), 140–51.

Wilson, Charles. "The Two Versions of 'Goyescas,'" *MMR*, LXXXI (1951), 203–7.

Winkler, Georg. "Das Problem der Polyphonie im Klavierschaffen Franz Schuberts." Unpublished dissertation, Vienna, 1956.

Winternitz, Emanuel. *Keyboard Instruments in the Metropolitan Museum of Art: A Picture Book.* New York, 1961.

Wolf, Johannes. "Zur Geschichte der Orgelmusik im vierzehnten Jahrhundert," *KJ*, XIV (1899), 14–31.

Wolgast, Johannes. "Georg Böhm." Unpublished dissertation, Berlin, 1930.

Wörmann, Wilhelm. "Die Klaviersonate Domenico Albertis," *Acta*, XXVII (1955), 84–107.

Wörsching, Josef. *Der Orgelbauer Karl Riepp (1710–1775): Ein Beitrag zur Geschichte der süddeutschen Orgelkunst des 18. Jahrhunderts.* Mainz, 1939.

———. *Der Orgelbauerfamilie Silbermann in Strassburg.* Mainz, 1941.

Wotquenne, Alfred. *Thematisches Verzeichnis der Werke von Carl Philipp Emanuel Bach.* Leipzig, 1905.

Wünsch, Gerhard. "Die Entwicklung des Klaviersatzes bei Max Reger." Unpublished dissertation, Vienna, 1950.

Wustmann, G. "Elias Ammerbach," *SIMG*, XI (1909–1910), 137–40.

Wyler, Robert. *Form- und Stiluntersuchungen zum ersten Satz der Klaviersonaten Carl Philipp Emanuel Bachs.* Biel, 1960.

Wyzewa, Théodore, and St. Foix, Georges de. *W. A. Mozart: Sa vie musicale et son oeuvre de l'enfance à la pleine maturité.* 5 vols. Paris, 1912–1946.

Yasser, Joseph. "The Magrepha of the Herodian Temple: A Five-Fold Hypothesis," *JAMS*, XIII (1960), 24–42.

Young, Percy M. *Tragic Muse: The Life and Works of Robert Schumann.* London, 1957.

Young, William. "Keyboard Music to 1600," *MD*, XVI (1962), 115–50, and XVII (1963), 163–193.

———. "The Keyboard Tablatures of Bernhard Schmid, Father and Son." Unpublished dissertation, Illinois, 1957.

Zimmermann, Franklin B. *Henry Purcell, 1659–1695: An Analytical Catalogue of His Music.* London, 1963.

Zöllner, Gerd. *Franz Hünten: Seine Leben und sein Werk.* Vol. XXXIV of *Beiträge zur rheinischen Musikgeschichte.* Cologne, 1959.

Index of Compositions*

* Indexes compiled by Dan Duffin.

General Index